Windy Thoughts

Joyce Green

Edee & Mike,
Always follow your
dreams!
God Bless.
Joyce Green

PUBLISHING

Eastsound, Washington

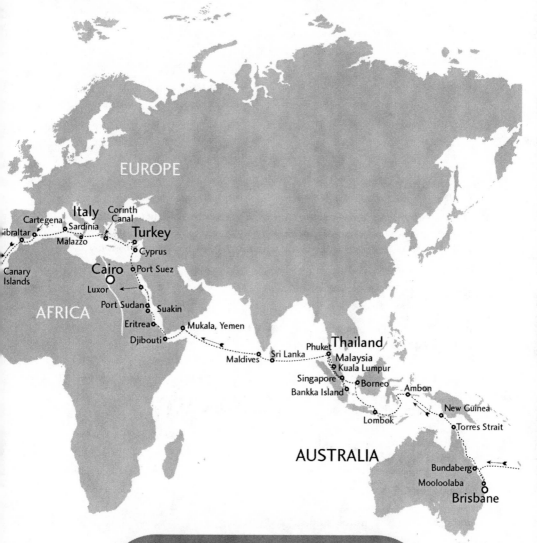

EUROPE

Cartegena
Italy Corinth Canal
Gibraltar Sardinia
Malazzo Turkey
Cyprus

Canary Islands
Cairo Port Suez
Luxor

AFRICA
Port Sudan Suakin
Eritrea
Djibouti Mukala, Yemen

Maldives Sri Lanka Phuket Thailand
Malaysia
Kuala Lumpur
Singapore Borneo
Bankka Island Ambon
Lombok New Guinea
Torres Strait

AUSTRALIA
Bundaberg
Mooloolaba
Brisbane

Voyage of Windy Thoughts

1986-1998

ANTARCTICA

First Edition

Windy Thoughts Publishing
P.O. Box 1604, Eastsound, WA 98245

www.windythoughts.com

Cover design by Mitzi Johnson, Ltd., Friday Harbor, WA

Maps, logo, interior design and layout by Bruce Conway
of Illumina Book Design, Friday Harbor, WA

Printed in the U.S.A. on recycled paper

Library of Congress Control Number: 2008930457

ISBN: 978-0-9802195-0-0

To Don, my husband and captain for life.

Windy Thoughts · *Seattle, Wa.* · 1986 - 1998

ACKNOWLEDGEMENTS
I would like to acknowledge the support of the following people:

Susan Brown, my dear friend who, unbeknownst to me, saved every letter written to her over the years of our journey. Out of her thoughtfulness this book was born, and out of graciousness and friendship she so skillfully took on the huge job of editing.

Bruce Conway, of Illumina Book Design, whose exceptional abilities turned my manuscript into a book. Bruce possesses more than mere technical expertise, as his graphic art abilities are top-notch. Sitting and watching Bruce perform his wizardry on the computer was an amazing experience.

Mitzi Johnson, of Mitzi, Ltd., who so artfully created the book's cover, making it just what I envisioned.

Judith Carter, Bruce's proofreader, who put the final polish on the britework of the book.

And finally, my husband, Don Green, who never allowed me to give up on the writing, and without who's optimistic outlook on life our dreams would never have come to fruition.

Front cover photo: *Windy Thoughts* sailing the Great Barrier Reef

TABLE OF CONTENTS

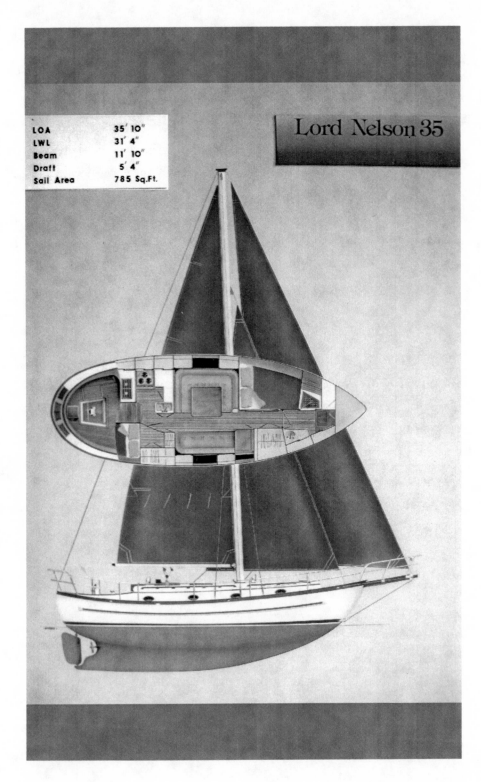

LOA	35' 10"
LWL	31' 4"
Beam	11' 10"
Draft	5' 4"
Sail Area	785 Sq.Ft.

Lord Nelson 35

FOREWORD

It was a complete stranger who first suggested that Joyce's book should include a foreword. My seatmate on a flight from Newark to Seattle had watched me working on my computer for several hours; finally curiosity overcame her and she asked "Are you writing a book?"

No, I laughed, I am not an author. But I was delighted to share with her my enjoyment at having been asked (allowed, really) to edit my dear friend's book. I expressed how honored I was to have been included in the editing process and how highly I regard Joyce, as the author, my friend, Don's wife and *Windy Thoughts'* first mate.

The conversation turned naturally to the subject of Joyce's book and I replied, "On the surface, it is a book about two people who circumnavigate the world in a small sailboat. But actually, it is much more than a book about sailing; the book has several significant themes, all very different but all interwoven in the most delightful way."

As I spoke these words, my seatmate nodded in understanding and identified herself as a free-lance book illustrator. We bonded instantly for that moment because we both have experienced firsthand the commitment and dedication needed from an author compelled to share a story with others.

We talked for the final minutes of our flight and I began to identify why Joyce's story is so meaningful, so worth writing and so worth reading. I spoke the reasons aloud as we were scrambling to exit the plane.

My seatmate looked at me and said, "You absolutely must write the book's foreword, both as a tribute to your friendship and to express just what Joyce's book means to you."

So, at the urging of a stranger and with the benevolent consent of the book's author, I have written this foreword with unrestrained admiration for Joyce, my passionate, humorous and uniquely wonderful friend.

The book thoughtfully explores both the romance and the reality of life afloat. The joys and wonders of offshore sailing are easily understood: breathtaking sunrises, starry night skies, peaceful anchorages and the solitude that only an ocean passage can provide. Less anticipated are the number of times such pleasures are quickly thrust aside. Any offshore crew must cope with the often dramatic and always unexpected events that come from mechanical failures, challenging weather conditions and arbitrary international bureaucracies.

Joyce writes artfully about the rich cultural experiences that are available to people with open hearts and curious minds. There are many deeply touching stories about people the Greens encountered in distant countries and I am in awe of their enthusiastic and respectful participation in local traditions.

The book is a story of friendship shared by two women who remain inextricably connected by letters written while literally a world away from one another. The communication between friends predates modern email technology and the depth contained in the letters is a testament to Joyce's innate candor and willingness to trust in others.

Windy Thoughts is first and foremost a love story. This is a story of the love, honor and trust of a first mate for her captain. It is a tale of two people bound by more than wedding vows. As Joyce's story unfolds, the synergy of their marriage is tangible, the reliance and faith in one another is irrefutable and the successful completion of their shared dream is an inspiration to us all.
— Susan Brown

Chapter 1

The Path Less Taken

Twenty years from now, you will be more disappointed by the things you didn't do than by the ones you did do. So throw off the bow lines. Sail away from the safe harbor. Catch the trade winds in your sails. Explore. Dream. Discover.   —Mark Twain

Don's six-hour watch was just nearing its end and I was waking up below, soon to join him on the approach to the last landfall we would ever make on our great adventure together. The morning sun was just softening the night sky with its welcoming morning glow as we sat a few miles off the entrance to San Carlos, on the eastern shore of Mexico's Sea of Cortez.

It was the last watch of twelve years of cruising, the last ten of which had taken us around the world in a circumnavigation that brought us more joy, wonders and challenges than we ever could have imagined back when our dream of the cruising life was first born. It had been years brimming with the very highest of highs and the very lowest of lows.

Excitement at being nearly home was mixed with a sadness that it was all about to be over in just a number of hours. Our world as we had known it all these years would rapidly return to what most people called a normal life. Memories were swimming in our heads—memories of years with an eye and an ear constantly to the weather, to the safety of the boat and to ourselves. Memories of those things that we dreamed of before our adventure began— pristine bays and white sandy beaches, with palm trees swaying in tropical breezes. Memories of people we met along the way, good friends made and cultures that amazed and enveloped us. Years that were filled with adventure that we knew we would never again experience.

It had been our practice over the years to await daylight before making an approach to land. A close watch was necessary as we hove-to off San Carlos.

During the black hours of the night we had contemplated throwing caution to the wind and working our way in slowly through the darkness. That wind to which we would throw caution had piped up and we were being uncomfortably tossed about in its accompanying seas as we awaited daylight. Calm waters, the hook down and a good night's sleep were so close.

The entrance to San Carlos' harbor appeared fairly straightforward on the chart, with a pass between two walls of rock, the large anchorage opening up just inside. But when our waypoint made no sense in the darkness and we could see no opening on the radar, caution overruled and we had turned tail to scurry back out to the safety of the sea, to continue our vigil those few miles off until those first rays of the morning sun beckoned.

The wind had been at our backs when we first sailed south to Mexico to reach latitudes where trade winds can be picked up to carry westward-bound boats toward the magic of the South Pacific islands and beyond. Mexico offers its own unparalleled delights in the plethora of cruising grounds found in the Sea of Cortez and on mainland Mexico's coast. After eighteen months of cruising in the Sea of Cortez, our sail around the world had started in La Paz, located on the eastern shores of the Baja Peninsula.

And now, only a few days prior to this last night at sea, *Windy Thoughts* had crossed her outward-bound track to complete a circumnavigation on March 20, 1998, just outside of La Paz, the beautiful city of peace.

So easily these words are written—a circumnavigation of the world—as though it had been just a pleasant vacation that had come along in the middle years of our lives. As though there was really nothing to it. In truth, it had been both the most difficult and challenging experience imaginable, but by far the most exciting and rewarding experience two people could ever share.

There were three weeks before the scheduled carrier was to take *Windy Thoughts* from San Carlos north to Seattle, eliminating a hard beat against headwinds that her little crew of two had no desire to undertake. We planned to make the 300 mile passage from La Paz to San Carlos with stops at the memorable spots that we had enjoyed ten years earlier—when this adventure was still in its embryonic state. Even with all of the wonders that greeted us in the years to come, our memories put the Sea of Cortez at the top of our list of favorite cruising grounds.

I wanted to collect more shells not as plentiful in faraway places. Don and I were eager to get back to snorkeling and diving in waters teeming with tropical fish of every variety and color. Don wanted a final opportunity to hunt for lobster. Such simple pleasures weren't likely to be an everyday part of our lives in just a few short weeks. We had big plans for a celebration dinner in La Paz to commemorate our circumnavigation.

On our arrival in La Paz we treated ourselves to a slip in the Marina De La Paz. *Windy Thoughts* lay on her anchor for the two winter seasons we had spent there. Resting in a slip and stepping off the boat onto the dock was to be a fitting closure to the years when most of our time was enjoyed at anchor, lazily bobbing about—or sometimes violently plunging about. Only at anchor can one savor the wonders of the remote world, and we had a lifetime of memories of remote little hidey-holes all over this earth.

Don made a phone call to the boatyard in San Carlos that would handle our haul-out, as well as part of the transit to Seattle. Don learned that the yard was booked heavily and would prefer to initiate the transit in one week instead of the scheduled three!

All plans for our celebration in La Paz were tossed aside when we threw off the dock lines and headed out. Northerly winter winds blowing down the Sea of Cortez hadn't fully abated, but the weather pattern opened up and gave us a flat calm to make fast tracks north under power. At our destination we would have plenty of work preparing the boat for the transit. There would be no time for any poking along and enjoying the Sea of Cortez's many delights.

Our weather window held and it wasn't until midnight on this last night at sea that the notoriously nasty winds gave us a last taste of their vengeance— building rapidly out of the north, producing those short and steep seas prevalent during the winter months that make for miserable and slow northerly progress.

And so, our last remaining hours of our time at sea were spent waiting off San Carlos. We weren't meant to depart from this cruising world without a final reminder of how uncomfortable the sea can be. However, we were almost home and had only hours left before the cruising life we had lived for so long would be over—over forever.

I crawled out of my sea berth and was rustling up some breakfast. Don was silently thanking God for bringing us safely around our world, gazing at the sea, experiencing many feelings about this final landfall.

Suddenly, Don's reverie was broken when the water exploded not ten feet from the boat and an Orca whale catapulted completely out of the water! Showing off his black and white glorious splendor, the Orca did a complete spinning roll in the air before plunging back into the sea, giving a second performance before I reached the top of the companionway stairs.

To this day Don maintains that Orca was giving us a special goodbye to our life at sea. Or—perhaps he was welcoming us home! In our northwest Washington waters, the Orcas had greeted us on numerous occasions. Was this a goodbye, or a hello?

Soon we were inside the calm harbor of San Carlos where several cruising sailboats peacefully shifted in the wind, their crews still asleep below. All was quiet. There wasn't one boat name with which we were familiar, no one known from somewhere down the line—or some previous year to happily call hellos to—no one on deck to call good morning to. These boats were all part of the fresh new group. We were just the old shoes now. We crept slowly through the anchorage and silently picked our spot.

And then the anchor went down for the last time of our great adventure. It was suddenly and abruptly over, and nothing would ever be the same again.

There were wonderful days ahead and the beginnings of a new life ashore that we love deeply and with which we are very content. However, our days aboard our dear *Windy Thoughts* and the adventures that we shared together will forever remain vivid in our daily memories.

Could we do it again? Not a chance in the world! Age makes for differing pleasures now. But to regain those halcyon days for just moments at a time—we would treasure the opportunity!

Chapter 2

A Dream is Born

Nothing happens unless first a dream.
—Carl Sandburg

It is often said that if you can dream it, you can make it happen. Not only had we not dreamt of sailing off into the sunset, we had never stepped foot aboard a sailboat. We were leading quite contented and comfortable lives in the home that we had worked so hard and long to build and were busy with jobs and land life. Living aboard a sailboat and cruising off to magical places was something that other people did, a life about which we knew next to nothing.

So just how did we end up selling the house and cars, giving up our jobs and all sense of security and moving aboard a sailboat well into the middle years of our lives? To say that our dream began one day and settled in to take over our very souls only begins to account for the demands that dream made of us from that day forward.

Perhaps it was the hand of fate, but in truth it was a sailing and cruising magazine that changed our lives. Don picked it up while perusing the magazine section at a bookstore during his lunch hour—a magazine never noticed previously and in which he had never had an inkling of an interest.

At the end of that fateful day in 1980, Don returned from work full of excitement, ready to show me stories of people "out there", doing something about which we knew absolutely nothing.

"This is what we should be doing," were his first words. Seven little words set the tone for the years to come—and so began our dream.

That evening found me with my nose buried in the pages of tales about people sailing to faraway places and doing it aboard their own little homes, a seemingly fascinating way of life.

Don claimed that if others could do it, why couldn't we? Figuring that we were normal and of average intelligence, why couldn't we too learn to sail?

It would be five long years before our dream of "going cruising" came to fruition—years during which we didn't learn to sail. But never once did I doubt that Don had what it would take to make the dream come true. Once setting his mind to something, Don simply perseveres and does what has to be done to accomplish whatever the goal may be. Never one to dwell on impossibilities, he instead focuses on the possibilities.

This was no husband's dream, however. The dream had taken over both our souls.

We lived on a lake ten miles outside of Spokane, Washington. In addition to the family awning business, Don was in the building business. The economy was going haywire with the high interest rates of the early 1980s, affecting a condominium project that Don was developing. I was teaching first grade at the nearby school on the lake—quite removed from business worries but very aware of Don's.

Much sweat and labor had gone into building our home on the lake amidst twenty acres of trees, a rural environment that offered the beauty and peace that we loved. Don cut cedar logs into bolts and hand split every shake for the roof. We pictured that we would live out our days there, never once imagining that our lives might take a different turn, or that we would ever willingly give it all up.

Prior to living at the lake we had owned *Donald's Duck*, an eighteen-foot cabin cruiser that we took on camping trips, enjoying many hours of fun. Our only water craft now was a canoe. Don remedied the situation by building a riverboat. The pontoons were twenty-five-foot long fuel tanks taken from airplanes, given to us by Don's friend. The rest of the boat was built from lumber. It had a big ship's wheel, blue outdoor carpet and blue and white captain's chairs. An old outboard engine provided propulsion. Don designed a blue and white-fringed canopy and a white "Donald's Duck II" proudly emblazoned on the canopy.

That first summer found us taking toots down the lake during breaks from the building process. A couple across the lake borrowed *Donald's Duck II* and held their wedding aboard. We may have been out on the water, but piloting a riverboat is a long, long way from sailing oceans.

It was six years later when Don came home with that magazine and something in us said, "That could be us."

Our destiny was set. We were going cruising!

From that day on, we began devouring every article on sailing that we could find and explored the public library for books written by people who had lived or were living the cruising life—names new to us at the time, but names known and read by every cruising sailor. Attempting to soak up every bit of vicarious knowledge, we pressed ahead, undaunted.

I was thirty-eight and Don forty-eight when the whole idea first took root, and it would be five years of intense planning and finding the means before we purchased our boat and moved aboard. Wanting to go before age might bring lessening interest and health, we were determined to make this total lifestyle change, a commitment to which we expected to last at least a few years. All available funds would go toward the ultimate dreamboat. Our house went on the market in 1981.

Over the years we have thought about what it takes to give up everything and move aboard a small sailboat to live out your dreams. As we made our way around the world and met up with other cruisers, some common traits emerged. First, there was desire coupled with a sense of adventure, followed closely by just getting out there and doing it! Others had found a way, just as we had. No, it wasn't easy to make plans, spend time acquiring the well-found boat and outfitting it for offshore cruising—and rearrange our lives. Financial planning was a major part. Our master plan centered on putting our very souls into just doing it.

There were myriad skills to acquire: navigator, pilot, sail repairer, diesel engine mechanic (most of your cruising years will be spent working on the engine), electronic technician, nuts and bolts expert, licensed radio operator, electric pump expert, sea water pump expert and on and on. Time spent reading the engine's manual will vie for attention with the many books stowed aboard for your pleasure. Manuals might win out in the end.

Few people cruise oceans without many years of sailing experience, some on open water. We had virtually none. Not for one moment did we expect any of this to come easily. It did not. As we wended our way around the world, cruising would require more than we had ever imagined ourselves capable of. It would humble us. It would humiliate us. It would try ever so hard to defeat us. With our eyes wide with wonder and terror, we would look Mother Nature in the eye and face off against powers that most never experience in a lifetime.

In the end, even with all of the challenges, it is the magic that grabs hold of you and remains embedded in your soul forever.

Certainly, we would have liked to set off with a comfortable bank account, but circumstances in the early 1980s (the prime interest rate leaping to unprecedented heights) changed our perspective. We would do it with the means we had and be thankful. It was not a grand "vacation budget", or a tidy retirement plan, but was instead a very tightly trimmed budget within which we were determined to live. It is a simple matter of perspective. If you want something badly enough you will do what you have to do.

We did what we needed to do and we did it successfully for many years, missing little that was important to us. We saw the same places, enjoyed the same wonders and sailed our own boat—albeit with few expensive dinners out and few trips back home. We all faced the same elements, the same problems and the same sole reliance on ourselves. Don and I were not youngsters who would return some day to the job market and begin our lives anew. We had built our lives and we were giving up much of what we had built over the years.

Still, in our estimation, we were gaining far more than we were giving up.

Our budget, though never opulent, was somewhat healthier for the last five years of our adventure, allowing for shifting priorities from absolute necessities toward more pleasurable amenities.

Many amongst the sailing/cruising crowd could fly home at least once a year, some more often if they could safely leave their boats. Most were on a limited time plan and would either retire or return to work in a short timeframe. For us, there were only four home visits in total, two of them in the last two years. But we made do with what we had and lived our dream comfortably and happily.

Cruising isn't a vacation, it is a lifestyle that we had chosen, truly a unique and wonderful one. It wasn't unusual to have people perceive the lifestyle a result of luck, as in, "You are so lucky to be doing this." Candidly, luck has very little to do with it. We believe that we pretty much get what we want in direct proportion to what we are willing to put into life. We believe anyone truly wanting to cruise will be out there cruising. Nothing about living life on the oceans brings people closer together than the stark realities of what is required to sustain the lifestyle.

What you have in your pocketbook doesn't make much difference when it comes to handling a small boat in a storm. In a well-found boat that is your haven in storms or good weather—and with the entire world as your oyster—there is really little more you need than the freedom to leave tradition behind and a unending love of adventure. Add in abundant good health and all becomes attainable.

On weekends we began to take little forays over the mountains to the coast, where we spent every waking minute walking the docks. Lists of attributes important in a well-found, offshore cruising boat were clutched in our hands. With stars in our eyes, we were certain we would find the perfect boat for us and we weren't planning to settle for less.

The first real blue-water boat that we looked at was a traditional double ender with beautiful teak work, the topside and the cozy cabin opulent in our eyes. I imagined myself making meals in the little galley, but followed Don back up on top to look over more carefully the actual sailing attributes of the boat.

Attempting—and utterly failing—to unite my strictly hands-off sailing knowledge with the bewildering array of ropes and lines before me, I looked at Don and asked, "Do you think we will ever become comfortable with all of this?"

Along with his work in the building trade, Don was part of Spokane Tent and Awning and F. O. Berg businesses in Spokane. His parents had started Spokane Tent and Awning Company in their early twenties, and when Don was young, one of his more interesting jobs was helping to put up a big circus tent.

And so Don's answer came very logically, "Sure we can, it's just basically blocks and tackle."

Basic was our knowledge as we headed feet first into the sailing world wide-eyed with wonder, confident that with hard work and determination we too could find ourselves sailors. But we had a lot to learn! No amount of book reading or insight from other sailors—though certainly very helpful—can take the place of experience and practice and we knew we fell far short and needed to get out on the water to learn to sail.

On a lovely summer day we jaunted off to nearby Lake Coeur d'Alene, Idaho to rent a small sailboat for a few hours. Despite our limited knowledge of sailing we somehow made it away from the dock, and the breezes carried us out onto the lake. But as we proudly looked back toward land and our accomplishment, we saw the bottle of wine and the lunch that we intended to take along for celebrating this auspicious occasion—still sitting on the dock! Unable to quite figure out how to get the boat back to the dock, they remained there until our day of sailing was over—when with antics that would have delighted any onlookers were they about, we somehow reached the dock.

While concern for the right boat occupied our thoughts, our house sat on the market throughout that first summer and then the following winter. With the high prime interest rate, the housing market in Spokane was virtually in the dumps but we were determined to stick to our price. All would be ours in due time.

Meanwhile, we began a celestial navigation correspondence course offered through Seattle's Castoff School of Navigation. Satellite navigation technology (SAT NAV) had arrived, but most felt it important to understand and master traditional navigation. Even today, with the technology advancing every year, learning to navigate celestially is considered an art wisely pursued by many who go to sea. Electronics break down. God's celestial bodies don't. A star to steer her by isn't without merit!

When we ended our cruising days in 1998, the majority of cruising boats were out there with back-up GPS units, but fewer and fewer were steered by sailors who were masters of celestial navigation. By 1998, we had three GPS units aboard ourselves, but Don diligently maintained his celestial navigation skills. The world continues to change as technology takes over our lives. But is it all for the better?

Don pursued his celestial navigation studies each evening after dinner, eagerly trying to understand this art form. My persistence doesn't run the same course as Don's, and not finding it easily understandable at first try I gave up on it for a while. Ultimately, it was agreed Don would tackle the celestial navigation and I would get the amateur radio license, better known as a Ham Radio license.

The Ham license involved a study of more electronics than I was anxious to delve into and was easily put off. While Don spent every single evening for five years working on some aspect of making our dream come true, I busied myself with the more interesting aspects of it, such as reading tales of others who were cruising.

Consequently, my indifference met with stark commitment two months before we actually went offshore—succeeding best under pressure. I could answer every question from the 500-question pool each for the Novice license level, the Technician level and the General license level. I practiced my Morse code for hours, days and weeks. The most technical questions or formulas were no match for this gal now on a mission.

I made little attempt to develop any true understanding of electronics, wanting only to know the right answers and secure the license. When we installed our Ham radio, Don had to tune in the frequency for me before I could talk. Then it was move over, Don—because legally he couldn't transmit on the Ham radio frequencies. For me, the talking part came quite naturally. Don maintains talking never was a problem for me.

Frantic phone calls to Mr. and Mrs. Williams in Seattle—the folks who both developed and were teaching the celestial navigation course, assisted Don as he fought an uphill battle toward the understanding of celestial navigation. He spent his evenings working out fixes for any number of scenarios suggested by the practice problems long after he passed the course.

In the end, Don was ready for the big time—the purchase of a sextant! He proudly called the classified department of the local paper to place an ad for one. The woman on the other end of the line told him, in no uncertain terms, that their paper didn't advertise for pornographic material and slammed the phone down.

Not many people on our side of the mountains seriously thought that we would ever follow through with this crazy idea, and we rarely brought it up in conversation. We had our dream, however, and would fulfill it come hell or high water. When we married in 1967, Don told me that there would never be a dull moment in our marriage. He fervently believed that when opportunity knocks it is best to take advantage, as there may not be another. Our life together had pretty well followed this philosophy.

And so, we forged full speed ahead with our plans, still never having actually done any real sailing ourselves—a rather major flaw in the plan that was yet to be remedied.

Don did find his sextant when doing some business and the talk came around to sailing plans. The customer had a very nice Tamaya Spica sextant that he was willing to part with—that had belonged to none other than the same Mr. and Mrs. Williams from whom the customer had taken their celestial navigation class!

One early morning when Don was taking a walk in our woods, he went to his knees and asked God to let him know if he was to go cruising, hoping that it would be soon or he felt he would be too old. Within a year it seemed that the dream that had never been relegated to the back burner was to become reality. It was as if the weight of the world was lifted from Don's shoulders.

In October of 1985, after five years of working toward our dream, our realtor stopped by with a couple up from California with a list of specifics they were looking for—the main requirement that their new home be in the woods and on the water.

They stepped through the door of our house and without a moment's hesitation stated, "This is exactly what we're looking for."

After breezing through the house and the surrounding acreage, all papers were made ready to sign and we were to be out by Thanksgiving, only six weeks away!

Excitement following on the heels of panic, Don ordered the boat the next morning with a phone call to the brokerage in Seattle. We had narrowed our choice to the Lord Nelson 35, measuring thirty-five feet, ten inches, with a seven-foot bowsprit. The Lord Nelson 35 presently being laid up could be secured for us—and before anything was finalized on the house, we signed away our lives for the boat.

There had not been one day in the five years since Don had first picked up that cruising magazine that he had any doubt that we would succeed, though there had been just cause for doubts. When interest rates hit twenty-two percent in 1980, the building trade was hit hard and dreams sat in limbo while business problems tormented Don—and neither the business nor the house sold.

Stunned that it was finally happening, we had to think fast about what we were to do with our entire household in the next few weeks. Because public storage was a bit pricey for people no longer part of the working world, we built our own storage unit—a metal building in the woods on ten acres that we kept. The builders arrived and laid a foundation in rapidly deteriorating winter weather while we began the unending job of packing up, sorting out and making major decisions.

Innumerable forays were made through the woods between the house and the storage building over a rather primitive rutted path, most trips made in the evenings after work in pitch dark. Snow arrived in bucket loads, making the whole procedure even more challenging. Somehow, all of our earthly goods ended up in that building in the woods. We locked the door behind us, hung the key on a tree and never looked back—for twelve years.

In addition, we needed to find a place to live until school was out in June and I would be free. Don was miraculously freed when both businesses sold, closing on the very day the house closed. On Veteran's Day weekend, we found a one-bedroom apartment and made plans to move in over the Thanksgiving holidays.

Our pets would need new and loving homes. Friends took Chako, our beloved dog, who was a mix of malamute and shepherd. A woman down the road took Kitty, the other cat Panda to go up the road to a farm. While I spent the last moments in our home mopping my way to the front door, Don spent his catching Panda. I drove while Don held tight to the box in which Panda was secured. When we arrived at the farm Don let Panda out at the barn door, only to see her take off into the woods, not in the least interested in the delights that we had presumed barn cats liked. Fortunately, Panda quickly made her way back to live happily with the barn creatures, well fed and loved by the farm's owners.

Living our dream vicariously and planning for blue water sailing while living inland without a boat, we read and studied in depth anything pertaining to sailing, boat handling, boat provisioning, or tools and parts. Files of articles and notes on every subject related to any of the above accumulated.

Somehow we made all the right decisions regarding what to pack up for storage, what to take to the boat and of what to rid ourselves. China, silver and stemware was packed up and carefully stored with Don's mother. Friends kept Don's motorcycle and the canoe for us. People down the lake were happy to take *Donald's Duck* off our hands and looked forward to many lazy summer afternoons out on the water.

With the boat's diagram and layout in hand long before seeing the boat in actuality, every locker available on the boat had plans for its contents. Meanwhile we had seen a Lord Nelson 35 only on paper and we were still non-sailors! Undaunted, we forged ahead. Having become familiar with the quality of the Lord Nelson 41, our decision to go with the Lord Nelson yard was sealed—a decision we would never regret.

We wouldn't lay eyes on our boat until it arrived from Taiwan, delivered to the port of Seattle in time for the 1986 January boat show, where it would be part of the Cruising Yachts display in the Kingdome.

Many had told us that the purchase of a boat always involved compromise, but not once did we find this to be true in our choice of boat. The Lord Nelson proved to be a well-thought- out, high-quality boat that never once let us down. It was designed by an American design team and built in an American-owned yard.

She was a cutter-rigged double ender, beamy at eleven feet, ten inches and thirty-one feet on her waterline, with an insulated hull. She had Burmese teak working areas on deck, a full teak cockpit, teak combing and rub rails, and high lifelines and stainless steel mast pulpits of the same diameter as on the forty-one-foot Lord Nelson. A seven-foot bowsprit with high and sturdy stainless steel rails allowed us to carry considerable sail area.

Her cabin was solid, hand-rubbed, beautifully finished Burmese teak throughout, including the interior recesses of all lockers. She had a teak and holly sole, ash cabin roof and a solid rosewood compression post with the mast stepped on deck. A roomy head with a tiled shower and a vanity top of Italian marble in the forepeak left that more uncomfortable area at sea to only its most necessary of uses! Located on the port side and just aft of the head compartment, our Pullman style master berth had built-in bookshelves and six very amply sized drawers below the bunk. Just opposite the berth was a hanging locker.

Moving aft, the main cabin had a traditional layout, with a U-shaped dinette to port, along with the galley located just at the foot of the companionway stairs. The Dickinson Marine cook stove proved to be worth its weight in gold, and there was an ample cavity for refrigeration.

A very comfortable starboard settee nestled opposite the dinette, with a wet locker separating it from the aft cabin. Forward of the settee and located on the opposite bulkhead from the master hanging locker was the chart table. A double berth was tucked under the starboard cockpit area, with another full-sized hanging locker and a door for privacy.

During the previous years of looking we sat down on many a boat's settees, always testing them out, and found those on our *Windy Thoughts* designed with live-aboard comfort in mind. Located mid-ship, they made comfortable sea berths, the double master berth generally reserved for when at anchor. More importantly, the settees would be our sofas in our little home. Don commandeered the starboard settee and I the port. They proved throughout the ensuing years to be the perfect spots to curl up with a good book, or more often to stretch out with that book.

An abundance of lockers stowed all of our goods, and ample bookshelves with removable teak rails held our many books at bay.

She was very roomy below and was always just right for us.

I was in my element planning for my galley, and we purchased a set of stainless steel Cuisinart Cookware with detachable handles for the pots that nestled into each other for storage.

The fellows at the brokerage had quite a laugh when Don came down the dock carrying the come-along and chainsaw that he insisted be part of his tool supply. How can you be a Pacific Northwesterner and not carry along your chain saw? Though he left it behind when we embarked on the big voyage, it saw much use during our first two years of cruising in the Pacific Northwest. He kept the come-along aboard, worth its weight in gold as well when, on two different occasions, the two of us alone took the engine out of the boat.

Lest we leave the impression that we were still unseasoned sailors, the prior year we had purchased a seven-foot, hard fiberglass sailing dinghy with teak trim, teak floorboards and seat— beautifully built and strong enough that in future we could pull ourselves up over the sides when snorkeling in warmer waters.

The choice of a hard dinghy had come as a part of a survival plan. If we had to abandon the boat, first to go off would be the life raft that we had yet to acquire. Circumstances allowing, the dinghy would be lowered into the water as well, with a chance that we might actively participate in our survival.

We named the dinghy *Breezy*, sailing her on camping trips in the summer to Priest Lake, Idaho and many a time on our own Lake Spokane. Seasoned sailors were we? Not by a long shot, but we were working our way through kindergarten.

The answer to the question of what to name our big boat was solved when good friends Jack and Elise Dean invited us to the horse races for my birthday. While sitting in their box seat and reading the racing form, we honed right in on a horse named Windy Thoughts—whose name rang a bell right there and then as the perfect name for the boat. After all, we would be living with the wind. Though the horse came in last, *Windy Thoughts* as a name stuck.

We had our dream, our dinghy, and our boat was arriving within a few weeks; our home was sold, an apartment was ready for us and a new life was just around the corner! Not once did we get cold feet and wonder just what in the world we were doing.

After busily settling ourselves in at the apartment over the Thanksgiving holidays, we returned to work. Don expected to be free at the end of January when the new owners were to take over at the business. But when they asked Don if he would stay on for the next few months while they looked for someone to fill his shoes, he agreed. After all, what did these two young upstarts from the banking business know about the tent and awning business? I wouldn't be free until June, so this offered us a good transition. It was a very strange feeling to walk through the doors of a business that Don's family had owned since he was a kid—and to suddenly work for someone else.

Several years earlier when architectural renderings for canopies and awnings became a huge expense, Don taught himself perspective drawing and did the renderings himself, working on this skill until able to produce professional looking results. Just when Don felt sure that his expertise was valued, the new owners invited him to lunch and he was given his walking papers. A replacement had been found for him, someone who could do the renderings and who was willing to learn to sell as well.

Arriving home that day with a stricken look on his face, Don announced, "I think I got fired today!" A lot of history had taken place between those walls over the years. But in truth, this was the last big step in the freeing of his soul to follow his dream.

Things were falling into place nicely. Our boat was arriving soon from the Lord Nelson yard. It was hull number nine and the first Lord Nelson 35 to arrive in Seattle. The rigging, mast and sails were American products and put on the boat after its arrival. Excitement ran deep in our veins and we could barely stand it until we could see the boat for ourselves.

She arrived by ship on January 14. The Seattle Boat show was to kick off the week of January 17–26, 1986, and *Windy Thoughts* was trucked to the Kingdome. Once there, the mast was stepped, the rigging installed and all surfaces and equipment readied for the big show. Working late into the night, the Cruising Yachts team built a first class display. *Windy Thoughts* shared the limelight with a Lord Nelson 41 and a Lord Nelson tug, all three boats guilty of stealing the huge show.

We would work the boat show for Cruising Yachts and we made tracks over the mountains from Spokane to Seattle the evening before the show's opening. On our arrival, we stumbled into a horrific windstorm. Driving over the mile-long bridge that spans Seattle's Lake Washington was becoming dangerous and we scooted over only minutes before it was closed to traffic.

Late that night, after checking into our five-star hotel that was compliments of Cruising Yachts, we tore off to the Kingdome where workers were frantically preparing the display for the next day's opening of the show. When we entered the huge dome we spotted our *Windy Thoughts* for the first time and burst into a run. She shone like the star she was amongst the others in the show.

She was everything that we had dreamed—and oh, so much more.

Sleep didn't come easily that night with the excitement and happiness that we felt. Not to mention that we were on the nineteenth floor of a hotel that was literally swaying in the big winds blowing outside. All part of earthquake protection built into the building, we were to learn the next morning.

Wild horses couldn't drag the two of us off our boat, and we spent the next days and evenings at Seattle's Kingdome. Don welcomed people aboard. Casually mentioning that this was his boat, any buttons may easily have popped, so proud was he. I was assigned the job of checking that all shoes were removed before boarding.

As a celebration of our boat's arrival, Don took me to lunch at a well-known Japanese restaurant downtown. Seated at a low table along with four Japanese men, we shared pleasantries, and they asked if we lived in Seattle.

This was Don's opportunity to explain why we were in town and he proudly told them that we had just purchased a new sailboat. The men smiled and said that they were in Seattle for a new purchase as well. Oh, and just what might that be?

A 747!

Our three days of glory now over, we headed back over the mountains to wait until June and to spend most weekends driving the 275 miles one way from Spokane to Seattle—and then back again. It never failed to blow a blizzard right up and over Snoqualmie Pass, when we could make the last hour in the more temperate climate of the coast. Arriving at the boat late in the evening we snuggled down into sleeping bags in our berth, to wake up the following morning ready to absorb everything new about what was soon to be our life.

After the boat show, the mast was re-stepped again when the boat was back at the dock. The mast stanchions, along with lifelines, mast pulpit and bowsprit, were tweaked. Also to be installed was the equipment that we had chosen: radios, roller furling, extra fuel pumps, Espar diesel furnace and on and on. The purchase of a new boat is just the beginning. The purse stays open as the boat gobbles up every penny!

Don was now free for the first time in his adult life and he began going over to Seattle for a few days at a time to learn all that he could while Barry McCormick commissioned the boat. Barry was an avid sailor who lived aboard his own boat in Seattle, and would become a good friend who remains so today. Don intently watched the installations of all this new equipment, knowing that there would be no repairmen at our beck and call.

Winter meant slower sales activity for the brokerage business but better winds in the Seattle area. The young salesmen at Cruising Yachts were apt sailors, ready and willing to go out on the boat with Don. The theory of sailing seemed logical to Don and he felt natural on the boat. He had piloted small planes in the past, and during our cruising years we were surprised at the number of fellow sailors who also were small plane pilots. Was there some connection in the brain with flying and sailing? Don loved every minute of his time in Seattle.

In the spring I drove over on weekends and we spent every waking minute sailing. The first time that we took the boat out by ourselves, we left our moorage at the dock only to have the engine quit once out onto Lake Union. Wide-eyed, I looked at Don and asked, "You know what to do, don't you?"

He just shrugged his shoulders. Did we learn fast!

The fellows at the brokerage often kidded us when we were about to leave the dock, reminding us not to pay any mind to the millions of dollars worth of boats that we would be maneuvering through as we worked our way into and out of the marina. Don did a masterful job of it all and I did a masterful job of jumping on and off the dock and fretting—fretting being my strong point.

We relentlessly practiced our docking skills on a large commercial dock across the lake, not in use on the weekends. Everything was a grand adventure to these two landlubbers from the opposite side of the mountains. The first time we crossed Puget Sound to anchor for the night in a little cove on Bainbridge Island, one might have thought we were crossing the mighty Pacific Ocean itself. Each weekend brought a new adventure and we practiced and sailed and worked our hearts out.

Don was raised in Spokane and spent his life loving anything to do with the outdoors—camping, hunting and boating, always having a taste for adventure and always willing to try anything new. He never had any doubt whatsoever that we were going to sail oceans. He had spent his life having to figure things out on his own, and it was solely due to his persistence that we ever got where we were at all—though we were embarking on an adventure for which we had no sailing experience and no skills.

I was raised in rural western New York State in the tiny town of Ischua, and had spent my childhood climbing trees, water skiing at our nearby Cuba Lake during the summers, sledding down the local hills and ice-skating on the local pond that we shoveled off during the winters. With the maiden name Shipman, I was convinced that the Shipman family history, that suggested the English name was derived from men of the sea, had some meaning for our aspirations!

Over my spring break from school we took as much as possible to the boat and headed out on a short cruise north, into Puget Sound. Sailing the few hours' distance from Seattle's locks north to Port Ludlow, we anchored in a small lagoon that wound in behind the marina.

Waking up at first light, Don eagerly got into the dinghy to play about the anchorage in the stillness, a harbor seal joining him to greet his day with its own playfulness. The day was spent in leisure, just enjoying the beautiful surroundings, the quiet and the peacefulness.

Otters played on the docks, sea gulls squawked their presence, and while we were underway the Dall's porpoises played about the boat as they zoomed across our bow, back and forth, back and forth. The Orca whales that navigate these waters each spring and summer cavorted about us, seemingly just wanting to communicate that they were there and to say their hellos. Their huge, beautiful black and white bodies skimmed the water near us, nosing in and out around us.

We were learning what a joy it was to be out on these incredible waters. Some of the most beautiful cruising in the world exists right here in our Pacific Northwest, from the south Puget Sound right up through the jewels of Washington's San Juan Islands where we now make our home. It doesn't stop here however, but the chain of islands continues to dot the British Columbia coast of Canada and then north through the spectacular beauty of Southeast Alaska's waters.

I was free on my last day of school, in June of 1986. Don was waiting for me in the parking lot. We set off for Seattle with anything left that was to go to the boat piled in boxes and stuffed in every spare niche of his car. With us was a beautiful quilt that my first graders at Lake Spokane School had presented me at a surprise going-away party the day before. Each child's name was stitched below a sailboat that was in each square on the quilt. It was used on our berth on *Windy Thoughts* throughout the years to come and is a wonderful memory of my teaching days.

My car was left with Don's sister to sell, and Don's pride and joy went to Seattle with us for those few weeks of summer preparation before it, too, ended its days with us. It was the last of the "spiffy" cars of a lifetime and we never looked back. There were more important things in life now.

Off over the mountains for the last time, this time to move aboard *Windy Thoughts* and officially become "full time live-aboards". Cars, a house, jobs and the conveniences of land life meant nothing to us now. We had our boat and our dreams. And we had each other. Who could want for anything more?

It never occurred to us to be concerned with the move to such small quarters. *Windy Thoughts* was well laid out and we never, in all of the years to come, felt crowded. As every boat owner knows, there is a place for everything and everything has its place.

While I was busy with the nesting instinct, Don was busy finishing the last chores to ready the boat for a summer cruise north to Canada's Desolation Sound, a huge area full of islands and mainland bays that give the boater no end of perfect cruising grounds. Its glory begins only about 275 miles north of Seattle, but may as well have been oceans away for the awe in which we held it. Three weeks were spent in this last preparation, installing the rest of our gear and loading up with provisions.

It was time for Don to drive his car back over the mountains to Spokane, leave it at the airport for a friend to pick up and sell, then hop a plane back to Seattle.

We were now jobless, carless and houseless—and the boat was our domicile as well as means of transportation. But, oh, what a beautiful little home she was already making for us. We were happy beyond belief.

Chapter 3

Goin' Cruising

Dream lofty dreams, and as you dream, so shall you become.
—James Allen

It was the first week of July, 1986, when we set off on our first "voyage", provisioned, fueled, everything shining like a new nickel. One of the delights of boating in the Pacific Northwest is the protected waters amongst the many islands. Boaters often trail their dinghy on a line behind the boat, impossible when sailing oceans.

As we left the dock our friend Barry was frantically gesturing and shouting to us. His voice could clearly be heard as he called to us, "Salvage rights! Salvage rights!"

We had failed to tie the dinghy on properly, leaving *Breezy* behind! We crept back to the dock with our tails between our legs to tie *Breezy* properly before our second bon voyage. Becoming separated right here at the dock was just one of our lessons never to be forgotten.

Our first stop was in the lovely lagoon anchorage of Port Ludlow, visited in April. Once through the very narrow and shallow pass entry, we chose what we felt was the best spot to drop the hook. Don let the anchor down and we were careful to adhere to our newfound anchoring rules. There would be no wild shouting back and forth from the foredeck to the cockpit. Instead, we would use hand signals, determined not to be a spectacle to those around us.

While we were feeling that all was going quite nicely, a boater aboard a boat still some distance from us called out, "Your anchor is right on top of mine!"

Nothing to do but to wave an apology, up the anchor and move some-place else. There was just one problem. The chain stripper didn't want to strip the chain properly as it came aboard. Don had to wrestle the anchor up hand over hand, as use of the electric windlass and a disagreeable chain stripper wasn't possible. The bottom was soft mud that came up with the chain in copious amounts and globs, and by the time he got the anchor aboard Don was covered with mud from head to toe, exhausted and more than a small bit embarrassed by the show he had made for those silently watching in the anchorage.

Tucking our tails between our legs once again, we got ourselves back through the opening of the lagoon and over to the well-appointed marina—never again envisioning ourselves as anything other than the two greenhorns that we were.

The next morning we set off for the quaint and charming town of Friday Harbor, on San Juan Island, where we ordered another chain stripper to arrive the following day by seaplane. There would be untold numbers of repairs to face in the years to come and this was just the beginning. The chain stripper was welded to the windlass and our problem was solved.

There is no end to descriptions of lovely passages amongst the jeweled islands in our Pacific Northwest waters, one lovely anchorage after another. As we ambled along we were very cautious and conservative in everything we did. We studied the charts and read the current tables to determine the best times to take the boat through the many tidal passes that exist in our Pacific Northwest. Each experience had our hearts in our throats, but with the successful accomplishment of each obstacle ahead of us we felt one more step toward becoming sailors after all.

To this day, we are quite sure the good Lord was sitting on our shoulders all of the way and did so for the many years to come.

The next obstacle presenting itself was the big Georgia Strait. After a lovely hiatus at Nanaimo, British Columbia, on Vancouver Island, it was time to take on the twenty-mile stretch looming ahead of us like a major ocean to reach Canada's mainland. Gads, twenty miles? A close ear to the morning forecast, as well as a walk up the dock to a point where we could see the smoke rising from the pulp mill, was our means of deciding if that morning was a go for crossing.

The smoke wasn't rising straight up as hoped for and there was wind from the northwest, the direction toward which we would be going. A low-pressure system forecasted to arrive the next day was to bring very strong southerly winds. The seasoned sailors were planning to stay put, so we felt that we best get moving and head across right then.

Windy Thoughts just leapt through the seas on a close reach, racing along like a purebred racehorse for the finish line. What a feeling of accomplishment! Wow, twenty miles!

With calmer waters, Don's fishing gear came out and he nursed his line in hopes for the big one while we headed across the Malaspina Strait toward Pender Harbor, on British Columbia's mainland. No fish tested his line this time, but there would be many successful opportunities to come. After tucking into Fisherman's Resort Marina we filled water and fuel tanks, washed the boat down, had showers and polished our thumbs as we prided ourselves on our successful voyage. We were really cruising!

After a comfortable night on the dock we headed out of Pender Harbor to make a side trip up Princess Louisa Inlet, whose name conjures up visions of crowning beauty. Up Agamenon Strait to Queen's Reach and on to Prince of Wales Reach, a forty-five mile stretch lined on both sides with steep fjords and mountains, offering up visual impact that stretches the imagination

Our destination was Chatterbox Falls at the head of Princess Louisa Inlet, located just three miles past the Malibu Rapids that we planned to traverse just past slack high tide at 5 pm. Dark clouds suddenly appeared ahead of us, and chop on the water increased to make very slow headway. Water depths were far too great to drop anchor and we didn't reach the Young Life Camp located right on the banks of the Malibu Rapids until 6:30 p.m., missing the slack tide. The non-denominational, Christian affiliated youth camp brings in young people for one week stays and is situated in one of the most stunningly beautiful spots on earth. With no access by roads, the camp is a wonderfully remote place for young people to experience the beauty of nature.

After tying to the dock, we went ashore to ask if we might be allowed to stay the night, hoping to traverse the rapids at the 6 a.m. slack water the following morning. One of the camp directors felt that if we were very careful we could make it right then—and pointed out the safest path. *Windy Thoughts* shot through the tidal rapids to the clapping and hurrahs from the many standing on the rocks ashore.

Six miles further up Princess Louisa Inlet itself, when coming around the last bend in the waterway, our eyes took in the long-awaited sight of Chatterbox Falls, water cascading down a huge fjord in front of us.

The Canadian Parks Service maintains the area and provides a long dock with water, free of charge. At the foot of the falls one can nose right up, drop the anchor and fall back to the rushing and thundering sound of the waterfalls—a sensory overload and an unforgettable spot. Boaters on the dock called to us. They would move a couple of boats about and make room for us.

Relaxing and reading our books in the evenings in our cozy cabin, we listened to music by the Seattle Symphony featuring John Weller on the violin. John has a Lord Nelson 35 sister-ship, purchased soon after ours. He remains a good friend and continues to play the violin and live aboard his *Poeme* in Seattle.

Princess Louisa Inlet, with Chatterbox Falls at its head, remains to this day one of our fondest memories of unsurpassed beauty. But there would be so much more to come during this summer's frolic about these spectacular waters.

The first sight of British Columbia's Desolation Sound comes when rounding Sarah Point and looking up into mind-numbing beauty that takes your breath away. Surely it is the profound sense of being blessed to venture into this part of our world that makes it all worthwhile. No challenge presented by the cruising life could possibly outweigh such rewards. This is what cruising is all about and why we venture out as we do.

We kept our bikes ashore against a tree while anchored off the lovely Marina Park beach on Rebecca Spit. With laundry bags tied behind us, we pedaled six miles from the anchorage around to the little settlement at Heriot Bay. Many explorations to other islands and bays followed, but we invariably returned here, thinking of it as our home base.

What followed was a perfectly glorious summer of cruising about Desolation Sound, anchoring in one spectacularly beautiful anchorage after another. The mountains reached high above us and the blue skies served up endless days of deliciously warm temperatures. We fished for salmon, set out crab pots at day's end, and marveled in the joy of life's simplicity as we experienced these waters, sights and wonders. Every step lent new challenges to face—tidal passes to traverse, an intense interest in weather, the constant learning about the boat, sailing, the workings of a diesel engine and the total enormity of what was for us a new task, a new way of life and a new adventure.

About the third week of August, boats had nearly cleared out of Desolation Sound as families headed home to prepare for the start of school. Our last weeks were spent in the solitude that early fall brings and were a beautiful respite from the summer crowd—a crowd that is easily forgotten even during the summer in the quieter spots.

With some nice following wind we retraced our steps south, making for Beach Gardens Resort and Marina, located at Grief Point, British Columbia.

The dock master introduced us to Bill Alexander, who moored his fishing boat in the marina. Mr. Alexander was an artist whose television program Don had faithfully viewed for some time. Don was thrilled to visit with Mr. Alexander, who invited us to his home the following day.

Mr. Alexander was originally from Germany, and he and his wife had developed their acreage into a park-like setting with a lovely cedar home, a studio and Mr. Alexander's own salmon hatchery—where he estimated that he had 50,000 young salmon.

Mrs. Alexander charmed us with her delicious Alexander cake and lemonade while we sat under their grape arbor. She shared her recipe, and Alexander cake shared many a meal's end in our future as *Windy Thoughts* wended her way around the world.

Summer's end found us moving on south, crossing the "big Georgia Strait" again to anchor off Newcastle Island, a Provincial Park located across the water from Nanaimo, British Columbia.

Breezy's engine had given us trouble all summer—limiting its use and giving us unlimited rowing experience. When we returned to Newcastle Island the engine gave up for good. The next day we rowed the long distance down the harbor to a repair shop where we were faced with the purchase of a new engine—only one in the long line of cruising costs to come.

On the last day of September, 1986, we arrived back on Vancouver Island at Canoe Cove, near Sidney, British Columbia. After a very pleasant night on the dock, it was only a short jaunt down the Saanich Inlet to Butchart Bay, sitting at the foot of the Japanese Gardens—only one of many in the well-known Butchart Gardens frequented by visitors to nearby Victoria.

We picked up one of four empty mooring buoys in the secluded cove, and a small dock gave direct access to the gardens. Looking down at *Windy Thoughts* from a lovely pocket vista in the Japanese Gardens, it was picture book perfect.

Summer had given way to fall and it was time to leave this beautiful spot and head south to home waters. San Juan Island's Roche Harbor Marina provided us with as easy a clearance into the United States as we had experienced when departing. Early in the morning, with fog obliterating much of the harbor, we were treated to the melodic sounds of the chimes from the little white chapel on the hill as it played old hymns resonating throughout the harbor.

Our cruise north had been filled with all of the pleasures and excitement available to everyone who ventures amongst these emerald islands. Sitting in the serene atmosphere of the quiet bay with the old Roche Harbor Hotel ashore, we reflected upon our summer—a time that only a few months before, we had looked upon with awe and wonder at what we might encounter.

Mother Nature had offered up a full plate of never ending and always changing wonders. Sailing up through Washington State's San Juan Islands, on north through British Colombia's Gulf Islands, and then up into the drop-dead beauty of Desolation Sound simply overwhelms the senses. Throughout our travels around the globe, we saw unending beauty, sometimes stunningly so—but never anything to equal the true mountainous, green, clean, beauty of our Pacific Northwest with its abundant and safe anchorages.

OUR FIRST WINTER HOME ABOARD

It was fall and I wouldn't be in front of a class for the first time in twenty-three years. Don was permanently retired, a situation in which he also couldn't quite believe himself to be.

Leaving lovely Roche Harbor, we sailed to Friday Harbor on San Juan Island and joggled down to the southern end of the harbor to drop the hook for what became a very uncomfortable night when the wind came up. Anxious to leave at first light, a very brisk sail in thirty-five-knot winds whisked us to neighboring Orcas Island for a stop at Rosario Resort Marina. The lively winds made the water in the small harbor lively as well, but the harbormaster and several others were waiting to help us with our lines.

Rosario was originally the home of Robert Moran, a ship builder in Seattle whose doctor had told him that he had heart problems and would likely live no more than four more years. Moran came to Orcas Island in 1906 to build a beautiful mansion for his family and lived on Orcas to enjoy this marvelous spot for forty more years!

Rosario passed on to other owners and in the 1950s was turned into a resort. The original mansion houses offices, a restaurant with spectacular views looking down Cascade Bay, the spa with the original pool in the lower level where Mr. Moran had a bowling alley—and, on an upper floor, the music room. From its upper balcony, Mr. Moran regaled his guests with concerts on the pipe organ that was also a player organ. His guests enjoyed the music from below, none the wiser that it wasn't Mr. Moran at the keys. The beautiful Steinway grand piano is still the center of the main music room.

It was the end of the season and we had yet to acquire moorage in Seattle for the winter. Plans were to leave Seattle early the following spring and expand our horizons north to Alaska before setting off across oceans.

One night at Rosario turned into two. Susan and Hal Brown, on *Nomad*, a beautiful Hans Christian Hansa 33 sailboat, introduced themselves and enticed us to spend that extra night.

Susan offered us a ride up to nearby Mount Constitution in Moran State Park, named after Robert Moran, who donated over 2,600 acres of land that became the first State Park in Washington. As so many before us, we were overwhelmed from atop this mountain where one can see the endless islands all about—north beyond Vancouver, British Columbia, and south to Mt. Rainer. We thought it a bit like standing up in heaven and looking down.

Susan and Hal had just sailed north that season from California and intended to make their home aboard in the Northwest. Little did we know that Susan and I would become fast friends, she faithfully writing me and sending us things to ports around the world, her letters often lifting my spirits for days. Unbeknownst to me, Susan saved every letter I wrote her over the years, presenting them to me at the end of our cruising days in 1998, when she and Hal arrived at *Windy Thoughts* in Seattle one day with a large plastic storage container. Inside were eight big ring-binder notebooks, each letter page inserted in a plastic overlay.

Over the years I wrote Susan often in great detail about where we were, what we were experiencing and just what my emotional state might be at any given time, that seeming to vary with the circumstances! It is those many letters to Susan, along with my journals, that form the basis for this book.

At the end of our second day, Rosario's harbormaster, Bill Mason, ambled down the dock to visit and offered us the opportunity to spend the winter at the Rosario marina. When Bill told us the monthly moorage would be $85 including electricity, we settled right in—with full use of the spa showers, the spa hot tub and the hotel.

Bill's wife, Gloria, also worked at the marina and could often be seen fishing for salmon off the end of the docks, a time when big ones were easily hauled in. Though Bill and Gloria no longer live on Orcas, they were central to introducing us to Orcas's many treasures and have remained dear friends ever since.

Rosario sits in a spectacular setting and provided us with endless chances to appreciate nature's beauty. Tucked into Cascade Bay on the east side of East Sound, the lovely Rosario mansion sits on the cliff above the marina. Emerald green hills surround it and the view is south toward the vista of the green islands.

The village of Eastsound is six miles from Rosario Resort and one day we decided to give hitchhiking a try. After all, we had chosen to jump into cruising feet-first and do without all of the amenities of land life the moment we moved aboard the boat. Orcas Island was certainly a safe place to stick out the thumb.

The first car to come along pulled over and when Don opened the door, an oxygen tank fell out onto the road. Don and I scrambled about on our hands and knees in attempts to find the cap that had been knocked off. The driver was taking the tank into the village to be filled at the Medical Center for her visiting daughter. Apologizing profusely, Don tried to lighten the moment with the comment that this would teach her to pick up hitchhikers. We checked with the doctor at the clinic and were relieved to find that no harm was done to the tank.

Later that evening we heard a knock on our hull. Pulling the hatch back, we had the pleasure to meet Earnie Granville, the husband of Elaine Granville, who had given us the lift into town. Earnie was Commodore of the local Orcas Island Yacht Club and invited us to the meeting the following night, kindly offering to pick us up.

Along with the Masons, the Granvilles remain a very special part of our beginnings on Orcas Island—a story that didn't end with this winter-over at Rosario Marina, but had more for us to come at the end of our cruising days.

Strong southerly winds blew into the bay during those winter months, often making it very uncomfortable in the marina, but giving us opportunity to regularly get out on the water and practice our sailing skills. Considerable time was spent studying charts and cruising guides for Alaska in preparation for our upcoming trip. We sailed down to Seattle to add radar and purchased a Loran C to assist in navigation. Satellite navigation would be added later down the line and GPS only a few years later. Everything that was possible had been added at the commissioning—but as anyone with a boat knows, the budget can and generally does go way over the top. Some things had to wait.

We rapidly became attached to the magic of the island, and it wasn't long after our arrival that we visited a realtor. Honoring our need to have something tangible to return to, we had kept fifteen acres at Lake Spokane—but with our eyes and hearts open to what the future may bring. Orcas Island was pulling us into her charms. It has all the natural beauty and peaceful settings one could desire and offered everything that we could ever imagine ourselves wanting in the future. Without a nickel to spare, we gambled and purchased a lot located not far from the resort.

A year later we felt that we had uncomfortably overextended ourselves and, with sadness, called the older couple from whom we had purchased the land and explained that we needed to turn it back to them. Though they didn't know us from Adam, they suggested we wait a year without making payments, time to see what transpired. Fortunately, we resumed payments within a few months, but we will never forget what their great generosity and kindness meant to us in the many years to come when we dreamed of returning to make our home on Orcas Island.

When we did return to Orcas Island these many years later after completing our circumnavigation, we sold this property and purchased eleven acres in the woods, offering us both the privacy that we loved, as well as another spectacular view.

Seattle To
Alaska And Back

Juneau

St. Petersburg

Sitka

Wrangell

Ketchikan

Neah Bay

Seattle

Chapter 4

North to Alaska

The journey is the reward.
—Chinese proverb

By spring we were up and ready for the big cruise to Alaska. While commissioning the boat we had installed an Auto Helm 5000 autopilot and now had our radar and Loran C. We had studied everything we could about cruising north and had talked to many who had been there.

We left Rosario on April 30, 1987, and sailed to Canoe Cove, on Vancouver Island, British Columbia, where we had the boat hauled and anti-fouling applied, finished provisioning and headed out. This trip was looked upon as the big time to us—even though we knew we had far bigger times ahead.

It is about 1,000 miles from Seattle to Juneau, Alaska, and we left in early May in order to have time to enjoy the summer and return safely before the strong southerly winds arrived in early fall. We took advantage of any southerly wind we did get heading north, averaging about seventy miles per day and seven knots of speed, often under power. We weren't heavily loaded, nor were we carrying the extra fuel cans, gear and provisions for extended offshore cruising. *Windy Thoughts* carried 80 gallons of fuel and 180 gallons of fresh water in her tanks. The farther north we traveled, the longer the daylight hours, and we made use of the extra time to get us quickly north.

Northwest waters have big tides, very heavy currents and deadheads of which to always be wary. Deadheads are the floating logs that loosen themselves from log jams and stand straight up just under the surface of the water. Other logs lie parallel to the surface and we kept close watch for such hazards.

Our eyes constantly looked up at mountains that were laced with spectacular waterfalls and verdant green that stretched as far as the eye could see. Secure, well-protected anchorages were available each night. Sometimes, fishermen sharing an anchorage also shared their catch for our dinner. Few other boats were seen—just unending mile after mile of solitude and beauty. When the anchor went down for the night, so did the crab pot in wait for the huge and delicious Dungeness crab. Crab omelets for breakfast, crab salad for lunch, crab cakes for dinner. Would it never end? Let's break this up with some salmon for dinner. Halibut, anyone?

Not to leave the impression that it was an easy life involving only pleasure and relaxation—we continued to be wide-eyed with awe and sometimes terror as we moved along. Tidal rapids whose timing must be figured carefully can sometimes reach speeds of twelve knots, much faster than *Windy Thoughts'* top speed even under power.

While in Canada, our stop at Powell River turned out to be a godsend when a trip to the local chandlers led us to purchase Mustang cruising suits. These resemble snowmobile suits with flotation built in—designed to stave off hypothermia for up to three hours. May's early mornings were very pleasant ashore but often cold out on the water. The suits were the first things we reached for before setting out for the day, peeling them off as temperatures warmed.

The Pacific Northwest enjoys a marine climate and is generally mild year-around, with winter temperatures in the lower forties and water temperature never much above fifty degrees. Our Espar furnace kept our cabin warm, and often all that was needed was the cabin's Trawler lamp to take the chill off early mornings or in the evenings.

Passing north through Desolation Sound, we worked our way through the Yuculta Rapids (running at nine knots) and then through the Dent and Gillard Rapids to Blind Bay. A restaurant kept by a German couple and noted by boaters venturing here in the summer was our destination. Though we were disappointed to find that the restaurant wasn't open, we tied up at the dock and settled in for the night. We would also settle for the fresh salmon that Don had caught earlier in the day, not a bad substitution.

Our departure from pretty Blind Bay had to be timed just right in order to traverse the Green Point and Whirlpool rapids before jetting out into Johnstone Strait. Very brisk winds met our attempt to make for Johnstone Strait. Even the big fishing trawlers were heading back into the anchorage. We joined them to wait it out for four days, staying below with our Espar furnace keeping us toasty as the torrential rain poured down on us and the wind blew its fury day and night. Not a soul was seen from the neighboring fishing trawlers sitting silently at anchor. We whiled away our time reading and creating culinary treats.

Soon we were able to move on to lovely Minstrel Island for a very peaceful stop tied to a small dock. After our fresh salmon dinner, we heard someone come aboard and, suddenly, the hatch was slid back.

The dock manager's seven-year-old son peered below and invited himself down to "inspect the boat", doing a very thorough job, opening lockers and checking everything out while keeping up a running conversation. He was a joy throughout and told us all about his schooling by correspondence from Victoria.

The following morning at 7:00 he appeared again, pushing back the hatch and inviting himself for breakfast. After cereal and toast, we followed him ashore to see his schoolroom in their living quarters behind the little store. A desk, chalkboard, typewriter, and ABCs on the wall provided atmosphere as we were invited to participate in the taping of an interview for Language Arts that he was to get on the mail plane that day. An eight-year-old boy was moving to a nearby logging camp later in the summer and our young host was very excited about the prospect of a friend. Gosh, we were meeting such interesting people!

Don's May twenty-first birthday was celebrated quietly at anchor at the head of Tracey Harbor. The day had become warm and sunny in honor of the occasion. After a dinner of freshly caught halibut, we snuggled in with our books and went early to bed. We planned a 4:15 a.m. start toward the southern part of the Queen Charlotte Strait with a run up to Blunden Harbor on the mainland side.

Eagles swooped about in the trees and Dall's porpoises played about the bow of the boat as we worked our way to the next day's destination. The charts showed many underwater rock hazards at the entrance to Blunden Harbor and we crept in slowly. Once inside the harbor, good anchorage was found off the beach of an old deserted Indian village.

Anxious for an opportunity to walk the beach at low tide on this glorious sunny day, we took *Breezy* down and headed to shore. We were excited to find five trade beads that had been spit up by clams, and Don wanted to have them made into a necklace for me. It never occurred to us that it might be wrong to take the beads—but we learned this very soon on up the line!

The crab pot went down and produced two huge Dungeness crabs for dinner. Is there anything better than fresh Dungeness crab? We were not missing the supermarkets at all.

Inside the bay, a small island was home to old Indian burial grounds where remains were still in the trees. Believing it to be a sacred place, we didn't go ashore. Our respect for the burial grounds aside, Don swears that our trade bead hunt was the cause of the events surrounding our departure the following morning.

I was on the bow, peering into the dark, when the boat suddenly hit an underwater rock, and a horrid crunching sound accompanied the sudden change in course. Don reversed in panic and, fortunately, *Windy Thoughts* came quickly back off the rock while our hearts did a flip flop. Rushing below to check through-hulls and bilges, we breathed huge sighs of relief when we didn't see any water. Don marked it on the chart and named it Joyce's Rock.

Blunden Harbor had certainly been a memorable stop, and those trade beads were indeed made into a beautiful necklace at summer's end.

After that little scare, we were out into the Queen Charlotte Strait running between Vancouver Island and mainland British Columbia. The morning's start only added to my nervous anticipation about the northern stretch of the Strait, open to the ocean on its westerly side. Heading north in fifteen knots of northwesterly wind, we were experiencing our first real ocean swells sweeping in and giving us a very rolling ride.

The wind increased and I radioed the light tender on Egg Island, a small island farther on in the Strait. He assured me that the swells would ease after we passed Egg Island. For 8.5 hours, I stayed glued to my spot, afraid to move when the wind not only didn't ease off, it increased.

When Don asked me, "Don't you want a cushion to sit on?", my answer was a quick, "No! That would make me three inches higher and I don't want to be three inches higher!"

Windy Thoughts loved it, however, and Don was enjoying the way she handled everything.

Once across the Strait and into the lee of Calvert Island, all eased to comfort again and we ran up Fitzhugh Sound and into lovely Pruth Bay, to anchor for the night. Our crossing of the Queen Charlotte Strait had left us exhilarated that we had been out in the "big stuff" and that *Windy Thoughts* didn't mind it at all.

Crab whetted our appetites for dinner while we watched three otters play about the shore. A walk across the isthmus took us to a spectacular unspoiled beach on the "outside", a wild and rugged coast. Awesome thoughts swam in our heads as we gazed out at the vast Pacific Ocean, knowing that we would be out there someday soon.

It was at Bella Bella, our next day's stop, that we learned of our error in taking the trade beads found in Blunden Harbor. Bella Bella is a small reserve of Heitlick Indian heritage and sported a brand new dock with fuel. *Windy Thoughts* was allowed to tie to the dock for the night, and we took on fuel and headed ashore to visit the local school which was also the local Cultural Resource Center. It was here that we learned one never takes any artifact found anywhere. Our happiness over having the choice blue trade beads, however, outweighed any feelings of guilt.

On our way back to the boat we were stopped by some locals who advised that it might be wise to pull off the dock and anchor across the way. At night the locals, buoyed by spirits of the bottled kind, were known to get off a few potshots with their guns at boats at the dock. We hurriedly took the advice!

Moving on north, our radar got a good workout when fog and drizzle reduced visibility to zero. We crept forward like a cat on the hunt, relieved when Bishop Bay began to appear in front of the bow. Bishop Bay had a float of logs and a rudimentary bathhouse ashore, built over a fantastic natural hot springs. Don had spikes along just for such occasions; he drove them into the logs, using weights to keep the fenders securely in place—and we tied right to the log float.

Soon we were joined by the *Sarah L*, a pleasure trawler out of Vancouver with Pat Lobsinger aboard. Pat was traveling alone, just back on his feet after a very long stretch of heart troubles solved with surgery. Pat's goal was to get into Alaskan waters.

A long leisurely soak in the hot springs gave us an opportunity to enjoy Pat's good company, and afterwards we invited Pat to dinner aboard *Windy Thoughts*. When Pat asked about the dress code, we laughingly replied that it was formal, of course. Were we ever surprised to see him working his way along the log in a suit and tie, drizzle surrounding him as he climbed aboard! Don and I were suitably attired in our warmest sweats.

The *Sarah L* and *Windy Thoughts* stumped along together to Prince Rupert, our last stop in Canada. Pat was an avid halibut fisherman and had a mold to make his own lead lures, heating the lead on his perpetually burning diesel stove in the cabin. Pat made it into Alaska and up to Ketchikan before heading on back south to a worried wife—to whom he hadn't let on that he would venture quite that far! His recipe for the "Best Boat Bread" is with us still, and we made it often as we wobbled our way around the world.

Prince Rupert is the northern terminus of road in this part of Canada. Our interests turned to the Dairy Queen, where we sank our teeth into double burgers—a real treat after so much seafood!

It was fully light by 3:30 a.m., and after a quick breakfast we were underway from Prince Rupert. A shortcut through the narrow and rock-strewn Venn Passage carried us out into Chatham Strait, and then out into Dixon Entrance—a ten-mile stretch of water open to the vast Pacific Ocean. Fog and difficult visibility had yielded to sunny skies, and any qualms that we had about Dixon Entrance disappeared as we headed out into beautiful calm waters—and motored the entire distance!

Ninety-three miles separated Prince Rupert from Ketchikan, but with lovely conditions we pressed on and made Ketchikan by 7 p.m., covering the entire distance in daylight. Alaska at last!

This small city is nestled at the bottom of surrounding mountains and is on the cruise ship itinerary. Three big ships were in the harbor, and we watched people herded into and out of the shore boats for their hour in town. Don and I were happy to be aboard our own *Windy Thoughts*, even if they may have been enjoying more luxuries.

Misty rain and fog had persisted throughout the trip north through Canada, but once reaching Alaska we met with a summer with predominant sunshine and lovely conditions!

But not quite yet, as we had a few ensuing days of rain as we made our way north to Wrangell. Its harbor was full of fishing boats rafted four deep and we too had to raft up. We didn't find the town appealing on our initial walkabout—but our attitude was to make a complete turnaround at summer's end when we stopped here on a sunny day. My, what a difference the sun makes!

During the inclement weather at Wrangell, we stayed below in our comfortable cabin. Don enjoyed books while I studied ham licensing theory and CW (Morse code). I wasn't to put in any great effort until forced to do in so in later months, when true offshore cruising suddenly loomed ahead. Don had shown much more persistence in learning celestial navigation!

The convenient and beautiful Wrangell Narrows are located between Wrangell and Petersburg, a truly narrow twenty-mile stretch of water with strong currents, frequent cruise ships and ferries that require close attention.

Sure enough, no sooner had we entered the channel when around the bend directly in front of us loomed a huge Alaskan ferry. Very fortunate to be adjacent to the first deep water turn off, we squeaked off to the side—where *Windy Thoughts* rolled heavily as the ferry passed us so closely it seemed that we could reach out with our boat pole and tap it on its side. The few passengers who ventured out onto her decks on this fine sunny day stared down at us as we waved hellos. Guess we little guys don't demand much respect!

With its Scandinavian heritage, Petersburg is known as Little Norway, a beautiful town where we went alongside a dock and were hooked to power for the first time in several weeks. I had cleaned crab while underway for a big crab salad for our dinner. We decided to stay an extra day just to enjoy the town, do laundry and meet locals—who gave us good advice about foregoing Glacier Bay, suggesting that we visit Tracey Arm instead.

In broad daylight at 3:00 the following morning, we were up and out into the channel to begin the trek to Tracey Arm, located in Holkam Bay—at whose head sits the South Sawyer Glacier. Just outside the entrance to Holkam Bay we met with our first icebergs. They dotted the entrance and their natural beauty simply overwhelmed us. The day was overcast, lending a deeper shade to their ice blue coloring. Range markers mark the course into the big bay. We lined ourselves up and followed them very carefully to cross a bar.

As we headed up into Tracey Arm we were surrounded by even more icebergs—some as big as houses and the most beautiful and breathtaking natural sight we have ever seen. Tracey Arm is formed by a fjord, with green mountains coming straight down to the water's edge and hundreds of waterfalls that pound at the senses. Between the icebergs and the scenery, we were in a virtual wonderland.

The old saying about the tip of the iceberg being only 10 percent of the whole is true, and it was necessary to work very slowly through the icebergs! Twenty-five miles up and at the head of Tracey Arm, we could see another sailboat in near the South Sawyer Glacier itself. We made our way closer to the boat and received a radio call asking us to pull alongside for introduc-

tions. The owner was a private charter out of Juneau with a couple from
California aboard. The captain told
us of an anchorage near the entrance
of Tracey Arm, in no-name bay, as it
is called by locals.

While taking in the wonders of
South Sawyer Glacier, we listened to
the story of a boat that was recently
anchored in the adjacent Endicott
Arm, at whose head is another glacier. During the night one of the big
icebergs moved right up the chain
and consumed the boat, slowly sink-
ing it. The fellow aboard was alone but was able to get into the dinghy and
get to shore—where he waited for a week before another boat came into the
arm.

When *Windy Thoughts* worked her way back out of Tracey Arm, we were
happy to find the little no-name bay. The boat from Juneau was already sitting
at anchor and the radio came alive with a call to *Windy Thoughts*. We were
invited for a steak dinner. Having already stuffed ourselves on my tuna noodle
casserole on the trip down the inlet, we had to politely decline. Don didn't
soon forget the foiled opportunity for steak verses tuna casserole—but we did
go aboard for a visit and found the California couple very curious about our
live-aboard life.

Juneau was just a couple days' travel north, and its nice marina, town
and fun gold rush history, added to a visit to nearby Mendenhall Glacier,
made it a fun stop. Though Don and I had thoroughly enjoyed the pleasures
of Alaska's wild scenery, Juneau was a good change of pace from our usual
days. And we had only to glance upwards to be reminded that we were in
Alaska, because those ever present mountains rose in their beauty right out
of Juneau's streets.

It was impossible to complain about summer weather in Alaska when we
were enjoying temperatures of eighty degrees with lots of sunshine! Juneau,
like Ketchikan, is a stop for cruise ships and they seemed rather monstrous—
even out of place, really, in so serene an environment.

We hoped to take the train up over the Chillcut Pass, but when we
learned the train wasn't running that summer we decided to forego Skagway.
We would instead make our way toward Sitka, giving us more time for the
west side of Prince of Wales Island.

One of the interesting stops along the way was Funter Bay, where an
abandoned cannery with an eerie and rather sad atmosphere whispered to us

of the past glory days. We wandered about an old cemetery where stones were etched with names of old sea captains and their ships. Such history this quiet, abandoned spot could tell!

Continuing on down Chatham Strait to Tenekee Springs, we came upon one of the most charming little spots in Southeast Alaska. Sitting at the water's edge, Tenekee Spring's homes and few stores perch precariously (it seems) on stilts over the water—or hang from the mountainside. A footpath winds throughout the town and beneath the mountainside buildings that offer the same simple dignity as those homes stretching their arms out over the water.

A Fourth of July celebration was to take place on our second day at Tenekee Springs, with a potluck dinner in town. Fishermen aboard the fishing boats that stopped here for the occasion brought salmon for the barbecue— and free hot dogs, buns, and tableware were provided by the local store. Invited to join in the potluck, I baked a chocolate cake to take.

The Fourth of July parade in Tenekee Springs goes down in our memory as certainly the best we have ever seen. It lasted fully five minutes beginning to end, with the one vehicle in town, a small local fire truck, in the lead—followed by three women cheerleaders, a mother pushing her baby in a dock cart and a small four-wheel tractor pulling a wagon full of hay, atop which sat a five-piece country band. Last and best, four women did a twirling routine with back-brushes in honor of the local bathhouse where the town bathes in steaming, natural hot springs.

A hike of perhaps 100 or more wooden steps up the steep mountainside brought us to the new school that was soon to open. Tenekee Springs had only eleven students, but the school was one of the most beautifully equipped and visually appealing schools imaginable, with full living quarters for the teacher. I couldn't help but wonder at the fun of living and teaching at a place like this.

Windy Thoughts would be passing through the Sergius Narrows on the way to Sitka. We had a book on Alaska that showed a picture of a huge red bell buoy, submerged by the strong current located in the Narrows. Ever mindful of that picture, the passage was timed very carefully and *Windy Thoughts* zoomed through to make it safely into Sitka. Just one more exciting part of the adventure!

The Old Russian Orthodox Church and the National Park Service's Totem Walk were two of the more interesting spots at Sitka, an amazingly interesting locale. Judy and Virgil Hennen of San Juan Island, a neighboring island to Orcas in Washington's San Juan Islands, were in the marina aboard their lovely *St. Jude*, a fifty-foot De Fever power yacht. What fun to meet them and to enjoy bumping along in tandem for awhile. After settling down to land life we have happily renewed our friendship.

Ell Cove offered us a picture perfect respite during a particularly uncomfortable day of southerlies. While the wind made the waters outside disagreeable, on the inside we were rafted up to *St. Jude*—and had only to visit across the rails to while away our time.

With *St. Jude*, we pulled up anchor the following morning and headed out of the entrance to find about 300 seiners working the immediate area. The salmon season had opened that morning—lasting only two days. The fishermen worked fast and hard, small tenders carrying the end of the net from the mother ship and making a big circle with the net to entrap the fish. The restrictions on fishing and its short season make hard and dangerous times for the fishermen.

Flat and calm seas made a comfortable passage to Baronof Warm Springs, our next destination. Just outside the entrance to the bay we were greeted by three whales, and inside there was more hectic activity. A float house was tied to the end of a small dock and, about an hour prior to our arrival, had begun to sink. The owners, with two small children aboard, had been towing the float house behind their small tug en route to Thorne Bay, no small distance. The tug blew an engine in Chatham Strait and the family had been in here two weeks, making repairs.

Everything they owned was onboard and the few boaters there were hauling all earthly goods off the float house and onto the dock. Piles of clothes were carried off and photos were lined up to dry on the dock. A big fish-processing barge pulled in directly behind us to lend assistance with a pump that didn't produce much in results. Thankfully, a Coast Guard helicopter arrived and dropped two additional pumps onto the tiny piece of beach, a maneuver that was heart-stopping to watch.

Frantic pumping resumed, followed by further sinking of the float house as well as hearts, until finally, water began to recede. The furniture was lost, but everyone helped to wring out their clothes before taking them to a lady living in a nearby cabin. There was no power in her house, but she ran them through her wringer before hanging all up to dry. Hearty people, these Alaskans are!

St. Jude left Baronof Warm Springs with us and, because they made one or two knots of speed on us, awaited us at anchor in Red Bluff Bay. Humpback whales gave us a real show for over an hour as we moved down Chatham Strait, and our arrival at Red Bluff Bay left us speechless at the beauty of the surrounding red rock inside the bay.

After a shared dinner, we slept well in the tranquility. In the morning

Don and Virgil took off to outer regions for halibut fishing in Virgil's Boston Whaler tender— while Judy and I baked ginger cookies aboard *St. Jude*. This gave us all energy to move on to Port Alexander the next day, where we found Haagen Daz ice cream, surely one of the highlights of the summer! Ginger cookies and ice cream—two special treats all at once! *St. Jude* was all-electric, and we bought as much ice cream as could be crammed into her freezer for later indulgences.

Fishing boats were rafted four deep, and with our boats on the outside we all went to bed early to get a dawn start around Cape Decision to Sumner Strait the next day. Once across Sumner Strait we worked our way through the narrow, rocky and shallow El Capitan Passage. It required careful attention and navigation but was incredibly beautiful. Two black bears along the banks seemed to want to pose just for us, giving us yet another spectacular camera moment. We were headed for the Hole in the Wall, an anchorage in the San Lorenzo Islands, on the outside of Prince of Wales Island.

The Hole in the Wall will live on in memory for the "big fishing story"— for it was here that Virgil caught a ninety-two-pound halibut. At five feet, it was a challenge to drag the big fish to a fishing barge at anchor where it could be weighed. Virgil gave it to a forest service boat skipper to take home for his family, and our men were high on their fish story for days.

The Indian village of Klawock, on Prince of Wales Island, was our final destination with *St. Jude*. These fun folks would be heading south and we would miss their good company. We walked about the Totem Park above the town, did laundry at the local Laundromat and celebrated my birthday aboard *St. Jude*. Another picture perfect setting kept us there for a few days before Don and I retraced steps to Wrangell, as we began our own journey south.

We were finding this life, with all of its perils and adventure combined, much to our liking so far.

It was the second week of August and precisely the time of the salmon's spawning season. Anchored in Anan Bay, we took *Breezy* to shore and hiked along a trail through the woods to a bear observatory located just above a set of falls. Salmon by the hundreds, if not thousands, return to these falls to fight their way upstream. Breakfast, lunch or dinner is mighty handy for the resident bear population during this time of year and the bears have a heyday.

We weren't disappointed as, just ten feet from us, a huge black bear came ambling along. The bear observatory was a small, deck-like structure with no walls for protection and we were a mere twenty feet above the falls. The bear headed right into the falls and was soon joined by two equally huge bears, one having ambled past Don within five feet! Fortunately, they were far more interested in the salmon than in us. Our boat horn had been brought along as "protection".

The falls were thick with salmon fighting to reach their spawning grounds just over the top in the shallow, calm creek. Once into the calm water the salmon spawn and soon die, and the water was black with their numbers. All a part of their species' life cycle, it is a wonder of nature that brings them from the ocean back to their origins.

Still full of wonder, we moved on to the fishing village of Meyer's Chuck and onto its beautiful Alaska State float, one of several found throughout the summer and well cared for. This tiny village had a charm all its own and, of course, sat in another spectacular setting that had us looking up at the surrounding mountains awestruck at the splendor that is Alaska.

Our plans were to head soon to Ketchikan, where we would prepare for our passage back to Puget Sound. We wouldn't be wending our way down through the islands as we did going north, but would head out into the open ocean for a 450-mile passage, a big change from the 1,000 miles going north through the islands. Our return would be a fast one, sailing south on the outside, the west side of Vancouver Island.

It was at Loring where we encountered our first mouse aboard. *Windy Thoughts* rested up against another state float, and a small village of six houses nestled amongst the trees. We met Sergio, a Brazilian who came aboard with his classical guitar. Who would have thought to be listening to this fine music in this remote little spot? Sergio invited us to his home to meet his wife Cathy, and we listened to the adventures they shared living here and relying on their high- powered open boat to take them into Ketchikan to work.

The following afternoon the wind began to pipe up—and with it big swells. *Windy Thoughts* began to bounce and buck like a wild horse. Worse would come as the waves built, and we moved off the dock and onto a float adjacent to a long forest walk. We were just behind an island in the bay, and there we found calm conditions. Two small powerboats from Ketchikan were also moored alongside the float.

That evening a little boy on one of the boats could be heard complaining that a mouse had gotten into his peanut butter sandwich. It was then that we learned that several mice were seen scampering back and forth on the dock! Don and I closed all up tight, but during the night could hear rustling in the chain locker. Sure enough, we had a mouse!

I rapidly put dry foods into the refrigerator and Don set traps in the lockers—and before very long we caught a little deer mouse. Little deer mouse or not, he wasn't welcome aboard and Don gently tossed him off the boat. The next morning I bleached every inch of each locker, not a difficult task at this point in our cruising life. It would prove to be much harder a few years later when faced with rat problems in Southeast Asia and lockers full to the hilt.

SOUTH FROM ALASKA

It was rapidly approaching time for the passage south and we left Loring for nearby Ketchikan to make preparations to depart by the end of the month. Along the way, we stopped at a state float at Helm Bay, where we sat in total solitude for four peaceful days while we studied charts and cleaned the boat. A small cabin ashore provided safe respite for anyone caught out in this remote area. A wood stove with a supply of wood, a bed with springs, and table and chairs all looked inviting should one come upon the cabin in time of need!

Lane and Sandi Findley, owners of Cruising Yachts, were flying up from Seattle to crew with us on our southbound passage. In civilized Ketchikan's marina, we made ready for our upcoming experience. I planned menus, did laundry, baked batches of chocolate chip and oatmeal cookies and made trips to the market. Don checked all gear and we spit-polished everything. Lane and Sandy were to arrive on Monday, August 31, 1987. Weather permitting, we would take off as soon as they were aboard. Don and I were nearly beside ourselves with both excitement and nervous anxiety about what was to come.

Sunday marked our catastrophe (as we then considered it to be), starting while we went to the market for some fresh things. Unbeknownst to us we hadn't completely blown out the trawler lamp when we left the boat.

On our return, we started down the companionway steps into a cabin whose every centimeter was covered with a thick, black, oily film from smoke that had been pouring out of the lamp for three hours. Nothing had escaped the oily black deluge. The only positive thing we could conjure up was the fact that there had been no fire.

The film didn't wipe off easily. Thorough cleaning with soap and water, and much elbow grease and sweat were needed, and needed fast! Don carried all cushions up to the cockpit and blew on them for hours; wiping them off was impossible, as rubbing only smeared the oily mess, but Don's blowing technique worked.

We cleaned from the ceiling right down to the cabin sole, sure that we would never be finished by the time Sandi and Lane's plane arrived the next day. However, by 11 p.m. all was sparkling clean, and I had managed to make a pasta salad, bake a corned beef casserole, a pan of Mexican lasagna, and two Alexander cakes. We collapsed into bed, bone weary with the effort. Tired enough that the prospect of setting off for our first ocean passage didn't even deter us from sleep!

The following morning dawned dreary with very heavy rain. A kindly, neighboring live-aboard sailor insisted that we use his car to get to the airport. Donning full foul-weather gear we set out. Sandi and Lane disembarked the plane from Seattle in shorts and T-shirts, big smiles on their faces and ready for the challenges ahead. The first step was to change into their own foulies right in the airport's lobby.

We were not to leave that day. Weather reports predicted a strong high-pressure system to come in the next day, bringing gale force winds out of the north and favorable for us.

On the following morning *Windy Thoughts* backed out of the marina as nice as could be, setting her sights for distant shores. We headed down Nichols Passage into Clarence Strait and sailed out into the open ocean. By now, we were experiencing big ocean swells, beautiful sunshine and clear skies. Sunshine does so much to soothe the soul when you are setting out on your first ocean passage.

Our watch system was set up for three hours on, giving each of us good rest time. Sandi and I rapidly succumbed to mal de mer, while Don and Lane ate their way through the cookies and the prepared meals. We started out with fifteen to eighteen knots of favorable wind, about perfect, and weather reports predicted much more in the next few days. I wasn't particularly excited about the predicted "much more".

Sure enough, by day two we were surfing along in thirty-knot northerly winds, with perfectly clear blue skies and sunshine all day as we sailed off the west side of Vancouver Island—getting pushed well out to sea. That sunshine does make all the difference, doesn't it?

Night watches were a new experience for Don and me, and I forged on with my duties regardless of occasional stomach reactions. Sandi was a real trouper as well, and we dutifully stood our watches as the boat crashed through the waves, marveling at how big they were as they unendingly rolled in from our quarter, seeming that they would surely come crashing down upon us. But instead, *Windy Thoughts* would lift to each one and ride up and over with the wave as we soared down into the trough of the next one.

As the forces of Mother Nature rained down around us, we were ever thankful for a strong, blue water boat. Neither Don nor I had experienced the open ocean before and this passage was preparing us for our journey from Seattle to San Francisco, very possibly in similar or far livelier conditions. Don was in his glory. *Windy Thoughts* was rolling along without much attention from anyone and we hadn't even taken a reef in the main or rolled in the head sail. Though the ride was anything but smooth, we were averaging better than seven knots over the ground most of the way.

Our Fleming wind vane steered for the entire 4.5 day trip to the Strait of Juan de Fuca. The vane held the course, worked flawlessly and stood up to its over-built, stainless steel construction. Peeking out of the companionway as the boat surfed down twenty-foot seas, we watched it dutifully working back and forth, back and forth—never seeming to mind the onslaught it was taking. Hanging on for dear life with the motion of the boat in these conditions was new to us, as was the difficulty accomplishing the simplest task—and all the while attempting rest when not on watch as the huge seas crashed and banged about us.

Windy Thoughts didn't seem to give the conditions a thought as she sailed along in total glee. I wasn't experiencing total glee, but I have to admit to being awed by the might of the ocean!

We were dead reckoning south from Ketchikan, as the Loran C was of no use. On Don's 3 a.m. watch on the fourth night out, he picked up a light from the west coast of Vancouver Island. Counting the flashes and seconds between, he got a fix of our position and we knew we were off Barkley Sound. Don set our course for the entrance to the Strait of Juan de Fuca.

A few hours later we entered the Strait in rapidly decreasing wind and were soon riding huge swells east, reaching Port Angeles at 9 p.m. that evening. A fishing derby would commence the following morning. The marina was full and no anchorage existed nearby.

Sorely tired, we were forever grateful to Dick Rasmussen, president of Northwest Hinckley sales in San Francisco, whose beautiful fifty-nine-foot Hinckley was tied to the outside end of one dock. He invited us to raft up to him, and we all got a great night's sleep before Lane and Sandi were off the following morning to Seattle and back to their Cruising Yachts business. They were a godsend to us on our first ocean passage. Mr. Rasmussen was a godsend to us on the completion to this passage.

This kind man had been in Alaskan waters for the summer and was awaiting crew for the passage back to San Francisco. We enjoyed the next two days with him in Port Angeles while he made meal plans for his crew and shopped for provisions. When I was able to show him how to operate the washers and dryers in the local Laundromat, I prided myself on something I knew about! And I would get so good at laundry chores in the coming years, but seldom with the luxury of a Laundromat!

Upon learning of our plans to be starting our offshore adventures the next season, Mr. Rasmussen generously offered us his slip at the St. Francis Yacht Club, in San Francisco, the following summer. His own boat would be out cruising during the summer months and the slip would be empty. He was even to mail us precise directions and an aerial photo of the marina, showing the slip's location. This kind and very generous offer would put us in good stead when we reached San Francisco, and without it we likely would not have had the enjoyment that we had in that exciting city by the bay.

Our first ocean passage was now successfully completed and we looked forward to the time when *Windy Thoughts* would take us much farther in the future. Our beautiful Pacific Northwest had been good to us, giving us pristine spots into which we poked our noses, green mountains to continually take in with wonder, waterfalls, abundant seafood, and small villages filled with amazingly able and stalwart people. This was our time to be together and to savor wonders such as we never had before experienced.

It was a wonderful beginning to a time that would give us even more wonder and joy, and we knew that the magic was only beginning.

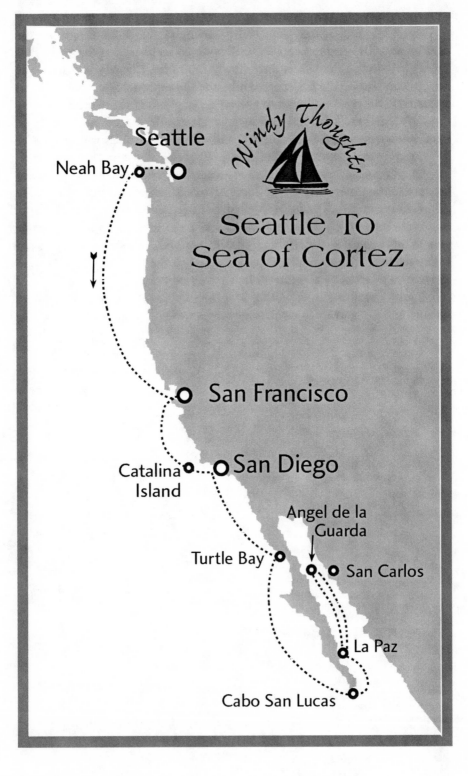

Chapter 5

Sailing Away From the Safe Harbor

The ship is safer in the harbor, but isn't meant for that.
—Anonymous

Our home from the fall of 1987 through August 1988 was Winslow Wharf Marina, located on Bainbridge Island in Puget Sound. The quiet Winslow village was within walking distance, and the Washington State Ferry carried us for a short thirty-minute ride across Elliot Bay into downtown Seattle.

Much preparation was underway for what Don kept referring to as real blue water sailing. We had the proverbial list that accompanies such events and which never quite seems to shorten. Dreams of basking in the warm Mexican sun kept the stars in our eyes.

Don had a thirty gallon auxiliary aluminum fuel tank built to fit in the bilge beneath the engine under the companionway stairs. Together, we took the several-hundred-pound engine out using the come-along that Don had insisted be a part of his tool supply—and that we would more than once be thankful to have along in later years.

In addition to purchasing *The Merck Manual* (a medical manual), we purchased the book *Where There is No Doctor*, written in the simplest of layman's terms to help with the most common medical problems and emergencies. On its cover, the picture shows villagers from a remote region carrying an ill or injured person across a river on a homemade gurney. Meant to aid people in remote places, the book proved our handiest reference. The chapter on the need to keep pigs out of the house proved that even the most basic facts weren't overlooked. The illustrations were simple and easily understood by anyone and it proved to be a wonderful reference to have aboard for the crew's use and for sharing with local people.

Seattle is known for its high ratio of CPR-trained people and it is said that if you are going to have a heart attack, have it in Seattle! We took advantage of the training offered at a local fire department, updated our Red Cross skills, and hoped that little of this knowledge would be called upon while alone at sea—or at anchor in a remote area.

A local Seattle pharmacist who was experienced in providing medical kits for fishing boats made up our medical kit, including morphine should one of us get badly hurt. Over the years we replaced outdated drugs and added new and, fortunately, needed very few of its contents.

Endless evenings were spent planning the contents of our overboard, or grab and run, bag—an orange, waterproof river float bag purchased at an Army/Navy surplus store. Much thought was given to precise items that might help us to survive if we had to leave the boat and resort to the life raft.

Don prepared a hand line for fishing and a small block of wood on which to cut, adding a sharp knife and various lures. Only one prescription drug was necessary and we added aspirin, seasick pills, vitamins, hydrocortisone cream and ChapStick. Various sizes of Ziplocs were added for catching drinking water, two collapsible water jugs, as well as a small solar distillation device. There was cotton underwear, cotton T-shirts, crushable sun hats, sunscreen and a package of baby wipes.

Basic survival equipment included matches, a smoke signal device given to us by the crew of a large ship, extra flares, a mirror for signaling, and pencils and paper. Don included his small handheld computer with a navigation module. We purchased a plastic Davis sextant just for the bag as well as a book on navigating using only positions of latitude.

Dugall Robertson's *Survive the Savage Sea,* was also included, chronicling the Robertson family's survival when a killer whale hit their sailboat off Panama, sinking it in a matter of seconds. With little time to gather survival gear they got both the life raft and the dinghy into the water—and towed the dinghy behind the life raft.

When the life raft began to leak water several days later, all five people had to move into the seven-foot dinghy that proved to be their lifesaver. The story of the family's survival for weeks on end in a dinghy with two adults, twin eight-year-old boys and a sixteen-year-old crewmember was filled with practical advice on how to survive when you have little else but your brains and a small penknife.

Drinking water was our number one priority, so in addition to the small solar distillation device, we purchased the Survivor 07 hand-operated water desalinator that produced a pint of drinkable water in thirty minutes of pumping. Granola bars were a priority but these tended to disappear on long passages, necessitating frequent replacement!

The responsibility to study for and pass the exam for my Ham Radio license was full upon me, and I diligently crammed technical theory into my head for the three weeks prior. During the Morse code section of the exams the messages must be rapidly decoded and written down. The General exam required proficiency at thirteen correct words a minute—no mistakes. I worked to make myself ready for this with hours of practice at twenty words per minute.

The opportunity to sit for the Novice level license came when a two-day crash course was offered in Seattle, given by an ace from California. I studied hard, was prepared when I walked into the class, and walked out with the license. Only one more exam to pass!

We sailed south to Bremerton where the various test levels were given in classrooms of a large church. I arrived early and wandered about the church, stopping to play old hymns on a piano, attempting to divert my mind from the business ahead.

As people arrived for the exams, we all took seats in the classroom, every one of us sweating in anticipation. After sitting for both the written part of the general exam and then the Morse code, our papers were checked, and I breathed huge sighs of relief to learn that I had passed the General Level requirements that would allow me to work the radio bands we would be using as we wended our way around the world. One more step towards becoming offshore sailors.

Meanwhile, Don diligently continued practicing his celestial navigation skills as the months flew by and we marked each completed task off the list.

Sandi and Lane Finley inquired about joining us on the trip to San Francisco, and we jumped at the opportunity to have these good mates along. Lane had fairly extensive offshore sailing experience and wanted Sandi to get as much as possible because they planned to be full- time cruisers themselves. This would be the last time we were ever to have crew aboard and from San Francisco onward we sailed our own boat. Sandi and Lane would meet up with us at Neah Bay, where we would hang a left and sail out into the open Pacific Ocean.

The moment that we had worked toward for so many years arrived on the morning of August 23, 1988. We threw off the dock lines at Winslow Wharf Marina at 3 a.m. in pitch black to catch the tide that would help to carry us north from the safety and comfort of the marina life toward Neah Bay. This little haven sits conveniently at the northeast point of the Olympic peninsula and at the outermost reaches of the Strait of Juan de Fuca. Fishing boats and other seafarers hole up in Neah Bay, awaiting good weather to either exit the Strait of Juan de Fuca into the Pacific Ocean, or to enter the Strait upon return.

Winds frequently blow from a westerly direction through the Strait, so a nice easterly breeze behind us would be our dream. Dreams aside, we headed into the Strait, and it wasn't long before our ride became bumpy with westerly winds right on the nose. It wasn't a warm morning and to compound our growing anxieties, fog began to roll in. Soon we could barely see the bowsprit—to say nothing of the ships plying the waters of the Strait. Both Don and I had our eyes glued to the radar as we listened to the big ships hail their warnings with foghorns, sounding forlorn in the murky environment, but oh so close!

I tried hard not to allow myself to dwell on thoughts of the what-if kind. What if our big adventure ended right here with a close encounter with one of these big ships? It was best to forge ahead with seeming confidence, so I did my best to hide my jitters. My stomach began to react to the motion of the boat as it punched into oncoming seas— and likely to nerves as well, as mal de mer did its best to defeat me.

We nervously tracked the big ships on the radar until it quit functioning in our first half-hour. Unable to slink below and curl up into the fetal position, my job was to share Don's vigil, keep us away from the ships and to do my part in this boating experience. This was our life now.

Windy Thoughts did not yet sport satellite navigation aboard, and the Loran C had been of little use on the previous summer's voyage to Alaska. It didn't give us any help now. I sincerely hoped we wouldn't miss Neah Bay and end up heading right out into the Pacific in the fog!

As the day wore on, the fog lifted, and jitters turned to enjoyment as we passed through this beautiful area. Neah Bay turned out to be exactly where the charts had indicated, and proving to be a snug village with a dock as well as good anchorage. With sighs of relief, we dropped the anchor, tidied up the boat and headed to bed for a good sleep. Our great adventure was underway!

Sandi and Lane arrived the following day. Good friend Barry McCormick drove them to Neah Bay and said his bon voyage, glad that this time the dinghy was secured on deck!

Over dinner, we all anxiously discussed the coming voyage. It definitely didn't look great for heading out in the morning, and we all snuggled down into our sea berths with plans to enjoy the village the following day.

Windy Thoughts lay ready to charge out into the Pacific Ocean and begin her blue water cruising. Don and I lay with excitement running through our veins, for our dream and all that we had worked so hard to accomplish had come true. *Windy Thoughts* had taken us on the most beautiful summer cruising and was now prepared to take us to more distant shores. We were nearly breathless with anticipation.

Three other cruising sailboats sat with us in Neah Bay, waiting for the weather window to make the same passage. Only one had a dedicated weather fax aboard and we all welcomed the shared weather information. Wind was blowing southwesterly at a steady twenty-five knots that would be against us heading south. What we needed was wind out of the northerly quadrant behind us to give us a good push south.

The next day, we eagerly listened to every snippet of predictions and final preparations were put in place. With predictions for the southwesterly to die down sometime the following day, it was decided that *Windy Thoughts* would jump off in the morning—with expectation that better conditions would await us as the day wore on. We would listen in to weather radio once more in the morning and make the final decision then.

I had prepared food in advance and had bins of oatmeal and peanut butter cookies ready for those with stalwart stomachs, a casserole for that first night's dinner, lots of sandwich meats and breakfast items in the refrigerator—and other food ready for easy but nutritious dinners at sea.

Sea berths were made up and at the ready prior to Sandi and Lane's arrival, charts were duly pored over, every line was ready, water and fuel were topped off—and there was little else to do now—but to do it!

We expected a passage of about six days, perhaps seven, and my stomach was in knots of excitement mixed with stark fear that I attempted to hide. What in the world could we possibly be thinking, that we could just head out around nearby Cape Flattery—and take on the Pacific Ocean as if we were heading out for a camping trip? Were we really ready for this? All of the things that possibly could go wrong tried to take over my thoughts but I pushed them aside, kept a smile on my face and told myself that this is what we had planned for years and that, yes, we were really almost on our way into the wild blue yonder.

The fact that Sandi and Lane were aboard was a distinctly comforting thought, as this leg of the journey is known to sometimes offer up some of the harshest conditions one may see in a circumnavigation. Four people to stand watches would make it ever so much more palatable. Even when the wind is with you, seas and swell can be mighty big out there when they roll all the way down from the far reaches of Alaska and north. Then again, for others it can be a gentle ride south. What would we be facing?

SAN FRANCISCO, HERE WE COME

The morning dawned partly sunny with weather reports predicting clearing and settling southwest winds turning to the northwest quadrant, just as we hoped. None of the other boats elected to leave just yet. The morning sun had burned off any fog and we motored out of safe Neah Bay with all hearts pumping overtime. Cape Flattery was just ahead to our port. Very shortly we would be rounding this Cape and southward bound for San Francisco!

It was a good morning with light winds and, as we rounded Cape Flattery, conditions stayed light. The excitement and thrill that filled us began to settle in with the rhythm of the boat, as *Windy Thoughts* dipped with the big swells and gently rolled off each wave. The ocean swells were not totally new to us now and the motion wasn't fearful; it was natural. We were bound for San Francisco and wouldn't touch land again for 5.5 days, a much shorter time than expected.

These were days that we were not to forget, as we would shortly encounter some of the heaviest winds and seas of our circumnavigation.

The first day and night were pleasant with a perfect fifteen knots of wind developing out of the northwest, just what we looked for during the first hours. Don was in his glory as *Windy Thoughts* cut through the seas, loving every minute of it and loving his *Windy Thoughts*.

With four of us on board, each stood three-hour watches, with a good break before our next watch was due. We sat in the cockpit that first day in sunshine and with easy stomachs. There was time for a rest when needed and good sleep on our off watches. Lee cloths held us in our sea berths and  we used pillows for fillers so that we could sleep with the motion of the boat as it met the seas and swells. The continuing rhythm that played its melodious song on the sea brought enjoyment and a sense of peacefulness that was mixed with the excitement of being on our way.

I took the first evening watch starting at 6 p.m. Don came on when my watch was over and carried us into the night while he marveled at the stars and the solitude of the sea surrounding us. Sandi followed at midnight and Lane took the dogwatch starting at 3 a.m, bringing us into the morning hours.

Don and I shared the aft berth, a tight double berth when we were in there together and we didn't roll about. When in the berth alone, a lee cloth that was hooked up from the middle was required to keep from rolling about.

Anything forward of the center of the boat becomes less conducive to comfort and sleep because it gets the most action. Our master berth, though just aft of the forward head, experienced more motion as well and we didn't use that while at sea. Sandi and Lane were given the sea berths on the port and starboard settees in the main cabin. Don made strong lee cloths from Sunbrella material, sewn on the old Singer sewing machine purchased back in Spokane. The lee cloths hooked on under the bottom settee cushion, came up and around the open side, and hooked with bungee cord to the bookshelf above each settee.

Because we were still in the northern Pacific, nights were cold. Sandi and Lane had Mustang cruising suits too, and on night watches we each sat in the cockpit bundled up against the night air and wind. Underneath the cruising suits, we wore long underwear and warm socks. This wasn't tropical cruising!

Getting out of a warm bunk to come up into a cold night cockpit with sometimes unpleasant conditions is a bit of a challenge—not only emotionally but physically. Imagine yourself rolling about in the sea—and even in the most pleasant conditions the boat gently rolls—holding on with at least one hand at all times while attempting to stand up in order to get into the suit. Then on with the wool watch cap, topped off with warm gloves, and followed last but not least by sea boots.

What a difference it is to sail and cruise in tropical latitudes, where bare feet and the very least of clothing suffice as you roll through the warm tropical seas. After leaving San Francisco, we never saw socks for years to come! Socks were for cold weather shoes. Socks were only thought of again for three very cold days in Australia, when the temperatures dropped down into the mid-seventies and we thought it was an Arctic chill!

The former watch has awoken you quietly so as not to disturb the others and with about ten minutes warning, so that you have time to get into the gear and perhaps heat a hot cup of cocoa. It is important that you perk right up and be ready because the last watch wants desperately to get below and into a warm berth—particularly during the night watches. Sleep is rationed out at sea, and the prospect of having to leave your own little cocoon environment is generally daunting.

Once off watch, the responsibilities of the boat are in someone else's hands. It is a wonderful, relieved feeling when the watch is over and you can get below and away from the weather and cares—much like entering different worlds.

One world is wrought with responsibility and duties to the boat. The other gives you an almost magical, free feeling as you step below to creature comforts of a berth and cozy cabin. No matter that your berth is rocking and rolling. No matter that the noise of the seas is dreadful. You are off watch and all the cares from just a few feet away are left to someone else. While it was much more pleasant to stand watches in warm climates, the chance to give all cares about the boat over to another was always eagerly awaited.

Just what do you do up there in the cockpit when you are standing watch alone? The person coming off watch generally goes over pertinent information, such as the sighting of a ship's light and the ship's track, the last calculated position on the chart, the wind and sea conditions. Then, suddenly, you are on your own.

There is little to do but to keep an eye out for ship's lights, occasionally check the boat's position, mark it on the chart, adjust a sail a bit in or out and keep a cursory check on things on top. If it is rough, there is a need to check for things like chafing on lines and to make sure that all loose ends of sheets are in the cockpit and tied off—and finally, that the boat is sailing at its best. If the winds perk up it may be necessary to take a reef in the mainsail, all of which leaves little room for boredom!

Big ships aren't looking out for smaller vessels. Their size and speed prevent the ability to quickly change course. A small boat must stay clear of the ships, regardless of the rules regarding the right of way. From the first sighting of a ship's lights on the horizon, it will generally be a fast fifteen minutes before it is upon you if on a collision course.

On the passage to San Francisco, we tucked ourselves into the forward-most niche in the cockpit, near the companionway steps. The dodger that covered the hatch and companionway gave protection from cold spray and colder winds. As it got rougher—and it would—Sandi and I found that we could achieve a sense of rest if we sat on the cockpit table (attached to the binnacle holding the steering wheel and compass) and lay with our heads in our arms on the hatch cover.

The doors to the hatch were kept shut, the weatherboards were in and the hatch cover was closed. It wasn't exactly comfortable in the cockpit in the rough seas and three hours seemed a very long time, but we each dutifully did our part. Sandi suffered terribly from seasickness the entire trip, but was always right there when it was her turn.

I joined Sandi in meals of saltine crackers, sometimes adding a little peanut butter for protein. Don and Lane made huge breakfasts of sausages and potatoes and eggs, no matter the conditions, ate dozens of cookies day and night and never suffered a moment from mal de mer. They insisted that keeping food in their stomachs was the answer. In the future, I was to find that this was best for me as well and over the years seldom again had a problem. Don maintained that it was a matter of IQ, but during a horrific storm in the Coral Sea between Australia and New Caledonia, he was made to eat his words, literally.

It was during our second night that the wind began to pipe up alarmingly—as did the seas. Weather radio was telling us what to expect, and it didn't sound heartening.

When the wind began to blow above thirty knots, it became very uncomfortable, though not dangerous, because the boat was well under control. Two men were in charge and Sandi and I had only to take our watches. Any major decisions could always be discussed and we had assistance if needed.

On a sailboat in twenty-five-foot seas and winds that increased to forty to forty-five knots, you become very aware of your small but immediate world! When at sea, crew members do their part no matter what is felt on the inside. *Windy Thoughts* was under control and she was sailing beautifully—but it was very, very rough.

The next few days were sailed under cloud cover, making a good sun or star sight impossible with the sextant, and dead reckoning became the order of the day. Dead reckoning utilizes the estimated speed of the boat over the ground and the boat's magnetic course between two points on the chart. In very rough seas and bucking like a bronco, we estimated our position on our fifth night to be off San Francisco. We could make out a blinking light that didn't match the chart or seem to make sense with anything in the light book. After repeatedly counting its flashes and the seconds between flashes we still couldn't make heads or tails, or locate anything similar near where we expected we were.

We made our way toward this light until we could read the number on it and then dashed below to look it up in the light book to find—to our horror—that we were smack in the middle of the Farallon Islands, about twenty-five miles off San Francisco. The Islands are literally a big rock patch, one in which no one should find himself even in daylight. Quickly plotting a safe course, we crept slowly toward San Francisco Bay.

Once sure that all was safe, Sandi and I went below to the comforts of our berths while the guys held vigil for the remainder of the night. We would help when we neared our landfall.

The passage from Neah Bay to San Francisco gave us two consecutive 200-mile days in 5.5 days total, and an average speed of eight knots, very good for a thirty-five-foot, heavy duty, blue water boat. The final 2.5 days were under double reefed main only, in forty-five knots of northwesterly wind on our starboard quarter. Over the years, 120 to 130 miles covered in twenty four hours was considered average.

The forces of Mother Nature had dealt much discomfort and it often seemed that we were in a big cement mixer, endlessly being thrown about. The noise of water as it hit the hull sounded much like huge semi-trucks were plowing straight into us, over and over again, frightening sounds. *Windy Thoughts* rose to the occasion as each wave rose precariously high behind her stern, seemingly ready to bury us in its watery vastness. She just tipped her stern to each wave and grandly rode it up until its crest rolled under her hull, proudly ready to take on the next wave building in its towering height just behind her.

Conditions were rough enough that we preferred to leave the steering to Flem, our Fleming Major wind vane. Flem was our stalwart fifth mate for the entire passage and seemed to love it the rougher it got. The vane was all stainless steel tubing, beefy, strong and never wavering in its duties. It rhythmically steered us south through the onslaught with its steady movement back and forth, back and forth—much like a metronome keeping time to the rising crescendo in the music of the thundering, crashing seas.

As the wind screamed in the rigging, coupled with the roar of the seas and the full might of God's mighty ocean, we began to internalize the difference between the truly dangerous and the merely extreme discomfort. *Windy Thoughts* seemed to love the challenge, but I would never quite feel as excited about rising wind as she did.

That next afternoon, we entered a small bay to port of San Francisco Bay itself and just outside the Golden Gate Bridge. As soon as the anchor went down, we all hit our sea berths for much awaited uninterrupted sleep. Not even the barking of the nearby sea lions prevented our sleep.

Excited to sail under the Golden Gate Bridge, we were up and off at first light on the following morning—a milestone that we had only imagined for so long. The berth awaiting us at the St. Francis Yacht Club was so very welcome. Once tied securely, there was no more motion. No more watches. All of San Francisco awaited us.

Sandi and Lane had to fly right back to Seattle, but Don and I spent a wonderful three weeks seeing all that we could of this beautiful city.

Two other sailboats arrived from our marina on Bainbridge Island, with our friends Jan, Dave and young Joel on *Moulin Rouge*, a beautiful Hans Christian Hansa 33—and Nori and Jim, a young couple on *Alele*, a lovely twenty-eight-foot Bristol Channel cutter. We all shared tales of the Seattle–San Francisco onslaught. *Moulin Rouge* had lost its steering cable. Nori and Jim had suffered a full knockdown and lost their dinghy, arriving shaken and exhausted. Tied securely in a slip, Nori and Jim stepped off the boat and kneeled down to kiss the dock beneath their feet.

The cruising crowd on the docks shared talk of equipment that worked and that didn't. No one had expected a wind vane to steer in such strong conditions, and most had steered by hand, not trusting their autopilots either. For us, these had been the exact conditions in which we fully expected and relied upon our wind vane to steer for us—and there wasn't a glitch in old Flem's workout for the entire distance.

From that point on we knew that Flem was a trusty mate—though in future we came to use the autopilot more frequently. The autopilot had the ability to steer the course with computerized ease, and the addition of solar panels kept batteries up without a problem.

The run south had gone well, but was more boisterous than we hoped to experience again right away. Occasionally, a boat arrives in San Francisco only to be put on the market, its owners having had enough! We were so thankful to have had no problems, no breakdowns and a rapid passage. We were doubly thankful to have shared the crewing with Sandi and Lane, who made a rough passage so much easier. We had made it through some of the highest winds and certainly some of the biggest seas that we would ever see.

Don's daughter Patti had lived in San Francisco and we called her friends Jan and Danny Peterson, who came down to the Yacht Club for a visit. When Don asked if they knew where he might get a nice piece of wood to make a seat across the stern of the boat, Jan and Danny surprised us with a lovely twelve-inch-wide piece of redwood, six feet long. Don installed it across the center rail of the stern pulpit, and it became our favorite "back porch perch", made even more comfortable with the addition of cushions that Don made later on.

These good people picked us up and drove us to the marina where they kept their own sailboat, with dreams of cruising very similar to our own. To top off our royal treatment, we were treated to a lovely dinner out on San Francisco Bay.

While here in San Francisco, we added a satellite navigation system (Sat Nav) to our inventory of equipment. There had been so many expenditures in Seattle, some things had to wait.

It was time to leave the luxuries of yacht clubs and land life in San Francisco. We were now on our own and ready to depart. In the stillness of night and taking advantage of the 3a.m. tides, I was to back the boat out of our berth while Don worked a line from the dock to get the boat headed the right direction. We were moored in a very tight spot that was difficult to turn in, and *Windy Thoughts* never did back for beans. In Don's estimation, it was to be a fairly simple and logical maneuver. But logic doesn't always fit my way of doing things—and we were soon backwards and unable to get turned around at all.

With a full five feet of water separating the dock and the wind vane, Don leapt right onto Flem. Never mind, we were on our way; though being on our way meant going backwards all the way out of the marina—in the dead of night—on a full-keel boat—and up and down three different legs of long docks filled with very expensive boats—in a very strong current.

Ah, but the world was our oyster. When we made it out onto San Francisco Bay and headed under the Golden Gate Bridge, we polished our thumbs—feeling like real seafarers after all. We were on our way!

Cruising boats don't head to Mexican waters until after the hurricane season ends in mid- to late November, so we had some time before heading south from San Diego. Catalina, the southernmost of the Channel Islands, was the perfect spot for us to spend time, and we anchored in Cat Harbor on the backside of the isthmus. With tourist season over, it was quiet and peaceful, with water ashore (available to haul by dinghy), a small laundry and even a small grocery store.

While at Catalina, we called several of the yacht clubs in Marina Del Rey to ask if they offered interim moorage to boats from other yacht clubs. One replied that no one had ever asked, but that they did honor other memberships. We had our membership card for the yacht club on Bainbridge Island. We had joined for a very nominal fee just for such occasions, though we had never actively participated in the club itself.

Our card would be accepted, and we set sail for a huge marina complex where we spent our first three days on the guest dock at one of the more exclusive clubs. Certainly, we were the only cruising boat there and were surrounded by huge power boats, most with crews taking care of the boats. We washed our *Windy Thoughts* down and she glistened as much as the others.

At the end of the three days we moved to a club that catered to sailors who were more of the adventurous type. When we asked how long we might use their guest dock, they replied that it was free until someone else came along. Not another boat showed and we spent two weeks here. Don's son Rick lived in Los Angeles at the time and gave us a wonderful tour of all the sights, treating us royally and even sailing to Catalina Island with us for a couple of days.

Rick gave us the video of the old movie, Rudyard Kipling's "Captains Courageous" starring a young Spencer Tracey. The video went around the world with us and many an evening was spent watching it with others. Everyone loved it. When we were in Australia a couple knocked on our hull one evening and asked if this was the boat that had "Captains Courageous" aboard. We invited them aboard for an evening of movie and popcorn, a great way to meet new people.

We bumped along toward San Diego—and chose to anchor just five miles north of San Diego, in Mission Bay. With very limited moorage in San Diego, all dock space was filled with local boats, and there was a backlog of cruising boats wanting to get a slip. Few houses or buildings dotted the shore of Mission Bay and it was a very quiet and secure anchorage. Bus service provided transportation to Shelter Bay, where boat chandlers and all things needed to outfit or repair a boat are located.

While we were still in Seattle, a couple had taken a test sail on *Windy Thoughts* and loved the boat so much that they immediately purchased a Lord Nelson 35 themselves. To our surprise and delight, they invited us to their home in San Diego for Thanksgiving dinner. How nice to be included and to share this special occasion with these warm and friendly people. It was only the first of many special holidays aboard to come, though only a few in the future would include a turkey dinner with all of the trimmings!

We did more provisioning and generated our Mexican crew lists, required documentation in every port in Mexico. Don and I were listed as crew along with our passport information, boat name, tonnage and other pertinent information. Crew lists were an important part of the clearance procedure in any country and we made up a model of the proper form for Mexico, in Spanish, and duplicated copies that were at the ready to fill in for every stop in Mexico.

Don continued his work on the boat and had stainless steel framework built for a bimini top to cover the cockpit. The covering would prove to be the single most important addition to our boat in terms of comfort. Without its protection, we could not have stayed in the cockpit more than five minutes in tropical latitudes. Fans that were added well down the line probably vied for second place, though by that time we might have had to toss a coin to make that consideration, as both the bimini and the fans were equal to our comfort. While in San Diego we also added two Arco solar panels that were attached atop the bimini framework.

Though boats were not allowed to anchor for more than seventy-two hours in southern California, cruising boats laying over here seemed to be ignored for a full two weeks before the Harbor Patrol arrived. Sure enough, at the two-week mark the Harbor Patrol made us leave immediately.

The Police Docks in Shelter Bay offered temporary moorage, and we managed to secure our allotted three days by waiting astern of a boat preparing to leave—and then received permission to anchor off the San Diego Yacht Club for three days while we finished the last minute provisioning, bringing fresh items aboard before heading for Baja.

The Baja peninsula runs between the Pacific Ocean on its west side and the Sea of Cortez on its east side. The Sea is a large body of water between the peninsula and mainland Mexico and is a fabulous cruising ground. We looked forward to exploring its many bays and islands.

Clearance from the United States was done efficiently in San Diego. We were informed about the proper procedures in Mexico and were prepared for the inefficiency that often accompanied the process. Though it all sounded a bit daunting, once you've been cruising in Mexico the process of clearance in the rest of the world is all downhill! In all other countries, clearance into a country is done once when arriving at a port of entry and again when departing the country. Not so in Mexico! You must clear into and out of each port, which is virtually every little village or big town. This procedure varies from slow and laborious, to slower and even more laborious.

We would soon learn that no one was in any hurry except us—and there was often a need to remind ourselves that time wasn't of the essence. Whole days would be spent going from Harbor Master, to Immigration offices, to Customs, getting the correct stamps of approval. There didn't seem to be any thought given to locating these offices even within some reasonable distance from each other, and the process was usually managed on foot under a relentless hot sun. But wasn't that glorious sun the reason we were all heading south?

Government reigned and if the official wasn't quite ready to face the day of work, you waited. Official fees varied and weren't strictly official. Our important papers would go into piles of papers heaped willy-nilly about the room. Any system of filing appeared non-existent. Officials laboriously typed in forms on old typewriters, pecking away one finger at a time.

Meanwhile, we assumed a friendly and cheerful nature. Perseverance and patience were necessary. Patience was something we were learning was necessary for nearly all aspects of the cruising life. Surely, this whole gambit has changed for the better, but we couldn't vouch for that—the process wasn't much different when we returned to Mexico in 1998.

Ah, but those experiences were still in front of us and a successful journey from Seattle was behind us, with only about 900 miles to go now to reach the tip of Baja, Mexico.

THAT WALL TO WALL BLUE BAJA

Armed with everything we could learn about cruising Baja, we departed San Diego early on the morning of December 18, 1988, with sunny skies and about fifteen knots of favorable wind. Setting ourselves out a bit to be safely away from land dangers, we rocked and rolled along, started our four-hour night watches, read, ate, sailed the boat and found our new Sat Nav to be a wonder.

How easy it was to get a position of latitude and longitude every few hours, marking the position on the chart as we watched our line move south in little increments. It would be a couple of years before we had our first GPS, and we felt the Sat Nav to be the piece of electronics we most feared breaking down. There is a saying amongst seafarers that whatever can break down likely will; we were ever conscious of keeping up with celestial skills.

Three days later and about three hours before dawn, we were off the entrance to Turtle Bay, Mexico. As we sat waiting for daylight to make our approach, I watched a light sitting close to the horizon that seemed to be another boat. When the light stayed directly in front of us I put out a call on the radio, but received no answer. With a huge sigh, Don informed me that I was radioing Venus, the morning star.

Our intention had been to sail without stopping to Cabo San Lucas, at the tip of the Baja Peninsula. But the day before leaving San Diego, we had learned that our good friends on *Moulin Rouge* had left their clearance papers in a copy shop in San Diego. *Moulin Rouge* now sat in Turtle Bay. A local chandler who ran a very active Ham radio net between San Diego and the cruisers in Mexico had received this message via radio, gone to the copy shop, found the important papers under a pile and called us on the VHF radio. Could we carry the papers to them? Of course, we could!

This break would turn out to be a wonderful layover in Turtle Bay for Christmas celebrated with seventeen other sailboats.

As we slowly entered Turtle Bay, Don radioed *Moulin Rouge* and announced that the *Windy Thoughts* courier service had arrived. As soon as our anchor went down, Dave was there in his dinghy to take us aboard *Moulin Rouge* for a delicious breakfast with Jan and their ten-year old son, Joel. What fun to meet up here and share tales of our passage down! Had it not been for our "courier service", we wouldn't have had this special time here with friends, enjoying a Christmas that we will never forget.

We would enjoy *Moulin Rouge*'s company on and off during our time in Mexico, and young Joel easily made friends amongst other young people of the cruising community. Both Jan and Dave shared in Joel's home schooling and continued for the next years to provide both an excellent education and a unique experience as they sailed to distant countries.

Turtle Bay was a small, dusty village with the most welcoming people. On Christmas Eve, we shared festivities aboard *Moulin Rouge* along with another couple and their young daughter from *Mary T*, bobbing gently at anchor nearby—and we all enjoyed Christmas cookies and goodies that were prepared while listening to Christmas carols sung in the little church ashore. It was a memorable Christmas and we realized how blessed we were with our boat, our dreams still so fresh, and full of wonder at all that lay ahead.

Three days after leaving Turtle Bay, a group of pilot whales appeared and sailed along beside us as we neared the southern tip of Baja. A huge welcoming party!

Our whales swam off as we rounded the point, but Cabo San Lucas's scenic (and never to be forgotten) pinnacle rocks rose up to greet us in welcome. We headed into the huge outer anchorage on December 29, 1988. What only a few years before had been a sleepy fishing village had blossomed into a very busy fishing and vacation resort, complete with very plush hotels, with many more under construction.

While we sat at anchor for three days, we were ever aware that it was here that so many boats were lost just a few years before in a sudden onshore storm. In Seattle, we met the owners of the only boat to survive, and with remarkably little damage. The owners had attempted to power against the seas to move the boat into deeper water and the safety of the open sea—but their propeller fouled on a dragging anchor line and the engine was lost.

With the boat heading for the beach and thrown onto the bottom repeatedly, the owners held hands while they jumped into the water and right into the welcoming arms of the Mexican people. Because the boat's hull had hit the beach facing the oncoming sea, the boat survived. But it took weeks to dig it out of the sand with the help of the Mexican people and a bulldozer, and still weeks more before it was ready to sail to La Paz for repairs.

Windy Thoughts was anchored well out from the beach, ever aware of the unexpected.

Our dinghy engine had packed up and when Don couldn't find the problem we took it ashore to a local repair shop. Fortunately, a shore boat made excursions out to the anchorage and back to shore frequently, eliminating a long and bumpy row in the dinghy. We mixed a bit with the cruising group and the tourists in town but soon we were ready to be off and headed north.

Strong northerly winds blow down the Sea of Cortez all winter, making sailing north unpleasant at best during the winter months. Boats usually hole up somewhere until spring brings lessening winds—and cruise mostly during the summer months.

After three days in Cabo San Lucas, we awoke around midnight to a silence indicating that the blustery and contrary northerly winds had stopped blowing. It was still, calm and even raining! While the stillness was a near miracle in itself, the rain was just an oddity in this season. In high gear, we upped anchor and were bound for La Paz, a popular destination for many of the southbound cruising boats coming from the Northwest or California.

La Paz is located about 150 miles north of Cabo in the Sea of Cortez, on the eastern side of the Baja Peninsula. We looked forward to the R and R there amongst others setting off for distant lands—as well as those who linger, never to leave the welcoming waters of Mexico.

Twenty miles prior to reaching La Paz, the contrary northerly wind reared its ugly head to give us an invigorating beat to windward. Our final hours were made longer by the long tacks back and forth that were necessary. When we finally putted into La Paz Bay and neared the anchorage off the main part of town, we could barely believe the number of sailboats sitting at anchor—with many other boats at one of the two well-appointed marinas.

The winds often blow opposite to the strong tidal current here and all boats at anchor were subject to the La Paz waltz. Boats moved about as if dancing, without heed to what they bumped into. Our first two nights were spent amongst the hordes of other boats off the main town, but anxious anchor watches and fending off boats in the night weren't to our liking—so we moved to the south part of the bay where there were fewer boats and more room to dance about.

We loved La Paz, a small city that welcomed all of the yachties with open arms. The city gave us many months of relaxation and there was pleasantly busy camaraderie. New friends were made and the cruising community felt like a big family. We rapidly became attached to La Paz and we loved the lovely, quiet atmosphere.

Food experiences became important to us. One of our favorite foods in La Paz was the most common: fresh tortillas. We made frequent trips to a tortilla shop run from a home where we purchased fresh, hot tortillas packed in big stacks and costing next to nothing. Too many to eat right away but plenty to share with others. Tortillas haven't tasted the same since!

One street vender sold fish tacos every noon. It was a family-run business, sparkling clean and known to be a safe spot to eat. A big cart appeared on the street corner each day with a variety of fish to choose from, as well as salad toppings. A meal of two tacos cost twenty-five cents, and fish tacos at this little spot became a staple each time we ventured into town. The lovely old Los Arbos Hotel sat right on the waterfront and was a very pleasant spot for a Sunday's treat.

Against our better judgment, we joined a group of friends for dinner one evening at a street-side spot. Pork was cooking on a vertical spit, ringed with pineapple, smelling succulent and making our mouths water. The others had eaten here frequently and lauded its culinary delights. So we threw caution to the wind and ordered some ourselves. It was delicious, never mind that we were ingesting pork off the streets.

By evening, I was so sick that I couldn't stand—and by the following morning Don was pouring me into the dinghy and taking me to shore, where he hailed a cab and took me to the local Military Hospital. Salmonella poisoning kept me under the weather for a few days. No more street pork for us.

There would be more parasite problems that summer when stopping in at the little village of Santa Rosalia, located well north in the Sea of Cortez. Don suspected that he had amoebas. Symptoms are elusive, ranging from none at all to extreme tiredness. Either way, if not caught, amoebas eat through the body's organs, and Flagyll is the only drug that will effectively kill them. Flagyll is powerful and not recommended without proper diagnosis. Local doctors even came on the morning radio net to warn the cruising group against self-medicating with Flagyll.

The local doctor's office was in her home in Santa Rosalia. Tests showed that Don didn't have the amoeba but did have a bad case of giardiasis, caused by another nasty little parasite, giardia. It required only a pittance to send him away with the proper drugs.

Meanwhile, we were happily exploring La Paz and sharing fun times with many friends during the winter. For the contingent determined to cross the mighty Pacific in March, there was much meeting of the minds and sharing of information. Anyone who had actually done it was looked upon as the consummate authority and eagerly plied with questions and asked for opinions. Most of us were very new to ocean crossings. Though we would be spending the coming summer cruising north into the Sea of Cortez and wouldn't be taking off until the following year, we attended and listened in with eagerness to every word.

Advice from an experienced fellow cruiser stood out in both of our minds when the group was discussing radio frequencies with which to keep in touch. He strongly advised that it wasn't necessary to "party line" your way across the Pacific Ocean, but that each should sail his own boat, using the radio for necessary communication but not as the local La Paz radio net was used.

In retrospect, we remember La Paz with great fondness—and for its famous morning radio nets. Perhaps in no other spot in the world do so many rely so much on what others are doing and thinking when planning their day.

Ham nets were our lifeline when out on the Pacific, but we sometimes found the daily chat on the morning net on the VHF radio in the anchorage in La Paz a bit useless. However, we might lose out on the latest gossip if we didn't listen!

We learned to look forward to communication with others when making ocean passages. Often, we were several hundred miles apart, but we found great enjoyment in keeping in touch daily via the radio. Advice and help from friends concerning problems that crop up is welcomed during radio contact. Just as the fellow advised in La Paz, we found that idle chatter isn't often necessary when out on the oceans, but informative and supportive "chatter" is most welcomed!

We carried Jimmy Cornell's book, *Ocean Passages of the World*, and it was of great help in trip planning. Twice during the coming years we chanced to meet up with the Europa Rally, organized by Jimmy Cornell. This large group makes a 1.5 year circumnavigation "together" requiring constant movement with little time in any port for anything other than refueling and provisioning. With a very strict schedule and great financial cost, the 1.5 year timeline is about as fast as a circumnavigation can be made and doesn't allow for much time ashore.

To us, cruising meant stopping to smell the roses whenever we could. Certainly, the opportunity to get a glimpse into other cultures, to meet interesting people and to see a bit of our world were our reasons for leaving home in such an unconventional way. The ocean passages in between places were necessary, sometimes enjoyed and sometimes just endured. We had our own food, our own bed, and our own books and music.

Spring brought the expected lessening of the strong northerly wind and we were making ready for the summer in the Sea of Cortez. In April, we set out

to enjoy the many mainland bays and islands that dot the eastern coast of the Baja Peninsula. It was time for the cruising part of the adventure again.

Villages were few and far between. The landscape is desert with high mountains striated with reddish lines of color gracing the coastal area. What we thought may be a dreary desert environment proved to be truly lovely, with the colors of the mountains changing in different light. A violet glow before sunset contrasted with the colored rock against the turquoise sea, making the end of day breathtakingly lovely.

There were abundant bays to explore, some with friends sharing our good times. It was here that we found the best fishing in our cruising experience. Don had two spear guns and we snorkeled for several hours every day. It was hotter than anything we had ever experienced. Our answer was to spend as much time as possible in the water, and we delighted in the wonders that the Sea of Cortez offered.

Though no coral, there were fish of every tropical sort imaginable to view and enjoy—and in such abundance that we often picked out what we wanted for dinner when ready to head back to the boat and call it a day. Our favorite eating variety was the Cabrillo, a member of the grouper family. It was just a matter of choosing one that was frying pan size—not too large— and dinner needed only to be cooked. Never again did we see such abundance. Lobster waited to be hunted—and we will never forget the thrill that Don had in getting his first lobster! The lion's-paw scallops provided a hunk of meat so big that one or two was a meal.

What the Sea of Cortez doesn't offer is nightlife, shore activity, sightseeing or mall shopping. Instead, it offers hundreds of miles of pure cruising, fishing, snorkeling and sailing in beautiful turquoise waters. All of this, plus lovely and abundant anchorages, pristine beaches and the opportunity to learn how to make 200 gallons of fresh water last for a couple of months—with our wardrobe of little other than a bathing suit and thongs. Who cared about hairdos? A sun hat was necessary at all times anyway.

One night we were tucked into a bight on an island north of Coyote Island. John and Francine from the *Red Baron*, out of Canada, were enjoying the quiet of the evening with us in our cockpit. While we were visiting, Don

noticed an amazing light in the sky, but, trying to put logic to what he was seeing, said nothing at first. Unable to contain himself any longer, Don insisted we look up to see a huge, white, and bell-shaped light—so large and so seemingly near that we looked at each other to be sure that we weren't suddenly out of our minds. Its size was many times larger than the sun, and also much closer.

After watching this amazing light for several minutes and discussing what it logically, or illogically, could be, Don and John jumped into the dinghy and sped to the other end of the bay where a power boat sat bobbing gently at anchor. Our men were sure the huge light in the sky was some unexplained phenomenon that someone other than the four of us should witness.

Don and John pulled alongside to rouse the folks aboard. No sooner had they started into their cockpit to take a look—when the light disappeared! The folks looked up and saw nothing.

Our men returned with tales of the looks they had been given. Soon after, newspapers reported that fishermen on Coyote Island had seen the huge light and were sure it was an angel in the sky. Perhaps it was! Don feels certain that it was.

In the huge natural wonder known as Conception Bay, we met up with another Seattle boat whose owners mentioned a small marina just north in Santa Rosalia. It would be a safe spot to leave the boat, and they told us about the bus that went back to the U.S. border. Right on the spot, we made the decision to visit home if a slip was available.

The marina had only twelve slips and we were fortunate to get the only one left. Within twenty-four hours (and after that visit to the local doctor), we were on a local bus and heading to the border with hurriedly packed bags—for a bus ride that took twenty-four hours and was an experience in itself.

We left at 6 a.m. and rode the bus all night until 9:00 the next morning. Going south by boat had entailed much more time and effort! There were rest stops where the men lined up on one side of the bus, the women on the other—other stops where the facilities were appalling, but nature's call doesn't bow to anything and we persevered.

A relief driver rode underneath the bus in the luggage compartment, where he slept until it was his turn to sit behind the wheel.

We reeled around curves without guardrails and our eyes looked down over steep drops as we wound up and over the mountains, lurching and groaning along. Babies and young children joined parents on the bus and yet it was noticeably quiet. Always polite and well behaved in public, Mexican children were a joy.

When we reached the border crossing at Tijuana, we collected our luggage and sped for the border on foot—where, just on the other side, we made fast tracks for a McDonald's. Yes, we were really back in America! Our stomachs growled with hunger because we hadn't dared to imbibe the foods at the local stops along the way. Not only was food on our minds, but a clean toilet facility was right up there on the list of expectations as well. It was most disappointing to find the opposite, and the deplorable conditions made us change our minds about eating there after all! Hunger pains would have to suffice.

A train running north to San Diego was leaving right away and we hopped on it for the short ride to the local Amtrak train station. Though we didn't have a firm plan for getting back to Washington, we quickly learned that an Amtrak train would leave within the hour for Seattle. Don raced out of the station and up the street to find an ATM to get U.S. dollars.

No sails to tend and we could sit back and relax. We were headed home!

One of our first encounters when we arrived in Spokane to stay with Don's mother was a visit to a local supermarket. Walking through its doors was overwhelming, and tears welled up before I was more than a few steps inside the door. Where to start? Just to walk the aisles and see so much abundance was more than my emotions could handle. Pushing the basket outside to load groceries into the car and drive home put me over the top.

In the cruising life, temporarily abandoned, the quest to find things from which to make a meal was laborious, usually requiring visits to several different shops. Purchases were loaded into our cart and hauled two miles through hot, dry and dusty streets, only to then be loaded into the dinghy and taken out to the boat. Once onto the boat, there was the chore of finding a place for everything and stowing it all so carefully.

Yes, cruising isn't all easy and sometimes you struggled to remember just why you are doing it after all! But suddenly, you know in your heart that you have made the right choices and that even with the stark contrast with land life, cruising is worth every effort and every sacrifice.

After 6 weeks of luxuriating stateside—the last three in Palm Springs visiting with Don's old friend Phil Klug—the return to Mexico and cruising seemed a bit less enticing.

While in Palm Springs, we enjoyed the luxury of our own car on loan from Don's old friend Bill Ingraham, who lived in Los Angeles with his wife Virginia. The car, a brand new Buick Riviera, belonged to Virginia and when our stay in Palm Springs stretched to three weeks, Bill told us that the next time we decided to linger we could catch the bus. Good that he and Don were old buddies from way back!

Very few people stay in Palm Springs during the summer, and we had the three pools in the condo development all to ourselves, basking in luxury as we wandered from one pool to the other. But was this really so much better than those pristine waters of the Baja in which we spent so many hours each day?

Phil very generously offered to drive us back to Santa Rosalia in his van, looking at it as an adventure—and his joviality and good company made the journey just that. Loaded with boat equipment purchases, Don and I were concerned for the security of our new treasures and we slept fitfully in the van during the two night journey while Phil slept soundly in a motel room.

Amongst our treasures was a new life raft. When in Spokane Don and I were walking through a downtown shopping mall and noticed a wildlife painting on display out in front of an art gallery. It immediately grabbed our attention because we owned Breaking Trail, a painting of buffalo pounding down over a ridge in the snow—and done by the same artist. Don mentioned this to the proprietor, who immediately offered a price for Breaking Trail that— though we parted with a favorite piece of art—would allow us to purchase our life raft!

At the Mexican border, officials didn't understand what was in the big white canister and insisted that we open it. With frantic gestures and drawings, we succeeded in efforts to explain that it was a life raft, avoiding its sudden explosive deployment—and we escaped a very expensive repacking that would require a return to San Diego.

Once reaching Santa Rosalia, we were tremendously demoralized to find *Windy Thoughts* covered with a thick coating of a hardened lime-like substance that originated from a nearby plant and rained down in certain wind directions. Sure that we would never get *Windy Thoughts* back to her original glory, we busily applied elbow grease along with Lime Off, given us by a fellow sailor.

The days were hot beyond belief. At first, Santa Rosalia seemed to offer little when compared to Palm Springs, where every amenity was at our fingertips. But there was good news! Water was available on the dock and a hose provided many showers throughout the day—and provided the means to make *Windy Thoughts* sparkling once again. We reminded each other that Palm Springs wasn't meant to be like cruising, and we worked on our attitudes about the charming village where *Windy Thoughts* had awaited our return.

The many bags were unpacked and new things stowed or installed. Our spirits picked up and we found ourselves happily ready for the lifestyle we had worked so hard to attain. The smiles and warmth of the people of Santa Rosalia went a long way to renewing our spirits.

We would cruise come hell or high water.

High water did play a small part in our story within the next few days. Don took the bimini top off for cleaning, and once washed, it lay overnight on the dock along with our cleaning supplies. As the dock moved up and down with the tide, the bimini managed to become tightly wedged between the piling and the dock. We awoke to find the dock listing heavily to port and our slip way out of line with the others. Everyone joined in the discussion on how to resolve this without cutting the material free. Losing the cockpit cover was decidedly not part of the plan!

Finally, Don stepped back and drawled, "Well, the tide comes in and the tide goes out."

Of course! Everyone waited with bated breath until the tide did change and, sure enough, when the dock began its drop against the piling we worked the fabric free—and without so much as a rip to be found!

When we left Santa Rosalia, we set our course for points north. Occasional squalls kept us on anxious anchor watches during the night. The intense heat would surely fry the proverbial egg on *Windy Thoughts'* topsides, were we inclined to experiment. Heat and humidity had us dripping twenty-four hours a day. Constant tasks kept us busy as we worked to keep everything in tip-top shape.

In Santa Rosalia, we purchased Vel bar soap that sudsed up in salt water, working wonders for baths and making our hair shine like the most expensive salon treatment. A spray bottle of fresh water was kept handy for a quick rinse after a dip in the saltwater. Followed by a good drying off, we felt fresh as daisies. We purchased enough Vel to last well into the future!

Laundry was the nemesis of this first mate, and keeping our clothes clean and in order was high on my priority list. Fresh water wasn't readily available, but we lived for the most part in bathing suits that could be washed out in salt water with Joy dish detergent. I discovered a spigot in a trailer park when we were anchored off a small village quite far north, and spent an entire day in the intense sun with laundry, buckets and toilet plunger tackling sheets, towels and everything I could get my hands on that needed freshening. We always had clean sheets, towels and clothes, but it was a chore of immense proportions at times!

Don wasn't relaxing on the boat while I labored away with laundry, as there was always a long list of maintenance jobs that required his attention. Chores aside, there was the constant quest to see what lay around the next bend, to savor the delights offered by this beautiful area and to enjoy warm waters, diving and the sandy beaches. Pleasures far outnumbered difficulties.

While at anchor off the pristine and lovely island of Angel de la Guarda, we enjoyed the company of a couple on a Canadian boat. Shore excursions were shared as were dinghy trips to a small island outcropping, where we encountered sea lions that sometimes used our dinghies for naps while we explored ashore. The creatures obviously found the dinghies to be comfortable beds and had to be coaxed out—by people very leery of the huge fellows.

The four of us were having dinner aboard *Windy Thoughts* one evening when the wind suddenly built rapidly from sea, our boats now on a lee shore. Always the consummate worrier, I would periodically pop up on top and then anxiously fly below to mention that things looked to be turning sour out there. Everyone else was content to enjoy the evening and pooh-pooh my concerns. Just a little wind—probably a squall coming up.

When the rigging began to whistle, the Canadian fellow poked his head up to take a look. Immediately, all hands were on deck. The Canadian boat was anchored close in to shore and had dragged dangerously close to the beach. Our little soiree came to an abrupt end as they high-tailed it home. We flew to the radio and learned that a hurricane was threatening. Anchored farther out and with room to drag, *Windy Thoughts* was all right where she was, for the time being.

It was an anxious night without sleep as the winds and seas built and poured in on us. But the hurricane and its fury were bent for Guaymas, across the sea from us and on the mainland. We received only the back side of the hurricane.

We had two CQR anchors aboard, a forty-five pound for our main anchor and a thirty-five pound as our backup. The forty-five pound anchor never budged, but there were long minutes that soon became long hours of anxiety as we monitored the hurricane's path. We were all relieved when all began to settle down and we realized that we were going to be spared the worst of the storm.

It was a blessing to spend time at this anchorage, one of most beautiful spots in the entire Sea of Cortez, and one of the most memorable stays in all of our years of cruising.

We relied on solar panels for our complete electrical/battery needs, choosing not to use our freezer and being grateful for a good refrigerator. The Frig a Boat refrigeration system, a DC compressor type, was eternally reliable and perked along for the twelve years of cruising—and for another two years of continued living aboard at the end of our cruising years. Many boats had engine-driven refrigeration with sometimes generous freezer capabilities. At times, we were a bit envious, but never of the need to run engines every day to keep the batteries charged. We wouldn't trade the diesel fuel for the freezer.

In Australia and Singapore we purchased vacuum-packed meats that stayed good in the refrigerator for up to two months. Otherwise, an abundance of good canned meats filled our lockers; we enjoyed the usual tuna, excellent white chicken with which we made many great curries and other dishes, and Libby's canned beef. The beef made great hot roast beef sandwiches and lent itself to a pot roast dinner when added to potatoes, gravy, carrots and onions. In La Paz, we found seasoned canned pork that was delicious in burritos, scrambled eggs and any number of dishes.

In addition to meats, pastas provided easy meals with the addition of canned sauces and bottled pesto. A top-of-the-stove waffle maker made delicious Belgian waffles, thick and fluffy, and oh what a treat they were!

My dear friend Susan Brown periodically sent us care packages from Seattle, with little treats such as fettuccine sauces and specialty bread mixes—all of which were saved for exclusive occasions. Crackers were a staple, as was peanut butter, the combination a healthy and nourishing treat at sea when in need of a quick carbohydrate and protein burst.

Mexico's Bimbo Bread was so loaded with preservatives that we crossed the Pacific to the Marquesas Islands, a twenty-seven day passage, without the necessity to bake bread—for we were supplied with Bimbo bread that held the entire distance!

When in Costa Rica many years later, near the end of our story, a fellow boater shared a song she had composed and recorded. It was hilarious, all about the merits of the unsinkable, un-moldable Bimbo Bread. She even sang it on Mexican television and her little jingle brought back all the old memories of that devoted, spongy, white Bimbo bread on which we all so relied. At the end of her song, her lyrics asked that she be buried in Bimbo bread, preserved for perpetuity.

Brown as berries, in mid-November we made a quick passage back south to La Paz on the first northerlies of the season, surfing down on the sea behind us.

In La Paz, the boat was hauled at Big Aborrah's Boat Yard, where our yearly anti-fouling was taken care of and the cutlass bearing replaced. The replacement proved to be more complex than we bargained for when the flange wouldn't come off. Not realizing the flange was threaded on, the yard took a torch and a hammer to it for the better part of a day—and in the end, the flange was broken.

A new flange was modeled after the old and made at the local Pepsi Bottling Plant. The local population was quite accustomed to making do with what they had and if you could show them a sample of what you wanted, they could generally make it. Before we got out of the boatyard, the second flange on the shaft broke clean in two and yet another was made. We never quite trusted it, and in fact had nothing but problems with it for the next ten years.

Our second winter in La Paz felt like coming home, familiar with it as we were by now. March's jump-off for the big voyage across the Pacific was just ahead, and we were loaded down with charts that could take us all the way to New Zealand or Australia. La Paz had good supermarkets for provisioning that looked more inviting to us after the remote areas of summer!

We spent time in the frenzy of preparation that always precedes an ocean crossing, no matter how long you have been at it. Don relentlessly checked out all systems. Our Fold-It cart made many trips along the hot and dusty streets to the Ce Ce Ce Supermarket, and more and more provisions were added to our bulging food lockers. We planned for a minimum of six months of self-reliance, knowing how expensive foods would be in the South Pacific. The cart served us well for more than groceries. Don could comfortably fit 4 six-gallon fuel cans or 4 five-gallon water cans in the cart.

Don first spotted the Fold-It Cart in a metal shop before we left Spokane. It was the first one made and Don didn't care what it cost; he wanted it. The shop owners had no idea of its value to the marine world and Don suggested they market it at the Seattle Boat Show. To this day the carts are found in marine stores and chandlers everywhere. Ours looks as good today, after all of its use, as it did when we first purchased it—and this can't be said for many things! It has been used relentlessly since moving ashore, and it makes a dandy cart for hauling wood or any number of things.

We shopped in La Paz's big Public Market for fresh foods. There were dozens of stalls filled with vegetables, fruits, fish, meats and fresh corn tortillas. We found the produce beautiful, the eggs plentiful and the atmosphere fun. Though much larger, this market was similar to the central markets in every country that we visited and generally where we did most of our shopping.

We were careful to dunk all produce in the water before bringing it aboard and then soaked it in a chemically prepared wash. We brought no cardboard boxes aboard for fear of importing the cockroach eggs that live in their corrugation. While we took special care to keep the cockroach population at bay, our efforts didn't always work.

During the summer we met an American from La Paz who had tried every chemical known to man to rid his boat of cockroaches—and eventually discovered his own sure-fire recipe for eliminating them. He shared this recipe with us: we mixed up a paste of Nestlé's sweetened condensed milk and powdered boric acid and put the paste in small cups made from aluminum foil. The cups were placed wherever cockroaches had been seen. Though it could take awhile to kill off the little fiends it always worked. Sprinkling boric acid around by itself didn't seem to make any difference, nor did mixing it with jam or some other sweet substance.

Safely past the hurricane season, March was the magic month to cross the Big Pond, as we had come to think of the Pacific Ocean. The trade winds that we would find south of us would be properly set to carry us west across the nearly 3,000 miles of open ocean.

We were as physically and mentally prepared as we could be. The boat was safe and in perfect condition. A local pharmacist had assisted us in re-supplying our medical kit with drugs that were a bargain in Mexico. We had four dozen fresh farm eggs, and food stores to carry us for many months. During the winter, *Red Baron's* owner, John, the consummate radio man, helped Don install a random wire antenna for the Ham radio, to supplement our Hustler antennas. There was really nothing left to do but last minute fresh food provisioning and topping off our water tanks at the very last moment.

It was time to make the voyage across the Pacific Ocean, to not make landfall until reaching the Marquesas Islands, in French Polynesia.

Mexico to French Polynesia

San Diego

La Paz

2,900 Miles

Marquesas

Nuku Hiva   Hiva Oa

Tuamotus

Ua
Pou   Fatu Hiva

Manihi Atoll

Tahiti

Chapter 6

The Magic of the South Pacific

The sea is the great consoler. She may beguile us, she may challenge us, she may destroy us; but she never refuses us. —Tristan Jones

The morning of March 7, 1990, dawned clear and wall-to-wall blue, as do most days in Baja—a perfect day with perfect wind conditions to start our long journey across the Pacific Ocean. Heading south in the Sea of Cortez with twenty-knot winds right behind us was the kind of start we dreamed of. With the Yankee poled out to starboard and the main out to port, we were running wing and wing.

Our plan had been to make a stop in at Cabo San Lucas to pick up skins, very lightweight wet suits ordered and sent to a cruiser's mail drop in Cabo. However, with these perfect sailing conditions, we decided it was best to continue on and forego the stop. When cruising, you must be ready to leave when conditions are best, day or night—and not just when most comfortable or convenient.

And so, we suddenly found ourselves on our way—with about a month at sea ahead of us. As we changed course to sail into the Pacific Ocean and begin our westward journey, we knew there was no turning back.

Friends in Cabo came up on the morning cruiser's net and agreed to pick up the suits for us. However, the package wasn't there, and though we left forwarding addresses, we never did see those skins!

Our next stop would be the island of Hiva Oa in the Marquesas Islands. We were anticipating twenty-five to thirty days of open ocean sailing—a long time at sea ahead of us with no land in sight and only the vast ocean as our surrounding vista.

Armed with radio frequencies for the Pacific Mariner's Net operated by a kind fellow Ham operator out of Hawaii, we were tuned up and awaiting roll call promptly at 7:00 on our first night out. When the net operator asked for new check-ins, we gave our boat name, our names, our position, weather conditions and wave and swell conditions. Once on the roster, each boat name is called in order of having originally checked in until making landfall. If someone doesn't come up for several days in a row, concern builds as to why and what has happened.

This evening schedule became the highlight of our day. We listened to boats ahead of us or behind us, extrapolated what we may be facing, compared present conditions—and knew where old buddies were, as well as boat names new to us but becoming very familiar as we listened with fervor each evening. It was contact with the "outside world" when our whole world was the boat and the sea around us.

We didn't yet have weather fax facilities, but had excellent weather reports given before roll call by the net operator, who was there for us every day, prepared with a very comprehensive weather report for the entire area.

When our boat name came up on the roll call, we gave the pertinent data and then could call out to other boats, and change to another frequency to continue our contact. I often made contact with my dear friend Susan Brown who lived aboard in Seattle and was also a Ham operator. These opportunities were the absolute highlight of my radio days.

Al, also from Seattle, was available each night to make any "two-ways" requested. Using a two-way into Washington with Al's assistance, we talked to Don's mother in Spokane. Al called Don's mom at home on his landline and then relayed our conversations back and forth by use of special equipment. The calls were a wonderful way to keep in touch from the middle of the ocean and no doubt eased her mind as to where and how we were. It was a wonderful comfort to us to hear her voice with nothing but the ocean about us.

Once the nightly net was finished, we began our night watches, usually four hours long on this passage. In future, we would change our schedule to six hour watches that gave each of us a better rest below. Don took the watch until midnight and I came on until 4 a.m. Don took his watch again until 8 a.m., when I got up and made breakfast before Don headed below to crawl back into his sea berth.

During the day we didn't stand watches, but took turns getting rest. We loved to read and had about 200 books aboard. During a special time each day I read aloud from a book that we both enjoyed. This broke up the sameness of our day and gave us something to look forward to. Don still claims that this was his favorite time of those days at sea.

Days passed and it grew hotter and hotter as we rolled along, the first ten days in pretty lively wind and seas. On the sixth day, we learned from the net that a nasty weather system was moving our way from Hawaii. Don had planned a great circle route for the passage. But the net operator advised us to head directly south and hang a right at about two degrees south of the equator. This route was meant to keep us away from the system chasing us—and give us better conditions. Though the advice was well intentioned, Don's plan would have provided a much better sail, as it turned out.

The brisk wind conditions soon changed to very light winds when we met the Pacific High. Put the whisker pole up to try to catch as much air as possible. Take it down when the sail flapped incessantly. Put it up again. Take it down. Reef the mainsail when a squall threatened. Perhaps lots of wind, perhaps not. Bring the pole in. Put the main back up when the squall passed. Reef again in a couple of hours when the next squall came through. This was our routine as we rolled and bobbed our way across the mighty Pacific.

The temperature was very high and the air equally as humid. Don had designed our bimini cover to allow us to tack, bringing the main boom through the wind and crossing to the opposite side of the boat without the bimini being in the way and without allowing the boom to hit us. The bimini was a lifesaver, because it kept us out of the direct rays of the sun. It would have been impossible to remain in the cockpit without it. Entering the cabin below was like entering a sweatshop, and we wonder now how we managed to sleep down below. It wasn't until we reached Singapore that we purchased the fans that changed life completely.

During the day we read and watched for ships, but didn't see one until about twenty-three days out of Mexico. We plotted our position on the chart and watched our line move slowly across in daily increments.

Reefing became a routine task and when heavy squalls brought rain, we stayed on deck to enjoy the wonderful fresh water shower. Ever mindful of our fresh water supply, I washed and rinsed dishes in salt water and then briefly gave them a fresh water rinse. We gathered salt water in a bucket and took saltwater baths in the cockpit with our Vel soap followed with fresh water from a spray bottle, just as we had in the Sea of Cortez—and we were able to keep refreshed and clean daily. Throughout our cruising years, it became our habit to conserve fresh water when making a passage—always aware that if disaster struck and we drifted for a long time we would have fresh drinking water aboard.

We never added a water maker. This equipment was expensive and required running the engine to make potable water. Like our decision to not use the freezer, we chose not to trade diesel for water. We found it easy to conserve water when making a passage, and we always arrived at our destination with our tanks at least half full of fresh water. As soon as we got in from a passage, no matter how short, we topped off our water tanks so that we would never face the necessity to suddenly up anchor and pull out of an anchorage without having done so.

Our approach to safety at sea was quite conservative. If in doubt about a black squall line's path, we reefed before it hit. Better to have reefed before the need, because shortening sail in high winds is very difficult. As the days and weeks passed, we got quite adept at tracking squall lines on the radar and could often tell whether or not we were going to be hit.

Don and I had a rule that neither was to leave the cockpit and go forward on the boat without letting the other know. When Don was on watch at night and found it necessary to reef the main, he was to wake me. I stood in the companionway and watched him carefully until he was safely back in the cockpit. It helped immensely when lying below in the stillness and blackness of night wondering, "Is he still up there?" He did the same for me whenever I went forward.

We shared all aspects of sailing the boat, including navigation. Don initially planned our passages, but as I felt more secure in my abilities, we shared all navigation responsibilities about fifty-fifty.

When he was hunting, Don had always looked to the North Star as his guide. When on watch he did the same—looking to the two outside stars of the Big Dipper that pointed to the North Star. Back home, the North Star sat way up in the heavens, but as we sailed into the lower latitudes, it dropped dramatically lower in the sky.

Sailing through the Pacific islands is often referred to as the Milk Run, with a fair amount of information available. We studied the cruising guides that we had for most of the island groups in advance.

Don spent time each day practicing his celestial navigation skills. He took sun shots during the day and during night watches took star sights and moon shots to confirm our position and to keep up with celestial navigation skills.

Sometimes we practiced together. Don brought the sun down to the artificial horizon through the lens of the sextant, and when he said, "Mark" I noted the exact Zulu time. We worked out the sight mathematically, reducing it down to our latitude and longitude. Don could work out any of the sights very proficiently. I could work out a sun sight and felt able to navigate celestially, if necessary, by myself. My hopes were always that the Sat Nav wouldn't pack in.

Don checked all systems each day, always looking for chafing on lines, any loose nuts or bolts, etc. We took good care of our sails and they served us well for the next ten years.

Making a meal at sea can be a daunting experience. Try opening a can when you can't set it down on the counter (even on a wet towel) and trust it to stay there long enough for you to grab the can opener out of the drawer. The gimbaled stove top had fiddles to prevent pots and pans from careening off the top of the stove. But getting that can's contents poured into a pan and then getting it heated up and onto a plate—or most likely into a big bowl (best, so the contents couldn't so easily fly off)—was a task not to be taken lightly.

Over the years, cooking at sea never became any easier, but it did become routine. We learned what worked and what didn't. When re-reading journals of our Atlantic passage many years later, a passage with strong winds and big seas, we note that we called it our best passage ever, and the meals cooked gave proof that we managed better after a few years of knocking about!

If it was really rough going, crackers and peanut butter were always available, though it was my contention that a good hot meal was necessary not only for the body but for the soul. During the times when you have had no real sleep for so long and are so tired and so exhausted, you wish that you could just "pull over to the side and park"—as easily as that would be in a car. But you must remain alert, think ahead, check everything constantly and take care of the boat. When your life is in your own hands, a good meal lifts the spirits.

On our twenty-sixth day out, on April 1, 1990, our position indicated we were thirty miles off the island of Hiva Oa, our landfall. Not wanting to make a night entrance, we hove-to, awaiting daylight. We had trusted charts and our navigation skills, and we sat in the cockpit straining our eyes, determined to see the island. Life had revolved around the two of us, sailing the boat and keeping her safe. Our horizon had been simply the vast sea about us for almost an entire month. All was about to change and the adrenalin was running high.

Just before sunset, we could see the faded shape of land rising up above the sea on the distant horizon—the island of Hiva Oa! Sleep didn't come easily that night, knowing that the next day we would be in! We each stood our watches while the other attempted rest below, anticipation bubbling over. The Net had resounded with glorious tales of an outdoor shower ashore, one that seemed to be the highlight of everyone's landfall. We were as anxious as everyone to enjoy that shower ourselves—and to enjoy the company of others after so long at sea.

The following morning our course was set for Atuona Bay, on Hiva Oa's south side—a Port of Entry and the island landfall for many boats. There isn't anything quite like sailing your small vessel for weeks across nearly 3,000 miles of ocean and making landfall at a magical shore of your dreams. As *Windy Thoughts* jogged closer and closer to Hiva Oa, the grandeur and tropical paradise far surpassed anything we could ever have imagined.

Just outside Atuona Bay's entrance, we lowered sails and motored in to find twenty-one boats at anchor. Boat names made familiar on the evening roll call, and that now seemed like old buddies appeared to dip their sterns to say hello as we passed by. Boats were arriving daily to make clearance into French Polynesia, rest up and then make their way amongst the delights awaiting them as they moved west toward even more exotic landfalls.

The bay wasn't big enough for so many boats to swing freely at anchor, so good friends came out in their dinghy to row our stern anchor out for us to keep the boat from swinging too close to others. Other friends greeted us with a fresh French baguette purchased that morning at the local village bakery. Smothered with fresh butter, it made our first meal in French Polynesia. To this day, nothing has equaled that fresh baguette!

At anchor. Our minds were suddenly relieved from watches, positions and weather. Sea berths were abandoned and we could go to bed and sleep the night through together in our master berth. In truth, the bay was terribly swelly and *Windy Thoughts* rolled from gunwale to gunwale. But we paid it no mind and it was a few days before the discomfort became critical to us. Twenty-six days of rocking and rolling at sea, lots of sleep deprivation and the constant attention to the boat were all nearly forgotten in the wonderful aura of "being in".

First things first: we zoomed off to shore to stand under that outdoor shower in a stone enclosure that was open to the skies —and we luxuriated in all the fresh water that we could possibly stand.

Outside this enclosure was a stone counter with two spigots where laundry could be done. There is probably no happier laundry memory in all of our years of cruising than right here on Hiva Oa. Would I remember this day when our adventure was over and the ease of dropping clothes into a washer and dryer was a mundane task to be grumbled about?

After sleeping straight through the night we headed back ashore —to stand fully clothed under the shower again before beginning the two-mile trek into town in the steaming hot and humid temperatures. The state of being wet or even damp was considered a luxury and a comfort.

The small, neat and orderly village was the administrative center for the southern Marquesas. The French officials were most polite. We first had to go to the bank to put up our bond and found the small building with one room and one desk. Bond was necessary to make clearance into French Polynesia—to affirm that we had means to leave the country and weren't planning to overstay our visas. It cost us each the equivalent of a plane ticket back home that had to be paid in cash. Bank cards weren't accepted. The money would be forwarded to Papeete, Tahiti, and returned to us there.

Obtaining a sufficient amount of United States dollars for this bond prior to leaving Mexico wasn't easy and took a period of several weeks and many trips to the local bank. They would give us only a small amount at a time.

On one of our visits to the Mexican bank, a fellow standing behind us in the long and slow-moving line asked us to come with him to his office where he would give us American dollars. We followed him into a well-appointed office, and he sat down behind his desk, asked us how much money we wanted, and proceeded to take out his wallet and count out the exact amount in dollars. He invited us to come back at any time. We did, and periodically took enough pesos with us to exchange $500.00 at a time until we had enough to make our bond on arrival in French Polynesia.

Following the very orderly and easy clearance process, we headed right for the fresh baguettes, baked in a grocery. Canned butter from New Zealand was available and we stocked up on it for the future. Everything was terribly expensive, $2.00 for one carrot if you even found one. Our purchases were meager, generally limited to the baguettes each day and we easily made do with the many stores we had aboard, truly wanting for nothing.

Fresh fruit hung invitingly from the trees as we walked along the road, but on private property. Little was sold in the market—what was there horrifically priced. When good friends John and Francine on *Baron Rouge* arrived, we presented them with fresh baguettes and two lovely oranges purchased from a woman who greeted us from her porch as we passed by.

On Sunday, we rowed to shore (conserving on fuel that was difficult to come by) in our Sunday best to stand fully clothed under that welcoming water before hiking into the village for church services. Several other boaters joined us, and the entire village met at the center of town to proceed to the church with the Padre in the lead carrying a cross. The service itself was long and hot, with much standing, to which we weren't accustomed. We did love the singing in harmony that was entirely a cappella and a real joy to hear. Young and old, men and women had their own harmony, blended to make the most beautiful, melodious and haunting hymn singing whose language wasn't necessary to understand to be moved.

A copra boat arrived in the bay and would sell diesel to the cruising boats at anchor. At first light the following morning, Don and I took the dinghy over to the quay where the copra boat was docked. Every boater in the anchorage was eager to purchase diesel, never knowing just when the next opportunity may be.

Each boater purchased a fifty-five gallon barrel, from which we each then hand pumped into our own jerry cans. Everyone remained patient as the day wore on. We carried 6 six-gallon jerry cans on deck for diesel, and it was a full day in the hot tropical sun ferrying them back and forth by dinghy to *Windy Thoughts*.

Each time our cans were filled, Don and I carried them to the edge of a small cliff. *Breezy* was anchored out from shore with a stern anchor to keep her from bashing on the rocks. Don climbed down and I let each diesel can down on a rope. Waiting for just the right timing in the surge, Don made a flying leap for the dinghy with a heavy can in tow. Then he leapt back to the rocks for the next, until he had all six aboard and could take them across the bay to *Windy Thoughts*. It was a considerable task to get them all aboard and emptied into the fuel tanks before heading back to repeat the process again.

Laundry was always a ceaseless task and here in Atuona Bay, each day would find many first mates at those two water spigots with buckets and soap. There seemed to be two methods of doing laundry, the foot stomping method, and the toilet plunger method. I subscribed to the toilet plunger method and was never without mine as I plunged and agitated my way around the world. Don concurs that agitating my way around the world came naturally for me.

The sailboats' lifelines made wonderful drying lines, and more lines were often strung from the mast to the forestay. Every boat was arrayed with clothes, towels and sheets blowing in the breeze. With much to catch up on after the long ocean passage we all chatted happily away as we stomped and plunged.

Cruising isn't all work and no play. Our visual senses were on overload as we took in the beauty surrounding us. The mountains of this volcanic island reached the heights of 4,000 feet and fell directly into the open sea. Jagged peaks at their tops were adorned with thick, verdant greenery. Flowers abounded everywhere and the scent of the floral heaven that encompassed the island bombarded our senses continually.

Paul Gauguin's final resting place sat high on a hill and looked down on the beauty that was Hiva Oa. Don and I paid a visit to this rather humble spot in a beautiful setting that must be very satisfying to the soul.

The temperatures stayed a constant eighty-seven degrees, but the humidity was much more prevalent. Wind came down from the mountains, keeping us all quite comfortable in the anchorage, and we slept well.

As we traded stories about our big passage, we found ourselves fortunate to have had no major problems. *Sloop du Jour* had turned back to mainland Mexico just four days out because of a serious leak in their rudderpost. Other friends blew out their mainsail in a particularly ferocious squall ten days out, and at the same time, the cable for their steering broke. They didn't carry any spare cable. The captain broke into the Pacific Mariner's Net, wanting to talk to *Windy Thoughts*. Though he didn't have a Ham license, the Net Operator allowed his call and we fell off to another frequency on HF radio and learned of their troubles.

Another boater, an engineer who knew their boat make well, broke in to tell them he would think through their broken steering cable problem. He gave a frequency to call him in the morning and told them to go to bed and just get some sleep. It was a very reassuring voice, and two very shaky people on their first ocean passage were able to do just that, even though the boat was completely out of control in very big and bouncy seas.

The next morning the concerned party (who became friends of us all) told the captain to take out a length of their lifelines to use for steering cable. He knew that it was the exact size of the steering cable and it made a simple solution after all.

By the time the boat reached Tahiti, the couple made plans to ship the boat home. We purchased two more Arco solar panels from them to install alongside the original two panels.

The boom was broken on another boat during a squall. On and on went the stories. It made our passage, one that we felt was wrought with ups and downs, seem so very mundane after all! We felt blessed that *Windy Thoughts* had made her ocean passage debut with nary a real problem. We breathed sighs of relief that so far, so good.

By the time we left Hiva Oa, there were twenty-seven boats in the anchorage from the United States, Canada, France, Switzerland and England. Most would wait out the hurricane season in either New Zealand or Australia. Everyone had glorious cruising grounds ahead.

Had we really sailed our *Windy Thoughts* all this way to make landfall here with others who also had sailed thousands of miles of ocean? A special camaraderie came from knowing what it had taken and what each had been through. We shared in something that was special to all of us and that couldn't easily put into words.

LETTERS TO SUSAN

April 16, 1990
Baie Hane Vave
Ile Fatu Hiva, Marquesas Islands
French Polynesia

Bon Jour!

Last Thursday at dawn we left Hiva Oa and beat south to Fatu Hiva, the most southern and most remote island of the Marquesas group in French Polynesia. It was only fifty miles, and you know that when I agree to go to weather it must be with stars in my eyes as to what is ahead! Few boats were going there. We made it into Hane Vave Bay (Ha' Nay Va' Vay) just before dark, and we aren't disappointed!

We would easily agree that this is perhaps the most spectacular anchorage in the Marquesas group—just shockingly beautiful, with a narrow valley that comes down to the bay between steep mountains with rocky, spirally, turret-shaped peaks that surround the bay itself. The tiny village is just ashore, with walking paths but no roads and no vehicles. Transportation is by pirogue canoes, the local outriggers that they build themselves—but with motors.

A footpath winds up the valley and through the village of about one hundred people. Homes are scattered about amongst the palms and the intense greenery. The people have very little as compared to the folks in Atuona Bay.

They live off what nature provides along with their chickens, pigs, wild goats and some fishing. A copra boat stops by once a month with supplies, though they make use of what the land offers for most of their wants.

The men asked for ammunition of twenty-two shells to kill the wild goat that they otherwise had to frighten off the side of the mountain in a fall, not easily done. The French government allots them each a specific number of shells for hunting purposes each year, evidently too often used long before the next allotment. Though we wanted to be of help, we don't carry twenty-two shells aboard and weren't at all sure it would be wise were we to be able to do so.

The young men have been taken in by the boom-box and wanted batteries for trade far more than they wanted fish hooks. Don is prepared with lots of fish hooks. Times change nearly everywhere you go in the world—even here—where cannibalism was still practiced up into the 1950s! We could see the archway in the rock formations high on the mountain through which marauding tribes used to pass to vanquish those on this side of the mountain.

The women seem always to be busy washing clothes, making meals over the outdoor fires of the outdoor kitchens and taking care of children. The men don't appear to be doing much other than sitting around, and seldom do we see them out fishing.

Tapa cloth is a popular art form in these islands and is made from the

breadfruit tree, its bark pounded to obtain the flat smooth surface. Designs are painted on the tapa cloth with the juice of the mulberry—the entire process a long and laborious one. A young woman invited us into her home and we purchased a sampling of this beautiful art practiced since ancient times. She had two babies and number three on the way, living in a home of one room with two mattresses on the floor and a table made from a board. Though our ability to communicate is minimal, I managed a teensy bit of my schoolgirl French, most of which I have long since foregotten.

Only three or four miles down the coast, another village on Fatu Hiva sits just ashore. With too much swell to get ashore safely we won't attempt a visit. On Good Friday everyone from that village hiked over the mountains to

Hane Vave for services and a shared meal. On Saturday those in Hane Vave hiked to that village to spend the night, returning in pirogues on Easter Sunday, right after services.

By now, three other boats joined us in the anchorage at Fatu Hiva. The local villagers invited all of us ashore for an Easter dinner on the beach, so special and so very thoughtful of them.

A young couple from Switzerland lost their autopilot when they left the Galapagos and had to steer the entire passage to Hiva Oa. Though Fatu Hiva isn't a Port of Entry, they were worn out with exhaustion and intended to stay as long as possible to rest up, keeping a low profile. Two French boats arrived and our little contingent was elated to be invited to share in the Easter festivities.

A wild pig was killed—and roasted in a pit in the ground. Breadfruit, taro, bananas and several unknown (to us) foods were cooked under the rocks with a fire of dried coconut shells. Raw fish with lime juice was served in coconut milk with salt and onion. We were introduced to the pamplemousse on Hiva Oa, in the grapefruit family but much larger and light green in color. One whole fruit made two meals for the two of us. It was one thing that we were familiar with at our Easter dinner.

I was offered something mushy and before I looked up, the fellow had scooped up a handful in his hand and plopped it onto my plate. Nothing to do but to eat it with a smile on my face and a heart that kept saying, "Just swallow, enjoy this and be thankful"—because there really was so much to be thankful for.

It was a wonderful meal shared there, amid nature like none we had seen before.

The French boats left, but two American boats brought friends who joined us one day on a long hike up the mountain—through thick greenery and lush surroundings in search of a beautiful waterfall, sweating absolute bullets the entire way. Clean fresh water awaited us at the end of the trek, such a treat after so much salt water. It was like finding that pot of gold at the end of the rainbow—and everyone jumped or dove into the lovely pool at its base. On the hike back down the mountain, we lay down in a stream fully clothed and let the

refreshing fresh water flow along around us. Next time you turn on the faucet, think of me.

Such beauty and such friendly welcoming people on Fatu Hiva made us want to stay longer, but we have allowance of only a few weeks to make it to Papeete, Tahiti, where official clearance actually takes place. We must be there by July 2, to apply for our three-month extension on our visa for French Polynesia. Before we left Fatu Hiva the villagers performed native dances for us.

We want to see more of the Marquesas Islands, as well as stop in at some of the atolls of the Tuamotus before sailing on west for Tahiti and other islands of the Society group. Passages are now only a few days in length between the islands, and it is a leisurely mode of cruising we are finally into as we bob along west.

April 24, 1990
Baie Hakahau, Ile Ua Pou, Marquesas Islands
French Polynesia

Bon Jour!

Still in the Marquesas group, we have continued on westward to Ile Ua Pou, where we met up again with George and Connie, aboard *Beleza*, out of California and first met back at Hiva Oa when getting our diesel. Many good times have been shared together and we hope to bump into each other more as we continue on.

Ua Pou has a lovely village with six stores, paved streets and beautiful land-

scaping. As in most of the villages, a real downtown area doesn't exist—but rather stores are scattered here and there in homes. An open door with goods inside welcomes you to walk right in.

When Don and I were poking our noses into the local school, a teacher introduced himself and invited us for a tour of the island in his jeep. Weren't we lucky? The views were spectacular up in the mountains—so lush and green everywhere.

One of the most interesting stops during the day was at the home of his friend, the local tattooist. In the past, entire bodies were covered with tattoos, and it is an art here that most of the local men still regard with high respect. Stunningly beautiful designs are commonly seen— but I was glad that Don didn't show any interest in doing the same himself!

At the end of our day with this generous fellow, he took us to his home to meet his family. He gave us a huge stalk of bananas before driving us to a friend's orchard where we picked pamplemousse, our favorite fruit.

A stalk of bananas can be seen hanging in our cockpit most always as we pass through these islands. I keep busy baking banana bread, banana cake, banana muffins, banana pancakes; you name it. These bananas are very sweet and so much more delicious than those we get at the supermarket back home. But having the oven on in this climate is a price we pay to enjoy this bounty!

May 5, 1990
Baie Taihoae, Ile Nuku Hiva, Marquesas Islands
French Polynesia

Bon Jour! Bon Jour!

This may be the last letter until reaching Papeete, Tahiti. We plan to leave Nuku Hiva for the Tuamotus on Monday, and we expect to be in Papeete around the last week of June in order to make it in time to apply for our three-month extension on our visas.

A lovely day sail of only twenty-six miles brought us here to Nuku Hiva, the capital of the Marquesas Islands and a Port of Entry as well, so there are many boats here—about twenty-five in the huge anchorage.

Before arriving here in Baie Taihoae we first went into Daniel's Bay, only three miles from here and named after a local Polynesian who lives ashore with his wife. He lets us use his water spigot! While there we hiked a path known as the old King's Highway to the second highest waterfall in the world. Along the way we passed many ancient stone foundations of four or five feet in height, as well as two original tikis that were sitting alongside the path. Most original tikis have now been removed.

Don and I wanted to get off the beaten path and were going to visit Keuhei and Fakarava. However, one fellow going to Keuhei has talked twelve other boats into going there. Surely, each of them has passed this on to others because it seems that everyone we talk to is heading for the "secret atoll". Perhaps we might stay on the Milk Run through the Tuamotus after all.

Because anything in the groceries in these islands costs about four times more than at home, we are happy that we have such an abundant supply of provisions aboard. However, we did purchase canned New Zealand butter at just $1.69 a pound. The dry mixes you sent us are certainly making a hit and tonight I used one to make lemon chicken. With the addition of cream of chicken soup to the lemon sauce, a fresh lemon squeezed into the mixture and a can of my excellent white chicken meat, it was absolutely delicious served over rice. Can you hear our "thank you" from there?

Though most are eating out frequently, we are saving ourselves for Papeete and only treat ourselves to a very expensive Coke now and then. Hiva Oa had one restaurant, as well as one in a home both on Ua Pou and here on Nuku Hiva. Both lunch and dinner are a standard $25.00 or $30.00. However, we adjusted to all of this, four years ago.

It looks like we haven't made a dent in supplies, and we are about two months into our eight month food supply on board—doing quite well as we ramble and rumble along.

We are gearing up for the Tuamotus Archipelago and looking forward to atoll life where we doubt there will be much by way of supplies available—though we can't imagine needing anything at all. However, a few Snickers bars would really taste good.

MANINI ATOLL: A NIGHT TO REMEMBER

May 15, 1990
Manihi Atoll, Iles Tuamotus
French Polynesia

Hello Dear Friend,

Experiencing our first atoll adventure has been a bit more of an adventure than we would have preferred, but well worth it!

We arrived the morning after our radio contact, May 10, the radio contact for me the highlight of many days. It was just so good to hear your voice and I am so glad you are a Ham as well!

I have just made us both lemonades after coming aboard from some snorkeling on the nearby reef that sits a bit too close behind us for comfort. Don dove on the anchor and it is hooked well, so the boat shouldn't move. We are relaxing in the cockpit under a perfectly clear blue sky that stretches from horizon to horizon, turquoise water shimmering around us in the bright sun shining down on us. Picture perfect once again.

Leaving the Marquesas with their lovely but generally very rolly anchorages, we have also left behind the tiny no-no flies that bothered many to no end. Luckily, I was never bothered by them and Don only moderately so. Little bites responded immediately to hydrocortisone cream and we have scads of this aboard. Never having had a mosquito bite in my life, perhaps these little fellows didn't like my blood either. The local people laughingly refer to the no-no flies as their own built in deterrent to tourists. But they seemed a small price to pay to be in these magical islands, an experience most of us will likely never have again—and we paid a grand price in adventure to get here.

Sailing westward in the Pacific to the atolls of the Tuamotus Archipelago required close attention to charts and our position, with coral reefs always a danger. *Charlie's Charts* was full of valuable information on how to best traverse the currents in the passes. The atolls extend only about three feet above water, making them visible only when nearly upon them.

In wind and seas, and when there are no nautical markings, it is very difficult to locate these breaks in the reef that form the pass. The Sat Nav gave us a fix about a half hour before arriving at Manihi Atoll, so we were able to determine where the pass should be—more or less. The guide said, "Look for a few sticks sticking up, placed by the fishermen on the port side of the entrance." Navigation aids of the more local kind.

Sloop du Jour is in the lagoon along with one other boat, neither in sight of us, as this lagoon is four miles across. They report nothing to see where they are but the outer reef off which they are anchored and waves pounding on the other side of it very close by.

Our entry into the lagoon was a major adventure of the kind that we didn't want to experience!

After making our approach, we hove-to at first light about three miles off and timed the pass for 11:30 a.m., with information passed on by *Sloop du Jour*.

Don took the precaution of having the anchor at the ready before we started through the pass. It didn't look very wide and there was some turbulence. But we would trust local knowledge and hoped to have something close to slack water. We rolled in the Yankee, dropped the main and secured it on the boom.

The currents in these passes are nothing less than those in our tidal passes back home, but without both tide and current tables there is no easy way to know what will be happening. Though there are numerous schools of thought on how to go about it, radio chat suggested that none of the theories seemed to work for anyone—even the moon-set theory that we planned to use.

One fellow suggested—after listening to varying opinions—that the best time to go through any of the passes is when you get there. We turned on the engine and headed right into the pass, hearts pounding.

Wouldn't you know that right in the middle of the pass—and with about five knots of current against us—the engine suddenly lost all power! I was on the bowsprit and up on the rails to get good visual on the bombies, those coral head tips that rose to the near surface all around us.

Don let go of the wheel, dove below and hit the starter for the engine while the bow swung right over the bombies. I felt sure that we were about to hole the boat right here in the middle of nowhere, our *Windy Thoughts* never to see civilization as she knew it again—instead, to grace this entrance with her forlorn body there for perpetuity—and us to catch the next copra boat out of here with likely few of our possessions in tow.

Windy Thoughts was reacting to the strong current with little bursts of energy from the engine that puffed a bit and then poofed out again, puffed to life once again and then poofed again. Don was running the Yankee out while doing all of this and hollered to me to stay by the anchor and keep watch for coral heads, the lot of them something about which I could do absolutely nothing.

I mentally readied myself to drop the hook if necessary, still watching those bombies as we swung above them—though suddenly in a way that was moving the boat back out of the pass nice as could be! Couldn't have done better with the engine on and control of the boat!

Once we were off far enough to begin to relax a bit, Don dove into the engine compartment, bled the engine once again and switched filters. Fortunately, the engine started up and he tried to duplicate the minutes prior—but still all was well.

Should we go ahead and start back in?

Well, of course, we would and we did, this time going through with nary a mishap—but my heart continued to beat frantically until I knew that we were out of the grip of the current. Though it is easier to control the boat with the current against you, five knots was giving us a very slow entry at about one- knot speed, tops. This seemed to take forever, more than enough time for the engine to do its thing again. But, hallelujah—we made it through!

Once in the clear it wasn't clear, because the lagoon is seemingly mined with coral heads. *Sloop du Jour* had radioed us with information from the head man on Manihi, who requested that we anchor in a different part of the lagoon off the small resort. I hung on the bowsprit rail and we slowly worked our way a mile and a half from the entrance.

So here we sit, right in front of a resort that is very low key and very expensive. Twelve small huts with thatched roofs sit out over the lagoon, with a restaurant in an A-frame building nestled in amongst them. For a while we saw neither hide nor hair of tourists, but learned they keep busy with snorkeling trips and various other adventures.

We have met nice people from both San Diego and Arizona, as well as most of the others at the resort, when we were invited to join the small group to do a drift-dive on the pass. This, the same pass through which we held our breaths for so long while going through on the boat! The French dive captain even pulled the launch alongside *Windy Thoughts* to pick us up.

The launch went right out to the outer pass through the reef and we jumped into the water to drift-snorkel back through the pass with an incoming current. Bruno, the dive captain, gave strict instructions to stay along the edge of the pass—and to stay with the current as well as with the group. With faces pressed against our masks, we viewed the other world just below the surface, and the dive boat picked us up before reaching the bar with its big rips. My, what a difference this was to bringing the boat through the pass!

Yesterday, the launch picked us up for a ride to the small village, too far for *Breezy* to attempt. With two stores to welcome us, I found flour that everyone had said wouldn't be available in the Tuamotus; dried milk and a few canned goods were available as well, though we needed none of these items. Of course, a few Snickers bars weren't available.

May 18, 1990
Still at Manihi Atoll

Bon Jour Again,

Looking about us as we sit off this atoll, we see a very harsh environment, with only coconut palms and some bushes growing.

Determining slack water in the passes is elusive, because there often isn't any slack water. Seas break over the atolls—and depending on the volume and the winds, it is frequently ebbing. Because there is always considerable wind, this produces considerable seas.

The San Diego people have been out to the boat and we have taken a shower in their hut. Such luxury! The rooms are small and not elaborate, but have the essentials and are very nice. The individual huts sit on stilts out over the water in the lagoon, with wooden walkways to each—a wonderfully private feeling.

A small round building with a thatched roof holds a bar. After treating ourselves to cold drinks, the proprietor raced down the beach after us to return our tip. It is the height of rudeness to leave a tip. How culturally inept we are!

One evening, Don and I got all spiffed up for dinner with the folks from San Diego and Arizona and went ashore to the very nice restaurant. Fish is on the menu every night and that night it was tuna, our least favorite fish. We paid a very hefty price for what we caught in abundance in the Baja! Still, we enjoyed a restaurant meal in a lovely atmosphere with lovely people—and must remember—all this in the South Pacific and in the Tuamotus. We aren't likely to pass this way again.

From Papeete, Tahiti, guests fly the several hundred miles to the small airstrip on Manihi Atoll in a little puddle-jumper plane. When we think of the cost of their trip as well as accommodations it makes us glad to have our home with us. Admittedly, they got here the easier and faster way—but certainly not with the adventure we have shared!

Yesterday, we came across the lagoon to anchor near *Sloop du Jour*. There was a reason for leaving our paradise and moving over here—where all we see is seas crashing very close in front of us on the reef off which we are anchored. But we are safe.

Near the resort, *Windy Thoughts* sat at anchor off the reef that gave us our private snorkeling experiences. Reef sharks whizzed about us to say hello, and the gaily-colored tropical fish nodded their welcomes as we cooled ourselves off in our own little paradise.

Several days later, when life seemed to be going very smoothly, the wind began to rise a bit about 4 p.m., setting the boat back toward a lee shore with reef only about fifty feet behind us. That same reef that we so enjoyed snorkeling was now looking rather threatening!

Surely, it must be a squall that would soon blow itself out.

It didn't. It gets dark about 6 pm in the tropics and by then we couldn't up the anchor and con our way across the lagoon to the protected side amongst the full garden of coral. We should have done so earlier. Winds had risen rapidly to thirty-five knots steady with gusts higher, and dangerous wind waves had developed in the lagoon. We settled in for a long vigil and anchor watch, anxious because *Windy Thoughts'* stern was now within a few feet of the reef.

I was well into red alert by this point.

Our vigil continued into the black of the night. Oh, how inviting those thatched-roof huts ashore looked. Just inside, people were safely tucked into their comfortable beds without a care in the world—and they didn't have to give the winds and seas any heed at all. Our situation was such a stark contrast that my heart ached for it to be over, for calm to once again descend on us. Would we ever again have that wonderful feeling of being semi-oblivious to the weather?

Windy Thoughts was encountering seas in what had only shortly before been a beautifully calm lagoon, battling for her life. Oh Lord, please don't let us end up on that reef! It was ever so close behind us. My stomach lurched with terror. At sea there were times when I would give anything to have land so nearby. Now, I would give anything to be out in the safety of the sea, with room to keep us safe.

With the bowsprit plunging into waves coming over us, our close proximity to the reef didn't allow us to put out more scope, and the ninety feet of chain in forty feet of water wasn't sufficient scope for the conditions. This unnerved us. The force of the water was putting very heavy strain on the anchor and chain, and the bow rose with each wave just as if outside at sea, pounding hard against the onslaught. Don started the engine and steered into the seas to keep the pressure off the anchor.

We always used a snubber on the anchor chain, and Don had made two in ten-and twenty-foot lengths of triple strand, one-inch nylon line as shock absorbers for the chain. The shorter one was much faster and easier to hook or unhook in the conditions. He secured it around the Sampson post and hooked it to the chain with a 3/8 inch stainless steel snap hook. At about 1:00 in the morning, the snap hook broke clean in two.

Seventeen hours later we were still with the same conditions, still in the cockpit and very worn out. *Windy Thoughts* had come very, very close to making a permanent home right in front of the resort—but we made it through the night.

The morning radio was alive with reports from other boats telling about the same wind conditions throughout the Tuamotus. It was called a Maramou wind and was expected to last for eight more days! Getting out of there was paramount. It was near impossible to get the anchor up under the conditions with just the two of us. Someone needed to control the boat, driving into the seas to keep pressure off the chain and someone needed to be at the windlass and—someone needed to dive on the anchor to release it from the coral head!

Knowing there was that professional dive captain ashore, I suggested that we ask if he might hire out as the third hand. The conditions prevented us from getting to shore in the dinghy, so one of us would have to get in the water and swim for it. Since the other would be responsible for the boat, I guess you know who volunteered to do the dastardly deed. I wasn't about to be left alone on a boat that was threatening to drag onto the reef at any moment! Wild horses couldn't stop me and I was into my shorty wetsuit (for protection when I expected to be bashed onto the coral reef), pulled on my mask, snorkel and fins—and was over the side before Don could argue the point any longer.

The coral reef was very close behind the boat, but actual land wasn't close at all. The seas were of the sort that made breathing, even with the snorkel, difficult.

When I felt the sand under my feet, I made a beeline for the beach and headed right for the restaurant—where I found the young and brawny Bruno at breakfast. He spoke just enough English to understand our dilemma and popped right up and led me to the launch, a Polynesian driver along with us.

The driver was expert at maneuvering the high-powered launch, so he managed to get us close enough alongside *Windy Thoughts* for both Bruno and me to jump onto the cap rail and over the lifelines. Both men agreed that we couldn't remain here at anchor.

Bruno would dive on the anchor, while I controlled the boat at the helm to keep the bow directly over the anchor, and Don worked at the windlass. The plan worked like clockwork and though it took a while to accomplish—with Bruno coming up for air and giving Don progress reports—the anchor was finally freed.

There was just one more favor to ask. Would they possibly be willing to guide us through the coral to the other side of the lagoon? The driver knew the lagoon like the back of his hand and the rough seas made it virtually impossible to see the coral heads beneath the water. Bruno kindly jumped right back into the launch and they headed out across the lagoon, slowly enough for us to follow along very directly behind them.

When we reached the lee side, it was as if heaven had dropped down and taken our troubles away.

Though Bruno refused any payment, Don stuffed a very healthy franc note for each of them into a Ziploc bag and passed it to him in a float bag.

Our vista now isn't exactly pretty as it was on the opposite side of the lagoon, but we sit in quiet waters—though with screaming wind, still. We are feeling precariously close to shore; the outer reef off which we are anchored is just a few feet away and we can see and hear the big seas crashing. But oh, does it feel good to relax! If only the wind would lie down, so we didn't have the constant screaming in the rigging.

Don's birthday is the twenty-first and we planned to have a nice dinner in the lovely restaurant ashore. Our privileged life while anchored off the resort has changed to sitting on the boat while waiting out "reinforced trade winds". The radio gives proof to the fact that many others are sitting in boredom in lagoons of other atolls as well. I remind us that boredom is better than that other situation.

We do visit back and forth with the folks on *Sloop du Jour*, as well as the folks on *Sarasen* who are faced with rebuilding their engine. Be thankful for boredom!

May 21, 1990
Manihi Atoll, still

Today is Don's birthday and we are still anchored off that reef here in Manihi Atoll. *Sloop du Jour* came over for dinner and we celebrated with chili and biscuits and birthday cake. Certainly not fancy fare, but I made the chili with some canned spicy pork from Mexico and some of our canned roast beef. It tasted great and we had a fun time.

The folks at the resort were kind once again to include us in a tour, picking us up in the launch to take us to a black pearl farm where the oyster beds are laid out in the lagoon. In a small hut just ashore, a Japanese specialist works at a very specialized and highly paid job. Armed guards stand at the door and no one is allowed to watch him work. The specialist spends his days planting or "seeding" the oyster that is then returned to the oyster beds, where it takes five years for the pearl to grow to maturity around the foreign substance.

Afterwards, we could purchase black pearls right here at a considerably lower price than up ahead in Papeete in the jewelry stores. They look like a little stainless steel ball to me and though Don wanted me to have one, I am sure he was secretly relieved that I didn't care for one. The fact that we didn't have $500.00 to grab one of the least expensive may have been a significant factor!

The waters of this lagoon are simply beautiful, but shelling hasn't been very good here or in the Marquesas—and I am glad that I made a point to make up a collection while in Mexico. I have them all sorted out by kind and color and stowed away in Ziploc bags.

Up until these past days, it seemed rather easy to nearly forget to pay attention to weather once we were in, because both the air and water temperature always stay in the upper eighty degrees—with steady trade winds. These reinforced trade winds are blowing up into the forty-knot range consistently and can let up any day now as far as we are all concerned.

Perhaps we might forego any more atoll stops when we can leave here and instead make right for Tahiti. We are ready for a change in daily life—perhaps restaurants! Just a little treat!

A few days later:
Somewhere between Manihi Atoll and Tahiti

Windy Thoughts is bobbing pleasantly along toward the Society Islands and we plan to make our landfall on Tahiti, going in at Papeete. I am on my night watch on our second night out. All is quiet and the sky is filled with every star up there shining right down on us. The winds are wonderful at about eighteen knots right on our quarter and the autopilot is steering us along nicely as *Windy Thoughts* reaches through the sea. I am much too relaxed and lazy at the moment to expend the effort required to give you a more exact point of latitudinal and longitudinal reference—but we will be in Tahiti tomorrow!

We thought that our entry and then the Maramou wind were enough drama in Manihi Atoll, but there was more to come before leaving there. When those winds decided to lie down after eight (very long) days, everyone was ready to be on the move, no matter in which atoll they were holed up.

By now, the fellow on *Sarasen* had spent eight to ten hours each day of the windy week rebuilding his engine and getting it functioning again. Luckily, *Sloop du Jour* has the same engine and David was able to pass along some important parts not in *Sarasen's* spares supply. *Sarasen* left the same morning and was right behind us. Don was at the helm as we neared the pass and I was again at the bow. The anchor was at the ready, the sail cover off, ready to set sail as soon as we cleared the pass. All of us had discussed the timing of the current in the pass ad nauseam. We planned it to be good this time.

As we started through, the current was very strong against us.

And then, drama struck once again about halfway through the pass when suddenly, the anchor began to run out! The dog was off to be at the ready, and I was keeping watch at the bow, sure that I didn't do anything to set all of this in motion—that is, unless I accidentally stepped on the pressure pad for the windlass. Would I have done that?

The boat swung rapidly sideways in the current, no matter that Don put every bit of power to it. I was once again face-to-face with bombies that were much too close to the surface and directly under me and the bow. However, this time I was frantically trying to put the dog back on while Don screamed forward, "Get the anchor up!"

While attempting to do just that, the chain ran out so fast that it might have been trying to beat all records. Gads, think! Is it, first stick the stick in to put the dog on? How could this not be automatic at this point? I've done this hundreds of times—but didn't want to stick my hand in there and lose any fingers with the chain's rapid descent over the bow of the boat! Brain kicking into gear and thankful for power windlasses, I did get the anchor up—while Don had his own drama back in the cockpit trying to control the boat and get us through the pass.

After a few very long minutes, we were through, Don remaining cool as a cucumber and me assuming the pose of one who takes such things in stride—just another day in the life of cruising.

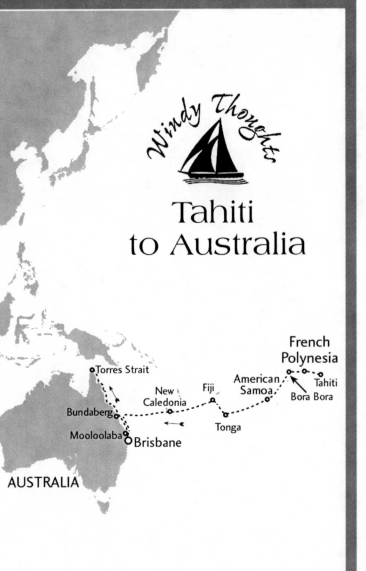

Windy Thoughts

Tahiti
to Australia

French
Polynesia

Torres Strait

New
Caledonia

Fiji

American
Samoa

Tahiti

Bora Bora

Bundaberg

Tonga

Mooloolaba Brisbane

AUSTRALIA

Chapter 7

Ironara, Malole Lele, and Bula Bula

Only at anchor can one savor the wonders of the remote.

June 6, 1990
Papeete, Tahiti
French Polynesia

Dear Susan,

Papeete is a far cry from the peaceful serenity of the islands that we have visited to this point—but we are thoroughly enjoying the "bright lights and city sights" scene as a huge change of pace. A modern, bustling city with lots of traffic, Papeete invites us to enjoy many good cafes, restaurants and shops.

Many boaters drop anchor out from the quay right downtown, and back down to the quay with sterns a jump or a board away for disembarking. Only fenders separate the boats on either side, lines criss-cross every which way in the process—anchor lines sometimes becoming entwined as well. The boats are a very narrow sidewalk's width away from the busy and very noisy traffic. Everyone seems to love it.

When we came through the pass in Tahiti's surrounding reef, the city of Papeete sat invitingly in front of us. Steering to starboard, we followed the lagoon just a few miles on around to the Maeva Beach Hotel, in front of which *Windy Thoughts* has rested on her laurels for the past week. For $3.40 a day we have use of the dinghy dock, fresh water, showers, garbage and full run of the hotel pool. We pick up "le truck" right in front of the hotel—taxis that are truck cabs with an elongated body and are open air, with long seats along the two sides and a covering over the top for sunshade.

We find ourselves keeping rather quiet about the peacefulness out here at the lovely hotel anchorage where we are enjoying such solitude. Many likely feel it is just too far away from the action, but with the le truck service, we don't find two miles distance to be any problem. A few other boats sit at anchor here as well and we meet ashore at the pool, where we visit and enjoy cold drinks and play tourists.

The cruisers have use of bathrooms ashore, lovely and clean with fresh flowers adorning the counters each day—and where we can stand under the shower to our hearts' content!

On arrival, we immediately headed for shore and indulged in the first hamburgers and fries we have had in a year. Fortified by our Visa, we are eating our way around Papeete, though sticking to lunches that aren't so hard on the budget. We wanted to develop the pictures taken during all of these last months, but the standard cost around town is $47.00 per roll of film so it may be Australia before we can get them developed!

A coral reef surrounds each of these Society Islands, but there is little current with which to contend. Papeete's pass is quite wide and has lighted range markers! We haven't seen the likes of navigation aids in a long time! Several boats have entered at night.

Good friends on *Beleza* arrived a few days before us, attempting the pass at 3 a.m. after several days out in strong winds and big seas. Their autopilot had packed up so, they were hand steering for days on end and were very tired. Unfortunately, they completely missed the pass, confusing the range markers with other lights of the surrounding city—very easy to do. The range markers were also solid green instead of occulting as is shown on the charts— that in itself very confusing.

With winds at around twenty-five knots, they drove the boat full force right onto the reef. The seas just picked the boat up and threw it on its opposite sides three different times. Connie immediately put out a radio call. George wasn't able to back the boat off the reef, so, figuring to have lost the boat by now anyway, he gunned the engine in forward gear. At that very moment a big wave lifted the boat—and he drove right over the reef! As it turned out, there was little damage aside from a small chunk out of the rudder. Now, how often could that happen?

On to more tranquil thoughts: big surf pounds constantly against and over the reef that separates us from the open sea where we sit at anchor. We look only ten miles distant at the island of Moorea, a simply beautiful sight. The sunsets are spectacular in color and mesmerize us nearly as much as they do when at sea; perhaps now there are too many other distractions.

We are so enjoying this time in Papeete, while we indulge ourselves in such civilized pleasures as meals out, wandering through the many stores and the fine, but very expensive, supermarkets so readily available. Thankfully, we stocked up well before leaving Mexico and have only to restock such things as flour, onions, potatoes and produce. Prices are very high and we wander the aisles in awe of the abundance of delicious things, amazed at the new things to see and at how our perspective changes as to our necessities.

At present, we are waiting for our mail to arrive and with it our insurance policy. We must come to some decision as to where we will hole up for the hurricane season. Suva, Fiji, is in the offing, as are Tonga and American Samoa. To top it off, this is supposedly an El Niño year, though it is impossible to tell yet where the problems will be. New Zealand continues to be right up there as well, but the passage down as well as back up can be a most unpleasant one. Perhaps Australia? We must be deciding soon!

Papeete is celebrating its centennial and beautiful Polynesian dancing and singing surrounds us. Practice for the pirogue races takes place right through the anchorage and we have a front row seat. Fete is in July and the Polynesians are preparing for the big festivities that always mark this occasion. Flowers abound everywhere, and as in the rest of Polynesia the women wear tiaras of flowers in their hair. All is so bright and colorful.

We are feeling quite continental now. The European women at the hotel go completely topless at the pool. Young and old alike, from nine to ninety and in all shapes and sizes, sun themselves and walk about topless all day. The bikini bottoms are so skimpy as to make one wonder if they are really there at all. I, of course, remain my conservative self and don't join in the local custom.

Thankfully, we have a good rowing dinghy; gasoline has been scarce and so expensive that we haven't used the engine during these past months. Gasoline at $4.00 a gallon is available at a very nice marina just nearby, where there are few, if any, cruising boats. An abundance of alternative anchorage space is available with good shelter.

I am very disappointed that we are having so many problems making radio contact together. Surely, we are just too far away now for boat-to-boat contact, but those conversations on the Pacific crossing were so dear to my heart! Not able to legally transmit while at anchor, I haven't even tried to make a phone patch through to you. I will get a call through to you just as soon as is possible and once at sea again.

June 17, 1990
Moorea
French Polynesia

Bonjour Once Again!

We join Captain Cook in thought as we sit in Cook's Bay, off the island of Moorea and only ten miles from Tahiti. Perhaps this is the real paradise right here! All of the beauty of the South Pacific as dreamed of, but with some subtle but very nice shore amenities.

We await extensions on our visas that should be ready by end of June. In the interim we will enjoy time here and will return to Papeete to pick them up. Though we were enjoying the liveliness that Papeete offered, we are quite sure we may never want to leave Moorea!

The small village of Pao Pao is just a walk down the road, with three very small, though very good, Chinese grocery stores. A few cafes and boutiques dot the road between us and the village. Tourism is way down right now in the Society Islands, very nice for us though not for the local economy.

Several unobtrusive hotels dot the island, all low-rise and of the bungalow type with thatched roofs. Though very upscale, they are nevertheless quite inconspicuous, nestled in palms and greenery. They sit right on lagoons that are a shimmery turquoise blue-green and that glow like a gemstone under these tropical skies. All seems to reflect a quiet village life.

Just ashore sits the Club Bali Hai that lets us use their shower facilities that are (again) adorned with fresh flowers every morning. A good dinghy tie up is available, all is immaculate and at no charge! The cruisers gather at the Club Bali Hai afternoons for visits by the pool. Don and I generally order cold drinks and often huge hot dogs that are delicious. Somehow, it doesn't seem right to have use of so many pleasures without giving them our business.

Perhaps you know the story of the three Bali Hai boys, Americans who came here in the 1960s, started the Club Bali Hai, and now have three hotels in the islands.

We have thumbed a ride in the back of the local garbage truck (largely used to transport limbs and tree cuttings) to get a tour of the island, standing up and holding on for dear life. It was pretty bouncy but sure gave us a good look about!

We also used our thumbs to get a ride to church, discovering that the lovely service that we attended in a little church amongst the palms, and where we were received so graciously, is considered to be "terribly fundamentalist", as it was put to us—evidently a sign that they may be devout Christians. It was, in fact, one of the most beautiful services we have ever attended, and the hymn singing in the native tongue was again a capella, with the haunting harmony that is found everywhere in these islands. On our arrival everyone stood outside the church and each person shook our hands in welcome. On leaving, we were treated to the same graciousness.

Our thumbs also did us service when a very elderly gentleman picked us up one day and gave us a ride to the rum factory for a tour. Of American descent, he has lived on Moorea for sixty some years, and lost his wife of those same sixty years only two weeks ago. The story of how he found her, married her and brought her here to Moorea to live was fascinating.

When our friend was a young man, his father sailed with his family from San Francisco to Moorea in their large sailing vessel. Falling in love with the island, his father purchased several acres that included all of Cook's Bay, as well as the equally large bay adjacent to it and the land surrounding both bays well up into the mountains.

The son fell in love with a young woman hired aboard as help for the voyage, and he married her when the boat returned to San Francisco. His father gave him all of Cook's Bay and a large amount of surrounding land as a wedding present. They returned and spent all of their remaining days, together, right here.

In the past they had copra plantations, a hat business and several small industries in which the locals worked. As the days of the locals wanting to work diminished, so did the businesses native to the island's natural surroundings. How fascinating a life he has led and how much change he has seen in the island and the lives of the people here.

You have asked about the cruising life and about how it is going. We do love the best parts of it and are coping well with those parts that are sometimes difficult—because the best parts of it far outnumber the more difficult! Though the passages can sometimes be challenging to everyone, all agree it is a necessary part of making wonderful landfalls.

You just can't live the dream without paying your dues.

Then again, passages often seem to be a microcosm of life itself. It is hard to pass up the joy of a simply drop-dead sunset observed while sitting in the cockpit of our own boat—with only the ocean stretching from horizon to horizon. I can't even begin to describe the total serenity and peacefulness of riding the waves in these tropical latitudes, our entire being centered just on sailing the boat and marking progress. It is good!

There is the opportunity to rid oneself of excess baggage that hangs about in the recesses of our minds. Maybe we have looked at the ocean as our entire world for so long that our brains go into a hibernation of sorts. If that's the case, it is a good kind of hibernation! It seems we find our joy in the simplest things nature has to offer—a beautiful sunset, a good night watch with stargazing as never experienced on land, and the soft sound of a bow wave as *Windy Thoughts* cuts through a gentle sea.

And, I must admit, there is a certain joy in having experienced the crashing sounds as she meets bigger seas pounding against her hull, with the wind howling in the rigging and the motion giving you no opportunity to forget for even a second that you are bracing for something that you never in your life thought you would experience. And you know that you chose this lifestyle and that you must pull from deep within yourself that which you never knew you were capable of. Perhaps the real joy of those conditions comes when all settles down again and you know you are part of something shared with others both in the present and the past. (And you lived through it!)

We have learned that there is a very distinct difference between extreme discomfort and the truly dangerous. *Windy Thoughts* just handles it all in her stride and we attempt to measure up to her standards, being ever so thankful for a strong and safe boat.

Don seems to have an inner strength but tells me that everyone gets afraid—and that fearlessness can mask stupidity. He has told me that his combat experience in Korea years ago taught him the absolute necessity of putting out of his mind the horror and the fear of the present to think clearly and concentrate only on what has to be done. Don encourages me to put fear aside and to deal with the moment, reminding me that I can be afraid tomorrow if I want. Today we have to get through this.

Sometimes I quiver inside with a terror unknown to me before and think I just won't be able to mentally and emotionally make it through the next five minutes.

It seems this is my recurring theme when I write to you. Nevertheless, Don assures me that my strength is that I am right there to do whatever has to be done. Of course, you can't just fall apart and stop functioning at all. That would surely be your demise! So often you simply act on instinct, so intent are you on doing everything right in order to take care of the boat. So you function—and with an adrenaline rush like nothing experienced before! It sure is a team effort, this cruising business, with both of us sharing the load, be it the good or the bad times.

It is just so very hard sometimes and then I wonder if I will ever adapt to the challenges. But I keep going. You know the old Norwegian proverb: "Heroism consists of hanging on one more minute." Well, it sure isn't heroism on my part, because I rate as the world's biggest chicken, but I do hang on just that one more minute at a time until I am looking forward to new horizons. But I hang on because I am terrified of what will happen if I don't, and not out of anything like heroism!

And then all is well and the emotions make a 180 degree turn. I leave the heroism to my captain and know that I wouldn't be out here with anyone else. It can be an agonizing kind of anxiety at times, but the good times and the rewards of living this life come only with having accepted and met those challenges. Isn't that true with everything in life?

Does this all seem so very self-centered when we sit here in paradise? Why is it that I feel compelled to sit down and write you every little thing that may have gone wrong when there is so much going our way? Most things that I worry may go wrong never happen—and we are very thankful that we haven't met with any big problems yet.

Two cruising boats were lost on reefs during the night in the past two weeks. The people are all right, one couple to arrive Papeete soon aboard a copra boat. Their boat was pillaged by islanders as it lay over on the reef, salvage rights assumed. They watched as people walked about wearing their clothes while they waited for the copra boat to arrive.

Our challenges have been the usual when sailing oceans—those moments of terror that always jerk your insides right up to your scalp—but perhaps I am just prone to these moments more than others. Still, with all of the challenges that this life presents, there isn't anything quite like sailing your own boat into magical places and having your own home with you—and, most importantly, doing so with the person with whom you share your life. It is an experience that neither of us would give up easily. Nothing with such rewards should come easily, should it?

Don has had lots of fun with very few big jobs on the boat to command his time so far. He spent so much of the winter in La Paz in preparation, to say nothing of the years of attention to every little detail. Don tries to stay on top of everything and I know that he went through so much to get us this far. The preparation never really stops, because you are always getting ready to leave a place and prepare for the next leg, long or short.

We accepted that it would be a challenging life. The ocean is a very hard environment on virtually everything on the boat, and the maintenance necessary to keep the boat in tip-top working order also comes with the territory. All of this is part of the adventure. It is the agonizing over what may happen that keeps my heart racing at times. Don tells me that I am paying debts that haven't even been incurred. I know he is right and I am working on this. I wish that I had his strength.

July 30, 1990
Bora Bora
Society Islands

Ironara,

James Michener claimed Bora Bora to be the most beautiful of these islands, and while the lagoon is large and rightfully quite spectacular in its beauty—with its deep turquoise waters so clear that we can easily see our anchor at eighty-five feet—we personally found the other islands even more appealing.

We arrived yesterday about noon after only a four-hour sail over from Taaha (Ta-a-ha), a tiny island in the middle of the same surrounding reef as Raiatea. Good wind during the season for sailing amongst these islands is sometimes quite boisterous, and we sat out strong winds at Taaha that kept us from getting ashore while there. *Beleza* was in the anchorage with us and we had great boat-to-boat conversations, even if no big shore excursions.

When last writing, our anchor had nearly grown to the bottom of the bay in Moorea after 3.5 weeks. Don and I both fell in love with Moorea and it is the place we would choose to return to someday—albeit by air, since we aren't likely to come this way again by sail! Meanwhile, we treasure every moment.

The opening of Fete on Bastille Day, July 14, was great fun and we spent it on the island of Huahine. Fete is a huge occasion in French Polynesia, and little Huahine has quite a celebration. Everyone was very busy preparing for the festivities. The women sat about in the shade under the palm trees, weaving large palm fronds to cover the outsides of several small stands built by the men.

There was a parade through the small town and a very festive atmosphere everywhere. A group of local ladies sang in that beautiful harmony that we ache to hear again and again. Their colorful long flowered dresses, the flowers ever-present in their hair and the haunting singing made this a memorable day that we won't soon forget. We are ever aware that we are building memories every step of the way.

A few little restaurants called Snack, several with palm frond roofs, were built along the beach just for this holiday. Hamburgers, sandwiches, salads, cold drinks and ice cream were available, along with roast pig and the trimmings to enjoy. The ice cream jumped right to the top of our priority list of things to enjoy on Huahine.

We rented a van for one day with Connie and George from *Beleza* and, along with another couple, took a tour of the island. Huahine is the site of the richest archeological findings in French Polynesia. In ancient times it was the center of Polynesian culture, ruled by a centralized government rather than by warring tribes, as were most of the islands.

Great exploring and hiking gave us opportunity to stop along the way at several ancient mareas, homes to ancient chiefs and a public place to worship their gods as well as make sacrificial offerings. As we walked among the well laid-out foundations of these mareas, we imagined the stories they could tell!

About a week later, we left Huahine and sailed the short day-sail over to the island of Raiatea, straight into deep Faaroa Bay that opened up right inside the pass through the surrounding reef. Just above us on a hill was the home of a couple who sailed to Raiatea ten years ago, fell in love with the island—and chose to make Raiatea their home. We were invited to their home for a visit and given a grand tour of the island that included explanations about the island's history as we rode along.

Raiatea was the center of religion in ancient French Polynesia and Mt. Temi Hane is believed to have been where the gods originated. The five-point orchid grows on its slopes, the only place in the world where it is found. In order to study this orchid, botanists have made numerous attempts to transport it off the island in acclimatized containers—but each time it was removed it has died.

Beleza arrived to also enjoy the hospitality of these kind people. Connie and I spent one day with our hostess, who taught us the process of photosynthesis dyeing that is so popular in these islands and is seen on many materials used for the paraeu.

Cotton voile from China was cut for each of us to make a tablecloth and four napkins. All of us collected leaves and ferns outside. We folded the material first diagonally over and over and then dipped it into dyes. After laying it flat out on the grass and in the sun we very quickly placed the local leaves and ferns on top in any pattern we chose. When the material dried we removed the greenery, and voila—the loveliest effect was left!

As soon as the anchor went down here on Bora Bora, Don unhooked the halyard to take a flying swing out over the water like Tarzan, bailing in for a good cool-off. The anchorage is deep, and we hope to grab a mooring off the Hotel Oa Oa as soon as one frees up. Unable to let out sufficient scope for the depth because of the proximity of so many boats in the anchorage, we feel a bit at risk.

Beleza is in and wanted us to join them for dinner at the Bora Bora Yacht Club to celebrate George's birthday. The Yacht Club is a mail drop for cruising boats and *Beleza* has mail waiting. They are on a mooring here at the Oa Oa, which caters to the cruisers and has showers available. The Bora Bora Yacht Club won't let him have his mail unless he pays for a mooring from them—and they have none available. George called the gendarme on them, so now doesn't dare go back there for dinner—and another spot will have to be chosen for the celebration.

Don wants to be off for American Samoa in the next four days to take advantage of the full moon for the first days of the passage. It should be about a ten-day passage, to us about the ideal passage length—long enough to have adjusted to the watches and sleep schedule, but not long enough to be tiring. Many fronts are popping up out there and for the past couple of weeks, boats have had no less than twenty-five knots of wind right on the nose. I remind Don that gentlemen don't go to weather, but he assures me he has no intention of taking off until those more appealing trade winds properly push us along, preferably right on our quarter for a lovely reach.

How we would love to loll about these islands a bit longer, but our visas won't allow for such and besides, who knows what pleasures lie ahead? French Polynesia has truly been wonderful cruising. The lagoons with their surrounding reef protection provide beautifully calm anchorages with no swell to roll us about, and there is the constant fragrance of flowers in the air or floating by on the water. Listening to the Polynesian music from ashore combined with these lovely amenities confirms to us that the long ocean passages were worth it many times over!

August 26, 1990
Pago Pago, Tutulia Island, American Samoa

Hello Dear Friend,
Somehow, the days here at Pago Pago (Pon-go Pon-go) have flown by

and this is the first day aboard in our week here. Our passage from Bora Bora was the nicest to date and took us ten days with wonderfully steady winds of fifteen to twenty knots right on our quarter—just our favorite point of sail. We read several books, cooked good food and stuffed ourselves, lolled about in repose when we felt like it, and at night got good sleep on our off watches.

Pago Pago is a large harbor surrounded by mountains, and some distance into its head lie all of the boats at anchor—in a harbor inundated with oil, fuel, garbage and blood from the adjacent tuna cannery. Customs procedures had to be taken care of before we could drop the hook and call it a day, so we ambled our way up against the Customs wall and tied *Windy Thoughts* securely, ran up our Q flag (the quarantine flag necessary to fly when entering a country) and waited for the arrival of the officials. Because it was a Saturday, we were to stay aboard until the officials arrived at our boat on Monday.

Others repeatedly called us on the radio to tell us officials had been none the wiser when they went ashore just to get some groceries. Hearing of a real Italian deli in town, we immediately set our sights on getting there. Hot meatball sandwiches you wouldn't believe! We sneaked back quickly, and though encouraged to join the others at the Yacht Club BBQ that evening, didn't brave it and stayed aboard.

By now, there were two other boats side-tied to us, an American boat and a Swiss boat, and we all stayed aboard to have our own little get-together. By Sunday, obeying the law was becoming boring, because we were so anxious to get off the boat, explore the town and exercise our land legs.

Monday morning greeted us with the arrival of the female Customs Official who may have made a good linebacker for the NFL. She looked me right in the eye and immediately chastised me for having left the boat. She said nothing of the sort to Don. They must have feelers out!

One of the more exciting assets ashore was a real Laundromat at which I spent much of my time. Terrific provisioning at a big supermarket, with American goods at prices that were the same as back home, excited everyone and for orders of $300.00, they delivered to the harbor..

The process of the shopping itself started in the early morning and took half a day to complete. When everything conveniently arrived at the sidewall by the anchorage, we hauled it all out to the boat via *Breezy*, a process that took numerous trips—and all done in the extreme heat and humidity. I shall never again grumble about shopping back home with a car and a fine supermarket at hand. How could I ever have looked at it as a chore?

The next day was devoted to stowing it all and miraculously, by day's end it was all put away and cataloged. How good it is to know there is food enough to last for months! Fact is, we had food for months before setting off on this provisioning excursion.

Lest you think that Don was lolling about in the sun, a cold drink in one hand and fan in the other, not so. He went along on the shopping trip and then helped to get it all back to the boat before busying himself with tiring refueling trips with our cart and the jerry jugs—the process by which he works up much more of a sweat than I ever could while agonizing over where to put each can.

This is the routine for him: Get the cart out of the back storage area (our aft berth). Load it into the dinghy. Row ashore, get the cart out and up onto the quay and set off for the twenty-minute jaunt to the service station. Fill the 4, six-gallon cans—and haul all back to the quay. Using a dock line secured to the handle of one fuel can at a time, let each can down in the waiting dinghy. The distance from the top of the quay down to the dinghy varies with the tide and it can often be a challenge getting into the dinghy if it requires hanging over the side of the wall and dropping down.

Row back out to the boat, lift each full six-gallon can from the floor of the dinghy up into the cockpit of *Windy Thoughts*, and laboriously pour each can of diesel into the diesel tank through a funnel, working carefully so as not to spill any on the teak. Begin the entire process all over again and again until the tanks are topped off and all the fuel cans are left full and tied on deck.

It is the heat and humidity that makes doing just about anything more than breathing in and out so difficult—and there are times when you do question if you are really in paradise. But only for fleeting moments, because yes, it is all worth it!

Don has also been pursuing with fervor the search for a new TV set and had his sights set on American Samoa as the spot where he would surely find one. While others are madly busy getting boat equipment shipped in, he says he does have his priorities.

They see him maneuvering the big box into the dinghy and say, "New radar? Where did you find that?"

"Nope, new TV."

He has brought back two thirteen-inch television sets so far, neither of which work on the boat. We need a larger converter. Everything on the boat is working at this point, just the TV that is dying a slow death. But this is serious and we shall have to wait.

Pago Pago is a smallish town, but strung out a ways and with several shops. The Samoans are robust, friendly and happy people to be about. It is a safe anchorage from the seas (though very questionable holding ground) and the possibilities it offers for work for United States citizens make it a spot where a few cruising folks hole up during the hurricane season. Most attempt to get on a mooring if planning to stay any length of time.

September 29, 1990
Latitude: 18 degrees 34 min. S

Longitude: 179 degrees 16 min. E
En route between Tonga and Fiji

Malole lele,

We have crossed the International Date Line and are presently en route from Tonga to Fiji, a short four-day sail. It is about 7 p.m., Don is asleep down below and I am on my watch until midnight.

When we left Hunga Island, Tonga, black squall lines darkened the skies and the rain poured down in torrents that made visibility virtually impossible. It eventually cleared and has been a perfect sail since. *Windy Thoughts* just rolls along comfortably in ideal conditions with seas of no more than four or five feet.

The latitudes and longitudes for about eight uncharted reefs between Tonga and Fiji have been passed around amongst the cruising group via radio. Five cruising boats were lost in the area in the past two months. We passed the worst area this morning, so are in relatively clear sailing from here on in and will be approaching Suva harbor, Fiji, by daylight in the morning.

The special young couple aboard *Hybrid*, from Seattle, left Hunga Island with us. They are the good company with whom we have enjoyed many fun times and have bumped into on and off since Mexico. Rob, Danette, and little Cassie (eighteen months) are wending their way to New Zealand.

Tonga was every bit the "Magical Kingdom" and we leisurely cruised about the Vava'u group—the most northern cluster of islands that are verdantly green and reminded those of us from the Northwest United States of the cruising at home amongst our San Juan Islands. Of course, our evergreens were replaced with palm trees!

The water is that beautiful turquoise that reflects from the sun, crystal clear as it laps white sandy beaches with coconut palms swaying in the breeze. Every day was another day in paradise—yes, again!

We checked in at the town of Neiafu, a Port of Entry on the island of Vava'u, and settled ourselves into the big protected bay amongst a large number of other cruising boats for several days before heading out to visit the many nearby islands.

We loved Tonga. A grocery of sorts in the village of Neiafu reminded us of those found in Mexican villages, and the few shops lent themselves to more local needs. An open-air wet market buzzed with people very early each morning and we tried to be there by 6 a.m. to peruse the best of the day's offerings. Piles of taro and breadfruit were in surplus, but we don't much care for either. We did purchase excellent tomatoes, potatoes and pineapples.

You would likely snub your culinary nose at some of the dishes I have created as part of this cruising fare. How I wish I had your talent in the galley! But it is fun to try different things we find, at least once, and especially to meander through the outdoor market stalls and take advantage of the beautiful produce found. When that longing for a supermarket pushes itself to the forefront now and then, I remind myself that we wouldn't trade any of these experiences just yet for the conveniences so accustomed to back home.

Cruising and convenience aren't exactly compatible! It has nothing to do with why we are living this lifestyle in order to see some of our world—and what a wonderful way to see it.

Two days after our arrival in Tonga, King Taufa'ahou Tupou IV and Queen Halawalu Mata'aho arrived in Neiafu for the opening of the Royal Agricultural Fair. Displays of quilts, as well as those of handwork, prized fruits, vegetables and fish, reminded us very much of any small town fair back home.

Large strips of tapa cloth, perhaps ten feet wide by twenty feet in length, lined the middle of the open field. It often takes a full year for the women to make each piece.

The King, a huge man in his seventies who has great difficulty in moving about, arrived in a Bronco that drove down the length of tapa cloths displayed—using them like a red carpet. The women who created the tapa were obviously proud to see it serve in this manner.

The Queen walked the length, waving to the people, while the King waved from inside the Bronco, all to the accompaniment of the local band playing "Roll out the Barrel"—such an unexpected choice that we all got a real kick out of it and wondered if they understood the English translation.

Under a three-sided enclosure of pretty material fashioned just for the King and Queen, two huge chairs that were all decorated up to serve as thrones sat awaiting the royal couple. The police, looking very natty in their black lava lavas, white jackets and smart black hats, seated all of us in the middle of the field and right in front of the ceremonial thrones—where we felt somewhat conspicuous because the townspeople were lined up at a distance around the edges of the grounds.

We happily sat ourselves down cross-legged on the ground. As the King approached the throne, everyone stood at attention and our entourage of about twenty popped up as well. At this point there was great consternation on the part of the police, who rushed over to us and with frantic gestures motioned our group to sit back down while everyone else remained standing.

Feeling it appropriate for a day at the fair, we were all attired in the cruiser's standard wardrobe of shorts and T-shirts and sandals. We learned that exposure of the knees is the height of disrespect to the royal couple. Thereafter, we spent the remainder of the presentations to the King in attempts to cover our knees as best we could with hands, arms and T-shirts pulled down over.

The King spoke to the crowd in what seemed to be a very revered speech. Of course, we didn't understand one word of his message, but surely felt the honor of being in the presence of true royalty.

The Tongan dress is much more conservative than that in the Society Islands, where the paraeu is all that many of the women wear wrapped around them. In Tonga the women wear street-length dresses over a long skirt, and over this a taovala.

The taovala is made of woven pandana leaves and might be as narrow as a couple of inches or down to the knees. Worn over the skirts much like an apron, the longer taovala is usually solid, while the shorter ones are in strips that hang down. Men wear a short, solidly woven taovala over long pants, or over the lava lava. A taovala is stashed away in the recesses of the boat to bring back wonderful memories of this beautiful kingdom.

Our most meaningful experience while in Tonga was the opportunity to meet John, a gentle man perhaps in his fifties who lives on a small island just near Vauv'u. One day while we sat at anchor in the bay at Vava'u, John came by in his small boat needing spark plugs for his engine. Don gladly searched some out below and John invited us to his village.

The next day, *Windy Thoughts* anchored off the nearby island where John lives with his wife, two daughters and a grandson in a village of about six homes.

John was very proud to show us his home and introduce his family. His home was devastated by the last hurricane and was rebuilt of concrete block, with a basement area to run to in future hurricanes. It is in this basement where the women work weaving the beautiful baskets for which Tonga is well known. We purchased several to send to family and a few to save for ourselves.

Upstairs, John's wife sat on the floor weaving a rug of pandana leaves, a healthy supply of the dried pandana heaped on the floor beside her. More pandana leaves hung drying in a nearby shed for later use in the rug weaving process. John disappeared outdoors to the kitchen that was housed in another small shed with a thatched roof, and sitting invitingly just outside their home under the profusion of palm trees that hung over all. He returned with a wonderfully refreshing drink of lemons and water for us.

We were invited on a very educational and lengthy walk through the fields, with John our guide and our mentor. Each common man is given seven acres to plant, the noble class eleven acres. Amongst pandana and taro, the green bean was grown on a vine that entwined around another plant—a unique and useful method of "killing two birds with one stone".

A small and humble building comprised the school that sat atop a hill and overlooked the bay in the most stunning setting. A husband-wife team taught here, the wife teaching primary grades one through three and the husband grades four through six. Great care was taken to make the schoolrooms look inviting with the children's work displayed on the walls, a few charts to add color, and artwork that hung from the ceiling. Desks were tables that each held two students.

The children were a joy. When invited into the classroom, we were surprised to see the words to "Old Susanna" written on the chalkboard in English—and then treated to a performance of the little ones singing it to us in English. John just beamed, and it nearly brought us to our knees with the amount of dignity and respect we felt for John's pride in his island's school.

The young woman teacher took us outside, her own two pre-school age children who simply joined her in the classroom during the day tagging along. She wanted to show us a one-room and very humble building next door, their pride and joy—the newly developed school library created with books sent them by a visiting English woman. At this point there were perhaps forty to fifty books and the library comprised their proudest possession. It was the perfect place to leave the box of primary storybooks carried aboard, and it warmed our hearts to be able to contribute this little bit to them.

An even more humble one-room building was the home of the teachers, this husband-wife team and their two little ones, one more on the way.

It was an eye-opening experience after having spent so many years in the classroom. Just to see what this couple was doing here with very little money and few supplies, but with much ingenuity, and to see the respect the children show their teacher and their happiness at the opportunity to be in school was a like ray of sunshine.

After our visit, we told John that we were going back to the outer islands and would stop back sometime by the end of the next week. When we dropped the anchor off his island on the following Friday, John was standing on the beach and waving to us

Do you ever wish that you had the opportunity to just go back and do something over again? As John helped us drag the dinghy up onto the beach, he told us that he had waited for us for two days after that Monday. The entire village had prepared a Tongan feast and we had missed it! This wasn't one of the Tongan feasts put on for tourists, but was special just for us. I know that we will always think back to this wonderful visit in Tonga with a feeling of great sadness, knowing that they had done this for us only to have us not show up. Would that we could only do it all over again and be there on Tuesday to honor their friendship.

Tonga has presented us with two very interesting and exciting cave adventures. The first was Swallows Cave that we explored by dinghy, using an oar to work our way slowly into what looked for all the world like it was right out of the Raiders of the Lost Ark. Working our way slowly through a narrow passage until we could go no farther, we climbed up on the rock surfaces to look all about us at the surreal surroundings. We felt like real spelunkers.

The other was a more difficult experience. Don and I went aboard *Hybrid* with Danette, Rob and little Cassie, as did the folks on *Namir* with their four-year old Ryan, a fiery little red- head who has personality to pass around and still have much left over.

Hybrid sailed to a nearby island and anchored off the spot we were to look for—the lone palm tree on the cliff above—under which the underground approach to the Mariner's Cave is found. There are lots of palm trees. Finding the exact spot wasn't quite as easy as directions would have it.

The trick was to dive down directly under the lone palm, a distance of no less than ten feet, and then swim directly in about fifteen feet before shooting to the surface to come up into a completely enclosed cave. The fellows went in first to test the waters. Don swam back up by *Hybrid* to excitedly tell us about a beautiful blue aura inside the cave.

I felt some apprehension about getting down deep enough, because I sometimes need weights. Is this because I am so full of hot air? Not to be outdone by the younger set, I gasped the deepest breath possible and went for it with Ryan shouting from *Hybrid*'s rail, "You can do it!"

Enough inspiration! Down and then straight ahead! Keeping deep enough and not beginning your sprint for the surface too soon was the key. Don was waiting for me inside the cave. Its size and circular shape was perhaps thirty feet in diameter and fifteen feet high above the water level. When the tide surges, the pressure turns the air into a mist. Sunshine filtering through the underwater opening turns the mist into this amazingly beautiful blue aura that fills the cave. We gals took turns staying with the little ones aboard *Hybrid* so that everyone could make the dive.

Gentle Tonga has been so good to us. What a perfect chunk of paradise! I believe that we both could happily come back here someday—but we won't be sailing back. However, flying in and staying at the hotel in Neiafu wouldn't be in any way the same experience as moving about these islands aboard our own boat, on which we paid our dues to get here, and meeting the local people as we have been so blessed to enjoy.

October 2, 1990
Viti Levu
Suva, Fiji

Bula Bula,

Windy Thoughts sits at anchor off the Suva Yacht Club amongst perhaps twenty other boats, in rain and drizzle that we understand has persisted for the past two months!

Arriving on Saturday, we weren't permitted to check in or leave the boat, but health officials did come aboard Sunday and gave us our Practique. Monday was a holiday as well, so, though still unable to make our clearance, we did sneak ashore to a real pizza parlor!

This morning, Tuesday, we upped anchor at 6:45 a.m. and moved to the Princess Wharf to begin our clearance procedures; it has been a regular fire drill since. There are many ships and smaller boats about.

Here is the procedure so far: Side tie to *Hybrid*, who in turn is rafted to a large local fishing boat third out from the big wharf. The fishermen tell us that they won't be leaving. It is very swelly and rolly and we anxiously adjust fenders as we await the officials. Security will board us here.

Then, the fishing boat to which *Hybrid* is tied does want to pull off. We struggle to get lines untied from both *Hybrid* and the fishing boat in now high winds that hold us on. We also struggle to maneuver about in the now dangerously shallow area at a very low tide that nearly puts us aground. It is managed—everyone reties—and we await Immigration.

Ten minutes later, the fishing boat returns and the fishermen want their spot back. We tied to a big tug farther back on the wharf, whose big black tires make huge marks on *Windy Thoughts*' hull. However, the fishermen aboard the tug are kind and tell us they aren't leaving. We roll around heavily, continue to attend to lines, and it is still drizzly.

At 10 a.m. the big tug decides to leave after all and the captain says he will be right back.

Hybrid, now on the outside of the raft-up, must get off first. Oh, what a scene we presented attempting to back up against strong winds in the continuing dropping tide.

The Port Captain calls us on VHF radio to tell us that since Immigration hasn't arrived, we can all get off the wall, drop anchor and go to shore to the Customs Office. Danette and I remain aboard to attend to the boats while Don and Rob head ashore in the dinghy.

Two hours later, Rob returns to let us know that Don is still at the Customs Office. Immigration procedures can be taken care of ashore as well, and Rob heads back to join Don on that mission.

The men return another two hours later, after which they start a diesel run. Diesel is $4.00 a gallon and must be ferried by dinghy from here to the Yacht Club.

That chore done still later on, we all up anchor and go back to the main anchorage. It is finally time for our much awaited "shore leave" and we are allowed to tie our dinghies at the Yacht Club. The luxury of a taxi awaits us and we taxi into town to enjoy our shore leave.

We spent about a week in Suva and it never stopped raining. Anticipating that the Suva Yacht Club would have a laundry, in my dreams it had surpassed all of my expectations. In reality it lacked this amenity. A laundry of sorts in town charged $16.00 a load. Consequently, our laundry buckets are in constant use, the five-gallon water jugs ferried back and forth from the Yacht Club dock. Don is none too happy about the necessity to string lines below in our cabin to hang the clothes to dry. But everyone else has the same problem, so I can't feel too sorry for myself.

In between, we are happily exploring Suva and find many restaurants and even computer stores and copy shops, the local Indians making up the entrepreneurial population here. Beautifully colored saris flow from all of the Indian women and the Fijian men wear long pants or the lava lava. Communication is easy with English spoken as a second language, and the atmosphere seems quite cosmopolitan to us after the months of simpler surroundings.

Obtaining our Australian visas was one of our main reasons to visit Suva. It seemed very uptown to ride in an elevator in the building where the Australian Embassy is located, a common event that took on an air of grand significance! My, when was the last time we saw an elevator?

Getting the Australian visa isn't easy and many must return several times after applying. One's financial stability must be proven with current bank statements and all manner of red tape. You must sign your life away that you aren't coming into Australia to obtain work of any sort. In addition, you must strictly adhere to the six-month visa—absolutely no exceptions.

Unable to prove their financial stability, one Canadian couple was denied visas today and will have to go to New Zealand instead. They had planned to sell their boat in Australia where the market is better. When we get our visas, we feel that we have passed another milestone. After this long (but adventure filled) haul across the Pacific, we look to Australia as our R and R and we have chosen it as our safe haven.

We rather enjoy this time in Suva, but will be happy to see the sun again once moving to the other side of the island.

Hybrid is bobbing at anchor nearby, as are others we have met along the way, and we enjoy the company of everyone, doing laundry chores, boat repairs and enjoying the town, with several restaurants to offer such treats after those cruising meals!

You have asked about our meals and how the eating plan is going. We eat well aboard, though certainly not gourmet. Our breakfasts are much as at home, consisting of fruit, eggs, cereal and toast, pancakes, waffles and French toast. If no fresh fruit, we have canned. The top-of-the-burner waffle maker might be our favorite piece of equipment, making the most wonderful Belgian waffles that we sometimes even have for our dinner.

Lunches are sandwiches with the bread I have made aboard, or purchased—often the case now as we move about these islands. Canned tuna, chicken salad, or the never forgotten peanut butter and jelly whet our appetites. Perhaps crackers and peanut butter with fruit or canned soup with crackers might be on the menu. I have learned to brush my fresh-baked bread with vinegar and it keeps fresh for a long time, with no vinegar taste at all. At sea and between island visits we are never without fresh bread.

Dinners may not sound elegant, but I manage to put together very tasty meals with the supplies on board and don't use our freezer. The excellent Libby's canned beef in gravy has made us delicious hot roast beef sandwiches, especially good with our own home-baked bread—and even what respectably tastes like a good pot roast dinner when served with fresh potatoes, onions and carrots. Sometimes we wonder if our cruising tastes just accept the lesser because we are so grateful to achieve a modicum of the original—but no—that roast beef and gravy is delicious!

The beautiful, canned white chicken works particularly well in a curry, as well as many other dishes. Canned vegetables fill out a dinner, though we are partial to only a few; canned peas just don't pass muster. Pasta keeps well and the jars of good sauces with perhaps the addition of a can of chicken or roast beef, topped with our Kraft Parmesan cheese, tastes like a very fresh meal. Pasta with pesto is another favorite and provides a variety in our pasta experiences.

I make an absolutely to-die-for pasta Alfredo with canned evaporated milk, New Zealand canned butter and our shake-on cheese that seldom makes us long for fresh parmesan, so thankful are we for this. The canned butter from New Zealand is a godsend, quickly identified by the picture of a cow on its gold can.

When we can find corn chips, nachos are enjoyed. Jars of salsa with the addition of melted Cheese Whiz—along with sour cream made from canned cream with the addition of some lemon juice or vinegar (much better tasting than it may sound)—topped with canned refried beans makes our mouths water. The Cheese Whiz part likely sounds revolting, but honestly is very good under the circumstances. Read on:

Cheese Whiz has become somewhat of a "gourmet staple". It is used in macaroni and cheese, spread on crackers, invitingly melted in cheese omelets with tomato sauce seasoned with Italian seasoning, and even for toasted cheese sandwiches. While I hear others on the radio speaking of taking a roast or steaks out of the freezer for dinner, I simply sigh and don't give it a thought. We aren't starving and certainly have no less than six to eight months of supplies right aboard *Windy Thoughts*—and are eating quite well, thank you.

As to your question, are we happy? Even with its challenges we love our life, both of us finding so much enjoyment and magic from this experience. Certainly, the support and camaraderie from other cruising people gives all of us morale boosts and a feeling of family when we are so far from home.

The cruising family has proven to play an important part in all of our lives, though we also enjoy our peaceful times swinging at anchor by ourselves. There are bonuses to both situations and it is always the balance that makes this life so interesting. Not to mention the importance of meeting and enjoying the company of local people—this one of the biggest bonuses of this life for Don and me, and the very reason that we chose to see our world in this way.

Our passages have been good ones so far and we have been fortunate to not suffer any serious breakdowns. Everyone else seems to spend an inordinate amount of time working on whatever has broken down at the moment. We know that our time will come. Sure, there have been moments of terror, but that goes with the territory, and I know that I suffer moments of terror far greater than are really necessary. *Windy Thoughts* remains the most safe and comfortable home. We have our own food, our own bed, our own music and books with us always. She is beautiful and strong and we are so thankful for finding what, for us, is the perfect boat on which to venture so far away on the sea.

Ever aware that this is indeed a unique experience, when feeling down we remind ourselves that we went through too much to turn back now. You have reminded us that we are unlikely to pass this way ever again.

Many left from French Polynesia and some plan to ship boats home from New Zealand. Though we don't know how we will feel a year from now, at present we realize that we would never see and experience the things we have in any other way than by sailing our own boat. It is still hard for us to believe that we are living what had been our dream, for so long. We are humbled, yet grateful for the blessings that have come our way.   .

December 2, 1990
Mooloolaba
Queensland Coast, Australia

G'day Mate,

Only by the grace of God, we have reached Oz! We are snugly tied off to a dock after 2.5 years on the hook, are at the lovely Mooloolaba Yacht Club located fifty miles north of Brisbane and have found a home for the next months while we wait for the cyclone season to pass. This is the quintessential spot for the perfect R and R—we are absolutely positive of this already!

Though my last letter had us making straight for Brisbane we ended up far north, and when stopping at Mooloolaba on our way south found that we don't want to leave this perfect spot. We are so very ready for a break after a stormy passage to Australia from New Caledonia—a passage on which I will elaborate. But because nothing made it to the mail after leaving Fiji, I will first tell you of our meanderings.

Before leaving Suva to head out to other Fijian islands there was an obligatory visit to the Tourism Minister, where we were politely but firmly told of our obligations and restrictions on non-tourist islands.

Each village chief must give us welcome and permission to visit and protocol demands that we share the kava ceremony with the chief before doing anything else. In addition, though a camera or bag can be carried, it is impolite to wear either over the shoulder. No hats are allowed and men must wear the lava lava. Don was prepared with his lava lava. He looks pretty spiffy in it, floral pattern and all.

One-half kilo of kava is appropriate to present to a chief, and Don purchased ours at Suva's open market that is huge and full of every variety of produce imaginable. Kava looks like a big, brown unattractive weed, but is boiled in a pot and said to have a narcotic of sorts in it. It tastes vile. For the kava ceremony, everyone sits cross-legged in a circle. The chief takes a first drink from the cup, after which everyone claps three times before the cup is passed to the next person and the same procedure is followed again.

Don and I were anxious to get over to the west side of the island and into some sunshine! With our Australian visas in hand, our laundry chores caught up and some good meals out—and with our kava at the ready—we finally hauled the anchor and made our way out of foggy, rainy and windy Suva Harbor along with *Hybrid*, and *Imagine* that hails from the UK.

Dealing with thirty-five to forty knot winds, we were all anxious to get the hook down at an island just a half-day's sail from Suva. There was no village ashore here so we were unable to try our wings at the kava ceremony, nor did the opportunity present itself at the next two island stops. Our kava went over the side. Perhaps the fishes had their own ceremony!

Once away from Suva our welcome sunshine prevailed, but strong winds kept us from "shore leave" each time we dropped anchor for the night. The British boat had us all over for cheese on toast. Never has cheese on toast tasted better! Cassie had the enviable position of caring not at all what was going on with the winds and we all enjoyed her sweet disposition.

We were headed for Musket Cove and its Yacht Club, on Mololo Lai Lai Island, located off the west coast of Viti Levu. It was a fine sail, still with very brisk winds, and finding our way into Musket Cove was somewhat challenging—because none of us had a chart telling us exactly where Musket Cove was, and considerable time was spent conning our way amongst the coral.

When we all carefully made our way amongst the coral to gain entrance to the anchorage, we dropped our hooks to settle in for a few days of leisure where so many have been before.

Joining the Musket Cove Yacht Club requires that you have sailed an open ocean passage of no less than 2,000 miles. Membership is opened on the spot, with a membership fee so small it would be difficult to imagine anyone turning it down! How does $10.00 sound?

We all got dinghies down and headed to shore to the palapa-style Club for cold drinks, sitting around a table together for great conversation—and glances up at the rafters where the names of members are carved. How exciting to find names of boats that we have only read about! Of course, we will never get back here to check but will go on faith that *Windy Thoughts* will be up there with the rest!

An exciting event took place the night before our arrival at Musket Cove. Though not expected quite yet, a new baby was born right here in the anchorage! As luck would have it, a pediatrician happened to be on one of only five boats in the anchorage.

When it became obvious that the baby wasn't going to wait for a more convenient time and place, the expectant father jumped into his dinghy and raced over to the doctor's boat. Blurting out that his baby was about to be born, the doctor told him to relax. Babies always take time to come into the world.

Not this baby; she was ready to make her debut right now!

The doctor hopped into the dinghy with the frantic father and returned to his boat to deliver a healthy baby girl right in the cabin. The family was flown to a hospital in Viti Levu. All went well and both are doing fine.

While at Musket Cove, we pulled *Breezy* up onto the sugary white sand, lounged at the pool of the lovely hotel just ashore, enjoyed lunches at the restaurant and played tourist again for a few days. Cassie loved the pool and Danette and Rob were wonderful companions as we enjoyed the leisurely life Fiji style. It was so relaxing, an engaging and beautiful part of this earth.

Clearance from Fiji could be made from Lautoka, north of us and on the west of Viti Levu Island. Because we didn't really want to spend an entire day sailing there and another sailing back, Don and I decided to use the little air service on Mololo Lai Lai Island. A small plane would take us right to Mololo Island, and we walked to the tiny, thatched gazebo-like structure that was the terminal, purchased our ticket and waited for the plane to land.

It was a very short trip of about twenty minutes to Viti Levu Island, during which we had breathtaking views of the ocean with its ever-changing turquoise colors varying with the depths—and reefs, oh, so apparent from this height! When our plane landed on the airstrip in Nadi, we simply stuck our

thumbs out and caught a ride to Lautoka. The driver acted as guide as we passed fields of sugar cane, an important export of Fiji, alongside the road.

When we arrived at the official offices in Lautoka I was very nervous. We didn't mention that *Windy Thoughts* wasn't actually sitting at anchor off Lautoka, saying only that we wanted to make our clearance from Fiji. We had all boat papers in order, the officials were most polite, and soon the paperwork was completed and we were on our way. The plane ride back to Mololo Lai Lai Island was just as grand as the ride over. What an exciting way to clear from Fiji!

We said goodbyes at Musket Cove to our friends on *Hybrid*, who would sail to New Zealand. *Hybrid* will be shipped back to Seattle from New Zealand. Rob is far too young to leave the working world—their life still in the early stages while ours is reaching the fall of life. It was sad to say goodbye and we look forward to connecting when we are home again. [We have done just that, and three lovely daughters now make up this beautiful family, and *Hybrid* is still a part of the family as well.]

It was time for *Windy Thoughts* to head for New Caledonia— called the Riviera of the Pacific and a stop that would give us a break on the way to Australia. You can well imagine our anticipation! It was a good, full week's passage with favorable winds that pushed us ever westward. Only our last two days brought livelier winds that kept us on our toes with little sleep.

Our landfall at New Caledonia was made after a long night, two very tired sailors wanting to make a very careful approach to what the pilot described as a difficult pass. But fog had made visibility so poor that we had great difficulty seeing the marker that was to mark the pass through the reef.

Don and I have always had an agreement that should one of us be uncomfortable with something, we would concede to that one's decision. Don caught a glimpse of the marker to confirm our safe course on three different approaches to the pass, only to lose sight of it. Though he assured me that staying on course would take us through the pass, I was uncomfortable with heading in blind, so we headed back out to the safety of the sea.

It was fully three hours later that our final attempt was successful. We breathed big sighs of relief and headed right for a nearby anchorage to drop the hook—and slept all day and through that night. It was an idyllic spot for respite. The trees ashore looked very reminiscent of our pine trees back in our northwest and were almost a touch of home!

The next morning we sailed into Noumea, the capital and a rather modern city. We spent a full week exploring the town and awaiting the weather window for our passage to Australia. Don and I pressed our noses to the windows of the good restaurants and inhaled the fragrances of various culinary delights, prices well beyond our budget. We needed to move on now before the cyclones started—and we were anxious to reach that land down under!

The yacht *God's Speed* was in Noumea, with Tina and Paul and their two young teenagers aboard. Paul had a dedicated weather fax, and we were planning to start the passage together and keep radio contact along the way.

Now comes the agony—or getting to Australia the hard way as, it will forever be ingrained on our minds!

As it happened, *God's Speed* wasn't quite ready on the morning we were set to depart. *God's Speed* would pull off the following morning and would catch up with us in a day or two. Both Australia Radio and Paul sent us off with good weather reports.

Windy Thoughts sailed out through the reef in lovely winds of fifteen to seventeen knots, skimming over turquoise waters as if we were on a magic carpet. We had to constantly pinch ourselves. Were we really in this far-off part of the world, and had we really sailed all this distance aboard our own boat? Will we ever find all of the magic a mundane experience? Our eyes are constantly wide with wonder. To think, we were on our way to Australia!

Though we expected the passage from New Caledonia to Australia to be five or six days, it turned into nine very rotten days.

Day two dawned cloudy with blackening skies. The Coral Sea can sometimes be nasty with lows popping up seemingly out of nowhere, but we had counted on the good weather to last for a few days while we skirted across to the Land of Oz. We expected that *God's Speed* was on its way. However, when Paul came up on our radio schedule that morning, he told us that he had received weather faxes that held them back.

Paul's next statement set our hearts to beating on overtime: "You're going to get hit and hit hard!"

Weather faxes showed a deepening low pushing its way up from the south and the notorious Tasman Sea. As our barometer began its rapid drop, I was wishing that I was anywhere but here in the Coral Sea, about to be hit with what in my mind might be the mother of all storms.

Mark Twain said it best and I quote, "I've suffered a great many catastrophes in my life. Most of them never happened."

As we meander across these oceans, does my correspondence seem to echo his very words? I was never like this in my other life! But then, our other life, adventurous as it always was, didn't involve this kind of day-to-day living on the edge and so often by the seat of our pants. Imminent boat sinking and/or drowning weren't an ever-present possibility! Though ever mindful that we are cared for and watched over, my mind and my emotions struggle.

Following were the most horrendous days—a blur of sleeplessness and more discomfort and noise from the mighty force of the winds and seas than I could even begin to describe. You know the old expression—when the going gets tough the tough get going. Trouble awakens in Don a tremendous capacity to deal with the matter at hand.

As for myself, I was overtaken by resoluteness in being right there with him, no matter the quaking in my body—because getting tough just isn't one of my strong points! Instead, I was absolutely limp with anxiety. I could never, ever do this with anyone else. Such is the trust that I have in Don's ability to do everything in his power to keep us—well—alive.

There are no breaks, no relief from the constant barrage of wind and sea—and our magic carpet isn't always a magic experience. You just have to deal with every second of every minute that faces you, around the clock, day after day. If you fall apart you simply will not be able to take care of the boat or make the decisions necessary to get through it. That in itself is always a great motivator!

Don has never experienced seasickness and I have dealt only with the occasional bits of queasiness. When crossing the Coral Sea I fell prone to its dirty tricks, though you can't let up the vigil of what has to be done, for even a few seconds. Don tried to humor me with comments as to how it was all a matter of IQ. I notice that he hasn't used that expression since he lost everything in his stomach right in the galley sink one extremely rough and frightful day!

With the relentless bashing of *Windy Thoughts* and with every drop of the barometer, our hearts dropped farther down toward our toes. We garnered every tidbit of new information from any available radio weather reports—constantly charting our position and recording every pressure gradient change. As the winds began to build in intensity that second day, we knew that this was going to be a big one. Before dark, Don reefed the mainsail down to the first reefing points and rolled in some of the headsail.

Neither of us could sleep, but to get below for a bit was a kind of mental and physical respite. Just to tuck into your sea berth and secure the lee cloth around you with pillows stuffed all about creates a great cocooning effect and this wonderful "off duty" sense—even though you are acutely aware of the goings on above and around you.

On Don's watch, I would invariably begin thinking, "Is he still up there?" At various times during the saga, I got up to take a peek to reassure myself that he was all right and that I wasn't all alone in the middle of the Coral Sea.

When the wind increased to upwards of forty-five knots during that second night, we were glad that Don had by now added a second reef in the mainsail—and that the head sail was further rolled in so that it too presented only a small portion of sail to the wind. Don ran a jack line to hook onto when moving back and forth on deck—the first time to do so since sailing south from Seattle to San Francisco. Though forty-five knots of wind keeps you on your toes and instills the fear of God in you, our barometer told us it would get worse. Anticipation of what is to come is, without a doubt, the most difficult with which to deal. For me that means intense anxiety. Oh yes, paying those debts again before they are incurred!

The boat was rolling and crashing very heavily now in the big seas—but Don reminded me that we were sailing along just fine, the boat well under control.

It began to rain, adding to the misery. These weren't the conditions in which to stand on deck, have a fresh shower and maybe wash your hair. The seas continued to build and by morning's light we judged them to easily be twenty-five feet in height at minimum—a very conservative estimate based on seas we had experienced, because we suspected they might well be much bigger. And they would increase.

As conditions continued to worsen, we decided to lie hove-to. Though *Windy Thoughts* always did her duty and rounded right back up to weather, she chose to fall off so that the seas were hitting her almost broadside—slamming over continually at the rate of once about every three seconds, like a metronome. Both of us harbored a dread that with every slamming we would surely suffer a total knockdown. Hoving-to is not always that pleasant respite that you read about in the books.

I just wanted to go home—but there was no easy way to get there from the middle of the Coral Sea in a small sailboat that was facing off with a full-fledged storm! Where was our magic carpet now?

As the wind increased, we listened to a fellow on single side band radio (SSB) talking to Australia Radio. He gave his position as only ten miles north of us! Don put out a call to him. When he asked about our wind speed, Don estimated it to possibly be as much as fifty knots, as we don't have a wind-speed indicator. The fellow replied that his indicator was topping off at a steady sixty-five knots, the highest it would read, and the needle wasn't wavering one iota.

It was worse than we thought.

The wind was blowing the tops of the waves off like an ocean of white foam, further indication that it was piping right up there on the Beaufort scale's range in which we didn't want to find ourselves. The noise was absolutely deafening. The rigging screamed and the big seas hit the hull as though a Mack truck were driving straight into us at 100 miles an hour. We are sure that the boat itself was far better at handling it all than we were!

It had become dangerous to be in the cockpit. Lin and Larry Pardey have written in one of their books that there is nothing that will keep you from disaster if you don't develop the most important seagoing skill of all—the complete fear of going overboard! Don would wait for the split-second chance to throw the hatch back before taking a rapid look about the cockpit and forward at sails and lines, ever worrying about something breaking or chafing on top. His leaps into the cockpit were short-lived, but necessary.

The steel framework for the bimini that is also home to many antennas was holding well, but there was a problem with the sun curtains that can be dropped from either side. Don had made them to roll up, with cording to hold the roll secured to the frame. Cording had come loose on one side, and as the material flapped about like a sail, the entire framework shook as though it would all let go at any moment.

Don hooked his safety harness to the interior companionway railing, pushed back the hatch cover—and at the opportune moment leapt over the weatherboards. Not taking even the few seconds necessary to roll it back up and tie it securely, with knife in hand he made a rapid slash—and the entire curtain was gone with the wind in a flash. The horrific shaking stopped, the solar panels seemed in less peril for the moment—and he was back below before finishing his second breath.

Don's mind was contemplating whether some little thing that he may have forgotten to do or had put off for another time may now start a chain of events that could lead to disastrous results. Oh, the things that could go wrong without a moment's notice!

Fifty long hours passed while we lay hove-to without sleep or rest of any sort—and without nerves of steel. At one point Don crawled into my sea berth with me and we held tight to each other, a direct line to God in full use. It certainly is a long way from home out there!

I had long since mentally flown through the mantra of preparation for leaving the boat. Any cash, credit cards and copies of our passports were put into one of our trusty Ziploc bags, then into another small waterproof float bag. This was pinned to the inside of my bra, which I hastily put on so as to be properly attired should we happen to be picked up someday in the life raft—or preferably in *Breezy* as we attempted to sail to some destination!

My mind played and re-played a routine that I hoped would become instinct: get the grab and run bag up on top first and secure it to something. Tie the life raft off before slashing it free; when it hits the water and inflates, lower the water jugs and grab and run bag into it. A knife is tied to the mast; slash the dinghy free and hope adrenaline provides enough muscle to get it overboard in any way possible. Remember to secure the lanyard first! Absolutely don't get washed overboard in the process!

Most importantly—don't leave the boat until we have to step *up* into the life raft!

Don was constantly listening for every little sound. What if that bolt that he was going to replace as preventative maintenance gives way in this? When the boat is taking a beating like this, the mind works overtime conjuring up any number of things that can go wrong. As you know, I have no problem with anticipating the worst.

We were far from land, so in that respect weren't in any danger. We constantly kept track of our position, needing to know how far north we were being pushed and just where we might be able to make another Port of Entry. In reality, *Windy Thoughts* was handling everything well. All was holding together and our job was just to hold ourselves together in order to keep her safe! We continued to be pushed north far off our course—these nasty winds right out of the southwest.

You will be proud to know that I actually prepared a hot meal during the worst of this. It seemed the thing to do to calm our souls and give us the nourishment that might go a long way toward calming stomachs. I somehow managed to cook rice and tossed in a can of roast beef. We plopped ourselves down flat on the cabin sole and braced ourselves between the two settees. With one big spoon to share, we took turns spooning our gourmet dinner into our mouths. A hot meal does wonders. It seemed so normal amidst all that was anything but normal—even if only for those fleeting moments.

Accomplishing something good for us was a huge positive during a time that felt anything but positive. Of course, there was an abundance of positives in our situation as *Windy Thoughts* took on the Coral Sea just as if it were just any day of sailing.

Darkness lasts twelve hours in the tropical latitudes year around, but in the storm it seemed to last forever. Seas continually bombarded us and though we have never had so much as a tiny leak below, the sheer force of the water sprayed through the sealed portholes. Thankfully, the amount of water was slight and nothing to be alarmed about.

Australia Radio called, and when we heard our *Windy Thoughts* hailed it was as if heaven itself was checking in on us. They inquired as to how we were doing and how much food we had aboard. I grabbed the mike and replied that we indeed were fine, and that if we were careful we easily had at least eight months worth of provisions—and God forbid that we should be out there that long. They likely won't forget that conversation. They asked that we report in to them regularly to let them know how we were doing.

Finally, the winds began to lessen, then dropped down to thirty-five to forty knots, coming around to a better point of sail. We began sailing our course again and drove through this for two days. Though very uncomfortable, it was rather a lark after the proceeding days—fine sailing in comparison. My, how one's perspective changes!

And then, the wind decided to give us more grief by turning right back out of the southwest and on the nose—and we beat into it for three solid days more. Now, you know that any time the wind goes even a teensy bit forward of the beam, I go into red alert. We were, by now, so very tired. It seemed a mighty bang, crash, shudder each time the hull met a wave head on—the noise never letting us forget for even a moment that we were going to weather. I hate everything about beating. But it wasn't sixty to sixty-five knots of storm force wind.

By the time we were able to lay a course for a new port, we had some repairs to make, all miraculously minor. The bolts were loose on the roller furling and Don checked out everything on top.

And now comes—the ecstasy!

The southwest winds had forced us north a good bit and Brisbane as a landfall was a long way south. If able to hold our course we could lay Bundaberg, north of Brisbane by a few hundred miles and reached after crossing the sixty miles of Hervey Bay and heading up a river.

Windy Thoughts did hold her course and once across big Hervey Bay, we dropped anchor inside the river's mouth in a small bay. It was nine miles on upriver to Bundaberg and all berths and moorings were full, so we stayed right here.

The officials would come to us if we could put the boat on the small wharf—no easy matter in winds blowing a steady twenty-five to thirty knots with a very tight area in which to maneuver. Somehow we managed it. I didn't miss the wharf when Don brought the boat alongside and told me to jump and get a line around something—fast. Gosh, it is a thrill when things go right! The officials boarded us and the clearance procedure was a pleasant one—but they took all of our popcorn and potatoes. Do they really dispose of it?

This crew was elated to be in, thrilled to know that we had actually made it to Australia, and I wasn't at all anxious to go one nautical mile further.

It seems that we were indeed fortunate to reach this safe harbor, as a sailboat that had left Australia with four men aboard went down in the storm.

Australia Radio picked up the Mayday and flew out, spotted them in the water and dropped down a life raft.

An American boat with two women aboard radioed a May Day after a total rollover, dismasting and one woman seriously injured. The plane flew out to rescue the women first, planning to return for the men in the life raft—but the men were never found. A very sad story that reminds us all of how perilous this life can be. And to think that I was agonizing over things that never happened, when it had gone so very well for us.

[We later met the women up north in Port Douglas where locals had taken up a fund to aid them in repairs. Fortunately, local fishermen who were familiar with the currents and winds went out and found their boat! The two women faced a horrendous expense to restore the boat to sailing condition, and the Australian visa's no-work restriction prevented them from taking jobs to help restore the kitty.]

As for us, we were cleared into Australia, I was more than a little shell-shocked and we were exhausted. Had it been only nine days? We sat at anchor awaiting good conditions in which to head south. A large portion of the anchorage dries to very low water at low tide, and while the anchorage looks large, we had to be ever aware of dragging.

An Australian boat arrived with a couple aboard who cruises from Brisbane north to the Whitsundays each season for six months. They were heading home to Brisbane and we enjoyed chatting with them and getting lots of information.

We took two trips by bus into Bundaberg, finding it the most delightful town with gabled roofs, looking like a picture from a postcard in the 1950s. Fortunately, there was a small grocery and a restaurant just ashore from the anchorage—where we were introduced to beetroot when we ordered long awaited hamburgers. Though beetroot is a popular addition to Aussie hamburgers, to us one beetroot experience was enough. Sliced onion and tomato probably wouldn't do from their perspective either.

A laundry was available in an RV park down the road. During our lively days at sea, what we were wearing hadn't been a high priority. But for two days I kept the machines going in what seemed almost decadent, absolute opulence! Though no dryers were available, there were lines strung that provided for drying out in the perpetual sunshine.

While I attended to this chore, Don worked on the many chores on the boat—refueling, preventative maintenance, the attention to every little detail never ending. We spent a week here at anchor keeping busy with boat chores, planning the next step and poring over charts. It was a great spot to catch our breath and regain that sense of normalcy.

Having attempted to give you a glimpse of life at sea in a storm without dealing too heavily with the emotions, I do feel an urge to be very honest with you. You are my sounding board and I must share that I was in an absolute agony of nervous exhaustion and anxiety—and was at a point where I felt I simply couldn't go back out there again. Seriously, in a mental and emotional stew that just overwhelmed my senses day and night, and out of which it seemed I just couldn't climb. While there are always conditions that try your sanity in this ocean sailing and cruising business, I seemed to be sorely lacking in confidence at this point.

Taking the bus down to Brisbane seemed the only alternative to me, as any thought to actually sailing *Windy Thoughts* south was seriously out of the question.

But reality always wins with me. And the reality was that I would never abandon Don to sail the boat himself, capable though he certainly was. We were in this together. After all, we had brought *Windy Thoughts* safely to Bundaberg, nothing bad had happened to us or to the boat and everything other than my anxieties had really gone well. But I wasn't ready to face "doing well" through anything horrific again just yet. I was in a real emotional stew—an awful anxiety was eating away at my insides.

So while on the inside I couldn't bring myself to even consider upping anchor ever again, on the outside I did all that we had to do, wearing my vulnerability on the inside as usual and discussing the trip south with the Aussie boat as we learned the ins and outs of getting to Brisbane. They went over the charts with us, explaining the most pleasant way to go about it.

Fraser Island, the largest sand island in the world, is located only a day's sail south of Hervey Bay. The easy trip is to sail behind Fraser Island and down through the Great Sandy Strait that forms a popular cruising ground for the Aussies.

However, once through this Strait you must cross over Wide Bay Bar at the south end of Fraser Island—a very shallow bar that extends out for fully five miles and often has rather miserable conditions, making its crossing less than something to look forward to. You can imagine how this next challenge hit me in my state of mind. Gads, so close to our R and R and now there was an often-nasty bar to cross? A bar that extends out for five miles!

Being somewhat shell shocked after the past few days that seemed like forever—well, very shell shocked—this bar loomed in my mind as the ultimate obstruction to what should otherwise be a nice passage south to Brisbane. Certainly, we would cross it and perhaps in lousy conditions. But I didn't want to have to go through the anxiety of challenging conditions just yet!

Nothing to do, however, but to forge ahead and get it over with, as we knew we had those much-anticipated months of R and R awaiting us. This thought alone kept me going.

The sail down to the Strait was lovely, with a steady twenty knots of wind that seemed so perfect after what we had been through. Once behind

Fraser Island and into the Great Sandy Strait, the seas and swell dropped to nearly nothing in the protection of the huge island, and we sailed along on water that was like being on a lake—ghosting along on our magic carpet once again.

This Strait is very shallow and to divert from the buoy system even a bit can abruptly put a boat aground, a common experience here and one that, before long, we were to find ourselves chalking up in our own records. The markers were a fair distance apart and we kept a constant vigil to focus in on the next one.

Merrily rolling along and sailing wing and wing with these steady winds right behind us, all was far better than the preceding days had been! I was working big time on the attitude and feeling that I could keep anxiety at bay through mind over matter. After all, conditions were perfect, the day was perfect, Don and I were together and what more could I possibly ask?

We joined the newfound Aussie friends in an anchorage for the first night and they joined us aboard *Windy Thoughts* for dinner and an early evening in the cockpit, with peaceful conversation and the camaraderie so enjoyed in this life.

We all set off the following morning for the next day's run. The Aussie boat was ahead of us and already in the anchorage when we came upon the big red bell buoy ahead of us.

The buoy system in the rest of the world is different from that of the United States, so you must be on your toes to remember that "red right returning" doesn't apply. The buoy sat right in the middle of the main channel—but was also centered just at the entrance of a channel leading up around to the north side of a small island to our port. We were to go up this channel to anchor on the north side of this island.

The buoy was clearly marked on the chart. Was it marking the main channel that we were in—or the entrance to the channel bearing off to our starboard side and into which we were to turn? The final decision was to keep the buoy to our port side as we went around it and then on up the channel.

Wrong decision—though we rounded it very closely just in case. It was definitely meant to be kept to starboard and we abruptly found ourselves hard aground for the first time ever.

Don first attempted to get us off by maneuvers back and forth under power that did no good at all. We called the Aussies at anchor and told them that we were close by but aground, and would hopefully join them soon. They wanted to up anchor and come down to assist us, as they knew that we were at the top of the highest tide in a month—and that if we didn't get off very soon we may be there for a while. Don asked them to stand by. We would attempt to kedge ourselves off first.

We untied the dinghy and got the thirty-five pound CQR anchor ready.

While making these preparations the wind picked up considerably and *Windy Thoughts* shifted just slightly. Don jumped back to the engine, gunned it—and suddenly we were floating free!

The Aussies couldn't believe it when we radioed that we would see them shortly! After a lovely evening sharing stories and dessert with them, we had a gentle night's sleep at anchor, ready to joggle on in the morning.

The next morning, steady twenty- to twenty-five-knot winds and little sea gave us a lovely sleigh ride south. We happened to gaze ashore at just the opportune time to see two dingo dogs standing on the shore and looking back at us. As they are not generally seen by "passersby", we considered it quite a privilege to give them a wave.

Just a couple of miles past the Wide Bay Bar's entrance (that would wait our crossing for a few days yet) sits a small marina in the storybook village of Tin Can Bay. What a treat to tie securely into a berth and to step out onto the dock!

Best, is what a memorable spot was Tin Can Bay. We enjoyed one of the finest evening meals ever experienced, at a small restaurant with live chamber music provided by three very talented musicians. The food was exquisite. We will likely never forget tiny Tin Can Bay, whose name belies what a special place this dot on the chart is!

One more night on the dock—an experience not had in years, we slept like babes, without an ear even cocked to the wind. I awakened with a start only a few times when my conscious mind thought about that bar just ahead.

Early on that next morning we were up and at 'em, and set off to take a look at this bar and its conditions. Conditions were very, very bad. We saw fishing boats anchored in the bight just adjacent to the bar's entrance and dropped our hook amongst them. When they headed out, we would be right behind them. They know the territory. We would hunker down for the day just as they did.

The next morning we started the procedure over again, up very early, eyes and ears wide open for any sign that it was a go. The fishing boats were upping anchor at first light, so off we went right on their tail. It appears that you are just sailing right into the open ocean—which, of course, you are—albeit with a very shallow and extensive bar right under your hull for a full five miles.

What silliness my fretting had been, as we now had probably the most perfect conditions one could ask for! In fact, the Aussies told us that of all the years they had traversed this bar, never once had they seen it this good! The swell was slight; there was little wind and little sea. Once again I had agonized in vain. Will I never learn?

Australia doesn't lack for steady sailing winds, which soon piped up to twenty knots behind us, giving us a great sail south. Setting our course for Mooloolaba, on the Queensland Coast, *Windy Thoughts* charged through the seas and we had nary a task but to keep the sails trimmed properly, chat with each other, eat, enjoy our lovely day and relax to our heart's content.

The Aussies had recommended the Mooloolaba Yacht Club as a fine spot for a rest up on the way south, located about a half-mile inside the entrance to a river whose mouth empties into the sea. While still a couple of miles off the river's entrance, we radioed the Yacht Club to request a berth and learned that just one berth was available.

With winds creating very lively seas that blew right into the river's entrance, we dropped sails, turned on the engine and bounced on in to find the Mooloolaba Yacht Club awaiting us on our starboard side. Assigned a berth on the radio, we muddled about to find the proper dock.

And then, *Windy Thoughts* was tied up to a dock for the first time in 2.5 years—other than that little respite at Tin Can Bay. Lying at anchor is the ultimate experience, but there comes a time when the comfort and security of a marina is heaven itself! Though we planned to roll on to Brisbane, about fifty miles south, plans changed in the wink of an eye. Immediately falling in love with Mooloolaba, this is where we will spend the winter—well, their summer—right here. The Mooloolaba Yacht Club is a first class club and, oh my, do we feel in the midst of luxury! What a great feeling it is to know that we don't have to leave in a day, or even in a few days!

There are several cruising boats in for the cyclone season and we have been welcomed warmly. The club is beautiful, with two nice restaurants. The entire area is pristine with the most beautiful, wide, white sandy beach just across the road from the marina—a beach that extends around the big bay and on north for miles and miles.

Mooloolaba itself sits with its beautiful esplanade directly across from the beach. A lovely grassy area between the beach and this esplanade sports picnic tables, and gas barbeques with twenty-five cent fee slots that give one-half hour of gas flame. As you likely know, the Aussies are well known for their barbies!

All is spotless; the small town has a resort atmosphere and many nice shops and cafes. The beach is likely amongst the loveliest we have seen in the Pacific—and that is saying a lot! The waves are just right for surfing and it seems that every local kid has a boogie board. Should we get one?

This area of Queensland is called the Sunshine Coast and is a popular family vacation spot, laid back and quiet. Brisbane is about fifty miles south. The Gold Coast, a few miles further south from Brisbane, is known as "Little Miami" with its party atmosphere and high rises blocking the afternoon sun. High rises aren't permitted in Mooloolaba and we find it the most perfect spot for us.

Windy Thoughts is located on D dock along with exclusively Australian boats and we enjoy the opportunity to mingle with local people. That's what we are here for!

Right next door to us is Kimmie, four years old and a very busy little girl starting at about 6:30 a.m., sometimes earlier. On the other side is a couple from Tasmania, here for the season with Madeline, who is a year old. She is a cutie as well and is put on deck, with safety netting enclosing all of the lifelines, by 5:30 each morning while mom and dad go back to sleep for awhile. She stands on the bow and screams her lungs out in happiness, just for the joy of it. She looks like pictures of the old-fashioned Gerber baby with those big round cheeks, but we can attest to the fact that she has the lungs of an adult!

Windy Thoughts sits only a few feet away, all of our ports and hatches open to the air and Madeline about five feet from our noses. We, of course, don't sleep through this. However, the people are very nice and so friendly that nothing could mar our happiness with this beautiful Yacht Club.

Lovely homes line the banks on either side of channels located off the river. *Breezy* takes us up one channel to another marina where we tie up and cross the road to a mall with two supermarkets. Think of that after these years of shopping at local wet markets!

Temperatures are in the eighties every day with clear blue skies, very comfortable with a constant sea breeze from the ocean just across the street from the Club. I refer to spending the winter here but it will be summer starting any day now, as we are "down under".

The temperatures dropped down into the low seventies for about three days and everyone here nearly froze. I rummaged in our lockers to find socks for our feet—not required since we left home on the passage to San Francisco.

We are up early with our alarm clocks on either side of us—and we work very hard all morning. I did ten loads of laundry in the first couple of days, cleaned the head, the galley lockers, the entire outside of the boat, and have still many chores ahead.

Don attends to his list, replacing the float valve to the automatic bilge pump, one spreader light, and has cleaned and worked on the battery terminals. He plans to send the chain to Brisbane for re-galvanizing, and all in all feels very thankful that we have had no major breakdowns.

At lunchtime each day we head for the showers and then begin exploring Mooloolaba. Across the road from the main shopping area is the grassy, tree-lined picnic area adjoining the wide, white beach with sand so fine that it squeaks when you walk in it. The water is pristine, azure blue and clean, with lovely surf pounding the beach.

Post cards with aerial pictures reveal that, once away from its coastal area, Australia becomes a vast, mostly unpopulated area. The population of the entire country is less than that of California!

January 1, 1991
Mooloolaba Yacht Club, Oz

G'Day Mate,

Your most welcome letter has been received and reports of your wintry weather make us question if we shall ever be able to face colder temperatures again! Summer vacation began here the week before Christmas and ends at the end of January. Many kiddies are seen about the beaches, all with their surf boards at the ready.

Thanksgiving arrived very soon after our arrival at Mooloolaba. Don and I celebrated with a chicken, turkey not being so readily available and the holiday not at the forefront for the Australians.

We had a lovely Christmas and invited a young American single-hander for dinner along with his mother, who had flown in from Oregon for the holidays. Tom is a very nice young man who sails a lovely and beautifully kept boat. A young couple from South Africa on *Six Pack*, aptly named for the generously stocked bilges, pulled in to join us and we all had a wonderfully festive day. I served cold ham and salads, and Tom's mother contributed the pumpkin pie and a vegetable dish.

For transportation about Mooloolaba and reaches further, we have purchased two bikes. Mine is an older no-gear bike that we call the Red Bomber, painted up a very bright red and in great condition. Don has already traded in his original for an upgraded black beater-bike with gears, and we are off and away every afternoon. The bike shop owner has offered to buy both bikes back at the end of the season for the same price as he sold them to us.

After the drama of the past months, we are captivated with our present life and find our biking excursions taking us to a video rental in Mooroochadore. We pedal along on the most beautiful asphalt bike and walking path that borders the ocean the entire distance, about ten miles up the beach. Our view is the ocean spreading east of us for thousands of miles—and on the land

side, the occasional beautiful up-market condominium whose owners wave hellos to us along the way here and there.

In America our televisions operate on the NSTC system, but in Australia the PAL system is used—so the videos are not interchangeable. Consequently, we have rented a fourteen-inch television and a video player by the month.

The owners of the bike shop have been down to the boat a few times and recently took us to see their fifty-foot cat boat under construction in a warehouse nearby. My, how huge it looked. We also recently joined them in their four-wheel drive for a ride at low tide to Double Island Point, about twenty-five-miles north, which we sailed past on our way down to Mooloolaba. It was a beautiful day and we picnicked at Double Island Point, looking down at the ocean just below us.

The beach stretches from Mooroochadore on north—so pristine and with no homes to mar its naturally spectacular setting. The waves crash and pound onto the beach with surf made just for boarding. Swimming can be dangerous to people not familiar with local currents and conditions.

Such good fortune we have had in meeting Jo Beard, from Brisbane and aboard the boat that her husband had sailed north to Mooloolaba a week earlier to moor at the Yacht Club over the holidays. She and two girlfriends drove up from Brisbane to spend a week aboard. David pilots a research ship up in the Great Barrier Reef in one-month stints.

Jo invited us for two different days of sightseeing and gave us the opportunity to see beyond our biking distances. We drove north about thirty miles to Noosa Heads, an absolutely charming town where we saw the sweetest koala bear in a tree right outside a shop in the village! Jo had never before seen one in natural surroundings so close in and the townspeople were surprised as well. Weren't we lucky?

We stayed to see some kangaroos that come out into the fields in the late afternoon and even walked closer to get some pictures—but it was considered unwise to try to get too near!

On another sightseeing jaunt, Jo took us to a National Park in the nearby Glasshouse Mountains, where we went swimming in a big lagoon in the natural rain forest. The teenage boys were jumping off a high steep cliff. Don felt compelled to join them—and with a running start, flew out over the edge in a perfect dive down into the glen below.

It was all such a fun day and we saw so much more of the area with Jo. She has invited us down to their home in Brisbane and we plan to visit there soon.

A BRISBANE WELCOME

When Jo's husband David arrived back at Mooloolaba to sail the boat to Brisbane, he invited Don to join him. It was good for Don to enjoy male company, and especially with such an experienced a sailor. David set the record for the first Australian to sail solo nonstop around both Australia and Tasmania inclusive. We found David to be a very humble and most interesting man.

About two weeks later Don and I took the bus to Brisbane, finding public transportation in the country very pricey at $50.00 each. Jo and David were very congenial hosts, and Brisbane proved to be a lovely, beautifully clean city with a picturesque river, no freeways and no heavy traffic. Had we not found perfect Mooloolaba, we would likely have been happy sitting on anchor here in this river, none the wiser.

On our first day, Don and I took a tour that included all of the sights one shouldn't miss. When our time ran short we missed the Maritime Museum—so we returned the following day in hopes to see it then.

Volunteers dressed most nattily in nautical attire listened politely, and then the woman told us that our tickets were good for the previous day only— and that it would cost us $1.50 each. Don didn't seriously question the meager fee and thought he was humoring her. When we mentioned that we were cruising people, presently visiting friends in Brisbane and didn't want to miss this exhibit, she promptly replied, "Oh, I know who you must be, friends of the Beards. We're coming to a surprise party for you tonight at their house!"

Aghast at our blunder, we tried desperately to pay the small fee but were denied the opportunity—and slunk in, duly embarrassed.

That evening, we put on our best faces for the Beard's friends who gave us such a warm welcome. The lady from the museum was there with her husband. The Gulf War had just broken out and was all over the Australian news. With a staunch British accent and his nose a bit in the air—having moved out to the "colonies" some time ago, he spoke up and claimed that our American boys would find themselves in way over their heads and didn't stand a chance against the superiority of Saddam Hussein's forces. A very few days later, he was proven wrong on that score!

We loved our season in Mooloolaba, though it passed much too rapidly. The boat was hauled and bottom paint applied, the job costing us U.S. $1,200.00, the most expensive haul out ever. But it was done very conveniently right next door to the marina and done well. Don sent the chain down to Brisbane with neighbors for re-galvanizing.

After a month of trying to ignore our two cute little alarm clocks on either side of us, the constant noise became a bit uncomfortable. As much as we enjoyed them, Madeline with her lungs exercised much of the day, and Kimmie with her entourage of little ones always about and aboard us as well, kept things fairly lively.

We privately asked the manager if we could be moved to a different dock, requesting that nothing be said lest we hurt anyone's feelings. Within days he had a slip for us and we found ourselves down amongst the cruising group again, definitely quieter and more peaceful.

New Year's Eve was upon us and we attended a party at the Yacht Club. Madeline was there and toddled right up to Don and crawled up onto his lap. Don suffered bouts of guilt concerning our departure from D dock in favor of more tranquil surroundings. Little did she know what exasperation she had caused!

Two more bus trips were made into Brisbane, one to visit the Beards and one to get our visas extended. Extensions were granted to cruising boats unable to depart during the cyclone season with sufficient time to make it north and out of Australia.

Don and I innocently waited our turn outside the official office. The couple before us stopped by us on their way out and whispered to us, "We sure hope you don't get the same fellow we had to contend with."

We did.

We walked in with big smiles on our faces and were met by a very sullen man who demanded to know, in no uncertain terms, just what we were doing in Australia. We mumbled something about visiting their country by sailboat and wanting to extend our visas in order to have time to make the long journey north to the Torres Strait, or to Darwin, to clear there.

He stood up, shook his finger in our faces and told us that once making clearance into Australia at Bundaberg, our Cruising Permit didn't allow any cruising at all—and we were to have stayed right in Bundaberg.

Had we done something wrong? We had exactly the same clearance and permit as all of the other boats strung out for hundreds of miles along the eastern coast of Australia—and who, for the most part, had been freely cruising about while in the country. Plunking ourselves down in Mooloolaba for the season, we hadn't even left the dock. We could make neither heads nor tails of his displeasure and were also told that we had applied too early for any extension. We still had two weeks and would have to come back—and were sent out the door. How did all those others get their extensions several weeks before their cruising permits expired?

Neither of us dared express any assertiveness, feeling like a couple of youngsters chastised by the principal as we skulked out with tails between our legs. We had neither an extension nor any idea that we may get one, and it would require another bus to Brisbane very soon, with no idea as to how to make our plans.

In the end, we did soon make that trip back down to Brisbane and were granted the same extension that everyone else had been given—this time without a hitch. Luck had it that another official was in the office, one who exhibited the welcome that we always found so evident in the Land of Oz. We must have caught the other fellow on a particularly bad day!

Planning to depart Mooloolaba at the end of April, by the end of March we had accomplished much of our preparations. *Breezy* zoomed about in high gear as we made numerous trips back and forth up the channel to the supermarket to take on those usual quantities of provisions—added to the quantities already on the boat. April saw more serious provisioning and as time pressed on there was the last minute provisioning—and then last minute provisioning again when something would stall our departure.

Windy Thoughts' mast sported a storm sail track but we lacked the storm sail. Two reefs in the mainsail had sufficiently reduced the size of the sail to get us through everything that had been thrown at us to this point, but after that storm experienced on the way to Australia, Don had a third reef put in the mainsail, to serve as our storm sail.

A large group of the cruising crowd gathered for weekly barbecues held on the beach. Everyone brought their own food and there was great camaraderie to enjoy. It was just another of the pleasant factors that made this R and R so special.

Our neighbors on the new dock were Valerie and Roger, on *Impetuous*, out of New Zealand. They sold us a nearly-new 150 percent Genoa sail and we purchased all new super braid to replace our original sheets. Plans to head up to the Torres Strait and on to Indonesia and Southeast Asia this year were discussed, and the folks on *Impetuous* wanted to buddy-boat with us to Singapore. It all sounded fun and would help to alleviate piracy concerns and give us company in the lesser-cruised areas.

Southeast Asia it would be, and we anxiously awaited news from our German insurance company about our coverage on ahead for the Red Sea. If not covered, we would have to go around South Africa. The investment in the boat was too much for us to risk total loss and we were unable to self-insure. To lose *Windy Thoughts* would be to lose our home.

We received a fax from Germany notifying us they could offer us coverage for the Red Sea—though unbeknownst to us, this decision wouldn't be necessary for a few years yet and our minds would be changed several times in the interim before the Indian Ocean beckoned us!

An Indonesian Cruising Permit was required, with an application fee of $250.00 and the application made several months in advance. The application must state very specifically each port to be visited, with the exact date of arrival and departure for each—an impossibility when at the mercy of weather conditions. We wrote down that we would make clearance into Indonesia on July 26, making guesses about our route and dates to the best of our abilities.

There would be many miles between Mooloolaba and Ambon, Indonesia, our planned Port of Entry, with plans to make some stops along the way north to the Torres Strait. *Windy Thoughts* would also have to make tracks heading north in order that we get cleared into Indonesia and still have our three months visa allowance to meander through that country and on to Singapore. Several thousand miles would pass under her hull before reaching Singapore.

On May 11, 1991, we were still in Mooloolaba with thirty-knot winds howling about us, but with all at the ready to jump off any day. We knew that it would be a push up and around Australia, but later season cyclones are generally the fiercest—so we felt the small delay perhaps for the best.

The *Impetuous* crew had gone for a visit home to New Zealand and so would be late in getting off, but would catch us up several weeks later near the top of Australia.

Don's Colt forty-five automatic was securely stowed aboard and he had recently purchased a twelve-gauge shotgun, more effective at close range. We were awaiting its arrival before heading into Southeast Asia's waters.

There is, of course, a much varied outlook on whether to carry arms aboard. Don is an experienced hunter, a decorated combat veteran from the Korean War, is comfortable around weapons and knows that if you own a weapon you must be prepared to use it. Though many consider a flare gun sufficient, Don didn't consider flares as adequate protection against someone intent upon causing us harm. We chose to be proactive rather than reactive.

We knew that we needed to take full responsibility for all risks inherent in ocean sailing, personal safety included. There is no 911 service to send protection. People unfamiliar or uncomfortable with guns may well have a different opinion. Considering guns on board to be a personal choice, and believing the need to use a gun to be unlikely, we put it all aside and moved forward with our happy and fulfilled lives.

REEF, REEF WHEREVER WE LOOK

With *Windy Thoughts* ready to jump off from Mooloolaba, we waited first for heavy winds, then rain and gloom to clear. Finally, we could wait no longer. The time had come to simply leave.

At first light on May 25, 1991, we threw off the dock lines and left the Mooloolaba Yacht Club to head north along Australia's Queensland Coast and through the Great Barrier Reef to the top of Australia—where we would pass through the Torres Strait.

Our Indonesian Cruising Permit would be in effect soon and we didn't want our time in Indonesia cut short. We were leaving good friends, good times and so many wonderful memories behind in Mooloolaba. We loved Australia for everything that it is. The months here left us refreshed and ready to venture on to new horizons. The southeasterly winds had set in, winds that would be right behind us. It was time to continue our adventure.

The first leg was a slog against a strong southerly setting current. With twenty-knot winds at our back and the strong current right on our bow, the seas were very confused and mighty uncomfortable. On the fourth morning out, we were relieved to clear the north tip of Fraser Island and break free of the current.

At 10:00 a.m. we motored into Roslyn Bay. Local boats were tied off bow and stern between pilings and we joined a handful of boats at anchor. Sleep had been elusive during our little jaunt, so after putting the boat in order we crawled into the welcoming cocoon of our master berth. How good it felt to snuggle down and let our cares melt away for a while.

Don stirred a bit later, and with sleep-laden eyes peeked out of the porthole over our bunk to check on things. With a start, he saw that we had dragged anchor clear to the back of the bay and were perilously close to the wall behind us! The wind was blowing about twenty-five knots, gusting frequently to thirty knots.

In a flash, Don was forward on the bow and I was at the helm. The windlass stuck when he started to take the anchor up, the chain stripper simply refusing to strip the chain properly. There was nothing for Don to do but to pull the chain up hand over hand until he had the forty-five-pound CQR anchor aboard. Its weight, along with that of the 100 feet of chain, was not a refreshing exercise in the middle of his treasured sleep!

Our day in Roslyn Bay was not to be spent in the prone position, sound asleep after all. During the next two hours, *Windy Thoughts* dragged through the silt again, the winds expediting her journey to the back of the bay. After two more re-anchoring sessions that also meant hauling the anchor and chain up hand over hand, we wrestled *Breezy* down into the water and headed to shore. We tied up at the wharf and climbed up a steep ladder to the dock. It was a huge relief to learn that a fellow nearby could do repairs on the chain stripper. *Windy Thoughts* would have to move to the jetty the next morning where power to make repairs was available.

Don let out more chain when we returned to the boat, and both of us stood anchor watches that night while the wind blew a steady thirty knots. In the morning Don had another opportunity to work the forty-five pound CQR anchor along with now 160 feet of chain up from the bottom and onto the deck of *Windy Thoughts*—by hand.

Once the boat was tied securely to the wharf, we walked about and stretched those sea legs while our repair was made. And when we left Roslyn Bay we had a properly working chain stripper and Don had a sore back—one that could take a much needed rest.

With these steady winds behind us, we sailed with beautiful clear blue skies and consistently ideal temperatures in the low eighty degrees. Turquoise waters surrounded us; *Windy Thoughts* gaily romped along north and all seemed about perfect.

Australia's Whitsunday Islands are prime cruising grounds, wooded, with many natural beaches. In season, the many island anchorages are enjoyed by both Australians and those who have come from afar. The community of Airlie Beach is a hub for the sailboat charter business in the Whitsundays and a popular stop for cruising boats. We were anxious to visit a small ten-acre wildlife park that was privately owned and had every variety of Australian wildlife to be imagined.

Australia does have some odd characters amongst its animal population and this was the perfect place to view them up close and personal. One of the more fascinating was the cassowary, a huge bird similar in size to an ostrich, but a very clumsy fellow and funny to watch. Then there is the Tasmanian devil, who isn't really a fierce devil at all—but instead, a rather timid little fellow. The wombats, koalas, and even the most poisonous snakes in the world, along with lots of lizards, birds such as parrots and cockatoos and, of course, the country's mascot, the kangaroo, gave us a day to remember.

Australia is home to the salt-water crocodile and feeding time at the crocodile pit left its mark on Don. He had been hoping to take the dinghy up a river farther north to view many crocodile located in the wild, anticipating it to be a great adventure.

While we stood by with noses pressed to the surrounding chain link fence, a sixteen year-old girl dangled a chicken on a stick out over the water of a pond about two feet deep. With a sudden ferociousness that made us nearly jump out of our skins, a crocodile reared up out of the water, its huge jaws opened wide and showing its fierce sharp teeth that made one big snap at the chicken—and in the blink of an eye the big croc was back under water.

Fast on the draw and it was over before we could catch our breaths!

More than once, the young girl had to make a dash for the big chain link fence and make a hasty retreat up and over the top. Don decided that close-up encounters with crocodiles in our dinghy might not be the adventurous experience he was expecting. Perhaps we should forego that river experience after all!

As we pushed north, we were within the protection of the 1,000 mile stretch of the Great Barrier Reef. The outer reef was about fifty miles to the east of us—but reef encompassed the entire area between those outer reaches and the mainland, and we were navigating through more of this reef than we ever wanted to meet with again!

No longer experiencing ocean swells, we bobbed along on only three to four-foot wind waves. Steady winds with these slight seas pushed us north in some of the most perfect sailing conditions we would ever experience. Lighted buoys made excellent references at night, marking the safe channel through the reef-strewn area. Most nights were spent at anchor, and good shelter was always available as we bobbed our way north—sometimes off the mainland, sometimes behind reefs and sometimes tucked behind a welcoming island.

Able to get into the very nice marina at Townsville, we took on water, did laundry, picked up some fresh produce and enjoyed some walking about this charming town. Townsville is a good place to effect boat repairs with the good marina and the availability of boat parts in the chandlery. It was also a good place to await parts being shipped in. Four nights were enjoyed while we worked on "the list" before moving seven miles across the bay to Magnetic Island.

Plans were to spend one night at anchor at Magnetic Island before making an early start the following morning for Palm Isles, just thirty-five miles north. But Don discovered a leak between the fuel pump and the fuel filter and we had no replacement hose. Plugging it with Marine Tex seemed to solve the problem temporarily. *Breezy* came down and we were off to shore. Don called the chandlery at Townsville, ordered the hose, and we planned to go back over the following morning to pick it up.

Meanwhile, we stretched our legs on Magnetic Island and came across a Backpacker's Resort, one of several in Australia. It was popular with the young crowd, with a pool, lovely grounds, restaurants and music at night. Accommodations were cabins with dormitory style sleeping, the going rate $5.00 a night. Included amongst the buildings were toilet and shower facilities as well as laundry facilities. In a lovely setting, it was almost comparable to any medium priced resort accommodation. A quiet atmosphere—but we reminded ourselves that it was 10 a.m. and perhaps many of the younger set were still asleep!

While in Townsville, we made radio contact with Roger on *Impetuous*. They were back in Mooloolaba and hoped to head north within a week, to make fast tracks in hopes of catching us and cruising Indonesia together. Roger learned that we needed visas if staying more than two months and our Cruising Permit was for three months. He suggested faxing our agent in Jakarta. The $100.00 for our visas would have to be sent, followed by a wait in Townsville—and we had already been here for a week.

This was June 18, 1991, and our security clearance would take effect within the month. We called the Indonesian Consulate in Darwin and understood that we could not take care of our visas by mail or fax, but would have to go to Darwin, 800 miles west from the Torres Strait. Fortunately, we would learn otherwise up the road!

When we finally headed north again from Townsville, our next stop brought us to anchor behind a little island a few miles off the small town of Port Douglas on the mainland. Several other boats sat at anchor and we relaxed in our cockpit and watched hydroplanes whiz past, taking tourists from Port Douglas to the outer Great Barrier Reef. A big, fancy-looking power yacht sat in the anchorage and Don intently watched the goings on through the binoculars. He could see huge spotlights and big movie cameras on deck, a hub-bub of activity—and then a small dinghy in the water with a deployed life raft.

Ah ha! He knew exactly what was going on! They must be making a movie about the Robinson family whose sailboat was sunk by a whale in the 1970s. We had Mr. Robinson's book, *Survive the Savage Sea*, packed in our life raft. This very story was unfolding right here before our eyes!

Later on we saw the movie and were aghast at how the reality of their ordeal was so different from the film. In the film the family lounged around in a huge life raft surely meant for at least twelve people. Filmed in the anchorage, there was barely a ripple on the water, only the chop from the wind, and we could see the mainland hazily visible in the distance.

Mr. Robinson was ingenious in survival skills at sea, and was able to determine their position with some degree of accuracy using two crossed pencils as a sextant to determine latitude for a sun sight. The movie only referred to his navigation skill once, but even then the position of longitude it stated doesn't exist—something that even a grade school child could catch. Theirs was such a fascinating story, full of so much human triumph, that a true portrayal could have made the movie far more interesting.

July 2, 1991
South 11 degrees 15 minutes
West 142 degrees 52 minutes
Great Barrier Reef

G'Day Mate,

Windy Thoughts is nearly to the "top" of Australia now, with only 150 miles to go to Thursday Island in the Torres Strait, where we will make our clearance from the country. Fortunately, we have learned that we need not go the extra 800 miles to Darwin after all and we breathe huge sighs of relief, because our Indonesian Security Permit took effect two days ago and we are behind schedule.

Two days ago, we left Lizard Island, where we sat for three weeks awaiting *Impetuous*. Val and Roger joined us and delivered batteries purchased for us in Townsville—where *Impetuous* was held up for ten days waiting for a new compass to arrive from England. Thank goodness for radio contact!

We lost the sealed Stowaway bank of batteries and the replacement batteries set us back hundreds of dollars, about double the cost back home. Never mind, we are so thankful for *Impetuous'* willingness to track down two 100 amp Johnson Control gelled batteries and then haul them along to Lizard Island. Thankfully, our main bank of Prevailer batteries just keeps perking along.

This respite from our rapid push north gave us the most delightful vacation on Lizard Island. Before elaborating on that piece of paradise and our escapades prior to cavorting with lizards, let me catch you up on our present status.

Windy Thoughts sits at anchor behind a point on the mainland around which sits little Restoration Island—the same island on which Captain Bligh made his landfall after his heroic small boat voyage following the mutiny on his *Bounty*. To get here he had to find a pass in the Great Barrier Reef.

Speaking of reefs, as we move north we must keep a very close watch. Just a few days ago we were sailing briskly along in twenty-five-knot winds when I happened to glance ahead at precisely the right time to see waves breaking over reef directly ahead of us, not more than 100 feet! Sailing wing and wing dead downwind, changing course was a wild motion of four arms and four legs flying to duty!

Outside of little wake-up calls such as this, the sailing is about as perfect as it gets with no swell and seas generally only about three to four feet. Sailing in depths of only thirty to sixty feet means that one eye glances at the depth sounder off and on just to be sure that the bottom isn't coming up much too fast.

Departure time has been 3 a.m. for the past few days in order to make the next anchorage before dark, as we don't want to make approaches amongst reef in the dark. Don truly wants to go in at Escape River, but if we make this overnight passage it appears that we would arrive at low water late in the day and wouldn't be able to get over the bar.

The channel is so well marked at night, the light markers actually making it easier to avoid the reef. These lights are located about ten or twelve miles apart, showing white if in the channel, red if too far to port, and green if too far to starboard. The channel is quite narrow now in spots, with reef surrounding us.

Today we are having a lovely sail in about twelve knots of wind, dead downwind again and only fifteen miles now from our next anchorage. Only a one-meter sea is running with no swell and all is so gentle. These light winds have been the pattern earlier in the day for the past two days, piping up to twenty to twenty-five knots by afternoon. Two days ago, it suddenly piped up to forty knots, somewhat stressful because of rocks to one side and coral reef to the other. Don had difficulty getting the pole down. That wind stayed up until we were in for the night—but once the anchor was down and we had our dinner, we went right to bed. Hooked securely—let it blow!

Just before heading to Lizard Island we were able to get a couple of nights on the dock in beautiful Cairns. We walked about the town to stretch our legs, and you can imagine our surprise when we came upon a restaurant with an American cowboy theme. Of course, Don was smitten right off and we stepped inside to a scene right out of our American West.

Settling in for big juicy hamburgers American style, we had the most interesting visit with the owner/manager, who hailed from the United States—and to our surprise was from Spokane, Washington! Don began asking the "did you know so and so" question, and to our further amazement we learned that he grew up and went to school with a fellow whose family are good friends of Don's!

Cairns is the last big center for provisioning and boat services, and sports a big hydrofoil business that takes tourists out to the outer Barrier Reef.

But it was Lizard Island that has stolen our hearts on our trek north, sitting a short ten miles from the outer Barrier Reef. At Lizard Island, we were enveloped in a wonderful remoteness, but with a very posh, small resort tucked away in the next bay over and just a walk away.

Eight sailboats sat in the anchorage, with the resort around the corner so that we had our privacy and they had theirs. All at anchor kept a very low profile, respecting the beauty and the serenity of the area. It was a quiet and magical atmosphere.

Not realizing that we were not allowed to venture onto the hallowed grounds of the resort, Don and I took a walk over there on our first day. The cook very kindly showed us about anyway and even allowed us to purchase cold Cokes on the sly from a cold drink machine in the back. They don't sell to visiting yachties. He told of catching a tiger shark just recently. He threw out a big hook with a leg of beef on it. The tiger shark was so big that it took them several days to haul it in. These sharks aren't a worry, as they are nocturnal creatures and our daily frolics in the water weren't a danger. Still, we are always aware.

While we awaited *Impetuous*, our vacation on this getaway island cost only the price of our Cokes, while guests at the resort pay upwards from US $450.00 a day per person! It is very private though I believe we enjoyed our time as much as, if not more than, the guests as we snorkeled each day and hiked about the island.

The water is crystal clear and the sand blindingly white. The resort guests seemed to prefer the pool, never venturing out to enjoy the beach or to even stroll in the sand. The temperatures are around eighty degrees, so comfortable that we sit on the beach in the afternoons with our books, something rarely done in our tropical adventures.

Don and I found a private beach where we cavorted with giant clams, five feet in diameter and well known characters here at Lizard Island. The coral garden was beautiful and the sea was alive with every manner of tropical fish, making for excellent snorkeling to while away the hours. Living up to its name, Lizard Island is home to big goanna lizards, two to three feet in length and harmless, rather shy fellows. This is also the black marlin capital of the world.

Don called the resort on the VHF radio to inquire about dinner reservations. Though they don't generally offer their services to the likes of the cruising folks, they would, upon reflection, make an exception. However, when we learned that dinner prices began at $75 a head and the wine list started at $80 a bottle, they were able to uphold their standards. We instead dined on the boat, making pizza.

With our beautiful surroundings and our own little home sitting right here amongst such beauty and peacefulness, what more could we ask for? *Windy Thoughts* is just the perfect venue for a good dinner, bobbing in the breeze. Don and I are sitting in our cockpit, a cool drink in one hand and a slice of pizza in the other. Isn't this what we dreamed about for all those years? Paradise is right here. We remind ourselves that fine dinners were taken for granted in our old life and were enjoyed in superfluous abundance. Dinners out will still be there waiting for us when our days in the sun are over, but the magic of sitting at anchor off Lizard Island in the Great Barrier Reef will never happen again.

Pizza never tasted better, even topped with fried Spam pulled from our lockers. Capture the moment!

When Captain James Cook's *Endeavor* explored these waters, it anchored here and he named the island Lizard Island after the Goannas. Cook climbed to the top of a steep hill abutting the anchorage, searching out over the waters for a pass through the outer reef into the Pacific Ocean. We did the same, a hot and long climb, but we were easily able to see the same pass through the outer reef, so clear are the waters. *Windy Thoughts* sat below bobbing on the turquoise sea, waiting for our next adventure.

Lizard Island has a sad story from the 1880s concerning the demise of a Mrs. Watson and her family. Don and I walked about the stone ruins of her home.

Mr. and Mrs. Watson ran a sea slug processing operation and when Mr. Watson was away, local aborigines attacked and killed one of the Chinese servants. Mrs. Watson grabbed her baby and the other Chinese servant and headed to sea in a big laundry cauldron. They washed ashore at a nearby island. Without food and water, one by one they all soon died. It is a sad and haunting tale.

We hiked over to the other side of the island to visit the Lizard Island Research Station, where we were graciously welcomed and given the cook's tour. It was all so very interesting and is a world-known research center with tanks full of every variety of sea creatures.

An amenity of the practical sort was a water faucet located back in the palms. It seemed a bit lonely, so we often trekked over there with a bucket and toilet plunger, keeping our clothes sparkling clean—laundry never a problem and no one the wiser! Don even hauled five-gallon jugs of this fresh water back to the boat, a heroic task, because the cart's wheels didn't turn in the sand and he had to carry the heavy water jugs.

Don has so wanted to make a stop further north in Cooktown, a little burg that developed after Captain Cook took the *Endeavor* into the river entrance to make repairs. A museum dedicated to Captain Cook is found in Cooktown, but getting into the river requires a high tide over the bar, with precise timing— and we won't be in the area in daylight hours. After foregoing Escape River and the crocodiles, this is another disappointment for Don.

Impetuous and *Windy Thoughts* anchored off the mainland and the four of us rowed ashore to explore—Roger carrying an oar as protection. It definitely looked like crocodile country and we're talking about the fierce sea-going crocodiles! It was somewhat disconcerting when, sure enough, we saw several big dragging marks made by their long tails on the sand. We decided to keep our hike to a minimum and to keep our eyes wide open lest we had to make a hasty retreat!

After today's great sail under a cloudless sky, *Windy Thoughts* has come to rest once again, just off the mainland and tucked into a secure little niche. We have just finished our dinner of pesto pasta, a salad made with long-lasting cabbage, and the bread that I baked yesterday. Sitting in the cockpit and watching the sun go down, we take deep breaths and savor the moment, and we wave to *Impetuous* anchored nearby, the four of us ready for a good night's sleep.

These waters are home to both the big tiger shark and the hammerhead shark. Aren't we in good company? Aside from the cute koalas and the kangaroos—who can be a danger themselves—it seems that most of Australia is infested with poisonous creatures or something that will eat you—as well as plants that can do you great harm! The Taipan snake, one of the deadliest snakes in the world, lives here—and then there is the sea snake. Still, few people meet their demise and these statistics are encouraging, so we choose to not worry ourselves. We love Australia.

Don just talked on SSB to another boater on Thursday Island who gave us scads of useful information. The Torres Strait area is full of reefs, and they had a horrid time with very strong current as well as winds at thirty knots—reminding us to definitely arrive on a making tide. Getting through these Torres Straits is one of the biggest challenges before reaching the open ocean. We have been advised to anchor off Horn Island, rather than Thursday Island itself. The fellow said to look for the resident crocodile that is often seen stretched out on the beach. Don may get his crocodile experience yet!

July 30, 1991

Windy Thoughts sits behind a small coral outcropping for the night, with a small bit of sand cay showing above the water. The wind is at about twenty knots at present and we are ready to tuck into bed. Don reminds me, as he has before, that we aren't setting up housekeeping here. It is a bit rolly but we're quite comfortable.

Both yesterday and today were beautiful days of only forty-five mile runs and in winds just perfect at about fifteen knots, *Windy Thoughts* averaging a steady 6.5 knots over the ground. With little sea and no swell it wasn't until we were near our respite for the night that the wind freshened to twenty-five knots.

The folks on *Impetuous* came over to *Windy Thoughts* for tea this evening. Mind you, coming for tea is Aussie and Kiwi for dinner, so I didn't have to put the pot on to boil. I learned that the hard way a while back.

Next day:

Mt. Adolphus Island is our shelter for tonight and we hope to get more sleep than any of us did last night when the wind increased to thirty knots for the remainder of the night. It was very uncomfortable and we kept an anxious anchor watch all night. With only coral reef in front of us, waves sloshed against the hull and we rocked and rolled heavily all night. Ok, so we weren't setting up housekeeping.

Today the brisk winds kept us on our toes navigating through this area and both crews arrived exhausted this afternoon. We picked up considerable current and after ripping along were at anchor at 1:30 p.m.! Forty-five miles in six hours—a speedy and good run. After all of the horror stories heard, it was definitely a good day for us. There is less outer Barrier Reef for protection now, just scattered reef throughout the area.

Tomorrow, we will leave at 10 a.m. to face the grand finale and most difficult part in getting to Thursday Island. The bar crossing awaits us, and proper timing is crucial, as is ensuring our arrival at Thursday Island at slack water—if there is such a thing in this area! Two islands sit west of Thursday Island, two miles apart. High water is at one island when low water is at the other—to give you a little idea of how crazy this area is. The bigger challenge of getting off from Thursday will still be ahead of us!

Predictions are for SE winds at fifteen to twenty knots, so all should be just fine. A front with very strong NE winds is arriving in the next twenty-four hours, so it is time to get cracking!

August 1, 1991
Thursday Island
Torres Strait, Australia

Continuing the quest....

Windy Thoughts has made it to the top of Oz!

She sits anchored off the preferred anchorage at Horn Island, only about 1.5 miles across the Strait from Thursday Island and amongst perhaps as many as fifteen other sailboats. Where did they all come from?

Just perfect conditions greeted us when plying the approach to Thursday Island with no more than twenty knots of wind and favorable currents. It is absolutely chock full of reef, most of which isn't visible. One buoy is missing and there was a bar to cross with only ten feet of water under our keel. The last four or five miles was the most difficult, but had we known last night that all would go so well, I know I would have slept much better!

A foot ferryboat runs between Thursday Island and Horn Island. We joined the schoolchildren aboard—lovely children—so polite and so eager in their excitement, their black eyes radiating happiness.

Thursday Island has a small grocery where we purchased vacuum-packed pork chops, steaks, chicken and some Aussie sausages. Imagine that! The meat will last about two months in the refrigerator without need to freeze it. My, the weeks ahead take on a completely new spirit!

Don and I also visited a doctor to purchase malaria pills to begin taking now. The scuttlebutt has it that it is important to get our systems adjusted before moving into Southeast Asia.

Extensive communication with Thursday Island Radio last evening provided us with great information. Today we visited the Thursday Island Radio station. The two fellows who man it keep ships and small boats like us out of peril.

The Coral Sea and the Aryufuru Sea meet right here in the Torres Strait, making tides and currents difficult to predict. One will frequently flow over the other and make for seas of two differing heights! So the pattern is very changeable with up to eight to ten knots of currents. It is full of treacherous reefs—and generally not less than twenty-five-knot winds. With all of this to contend with, the crews of both *Windy Thoughts* and *Impetuous* are a bit on edge, as are those on the other boats who sit here readying to face the final challenge.

Don and I took the dinghy down the beach a ways, staying close in where it wasn't so rough. You might guess what we were looking for—yes, that resident crocodile. Sure enough, the big salt-water croc was lounging about in the sun on the beach. Don wanted to get in closer for a camera as well as a video moment, but as we cautiously approached, the croc slid into the water and headed straight toward us. *Breezy's* motor went into high gear as we made a hasty retreat and Don has again missed his close encounter with crocodiles.

Only the previous day, locals had told us that there had been two crocs until very recently. But one was threatening the school children so it was necessary to do away with it. This was his buddy and he did look rather lonely!

Our day-sails have made it easy to sail in tandem with *Impetuous* and we have enjoyed their company these past days. The radio is humming with boat chatter about getting through the Strait. We eagerly listen in to everyone's conversations, hoping for a new tidbit of information.

I will certainly be happy when we are out at sea again, away from coral reef and with miles and miles of sea room surrounding us! Don and I are ready to move on now, ready for new adventures, and anxious to see what awaits us around the next bend.

Torres Strait to Thailand

Thailand

Malacca Strait — Phuket   Malaysia

Kuala Lumpur

Port Klang —

Singapore

Borneo

Bankka Island

Suluwesi

Ambon

New Guinea

Gili Air

Torres Strait

AUSTRALIA

Chapter 8

Southeast Asia Captures Our Hearts

*Cruising gives you a new and different platform from which you
judge what is necessary in life and what is not.*

Indonesian visas in effect, we were anxious to get to Ambon, Indonesia,
knowing that our allotted two months would pass quickly. Many nautical miles faced us before reaching Singapore and we would choose our stops
along the way—in what we were soon to learn would be one of the most interesting and welcoming countries that we would visit in all of our years of
cruising.

We did have a bit of apprehension niggling at us: this Torres Strait. We
pulled up anchor, left our haven off Horn Island and set off with as much
information as possible from the kind operators of Thursday Island Radio.
Morning's light gave us fair winds of fifteen knots. *Impetuous* stayed behind
for one day; all assumed that this faster boat would catch up and we would
arrive at Ambon about the same time.

The Sat Nav system was our lifeline when calculating position, but we
would be lucky to get one reading while navigating through the Strait. Exercising every bit of navigational skill we possessed, we zoomed along in increasing winds, while tending sails and keeping a constant vigil for reef—and
closely watching our depth sounder. The currents plied their way about us
and very confused seas came at us from several directions.

When we cleared the Torres Strait and were into open ocean again, we
both breathed sighs of relief and settled in for the anticipated week's passage.
The wind had picked up to a steady twenty-five knots directly behind us as we
set our course for Ambon.

Don went forward to set the long whisker pole and we readied the big
Genny. I let the sheet out until the sail reached its white arms out to our
port side, the full main reaching out to starboard. The sails looked like two
huge wings on either side of the boat, catching the wind as we sailed wing
and wing. We rolled out the smaller staysail and hauled in on the sheet until
the sail was tight to the mast, helping to reduce the roll of downwind sailing—somewhat.

With the currents in our favor, we were making good time but in less than comfortable conditions. Running dead downwind as we were in twenty-five-knot winds, we still rolled from gunwale to gunwale, and the only place that we felt comfortable was tucked firmly into our sea berths. The humidity and heat increased our discomfort as we lay below. Our clothes stuck to our skin and we stuck to the sheet beneath us.

Radio contact with *Impetuous* let us know that they were having a much more difficult passage when they headed through the Torres Strait. The heftier winds and crashing seas that we were now experiencing were the ones on which they departed, and without knowing their exact position, it all added up to a very frightening experience. Relief was in their voices when they too had cleared the Torres Strait. It is always a good feeling when you have sailed the boat considerable distance from land and are away from its dangers.

Impetuous never did close on us, but stayed about a day behind. We kept radio contact in the morning and evening, sharing our positions, wind and sea conditions and general chitchat. Our conversations centered mainly on our mutual discomfort, and we commiserated on whose back was hurting the most from the constant supine position. What was the other managing to put together for a meal? When standing at the stove seems more than you can manage, peanut butter and crackers sometimes suffice to make a wonderful meal. Any granola bars in the locker surface at these times as well. We even sneaked a few out of our grab and run bag.

Don and I listened to books on tape or read, and generally felt time was passing much too slowly to suit us. But patience is nothing but that old adage—a virtue when at sea. If boredom was the only complaint on an ocean passage, we must consider ourselves fortunate.

Concern built as our course in the Banda Sea brought us in close proximity to the west coast of New Guinea. With high piracy reports in this area, both boats ran without running lights in order to be as inconspicuous as possible.

In Thailand, we would meet a couple who, with their eleven-year-old daughter, were boarded and attacked off the northern coast of New Guinea. While the captain was held at knifepoint, both his wife and little girl were assaulted in front of him. They were very thankful to have come through the experience with their lives and were continuing on with as positive an attitude as possible.

An older couple was boarded by pirates off New Guinea's south coast, and though they were not personally harmed, their boat was ravaged and equipment was taken. We were ever wary and uneasy.

Navigation chores and simple boat chores had to be attended to as did the sails and the attention to weather. Other than that, we were flat on our backs, often with our books on tape to help pass the time. It was very hot and humid and every centimeter of our bodies in contact with the berth or lee cloth was sopping wet with perspiration. Meals were simple ones, requiring the least preparation. We were thankful that our discomfort was due only to the downwind sailing in heavy seas and not to bad weather.

Though we didn't see any lights from fishermen, when further off the coast of New Guinea one night, we did see lights from a completely different source, Mother Nature herself.

Don was asleep below and our night started out like so many others while we followed the routine for standing our watches. I lazily lounged in the cockpit with eyes partly closed, getting up about every ten minutes to look around us for any ship's lights.

Suddenly, my senses were overcome with the most astounding sight! The sea was alive with a vast bright green glow of bioluminescence that was often experienced in the boat's wake—but this was an entirely new phenomenon. *Windy Thoughts* sailed into a sea that was literally alight from horizon to horizon with a bright luminous green glow as far as the eye could see. Amazingly, the sky around us was aglow as well.

When Don came on watch two hours later he couldn't believe that I hadn't wakened him. But, covering an area beyond our imagination, I knew that this magic would still be there awaiting him. All was dead quiet, the wind and seas calmed considerably. And yet our speed increased as *Windy Thoughts* sailed along in silence, not a sound of a wave breaking on her hull, not even the sound of the bow wave as she cut through the water—and not a whisper of wind was heard. It was surreal. Don spent the rest of the night sitting in the cockpit surrounded by this magic.

We would learn that this extreme show of bioluminescence occasionally occurs in the Banda Sea. Weren't we the lucky ones? It will be remembered always as our own personal Never Land experience, just for us.

During the wee morning hours on the eighth day out, the welcoming sight of landfall greeted us. A few miles out from Ambon *Windy Thoughts* lay hove-to, waiting for *Impetuous*. Our friends on *Impetuous* wanted to make an afternoon arrival together—presuming the officials would quickly complete their duties for the day and our time exposed to harassment would be lessened.

Impetuous pulled out all the stops and, several hours later, closed with our position a few miles offshore. Beginning our approach, we left the big seas and swells behind and rejoiced in the calmer waters. Sailing into Ambon's harbor took some time, and as we passed outrigger canoes with houses atop people waved their greetings to us. So far, nothing seemed at all foreboding to us and we happily waved back, eager to see people again and to be a part of their world.

By the time we worked our way in to the main harbor, it was after 5 p.m. Several ships sat at anchor in very deep water but we couldn't find depths suitable for us. We moved further into the harbor to find refuge for the night. Darkness drops like a veil in the tropical latitudes, coming on in a matter of just a few minutes, and our path was filled with small boats anchored hither and yon. None carried an anchor light and they were difficult to make out in the blackness that descended upon us.

Finally, we found a small indentation near the shore that was welcomed with joy because we were all ready to get the hook down. Both anchors went over their bow rollers and settled on the bottom. Both were set securely and four very tired people were ready to call it a day.

There is just nothing quite as welcoming as the conclusion of a passage, even the most uneventful and pleasurable ones. The soul rejoices in another job well done and you know that you have earned the right to relax your vigil—and to sleep all night.

No sooner had we finished our respective tasks with anchoring but we were approached by a fast boat carrying naval personnel. They first pulled up alongside *Windy Thoughts*, returning our smiles and hellos with displeasure. The officer who could speak a few words of English made it clear that we were to leave immediately. This was naval property!

Attempts to explain that we had been trying desperately to find a spot with depths suitable to anchor were only met with the stern demand "You leave! Now!"

Not a smile broke any of their faces and they left us to head over to *Impetuous* to deliver the same message in the same manner.

Up came the two anchors and back through the black of night we slowly wended our way, returning to the city breakwater. After making several passes amongst the ships, we eventually found a depth of eighty feet, deeper water than we would like, but we hunkered down for the night.

With all number of derelict-looking ships surrounding us, Don slept in the cockpit with a knife at the ready. We felt very vulnerable. Prior to heading for Southeast Asia, we had heard so much about piracy. Roger and Valerie had grave concerns and had prepared us for the worst!

We awoke to the call to prayer from the mullah at the local mosque, broadcast throughout the city via loudspeaker. In the months ahead, we would awake to this on many a morning—and hear this call to prayer several times a day. Men looked down and called greetings to us from the ships so near about us and no one looked threatening in the least. Don and I returned their greetings with our own and waved to them with big smiles.

Don and Roger went ashore to find the Port Captain's office. Val and I stayed aboard to watch the boats and the show before us. It was a cacophony of noise. Horns honked continuously as cabs maneuvered about—somewhat like the old rickshaws but drawn by motor bikes or bicycles. Music blared, people milled about and women carried big baskets on their heads, filled with produce and their daily market purchases.

The new sounds and smells awed us, and not all were pleasant! With public toilet facilities absent, men passed back and forth under the nearby bridge. In contrast to the busy city life, the surrounding countryside was mountainous and extremely lush with greenery.

Our men eventually called to us from shore, encouraging us to come ashore to look about while they finished the clearance procedures. What—by ourselves? After all, Don had slept in the cockpit last night with that knife! *Impetuous* had approached this part of the world with much trepidation and by now had us wary as well, a rare feeling throughout our cruising adventures. We were soon to find just how mistaken we were.

I rowed us ashore in *Breezy*, coming up to cement steps in the quay within three feet of an open sewer line six feet in diameter. Our men expected us to just step into this? Well, cruising doesn't always present you with the expected and if we wanted to continue the adventure, there wasn't anything to do but forge ahead.

Trying to get as close as possible, we maneuvered between several canoes and bumped smack into the sewage drain. Holding our noses, we stepped out into the water, got ourselves on land, wiped off our feet and shoes as best we could with paper towels from our packs—and were pleasantly surprised to find that Ambon was as bustling as it appeared from the boats—and that the market was huge and fascinating.

Shouts of "Hi Mister" surrounded us wherever we went and the children made a parade behind us, always followed by twenty to thirty adults. When Don and Roger caught up with us, we learned that this market area wasn't the true city center after all. So we headed there to wander its streets and in and out of shops, always surrounded by a crowd of young and old alike and feeling like Pied Pipers. When we passed a school the children ran to the fence along the sidewalk, climbed up on it and called their greetings to us. It just tugged at our hearts to be so welcomed with such friendly faces and we will carry that with us always.

The fellows had not met with any problems with the officials. In fact, we were to find that our arrival at Ambon marked the introduction to some of our finest and most memorable cruising days. Seldom in life have we met with such warm and friendly people as Indonesians or traveled through such beautiful country.

The consensus on our arrival had been to up anchor as soon as proper clearance into Indonesia could be made. However, we instead enjoyed Ambon for five more days—though moving to a quieter spot down the bay and off a quaint hotel.

While walking along the road one day we noticed some women busily doing laundry in a stream that tumbled down the lush mountainside. The clean clothes were spread out on the bushes to dry and it appeared to be a social gathering for them as they cheerfully chatted away.

We stopped to visit, and pointing out toward the boats and then to us and our clothes, our sign language was sufficient to ask if they might do laundry for us. Smiling broadly, their heads nodded up and down. We knew the phrase "how much" in Bahasa Indonesia and they replied with fingers up to show that it would be US $7.00. Somehow, we understood that a husband would come out later and get the laundry.

Indeed, he did—and it arrived back the following day all clean, folded and smelling fresh as a daisy. What a treat not to have to face the laundry task myself!

Don had a poignant visit with an older man who spoke some English and had lived in Ambon during the Japanese occupation of WWII. The suffering of the local people while under occupation was difficult to comprehend. The occupying forces had committed horrific atrocities and had confiscated all of their rice as well. People starved to death, including all in his immediate family.

The gentleman took us to the cemetery and memorial. Don had tears in his eyes as he walked amongst the headstones; many of the graves were of young Australian soldiers taken prisoner, every one of them having died in captivity just months before the war was over.

Ambon was a fascinating introduction to Indonesia, and when leaving we sailed west toward Sulawesi Island, anxious to take in more of the pleasures of this phenomenal country. Nearer Suluwesi's southeast side we sailed down a channel that stretched sixty miles between Sulawesi and Buton Islands. The channel was well protected, flat as a lake and offered calm and peaceful anchorages every night—a wonderful reprieve from the usual passage making.

We passed tiny villages with thatched-roofed homes that sat high on stilts.

Farther up the mountainside a few homes sat atop even higher stilts amongst a profusion of lush greenery everywhere. It is strikingly beautiful country.

After dropping anchor one day, we sat in the cockpit with our lunch and took in the vista surrounding us—that lush greenery of the island, a sugar-white beach and a spattering of thatched roofed homes amongst the palms. We were protected from the glare of the sun by the bimini and were lazily enjoying our good fortune. This was perfect—the right here and the now.

Our lunch was slices of fresh pineapple, and toasted cheese sandwiches made from bread baked en route the day before—with Kraft Cheese Whiz that comes from a jar. Lemonade from a container in the refrigerator quenched our thirst and we might have been enjoying the most gourmet meal at a fancy resort.

We saw no high-rise hotel ashore, however; just a peaceful village nestled back in the palms. No pool enticed tourists from the ocean itself, but instead just God's unspoiled beauty spread out before us wherever we looked. Could we ever be more content? We relished the moment, and yes, this is the dream—this is the moment that makes it all worth it.

It wasn't long before we saw a hand-hewn canoe coming from shore. A little girl of about seven, with snapping black eyes and a big smile stretching from ear to ear, was calling to us, "Hello, Mister."

We waved back, calling hello to her as she pulled up alongside *Windy Thoughts*. As soon as she had a good hold on our cap rail she thrust a pretty shell at us, obviously wanting to trade. The shell still had its live animal inside, not how we like to get our shells, as the process of eliminating the animal is rather lengthy and smelly. But we smiled in happiness just the same.

What to give her in trade? She seemed enthralled with some hair combs that held my hair away from my face. Aha! Down below I found two more with pretty flowers attached—and when I put them in her hair, she beamed and giggled gleefully before paddling off to shore.

Being very enterprising, she soon arrived back with her friend, making it apparent through sign language that they would like a book. With no children's books left, Don suggested some cookies that were a hit. But I felt obliged to find more hair combs for the little friend and to put them in her hair and exclaim on how pretty she looked. Two very happy little girls left us, one paddling and one bailing water out of the little canoe with a half coconut shell.

Our American flag flew from the spreader in its proper position below the Indonesian flag. It wasn't long before several other canoes with entire families began to arrive, coming up beside *Windy Thoughts* to hold onto her sides while they peered at us, very curious but very friendly. They were not anxious to make it a short visit and we felt compelled to leave our books and sit and smile along with them. They smiled at length. We smiled back. We passed out peanuts from big bags purchased in Ambon—and continued smiling. If there were little ones aboard, we admired them and cooed at the babies—international language.

Though our ability to converse in each other's language was nil, there was eventually some understanding that we were invited ashore for "maundy", a bath and laundry at 11 a.m. the next day. They pointed to *Impetuous*, sitting at anchor not far from us. Our friends were below, not wishing to have any boats come alongside, but we understood that they were invited ashore as well.

We invited our visitors aboard and they quietly stared with awe at our little home, surely wondering at these two people who chose to come from the other side of the world to visit them on this boat that made a home so different from their own. These are the moments remembered and cherished—the moments shared with those who welcomed us into their world.

At 11:00 sharp on the following morning, both dinghies were off for shore. As we neared the beach, the entire village converged on us. There were smiles from everyone, shouts of "Hello Mister" and a rush into the water to help us bring the dinghies up onto the beach.

The boys grabbed the laundry bags, buckets and soap and led us along a path through the small village of thatched homes on stilts. Each had one room and no furniture, but lovely woven mats on the floor provided for sitting and sleeping. The village was neat as a pin.

The path continued through the jungle some  distance to a fresh water stream. A monkey chattered in the trees above us. The entire village followed along.

Val and I had discussed just how to dress for our baths and decided to put our bathing suits on under our sarongs and shirts. Not wanting to offend the modesty of the women in this culture, we ultimately just headed into the water fully clothed.

The teenage boys took over our laundry chores, taking the clothes bags well out into the water where they happily sloshed our clothes up and down and rubbed them together with soap—and were very intrigued with my toilet plunger! Meanwhile, about ten of the little boys frolicked about in the water, completely naked. Throughout the whole procedure, the women remained on the banks and laughed hilariously as Val and I scrubbed ourselves as best we could while fully-clothed. We were in hysterics ourselves at the picture we likely made.

The little girls looked on with envy as the boys cavorted in the water, surely wanting to be in there having fun as well. The fresh water, a bit muddy by now with the boys splashing about, felt so good, and we felt sure that we were cleaner than before, as surely were our clothes.

When baths and laundry were finished, we all trooped back along the jungle path to the village, everyone happily chatting and understanding how appreciative we were for this opportunity for fresh water baths and laundry. Isn't that a universal need?

Back at the village, we watched a woman grinding corn with a big stick in a dug-out log, and we realized that the crops we had seen on the mountainsides from a distance on the boat were most likely corn. Fishing is very good, coconuts grow in abundance and the neatness and orderliness of the village proved that they live a very simple but good life in these peaceful and stunningly beautiful surroundings. There were very few material possessions, but they obviously needed little not provided them by their own efforts.

On our last morning, when preparing to leave, we looked up from the cockpit to see a man frantically waving at us as he paddled furiously out to *Windy Thoughts*. He wasn't alone. He had a pig in his canoe—a very healthy pig that he wanted to present to us as a parting gift. Now, just how do you refuse such a grandiose gift as this?

Don and I both exclaimed on what a beautiful pig it was and how very generous a gift! There was just no room aboard for so fine a pig as this and surely, he would meet his demise on a rolling boat at sea. In addition, we had no proper food for so fine a pig as this.

Not wanting to offend the man's feelings for this very generous offer, we did our best to let him know how truly pleased we were with his kindness—but assured him that we wished that he keep the pig, and we would keep the memory of his beautiful offer in our hearts. He seemed to understand and paddled away with a huge smile on his face, hopefully happy with the resolution. The pig seemed happy that he wasn't going to sea as well, but may have made a good crew mate.

As we glided along on quiet waters amongst the islands that sit off Sulawesi's southeast coast, *Windy Thoughts* slowly meandered along in light winds and rested up at the end of each day in another quiet and calm anchorage. Small village after village welcomed us with open arms. One early morning we awoke to find a small canoe quietly waiting for any sign of life aboard *Windy Thoughts*. When we stepped up into the cockpit, four young men dressed in their best clothes were waiting to invite us ashore.

They hadn't seen another sailboat in three years and wanted to show us their village, as well as take us to a cave that we understood was a sacred place. They jumped aboard to assist in getting *Breezy* down and we followed them ashore, where many of the villagers helped to bring *Breezy* up onto the beach. About seven young men led us some distance into the jungle, monkeys squealing at us from above.

When we reached the cave, the young men climbed down into it and motioned for us to follow. Stalactites clung from above and stalagmites pushed up from the cave's floor. It was obvious that this was an extraordinary place and Don and I understood the importance it had to the villagers. We were simply awed by the unexpected beauty that this cave provided tucked into the jungle.

The young men led us back to the village and when we passed the school, the children ran out to call, "Hello Mister!", the national greeting in English. Stilts held the simple thatched roof homes above the ground and the entire village was orderly and clean, with obvious attention and pride taken in their homes.

The generous hospitality extended us wasn't over yet and we were invited to lunch in the home of one of our guides. We climbed a ladder made from tree limbs, and were once again welcomed with a generosity of spirit almost unmatched in our travels. Inside, a kitchen took up one corner, with a sand pit built in on which to lay the fire for cooking. We sat on the floor to enjoy a

delicious meal of rice with some baked yams.

After our lunch, we climbed back down the ladder to watch canoes being built under the palm trees nearby. It was fascinating to watch their expert work using the materials that were naturally available to them in their surrounding, and they took great pleasure in sharing their expertise with us. Before we left, one of the men gave us a stalk of bananas to hang in the cockpit of *Windy Thoughts*—and delicious bananas would once again be on the menu morning, noon and night!

We were learning that the simplest lives seemed often to be the happiest—and that the people living as such seemed always to be the friendliest and most willing to share their bounty.

As we anchored off the town of Raja, on Muna Island, a few days later, a sharp contrast to the simple village of thatched roofed huts was replaced by concrete buildings and a main business area that extended two blocks. Just at its edge was a huge public market where people did their daily shopping.

The public market was filled with hundreds of little stalls, all selling various and sundry items, from fresh foods to canned goods, to soaps and clothes. Outside, more people sat on the ground selling their wares, often a pile of fruit or vegetables. The wet market is always a busy hub of activity and as we wandered through, we gathered a large crowd of people behind us calling, "Hi Mister!", and again we felt like Pied Pipers.

Most tourists flock to the destination island of Bali. But there are more than 3,000 islands in this emerald island chain that makes up Indonesia, sitting like jewels dotting the sea and making our experience all the more special. We love to mingle with people, to get a glimpse of their culture and their lifestyle—and we found the Indonesian people kind and willing to have us peek into their world. Their graciousness and generosity of spirit warmed our hearts over and over.

All cultures have fishermen who deeply respect the sea, and it seems that people have a respect for the way we chose to travel. How we wished that we could communicate beyond our Bahasa Indonesia phrase book. Fortunately, a big smile always works and is easy to keep on your face—for we were literally bombarded with smiles all about us in Indonesia.

At the wet market Don and I purchased fresh pineapples, bananas, tangerines and oranges—but only perused the fresh fish stalls where fish was displayed right out in the intense heat with no ice. We treated ourselves to the national dish, Nasi Goreng—fried rice with bits of fish and vegetables with a fried egg on top. It was delicious and enjoyed often as we wended our way through these amazing islands. Cold drinks weren't cold, as there was no refrigeration. But the intense heat and humidity called for anything wet and we didn't in the least mind.

Cruising gives you a new and different platform from which you judge what is necessary in life and what is not. Our experiences went deep into our hearts and we hoped all would be remembered long after our days of cruising were over.

On our second day, rain came down in buckets and we kept busy aboard with the rain catcher, adding many gallons of fresh water to our tanks, as did our friends aboard *Impetuous*.

Our third day was devoted to topping off our fuel tanks. All fuel cans were untied from deck and the diesel was poured into the tanks before loading the empty cans into the dinghy. The heavy-duty, black plastic cans purchased at a boat swap back in Seattle had already ventured offshore from Seattle to Hawaii and back twice before we took possession. Don had made nice covers for them out of blue Sunbrella material to match the sail covers and they were kept on deck, tied securely to the stanchions.

The wharf was full with fishing boats, and ferries that were crude but efficient wooden boats with cabins of about three-foot headroom—and one big area with people sitting cross-legged inside, heads ducked in the cramped space.

The tide was down and there were no ladders to climb, nor could we find a spot to tie the dinghy. Not to worry. People waved and called to us and fishermen wildly motioned for us to tie up to them. The fishermen grabbed our lines and helped us aboard—and then grabbed all of our fuel cans, eager to give us a hand. We crept on our hands and knees through the warren of rooms in the boat, emerging on the bow to walk the plank that was nearly straight up to the wharf. Many hands reached out to us and made it a quick and easy maneuver.

Nothing to do but to follow them down the wharf to some old and rusty-looking drums. They smiled profusely, repeating "diesel" when Don asked about it, and nodding their heads to let us know that they understood what we wanted. By now, we had about fifty people surrounding us and happily watching the show. Our six cans were filled for us.

After Don paid for the fuel he gave each of our helpers some rupees, being very appreciative of their help. They were absolutely delighted, took right over for us and lugged the full fuel cans back to the wharf, down the plank, through the boat and down into *Breezy*.

On our return to *Windy Thoughts*, we passed Roger in his dinghy filled with fuel cans as well, off on his trip to shore for diesel.

After unloading all the fuel cans onto *Windy Thoughts*, Don had already laboriously poured about seventeen gallons into the tanks when Roger came rowing back from shore with his filled cans. He slowed down just long enough to comment that they had first started to give him gasoline instead of diesel.

Don looked at him in horror. Gasoline? This was the first time ever that Don hadn't smelled the fuel to be sure it was diesel, and our hearts sank at the prospect of what we might be putting in our tanks instead! Sure enough, we had gasoline!

With forty gallons of diesel already in our tanks before adding these seventeen gallons of gasoline, Don did some panicked thinking on how the two would mix—ultimately deciding to add a quart of outboard engine oil to the fuel tank.

We loaded the fuel cans back into the dinghy and headed once again to shore. Repeating the same routine, we climbed through a welcoming fishing boat and then up the plank, with the fishermen hauling the cans down the wharf for us.

Don had quite a time explaining that we didn't want gasoline, and we learned that the word for diesel is solar.

"Solar, solar," Don repeated over and over, and they laughed uproariously at our mistake. We took solar back to *Windy Thoughts*, and radio contact with a fellow sailor that evening assured Don that the addition of the engine oil was just what he would have done. This settled Don's worried mind and he slept much better!

Dugout canoes frequently visited us while we sat here at anchor. Their sails were always homemade and generally a patchwork of various materials where repairs had been made, looking like they surely wouldn't make it very long if a good stiff breeze came up. But the sails did amazingly well as the boats sailed merrily about. We loved trying to communicate and our conversations were based on our three Indonesian phrases, along with hands gestures and smiles.

One older fellow came alongside and held up a jar containing four pieces of what looked like white marble. He wanted to sell these interesting pieces to us for 25,000 rupees, about $12.00. He eagerly accepted two T-shirts for one piece but we gave him 2,000 rupees in addition. Don learned from a gold merchant in town that one of the pieces was the back tooth of a whale! It remains one of his treasured mementos.

September 30, 1991
Gili Air Island
Indonesia

Dear Susan,

For the past three weeks we have luxuriated in peacefulness with good eats while anchored off the tiny island of Gili Air, sitting just off the northwest coast of Lombok Island. Lombok Island is sixty miles across the strait from Bali. We are enjoying a little vacation at no cost to us, other than the lifestyle change required to get us here!

It wasn't a simple passage here from our last overnight anchorage off a reef. However, it had been a peaceful evening there before tucking below for a very restful sleep, the water turquoise blue and refreshing for a dive over the side—and all was again picture perfect.

When we turned on the windlass in early morning to up anchor, the anchor flukes were simply not going to break free of the coral head. Don didn't feel comfortable with diving on the anchor in ninety feet of water, but about this time a little fishing boat moseyed by and upon seeing our dilemma, took right over; one fellow free dived, coming up for air and diving down three more times before he had the anchor freed. Not only were we amazed at this feat, we were very thankful for his help.

This little scenario took two hours from start to finish, so we were off a bit later than planned. Not to worry; we still had plenty of daylight hours to reach Gili Air.

The Pilot indicated that winds could be expected to come up about noon each day—but these winds would come from the direction in which we were heading! No one else was terribly interested in my reports, but wind on the nose sends me into red alert just at the thought.

Sure enough, at noon on the button we spotted white water dead ahead of us—water that was actually a bit more than white caps. It was big, white water rolling right toward us, almost like seeing surf rolling in at us! Less than one minute later the wind direction changed and we hit twenty knots of wind bang on the nose—and with it its accompanying seas.

A mad scramble of hands on lines and boom and sail adjustment followed as *Windy Thoughts'* bow plunged into the seas. When we got the boat close-hauled, we were heeled over and headed on a course that wasn't going to get us to Gili Air without lots of tacking back and forth, making our passage much longer than planned. My heart dropped as I watched our speed over the ground reduce to a crawl while we beat into the wind and seas. Does anyone really enjoy beating? Since *Impetuous* was a couple of miles behind us, Don got on the radio and let them know about the wall of water that they would be sailing into momentarily.

I suppose that I silently held myself back from shouting to all, "I told you so."

Our day was spent making our way slowly toward Gili Air. An Australian already at anchor radioed an alert that our intended spot to anchor was totally untenable. He gave us coordinates for getting through the reef and into a lagoon anchorage with good protection. *Impetuous* had managed to pass us up and squeak in just as the sun was setting.

With darkness dropping like an old shoe, we knew that *Windy Thoughts* would have to lay the entrance through the reef on the next tack—and if the light failed we were out of luck. *Windy Thoughts* beat masterfully toward that break in the reef. We were so close to getting the anchor down, having a good dinner and a good night's sleep, and we certainly didn't want to bash about out here at sea all night in this maelstrom!

But as *Windy Thoughts* lay over nearly on her beams, we lacked about 100 yards of clearing the entrance and frantically scrambled to tack back out again. About five miles out, to be safely off the island, we spent the night hove-to in plunging seas and sleeplessness.

In the morning, *Impetuous* gave us coordinates on the blue roof of a small building on the beach. Lining ourselves up, we came right through the pass to calm water in the lagoon, at last. Don dove on the anchor to be sure that we were hooked securely and we cleaned up lines, put the boat in order and got the dinghy down. Then we joined *Impetuous* for breakfast ashore.

My, what a difference a night makes! Nasty night—absolute paradise in the morning!

We have decided against going over to Bali, preferring to enjoy this little spot rather than join the crowds at anchor in Benoa Harbor. Radio conversations tell about the lousy anchorage and the touristy atmosphere. We just can't give this special little spot up for that. Not to leave the impression that Gili Air is totally tourist-free; a small number of tourists come from Bali to Lombok on a large ferry—and then to Gili Air in little fishing boat ferries. Lombok is very close and only about one mile across the water from us.

A few very small resorts dot the beach here on Gili Air, all with little one-room thatched- roof bungalows and outdoor showers. They aren't the expensive doings as seen in French Polynesia, or even such as are found on Bali,

but are of the simpler sort that are lovely and go for $6.00 to $8.00 a day including breakfast, lunch and dinner!

The beaches are exquisite, with pure white sugary sand meeting the most turquoise waters imaginable, framed by the lush mountainsides and hillsides of Lombok in the near distance. We don't think that a more pristine and perfect setting could be found at any expensive resort, where the natural beauty is often compromised by the materialistic atmosphere. It wasn't easy getting here. We will cherish every moment!

Both our breakfast and dinner are taken ashore where the food is very good, prepared in one or two woks in the open-air restaurant for $1.00 each. Though bread isn't a staple here, they know how to do western style toast, and eggs are plentiful. Chickens peck about at the back door, ready for any chicken dish on the menu. Produce comes over from Lombok Island, as do most supplies. The local Indonesian dishes are the big hit with us and fresh seafood is readily available.

Only three sailboats enjoy this little paradise: *Windy Thoughts*, *Impetuous*, and after the first week an Australian boat, *Sousa*. The winds come up by noon each day and blow hard, putting us on a lee shore with reef right behind our stern. We also share the anchorage with four large, floating dock-looking structures recently placed here by the Indonesian government, anchored to the bottom with big fisherman-style anchors. They will be oyster-farming equipment and they look like very fancy structures.

It is easy to walk around the entire island, and homes with thatched roofs are clustered in the mid part. Air freely flows through them and mats on the floor provide for sitting and sleeping. Cooking is done outdoors and life appears to be very tranquil.

Sometimes in life you meet someone who you instinctively know has touched your life in an important way. We have met just such a person here on Gili Air. Akwan, a most interesting young man of nineteen, works at the restaurant and shares a bungalow with another worker. He has rapidly become very dear to us.

Akwan is very talented and has painted a watercolor of *Windy Thoughts* sitting at anchor and surprised us with it as a gift. His greatest desire is to go to University, a dream realized by few. He works waiting tables many hours a day, seven days a week. Presently, he is trying to establish a dive shop so that visitors can rent equipment for snorkeling on the fascinating reef. He has befriended us and helped us more than we could ever describe, a very special young man.

Akwan has been instrumental in getting diesel to top off our tanks. He arranged for four fellows to take a boat over to Lombok, fill a big drum and return to Gili Air. Pumping from the drum into our tanks was quite a procedure, with a good deal of diesel spilled on the teak. I stewed a bit, but there is nothing like Joy dishwashing detergent and salt water to make the teak look like new!

Akwan invited us to meet his family on Lombok. A small boat took us the mile across to Lombok where we caught a bus to town—and a little donkey cart carried us to his village. Brothers and sisters, as well as the entire neighborhood of children and adults, converged on the family home soon after our arrival. How privileged we were to have this special day with Akwan and his family.

Today Akwan told Don that he had something special to tell him. He is getting married ten days from now and hoped that we could stay for his wedding. Don said that he suspected that she was pretty and Akwan replied that she was beautiful in his heart.

Akwan's lovely Sameda lives with her family on Gili Air and we were honored to have the opportunity to meet her today. Both Don and I would love to stay for their wedding and are disappointed that our Indonesian visas are rapidly coming to an end—and there are 1,000 miles to go between Gili Air and Singapore. Sadly, we must be on our way and will leave tomorrow.

[We have kept in touch with Akwan, and he and Sameda have two children, a son, Budi and a daughter, Hasmi. Akwan graduated from University on the island of Lombok early in 2008. We are proud of his determination and hard work. He is doing very well, as we always knew he would.]

While here on Gili Air our friends on *Impetuous* decided to go over to Bali to pick up mail hopefully waiting for them. It would require an overnight stay, and their plans were to return the next day. We agreed that we would watch their boat for the two days they were gone, and then would have to be on our way as our visas would expire soon.

Early in the morning that they departed Gili Air they re-anchored nearer us in the lagoon. Don took them to shore in our dinghy to meet the little fishing ferry that would take them to Lombok Island, where they would pick up the big ferry to Bali.

That day, the winds came up with a vengeance and we didn't dare leave our boat to go ashore. *Impetuous* swung perilously close to *Windy Thoughts*. Worse yet, the anchored oyster structures began to drag about the anchorage. The local people dared not touch them because they were government owned.

That night the winds increased in strength and it was a sleepless night as we stayed on deck fending off both *Impetuous* and these docks. The following day was no better, and Don and I would have left and set sail for Singapore, the wind and conditions making the anchorage so unsafe. We expected our friends back late in the afternoon and eagerly awaited their arrival. The day wore on and they didn't return from Bali.

Up again all night, we attempted to keep both *Windy Thoughts* and *Im-*

petuous from being holed by these structures dragging wildly about the anchorage. One of them had come up under *Impetuous'* hull, and her bow was coming down on it as she rose and fell with the waves that had formed even here in the lagoon. Hard as we worked, we couldn't break it loose.

In the middle of the night we realized that we needed at least an extra hand. Don got into *Breezy* and made it to shore in very perilous conditions for the dinghy. He awoke both Akwan and his friend and asked if they could help. They eagerly returned with Don, and it took two hours to break that structure free from the bow of *Impetuous*. The boys stayed aboard her all night, fending off while we attended to *Windy Thoughts*.

Each day we eagerly awaited the arrival of the folks on *Impetuous*, but it would be five days before they returned. They had decided to stay on Bali for a little vacation, unaware of the drama taking place back on Gili Air. Fortunately, their boat was safe.

Windy Thoughts made plans to leave the following day for Singapore, while *Impetuous* wasn't pressed for time and preferred to hold back and move more slowly, to soon catch us up the line. The couple on *Sousa* had given us much help, and we would be making the passage to Singapore together.

October 17, 1991
Singapore

Dear Susan,

Windy Thoughts has passed from peaceful villages and mountainous green vistas right into the bustling city of Singapore. We are, however, anchored in a quiet spot off the northeast side of the island.

The ten-day passage from Gili Air, with a two day stop on Bauwean Island, was filled with more "intrigue", for lack of a better word, than we ever want to face again! *Sousa* had accompanied us north through the Karimata Strait. Both boats sailed about the same and we were always within a very few miles of each other.

Impetuous joined us at Bauwean Island, where we were once again met with the hospitality and generosity that we had come to find in Indonesia. Large groups of people quietly followed us through the village, waiting outside the shops or often coming inside with us to watch as we perused the shopkeeper's goods. When we passed the school, children ran out to call, "Hello Mister" in those happy voices that lifted our hearts over and over.

We marveled at the beauty of this village and its surroundings. While walking back to the anchorage we stopped to watch women working in the rice fields. They carefully gathered the cut stalks into neat bundles, and shook the rice kernels from these bundles within a three sided canvas enclosure that kept the rice from escaping. Never again will we eat rice without thoughts of the labor intensive work that goes into putting it on our table!

When *Windy Thoughts* and *Sousa* left this lovely island *Impetuous* dallied, but caught up with us in Singapore.

Moving on toward Singapore again, one night at 1 a.m. Don sighted a large powerboat on radar four miles behind us, running without lights. Don carefully monitored the situation as the boat maintained its course and closed with us. *Sousa* was sailing two miles ahead of *Windy Thoughts* and Don and Fran were on their night watches. Lyle and I were sound asleep below. *Sousa* held off, waiting for us to catch up, and by now both Lyle and I were fully awake as well.

When the mystery boat was about thirty feet off our stern, Don felt it possibly intended to board us and turned the million candle-power spotlight on it full force. At that moment, the boat's big spotlights came on. How vulnerable we felt as we looked up at this looming figure, its huge lights bearing down on us! A scenario of piracy was all too real in our minds and we both fully expected to play a major part. Suddenly, the mystery boat backed off, turned off all its lights again and pulled up ahead of us three miles to wait.

Lyle carried an AK 47 aboard. Don had so wanted one aboard, but let himself be discouraged by opinions of others who felt it unwise. Who else but ourselves to ensure our own security? Don did have the shotgun and the Colt 45 automatic at the ready—and though I was nearly frozen with fear I do know how to use each. When we set off on this adventure I knew that Don would always instinctively do whatever he had to do to protect us—and it was then that I knew that I would as well! I was mighty glad at the moment that he didn't assume a flare gun to be appropriate protection!

Expecting something to happen at any moment, we switched to our prearranged "secret channel". It would take eavesdroppers a bit of time to scroll through all of the frequencies to find us. We hoped to talk to one another before the mystery boat located our frequency.

As we closed with *Sousa*, the big boat closed with us again and very closely paralleled us for several minutes before shooting up in front of us again. Its next tactic was to turn around and shoot past us and then draw very close behind again. It repeated this pattern for over four hours—never making an overt attempt to do harm, but never moving off either. It certainly helped that

Sousa was out there with us, and lessened the feeling of being so alone. It also helped knowing that Lyle had that AK 47—and that he had no qualms about using it if necessary!

Just what did they want and why weren't they boarding us if they were up to no good? They kept their lights off during this cat and mouse game.

Finally, when they were waiting just ahead, our boats fell off on a different course, knowing they would likely track us on the radar and be on our tails again. Oddly, as time wore on and they didn't appear again, it seemed the game was over.

Slowly, we made our way back on course and shared a long night of worry. When first light came and we were still alone, we all breathed huge sighs of relief! Others haven't been so fortunate.

That next night Lyle found a little niche on the chart on the coast of Borneo, protected from the prevailing winds, that would give us a chance to get the anchors down and rest for a night. *Sousa* was in first, maneuvering slowly with lights off and using radar. *Windy Thoughts* soon joined them, using our radar to creep in with lights off as well. Lyle shined a small light to help us get our bearings. As soon as we got the hook down we kept as low a profile as possible. It was a relief to get a night's sleep after our frightening ordeal.

A few days later we faced the very last day on our Indonesian visas. *Sousa* made a stop for a few days, while we pressed forward to a port on the west side of Bintan Island, ten miles south of Singapore. The Pilot indicated that it was a Port of Entry with Port Captain, Customs and Immigration.

It was early in the day and we figured to make our clearance from Indonesia and get across the Singapore Strait that same day. Fortunately, a wharf tie was available, eliminating the need to anchor, get the dinghy down, row to shore and reverse the process on our return. Knowing that we had an all day trek to get around the east coast of Singapore to the Changi anchorage, we were glad to be able to exit Indonesia expeditiously. So we thought.

Though we found the proper offices without difficulty, for reasons unclear to us we were unable to make clearance. No official could speak enough English to explain, but with gestures pointing south and at their watches, Don understood that he could complete the clearance process at a town south of there. That office closed at 11 a.m. so he would have to hurry, because it was some distance away.

The officials dashed outside to get a taxi for Don, told the driver where to take him and to go in with him to interpret—and then to bring him back. It was a two-hour trip one way on roads that Don describes as a race at death-defying speeds, the taxi passing anything in its way—no matter that something may be coming toward them in the opposite lane. The driver got there just before the offices closed and ran in with Don.

Don obtained our proper clearance—and the taxi headed back with total disregard for anything else on the road once again.

I stayed aboard the boat and as the tide changed adjusted fenders and lines. People from the town came to the wharf to wave hellos. I kept up with social duties, the best part of my day.

After about an hour, a huge squall came up. With the darkening skies, the villagers scattered to their respective homes and the best part of my day was over. It wasn't one of those quick squalls; it lasted about an hour. High winds made the water rough, the pilings offering no protection as the seas simply flowed under the wharf and around them.

I frantically tried to keep the fenders between the boat and pilings as *Windy Thoughts* rose and fell. I was anxious about one piling in particular. It was cut off with its top just a few inches under the surface of the water, and so close to our hull that as we bounced and rolled about I was sure that *Windy Thoughts* would be holed at any moment. What if Don returned and the boat was sunk right here? Certainly, I had to handle this!

I ran up and down the deck, constantly lifting one fender momentarily to keep it between the hull and a piling—and then dashing to another. There was no question of me moving the boat off the wharf, because just getting on it had involved more maneuvering than I want to describe—with both of us wondering just why we had even attempted it in the first place. It was now blowing like stink.

Opposite us on the wharf was a good-sized Security vessel, but no one seemed aboard during my little crisis. When at my wit's end, I climbed up a few nails sticking out on a piling and pulled myself up onto the wharf.

Attempting to appear lady-like, cool and collected, I frantically knocked on the hull. A nice fellow came out, and seeing the state I was in, he climbed right down onto *Windy Thoughts* and helped me rearrange fenders and adjust lines. As the squall began to pass he told me to come and get him if I needed help. I thanked him profusely.

When Don returned late in the afternoon, all was well and we both had our stories to tell—my dilemma surely far worse than his!

You don't want to know the choreography necessary to get off the wharf in strong currents, as it wasn't pretty! Dropping anchor out just a few hundred feet, we would be ready in the morning to set off for the final leg to Singapore.

Forest fires that burn out of control on Kalimantan, Borneo, at this time every year have created thick smoke that made visibility about zero within a couple of days out of Gili Air. When we left the next morning we wended our way via radar across the Singapore Strait in this same zero visibility, the radar showing a plethora of big ships surrounding us. It was unnerving. Singapore is the busiest container port in the world. Two ships arrive and two depart every five minutes!

Ten miles into the Strait, traffic eased off as we worked our way toward the Changi anchorage—taking us all day with currents against us fully half the distance. We passed by the Changi Sailing Club, but aren't allowed moorage there. Not having seen many cruising boats for some time we were amazed at the large number sitting at anchor when we finally reached the Changi anchorage.

Once the anchor went down, setting it was near impossible. We dragged along the silt-covered bottom when we backed down on the anchor, but since we were in civilization again I wasn't going to spend a lot of time worrying. Well, not too much.

Immediately, we learned the ropes from others; we could use the dinghy dock at the Sailing Club for $40 fee per week—but no laundry privileges! A bus was available up the road from the Club. It would take us to the nearest MRT station, Singapore's mass rapid transit system that is clean, quiet and very, very efficient. A card is slid through a reader when getting on either the bus or the train system.

Singapore is an island city. In order to monitor the number of cars allowed downtown, and to control pollution levels, all vehicles must purchase a daily pass before entering the city limits. We jump on a train and in a flash are in whatever section of Singapore our daily errands may take us! One could walk anywhere in the city, even at night, and not be worried about crime.

Each MRT station is named for the original neighborhood or village in the particular area before Singapore's modernization. Each neighborhood now consists of clusters of tall apartment buildings, with the first floors housing shops, medical facilities and schools. Our favorite area is the centralized food court, always frequented by the local people and making meals easy!

The marina manager at the Club always shares information on where to go and how to get there. He feels that even though the old, charming villages were sacrificed to build highrises, life is better for everyone. Still, it is fun to get a taste of old Singapore where some of the neighborhood shops reflect the older ways.

Don and I have a favorite area that we refer to as the electronics capitol of the world, several multi-storied buildings with open malls that look up to floor after floor of electronics stores. We purchased a Micrologic GPS, teaming up with three other yachties to get a better deal. We can't wait to try it out when we leave, though we are unsure when that will be, as several things are holding us up.

At this point considerable time has been spent trying to get our Auto Helm 5000 autopilot repaired. We left the unit with an Auto Helm dealership and service center. The dealership was in a high-rise mall and a very fancy looking office that had us polishing our thumbs at our good fortune to find this right here in Singapore. We picked the autopilot up a week later and Don re-installed it. Now it doesn't function at all!

It was an all day procedure returning to the dealership, where they questioned that the autopilot didn't work and wanted to come out to the boat to see for themselves.

Representatives arrived at the boat a few days later and we set out for a few hours of tooling about off the coast of Singapore. Don explained again that before bringing it in to them, it had only a few glitches now and then—and it was these glitches that he had requested be put right. Don asked repeatedly and politely what work had been done at the shop, but it seems no one knew.

After a two-hour trial, the experts looked at us and said, "It doesn't work."

We kept our opinions to ourselves with smiles on our faces. Back at the anchorage, Don unhooked the autopilot and the representatives took it back to the shop with them. We weren't feeling too confident about our autopilot.

The scuttlebutt around the anchorage included similar experiences with the dealership and we lowered our expectations. When we made the jaunt into the city to pick up the unit the following week, no amount of questioning produced any explanation about what had been wrong or what had been done to remedy it—nor was there any paperwork.

The following morning, Don re-installed it and we headed out into the Strait for a trial run. When the unit kicked in we were ecstatic. Should we trust it?

With so much to take care of while in Singapore, we find time slipping by us. Our ventures into the city have been almost daily and are an all-day process that includes provisioning, eating meals out and enjoying this beautiful, bustling city that keeps us busy and happy.

Changi Village is just a short walk from the anchorage, past lovely old homes surrounded with stately trees in a quiet part of the island and far from the hustle and bustle of the downtown. Changi Village's several small shops, along with its food court that is a popular spot for the cruisers, gives us the best of both worlds. Don found a little restaurant that served New York style conies with an ice cold beer. It has become one of our favorite spots while in Singapore.

The latest addition to equipment on the boat has been cabin fans that provide comfort for the first time in three years! Well, we did try the nice Hella fans awhile back but the limited lifespan of their motors prevented any efficiency for the cruising life, and any comfort enjoyed by them was very short-lived. When we were riding in a taxi one day, Don asked the driver about the efficient fan that was mounted above the dash. The driver explained that it was a DC Sanyo fan that had run continually for a full year. We purchased four of the same! Don has mounted one to blow on my settee, one above his settee, one above our berth and one for the galley area.

As we recline on our settees with our books, air blows directly on us. At night, we sleep like babies. The difference this has made to our lives is indescribable and puts the top-of-the-burner waffle iron in second place as our favorite piece of "equipment".

Our time here is not totally spent ferreting out parts and working on the boat; Singapore has offered us so much sightseeing. A visit to Raffles Hotel to soak up its history and enjoy a very nice lunch was tops on our list. Don and I dressed up and felt like royalty as we lounged around in such luxury. Nattily dressed doormen wait at the entrances and the whole place reeks of old Singapore's moneyed class.

Singapore has a very nice zoo that is easy and pleasant to walk about, the animals are well cared for and the zoo sits in beautifully kept surroundings amongst trees and verdant greenery. A big orangutan with long shaggy orange hair loves to get his picture taken with people and will pose with his arm around anyone brave enough to snuggle up with him.

One day we visited the nearby Changi Prison, where pictures on the cell walls made by prisoners during the Japanese occupation document some of the occupation's horrific abuses. Though the most telling were recently taken down, what is left is still a testament to the cruelty suffered.

Provisioning was ever on my mind and many of the yachties were using a particular supermarket that delivered to the Yacht Club. With my list and our available cash in hand I set out to further prepare for the months ahead. Fortunately, once I arrived at the supermarket I had the good sense to ask first about the delivery service. My inquiry met with a blank stare and a shake of the head. No, they would not deliver!

The long journey by bus and then MRT had made it too late to alter plans, so I reversed the process and headed back to the boat. Don and I walked down to Changi Village, leaving provisioning for another day. When I pulled out my wallet to make a purchase in one of the shops, to my horror I discovered that my provisioning money wasn't there!

Though we searched every shop previously visited, the money was never found. In the end, we scraped together our reserves and did some decent provisioning at Jacob's, a much better supermarket as it turned out, one that carried many of our favorite American products as well as good meats and cheeses.

The supermarkets in Singapore are not surrounded by big parking lots as they are at home, and are located on either an upper floor or perhaps a below-ground floor of the high-rise malls. More people use the MRT system for their shopping needs than do by car, and most purchase their produce, fish and meats at the wet markets in their neighborhoods.

Laden with mountains of groceries, we planned a taxi ride to get it all back to the Club. Jacob's is located in the lower level of one of the huge, multistoried malls. This required hauling all sacks of groceries up a set of stairs to the street level and leaving them there unaccompanied while we went back for more. People stared at the amount of groceries, as this is not how the local people shop! We raced back down below at breakneck speed, ever worried about our sacks sitting up on the busy sidewalk or unaccompanied in the baskets below. Once all was safely on sidewalk level, we got into a queue for a taxi. One thing they do here is politely queue up for taxis. They do *not* do so for buses.

Once back at the Changi anchorage, we made several trips—hauling sacks the rather long distance through the club and down the long walk to the dock where the dinghies are located. It is very hot and humid, adding to the sweat factor. The Club is far from the anchorage, so the dinghy ride is a long one.

The real battle begins when getting all onto the boat, and the thrill of finding everything right here in Singapore begins to rapidly pale when faced with the daunting prospect of marking every can top and bottom, repackaging anything that is in boxes—worries about those little bugs who love to live in the corrugation—tearing the cabin apart to expose all stowage lockers—and then making decisions as to where to possibly put any of this! There is little room to maneuver about our cabin and normal living is turned upside down until all is put away.

It is the transition period between the SW monsoon and the coming NE monsoon and squalls can be expected. The holding ground is awful and there are many boats here, perhaps forty. The Sumatra, a particularly vicious westerly wind that comes from the island of Sumatra, is a fast and heavy squall that often creates a white-out situation if underway—and a very dangerous situation in this anchorage. The winds rapidly reach strength and can last for an hour or more, as we were to learn.

Sure enough, in the middle of two consecutive nights we experienced these Sumatra winds. I awoke the first night to the sound of the halyard beginning to slap on the mast, usually tied off when at anchor but neglected this time. I raced up on top, and thanks to the lights on the island I could clearly see a very black line in the sky coming from Sumatra to the west of us.

Don was sleeping soundly and I dashed below to wake him and suggest that he get up too—that I was sure a Sumatra was bearing down on us. The anchorage was quiet and no one else seemed aware. Disgruntled, Don thought I was overreacting until his senses suddenly came alive to the sound of the banging halyard.

He leapt out of our berth and into the cockpit to see the mammoth, dead black ominous line across the night sky. It was beginning to rain. The anchorage was rapidly beginning to take on the appearance of the sea and *Windy Thoughts* began bucking up and down. Don hit the starter switch on the engine and kept forward power on as the squall hit full force with winds at forty knots and gusting higher within seconds. Sleepy people from other boats were now dashing about in a frantic attempt to get second anchors out and engines engaged.

Everything occurred within a few seconds and *Windy Thoughts* was slipping backwards fast—but we weren't the only boat to be making a hasty retreat, as every boat at anchor was on the move!

Those attempting to get another anchor out found it a fruitless task because of the poor holding ground. Even with the throttle in full forward position we still continued to move backwards at an alarming rate. I hurriedly tied fenders on and we felt helpless as we rapidly approached a beautiful big schooner (originally owned by Errol Flynn) on a mooring.

As *Windy Thoughts* passed alongside within an inch of its hull, the two young crewmembers aboard screamed at Don to turn on our engine—and Don screamed into the wind that we had our engine on. They fended off our bowsprit as we whizzed by—and by the grace of God we never touched at all!

By now, we were staring at another sailboat behind us on a mooring with no owner aboard. When we were no more than ten feet from making contact, *Windy Thoughts* was suddenly brought up quick when our anchor caught on a cable stretching across the anchorage from a dive platform near shore.

Miraculously, not one boat ended up on the extensive rock reef located directly behind the boats dragging through the anchorage. Not one boat collided with another and after an hour of intense activity, all suddenly came to a stop. *Windy Thoughts* sat securely hooked on the cable, and unable to free the anchor we felt safe for the night.

When morning arrived we decided to stay put, feeling it was safer than re-anchoring! That night at exactly 3 a.m. once again, another Sumatra hit. This time everyone was up in their cockpits the very moment the first breezes passed through their riggings, in full rain gear and at the ready. It was another active hour or so but we all made it through unscathed.

After these experiences, I slept with one eye and ear open.

Singapore seems to be where everyone suffers breakdowns, and we are all getting one thing or the other back in working order before heading out again. For us, that meant the purchase of a worldwide TV so that we can watch videos from any country we are in. Ok, so maybe paradise shouldn't include TV, but we do enjoy a movie now and then!

Two-week visas are issued in Singapore but with our Auto Helm problems, we weren't at all ready to leave within the first two weeks. So, we upped the anchor and in less than an hour had moved across the Strait to anchor off a small town with a Port of Entry on a neighboring Malaysian island—where we received clearance both into and out of Malaysia before returning to Singapore. Another full day's procedure followed in downtown Singapore, but we are legal again. We had to repeat this formality three more times in the next few weeks, providing work orders and bills as proof that we weren't settling in as permanent residents.

November 25, 1991
Singapore

Dear Friend,

The time to bid farewell to Singapore finally came four days ago and we were off for points north in the Malacca Strait—so we thought.

Don dove on the anchor with tanks to get the anchor unhooked from the cable. Just as this task was completed the sky filled with black clouds and we departed on a nasty squall. More disquieting was the fact that the autopilot now refused to kick in. The new GPS didn't want to give any readings and we were feeling a bit dispirited.

By late afternoon, we had ducked behind one of the little islands off the south side of Singapore, all around us busy with big ships at anchor and workboats buzzing back and forth. The hook down, Don worked with the GPS all evening but still received no information. It was such a thrill to have a new GPS but we especially didn't want to set off from here without the autopilot—still thinking to head across the Indian Ocean very soon. Don was afraid the autopilot needed to be sent to England.

There was nothing for us to do but return to Changi, a full day's work with strong currents against us at least half of the way. How long would it take to solve the problems we had now? We planned to spend Christmas in Phuket, Thailand, with the many other boats.

The GPS problem was solved when we learned that all satellites had been down for the past few days! As for the autopilot, we have started all over again at the dealership, but with little hope for any help from them, and we are unsure what to do. To top it all off, the VHF radio started acting up on the way back to the anchorage.

It is necessary for me to nearly cry as we plead our case with the officials in order to get two more weeks on our visas. Don has instructed me to do so if necessary—but about now I doubt I would need any prompting. With all of this to contend with, we are well aware that we could be held up in far worse places.

January 13, 1992
Langkawi Island
Malaysia

Happy New Year from Malaysia!

We finally got off from Singapore shortly before Christmas. And with a working autopilot, thanks to a kind American boater who has a shop just ashore from the anchorage—a little miracle that just popped up for us. He traded his own Auto Helm 5000 control box for ours, and would keep the parts ordered to repair ours. How we wish we had learned of him earlier!

Suddenly, the lines to the toilet plugged up with hard scale after four years of life aboard. Because the lines were absolutely impossible to reach, Don ultimately had to remove the shower pan, a few inches of the tile from the pan up the wall all around it, and all floorboards in the head. Both of us struggled for hours to feed new lines through unseen channels in the bilge, and are quite sure that the boat was constructed around the head.

Meanwhile, boat work was mingled with more excursions about Singapore and good times with other boaters.

The big push for the Indian Ocean crossing is now old news, as we have decided to spend a year in Southeast Asia, meandering up and down the Malacca Strait between Malaysia and Thailand. Having heard so much about this beautiful area, rushing through and seeing little would be a mistake. After all, what are we cruising for if not to linger in places and to get to know the people?

Ah, but that is truly not the biggest story in this saga of *Windy Thoughts*, for she has met with piracy in the infamous Malacca Straits! And this is how it transpired:

We got off from Changi for the final time about a week before Christmas. The current was against us and it was slow-going in rather gloomy and grey weather with light rain. When we came around the bottom of Singapore and headed north, the wind came directly out of the northwest at about twenty knots.

An uninhabited island that lay just a few miles off the coast of Malaysia and about twenty miles north of Singapore looked on the charts to offer good protection on its eastern, leeward side. In late afternoon we headed in there, having taken about nine hours against the wind to get this far. After dropping the hook, I made a good dinner and we curled up with a movie on our new worldwide TV—our world now such a contrast to the one lived in all day!

After such a pleasant evening tucked below while the wind roared its vengeance about us, we crawled into our berth, hoping those winds would die off by morning so we could be on our way—for we were anxious still to make Phuket, Thailand, for Christmas. Though there were no visions of sugarplums dancing in our heads, there certainly were visions of palm trees swaying on the beaches and a Christmas spent with other cruisers.

About midnight Don awoke to the sound of a boat's engine rapidly coming up alongside. Sitting upright in bed, he caught a glimpse of a foot and leg just boarding us right next to the porthole. Stark naked because of the extreme heat and humidity, he leapt out of bed, rapidly dug for the Colt 45 kept hidden but handy, grabbed the million candle-power spotlight, and flew up the companionway steps.

By the time he reached the cockpit, one man had already boarded *Windy Thoughts*, one was climbing over the lifelines and two more were readying to do so. Don instinctively went into survival mode. Make that combat mode!

As he reared up into the cockpit, focusing the high-powered spotlight directly on them, he saw the big knife in the hand of the man already aboard. Screaming some rather vile profanity that he says just rolled off his tongue, he told them in no uncertain terms to get off his boat!

Were he to have been more reticent, things may have played out far differently. However, he didn't greet them with pleasantries. Instead, a stark naked determined man holding a 45 automatic in one hand and a blinding light in the other produced the desired result. They didn't know what hit them and this was the one chance that we had.

The last two men didn't move further to get aboard and the first two stopped dead in their tracks. While Don was yelling at them just what he would do with the 45 if they didn't get off his boat, they stared at him in apparent disbelief that he would resist—and immediately jumped back into the boat to speed off into the night. It wasn't nice weather out there and no one would be venturing out in a small, open boat unless up to no good. Nor would they be boarding our boat uninvited in the dead of night—a big knife, the parang that is often used in piracy attacks, in hand.

It could have been far different circumstances. Possession of firearms, even so much as a bullet, is against the law in Malaysia. However, I know that Don would do whatever necessary to protect us without hesitation. Our life is so full of joy amongst the people we have met. An incident like this is so unexpected.

Oh, the best laid plans of mice and men. Don spent the rest of the night alert in the cockpit before we upped anchor at first light—and it was a slow slog as we set our sights north. With 500 miles yet to go, we knew that we wouldn't be spending Christmas in Phuket. We would instead set our sights for the Royal Selangor Yacht Club in Malaysia, about three days sail north.

The Strait is very busy with shipping traffic and we saw lights of no fewer than ten big ships close about us, within 1.25 miles, at any one time. The fishing boats and nets strewn about kept us on our toes as well! The night temperatures are quite comfortable in the mid to upper eighties, and on a few occasions we have even pulled a sheet over us. It must be our new fans!

Port Klang is a good-sized town located about ten miles up the Klang River. With the new GPS, we zeroed in on the entrance to the river exactly. The entrance channel is out in open water and there were ships anchored, waiting for pilots to guide them up river, so we knew we were in the right area. It was Christmas Eve and we sang Christmas carols all night on our watches. We were determined to be at the Yacht Club for Christmas, have a good dinner and call it our celebration.

The Royal Selangor Yacht Club sits on the river and has guest moorings available. We made it in on Christmas Day, although the trip up river took an inordinate amount of time with the current against us. I baked a pumpkin pie as we punched along.

The first thing we did once *Windy Thoughts* was secured on the mooring was make for shore and our Christmas dinner, where all wished us a Merry Christmas. The Royal Selangor Yacht Club is an old club, lovely and reeking with old charm—and with the most congenial atmosphere. We were welcomed warmly and our Christmas was spent in such a peaceful and friendly place.

Because of the strong tidal flow several miles upriver, using the dinghy is a bit untenable. Fortunately, there is a jingo boat running every half-hour. *Breezy* never came down, so we felt rather spoiled.

The ringgit is $2.75 to our dollar and meals at the club were a real treat. The food was delicious, with Malay and Chinese dishes as well as many western dishes. A very nice pepper steak dinner that included our drink was $4.00, fried rice with bits of chicken or seafood, $1.00. Mind you, hot chilies are used in everything and we will have to get accustomed to the heat, because we have Thailand to come! There were even ice cream sundaes, as well as French fries, no hot chilies served with either.

Most of the club members are Chinese and native Malays and live in Kuala Lumpur, the capital of the state of Selangor about twenty miles inland. Very comfortable buses run all day from Port Klang into this beautiful city.

We were very fortunate to meet Jimmy Tan, a Club member who set us up in a hotel near his business right in Chinatown, where we stayed for three days to see as many sights as possible. K.L. (Kuala Lumpur) is a lovely city, with beautiful architecture in the older sections and newer buildings that are uniquely designed and equally beautiful.

The population is a mixture of native Malay, Chinese and Indian. The large Indian population supports its own

commercial district, its streets adorned with temples and many shops selling everything imaginable from India. Chinatown is glorious and has a night market right in streets that are cordoned off from traffic. Kuala Lumpur's main downtown is full of lovely stores and hotels, an exciting and remarkably beautiful city.

The Batu Caves that house a Hindu Temple are certainly one of the most interesting sights, located just outside the city. We made the long climb up 272 steps to the entrance. Each January, Hindu men make a pilgrimage to the Temple during the Kavali ceremony. The men enter a trance state when skewers are literally pushed through their cheeks and tongues and then out the other side—and large barbless fish hooks are hooked into their backs. Items of all sorts are attached to these fish hooks and are dragged on long lines up the steps to the temple.

When we left Port Klang we traveled north to the Perak Yacht Club at Lumut, Malaysia, with two French boats met in Singapore. A young native woman from Wallace Island was purchased by the much older captain of one of the boats. She has a tiny three-year-old daughter with her and evidently other children left behind. She could neither speak nor understand English. Life won't be easy adjusting to cruising and unable to communicate.

We have enjoyed time spent with the family of four on the other French boat, the parents and two young daughters. With the threat of piracy ever on one's mind, the French boats were interested in sailing in tandem, especially during the night hours—and this suited us just fine!

The Perak Yacht Club at Lumut sits on a river and is a lovely spot that is very popular with the cruising crowd. The small restaurant is run by a Chinese couple who live nearby with their two pre-school children. The chef has put moorings down and built the club where he does the cooking. Since this spot offers such good protection, we may return here for the SW monsoon season after spending the NE monsoon season in Phuket.

Brisk northeast winds are prevalent now and our course puts these winds forward of the beam. On a close reach with winds at twenty to twenty-five knots, the sailing gets pretty bumpy! To reach Langkawi Island, Malaysia, we pointed up as high as we could, just squeaking into the channel near the southern end of the island. It was a real slog going up the channel to Kuah Town.

Breezy is left on a lovely beach, pulled up above the high tide line. Kuah Town is just a two mile walk, or a taxi ride. It is a duty-free port, not a large town but rather interesting with lots of small shops. With only about 300 miles between Langkawi and Phuket, many of the cruisers in Phuket have parts shipped here—and sail back and forth to pick them up, or perhaps to reinstate their Thai visas.

As in Port Klang, the Muslim Malay women wear colorful, patterned long skirts with the matching long tunic and equally colorful head scarves. The Indian women dress in beautiful saris of all colors of the rainbow and the Chinese women dress western style. Little girls wear frilly dresses, no long pants or shorts.

The Muslim call to prayer is broadcast five times each day from the local mosque, easily heard throughout the town and out to the anchorage, and we are enjoying the different culture.

The French family joined us on an excursion to a bay on the west side of Langkawi. A very posh hotel sits ashore, and we had to anchor well out and behind a little island because of shoals that extend a long distance out from shore. With swimsuits in hand, Don and I jaunted off to the hotel. We always attempt to dress a bit above our usual cruising mode when we "resort it", wishing to show respect for the establishment into which we are sneaking!

After lunch at the beautiful poolside restaurant, we changed into our swimsuits and waltzed out to the pool, attempting to appear that we belonged, settling in for the afternoon on the chaise longues. When at a resort we have the routine down pat, especially cognizant of paying the fee for a hotel towel. This one acquisition puts us right up there with the moneyed class, hotel guests—or so it feels. It makes us feel somewhat less guilty to always purchase a nice meal whenever we take advantage like this!

Our French friends arrived and headed right for the pool, but, not interested in disguising themselves as the cruising folks that we all were, they spread out on lounges and casually strewed their clothes about them. They didn't have the hotel towel, the big give-away. The hotel staff came over to our group to ask if the French family was staying at the hotel, and unfortunately, they were asked to leave. Don and I kept a very low profile, slinking back into the pool.

There were more adventures here with these friends when the captain asked Don to join him in his dinghy for the ride a long distance across the bay in hopes of getting petrol. Claiming he had enough to make it there, he refused to take any spare fuel from Don. Don was hesitant. It didn't sound wise to make an excursion that far in a dinghy without a spare fuel can—but against his better judgment, Don headed out with him.

When, after two hours, they hadn't returned, the wind began blowing about twenty knots from shore and we couldn't see them anywhere. The bay had become very choppy and I was sick with worry that they might be pushed out to sea. Should I up-anchor and go looking for them?

About this time we saw them in the distance struggling against the wind and sea, the French fellow rowing for all he was worth and having a very difficult time making headway to clear the island—on our side. They took turns rowing throughout the harrowing experience and were two very exhausted men when they finally made it to *Windy Thoughts*. Neither was at all sure that they would get safely back to our boats.

The engine had run out of fuel on the way over to the other side of the bay. Closer to land than they were to the boats, they continued on. When they reached shore, the establishment had no petrol after all—so they thumbed a ride to a petrol station several miles away, filled the can and thumbed a ride back to the dinghy.

They started off with the wind rising. When they were well underway, the engine quit. Neither could get it started. While they rowed, the wind pushed them out to sea faster than they could make headway forward—and with every pull on the oars they were working their way farther toward the outside of the island. Only adrenaline from sheer terror got them to the boats.

It was a lesson in listening to your better senses from the start. Don could see them disappearing out to sea and didn't think I would notice how long they had been gone. Such little confidence he had in me!

February 1, 1992
Ban Nit
Phuket, Thailand

Dear Susan,

It was long after Christmas when we finally reached Phuket, Thailand, four days ago—but oh, the wonderful adventures we had getting here!

Sailing from Langkawi Island, Malaysia, we made a little diversion to Ko Phi Phi Don Island, Thailand—not long ago reputed to be one of the three most beautiful islands in the world and a "not to miss" spot.

Koh Phi Phi Don sports a couple of hotels, the once pristine island paths

leading to any number of ticky-tacky tourist shops. It will likely get worse in future. Still, it would be a misstatement to say that it is not a quintessential island paradise.

Ko Phi Phi Don presented us with our first opportunity to eat Thai food. Don's curry cooked in a clay-pot about took the roof of his mouth off, as did my chicken with cashew, but both of us fell in love with Thai cuisine on our very first try.

You may have watched documentaries that recount Thai men collecting bird's nests while hanging from the sides of cliffs on bamboo ladders. The big rock formations sticking up out of the ocean around the bay of Koh Phi Phi Don Island are not only beautiful—they are home to the birds whose very nests are a delicacy in bird's nest soup! *Windy Thoughts* looked up at these rocks while she sat at anchor, though little did she know of their significance!

We now sit at anchor at Ban Nit Marina, in Au Chalon Bay on the south side of Phuket Island. Ban Nit is a marina of sorts, without docks but with good moorings and room to anchor. The marina was developed by an American who was an engineer instrumental in building the first road out of Bangkok. He has lived here for thirty-five years, and did the work of developing this marina himself. Not only does he speak flawless Thai, but he writes it as well. He is also a wealth of information on where to find things and what to see of interest.

Shore amenities are simple, with two showers in a wood building and a restaurant that offers delicious and beautifully prepared Thai food. A water spigot provides potable water to fill our jerry jugs. I take laundry ashore and slosh up and down in my buckets right there—my own private Laundromat! Availability of the showers is a godsend and we all appreciate this more than you can imagine. Of course, there is no hot water, but who would want that in this hot climate?

The coral bed between *Windy Thoughts* and shore dries at low tide, and getting to shore is a matter of playing the tides. A channel dug through the coral by the owner can be traversed to about one-half tide—if you don't mind walking and lifting the dinghy now and then! Phuket Town is located about five miles from Ban Nit, necessitating a taxi ride that isn't always convenient because we aren't located on a main road.

February 16, 1992

Phuket is rapidly growing on us—what a spectacular island! The good sized Phuket Town is the main center, with any number of shops and restaurants and a huge wet market for fresh produce, fish and meats.

Don rented a new Honda 100 motorbike for $5.00 a day, with a seat for two people just as those ridden by many of the locals. You have to experience trying to cross the street downtown to begin to have an idea of what it is like to drive here—and on the opposite side of the road—in traffic that doesn't give too much attention to the rules of the road, if there are any. There seem to be as many bikes as cars. Whole families hang off one bike, dad driving and mom hanging on behind him, junior scrunched between and another little one in a basket off the front.

Though Don has ridden larger bikes for years, he had a bit of trepidation at first but repeated to himself, "Keep the center of the road to your right. Keep the center of the road to your right."

With no map and no idea of how to get back to the anchorage we were off, free at last, following the flow of traffic and happy just to be on our way "somewhere". Joining right in with the locals we do it their way, no helmets and dressed in shorts and sandals.

Phuket's western side consists of one magnificent bay after another, each with a spectacularly beautiful beach that makes this side of the island the most visited by tourists. Patong Beach, in Patong Bay, is probably the most popular with visitors and always has a ton of tourists on the beaches—as well as a ton of boats anchored in the bay. We much prefer beautiful and quieter Kata Bay, or any of the other fabulous bays without the honky-tonk atmosphere.

Thai food is exquisite—and most often very inexpensive. Everywhere, we are amazed at the wonderful dishes created from vegetables and bits of fish or chicken, always beautifully prepared and served.

Eating out is much easier than hauling bags of groceries, though a huge public market in town has all the fresh produce one could possibly want, with a new butcher store right next door that has stainless working areas. The supermarkets are full of every manner of paper goods, bottles of various seasoning sauces, cookies, etc.

When we want to purchase more than a few things at a time we take a taxi, and have befriended a young couple who have their own Tuk Tuk, a small Toyota truck with benches along both sides of the bed and a cover over the top. When in Phuket Town we always look for the owners, considering them our personal drivers!

The west coast beaches have become untenable anchorages this past week, so we will stay right here in this nice community of cruising people where it is very quiet, very safe. With a good restaurant, showers and water available, who could ask for more?

Windy Thoughts' bottom has growth reappearing within one or two days after cleaning, a disappointment after the $1,200.00 haul-out in Australia. Many of the yachties are using the only available anti-fouling, a Thai brand used successfully by the fishermen, and that repels barnacles so well it would definitely fail to meet regulations back home. Thankfully, color is irrelevant as it comes in a dark red only. As long as it gets us through the next year, red will do and should rather brighten up *Windy Thoughts'* bottom!

Don just purchased four gallons at only $50.00 a gallon. Shall we send you some? Once back to the boat, he stood precariously in the dinghy and handed the first box of two gallons up to me. Both cans tipped out and went straight to the bottom. My hero immediately tore the back berth apart to get his tank out, donned his fins and headed for the deep. It didn't appear that he would find either can in the mud bottom, but though it took quite some time and all of his air, Don retrieved both!

Crazy lady is in the anchorage with Elizabeth aboard—a retired lady who set off from California and has been single-handing much of the past eleven years! Elizabeth is a very classy lady who can work on her engine, fix anything and get herself across oceans on her own, thank you. She went into Phuket

Town with us on our first day to show us where officials were located and then introduced us to a wonderful restaurant where we all had lunch, and that we now frequent whenever in town. Elizabeth is a fascinating and very attractive woman who is truly living her dream.

I have rapidly developed a passion for chicken with cashew nuts, tried first over on Koh Phi Phi Don Island, and Don has fallen in love with lemon grass chicken. Both are so good that our mouths water just thinking about them. Our palates are adjusting to the hot spices and in fact, we are beginning to crave them!

Our visas are for thirty days, renewable for thirty more days, but we must report into Immigration every ten days. We plan to cruise nearby Phang Nga Bay for a few days—a lovely bay that sits between Phuket and mainland Thailand. The entire area is very protected and dotted with several uninhabited islands that are all of limestone formations.

Plans for the upcoming monsoon season are very loose, but with our anti-fouling at the ready we are thinking to head 500 miles back south in the Malacca Strait to Port Klang, where we hope to haul the boat and get the bottom work done. Once this work is completed we still foster thoughts of heading north to Lumut, to spend the SW monsoon season at the Perak Yacht Club with several others.

Phuket Island stretches about thirty miles north to south and our jaunts on the bike take us all over the island. Little villages here and there always provide a spot to stop and get a cold drink or something to eat. Don and I would easily put Thai food up against an expensive gourmet dinner in any five-star restaurant—and would take it every time. It is that good.

The countryside is stunningly beautiful. Riding along on the top of a mountain and looking down at any one of the most beautiful bays and beaches just takes our breath away. The South Pacific was very special, but so expensive. Here, one island paradise after another confronts us—and with the friendliest and most welcoming people imaginable.

As we ride along we see lovely Buddhist temples, rubber plantations, water buffalo and people working in the fields, all such a contrast to the west coast beaches heavy with tourists. We much prefer our quiet anchorage, and we are happy to visit the west coast on the bike and then return right here.

Those good Aussie friends on *Sousa* are now at anchor up on the northeast side of Phuket, by themselves and off a tiny village. They seem to have settled into the local scene, and plan to stay right there where they have made many friends of locals ashore. They can turn the boat over to the government and put up a substantial bond of $1,000.00 each—then fly down to Penang, Malaysia, every three months to renew visas. This is the common way in which many of the other boaters stay here, finding it difficult to leave this area and the perfect spot to set up housekeeping.

March 27, 1992
Langkawi Island
Malaysia

Salamet Pagi,

Before setting our course south again to Malaysia, we headed up the east coast of Phuket to Phang Nga Bay with intentions of inconspicuously cruising these island jewels for a few days.

What was to be a very quick stop to say hello to the folks on *Sousa* was, in the end, a two week stop when engine problems would not allow us to leave. After spending hours of investigation, Don turned it over to a Thai engineer who had formerly worked all over the world on diesel engines—and now runs a tiny restaurant just ashore! When the engineer told us that his work would be rather expensive, we were very happy to pay his bill of 150 baht, or $6.00, for five hours of work that remedied any problems with the engine for the present.

We enjoyed dinner aboard *Sousa* with their Thai friends from the village as well as a young American couple who work at the Seventh Day Adventist Hospital.

The doctor looked at me and said, "You have a pterygium don't you?"

"Huh? What's a pterygium?"

It is a rather massively large and yellow growth at the inner corner of my right eye that is growing toward the cornea and is caused by sun and wind. Neither Don nor I had paid it any mind; it had likely come on little by little over time. This eye does give me trouble, especially while whizzing about on the bike.

The next day we went to an eye doctor who frequently removes pterygiums and could do it right there in his office for $500.00. We decided to wait until we reached Port Klang and I could go under the knife at a real hospital in Kuala Lumpur.

Once underway again, all of Phang Nga Bay awaited us, its many islands of fabulous limestone formations sticking their heads up out of the sea in the most unusual shapes. Many of these limestone formations have caves within them—and hongs, inland seas formed when the top of a cave has fallen in. *Breezy* took us in through a cave entrance to slowly work our way into the center that is open to the sky and forms the hong. Lush greenery covered the sides and it was absolutely magical—though it is necessary to time the tides, as you don't want to be inside when a rising tide precludes getting back out soon!

After cavorting in Phang Nga Bay it was time to sail back over to Langkawi, Malaysia, to take care of our clearance procedures, as well as to pick up mail waiting for us at Kuah Town. With a full moon to aid us as well as some familiarity with a lovely anchorage on the west coast of the island, at 4 a.m. yesterday we worked our way slowly into the bay and got the hook down for a few hours of sleep.

Langkawi is a duty-free port and by international law we shouldn't pay duty on needed boat parts in any country, though that doesn't always hold true. Before leaving Phuket, Don had ordered a stuffing box replacement on February 26, to be shipped to an agent in Kuah Town by DHL Fast Carrier and to have arrived within three or four days. The agent had been notified of its presumed arrival date and a second fax let him know that we were delayed, asking that he hold it there for us. When we set off to pick it up today, not only was there no parcel, but according to the agent no fax as well. In addition, a depth sounder that Don also ordered to be shipped to the same agent wasn't there either. Both units need to be installed while the boat is hauled at Port Klang, so we wait for them here before heading south again.

A good hike from the anchorage brings us to a very nice resort, and shower bags and bathing suits in hand, we relax around the nice pool, blend in with the guests and, best of all, enjoy a wonderful shower afterward—the highlight of our day.

The air temperatures make heating the pool unnecessary and the water is still much too warm to be refreshing, but just getting into fresh water feels so good to us. A pool bar offers a pleasant spot to cool off with a tall, cold drink.

One day when we were in the pool we overheard tourists speaking English and excitedly joined in their conversation. They were from the United States and were meeting their daughter and her husband, in from Saudi Arabia where they teach in an International School. Malaysia was holding a teaching conference and the school had taken care of the airfare and accommodations for the trip. Where was I all those years of teaching? The International Schools sound very interesting if you are single, or a married couple who both want to teach.

The *Hati Halus*, a seventy-foot schooner, makes its home anchored off Kuah Town. The *Hati Halus* is a true Indonesian perahu that its captain had built for him in some remote islands of Indonesia. Hugh and Joanna are from Singapore and do sail repair aboard. They will repair our dodger with new zippers and new plastic for the windows, and re-sew the seams.

Hugh and Joanna invited us to join them on an hour's ride on a hydro-plane ferry to Alor Star, a city forty miles south on mainland Malaysia where we were treated to all the sights and had delicious curry chicken at their favorite spot. The bathroom in the restaurant was for men and women, but without the usual potty in the floor with the platform for your feet. There was instead just a drain in the tiled floor with the usual reservoir of water next to it. The plastic dipper provided "manual" flushing—which we understand. I checked with Joanna about the proprieties of using the facility and learned that you simply use the floor. New experiences!

These new friends also invited us to join them for the Hindu Kavali celebration while on Langkawi Island. They introduced us to their Indian friend who would be our host for this auspicious occasion—and what an experience it was!

We first went to a luncheon at the Hindu temple. The ladies were dressed in their best and most beautiful saris, the little girls in their frilly dresses. Tables were set up under a covered but open-air area. The four of us were the only non-Indians in the crowd.

Our plates were banana leaves and we ate with our fingers in the local tradition. Men came to each table with colorful plastic buckets filled with curried rice and pickled vegetables, amongst many other things, and a dessert of tapioca with cashews. Some of each was dipped onto each banana leaf plate with a big dipper. Everything was somewhat soupy. You can imagine how difficult it was for those of us not accustomed to using our fingers as utensils!

A water tank was brought in for washing hands, and then we observed how the others ate and got a few tips from Hugh and Joanna. You use the first three fingers of your right hand to pick up the food—and push the food into your mouth with your thumb. After taking a deep breath, we dug right in. It works!

After the luncheon, we followed the crowd to a park on the other side of town. The Kavali celebration that we had first learned about when visiting the Batu Caves in Kuala Lumpur would take place here. At the Batu Caves we had seen photographs of a bicycle hanging from one fellow's face, the bar having been skewered right through his mouth! Here, three men amongst about 100 local Indians were being prepared one at a time for this annual ritual. Everyone stood by and watched.

Eight large, barbless fishhooks were hooked into the flesh of the first and younger man's back. There was no blood. Hanging from each fishhook was a string of about eight inches. An old woman near us had built a fire of hot coals. With her bare hands she held a lime in the searing coals for several seconds before it was attached to those strings hanging from the fishhooks in the young man's back. She then picked up some of the red-hot searing coals and popped them into her mouth—and proceeded to dance about with the burning coals remaining in her mouth. She wasn't burned. We were allowed to film all of this.

Following this, a large colorfully decorated contraption was placed over the fellow's head, supported by one circular structure that went around his waist and another on his shoulders. The somewhat complicated structures stood about four feet above his head, with lines running from them to more hooks that were pierced into the fellow's torso.

This all took considerable time and the fellow was stoic throughout. The chanting continued around him and we were fairly certain that he was in some sort of a trance.

When the second fellow was brought forward, we noticed that he was well into middle age. His preparation took more time and involved much more body piercing and the same ritual with the limes.

The next phase of the ritual will sound gruesome. A steel skewer of about twelve inches was suddenly shoved through the man's tongue. There wasn't a drop of blood. All was accompanied with heavy chanting and beating on drums. Once the decorated structure was secured on his shoulders with the lines and fishhooks, he danced about.

Then the third fellow, much older than the other two, was prepared. It seemed that with age and experience the level of mutilation increased, and many more fishhooks were hooked all over his torso, arms and legs, all of them with lines connected to the contraption on his shoulders. A long skewer was pushed through his cheek, then through his tongue and through the other cheek. The ceremony appears to be a form of self-sacrifice and a confirmation of their aim to be a better person in the year to follow.

The preparation took over an hour, and when the three were ready they led the crowd in a procession back through Kuah Town to the Temple, barefoot on pavement so hot that people threw buckets of water on it to keep their feet from burning. We followed along. When they were gathered at the Temple about an hour later, the skewers and fishhooks were removed. There wasn't a drop of blood—but even more interesting, not a sign of a wound on any of them.

It was difficult for us to understand much of this, but it provided us with a very close-up encounter with this interesting culture and practice.

May 14, 1992
Perak Yacht Club
Lumut, Malaysia

Susan,

After a six-week wait for our parts, we finally got away from Langkawi Island! Both the permanent PSS Shaft Seal (stuffing box replacement) and the depth sounder finally made their respective appearances, but not without many hot hikes to town and back.

It turns out that the PSS Shaft Seal was sitting at the airport in Langkawi since the last week of February, though addressed to the agent's office. The agent claims to have checked at the airport three times, even searching the Customs area. Shipping costs were $95.00, with an additional charge of $100.00 for the agent. Ah, but no customs charge! The depth sounder was shipped Air Parcel Post and took five weeks to get here.

The month of March was the Muslim Ramadan, perhaps partly responsible for the mix-up with the mail service, as so much else gets ignored. After a fast from sunup to sunset, several small food stalls were set up in the streets, and we often ate barbecued chicken. The call to prayer begins at 4:30 a.m. each morning, again at 7:30 a.m. and three more times throughout the day every day, giving us an early morning wake-up call!

Ramadan ends with the Hari Raya celebration, officially beginning when the first sliver of the new moon is sighted. Since there was a cloud cover all night, the moon wasn't visible and Hari Raya was postponed for a day. Prayers from the mosque just ashore from the anchorage were broadcast via loud speaker all night. Thank goodness the moon was seen the next night and Hari Raya could be celebrated.

April and May are the transition period between the NE and the SW monsoons and it has been relatively inactive weather-wise, with heavy squalls and thunderstorms beginning in late afternoons and at night during our last week on Langkawi Island. Squalls kept us on our toes when sailing the Malacca Strait. The violent lightning was scary, with huge jagged bolts that traveled from the sky to the water. It isn't unusual for boats in this area to be hit by lightning and often electronics are blown out. We keep our fingers crossed!

Just before leaving Langkawi Island, Don and I took an hour's ferry ride to Satoon, Thailand, to reinstate our three month visas, starting over while we had the opportunity. We found the officials set up at the ferry dock and easily had our passports chopped, and we returned on the same ferry.

The reinstatement gives us until July 23, when we must leave and enter Malaysia again. The boat isn't involved, making the whole procedure an easy one with just a trip out of the country for ourselves. Train travel is very inexpensive and a sleeper on a night train from Lumut arrives in Singapore in the morning.

Anti-fouling and my eye are the two priorities at the moment. Our haul-out date in Port Klang is June 13, and if we can get there about ten days earlier I hope to get that pterygium removed in Kuala Lumpur.

While here in Lumut we have visited Dr. Wong, a dentist who was high-ly recommended by others. I had a complete checkup with no cavities for a grand total of $1.60. Don had not only a complete checkup, but had a wisdom tooth pulled, all for $7.00. Dr. Wong is board certified and went to dental school in England. Come on over!

Windy Thoughts is on a mooring here at the Perak Yacht Club along with several other boats. Not sure that the moorings are serviced often—if at all—there is a bit of worry about a Sumatra wind hitting. Evidently, if it ain't broke, don't fix it. Our mooring is close in to shore, so I, of course, have to worry about breaking the mooring and being on the beach in no time. Don tries to convince me it is better than being on the outside—where one of the big barges occasionally breaks loose from its mooring and with the strong river current goes walk-about. We have witnessed this twice and don't want to be in their path!

The Yacht Club burgee sports a huge jellyfish in black on a yellow back-ground. We have personally seen jellyfish up to three or four feet in the river, though they're known to be six feet in diameter. Guess we won't go swim-ming!

The town of Lumut is charming, with several shops and restaurants. As for our social life, the cruisers gather at the small club ashore. Sometimes we join another couple for a taxi to Sitiawan, a bigger town four miles down the road. A Kentucky Fried Chicken in Sitiawan is the hot spot for the locals, though we fail to understand how it compares to the excellent local Malay chicken dishes. However, the ice cream sundaes do lure us there whenever possible!

Cooking aboard is not a big priority here in Southeast Asia, since we all eat so many of our meals ashore. It is inexpensive, the food excellent and our cabins aren't rendered even more uncomfortable by the added heat of stove burners. Breakfast is always aboard; for lunch and dinner we enjoy Chinese, Indian, or Malay food available in the many restaurants or food stalls ashore. One of our favorite dishes is the Indian roti, a common breakfast food that we like for lunch—the flat roti spread with a thick split-pea soup-like mixture tastes quite delicious.

Lumut is home to the Malaysian Naval Base and our first week here of-fered excitement and intrigue beyond our expectations. Last week two United States LSDs arrived to render good will with Malaysia and to review it as a prospective port as an alternative to the Philippines. The ships carried Ma-rines as well as sailors and were part of a fleet of five, the other three ships in

Singapore—offering a great deal more for the boys to do ashore.

It seems that Malaysia doesn't stand a chance. The navigator came in ahead of the bigger of the two ships, *Fort McHenry*, in a small boat, using a lead line for soundings. When depths dropped below thirty feet in a matter of seconds, bringing the LSD up river was the worst experience ever—and the captain knew that this would be his farewell voyage if they went aground. When finally moored at the base, a diver was sent down, and he could put only an arm between the bottom of the ship and the river's bottom. Were this base to be considered, an LSD could get out on a rising tide only, negating the possibility of being considered alert-ready!

When we came in our depth sounder was on the fritz and I was on the bow with my trusty lead line, just like the big guys! With only one green buoy marking the river itself and our chart for the area barely readable—because it was a copy of a copy of a copy—the entire procedure was rather nerve-racking.

On the day the big ships arrived, I was at an evening meeting in Sitiawan with Tina from *God's Speed* and Barb from *Kelly Marie*—first met in Australia. Tina had come to know a woman missionary in Australia who was speaking in Lumut that evening, and she invited us to the meeting held above a Chinese store.

Afterward, we were walking into the center of town in the dark to ferret out a taxi. Imagine our surprise when we saw three American boys coming toward us on the sidewalk! In a Southern drawl, one asked if we knew where they could find a phone to call home to the United States. The only place to make an international call was at the Telekom office. It takes about fifteen minutes to book a call and has only one phone available, but was closed for the day.

They were also looking for a bit of nightlife, and the Kentucky Fried Chicken restaurant was the only action in town. Headed there ourselves, we had a nice visit and invited the three of them from the *Tuscaloosa* out to the Yacht Club for dinner the next evening.

The three young officers all came and seemed to enjoy a chance to mingle off the ship and to soak up some local culture at our Yacht Club, and everyone thoroughly enjoyed their company.

The next morning we awoke to find our dinghy overturned, the engine immersed in the salt water. An Australian fellow on a nearby mooring called over to tell us he had seen two other young Marines, guests of another boat the night before swimming out to the boats after imbibing a few beers at the Club. They were headed to *God's Speed*, where Paul's lovely sixteen year-old daughter was aboard with her family—but Paul didn't take kindly to their plan to see her and sent them on their way. Mind you, the river is full of strong currents and those jelly fish.

The Aussie saw the two fellows swimming about our dinghy and attempting to pull themselves up into it. The consensus was that they overturned it in their efforts. Though attempting to do just this to test the stability of the dinghy, we have never been able to accomplish it—but two strapping young Marines might if they were trying to climb in simultaneously on one side.

Don took the engine apart and worked on it for hours to no avail. Everyone tried to convince him that he should do something about this. Finally, armed with the names of the boys as well as the Aussie witness, the three of us trooped out to the Naval Base.

At the entrance, Don got one of the young men on the phone and explained that he would like him to come out and talk to him about the incident the evening before. Getting a negative reply, Don calmly told him that he could either talk to him, or he could speak to his commanding officer. The young fellow would definitely prefer to speak to us and would meet us at the gate when he was off duty at 4 p.m.

The Aussie fellow was unable to join us this time, and the young Marine was a no-show. Don called the ship and asked to speak to the officer on duty and explained our predicament and the expense of losing an engine. When the fellow replied that they didn't have the time to deal with us, Don said if that was the case he could take the matter up with the Malaysian police.

They weren't about to deal with the Malaysian police and the officer asked us to wait right where we were for an escort, two nattily dressed Marines who came right out to the gate to escort us onto the ship and to the Captain's office—with the Marine Commanding officer waiting there as well. Beside them stood a very alert and at attention young corporal who had spent some of his evening in the river by our boat. The other young Marine wasn't present.

Don explained what had happened to our engine and spoke about responsibility, saying that if they didn't want to wake us up, had they told anyone in the Club someone would have come out to wake us—and we could have retrieved the engine right away, not allowing the saltwater damage.

The young corporal didn't utter a word and was rightly very nervous after his one social evening in Malaysia had now been spoiled. The officers said that this would be resolved and asked the amount of damage, and that we call at 9:00 the following morning.

The result of that phone call was an invitation to lunch in the officer's wardroom on the ship that next day, where we were seated at the head table! With everything from steak to lamb on the menu, we ordered the first salads seen in a year—and big bacon cheeseburgers. The officers were interested in our cruising and not a word was mentioned about the incident that brought us there.

The two young corporals who were the unfortunate culprits were brought in after lunch and left alone with us. They both stood at silent attention and stared straight ahead. After some friendly attempts at chat, Don brought the subject up, explaining that he didn't want them reprimanded or to lose shore leave—but wanted them to accept responsibility for our engine, a very real loss to us.

Without a smile or a word, they both reached into their pockets and pulled out $420.00, advanced to them from their paychecks and the exact amount needed to buy a new three-horsepower Yamaha engine in Sitiawan.

Two officers gave us a complete tour of the LSD that carries two amphibious landing craft below decks, along with dozens of vehicles and tanks. When he took us to the bridge to introduce us to the navigator, we were given ten original charts for the Indian Ocean! Like most out here we work off copies, as the cost of charts is so very high—$30.00 each in Singapore.

Two days later the navigator came out to the Club with two other young officers and brought us two more original charts. He repeatedly told Don not to be bashful but to just tell him what we needed. Blessed far beyond measure, we wouldn't ask for more. When the ship left port, I believe we had tears in our eyes and practically stood at attention ourselves, pride welling up in us to see our American flag flying over the bridge. The benevolence of our good old USA, so well known around the world, has been bestowed on the likes of us and we won't soon forget it.

Along with entertainment of the United States Navy and Marines this past week, Don has also installed our new depth sounder using the inside-the-hull method, and it is actually working! Now we can safely leave Lumut and get ourselves down to Port Klang.

June 22, 1992
Royal Selangor Yacht Club
Port Klang, Malaysia

Hello friend,

It was wonderful to receive your letter yesterday and know that you are ensconced in that lovely marina at Semiahmoo and looking out at the mountains. It sounds luxurious and Don maintains that since you only live once, you may as well live where you want.

How he misses his mountains, and at times we do feel homesick for our beautiful Northwest. Don has a constant heat rash, it is ninety-five degrees day and night and any real exercising is out of the question, with humidity thick enough to swim through. A walk to the market nearly brings on a heat stroke.

Am I complaining? In truth, we know full well just how blessed we have been to have our eyes and our minds opened to so much in this world. We have made so many friends, seen so many interesting and beautiful places, and learned to get ourselves through whatever faces us.

However, it can be difficult sometimes, exasperated as I am by my worrying about every little thing. I know that we are watched over, always. Why do I fret? Here at Port Klang, we are well upriver with nary a ripple on the water, no matter how strong the wind may blow during a squall. Our mooring seems safe and it is a relaxed and secure feeling—one that I highly respect and for which I am thankful. But read on.

It is presently 8 p.m, and exactly forty-seven hours ago we sat on our mooring in the river off the lovely old Royal Selangor Yacht Club, comfortably curled up with books. Suddenly, there was the most horrendous and violent explosion, shaking *Windy Thoughts* to the core and actually heeling her over.

We both raced up on deck to see a huge tanker blowing up near us. It was berthed at the Shell Fuel Depot next to the Yacht Club—between our

mooring and the Yacht Club itself. Don saw flames running up the line from the ship leading to one of the big storage tanks that immediately blew up, followed shortly by the other nearby storage tanks.

It was frightening, and we wanted to get out of the river but didn't dare take the boat past the burning ship, nor did we want to make our way out of the tricky river channel in the dark. Our tall mast precluded heading up river, because of a bridge. What to do?

The tanker was burning furiously and we really feared that the mooring lines would burn through and the tanker might fly down river on the current—and right into us. Maybe it would roll and spill its contents into the river, the river then aflame and all of us in big trouble. What we didn't know at the time was that the tanker was carrying Zylene, a highly flammable fuel, and hadn't received proper clearance and permission to dock at that depot.

Most boats belong to Club members, with only four cruising sailboats in and with people aboard. A Swiss sailboat with Rudy and Evelyn aboard was just adjacent to the ship and Rudy was able to rescue the Captain from the water, the ship's papers with him. A small island just adjacent to us with homes and a restaurant was evacuated.

Don and I got the dinghy down and put passports, money and ship's papers into our waterproof shore bag, along with a change of clothes for each of us, and readied to get to shore if we had to leave the boat. The other four sailboats moved near us, as we were the farthest from the burning ship.

Thankfully, our boats were all fine through the night; we were just worried about what may be happening to people ashore and unsure as to how the disaster was being handled. The flames rose in huge, billowing, black mushroom-like clouds high above the tanker and the storage tanks.

By first light the next morning the tanker was still burning furiously and listing precariously. Don and I decided to get out. The big fire-boat tugs were still shooting water onto it and billowing black smoke still poured out of it. Though we weren't excited about passing close by, in the daylight we could see our way to get down river.

As we were readying to drop our mooring, a Club Jingo boat came by, the driver yelling to get out fast because they expected the tanker to roll and fuel to ignite the surface of the water at any moment. Club workers began to furiously move the members' boats out of the mooring area and down river about a mile, where they rafted them three and four together at anchor.

Wanting to get safely away from the scene, we passed the burning tanker very carefully and headed down river to anchor for the night. Friends arrived from Lumut the next morning and anchored within view of the club and the burning tanker, waiting to see what to do. By afternoon they radioed to tell us that the tanker was sinking and fuel igniting on the water.

The Yacht Club sits out over the water on steel piers. When the burning fuel traveled under the Club, the Club ignited and flames engulfed it. Our friends immediately headed down to anchor near us where we felt relatively safe from danger. Five big ships moved down to anchor by us as well.

At low tide the tanker sunk completely and the concern was now for the high tide. We headed back up and anchored amongst the boats rafted closer to the Club where it is an easy dinghy ride to shore.

The Yacht Club is still standing but is completely burned out. The mooring area is off limits until it is safe to put boats there again. The pontoons in front of the club, and to which the Sultan's big yacht was tied are charred black. All metal walkways going from the pontoons to the Club are completely melted, the windows in the Club are all gone, the front door is burned out and tables are burned up. Walls are black from floor to ceiling. Water and power weren't available this morning, but by afternoon were restored to the bar in the pool area. The shower/toilet rooms located in the back by the pool weren't affected. Everyone is in shock.

The real tragedy is in the lives lost. A Jingo boat pulled up while we were talking to some of the workers at the slipway this morning. It was dragging a body found on the water, only one of thirteen lives lost, and this has affected everyone here. Due to problems with the legality of the ship having docked there in the first place, the story will surely continue for some time.

On to more news that isn't so tragic. Five days ago I had that pterygium removed from my right eye. Our friend Jimmy Tan set us up with an excellent surgeon at Subang Jaya Hospital, a top rated hospital located about ten miles from Port Klang. All went well and I was awake for the thirty-five minute surgery, the eyeball deadened by a shot. The entire pterygium was cut out and a patch put over the eye.

After about an hour's rest back in my room, Don and I walked out and headed for the mall, returning to the hospital the following day for a checkup. I am to go back twice this week. We were very impressed with the hospital, the nurses, and the doctor, and I am very thankful to Jimmy Tan.

As for our social life, you may be interested to know that we have found a Hard Rock Café in Kuala Lumpur with all food flown in from the United States. Though it is adventurous, fun and tasty to eat the various ethnic foods that are so delicious, there is nothing comparable to real salads with blue cheese dressing, American bacon burgers and real strawberry milkshakes—a taste of home for the soul now and then.

Kuala Lumpur has lovely malls and we wander about and window shop. Very nice air-conditioned buses leave Port Klang for K.L. about every half-hour and make one change in Klang, four miles up the road, the trip taking about an hour to accomplish. A movie generally accompanies our ride, interrupted by the Muslim call to prayer on tape. The trip home is most often in the late afternoon when the buses are packed to overflowing, people standing in every available inch of space, even in the stairwells.

The locals don't queue up for buses. Everyone stands around quietly and politely waiting, but when the bus pulls up there is a rush toward the door, arms extended to grab the side of the bus by the steps to keep anyone else from getting in front of them. We are learning to approach this part of the journey with aggression if wanting to make it home that day! At the end of our adventurous day, on our arrival back at Port Klang we drag two very hot and tired bodies back to the Yacht Club.

As to daily living, our refrigeration is perking along beautifully thanks to the two additional Arco panels added in Tahiti. Water is no problem and has been plentiful since Singapore. Good showers were available at Lumut and Phuket and we enjoy the same here at the Yacht Club—we luxuriate.

Though laundry is always the perpetual chore, that ever-mushrooming pile is taken to the Chinese laundry in town where it is hand-washed in big tubs and hung to dry on lines running in every direction inside the big building. Everything is ironed—including underwear, socks, towels and washcloths. All is folded beautifully and packed back into the sail bag, the bag laundered and ironed as well. It is ready within two days and we take the cart back into town to collect it. With city visits to K.L., laundry chores in the hot sun have fallen into the background.

The boat haul-out went very well on the slip-way next to the club, a tide grid that *Windy Thoughts* moved onto at high tide. The boat-yard boys dove to check the bottom and to make sure that we were positioned correctly on the grid. Don checked all the thru-holes and changed all the zincs and the yard did the rest of the work. *Windy Thoughts* now sports the basic dark red bottom paint purchased in Thailand and seems ready to show it off. It looks good on her!

Next day:

Don has just been on the phone to his mother back home and learned that a tract of land on Lake Spokane that we sold has just paid off—and we have a little bonus in our kitty! Don talked about either coming home or making a trip to Bangkok, and his mother strongly advised us to go to Bangkok—because we are here and may never get the opportunity again.

Bangkok it is and plans are to take the train, with advice given to us by friends about the ins and outs of doing so. Tomorrow we will go to the train station in K.L. to make arrangements, hopefully leaving within the next week for three or four weeks. It will be a "grand vacation"!

August 4, 1992
Royal Selangor Yacht Club
Port Klang, Malaysia

Hello Dear Friend,

Four days ago we returned from nearly a month's land trip that included Bangkok and Chiang Mai, Thailand, a wonderful respite from our cruising days and a cultural experience that Don and I will remember forever. It was filled with new scenes, new foods and new experiences.

Life is rather rudely back to "normal" boat life again here in the Klang River on our *Windy Thoughts*. But it is good to be back in our own bed and back to Mr. Lin and the Yacht Club and all of those smiling faces that we have come to know and love here. It does feel like home!

The train was taken both ways, the entire cost for the two of us $80.00. Small, economical hotels with good restaurants provided accommodations, and we played tourist and did as much sightseeing as possible.

Our train passed through beautiful fields where people stopped their work to wave at us. Sometimes, locals boarded at designated stops and walked the aisles with trays of lovely treats to purchase. There might be sticky rice wrapped in leaves, or chicken satays with peanut sauce, or cool drinks to sooth our thirsty palates. We passed beautiful small Buddhist temples alongside the fields. We consumed wonderful food, luxuriated in a comfortable bed every night, fresh showers whenever we wanted them, meals out three times a day—and it was all a dramatic contrast to life aboard for the past four years.

We loved every minute of it—a total release from the cruising life.

Traveling light, we carried our leather backpacks and just one small bag each with an extra pair of shoes as well as important papers, a bar of laundry soap, toiletries and a small bar of soap and a washcloth. We packed a minimum of clothes and kept them washed.

Off we went, backpacks on our backs and feeling like newlyweds. Leaving the strikingly beautiful train station in Kuala Lumpur with its turrets and storybook architecture, we anticipated our sojourn with much excitement.

First class has sleeper compartments with air-conditioning. Second class has Pullman berths with or without air-conditioning, those without having fans. Third class was no sleeper at all, no air-conditioning and no fans. Friends advised us to get the more economical second-class with fans that they had found very comfortable. So, we purchased tickets in second-class with fans for the first leg—but when we boarded our car we found it stifling hot and filled with people, their luggage and baskets piled in the aisles, everyone trying to settle in for the night.

Our car was packed to overflowing. Don and I had upper berths across from each other, our bags in bed with us. The fans didn't work, but we expected they would when the train left the station, which wasn't for another long forty-five minutes. When they didn't, we lay in the upper berths feeling very claustrophobic from the intense heat and humidity. Little ones cried some initially but were quickly soothed; the children were very quiet and polite and must have slept through. Sleep always comes easily to Don, but I didn't crack a wink, instead concentrating on just breathing in and out in the stifling air.

Having witnessed the state of the bathroom during the night we decided to forego a wash up and try to deal with it off the train. So, we combed our hair, plopped on our sun hats and followed the people disembarking from the train in Butterfield the next morning. We changed our arrangements for the next two nights of our journey to Bangkok—from Pullman with fan to Pullman with air-conditioning.

A three-hour layover gave us some time to visit Penang Island, just across a bridge and a popular vacation island for Malaysians. A taxi driver was happy to escort us about and gave us a running description along the way.

We desperately needed to wash up, and when we got to Penang Island the driver drove a few miles up a hill to the oldest Buddhist temple in Malaysia. After leading us upstairs and around and through winding hallways, he spoke to one of the several monks he knew.

The monk smiled and led us down another hallway and into a big open room, pointing out some spigots on the wall over a big cement area into which we think we were to climb. Out came our toiletries carried in our fanny packs, and we washed in the cool, fresh water—but didn't climb in.

Feeling much fresher, we rejoined the driver and the monk who took us on a tour of the beautiful and ornate temple. As we walked along, the monk explained the temple's history and pointed out interesting aspects.

After leaving the temple, the taxi driver took us for a drive around Penang, and we readily gained an understanding of why so many come here for vacation, a lovely place.

The next two days on the train were adventuresome and we were like those two kids in a toyshop. Our second-class car with air-conditioning was beautiful, with comfortable seats by day that had footrests, and little tables pulled out for meals. At bedtime porters came through and made up our Pullman berths with crisp, white, freshly-ironed sheets. The car became a two level hotel with curtains to cordon off each private area. Above each berth was a light for reading.

Meals were a delight. We met a Thai family who were returning to Bangkok. The father spoke English and when we were passed cards to choose our foods at dinnertime, he asked us not to mark them, but to join him and his family in the dining car—whose existence we were unaware of. It was in the back of the train where all food for the hundreds of passengers was cooked in a few woks in one tiny kitchen at the end of the dining car. It was a long train, with perhaps ten passenger cars full to the brim. The Thai cooks kept busy preparing the most beautiful Thai dishes, all in a timely fashion.

Our Thai friend ordered for us and we sat at a table with a white tablecloth. The only others in the dining car were wearing uniforms of officials or the military. When the food arrived at our table, there were platters of six different Thai dishes, each heaped full to serve the six of us. More chicken with cashews, lemon grass chicken, Pad Thai and other dishes new to us. What a treat this new adventure was for us!

At the Malaysia/Thailand border, everyone had to disembark the train and passports were checked and stamped. A young American couple was pulled aside, their luggage opened on the ground and gone through and their papers found not to be in order. Something about their passports wasn't right. When we boarded the train to continue on, they didn't board with us but were taken inside the station with the Thai police.

For our first night's stay in Bangkok, we had our little slip of paper with the name of a hotel recommended by those Americans we met in the pool back on Langkawi Island. Our taxi was a Tuk Tuk with two covered seats behind a motorcycle. Bangkok is a huge city and traffic is unbelievable. Often, the Tuk Tuks can much more easily dodge in and out, going around the outside of a line of cars whenever necessary.

Our hotel appeared nice-looking and when we checked in the clerk asked Don how many hours we wanted the room. Puzzled, he told him that we wanted it for three nights for starters. The clerk's eyes grew big, but he nodded his head and made our arrangements.

Once upstairs in our room we freshened up, laundered the clothes worn so far, hung them up to dry and headed back downstairs to the restaurant for an early dinner. Bangkok sports some international cuisine and this restaurant specialized in authentic Louisiana Cajun food, prepared by Thai cooks!

About twenty waitresses, all young and lovely Thai women stood about. It was only 5 p.m. and we were the only patrons in the restaurant. I asked Don why they had so many waitresses.

The rooms were obviously rented by the hour, but we were a bit slow on the draw—though by now Don had a fair idea of where we may be. Still, our meal was exceptional, our room was good, and when it finally dawned on us what business the hotel catered to, we checked out the next morning. It wasn't an establishment where people checked in for more than a few hours at a time! A taxi drove us a long distance closer into the city and recommended another small and very reasonably priced hotel that turned out to be very pleasant.

This busy city has an amazingly continental cuisine and we decided to forego our daily rice and indulge in French, Italian, and good American food as well. That excellent Cajun meal had started us on a culinary binge. While taking great care of our stomachs, we also tried to do and see as much as possible.

Our first jaunt was to the Imperial Palace, arriving outside the gates at opening time in the morning to have the entire day to explore. When we stepped up to the guard, we were dismissed with the news that one does not visit the Imperial Palace wearing shorts! You cannot imagine the embarrassment we felt—and with tails between our legs we slunk off, to come back the next morning properly dressed. And it was an awesome day spent at this magnificent place.

Bangkok offers gilded Buddhist temples that dazzle the eyes—and we visited many of the more well-known, which have fascinating histories and are ornate beyond belief. Most impressive to see was the largest Golden Buddha in the world.

After five busy days in Bangkok we were back at the train station for the next leg of our adventure, heading further north to Chiang Mai, near the Burma/Myanmar border. This time we would have a first class compartment.

As we walked along the length of cars to reach our car at the back of the train, we noticed how sparkling clean they all were—until we got to the first-class cars that hadn't been washed down and looked very dirty. Our hearts took a nose dive. What were we in for?

After boarding, the interior of the train was as sparkling as we expected and our small compartment very nice after all. Our favorite activity was sitting and gazing out the window, watching the countryside pass by, watching the people working in the fields and pointing out to each other lovely, small Buddhist temples seen now and then amongst the green and lush scenery.

At meal times we were served in our own compartment on the tables that folded down, always a crisply ironed white linen tablecloth first placed ever so nicely on our table, followed by crisp white linen napkins placed in our laps—and then the most delicious piping hot food placed before us. If it was to be cold, it was crisply chilled.

For breakfast there was a choice of the more traditional Thai dishes, as well as eggs and toast. Always, there was freshly squeezed juice, fresh fruit and hot coffee or tea. For lunch we enjoyed a lovely Thai dish with rice, served with the same white linen service. At dinnertime we had a choice again of several dishes, along with that white linen service and cold drinks, as well as hot coffee or tea offered. Dessert was as beautifully prepared and served as we had become accustomed to expecting.

The Thai people greet you with genuine smiles and kindness and go out of their way to make everyone feel special, and our treatment on this train was only another example of their genuinely generous spirit.

Chiang Mai was fascinating. Numerous Buddhist temples beckoned us once again. At one temple we paid to set a caged bird free; another was a beautiful, ancient teak temple.

Lest you think that we saw nothing except every Buddhist temple in Thailand, we also visited an umbrella factory. Not the kind of umbrellas used when it rains but the beautifully painted decorative ones, made by people from the mountain villages who work at the small factory. Their skill and artistry are fascinating and this labor intensive work is performed with great pride.

Chiang Mai is the origin for trekking tours to visit the hill tribes of northern Thailand, but we decided to leave trekking to the more youthful backpackers, who described trekking up to their knees in mud, hiking up steep hills and riding on elephants. Don and I think about the indulgences of a hotel bed and the restaurant meals, and decide that the cruising life gives us enough adventure as it is!

Of the several different tribes, the Hmong tribe that helped the United States so much during the Vietnam War has their largest settlement just a day trek out of Chiang Mai. Each tribe is much like a country unto themselves, are all somewhat remote, and each has its own language, culture and dress. The trekking tours are in groups of four to eight people, as it isn't advisable to go on one's own into the Golden Triangle area.

When we boarded our train south toward *Windy Thoughts*, we headed to Lumut, Malaysia, in hopes that a mail package would be waiting for us. That night was spent at a hotel in a room on the second floor that had no windows. With the halls not lit at night, it was an eerie feeling, and we worried about waking up in the morning in time to catch our 7 a.m. train that would carry us south to Port Klang. With no phone in the room, wake-up calls were nonexistent, and we had to rely on our inner clocks. But we didn't miss our train!

August 15, 1992
Royal Selangor Yacht Club
Port Klang, Malaysia

Dear Friend,

Don called home today and, after hanging up, turned to me and asked, "Would you like to go home?"

Home! It has been three years since we last saw home and I am nearly physically ill with excitement! So what if we have no physical home there to call our own anymore—just setting foot on United States soil is home!

This is a safe place to leave our *Windy Thoughts*; she is our home now and we love her dearly. It will take at least a week to make all arrangements and by the end of August we should be back in our beautiful Washington, with family and friends. Don is aching to see his mountains.

I know that people think we are on a perpetual vacation on the boat, seeing the world. Lest we ever forget that it took so much to make this happen, or the blessings that we enjoy daily just to be here—there are many sacrifices required to float freely about out here. It sounds so blissfully easy, but can sometimes be so very hard. While we are ever thankful for everything that has come our way, for the enrichment our lives have experienced in seeing the world on *Windy Thoughts*, for every new experience—we want to come home, just for a while.

We want to drive around and cover lots of miles in a short time without planning and setting waypoints and poring over a chart and worrying about the wind and the weather. We want to sleep all night without standing watches, without any worries. We want to turn on a faucet without hauling every drop of water to and from the boat, after first finding places where we can even get potable water. We want to brush our teeth and let the water run—maybe just a little bit. We want to take all the showers we want when we want to take them.

We want to be with family again. We miss them terribly and have not had the luxury of flying back and forth for visits as many do. We gave all of this up to go cruising. After having some time to indulge ourselves in land-life's pleasures, we will long for this life aboard *Windy Thoughts* and the wonderful simplicity of cruising once again. We're coming home!

Chapter 9

Return to Malaysia

When you reach the end of your rope, tie a knot and hang on.
—Thomas Jefferson

Before we would face the realities of a return to Port Klang and those good people at the Royal Selangor Yacht Club, there would be far more time spent back home in the States than we could have anticipated when we boarded that plane in Malaysia.

Upon our arrival in the USA, we purchased a used car, giving us our own wheels without needing to depend on others for our transportation. Don's mother opened her home to us in Spokane and it was a wonderful few months with her.

When she left at the end of October to drive south to Mesa, Arizona, for the winter, we planned to close her place up and fly out two weeks later, to return to *Windy Thoughts* waiting for us in Malaysia. Don's mother left in good health and good spirits. Only a few days later a phone call from a hospital in Reno, Nevada, changed everything. She had suddenly taken ill during the night and was air-lifted to a hospital in Reno, where she passed away before Don and I arrived.

We stayed on in Spokane to settle all of her affairs. It was a difficult time emotionally for Don, for both of us. As time passed we began to see our way through the maze of paperwork and phone calls and life settled into a routine.

Winter brought snow in heaps and we got our skis out of storage and hit the slopes one or two days during the week when there were no lift lines—something not often experienced during our work lives when we skied on weekends.

Don often commented on how we were meant to come home when we did. We had those precious weeks with his mother and we had time with his friend, Jack Dean, before he too passed on after a battle with cancer.

As spring began to make way for summer, we had acquired considerable goods to haul back to the boat in Malaysia, four hundred pounds' worth! Not only were there the proverbial boat parts in great number, but there were all number of items such as canned foods, our Zip-loc bags, new clothes, and a new computer and printer, just for starters. So much accumulated that it would require boxing up and shipping it all back.

We did our homework and found that the most inexpensive way was by container ship. Weight wasn't a factor and an acceptable cubic space cost $250 shipped to any destination in the world. Six big packing boxes from U Haul filled the bill and considerable time was spent in the last weeks organizing and packing.

The boxes were shipped from Spokane via truck to a shipping company in Vancouver, British Columbia, Canada. A visit to Vancouver in person to speak with the head woman gave us confidence that they would take good care of our things. We had all of the paper work, the name of the ship and the date the ship was to leave Vancouver—everything in order on our end—so we thought. It would be shipped right to Port Klang, Malaysia. How fortuitous was that?

Shipping would take six weeks. To insure that it didn't arrive before we were back in Malaysia, we arranged to have it arrive in Port Klang about two weeks after our return. We thought that we had everything under such good control. After all, we were dealing with Canada and my—wasn't that easy for a change?

Its actual arrival, however, would be one more thorn in the flesh of our cruising life and we would have cause to expect that we may never see any of it again. However, that debacle comes after facing the results of *Windy Thoughts* sitting in the Klang River for so long.

For our last month at home we rented a small apartment in the lower level of the home of friends, Wally and Jim Coryat, in Seattle. Wally could be seen most days tending her flowers as we busied ourselves running to and fro for those last minute boat parts to add to those already shipped. These purchases had to be stuffed into sea bags to go back on the airplane with us.

It was also a particularly poignant time for us. Don's daughter Wendy lives in Seattle and our little grandson Taylor Scott was just two years old. Malaysia was a long way from someone so precious, and we knew that we were on borrowed time with opportunities to see family. That was the hardest part of the cruising life for us because we missed so much of their lives.

Don surprised me on my birthday near the end of July with a "Day of Beauty" at the Four Seasons Hotel in downtown Seattle. He dropped me off in the morning and I was treated to a full day of pampering, with a full facial, a full pedicure, a beautiful lunch—and then my hair was cut and styled before he picked me up at the end of the day to take me to a very special dinner.

As we sat by candlelight at the lovely restaurant, we just breathed in the ambiance. Very soon, we would be back on a plane and heading for our *Windy Thoughts* on the Klang River—and fried rice would be our choice as the order of the day. But oh, how good it would be!

And yes, it wasn't long before we were on our way back to our home afloat. Jim Coryat drove us to SeaTac Airport in the early morning of August 23, 1993. My dear friend, Susan, surprised us by being there to see us off. When she saw me carrying my three-piece suit from Bangkok back with me she asked whatever for? She would keep it in storage for me until we returned to land life. What would life be without dear friends like this?

Suddenly, it was time to step back into our cruising life again, to pick up where we had left off all those months earlier.

The first leg of our journey was the long flight that carried us from Seattle to Bangkok, Thailand, arriving in Bangkok at 11:30 p.m., Bangkok time. Blurry-eyed, we passed through the long procedure of Immigration and Customs, to get into bed at the hotel at 1 a.m. with a wake-up call for 5 a.m.

A nice buffet breakfast in the hotel helped to refresh us before readying for the flight to Kuala Lumpur, Malaysia. We were nearly back to our home and had transited the Atlantic and the Indian Oceans by plane in far less time than it took us to go the 300 miles from Singapore north to Kuala Lumpur, Malaysia, in the boat!

We had much more baggage than we had left with one year ago, but getting through Customs on arrival at the airport in Malaysia only took one minute. Don had a few boat parts in the bags, intending to get going on their installation before the big shipment arrived. A cruising sailor always has a "few boat parts" in his baggage. Anything that doesn't presently need fixing or replacing soon will, sometime down the line. Being prepared for the next small or the next major crisis is always right up there on the decision tree of what to bring back from points of civilization that you haven't seen in some time—and may not again in the foreseeable future.

When we arrived at the curb outside the airport, facing the temperature and humidity was a shock to the very core of our beings. Had we really lived in this same climate for the past years? How would we ever adjust to it again?

Pressing on, Don approached one of the taxis in the line at the curb. The driver took one look at our big cart piled high with the six large pieces of baggage and insisted that we needed two taxis. Don explained that it had all gone to the airport in one car and it could again. No deal with the driver—two taxis or nothing. But when Don walked over to another taxi, the driver changed his mind. And everything did fit into both the trunk and the back seat—as long as I lay precariously on top of the bags in the back seat.

Off we headed for the ten-mile trip that would take us back to Port Klang and *Windy Thoughts*. With no air-conditioning in the taxi, the windows were down, the hot and humid air rushing past our dripping bodies. Don sat in the front seat with one huge bag on his lap that obliterated his forward view and I, in my prone position in the back atop the other bags, held on and just concentrated on breathing in the sultry air.

Forty-three long hours after leaving Seattle, Washington, on August 23, 1993, we arrived back in Port Klang and the Royal Selangor Yacht Club in the mid-afternoon.

We were anxious to see how our *Windy Thoughts* had fared and were wondering just what we were coming back to. The Klang River is tidal, so isn't a clean river. Black soot, from a factory upriver, filters down onto the boats when the wind is just right—or even when there is no wind, to be honest.

Our Canadian friends, John and Francine on the *Red Baron*, passed through the Yacht Club in December. They faxed us in Spokane, reporting that they went aboard and all looked fine. We had them open lockers, lift cushions and just release the locks on the port in the head to let in some air.

The French friends were back at the Yacht Club in May and sent us a picture of *Windy Thoughts* on her mooring. The awning that Don had tied down as securely as possible over the boat did look droopy and the boat did look a bit forlorn. It was hard to tell a lot from the picture. Though our expectations were not particularly high for the state of things after a so many months of neglect in this climate, nothing prepared us for just how bad things would really be.

Prior to leaving home we faxed Saroja in the office, asking her to get us a room for our first two nights. She arranged a spot at the nearby Mariner's Center, a private club for the big ships' crews with a restaurant and pool.

As the taxi traveled along familiar roads and scenes on the quick trip to Port Klang, the months at home began to slip rapidly to the back of our minds. Within a few minutes we were pulling into the Royal Selangor Yacht Club, so far from our home country but back to our real home. Sparks of excitement began to share our exhaustion.

It was good to see familiar faces welcoming us—Saroja and the other women in the office and Mr. Lin in his spot now behind the bar at the pool. Tables were set up in a covered area  around the pool, forming the very nice main dining area since the fire in the Club. A kitchen was set up in a small bungalow nearby, and all was in good order and functioning nicely.

While gone, we had high hopes that a new Yacht Club would be underway. Instead, the remains of the old burned-out Club building still stood, the new to be underway soon. Problems with determination of liability for the fire stalled progress, and Shell Oil was taking no responsibility.

The Jingo boat drivers welcomed us back and helped us to load everything before setting off for our *Windy Thoughts*. She was visible from a distance, but we were unable to tell the state she was in until we approached closer.

Our wildest imaginations could not have prepared us for how bad she looked—forlorn and filthy beyond description. A thousand birds must have made her their home while we were gone, and bird droppings covered every centimeter of her exterior. Black soot and grime mixed with the droppings, and it looked as though the boat had been there for centuries. She was so filthy that we found it hard to even step aboard!

All bags were handed up and plopped down into the cockpit. When the Jingo driver left, we looked at each other and would have just bawled our eyes out right then, had we not been mature adults—at least one of us was.

As for the other—who would be me—I would be in tears in a very short time. It seemed that we had morphed in only seconds from the ease and pleasures of home—and the elegant goodbye dinner shared with Susan and Hal Brown just two nights before—into this steamy, hot and dirty environment of our home sitting in the Klang River, with no hope of things getting any better for a long time.

Don unlocked the companionway doors, uncertainty as to conditions below weighing heavy on our hearts—though with hopes it would be better. It didn't take stepping one foot below to know that we were mistaken. Everything smelled. A quick glance at the interior told us that there was a light film of mildew on every surface, as well as soot that must have made its way in via the forward port left slightly open. Mildew was literally everywhere, covering everything in every drawer, every locker, every nook and cranny. It hit us in the face and in our hearts. Our dear *Windy Thoughts* had suffered horribly from neglect.

Before leaving we had left the top of the refrigerator off to keep the box aired out. Someone had put it back on—Zainel, in his kind efforts to help when he checked on the boat— and its interior was a box of mildew.

We had given up the easy life back home and returned to something that, just then, seemed almost beyond our abilities to cope with. Because we were tired, jet lagged, and wilted from the heat and humidity, our spirits dived to an all time low. In addition, we sat in what right then appeared as the filthy Klang River. No matter that the beautiful old Royal Selangor Yacht Club was just ashore. Well, what was left of it—that being the pool and the eating area around the pool.

Leaving the bags in the dirty cockpit, I sat on the companionway steps and cried my eyes out—no longer the mature adult. Don's spirits, at a low point as well, didn't deter him from doing his best to try to look at the positive, reminding me that it would all be just fine and that we had so much to look forward to. I knew this intellectually, but emotionally was very aware of what lay ahead for us.

We were halfway around the world from that home we had left just forty-three hours ago and the contrast was so stark it had our heads spinning. These moments were just one of many low points in the dream. But then, it was sometimes necessary to remind ourselves that the high points were oh so high and so glorious in number.

We had chosen a different path than the easy and predictable one. It was that contrast to what we had always known that we had gone cruising for. We had chosen adventure and an opportunity to see some of God's great world. The only way we were to accomplish this was by pulling ourselves up by our own bootstraps. We were reminded once again that nothing in life worth doing comes easily. Things could be much worse—the boat hadn't sunk. This too shall pass!

The Jingo boat came around once again a half-hour later, and we were standing at the ready to board and head right back to shore, to face all of this the next day. The new hair-do that I had been so happy with in Seattle lay flat to my head with perspiration, not likely to look again as it once did. Cold drinks at the Club and relaxing in its nice surroundings in a stupor of denial of what awaited us in the next days raised our spirits enormously.

We hiked to the Mariner's Center and found our room was air-conditioned, with twin beds and a bathroom with a shower. Air conditioning, a shower and a bed seemed just about heaven itself to us just then.

Because it was Friday, the Muslim holy day, there was a plethora of food stalls, as well as the Friday night market on the streets in town. Though exhausted, we had a kind of nervous energy to burn and headed into town to get ourselves some supper and to renew our minds and spirits in this culture. It was good to see the sea of faces so missed for the past months, the beautiful and colorful dresses of the Muslim women and the lovely saris on the Indian women. The ever present smiles on the Chinese faces made us realize how fortunate we were to be back.

Easing right back into this fascinating culture, we found ourselves excited once again to be so far from our own. Plastic buckets, brushes and cleaning supplies were easily purchased for the cleaning projects to come.

Back in our room, we collapsed into our beds at 6 p.m. and slept like the dead until 6:00 the following morning. The Mariner's Center had a nice restaurant where we enjoyed eggs and toast for our breakfast, perking up already to face the day before trudging back to the club with buckets, brushes and cleaning supplies in tow.

When we reached the Royal Selangor Yacht Club, our spirits took a giant leap upwards when we found *Windy Thoughts* alongside the pontoon in front of the club! Unbeknownst to us, Zainel had towed her from her mooring and tied her to the pontoon when he arrived at 6 a.m.. There would be water hook-up for a hose! This kindness nearly brought us to our knees.

Overwhelmed, we had been unable to comprehend just how we could accomplish the enormous job with five-gallon jugs of water carried back and forth from shore. Right back to the basics and nothing like water, a hose and a dock right then could have been any more appreciated. The pontoons are for the Raja Muda and the Sultan's yachts and not for itinerant moorage, so we knew it was a privilege to be here.

Zainel made two boat boys available for hire and we had the privilege of working with both Mon and Morka for the next three days. They were waiting for us on the dock on Saturday morning and we began washing down the exterior of the boat.

Don took every bit of fabric off the boat—sail cover, awnings, bimini top, fuel can covers and life raft cover. The boys put all of this to soak in barrels of water with soap. Thankfully, everything was of Sunbrella, a material that can withstand about anything. Don's love affair with Sunbrella goes back a number of years. His Spokane Tent and Awning Company sold more than any retail company in the country when it first came on the market.

Then, Don took everything out of the aft berth, including the mattress, and piled it all in the cabin in order to get at the diesel fuel tank located under the aft berth. Our cabin was now not only dirty and grimy, but also near impossible to traverse from stern to bow without some gymnastics that required climbing up and over or under many items. There would be lots of hosing topsides so those six large sea bags were now amongst all of this. All ports had to be tightly closed and Don worked below in an unbearably hot and humid environment.

But as always, you do what you have to do.

For the next two days, Don barely saw the light of day as he worked below, pumping eighty gallons of diesel out of our tanks by hand with the hand pump into the five-gallon jerry cans. He lugged them one at a time up to the yard and dumped the diesel into barrels for the boys working in the yard who wanted it for some diesel machinery.

Mon and Morka called us Mr. Don and Madam and were there by 6:00 each morning to work alongside of us. That first day the three of us scrubbed our hearts out until 4 p.m., when we collapsed in joy to see that *Windy Thoughts'* topsides were actually beaming again! The dodger looked beautiful and her teak gleamed like a newborn baby.

As for Don and me, we looked like two shipwreck victims, our clothes sopping wet with perspiration as well as water from the hose, our hair just a wet mop plastered to our heads—and we were beyond exhaustion. It was exhaustion, however, that comes from hard work. Neither of us is susceptible to sunburn, but so much time away from the tropical sun's rays had produced some reddened skin.

Gathering our shower bags and clean clothes, we high-tailed it up to the showers to stand under fresh running water to our hearts' content, scrubbing ourselves until our reddened skin could stand no more. Donning clean clothes, followed by a good meal by the pool and socializing with others there, we were feeling nearly normal. We were home again.

Then we dragged two very tired and sore bodies the two miles back to the Mariner's Center on foot, to collapse into bed at 6 p.m. and to sleep once again like the dead.

Back at the boat by 6:00 the following morning, we had already worked ourselves into a sweat just walking to the club in the heat and humidity. Mon and Morka were waiting for us, and they spent the day waxing topsides. Don was below at his post, upside down in the fuel tanks. He managed to finish pumping out diesel as well as haul gallons and gallons of new diesel—and to fill both of the tanks and the jerry cans, an all-day job for him.

By the end of day two, *Windy Thoughts* was smiling at us. Could this all be happening in just two days? Certainly, without Mon and Morka it would have been many days for just Don and me alone.

Hope springs eternal with good old elbow-grease. When it gets right down to it, much of cruising life is just a healthy dose of that good old elbow-grease along with an intense desire not to drown.

Don made it known that he wasn't going to spend another night in the Mariner's Center. It had been an oasis for two nights, but he was ready to sleep in our own home. So Sunday night we stowed everything back in the aft berth, put the six sea bags up in the cockpit and made up beds on the settees. After showers, we emerged two normal-looking people once again, ready for a good dinner at the Club before falling into our own beds this time, bone weary, bruised and sunburned once again.

Ah, yes, back to the cruising life! But I wasn't cooking and we had this wonderful Club to adjourn to at the end of each day's work—with beautifully prepared dishes that set our hearts and stomachs right again as soon as we morphed from the realities of boat work into the pleasures of Club food and relaxation. Yes, there were blessings!

On our third day at work, Mon and Morka washed out all of the fabric soaking in the big barrels and hung it to dry. Don put it back on the boat before making two trips on foot to the hardware store in town, a half-hour hot walk going, an even hotter one on return. He was about the business of unpacking some of the spare parts and things that needed installing—and then beginning some of these projects.

I headed below to take all of our clothes out of the hanging lockers and drawers and sort what to keep and what not to keep. Every drawer was scrubbed with bleach before our home was ready to move back into properly!

By Tuesday we were attacking the next round of chores in our attempt to make *Windy Thoughts* livable again and ready her for her delight, sailing oceans and cruising to magical places. Don dove on the boat, not a pleasant chore in this river with its strong currents and zero visibility. Barnacles had grown over the thru-hull for the sea-water pump and scraping them off and cleaning that up while down there was added to his list of jobs in the deep. He checked all thru-hulls, as well as the condition of the bottom and that of the prop. All was a merciless mass of those full-fledged barnacles that had made their home on *Windy Thoughts'* bottom and would need his undivided attention.

While down there, he cut off a rope found wrapped around the propeller. The engine had started up on the first try, but with white smoke and then very black smoke coming out the exhaust. Though he made a very thorough check on the engine, he hoped that finding this wrapped rope solved that problem—not yet aware of serious engine problems that lay ahead.

Every inch of the cabin's interior was scrubbed, including the inside of all lockers. Hundreds of cans were taken out, each one scrubbed thoroughly and sorted into one of three piles—one pile for what we would save—one pile for what we would throw out—and one for what we would give away, this last group turning out to be a substantial amount.

Zainel put the big Yacht Club dinghy behind us and we loaded big garbage bags full of canned food into it. It was time for a turnover and we had this huge shipment coming—part of which was canned foods that we couldn't find here. It seems that if you purchase things whose appeal you question but feel might fill in to make a meal or provide some variety, it probably won't be used. There were those canned peas, for one. What was for give-away went to the workers' coffee room and disappeared rapidly.

The prior year I had made friends with Talianna, a Tamil Indian woman who cleaned at the club. She was the recipient of as much as was possible. Talianna's husband was in a recuperation facility and she was the sole support of seven young children. She worked thirteen to sixteen hour days, seven days a week, but remained so very cheerful and friendly. Each time that I took something up to her she would get all teary-eyed and I would follow suit, unable to keep the tears at bay.

Zainel moved us back a boat's length on the pontoon and we didn't have to go back to the mooring as soon as we thought. Still, we didn't want to push our luck—we weren't members and rightfully shouldn't be on this pontoon.

Don faced his tool drawer and tool lockers, every tool covered with a film of mildew and needing a cleaning. The water tanks would have to be emptied and their insides cleaned thoroughly, not an easy chore.

Every dish, pot and pan and piece of silverware would need a wash in bleach and each locker in the galley needed a scrubbing. All of our meals were eaten at the Yacht Club, where very good food was available in a nice atmosphere and at a very reasonable cost—a treat for us as well as an escape from our chores.

Unable to go a day here without our rice, for only $2.00, we enjoyed our favorite lunch of fried rice, delicious, always with bits of chicken or seafood, and served with a bowl of the hottest of red chilies. Don found one bowl sufficient to fire up his palate, but I always required two, having become immune to the effects of one bowl.

Zainel would put us back on our mooring on Thursday at slack tide. Don was anxious to start the installation of both the new autopilot and the windspeed indicator that he had carried back on the plane, and to get the engine fixed and re-aligned—this all to be done before the container shipment arrived full of more work for him. Some projects were easier to attack at the dock with electricity available, so he worked on these first.

MINGLING WITH ROYALTY

September 3, 1993
Royal Selangor Yacht Club
Port Klang, Malaysia

Salamet Pagi,

Life aboard is looking up tremendously, though we are still rising at daylight and keeping our sore muscles busy until dinnertime. The high point of our days is when we head up to the showers and then relax over some good food. Oh, for those pristine beaches and quiet anchorages of cruising again! There is so much to be thankful for right here, however, and we don't forget our good fortune that *Windy Thoughts* sits safely where she does, that we have use of so much fresh water and that we have had so much good help.

Imagine how relieved we were to learn from Zainel yesterday of a place right here in Port Klang that repacks life rafts! We thought we would have to fly to Singapore to have it done.

Next thing we knew, Zainel made an appointment for us and a man showed up at the boat to take both the life raft and us in tow to his service center. When he opened the raft for inspection, all was in excellent condition—other than flares that were outdated and needed replacement, as did the water packages, first aid kit, etc. We looked at the pitiful amount of life saving supplies that came packed with the life raft and wondered that anyone could survive more than a day or two. Thank goodness for our grab and run bag.

In the end, it was no cheaper for the repacking than in the United States, so it was a very expensive service, but one that is vital. To think of the thousands of dollars we spend on something that we sincerely hope and pray never to have to use!

Yesterday, too much sun along with an apparent bug had me collapsed on the settee in the afternoon. A distinguished-looking gentleman came by to invite Don and me to a christening party that evening for the Raja Muda's new fifty-five-foot Beneteau sailboat that has been on the pontoon all week. The huge power yacht belonging to the Raja Muda's father, the Sultan, was just opposite us on the pontoon. *Windy Thoughts* did look a bit derelict in her deplorable condition when she first arrived on the pontoon next to the Sultan's yacht, but we believe that she need not be ashamed of herself anymore.

Not wanting to miss an evening with royalty, I foraged about in the newly packed drawers and lockers for appropriate clothes. Out came the little DC iron and the little tabletop ironing board. Dirty hair, broken fingernails and chipped toenail polish were not about to deter me—though I was finding it difficult to even stay on my feet due to the nausea. Don was just as excited about the evening. This would certainly be a change in pace from our past few days!

After 1.5 hours in the shower room for me, much less for Don, we emerged presentable, Don looking downright spiffy in his perfectly creased new microfiber slacks and new silk shirt. I wore a new outfit brought back from home. My, it was good to have my new hairdo, a bit of make-up and a new outfit—and real shoes instead of thongs. I know—someday we will long for those barefoot days in the sun!

By now, large buffet tables as well as chairs were set up on the pontoon. Mr. Lin and the others were working hard to bring this all together, with many trips up and down from the Club with drinks carried on big trays from the pool bar.

They work very hard here. Mr. Lin starts work at 7 a.m. and quits at midnight, seven days a week. He stays in a small cottage behind the club and has three days off every month, when he drives down to Malacca to his home and his wife and children. He kids about being the F& B, or food and beverage man, has been working at the club for years and is very highly respected.

Don and I sat at the Club watching guests arrive before making our way down the ramp to the party. Of the approximately 100 guests, we didn't know a soul—but with a glass of champagne in one hand and an appetizer in the other, we set off to try to blend in with the upper crust.

The royal as well as governing class must be a Bumiputra, or native Malay, and we perused the crowd to try to pick out the Raja Muda. When we saw a jolly fellow who seemed to be the life of the party, I blithely stated that I knew royalty when I saw it. We wanted to thank him for our invitation, but weren't sure just how to properly address him. Do you say, "How do you do, Raja Muda" or "How do you do, your Royal Highness?"

We decided on using the Raja Muda form of address, introduced ourselves and thanked him for inviting us to the christening of his new boat—commenting on how beautiful it was.

He roared with laughter, introduced himself as Jo Jo, and explained that he was the Raja Muda's finance and business manager. Because we were visiting cruising people, he was curious about us and wanted to know about our cruising life.

Then he grabbed us and took us over to introduce us to the Royal Prince himself, who along with his wife and little two-year old son had been sitting up at the club very near us prior to the party. Perhaps we might have exchanged pleasantries had we known who they were.

The Raja Muda was welcoming, very open and easy to visit with, and it wasn't  hard to understand why the Malaysian people like him so much. His wife is an American from San Francisco. He wanted to know all about our cruising and our boat and even wanted to see *Windy Thoughts*. Think of that! We gave him a tour and afterward toured his new boat. We admired the gear topsides, commented on the electric winches, the anchor and other things that were so impressive.

Then we went below. What opulence! It was a stock hull, but with a custom interior that had every amenity, including air-conditioning. The master cabin had a round bed that Don and I knew would be difficult to stay on at sea. Don drooled over the navigation station. It was a beautiful boat—but we were happy with our own *Windy Thoughts*.

Jo Jo invited us to see the Sultan's yacht, which was off limits and not open for visitors. We boarded and gazed around with wonder at what was truly opulence here. We were shown every nook and cranny, including the Sultan's private stateroom. His and her baths were connected in the middle with a big spa, all fixtures in solid gold. You can imagine it as like one of the coffee-table books entitled *Fabulous Yachts of the World*.

All in all, our "high society evening" was a radical departure from our daily life thus far in Port Klang.

This morning we awoke to reality, gathered up scrub brushes, polish, screwdrivers and wrenches, and normalcy is returning to our lives aboard. We will keep you posted should there be any imminent changes in our social lives here from deck hands to personal protégés of "the Raj", as we are now privately referring to the Royal Prince. Since this doesn't appear too likely, we continue life here in Port Klang as usual. It is good.

September 28, 1993
Royal Selangor Yacht Club
Port Klang, Malaysia

Hello Friend,

Things are quite normal now and as of yesterday we are out of the water, on the hard stand and can sleep aboard right here. *Windy Thoughts* went on the tide grid at high tide at 5 a.m. and is ready for new anti-fouling. Barnacles have been scraped and today she should get a new bottom. Don is replacing zincs and I have done my share of scraping barnacles on the thru-hulls. Meanwhile, the adept yard crew is going at it full bore.

Last night we got a horrid Sumatra wind of 50 knots that had me nervous as a cat. I worried that the boat might be blown over on the hardstand, and instead of us dying at sea we would die right here in the boatyard—crushed, under 20,000 pounds of boat. Only a few two-by-four boards propped us up along the sides.

Don only sighed, turned over and went back to sleep. I made my way down the ladder and over to the shower room to wait it out—much safer there, I was sure. He could go down with the boat if he chose.

Au Chin, the diesel mechanic, worked on the engine all day. Hopefully, he is aligning it. Au Chin comes from a fishing village on a nearby island and grew up working on fishing boats. He seems to have a slight neurological problem that makes his movements somewhat spastic. Each time he comes aboard we worry that he will misstep and fall off the ladder or the boat—more on falling off the boat to follow. Don is a bit worried about the alignment, as Au Chin has great difficulty in holding any tools steady, but forges full speed ahead.

I stayed at the club all day, reclining by the pool in a comfy chair positioned so that a fan blew on me all afternoon. Tomorrow the fun is over and I will get busy cleaning the bottom of the dinghy and then painting it. The boys are busy with the hose today and so I repose.

Don remains so understanding of the difficulty of shopping for food and then cooking, with the boat in a state of disarray that seems to be the norm rather than the exception. We continue to eat at the club. The companionway steps are taken out while Au Chin works on the engine, so we can't even get below. Otherwise, Don is working on the engine and in my way, his legs sticking out right into my little galley. What a shame that he can't multitask while there!

Not only that, we have found the bigger markets at Subang Jaya or at

Kuala Lumpur to have better food selection. If you want anything refrigerated, you may as well forget that in the time it takes to get it back to the boat. A small grocery in Port Klang provides some basics, and the huge wet market is very good—but with the prices of meals so very inexpensive at the club and the food so good, we can hardly justify not eating right here during the boat turmoil.

I don't argue the point! We are experimenting with ordering new and different foods, but there is always some western style food on the menu. The one dish that we can't tolerate is a delicacy here, made with shrimp that is put out in the sun until it rots and then stir fried with chilies. The smell from the kitchen literally drives us right away from the club. It is a popular dish on Saturday nights, and perhaps a try at it would change our attitude, as it is said to be truly delicious.

Don had what could have been a very bad mishap here yesterday. When checking something out on the bow of the boat, he swung a leg over the lifeline—and somehow lost his balance. Suddenly, there wasn't anything to grab onto and he fell from the bowsprit of the boat down to the asphalt, a good ten feet or more.

Sure that he was badly hurt, everyone came running. Miraculously, he wasn't hurt at all, but had broken his fall with his hip on a can of bottom paint and was covered nearly head to toe with it. The worst that happened is that the anti-fouling immediately reacted on his skin—and while we were all concerned for broken bones or concussion, he was suffering from burning skin. He headed right into water that you don't even want to splash on you while riding in the Jingo boat.

The salt water only made it worse so he ran straight up to the showers, where I stood him under the water and scrubbed him down as best as possible. After cleaning up, he was left with reddened skin that burned for the next few days. Mr. Lin gave him some ointment that Don reports to be very soothing, some Chinese remedy. His hip was sore and very badly bruised and other bruises began to appear soon after the event, but he was whole and not hurt.

We were invited to spend a few days in Malacca with our friend Jimmy Tan, a club officer and a very active angler in these waters. He has a Nestle distributorship in Kuala Lumpur and had to go to Malacca on business. His son, Simon, home on break from Edinburgh University in Scotland where he is studying architecture, also joined us. Simon would prove to be a great guide for us in historical Malacca.

After arriving on Thursday evening, we all enjoyed Portuguese food at the Portuguese Center, located at a very scenic spot right on the ocean. Jimmy and Simon introduced us to so many interesting new dishes.

Jimmy also arranged for our hotel, a small and reasonably priced place that was very nice. He had a conference to attend on Friday, so arranged a driver for us from Nestle.

Malacca is a beautiful and very interesting historical small city. Simon provided a fascinating lesson on the Portuguese, Dutch and British influence in Malacca while we visited many lovely buildings that are 500 years old. Both Simon and our driver were a wealth of information.

One of the more interesting sights is the old historical fort. After dark that evening, we all attended a light show depicting the captures of the fort constructed by the Portuguese after capturing the harbor in 1511. Later, the fort was captured by the Dutch in 1641, giving them exclusive lock on the spice trade until 1785, when the British East India Company, wanting a safe port for their ships on the way to China, was allowed to build a fort on the island of Penang.

The competing European powers needed an open trade route to the Far East, wanting to establish their own trading ports at the source. At the beginning of the sixteenth century, the spice trade was routed through Egypt, and no non-Muslim vessel was permitted to dock in Arabian ports. Consequently, the Malacca Strait became an important trade route. With its rich and fascinating past, we were indeed fortunate to have this opportunity to be reintroduced to history right on the spot!

On Friday we were introduced to another sort of history, in the form of 100-year-old eggs, during a dinner enjoyed at a Chinese restaurant owned and operated by a friend of Jimmy's. The eggs were black, in brine and considered a real delicacy here. Jimmy purchased one for each of us, and we won't soon forget 100-year-old eggs!

It has been a joy to experience the different cultures and foods in Malaysia: native Malay, Chinese and Indian—all so different and each culture blending with the others, making the foods so delicious. Jimmy has often introduced us to Chinese dishes that we would never have opportunity to enjoy were it not for his kindness. It is an enlightening experience for two untraveled people who remain like those kids in a candy shop, enjoying every new experience.

Jimmy has gone out of his way to be kind to us and bought me a beautiful Chinese tea set made of clay pottery, explaining how to properly make tea. First you must pour boiling water over the very proper teapot, so diminutive that it looks like a child's tea set. There is a particular way to do all of this and certainly, I must learn to imbibe tea in a more delicate and well-mannered fashion!

Before leaving Malacca, Jimmy purchased a special gift for Don as well— a gold ceramic toad with a coin in its mouth, such as the Chinese business people often have in their shops. In the morning, the toad is turned so that it faces the door to let wealth in for the day. At closing, it is turned with its back to the door to keep the money from going back out during the night. Will it work for us?

The night before our vacation we had gone into Kuala Lumpur, to be ready to leave from there with the Tans on Friday morning, and stayed that night with young friends. Eric Oh is a club member who showed up at our boat that first week when back in Port Klang, remembering us from a Ham radio contact fully two years ago. He has his own Ham station set up in his home and back then heard us calling on the radio when approaching the Yacht Club and made radio contact with us. We have frequently enjoyed his company since.

Eric lives in Kuala Lum-pur with his wife Cathy and two year-old Johann, a delightful little bundle of energy. Their home is in a young neighborhood of terrace houses with three bedrooms, three baths and tons of toys! Johann is already an ace on the computer and loves his computer programs for little ones. Eric and Cathy have given so much of themselves to make us feel welcome in their country.

[We have kept in touch with the Ohs over the years and consider them a very special part of our Malaysian memories.]

Our experiences have been varied and we have been privileged to meet many interesting and friendly people who have all been so good to us. We greatly treasure the friendship of Jimmy Tan, who has introduced us to new foods, new people and new places—and with whom we have shared many a good conversation and meal when he is at the Club on Sundays. How honored we feel to be invited to join him at his table. We treasure the friendship of Zainel, a capable and hard worker who is in charge of the boat works. Mon, the boatyard boy, is never without a smile and has gone out of his way to be helpful to us. We appreciate the opportunity to share a friendship with Eric and Cathy Oh, who seem to have taken us under their wings.

Mr. Lin is always a joy to be around and never complains about the hours or the hard work. One day he told us of how, at seven years of age, he escaped China along with his mother and father and three siblings, one a baby, the other two younger than him. It was a heartfelt story of deep sadness, though he didn't try to make it so.

He spoke of the freezing cold in China when they didn't have coats or shoes. He told of a very small boat into which they bravely set off into the

South China Sea, the drowning of first the baby and then his mother, and the starvation of his other siblings on the long trek to freedom without food, water, or shoes—and with only the clothes on their backs. They survived under the most horrific of conditions and only he and his father were alive when they reached Malaysia. It was many years before he had his first shoes on his feet, and he told of the rats nibbling at his toes during the nights of his childhood, a childhood that was a nightmare difficult for most of us to comprehend.

We thought his life here rather sad, away from his family in Malacca most of the time and working such long hours—until we heard his story and realized how good his life has become. He has a highly respected job here at the Yacht Club and told us that he has no longings for anything more. He and his family have food on the table every day—and shoes on their feet.

The container shipment is still held up. We were hoping to be out of here and headed back north to enjoy the islands again before setting off across the Indian Ocean from Phuket at the end of December or early January. The most recent of many faxes to the shipping company in Vancouver was finally answered, telling us there had been a "slight delay". The ship should now arrive about October 16. So we hurry up and wait.

Meanwhile, we have kept very busy with boat chores, daily life here, and enjoying our forays into K.L. We are never bored and have lived through the worst to face us on our return, to emerge intact and still capable of having much fun and enjoyment too! Weekends are the busy time here when the club members come to spend all day Saturday and through dinner Saturday night, or to spend all of Sunday. We have met several and enjoyed their company thoroughly.

Evelyn and Rudy, the Swiss couple on *Scorpio*, went back to Switzerland for a visit but returned a week after us, and the four of us are the only cruising folks here. By the end of October and into November the cruising crowd will begin arriving as they make their way north toward Phuket and then points west, for those going on this year.

Many join the Raja Muda Race at the end of November, starting here at the Royal Selangor Yacht Club and ending in Phuket, with a couple of stops in between for dinners and parties. It is a very well organized event and done up big time for all who join. Many join to be in the company of a large group out of fears of piracy in the Strait—not a bad idea! Following this auspicious race event is The King's Race in Thailand, set for the King's birthday on December 5, and many boats combine the two events. We still prefer going on our own cruise or bobbling along with another boat or two, and have difficulty living with someone else's schedule, or converging on some remote spot en masse.

I have oiled and rubbed down all of the interior teak; we hauled the rugs into Kuala Lumpur on the bus to a professional rug cleaning business and will soon take the cushions into the city for reupholstering. Almost new!

Any boat part shipped in and marked in value less than $50.00 is by law to carry no customs duty. A starter switch just arrived with two engine hoses from Doc Freeman's in Seattle. This small package was marked $38.00 in value but was held at UPS until we paid $163.00 in customs duty!

A club member is acting as our agent for our shipment's arrival and assures us that we are not to worry about any duty—he says he can handle everything. We keep our fingers crossed.

It appears that we will be here much longer than anticipated, but we will make the best of the amenities offered. Though we may not be sitting in turquoise waters off a pristine beach, we won't have this ease of life for a long time to come, once we start the trek across the Indian Ocean and up the Red Sea. But ease of life is how you look at it and cruising again has its own ease unlike any other lifestyle.

November 6, 1993
Royal Selangor Yacht Club
Port Klang, Malaysia

Salamet Pagi dear friend,

Yes, we are still here and awaiting our shipment that seems to be out there in La La Land somewhere. That is, we hope it might be.

Meanwhile, the new autopilot that Don carried back on the plane from home doesn't work and we await a replacement from England—make that a replacement for the replacement that didn't work. The Auto Helm representative in Kuala Lumpur was busy and couldn't do the installation of the first replacement autopilot himself, but came out to the boat to do the calibrations on the new one after Don spent two weeks installing it. The warranty is void if anyone other than a Nautec engineer does the work, but John would sign off after doing the calibrations.

The outcome was that there was something wrong in the computer box and an entire new unit was sent out from England. After installing this new one there was something wrong with the ram—that has now also been sent to England. Meanwhile, we pay for the shipping back and forth of these replacements, as well as very high duty each time.

As to our shipment of goods, it seems it is a fight to the finish on our part though we are not sure an end will be seen. The woman with whom we originally made shipping arrangements in Vancouver won't take our calls, nor answer faxes. Our shipment is out there somewhere—maybe in Hong Kong—maybe in Singapore. No one knows for certain and there appears to be no way to find out.

Through no small effort on our part, we have finally learned that Vancouver shipped via Hong Kong, and not through Singapore as it states on our

Bill of Lading. Communication with Hong Kong is very difficult and trying to find out anything from the shipping agent here in Port Klang gets us nowhere, because they know nothing about it.

Now we are told that the shipment "might be" in Singapore, but the woman I talk to in Singapore has a heavy Mandarin accent and I understand little of what she is saying. In turn, she doesn't understand what I am trying to tell her, and when asking to speak to a superior he is unable to give us any information. They just don't know where it is. Could they find out? Probably not. Who could we talk to who might be able to help us? Don't know. Ships come into Port Klang from Singapore every day. Might our goods be found if they are there and then shipped up here? No one knows.

If you wonder what I do every day, I stand at the pay phone—because Don can't understand a thing she says, nor can he even hear her very well. He ultimately encourages me to become the ugly American because we are at the end of our rope. But our countrymen aren't really like that. Wherever we go, without exception, we are repeatedly told how friendly and generous Americans are. Ugly American seems largely a term conjured up by those back home.

Forging ahead with the problem, I do, however, become somewhat impolite and demanding and it has now been determined in very short order that our shipment is in Singapore—well, maybe—and it will arrive here on November 12—maybe.

After that phone call I am filled with shame, because rudeness and confrontation are neither a part of this culture, nor a part of my make-up. It seems that the problem with our shipment stems directly from Vancouver's initial foul up. They issued us the wrong booking number and sent insurance papers for half the amount that we paid for, stalling everything—somewhere.

We hired a boat boy who washes member boats—a new experience for us. It is difficult to keep the boat clean out here on the mooring with the soot that collects, and this was to keep it up after all the work put into getting it looking so nice again. The agreement was that he would come one day a week for $20.00, a very high wage here. We didn't expect there to be a number of weeks before we would be out of here. It was agreed that he would keep the gel coat polished as well as the stainless and would also clean the water line each week.

He has been coming two times a week, sometimes three, staying for perhaps an hour one time, two hours the other times and charging us the $20.00 each time—but never cleaning the entire boat. The first week we paid him $60.00. Will we never learn? We felt sorry for him and thought that we were helping him. He is from Burma and seemed a nice young man. He has a cell phone and spends much of his time making long calls back to Burma (make that Myanmar—I can't get used to these changes). The phone belongs to his boss and he isn't to be using it. He has also lied to us about his time that we have carefully tracked.

Don handled the matter and fired him, tactfully explaining why in a not to be misunderstood manner. It was a few days ago, when I wasn't yet in the fighting mood that I worked myself into today while handling the shipping business.

On a much happier note, last Sunday we attended a traditional Muslim wedding down in Malacca—where Zainel's family lives. Zainel's sister was the bride. He invited both Don and me along with Rudy and Evelyn from *Scorpio*, and the four of us traveled together in Rudy's car for a weekend that was a very memorable experience.

We drove down to Malacca on Saturday morning. Our accommodations were on the top floor of a small hotel that was literally no more than twenty feet in width, but rose up four stories. Going up the stairs we had to turn side-ways in order not to bump against the walls and were all in hysterics by the time we reached the fourth floor. It takes very little to entertain us. It worked best to approach the bed from the foot and climb aboard that way. We could roll over and bump against the wall of Rudy and Evelyn's room.

Evelyn had never been to Malacca, so she joined Don and me in jaunting about for the day. Rudy wasn't interested in antique shops and museums and went back to the room to take a nap—but got claustrophobia and found a place to sit outside and enjoy a cold beer.

Zainel had given us directions as to how to get to the "wedding place" and we called him Saturday night to double check on time and directions. All was set and we were to arrive at 11a.m. It was about eight miles out of Malacca in Kampong Tudong, a traditional rural village set amongst palms and lots of foliage. Traditional Malay houses sat prettily up on stilts with their colorful curtains dancing in the breeze.

We didn't witness the wedding ceremony itself, nor apparently did anyone else. The celebration afterwards was for the gathering of family and friends and is traditionally at the groom's family home. Zainel is one of ten children and we met all of his family, including that of his wife, Hattia, a sister of the groom.

Long tables were set up outside and the women of the village had been preparing food for a week. The men of the village slaughtered a cow on the previous day and huge cooking pots sat over open fires—the men gathered there in charge of the beef curry. Because we didn't know when or if we might be eating at the event, we had downed a big breakfast prior to leaving the hotel. The very moment we arrived at the wedding event, we were seated at a table and women started bringing food to us.

There were huge platters of rice, dishes of the beef curry, plates of cucumbers, and salads of every kind imaginable. Having given it a whirl during that Kavali ceremony, we felt quite adept at using our fingers as utensils and bravely dug in. They brought on more. We smiled and tried to explain that we were full to the limit. The curry was delicious. They brought yet more, wanting to please us, and we didn't want to offend anyone. We smiled and tried to appear to be eating while licking our fingers—and they still brought more. Somehow we found room to enjoy much of the good cooking, a wonderful culinary pleasure for all of us.

We were invited into the home of the groom's father where the newlyweds would live. Two very nice chairs were all decorated up like thrones awaiting the bride and groom. People sat on rugs on the floor.

Then the bride and groom arrived—the big moment of the day! We rushed up the village path with the others, cameras at the ready. The young bride and groom walked slowly as if down the aisle, with several young men chanting and beating on drums.

When the newlyweds reached the house they were ushered in and sat in the chairs, just like a king and queen, looking like royalty in their beautiful traditional wedding attire. Everyone sat on the floor looking at them—including the four of us. The newlyweds didn't crack a smile, surely uneasy at being on display, though perhaps this is the custom.

Don and I thoroughly enjoyed the day. Rudy was bored and would have preferred to be having a cold beer. Zainel solved the problem when he invited us to meet him in the jungle where he had a cooler full of cold beer. He may be Muslim, but beer is still his beverage of choice. Don and I declined the offer, feeling it not appropriate, and opted to stay at the wedding event and visit with the sister, who was showing us about the kampong. Rudy and Evelyn were ecstatic and were off to the jungle in a heartbeat. Everyone had a wonderful day.

Gifts are not given to the bride and groom. Instead, money is placed in a green packet traditional for Muslim weddings. Red packets are for Chinese celebrations and yellow packets are for Indian events. The green packets were presented to the groom's father, and we wondered if it was to pay for the food or if the newlyweds received it.

Kampong life is quiet and peaceful, a stark contrast to Kuala Lumpur. Both Zainel and Hattia want to go back to the kampong to live, but there is little to offer young people who need and want jobs. It is a lovely and traditional

Malay way of life that is disappearing as the country progresses. The progress is generally positive, and the rise in living standards, job opportunities and educational opportunities is noticeable throughout this country.

We drove home on Monday, taking the long way home and passing by dozens of oil palm plantations. It had been a glorious wedding.

Several cruising boats passing through the Yacht Club have headed on north. More should be arriving for the Raja Muda Race scheduled the week of November 22. A yacht from Hong Kong is in, as well as *Australian Maid*, the winning yacht last year. It gets pretty wild around here that week, difficult even to get in the showers. It is a fun time for everyone, but I believe that somehow we feel this is our own private spot now!

We are again in the transition period between the SW and the NE monsoon seasons and though the temperature doesn't change, the violent thunderstorms and lightning are startling and earthshaking. As I write this, the halyards are beginning to bang along with my heart. The wind is picking up very fast. I just peeked out to see if there is the dreaded black squall line of a Sumatra, but don't see one.

Now I have to wonder if this mooring really is safe. What if we break loose? A barge broke loose upriver last week and came roaring down the river with the current, big scary thing that we were sure was to be our demise. Miraculously, it made a path right through all of the boats, missing each seemingly by centimeters! Other than the wind, we sit in calm water here in the river and are very well protected.

Rain is coming down in torrents. Unfortunately, a good rainstorm doesn't wash down the boat, but instead turns the soot into caked-on, slimy grime, much worse than before the rain. A mad dash has closed all ports and hatches, so it is stifling hot down below. The lightning is violent and big bolts strike the water all around us. It is quite scary and we worry about the next one hitting the boat.

December 4, 1993
Port Klang, Still

Happy Thanksgiving and Merry Christmas!

Our shipment has arrived as of last week! The club member who would act as our agent arranged to have it delivered to the club and came personally to take care of the officialdom. A big truck pulled in and the boxes were unloaded right near the ramp leading down to the pontoon and the Jingo boat.

Alex had explained to Don that $20.00 would be the expected amount in "tip" to alleviate any concerns about customs duty. It should be given directly to the Customs Officer. Alex is a businessman and knows how things are done in business here.

Don just innocently peeled out his $20.00 bill and openly handed it to the Customs Officer as soon as he got out of his car and introduced himself.

The Customs Officer put up his hands, emphatically stating, "No! No!" and made wild motions not to take the money.

Don smiled and tried to make him take it, thinking this was how it is done. This isn't how it is done!

Alex was standing just out of the Customs Officer's line of vision, wildly flailing his arms at Don and shaking his head dramatically, mouthing, "Not now. Not now."

It is to be done in the underhanded way, so that it isn't obvious to anyone. Don caught on quickly and very obviously thrust his hand back into his pocket until he got the all clear from Alex and could slip the $20 bill to the Customs Officer—who eagerly snatched it and slipped it into his pocket. This is how it is done. We learn something new every day. Now, how did we make it this far with all of those other "tips", to be so unschooled in this?

The Jingo driver was right there to help load the big boxes into the boat and then to get them up into the cockpit when we got out to *Windy Thoughts*— not an easy chore, and we are most thankful for the kind and helpful people here at the Royal Selangor Yacht Club.

Then the fun began. It was like no Christmas either of us had ever experienced. We unpacked the new printer right away and are happy with its small size.

The canned goods are all stowed and we look with glands salivating at the cans of roast beef, the chicken, the pasta sauces and the salsas. And Zip-Loc bags—a wonder on a boat and used to store most any manner of items, from food to parts. They keep moisture out; the humidity is enough to keep you wet twenty-four hours a day.

I imagine being at anchor in some pristine bay with turquoise waters surrounding us and white sandy beaches just ashore. We will be listening to "Beethoven's Fifth", booming out to lift our souls while we play cruising—for the moments that we aren't working on the boat.

I will just open lockers and be overwhelmed with decisions as to what to prepare for our next meal. Will it be Cheese Whiz macaroni and cheese, or maybe pasta with pesto? Perhaps spaghetti with a jarred sauce and a can of chicken added. Or maybe chicken curry over rice. I might bake Don's favorite biscuits and have a can of Swanson's Chicken a la King on top. Perhaps I will open a can of corn tortillas, mix up a package of dried sour cream with my dry milk mix, and along with a can of Mexican chilies and a jar of hot salsa we will have a cruising version of nachos. There will be so many choices—it will be difficult to know where to begin! I can almost see the horror on your face as you read this.

Don has replaced the old bronze galley pumps with the new stainless ones that simply gleam. Our settee cushions were re-upholstered in K.L. and new covers were made for the settee pillows. All is fresh and new looking. It wasn't easy, as we had to live without cushions for a few weeks. The trick is to spend as much time off the boat as possible!

Don has made a big push to install all of the new equipment and spends his days bending over the engine, or over the head, or topsides working on some new installation there. He has replaced fuel pumps, filters, parts to the head, etc. and keeps going from morning till night.

If you aren't fixing something on the boat, you aren't really cruising.

That old division of labor seems to naturally assume its position on the boat. My specialties are provisioning and then stowing everything, and keeping the dirty laundry at bay. Most goes to the Chinese laundry, but I do out a small amount in a bucket on the pontoon most days.

I have hauled all of the dock lines and sheets ashore, laid them out on the pontoon and along with my bucket and brushes have scrubbed every inch of each one. Following the laborious chore of getting the soap out, they look like new again. We loop them over the lifelines to dry.

In preparation for leaving we have made one bus trip to the supermarket in Subang Jaya for provisions. While we stood in the taxi area outside of the Subang Jaya Shopping Center this past week, red ants suddenly made their way into my sandals and up my legs, biting with a vicious sting. The ride back to the Yacht Club was very uncomfortable, even though I slathered on an ointment that the driver pulled out from the glove compartment. Don't mingle with red ants in Malaysia!

The replacement autopilot computer box arrived today, but the new replacement ram is burned out. It goes on and on. We just sigh—and tell ourselves that this is all part of the good life. A fellow thinks he might be able to get a ram out of Singapore, or perhaps a motor. We have hope.

Don's heart is in the dumps because very bad black smoke is suddenly coming out of the exhaust along with very greasy stuff. The consensus is that it might be bent valves and that the valves should be ground down. Au Chin, our faithful diesel mechanic, found one injector that was bad—the same one that Don had so much difficulty getting off in Singapore.

Recently, when we were in Kuala Lumpur, we headed for the Hard Rock Café at the Concorde Hotel. Walking in, a sea of familiar faces surrounded us—Yacht Club members right in the middle of a press conference prior to the upcoming Raja Muda Yacht Race. We tried to slink away, but Jo Jo saw us and invited us to sit with him.

He offered us tickets to the Tony Bennett show the following night at no cost to us! Tickets are running a very expensive RM 400.00. After the press conference, we went right into the hotel and booked a room for the following night as our own big treat to ourselves.

This meant something special to wear, and we had to bus back to Port Klang to get our dress-up clothes and then the next day bus back into Kuala Lumpur, overnight bags in tow and our spirits in high form—for we were heading for a night on the town—no matter that it involved a mighty push in the rush to get aboard the bus and not be left behind.

After checking into the very posh hotel, we luxuriated in the surroundings before getting ready for the dinner show. Our table was next to the Raja Muda's and we were seated with his right hand man and his wife, along with others of his entourage. Tony Bennett was absolutely dynamite; we weren't aware that he was still performing. Our elegant evening was over all too soon, but we had the pleasure of retiring to our luxurious room before returning to the realities of life aboard.

The next day we were back on the bus and hoofing through Port Klang. The Raja Muda's right hand man and his wife had invited us to their home for dinner the following week, so we still had something special to look forward to and that made us happy.

The following Saturday evening we were picked up for our special dinner date at their home, located not far from Port Klang, in Shah Alam, within the Royal compound. It looks out over the Blue Mosque that is lit at night with thousands of lights, every turret's shape outlined by twinkling lights on every surface—a stunningly beautiful sight.

The meal was a delicious traditional Malay dinner with beef curry and salads. The house had a western style kitchen, as well as a traditional kitchen in back for the maid who did all of the cooking.

After dinner we were invited into our host's study that was devoted to the American West—an entire room centering on John Wayne! There were pictures of John Wayne and every manner of western art, posters, bronzes, a saddle with a holster and six-shooter hanging over it—Don loved it.

The evening was over all too soon, and we have invited them to the boat next week to get a peek into the way we live on our little home afloat.

We only gave a nod to Thanksgiving, as the week prior we took the night train to Singapore to renew our Malaysian visas. We enjoyed a good dinner of chili crab before climbing between the crisp white sheets in our own compartment, with air conditioning to keep us comfortable. When we awoke the next morning it was time for breakfast before arriving in Singapore. What a perfectly enjoyable way to travel south to this lovely city!

Cruising friends suggested cheap lodging at the YMCA and we headed there in a taxi. The first room that we were assigned was a bit disgusting and we requested to see another. It was marginally better and we just made do—choosing to not sleep between the sheets. The Concorde Hotel had spoiled us.

Regardless of our questionable digs, we had such a good time and shopped for Christmas presents for the little ones at home. After all of the time away, we had nearly foregotten what a beautiful city Singapore is—and the elaborate Christmas lighting in the city center put us right into the Christmas mood.

Seven boats at the Yacht Club were hit with lightning last week, one of them the Raja Muda's. We happened to be on the pontoon for the night to use shore power for equipment installation the following day. The next morning Don told Affendy, hired out of the Commandos in the Malaysian military to be Captain, that he thought the Raja Muda's boat was hit. Affendy asked Don to go aboard with him to check things out and they found several of the electronics blown out. It has been a mad scramble to get new equipment from Singapore installed in time for the race.

Oz, a beautiful sailboat belonging to good Australian friends who live and work in Kuala Lumpur, lost every piece of electronics. One thru-hull blew partially out and *Oz* was taking on water very slowly. The electrical panel blew off, as did half of the epoxy around the transducer. They discovered the damage this weekend, fortunately just two days later. *Oz* left Australia two years ago and Jo, Mike and seven-year old Jenna have become our good friends. Mike is an engineer, Jo teaches in the International School and Jenna is in second grade, a real cutie.

Jo tells amazing tales of how easy her job is at the International School, where she teaches Physics and English. The need for discipline is non-existent. When she walks into the room they stand. When they have a question they raise their hands and when called upon they stand. No one interrupts. The notion of turning an assignment in late, or not doing it, doesn't exist. Talking back is neither allowed nor accepted. Respect is of the highest order. In turn, she has the highest respect for the students. Does this sound like the dream teaching job?

These horrendous lightning storms should be over soon. We have discovered that we did take a hit, but it only shattered the insulator on the random wire for the Ham radio. It is a very frightening experience to watch the huge bolts hit the water around the boat. Don has run chain from all of the shrouds over the side and into the water—and from both the bowsprit and the wind vane paddle down into the water. Our hull is well grounded. Some boats have invested in high-tech lightning proof equipment—including the Raja Muda's boat that has everything possible to deflect lightning, no expense spared.

Here we sit with a tall mast and our chains running to ground all over the boat. I call it Don's budget lightning protection.

January 1, 1994
Royal Selangor Yacht Club, Still
Malaysia

HAPPY NEW YEAR 1994!

Thinking that we would be underway right after Christmas was a bit of wishful thinking. Au Chin was not able to find out what was wrong with the engine, but declared that the head was warped. Our hopes are slipping away along with the days, but Au Chin is the only game in town.

When replacing the injectors and grinding down the head didn't work, Au Chin decided that the engine should be completely overhauled. He dismantled the engine and threw all the nuts and bolts into a bucket on the galley sole, where they sit still.

Don and I took the engine out of the boat ourselves. It probably weighs 400 pounds. Again, we attacked the job with the trusty come-along, ropes, the boom and a good deal of sweat. Once getting the engine up into the cockpit, it sat precariously but ready to disembark the boat. The Jingo boat came alongside and with the boom, as well as many orders shouted, it landed down in the Jingo boat.

Au Chin has the engine ashore, we aren't sure where. Combine his neurological problems that make understanding him somewhat difficult with the language differences, and our communication about the engine runs mostly on trust. He is re-building it, to the best of our knowledge.

Of course, this process required that we order a new overhaul gasket as well as many other new engine parts from Seattle, all at great expense and arriving via Federal Express two weeks later at even greater expense for shipping and customs duty. Presumably, Au Chin is getting the engine back together and we press on with our plans. The ram for the autopilot is in Kuala Lumpur with the dealer, who has been on holiday.

Eric and Cathy Oh invited us to spend the night at their home in Kuala Lumpur, to attend an evening program at their church the week before Christmas. A very nice home was converted into a church by the congregation and without a cross on the exterior, no one would take it for a Christian church.

There was a cute program by the children, with two American ex-pats playing Mary and Joseph, and a tiny Chinese baby portraying Jesus in the manger. Refreshments and a gift exchange followed, along with the singing of Christmas carols—and it was wonderful to be amongst this fellowship. A handful of other Americans, two young men from South Africa, a number of Chinese, several Filipinos and Don and I rounded out the gathering.

Interesting rustlings on board consider making changes in our cruising plans for next year that fit in with the "we're not out of here as yet and don't know when we will be" frame of mind in which we presently find ourselves. We are thinking of heading to Chagos until April, then on to Madagascar, the Comoro Islands, Zanzibar, and settling in Kenya for the season. The Red Sea could be delayed until the following year, when we could leave Kenya in April and make it up to the Red Sea in a tiny window of time. This new route could be undertaken anytime between now and the end of February with fair to good winds.

A live-aboard Australian fellow who has been here for some time has roused our interest. Jungle Jim (the name Don and I have privately given him) is in his seventies

and has spent the past twenty years sailing back and forth between Singapore and South Africa and knows the area well. Jungle Jim has sailed about all the coasts of Africa and has no doubt that we would find it far nicer than rushing into the Mediterranean.

Don has copied all of Jim's charts, as well as his two British pilots for the South Indian Ocean. The pilots are thirty years old but will have to suffice. The ocean hasn't changed that much in thirty years. This new plan intrigues us and sounds so much more delightful than slogging up the Red Sea. Which way to go?

Jim is an extremely interesting fellow who has been a war correspondent in any number of wars—that number varying with the number of beers he has imbibed during the telling. He worked with Huntley and Brinkley during the Vietnam War and has pictures of the three of them together. Also, according to him he parachuted into Singapore in advance of the Japanese invasion of World War Two and warned everyone. Unfortunately, history doesn't record his brave dealings and the British obviously didn't heed his warnings.

Our first meeting and conversation with Jungle Jim, though memorable, wasn't a particularly good one. He invited us to join him and a few others at his table at dinner one busy weekend and his conversation soon steered to war-related topics and his experiences as a war correspondent. He began to relate wild tales of American troops dumping bodies out of airplanes and everyone listened, dumbfounded. He soon started in on Korea, Don's old combat stomping grounds, and began to denigrate our American troops who fought there. This was the breaking point. Don was up and out of his chair so fast that his chair fell over behind him.

"Come on, Joyce, we're going home. We don't have to listen to this," was all Don said as he awkwardly righted his chair, grabbed me by the hand and hauled me off toward the dock and the Jingo boat.

Jungle Jim is quite a crusty character. A club member has informed us that a book was written that reveals his drug smuggling in the South China Sea. Nevertheless, our paths cross at the club daily and after a first few uncomfortable moments we have found him an interesting and friendly soul.

Jungle Jim can rattle off the prevailing winds and currents for the entire Indian Ocean for any month, the information at his fingertips. If only a fraction of his stories are true, he has led an adventurous life!

Rudy and Evelyn first met Jim when spending four months on Chagos a couple of years ago. Chagos has become a paradise in the middle of nowhere where cruisers stop and stay for sometimes months. Evelyn tells of a place ashore where they baked bread in old catchments. They gave us a map showing where to find fresh water on a nearby island, carefully marking the path from shore—just like a treasure map. The American Naval Base is located at Diego Garcia, well south in the archipelago. Though it is off limits, its close proximity gives a sense of security. We hear reports of excellent fishing and diving and a perfectly picture-perfect lagoon. Robinson Crusoe, here we come!

Jim laid the moorings at a yacht club that is eighteen miles up the coast from Mombasa. It is a smaller but much nicer club, located in a creek and a safer place to leave the boat. We listen with rapt attention and take notes, sketching out diagrams and maps. So much for cruising guides!

The choice of going around the Cape of Good Hope and forgetting the Mediterranean is always in the offing. Certainly, once around the Cape this route could provide some fascinating cruising. A meeting of the minds in Port Elizabeth gives lectures on how to round the Cape and make it both alive and with the boat intact. It seems that the Argulla Current, combined with southwesterly gales, can make the trip seem death defying for a good part of the time. This prospect sounds far more challenging than the Red Sea, though the Red Sea could take far longer to transit. We hold all options open.

Amongst all of the preparation, we celebrated our twenty-sixth anniversary yesterday. It occurs to me that cruising either makes you much closer as a couple, or else is the straw that breaks the camel's back in a very short time. Any problem can rapidly bloom into a crisis when you live by the seat of your pants while joined at the hip twenty-four hours a day! Secured to a mooring here, there aren't the life and death worries to share. Still, there have been the ups and downs of daily life in readying to leave that have been somewhat trying. We are so reliant upon one another, bringing us so much closer. For others, it has the opposite effect. Fortunately, we are still holding each other up and becoming two old salts together.

We talk about the first years of cruising and we marvel that, had things gone south right from the start, we possibly wouldn't still be out here—but instead would have thrown in the towel and found some way to get *Windy Thoughts* back home and returned to land life long before this. Frankly, when the cost for shipping her home would be $25,000.00 or more, there is nothing to do but keep on sailing!

The good Lord has offered reality to us in bits and pieces until He felt that we were ready to cope with more. He has been right with us every step of the way.

Our anniversary was celebrated by taking the bus to the new Pizza Hut at nearby Klang, four miles up the road. It may not have been an elaborate candlelight dinner, but there have been many of those and we may not again have the opportunity to celebrate our anniversary by jumping on a bus and going to a newly discovered Pizza Hut in Malaysia!

In K.L. we always order double cheese, double pepperoni and double pineapple—our preferred way to add calories and cholesterol. Cheese isn't on the diet of people here and in fact, most find it distasteful. So it is a joy to order as much of it as we possibly can when the occasion arises. We explain at great lengths that a double order means twice the cheese, pepperoni and pineapple. We even refer to a "make your own pizza" section on the menu, making it clear that we will pay for the extra toppings.

Without fail, our order always comes with single toppings only. We engage the manager, show him the menu and refer once again to the "pick your own toppings" section.

Yes, they understand.

Yesterday, we even had it written down on paper for our anniversary celebration at this new spot. Our waiter nodded his head up and down and repeated, "No problems. Double cheese, double pepperoni, double pineapple."

It came with single toppings. The manager came to our table, and with big smiles we patiently explained to him what we had ordered. He told us that he would personally make us a fresh pizza with double toppings.

It arrived with single toppings. We give up.

Then there is the sandwich that Don has taken to ordering here at the Yacht Club. The food is delicious, but you must understand that a sandwich is very uncommon here. It can be ordered with chicken or beef and Don prefers to order his sandwich with double chicken, or double beef. It arrives on one slice of bread, open faced and with a truly miniscule portion of either, perhaps a tablespoon of each.

Don has now taken to asking for his sandwich on toasted bread and explaining that it can have another piece of bread on top—demonstrating how a sandwich fits together. Expanding his horizons, he requests cheese and tomato as well—and has been receiving quite a respectable sandwich for the past week.

Today it arrived open-faced, with the cheese and tomato on the side, a spattering of beef on one piece of toast, chicken on the other. I tell him to stick to fried rice! Don says that he will truly miss it here.

Jungle Jim's wife is here from Singapore for two weeks. She is much younger than Jungle Jim. We are unsure of their arrangement. She absolutely hates anything to do with cruising. She did spend several months on Chagos when Rudy and Evelyn were there—and loved every minute of it—which bodes well for Chagos. She evidently pursues her career of travel writing and photography while Jim lives aboard and on occasion sails to Singapore and back. She is presently consulting with the Sultan of Brunei about a book she is writing about Brunei.

Things have become so topsy-turvy. All was in order for the Mediterranean. Now we are thinking about Africa and even these plans are subject to change as the season progresses. I feel a bit overwhelmed lately with the boat in constant disarray.

Three days before Christmas I came down with what I believe was salmonella. I was sitting in town with an iced lemon tea and ice cream that tasted odd that first spoonful. When I later began to feel quite ill, with a fever sharply rising, Don hauled me ashore, called a taxi and took me to an Indian doctor who wanted to give me a shot. The syringe was taken from a bowl of used ones, so we politely refused. It was very disappointing to have to cancel plans to spend Christmas Eve and Christmas day in K.L. with the Ohs again. I instead spent Christmas and two days after in bed.

I have revived, and tonight is New Year's Eve with special doings at the Club. This means dressing up, fixing hair and wearing real shoes, and we are both looking forward to the evening. Real shoes are beginning to feel a bit tight, what with the constant sandals spreading out our feet.

There will be a nice dinner tonight. Don is dying for prime rib, baked potato and a salad—any kind of salad. We realize that it won't be a western menu and so we await with bated breath our New Year's Eve dinner, knowing that it will be something very special. Tomorrow, our friend Jimmy Tan is taking us out to Crab Island for seafood, a 1.5 hour ferry ride that should be fun. We look forward to a new adventure to start the New Year!

Plans are to leave here and sail north 200 miles to Langkawi Island, Malaysia, a good jumping-off spot. From there we will sail across the top of Sumatra, drop down to pick up the top of the SE trade winds, and ride the winds and currents across the Indian Ocean

It is the "seventh year" syndrome according to Jungle Jim, and the trade winds may be high this year. Presently, the northeast trade winds that would take us to Sri Lanka and on toward the Red Sea are up in the South China Sea. Either way, all isn't quite right as the NE monsoon seems not to have properly set in. It should be sunny and clear, but is cloudy with lots of rain.

Jungle Jim has transited the Red Sea six times and tells us that he definitely wouldn't make the passage this year. I hang on every tidbit of information, but Don rolls his eyes and reminds me to keep an open mind.

January 23, 1994
Port Klang
Malaysia

Hello Friend,

Au Chin completely rebuilt the engine and put it back in the boat two weeks ago; it now refuses to turn over! Au Chin returned to work on it several times the first week, but we haven't seen him this week. Don says he has lost face. Even Rudy, a former engineer, has given it a go and can't figure out what is wrong. What to do now?

Don doesn't want to cope with the engine problems that have plagued us for so long now and says we aren't hanging out here and missing the season to cross the Indian Ocean again. He is concerned about the times ahead when we will definitely need the engine. Consequently, we have ordered a new engine from Doc Freeman's in Seattle, another Yanmar, but a forty-eight horsepower turbo engine. A Yanmar dealer in K.L. can't get us an engine for four months, Singapore the same.

Don faxed John in the engine department at Doc's in Seattle and within a few hours we had a ten-page return fax with all information and prices. A new engine can be shipped out of Seattle immediately and at less cost than purchasing it here in Asia! Ordered four days ago, it is to arrive in Port Klang today. Our agent should have it to us in a couple of days.

Because of the higher horsepower, Don specifically asked John about the mountings and was told that it should fit the same engine mounts with only slight adjustments made. Because of a displacement hull, going from thirty-five horsepower to forty-eight horsepower won't provide any gain in speed. Don's choice was made on the theory that we would have more power in strong currents—thinking ahead to when we would be motoring considerably more in our own Northwest waters.

Don has taken our present engine out and re-installed it himself several times. But with the need to make the mount adjustments, Don asked around for qualified diesel mechanics. A highly-recommended Aussie diesel mechanic has newly arrived to work for Bayliner, in Kuala Lumpur! Jason came out to the Club to look things over. Don is so relieved, as he wants it done professionally and frankly is up to his eyeballs with everything else. The young fellow isn't available until February 6.

(In the aftermath Don would come to realize that another Yanmar 35 hp engine that he could have installed himself would have been a far better decision.)

A tragedy at the Club occurred this past week when a young worker on the new construction was killed. A family of four contracted from Burma is managing the piling work. The crane that drives the pilings suddenly toppled off the platform and into the water below. The driver jumped off, but the young sixteen-year-old working below was caught beneath the crane.

Don was reading the paper at the club after returning from town and I was on the boat. It was about 1 p.m—a busy time with many members at the

Club for lunch. Tables are set up around the pool area and dining is within three or four feet of the construction area. The huge crash occurred during the buzz of lunch conversation and everyone jumped up from tables and ran out onto the platform.

When no one moved to take any action, Don called down that they had to get the boy out of the water. While he was removing his shoes to jump down into the water from the platform, Mr. Lin ran out to warn Don of sharp metal under the water. At this point two construction workers went into the water to pull the young fellow out, while Don made a run for the parking lot and the ramp that led down to the pontoon.

The ramp had been taken out temporarily for the construction, and it was necessary to hop into a little aluminum boat and use a rope to pull the boat from shore over to the pontoon. Don repeatedly slipped and fell in the slippery mud that had accumulated in the bottom of the boat, creating a source of amusement for those above.

About the time that Don was running along the pontoon, Jungle Jim was approaching in his dinghy. All blood and guts, Jim joined Don to work on the boy on the dock. Don got the water out of him and performed CPR for forty minutes while Jim checked his pulse, and they were able to get him breathing on his own six different times.

Affendy arrived and held the boy's head. All felt that his neck was broken and as it turned out it was, and his thorax was crushed.

When the ambulance finally arrived, there was more time lost as the two men negotiated getting the dinghy to the dock. Only after they had reached the pontoon did they finally go back to the ambulance to get oxygen. They performed CPR for two minutes before pronouncing the young boy dead.

Don screamed at them to not give up on him. Jim yelled, "Get away from him and let Don and me keep working on him."

One looked at Don and replied, "We're doing the best we can."

Don replied that he knew they were, realizing that he and Jim were just overwhelmed with attempts to keep the boy breathing—and that it was now useless to continue.

Jim and Don went back up to the Club, both deeply affected. Mr. Lin made a special point to thank them for trying to help. Don was unable to talk about it and didn't sleep last night.

This morning the construction manager, who wasn't there during the accident, thanked Don for trying to save one of his workers. Tears ran down both his face and Don's. The other workers burned Joss sticks at the scene of the accident, a solemn occasion and one that left both Don and Jim saddened.

About two weeks later we had just arrived at the Club, and Jim was sitting at a table by the pool when we all heard an explosion coming from somewhere down the river. Jim jumped up, yelling, "Come on, Don, we better get down there." Jungle Jim and Don were mates now.

March 6, 1994
Same Ole Place

Hello Again,
Hallelujah! The engine is in!

Jason just needs about four more hours of work to finish the job. He hasn't been able to get here very regularly. In addition, the new engine mounts didn't fit after all and new ones had to be made, to be ready in six days. This was all at the start of the Chinese New Year that has everything a bit upside down with all of the festivities. Eighteen days later the mounts weren't ready yet. The fellows had gone bankrupt and were no longer in business. But Jason found another who could manufacture them in one day.

In addition, Ramadan held things up. Affendy invited us to his home for Hari Raya and came out to the Yacht Club to pick us up. He has a lovely wife and three darling very young children—a little boy and two little girls—all with big, snapping black eyes. Friends came in and out of their home during the day and lovely foods were served. When it was time to leave, the little girls cried and vied for space in the car to sit by us! My, we did feel special!

We felt especially privileged to be invited to spend the Chinese New Year celebration with Jimmy Tan and his family, a major event on the Chinese calendar and the main holiday of the year.

At the gathering at the family business in Kuala Lumpur, Jimmy introduced us to his father, a distinguished gentleman who told us about the death of his own father when he was only a teenager. After looking at the fourteen pairs of shoes lined up outside on the doorstep, he realized that it would now be up to him to take care of everyone in the family. He never forgot that feeling and the awesome sense of responsibility. Now, he is in the later years of his life and people paid their respects to both him and to Jimmy.

Jimmy took us to his parents' home afterwards, where the family gathered for food and more celebration. It is an important family event and both Don and I felt honored to be a part of the day.

(Jimmy was to become Commodore of the Royal Selangor Yacht Club after we left Malaysia).

We bit the bullet and purchased a feathering prop brought back from Australia by an Aussie who comes into the club when he is in Kuala Lumpur on business. Don will install the new prop when the boat is hauled for new anti-fouling two days from now.

Jason is here one hour on one day, gone four days, back for two hours another day and has to leave here and go into K.L. to purchase anything needed.

This whole scenario with the engine has required patience, said to be a virtue. Following the engine installation, we must put a number of hours on the engine to check it out and must run the new autopilot for checks as well. Our departure date remains, as always, "within the month".

Sailing south to Singapore and then following the east coast of Sumatra south and through the Sundra Strait should put us into the southeast trade winds shortly after heading into the Indian Ocean. May to October/November finds the best winds, so the timing should be good anytime. On to Chagos!

Along with the engine saga and our other matters to attend to, we have suffered the final degradation: *Windy Thoughts* has been home to a rat!

Don discovered a hole chewed through the screen on the companionway steps one morning about ten days ago. We were horrified to think that we may be sharing our little home with the likes of a rat from the Klang River! Though confident we are rid of him, it has been an all-out battle.

Mr. Lin gave us some salt fish from the Club kitchen that went into a trap the first night. No luck. Traps here are big, box-shaped cage structures. We are told the snap kind won't catch the likes of an Asian rat. Rats here are huge, apparently thriving on the warm climate. Dried squid, called sotong, was used the second night, but still no luck. The next step in the hunt was rat poison amongst a concoction of rice and crab from the Club kitchen, tried for two nights. We moved on to rat glue—a thick black glue globbed onto the center of a pizza box cover, the pizza having been consumed for our dinner. In the morning, we discovered that the rat had moved the cover of the pizza box over onto the rest of the cardboard to safely get to the goodies without stepping in the glue. One smart rat!

It seems he must have swum upriver for better lodgings. I have been very busy with bleach—disinfecting, scrubbing and cleaning every nook and cranny for the past several days.

Last week we attended a very nice dinner show in Kuala Lumpur with British friends who recently visited at the Yacht Club. We spent the night at their lovely condo that has maid's quarters, as do most—though she doesn't want a maid living right in with them. I wonder if I could give up that opportunity.

A lovely dinner was also enjoyed at the home of their Indonesian friends who work here and have just returned from thirteen years in Calgary, Alberta! The man offered to speak to a friend in the Indonesian Consulate for us, to inquire about the necessity of the Cruising Permit as we sail down the east coast of Sumatra. Though we don't plan to go ashore, we would like the option of anchoring a few times and perhaps taking on fuel once. The Permit must be obtained in Jakarta, applied for two months in advance, and is expensive. We have done this before and the requirements can be complicated.

April 18, 1994
Yes, Port Klang
Malaysia

Susan,

Things have definitely taken a turn for the better and this should be my last correspondence from Malaysia! We leave here on April 23.

The engine installation ultimately took six weeks. But we had to have a new shaft manufactured in a machine shop, requiring another haul-out ten days later. The new feathering prop was installed at the haul-out and looks impressive with its many gears. *Windy Thoughts* has been out for a spin each morning to put the first thirty hours on the engine, enough to tighten the heads. Supposedly, she would back up great with this new prop—but she still doesn't back for beans.

Don found the prop pitch is set too high, necessitating another haul-out to change the pitch. He prefers not to think of the problems that the abundance of the little parts could cause should he have to work on the prop at anchor. Both the engine and the autopilot work—surely something to crow about!

Approximately a thirty-hour sail should bring us to Singapore and this time we will head right for Raffles Marina on the west coast; it is new, deluxe, and a bit pricey, but we intend to make it a short stay of a few days. This will be our last touch with the civilized world until Mayotte Island off the African coast—and that after several more months.

There is never a dull moment! While leisurely having dinner with friends at the Club, having left the boat on the slipway, Zainel ran up to announce that they had misjudged the tides and *Windy Thoughts* had to go back into the water immediately—rather than an hour later as planned. We leapt up, ran to the boat and frantically readied everything.

When back on our mooring in the river, we took the next Jingo boat back to finish our evening with friends who had come out from Kuala Lumpur for a goodbye dinner.

Later that night Don got out of our berth and stepped into ankle deep water! The automatic bilge pump hadn't come on. Don hit the electric pumps and we were very relieved to see how rapidly the water receded. Though we didn't know where the water was entering the boat, when it receded we could hear water gushing in through the shaft.

Instantly, light bulbs went off in Don's head. With all the scurrying about to get the boat off the slipway, the necessity to compress the newly installed Shaft Seal before the boat went into the water had totally slipped his mind. We did some intense cleaning for the rest of the night to purge the boat of Klang River germs.

The folks aboard *Blackjack*, an American boat that arrived this past week, are also seriously considering sailing to Chagos and Africa. We would all like to keep radio contact along the way. However, they need two weeks in Singapore and plan to stay at Raffles Marina. Our budget could allow for a few nights of luxuriating there with them, before moving on to dear old Changi anchorage until they were ready. We will keep you posted on our imminent departure from Singapore.

April 28, 1994
Raffles Marina
Singapore

Dear Friend,

After two weeks of luxury in this new and decadent Raffles Marina, we have made no move to head around the north side of Singapore to Changi anchorage. *Blackjack* is here with us.

The trip down from Port Klang took thirty-nine hours, much of it very unpleasant, and we arrived on Singapore's west side at midnight in twenty-five-knot winds. *Blackjack* gave us a fix on a wharf behind which we could anchor if we made our approach at night. The wharf wasn't all lit up as they had described.

"Do you see those lights all in a row that they told us to look for?"

"Nope, don't see anything."

We roamed around back and forth until we finally found the wharf, ducked behind it and got the hook down. Mind you, it wasn't great protection with the wharf very high above us and it was a very uncomfortable night, during which I fretted about dragging anchor and crashing into the pilings at any moment. Don slept like a baby, knowing that I would be the alarm.

First light found us still there, but we upped anchor to make our way amongst the many fish traps in the channel. Once nicely tied to a berth at Raffles Marina not one word was mentioned about leaving in three or four days—and Don immediately signed us up for another week. *Blackjack* is busy attending to refrigeration re-pairs as well as the GPS lost on the way down. Here ten days now, we have another list of things to accomplish.

The marina has five restaurants, and in the main area fountains, circular staircases winding up each side, and a grand piano that is always playing and is centered in front of a huge curved window that looks out at the boats. Everything is more deluxe than most five-star hotels. Amenities include a theatre, a bowling alley and a beautiful swimming pool that winds here and there and into the main level restaurant.

The showers are truly luxurious, with lovely green glass doors and solid teak interiors, each a little room to itself. We think we may never leave. It will be a long time of "roughing it" after this. Ah, but we will be jumping into those pristine turquoise waters!

Chris, the bubbly young woman from *Blackjack*, has a rental car and has invited us to ride into Singapore with her the last two days. We have hit all the electronics stores and found many items to further enhance our life aboard.

After all the time in Port Klang there were a few glitches on the trip down to Singapore, hair-raising ones, actually. So, along with a venture up to Changi Village for those real New York conies that we loved so when here before, our social life includes visits to chandlers to insure that Don isn't without something to attend to on the boat.

It was a very sad goodbye back at the Royal Selangor Yacht Club. We were overwhelmed when we received several gifts at dinner the night before our departure. Nothing was said until we rose to leave, and then we were converged upon with gifts of a lovely Chinese tea set, a beautiful Royal Selangor pewter bud vase, some heavenly scented powder, a fragrant fresh flower and a delicious bag of fresh fruit. I couldn't hold back the tears. We will truly miss these people and this wonderful spot and hope to return someday in the next chapter of our lives.

Ready to pull off with the outgoing tide at first light, we were just about to let go the mooring when a little boat came out from the Club with Mon and another worker aboard. They carried a stalk of bananas for us—the straw that broke the camel's back for my emotions. Mon didn't work that day, but rode his motor bike out to the Club in the wee hours before dawn to bid us a special goodbye. The other fellow was a coin collector to whom Don had given a silver dollar that his mother gave him years ago—and that he had carried with him always.

Even with all of the holdups there, we will never forget the good times, the people we considered as family and the special way in which we were treated by everyone. There is a joy in finally getting underway, but this joy was mixed with sadness in leaving this country and these people who have touched our lives in ways that cannot be adequately expressed.

April 13, 1994
Raffles Marina
Singapore

Hello Susan,

As of today, the folks on *Blackjack* had a sudden change in plans and will leave *Blackjack* on the hard here at Raffles Marina, to fly home immediately. Chris had vacuum-packed meat for forty-eight days. I will take some of it and they will give the rest to the dock master.

All four of us went to the hospital to get shots for yellow fever, cholera, DPT and typhoid. Chris is a nurse and will give us the cholera booster and shoot us with gamma-globulin this evening.

We are ready to go; every last detail is carefully taken care of, fuel topped off, more provisioning done in view of the months ahead, everything stowed for sea again and we are ready to throw off the dock lines tomorrow morning. The weather is very blowy and nasty today, though it remains extremely hot and humid twenty-four hours a day.

With our late departure, we will likely be using the engine to buck against southeast winds that are developing now. However, we can top off our fuel tanks in a small marina that sits in a bight right on the Java side of the Sundra Strait, located between the southern tip of Sumatra and Java. Then—off across the Indian Ocean to Chagos for a lovely stay for several weeks before sailing on to Mayotte, the French island west of Madagascar. I will send the disc with letters as soon as we arrive at Mayotte, probably about two months from now.

Chapter 10

When Dreams Come Crashing Down

If I take the wings of the morning and dwell in the uttermost parts of the sea; Even there shall thy hand lead me and thy right hand shall hold me. —Psalm 139: 9-10

Bankka Island
Indonesia
May 21, 1994

Dear Susan,

Today is Don's sixty-second birthday. It hasn't been very celebratory for him, but is much more relaxing than the past days have been. Someday, we will look back on this and find it all seemingly minor, but right now are feeling pretty low. Things have gone so very wrong to this point, almost as if we were not supposed to have set off on this passage at all.

As expected, we bucked into head winds from fifteen to eighteen knots that, had we left Singapore two weeks ago, would have been behind us and provided delightful sailing south in the Bankka Strait. Making fairly good time under power, we bumped along to get down to the Sundra Strait as soon as possible.

For the most part our complaints were not of the life-threatening variety, but it is hard to believe that so very many things could go wrong after all of the months held up replacing the engine, the many autopilot problems, and then all of Don's time spent checking every system over so many times with a fine toothed comb before we set off for the long voyage ahead.

When a freighter was approaching very closely the first night out and didn't respond to our radio calls, we flipped the switch to turn on the spreader lights to really light us up—only to discover that the starboard light was out. It is always up to us to stay clear of big ships, who seldom notice small boats such as us. Not a big problem, because the port spreader light replaced in Malaysia worked, so we thought. But it suddenly went out as well.

We wanted to run with both the running lights and masthead light while under power. The fishing boats see the combination of lights and don't know what is coming, so are more likely to notice us. The tri-color light that is just always up there faithfully doing its thing was suddenly turned sideways, so we couldn't run with that at all. How in the world did that happen?

To top all of this, the compass light suddenly decided to give up the ghost. Well, a compass light isn't absolutely necessary—unless you are hand-steering the boat in the dark. We had the new autopilot.

As for the new autopilot, it went on the fritz on the second morning out, refusing to stay in auto mode for more than two minutes at the outside. Don had already reprogrammed it when we crossed the equator to the southern hemisphere—but did so once again to no avail. There is no trouble-shooting information. Any problems are to be referred to a Nautec engineer, not handy at the moment. We would just continue to hand steer.

Don replaced the bow light during that second day—out on the bowsprit with the bow plunging under water repeatedly, his safety harness hooked to the bow pulpit. I pictured him getting washed off and hanging from the bowsprit, dragged along under water as I busied myself with keeping the plunging boat on course, unaware of his plight. Could he yell loud enough?

When his chores were completed we took turns at the helm for the day, very tired by nightfall and facing another night at the helm. We shortened our watch schedule to two hours on watch, two hours off, and neither of us really got any sleep. The large amount of shipping traffic in this Strait constantly keeps you on the alert.

It was in the black of Don's night watch when he intently watched both a red and a green light, one to our port, the other to our starboard side. Because the two lights were so far apart he assumed they were from two different sources—though thought it strange that he saw no white stern lights—and it was puzzling to determine their course.

Suddenly, he was looking up at a supertanker directly in front of us—with four men distinctly visible on deck above and looking down at him!

The supertanker was so huge and so close that its red and green lights that should have alerted Don to a collision course, were so far apart that he mistook them for lights from two distinctly different sources! In shock, he turned *Windy Thoughts'* wheel and made it just out of the supertanker's path by such a slim margin that we rocked violently in its bow wave. It was a frightening, hair-raising few moments that left us safe under circumstances that came very close to the demise of both the boat and us.

A cloud cover had chosen to settle in just for the dark hours and we were unable to see the southern hemisphere's constellations in the night sky. Don rigged up an Itty Bitty Book Light over the compass, purchased for reading in the cockpit on night watches. They haven't proven to be the answer to our reading dreams because they last only four hours on one set of batteries, but our battery supply was sufficient to make us thankful that we had them along!

When a big ship changed to a collision course with us we frantically grabbed a new high-powered spotlight and shined it directly on *Windy Thoughts*; the new spotlight suddenly chose not work. Are the electrical gods trying to tell us something?

It was the around-the-clock hand-steering in busy shipping traffic and bumpy conditions that really got to us. We were tired and wanted to find a spot to drop the hook. Several islands dot the coast of Sumatra but reef, shoals, rocks and very shallow water surround them. The Sumatra coast it-self offers little shelter, shoaling out two to seven miles and exposed to the southeast winds. While Don was steering that third day, I pored over the chart looking for some little spot that might give us shelter.

Now, we sit peacefully at anchor at the northwest entrance to the Bankka Strait, off the north Coast of Bankka Island. It is about twenty miles out of our way, but we headed in for a spell to make repairs and give ourselves a break. Are we becoming wimps? Don was particularly tired, having spent most of his time on repairs since we left Singapore, with little relaxation or rest.

Changing course for Bankka Island put us on a close reach. While Don got some much-needed rest that afternoon, I sailed *Windy Thoughts*—who being the little lady that she is just dipped her rail down and headed right up as close to that wind as possible. It was so good to be sailing again, and instead of two or three knots we skimmed the water at six knots plus. Even heeled as we were, the ride was actually fun because we were headed in!

Don was dead to the world below and didn't notice that his lee cloth was the only thing keeping him from rolling onto the floor. I didn't wake him until we were into the lee on our approach and our world wasn't quite so topsy-turvy.

Here we sit in a big, beautiful bay, one that we would enjoy so much more were our tasks and hearts not so heavy. I neglected to mention a few other things that went wrong, the lights being minor though a very necessary component for safety amongst such busy shipping traffic, the autopilot not any disaster.

We took on copious amounts of water through the starboard chain plate. Water that soaked into all of the computer books and any other of impor-tance—such as the GPS manual, the engine manuals and others in that book-shelf. Books were literally awash. Water drained down under the settee and through all of the spare parts storage, then out onto the cabin sole, making it like a pond to wade through. Mind you, we weren't aware of this until the water reached the cabin sole, because I was busy steering and Don was lying over the engine.

Just what was Don doing lying over the new engine instead of resting or sleeping? Did I mention that water was gushing through the stern gland to make us *seriously* wonder if the boat might sink? That started during the first night out, when the engine mounts worked loose about every two hours around the clock. Each time, we shut the engine down and Don lay across the hot engine on a pad, with the boat rolling heavily in the seas while he retightened the engine mounts as well as set screws on the Stop Leak—assuming it to be the problem again.

Just when he thought the problem solved, water would come gushing through once again. Meanwhile, the new automatic bilge pump refused to work, significantly adding to the drama. So when Don wasn't steering he was trying to keep the boat from sinking.

When Don was steering, I removed all the books from the starboard bookcase that were soaked through to the point of dripping copiously—and assuming them ruined, stuffed them into big garbage bags until we could better cope. Every one of our bath towels was put into service to soak up the water. Water leaking through a chain plate can be nasty, but much more seriously gushing through the stern gland is enough to ruin your day. And it wasn't even bad weather or strong winds—just the bashing into head seas.

Once in the anchorage I continued sopping up sea water, cleaned with fresh water and then began the tedious job of separating every single page of every book—about thirty books for starters. We hung them out on the lifelines to dry with hopes that we could save them. Don took everything out from under the starboard settee, all well soaked through, and put it all up on top in the sun to dry out. This happened to be all of the spare engine parts.

As we sit in this peaceful, calm anchorage I have winched Don up the mast in the boson's chair to work on lighting; he has repaired the new automatic bilge pump, searched out and repaired the leak at the chain plate and then spent two full days installing, taking out, and re-installing autopilots. Not lacking for anything to fill his days. Isn't cruising fun?

He took out the new Auto Helm 7000 autopilot and completely installed the old Auto Helm 5000, stowed for just such an emergency. When it refused to kick in he spent hours checking out everything on that unit. Everything from the cockpit locker is in the cockpit, because he has to crawl down in there to take out and install—and then take out and reinstall rams to the units.

He reinstalled the new Auto Helm 7000 autopilot, and after reprogramming it yet once again for the southern hemisphere (having crossed the equator) was hopeful that this would solve the problem. Our hopes soared when it kicked in! We upped anchor and took the boat out for a little spin—and for that hour had a working autopilot.

Thinking about setting out for the 4,500 miles ahead of us with so many things going wrong right from the get-go had put us into a real blue funk. Having water pouring through the stern gland with threats of the boat sinking was the real stinker, but things were improving now that we wouldn't have to hand steer.

We knew that once through the Sundra Strait and out into the Indian Ocean we would be under sail again, and we could put the wind vane to work. Old Flem would love that broad reach across the Indian Ocean—but we have invested so many dollars in getting this new autopilot. An autopilot makes life on the sea so much easier and holds the course so perfectly—when it works. It is definitely our third mate.

After three nights here we thought things were going along pretty well; the autopilot was working, stern gland problems were solved, books and parts were drying out and the boat was cleaned of salt water below. Could anything else go wrong?

I may have neglected to mention that the refrigerator bit the dust for the first time ever on the first night here at anchor. Remember all that vacuum-packed meat that *Blackjack* gave us in Singapore? At ninety-five very humid degrees it doesn't last long without a working refrigerator. Fortunately, we purchased a big tank of Freon in Malaysia, no longer allowed in the United States. Don gave the refrigerator a good shot and got it cold again.

Unfortunately, we found the fridge packed up once again the next morning—so we were faced with this utopia of meat and no way to keep it. Many beautiful big boneless pork chops, each 1.5 inches thick, that had already started to go bad went over the side. I cooked up some of the mince and we had spaghetti for dinner and Italian omelets for breakfast. We ate the big sausages with potatoes and onions for two meals and again with sauerkraut for another meal. Two pounds of bacon were cooked up and one pound went down with pancakes, another in a quiche. The chicken, lamb, steaks and packages of beef cubes went overboard, not fit to pass to the fishermen ashore.

I cooked up what we felt could hold over in warm conditions for a short time and we took in as much protein as our bodies could humanly consume. Never had we had such manna in the way of meat aboard—for a few days anyway.

Don has kept very close records of fuel consumption with this new engine, finding that we burn about .75 gallons an hour. According to the tank tender, it appears we are now burning one gallon an hour, perhaps more. Certainly, the fact that we are punching into seas with the RPMs much higher than normal accounts for much of this. If we just bash on ahead in the Bankka Strait for thirty to fifty miles, we can sail all the way down to the Sundra Strait with the wind about fifty degrees off the bow—but fifty degrees off the bow is my limit!

I baked a cake for Don's birthday today and we are having one of the lovely Hormel canned hams and some scalloped potatoes for our dinner. Using the oven is a compromise to our comfort because it is so very hot and humid that you could easily wring each of us out like a wet sponge. The fans below are the only thing keeping us sane and run twenty-four hours a day. The one installed over our galley blows right on me while I attempt to perform miracles there.

Relaxing today, we will take off tomorrow to head south twenty miles, where we hope to anchor off a little point about a mile out, putt in to shore in the dinghy and purchase diesel. In readiness, diesel has been transferred from the jerry cans into the tank.

The fishermen who have a small hut ashore here at Bankka Island use sticks for anchors for their boats. Don and I took dirty laundry, buckets and soap ashore and the fishermen led the way up a path some distance into the jungle to a six-foot-square pool of fresh water in  a little swamp of sorts. It was really quite beautiful, with big towering palms all about. We set up shop right there.

Just to get clothes, bedding and all of those towels clean again was one thing over which we had some control. We sloshed away together, depositing this experience into our memory banks to pull out someday when back to what most call a normal life, one that didn't require a little swamp in the jungles of Indonesia. Would it really be better than this? It was a big contrast to our past days in Raffles Marina with a professional laundry service at our beck and call.

But we are cruising again. And we have fresh, sun-dried laundry. Who could ask for more?

There is more: the windlass broke and Don has spent hours fixing that. The GPS has blanked out four times and the new handheld GPS refuses to work at all. The Prevailer batteries are suddenly showing signs of serious problems. They have been reliable all these past years, so Don hadn't planned to replace with new until we reached Africa. Though a little life is left in them, suddenly they won't start the engine. We are using the other bank of Johnson Control batteries but won't be able to run all of the electronics. I believe the use of fans is now out as well. Oh, woe is me!

There is good news: the books did dry out just fine, every single laboriously separated page. The bookshelves are clean and dry and books properly stowed again. The spare parts dried out; Don has cleaned up and oiled each for protection and has properly stowed each. We have clean clothes, sheets and towels. The boat isn't taking on water. Most importantly, it isn't sinking! We'll have a good dinner. We sit in a lovely spot that, were our hearts not so heavy with concerns, would be the tropical paradise that we dreamed about before this cruising adventure ever began. And we have each other. Now, what more could we want?

I feel a strong urge to share some feelings with you—because they are so close to the surface that I can barely breathe. Even though lights failing and refrigerator packing up are certainly minor, the worry about the more serious matters—such as those copious amounts of water pouring into the boat—really wore on both of us with so many thousands of miles ahead of us. We were somewhat stunned to find so many little as well as big things going wrong all at the same time. And it is this abundance of problems, small and large, that is laying us low.

You don't start out on a major ocean passage without every little detail having been attended to and gone over a hundred times before setting off, without knowing that your equipment is working and ready for what is ahead. Without being as prepared as you possibly can be for any unforeseen event.

Don is so very diligent in his preparation and upkeep of equipment and the things on the boat that require more than my very limited knowledge of electronics or mechanics. I know that he has been feeling overwhelmed and actually has chest pains—this worries me to no end. My other fears pale in comparison.

We are setting off for months away from any kind of civilization as we know it and this start to our voyage just isn't adding up as to how things should be going. Something is very wrong with this picture, no matter that it appears we have set many things right now.

The batteries worry us. There will be no refrigeration—rightfully not the end of the world. Don isn't concerned about the GPS not working, and the handheld isn't going to be our backup after all. We do have the sextant and every set of sight reduction tables known to man, but we don't really want to do it like Joshua Slocum! Pinpoint navigation is just so wonderful when there are reefs and the like to worry about, or a pass through an unseen reef that must be exactly located in the midst of thousands of miles of ocean.

So many thousands of miles lie ahead of us and we were so happy to be setting off to new horizons again. Something in my soul, deep down, is hammering out a big warning. Is it just my hormones again, or are my intuitions telling me something? It truly seems that this voyage was destined not to be, for some reason. I have such a heavy feeling in my heart about setting out tomorrow morning with all so seemingly fragile now. Don insists that his chest pains were nothing and that they have stopped. My mind wanders constantly to various scenarios that all center on something happening to him. This is my major concern.

The coup de grâce has only just occurred. A cockroach just went scurrying across the galley counter!

Ah, but tomorrow is another day and the Indian Ocean beckons us once again. We will be off into the wild blue yonder with or without GPS and a refrigerator and maybe a few other things. After all, Columbus didn't have any of this. But we do have our autopilot for our third mate, as well as an adventurous spirit, one that I am working very hard on reviving right now. And the good Lord is still sitting right on our shoulders. This too shall pass.

May 29, 1994
Raffles Marina
Singapore

Susan,

Yes, this finds us back in Singapore once again. After crossing the equator twice in the past few days, we have learned that being forced back here was the best thing that could have happened to us.

On the day after Don's birthday we did leave that lovely anchorage at the tip of Bankka Island at 3:00 the next morning, on May 22. We hoped to make it to that town farther south before the headwinds blew strong. It was relatively calm, the first calm we had seen. We needed about eight or ten hours minimum, wishful thinking perhaps, but off we went with a good night's sleep and renewed spirits. And to think—we usually wish for wind!

We were on our way! Chagos, here we come! Africa and Cape Town here we come!

Once out of the bay we turned on the autopilot and our hearts sank. The words "Drive—Stopped" flashed—same old thing. Don worked on it to no avail.

We worked out a plan: we would persevere to the Sundra Strait, only three more days and nights of hand steering, get to the small resort, take the unit out of the boat again and ship it to England.

If this wasn't possible, we would get ourselves to Jakarta and ship it from there. There must be a bus, a motor bike, or a donkey cart available. Without Indonesian visas or a Cruising Permit, should we be stuck in Indonesia for awhile we would beg for mercy and do anything necessary to make us legal—and our westward journey would prevail!

If we managed to get the autopilot shipped to England, repaired and returned, Don would do the installation himself—invalidating the warranty, but warranties seem to be elusive contracts. Our best chance to make things right was before leaving Southeast Asia.

With a plan, we set our course and started our voyage. With calm waters, steering was easy and we lazed along with spirits rising at the prospects we had set forth in our minds.

Underway for no more than thirty minutes, sea water started gushing through the stern gland. Don turned the engine off and dove into the engine compartment to find the same problems, yet again. He did his thing lying over the engine and we set off again, concerns about serious issues at the forefront—pictures in our minds of making it to the bottom of the Sundra Strait only to be stuck there for the foreseeable future, broken down—or perhaps getting to Jakarta. Lord, please don't let us be stuck in Jakarta!

Two hours later the same scenario played itself out once again, and I will never forget the look on Don's face when he emerged from the engine compartment and looked at me to say, "Turn the boat back. We have to go back to Singapore."

Windy Thoughts was turned about and set on course for Singapore. My feelings mirrored Don's in many ways, but were mixed with a deep sense of relief that we weren't setting off on the 4,500-mile passage just yet. Too many things weren't right and a feeling of foreboding centered deep within my soul—as if some monster had taken over my insides and an elephant was sitting on my chest.

There could be far more serious things to contend with and we are well aware that we have been so blessed out here. But sometimes it is just so hard to keep going on when the going on requires so much of you. We have rallied our resources and spirits over and over for the past two years. Still, were it not for these setbacks, would we ever have had the opportunity to make the friends and have the experiences we have had in Southeast Asia? But it is time to move on west about now and we are ready.

It is only 600 miles from Singapore south to the Sundra Strait and a beautiful broad reach from there all the way to Africa. But after time spent working on the boat in Singapore, we would be that much further into the SW monsoon season. Right now we cannot even imagine having to start out all over again.

We discussed some options—one to ship the boat home from Singapore—and this shows you just how low our spirits actually were. Don didn't want to be held up for another year and agreed to explore the option. The prospect of shipping the boat home was enough to raise my spirits to an all time high. I could barely believe he would even entertain the thought!

Within an hour, the wind came up, but not out of the southwest as expected in the SW monsoon season. Yes, right out of the north and we were once again slamming straight into it. No rest for the wicked. Maybe the good Lord didn't like my attitude after giving us so many years of magic and seeing us through every step of the way. Here I was, questioning what we had worked so hard to be doing in the first place. Could we really give up our dream just because of a little setback—well, several setbacks over the past year—just because it is so very hard at times? Weren't we made of stronger stuff? I knew that Don was, but I wasn't at all sure that I was.

The wind direction was such that we were able to sail the boat on a close reach. After jigging along for the day and then into that night, the winds flung themselves back into the southwesterly quadrant with twenty knots of wind behind us for a glorious sail, sitting back and steering with feet on the spokes of the wheel.

"Sailing takes us away to where we always want to be," rang through the air while we surfed along. How could one's attitude make such a 180-degree turn in seconds? Thank you, Lord.

By late afternoon on the next day we explored the charts for a place to anchor. What if this really was our last touch with the real pleasures of cruising? If we actually did ship *Windy Thoughts* home, this could be our last hurrah. A sobering thought. The chart showed good protection between two small islands, and we set our waypoint for the pass between, images of the best parts of cruising filling our heads.

As we slowly made our way in we could see thatched roof huts forming a small kampong on the shore. A little rickety wharf with fishing boats tied alongside wobbled its way out onto the water. It seemed that an entire village was standing on that wharf and waving at us.

It looked perfect in every way.

Several people jumped into canoes and paddled out to *Windy Thoughts*. One old fellow waved and shouted at us, motioning to us to follow him—and we knew that he wanted to show us the best spot to drop the hook. Our hearts were buoyed beyond belief. Back to cruising again!

Smiles and shouts of "Hello Mister!" filled the pristine bay as the other boats pulled alongside. Soon, everyone was aboard *Windy Thoughts* and there was the absolute joy of smiling faces and the jabber of conversation in two distinctly different languages. Babies were bounced up and down, parents beamed proudly, and we were once again living the very reason that we took up this cruising life to begin with. What a difference a day makes! Thank you, Lord!

Don and I were tired from the hard work of the past few days, as well as the emotional anguish and the worry of setting off for months away from any kind of civilization—with water cascading into the boat the major consideration. We just wanted to get the hook down and sleep for about fifteen hours.

But the warmth of these people was much too welcoming to hurry them off. After a polite and enjoyable time had passed we made motions of sleeping, telling them we would see them "Pagi", in the morning. Many bodies climbed down into their boats, babies and little ones were handed down, little boys and girls who loved exploring and climbing about the topsides of *Windy Thoughts* joined them, and waves and shouts of "Goodbye" and "Pagi" could be heard as they made their way back to the wharf.

We were exhausted and happy. These smiling faces and happy people had been a gift to us when our spirits were sorely waning.

The next morning we peeked out of the cockpit to see the whole crowd was on the wharf, watching to see any sign of life on *Windy Thoughts*. We waited until our breakfast was finished before stepping up into the cockpit, and the people swarmed into boats and paddled furiously out to us.

"Salamet pagi," we called to them. "Salamet pagi," they called back to us.

This time I had several large packages of peanuts ready to give away. We weren't going anywhere for a while, if ever again. No need to save them for the long passages ahead. Don's big stash of red licorice went to the little ones and granola bars were passed out.

About ten young fellows wanted to help us to get *Breezy* down. Two went ashore in our dinghy with Don and one took over driving the outboard. Legs straight out in front of me in a narrow canoe, my ride was provided by a fellow bailing furiously the entire distance. The whole village awaited us on the pier as we climbed up steps made with tree limbs.

We heard greetings in English and were surprised to meet Kamla, who was raised in the kampong but had lived in Singapore for some time with her husband, a professional diver who has worked all over the world. They moved back to the kampong fifteen years ago, preferring the quiet and simple life to the cacophony of a big, modern city like Singapore. Kamla has relatives in several of the kampongs scattered over the island and her grown children live and work in Singapore. She also has three little ones who were given to her when just a few days old by three mothers here who had many other children.

With Kamla as our guide we set off to visit the headman of the village, about twenty others following along and all joining us in his home. We sat on the floor, Don and me seemingly the guests of honor and everyone else sitting around us while Kamla interpreted for us. Though we were here without visas or the proper Cruising Permit, the older headman sat cross-legged, smiling at us while we wrote our names, the name of our boat and the date in his little spiral notebooks. Our passports were never asked for.

After taking care of proprieties we all went off on a trek about the entire island, dozens of happy children skipping along beside us. We eventually arrived at the kampong with the school that goes up to Form Two. All of the children as well as their teacher came out to greet us. Shouts of "Hello, Mister," filled the air.

It would be an understatement to say that we were feeling overwhelmed with the greetings and the friendliness that echoed to earlier days in Indonesia.

Kamla had bought up much of the land on the island, wanting to preserve the way of life that is so special. She led us to her house, where we sat on the floor and drank from fresh coconuts that one of the boys cut after scampering high up in a coconut palm. They learn to do this at a young age.

As we walked to the opposite side of the island with Kamla as our guide, we visited five different kampongs, each with their spattering of thatched-roof huts, all clean and neat and in storybook settings beneath tall coconut palms, the earth around the homes swept spotlessly clean. Fresh and plentiful water comes from wells that aren't deep at all, and there is no electricity. We were served fresh pineapple and given more coconut milk to drink—so refreshing in the heat and humidity. We knew how to cut off a piece of the shell and use it as a spoon to take out the lovely soft meat just inside. We chewed on sugar cane and by day's end had our fill of the island's bounty. Who needs a big supermarket?

Just when our tired bodies felt that we couldn't go any further, we learned that we would return to the other side of the island in a boat. It was happy goodbyes when we reached that other side again and headed back out to *Windy Thoughts* at the end of a perfect day. "Pagi" was shouted back and forth. We would see them in the morning.

Pagi and our appearance in the cockpit brought everyone out to *Windy Thoughts* once again. We were sitting between (and very close to) two small islands. Today we would get the cook's tour of the other island and this time a group of young men led the way.

When thirsty, a fellow scampered up one of the hundreds of

surrounding coconut palms to cut coconuts for refreshing drinks. We swam on a beautiful beach and joined them in the most delicious refreshments of pineapples, coconuts and sugar cane, just as the day before. No one was along to interpret but understanding and enjoyment came naturally.

When we arrived back at the beach near *Windy Thoughts*, most of the people from the kampong on the other island had boated over. It was time to say our final goodbyes. We would be off first thing in the morning. We shook hands with each one and felt a bit forlorn while we stood on the beach waving as their boats headed back home. Emotions had run so high the past few days and the happiness of the past two was suddenly mixed with sadness, knowing that we were turning back with no sure plan ahead.

At 5:00 the next morning we hauled anchor. Tides were at springs and, not sure of the currents, we wanted an early start. Only fifty miles from Singapore, we would be leaving this island paradise that was like a step back in time, and heading back into a very first-world city. We wanted to make Raffles Marina before dark, which comes fast and early in the tropics.

It was still dark as we slowly made our way out into the Strait. A big black thundercloud was visible off to the west, but it didn't look like a fierce line squall at all.

Just nicely underway, it hit. With a sudden ferocity that we have seldom experienced before, we had forty knots of wind within thirty seconds—very close to being directly in front of us. It was the dreaded Sumatra wind that we had hoped to avoid. We couldn't run back to the anchorage in the dark, as getting in required some close navigating.

With Don at the helm, I dashed below and grabbed the safety harnesses. The Strait was suddenly boiling with seas that built rapidly and *Windy Thoughts* rolled violently in their disorientation. The rain was torrential and didn't let up; the winds continued to increase, the rain to devour us. Big ships as well as several fishing boats surrounded us within a quarter of a mile, few of the fishing boats carrying lights of any kind.

Don and I both hooked to the eyebolt just below the little cockpit table on the binnacle. While Don steered, I was on my knees with one arm wrapped around the binnacle, the other holding a flashlight on the compass for Don—because the compass light wired directly to the batteries in hopes that it would get us back to Singapore had chosen that moment to go out. About then the flashlight went out. I unhooked and frantically dashed below for another, giving myself what is now a black eye on the way.

Don became totally disoriented during the seconds I was gone, going on feel alone. In open seas this wouldn't have been so alarming, but here in the Strait we were surrounded with any manner of big ships and small boats very close by.

Windy Thoughts turned south with the sudden onslaught of the wind and seas and Don had great difficulty bringing her around. The squall had totally obliterated the radar screen and our greatest concern was the other ships and the boats, as the seas built up so fast our heads spun.

After the first hour without let-up, Don yelled through the wind, "That's it! We're going home!"

Home! After the past ten days, I can make it through anything just to make it back to Singapore. I will never set foot on the sea again. We're going home!

You might have been able to hear my joy from there, as you can likely imagine what a change in spirit this little announcement engendered.

Though it seemed the Sumatra wind would never end, after two hours it petered out and the seas gradually settled into a sloppy mode before finally returning to normal. The sun came out, the current was with us and once again the entire scenario turned 180 degrees—and we were two happy sailors under the sun, making the entire fifty miles to Singapore in six hours! Was it only a few hours ago that we were experiencing such despicable conditions? Life is good, isn't it?

And then we were back at the entrance to Raffles Marina. Just when we were making our way into the marina under power, Murphy's Law took over once again. The shaft slipped and began free spinning—and Don suddenly lost all control of the boat. Lots of big expensive boats to bang into—Raffles Marina to our rescue! A marina boat was immediately at our side to lend assistance and get us into a slip.

Once securely tied to the dock, we decided to forget our problems for just a little while and made a dash for the restaurant by the pool, the pinnacle of decadence at the moment and just the thing to pacify our weary selves. To think—just that morning we had left a remote kampong, only to have our dinner in surroundings so foreign to those of a few hours ago.

But was the big, fancy marina complex really better than that pristine anchorage with the beautiful kampong? Such a contrast between the two worlds that were only fifty miles apart! Could we really give up the world we had just left and the life we had chosen—just because we were dispirited and had been tried and found lacking?

Now that we have been back for three days, Don has found that the other two engine mounts are loose, one nearly wearing a hole through the oil filter!

I have called shipping companies to check on shipping costs. Very discouraging, $25,000.00 for starters and that only includes the shipping—not the cradle costs, ten different taxes, freight costs and then the costs at the other end. If we choose this path, it is final—and I believe I must regain my adventurous spirit. Don is rebounding. So many places loom over the horizon to see and explore and we would never start out again. At the same time, continuing on just seems so very, very impossible to have to contemplate at the moment.

The people next to us on the dock were picked up by a Japanese freighter when they lost a boat on a reef in the Red Sea. They have purchased a thirty-foot Cheoy Lee in Singapore and plan to sail it back to his home in Mauritius. I just want the good parts of cruising. I know that it will be too late to start down the Sundra Strait again this season and haven't a clue as to our next step.

Don is forging ahead as always, trying to get problems solved and doing what simply has to be done. I am an emotional basket case, but can't just throw to the winds everything that we both sacrificed for and chose for our life—all because of setbacks that are a part of the cruising life. Gads, this life certainly shows you up for what you really are, and I am not coming out too well. Anyone can sail around the world. It is taking the @#$#$ boat with you that is so very hard! I read that somewhere. Believe me, it is true. I may never leave Raffles Marina.

Though Singapore is an oasis in the middle of our troubles, we can't stay any longer than it takes to get everything fixed. The moorage fee is high, though we enjoy a five-star resort atmosphere, the likes of which we are unlikely to see again.

It will now be too late into the season to start out for the Indian Ocean. For us, this means another year in Southeast Asia. But we're together, very safe, and blessed with an abundance of memories behind us and the potential for even more ahead. The highs are so high, but the lows are so low.

June 4, 1994
Raffles Marina
Singapore

Continuing the saga…

The local Auto Helm fellow has been here and the dealership is under different management. Thank goodness, we think. He announced that our autopilot computer box has a problem. I replied that we were well aware of this after hand steering for six days. Another computer box has been ordered from England and should be here in about two weeks.

An Australian boat with six strapping young men as crew is having the exact same problems with the same autopilot, though theirs has never worked.

Having faxed all over, we are finally getting some movement. The U.S. head distributor for Auto Helm sent a copy of my fax on to the Singapore dealership. The next fellow sent out is the same one with whom we dealt two years ago. He had our unit for six weeks the last time and when it was returned he didn't know the ram from the computer box. This time we had to show him how to turn on the unit. Don tells me it isn't a major issue. We have only to plug in a new computer box and he will install a new ram himself.

Don's spirits are rising as he works every day, making progress resolving the many problems. The prospect of giving up is definitely not high on his list anymore. He reminds me of all we have gone through and how we could never have done any of this were we not working together every step of the way.

My chest hurts all the time and I have actually made an appointment with a cardiologist, wondering if I've worried myself into something wrong. Doesn't this all sound just so totally unlike me? I think it wise that Don should have a checkup as well, but having always been hale and hearty he sees no need to worry further.

We go to the pool each day for a break, then to the lovely showers, followed by a jaunt up to the chartroom to read the paper in air-conditioning. Easy chairs and televisions along with shelves of videos are at our service in the beautiful big room with solid wood paneling on walls lined with bookcases. We have our own private library since no one else ever uses the room. A very nice theatre offers free movies every weekend. If I were stuck in Jakarta, I might just go off the deep end. How can I be filled with concern amidst this opulent environment?

Raffles Marina is a gift to us amidst our problems.

Meanwhile, Don is working on the boat every waking moment of each day. When Don started the engine this morning it vibrated so badly that he dove down to check the stern gland. With the bolts on the engine mounts continuously working loose and the shifting of the shaft as it moved back and forth through the stern gland, the rubber teeth inside the stern gland were almost completely worn away! When Don took off the flange and examined it, he discovered that the keyway is completely stripped and the key is cracked! We are lucky to have made it here.

Two marine engineers have looked at it and have distinctly differing opinions, but neither will be available to do any work. A big mega yacht recommended an American diesel mechanic, who also looked at it today and will return later. The boat yard has no clue as to where we might find a qualified diesel mechanic. *Windy Thoughts* will be hauled here so this isn't reassuring. Hopefully, the fellow who looked at it today will be here long enough to see it through.

Did I tell you that the new Auto Helm wind/speed instrument installed back in Malaysia has never worked either? Maybe I left out that little expensive piece of news about our electronics.

July 21, 1994
Raffles Marina
Singapore

Hello again,

The British Auto Helm dealership's only response to our many faxes and phone calls is to reply that their autopilots don't have problems and they have no intentions of replying further. Even our American mechanic tells us to stay as far away from the local dealership as possible. Very reassuring, though we had already made that observation for ourselves.

One boater at the marina has replaced his three times and we witnessed him literally tearing the latest new 7000 (the one we have) out of his boat and throwing it overboard! A French fellow having the same problems is finished dealing with England and is suing the company. It seems that the lemon law clusters around us, but doesn't offer resolutions.

Having been talked into the Sea Talk combination system in Seattle, we are without depth sounder and all other instruments, since all are tied into the same system—an idea whose logic we failed to understand in the first place. I probably didn't mention that small fiasco. We have no intention of sailing around the world with my lead line only—even if Columbus could do it.

Enough about equipment failure! Life goes on.

The people at Raffles Marina are friendly, but due to its size the complex doesn't have the warm feeling of the Royal Selangor Yacht Club. It is a private marina and there are twenty-four rooms available for those wanting to spend a weekend. The workers arrive on private buses and are deposited in front of the laundry, where each day they pick up a cleaned and pressed uniform specific to their job. They have their own cafeteria, so there is no real intermingling with them.

Only recently have we learned that we can ride the staff bus to the MRT station, saving us considerable taxi fare.

Next day:

The American on the big mega-yacht didn't show yesterday or this morning, so Don and I dropped by the boat. The Captain and his wife are from Galliano Island in British Columbia! It was only a few years back that we were there on *Windy Thoughts*! The owner is Italian, and the crew who will deliver the new boat to Italy have been working on it for the last three months in Singapore.

They plan to leave on August 1 and it was proposed that we might like to join them, passage provided for helping with the crewing. We could ship *Windy Thoughts* home, go with them as far as the Mediterranean and then do some sightseeing before flying home ourselves.

The boat is big at 140 feet and has nice crew quarters, a separate Jacuzzi and sauna for crew and two washers and dryers. No buckets and toilet plungers for this crowd! And the gal hired as "stewardess" does all of the laundry! Imagine that!

Frankly, a part of us wants to believe that this just jumped into our laps at an opportune time, but we don't even know these people, and there are questions about insurance, as well as several other things. They are a younger group. Don sat up on the bridge at the navigation station and I could see him dreaming big dreams about night watches up there in air-conditioning with every amenity known to man at his fingertips.

This sure would be a much easier way to get up the Red Sea, but could we ever forgive ourselves for leaving *Windy Thoughts* in the lurch and doing it the easy way?

The news on the engine so far is not good. The grub screws are shirred off and embedded into the shaft. The flange is ruined, the new cutlass bearing must be replaced, the bolts on the engine mounts are too small and of stainless, which isn't proper—and the whole engine has shifted position and is ready to fall through the bottom of the boat. They tell us that it was the engine installation alone that caused all of this mess—and we are waiting for a haulout date right now.

It appears that we may be here in Singapore for some time yet and will be busy keeping Immigration happy with visits every two weeks, carrying letters from various establishments doing work on the various things going wrong. Meanwhile, we remain here in the lap of luxury.

Raffles Marina has been open for a year but in full force only since January. The grand opening is this weekend and all are asked to dress ship for the occasion. We received a letter stating that a S$500.00 goody bag would be given out to all boats that did, and would even include a set of signal flags. We agreed to have our boat open for visitors, but when we went up to get our goody bag were told it was for members only—though they would like us to participate in dressing ship and keeping our boat open for visitors to board.

The only blue water boats in the marina are *Windy Thoughts* and a couple of other cruising boats—and *Windy Thoughts* can proudly stand her own against any of the member boats. Most of them are fully crewed power boats whose owners seldom make their appearance.

Two fellows from the local Auto Helm dealership have been here and installed the new units. On their first visit they arrived with the ram only, denying that anything else came or was to come. Don had them call the company on their cell phones right there in our cockpit to find out where the other two parts were. We had our fax in hand with serial numbers listed of items sent and with verification that the parts were here. I called the manager, reminding him that the parts were in Singapore, we had paid for them—and we would like to have them.

On the opposite side of our dock is *Dream Weaver*, with the couple aboard who lost a boat in the Red Sea. He is native Mauritian, she is British, and they have sailed together for some time. They were married yesterday and we were invited over for a champagne toast to their happiness. They will sail *Dream Weaver* back to Mauritius where they plan to live.

They left this morning. Just last evening, he asked Don to put waypoints into his new GPS for our two anchorages in the Bankka Strait, and any others available. Don would be much more comfortable showing him how to put the waypoints in himself, but did his best to be of help. When Don found them without a proper chart from here to the Sundra Strait he gave them ours, purchased here in Singapore and the one chart that we really wanted to save—because it marked our sorry progress as well as our good anchorages, and was the only original used in some time now.

Something just doesn't seem right. We never saw provisions going aboard the boat or any of the normal kind of jumping-off business. Then again, who are we to question? They are a quiet couple, who kept to themselves.

September 26, 1994
Raffles Marina
Singapore

Dear Susan,

After two months in the yard here at Raffles Marina we were finally launched back into the water two days ago! Because the American mechanic couldn't do the work after all, we were left to work with the mechanic here at the yard—a beautiful facility—and living aboard certainly wasn't a hindrance to our daily activities in the least.

As for the work, it has been a battle all the way and we are biting our nails in anticipation that all is right. The total bill on top of the cost of the new engine was enough to make us gasp for breath. Thankfully, the American mechanic had done a thorough check on the engine and made a very concise account of the problems. Virtually everything that Jason did in Malaysia to install the new engine was done wrong and caused no end of problems. If we had only known! But we had trusted his abilities—and thought ourselves so fortunate to have a legitimate diesel mechanic do the work.

Vincente, our present mechanic, insisted on payment before we went back into the water but Don held back $1,000.00 until the work was finished. Vincente is very upset. There was a problem with the way the electrician hooked up our battery banks and Vincente felt that we should pay for resolving this. But Don resolutely told him that the battery system was correctly installed when we came to the yard and we wanted it back the same way. The head electrician found that the fellow doing the work had hooked up everything wrong. Don has tried to humor Vincente, but Vincente has lost face and doesn't like us anymore.

Unbeknownst to us, Jason installed all stainless steel bolts on the engine mounts, inappropriate for this use and the reason that the mounts worked loose repeatedly. He also used the wrong thread for the drilling and tapping. In addition, he insisted that the exhaust system didn't need changing. Don clearly understood otherwise and had discussed it with him several times, ultimately deferring to Jason's knowledge and supposed better judgment.

It turns out to have been a huge problem and Don was able to persuade the local Yanmar dealer to come out to the yard and give them written instructions on what needed to be done. The yard tore out the entire exhaust system and installed a new one. The downer is that they installed the new system wrong. Not just a little wrong but big time wrong! Many hours of labor added up for which we pay dearly.

Don had them tear it all out, after which he did the work himself. Feeling that he had to stay on top of everything, he learned to never leave them alone when working. At the same time he kept a jolly and determined demeanor to maintain something of a relationship with those into whose hands we were placing our lives. It was a delicate balance!

The yard management very much dislikes anyone telling them what they want done. The mere suggestion that we might be included in any discussion as to not only what they are going to do, but how they are going to do it, is very offensive. All manner of business is treated with as much secrecy as is possible—other than how much money we owe. We persevere, remain calm and hope for the best.

I mounted a campaign to get a $2,000.00 refund on the original engine installment alone, though there is no one to whom to appeal. The Bayliner business for which Jason works didn't respond to our faxes and phone calls for several weeks. When they did respond they said they would require an out-of-the-water survey by a surveyor of their choice. We happily replied that since we were here in Singapore on the hard, we would eagerly look forward to their surveyor. When could we expect him? Not one word in reply. Jason has gone back to Australia.

The good news is that my campaign has paid off and they are refunding the entire amount! I had to appeal to both the Prime Minister and the Minister of Transport. In addition, I wrote a letter to every boating magazine in SE Asia, made many phone calls and sent many faxes. Don thinks I deserve a medal for being so persistent, because neither he nor anyone else expected we would ever get a refund. Should I polish my thumb? No, just huge sighs of relief are fine for me.

We have been insured for the past two years with the company set up through the 7 Seas Cruising Association, whose monthly pamphlets have been so informative. When the June issue caught up with us at the end of July, we learned that the underwriters were in bankruptcy and our insurance was no longer in effect—and hadn't been for two months!

Thirty different companies have been faxed, but we have received replies from only six, all of which require a crew of three or more aboard. British friends who live in Singapore took our information home and made some phone calls. Within twenty-four hours we had quotes from two British companies, one whose premium is attractive and Lloyd's is their underwriter. However, unlike other policies with Lloyd's, crew of more than two isn't required.

The boatyard writes a letter for us every two weeks, after which we spend an entire day in downtown Singapore doing the Immigration thing to keep us in the country. They know us at the official offices now and we are quite sure that we can hear a huge sigh when we walk in. Here they come again—they are still here.

We need to get visas renewed once more and Don expects that Vincente may not write any more letters for us. Vincente is very unhappy about not receiving the pay in full before the work is finished. However, we are learning, if slowly! It takes a lot of patience.

Meanwhile, amidst the ordeal of getting the boat in working order, we have been to both the Hungry Ghost Festival and the Moon Cake Festival. We purchased some moon cakes put out by the marina in lovely boxes, but they are made from bean paste and not very tasty. Still, it is fun to be a part of the festivities.

October 7, 1994
Raffles Marina
Singapore

Dear Susan,

This week has been a very busy one, running into the city every day for doctor appointments and dental appointments. I visited a cardiologist after we arrived in Singapore, had a full workup and am in good health. It was just stress. Imagine that!

Though hot and humid around the clock, it is comparatively cooler in the early hours and our brisk four-mile daily walks begin by 6 a.m. or earlier. After showers, Don often uses the weight room, feeling that he has his own private gym. Swimming in the lovely pool later in the day after our chores are finished, we attempt to stay in shape as best we can.

It would be easy to feel that we were on vacation at this beautiful place if we didn't have to return to the yard and climb a ladder up to the boat. And then climb down that ladder and hike through the yard when we need to use the facilities. Ah, but never mind that. It is an easy life—if we discount the many issues involved in getting the work on the boat done!

We recently made a trip downtown to the Board of Censors to pick up a package sent by mail from friend Benny Benson. It contained three video tapes with local Spokane news footage of a firestorm that came very close to our property and the storage that holds all of our worldly goods.

Censoring is required of all video tapes before they are allowed into the country and the charge for ours was US $96.00. Don explained what was on the tape, and when they learned that it was news footage they were very suspicious. Not happy about having to pay, we decided not to accept the tapes and went home to the boat.

At the end of the day and with more thought, we decided to persevere. Benny has kept in touch and done special things like this, just as you have. Our consternation was overruled by our desire to see the news of the firestorm.

The next day we were back at the Post Office, pleading our case. It was decided that if we would meet an official at the downtown Post Office the following day at exactly 3 p.m., the package could be passed to us and then mailed to Malaysia, where censoring isn't necessary.

So we trooped into the city again on this third day of the saga and met the uniformed official at said time and place, feeling that we were part of some clandestine arrangement. After we showed our identification, the package was passed off to us. The official followed right at our heels in order to personally witness that it was properly sent via registered mail to Malaysia, and we had to provide him with a slip of proof for official records.

Our British friends living in Kuala Lumpur are the recipients and will surely wonder why they are receiving news videos from Spokane—and will also wonder just where in the world Spokane is. Friends going there soon will pick the videos up and bring them down to Singapore. This cruising life does present its variety of problems!

The time in Singapore has passed fast. While on the hard stand I spent ten days in intense labor detailing every square inch of the boat's exterior, beginning at the crack of dawn when the temperatures are down into the low ninety degrees, spit polishing the hull and every bit of stainless, and quitting at noon when I could stand it no more.

Don wasn't lounging about the pool, as he had his own laborious chores to accomplish. He keeps very busy mucking about with filters and engine business and details, never having time to wonder what to do.

Not to give the impression that all we do is work on the boat, we have had much time to explore Singapore—albeit often in pursuit of one of those nuts or bolts, so to speak. We have enjoyed an abundance of good meals out that we will look back on with longing when rolling about at sea, and many an afternoon relaxing around the pool when work and chores are done.

Singapore has luxurious movie theatres, requiring prior reservations at the theatre as well as seat assignments. We recently enjoyed *Forrest Gump*. No one caught onto the American humor, and they laughed in all of the wrong places, not cracking so much as a smile at the humorous parts. We loved the movie.

Any activity such as this takes up an entire day. We must bus to the MRT station closest to us and then take the MRT train to the section of the city that we wish to visit. Even so, both systems of transportation are reliable and well run, whisking about thousands of bodies very efficiently.

We have started the provisioning for the many months ahead, as Singapore will be the best spot for that. With our original plan for Africa aborted, the latest plans are set to head across the Indian Ocean and up the Red Sea and into the Mediterranean.

Shouldn't I know better than to detail future plans for you, by now?

I can stuff thirty-two rolls of paper towels into the back of our hanging locker. By taking out the cardboard from each roll of toilet paper and then sitting on each roll to flatten it, I can stuff fifty rolls into the starboard locker in the head, our towels occupying the locker on the port side. Twelve tubes of toothpaste are stowed away, as are vitamins, sun block, you name it.

Don stocks up on the necessary greases, nuts and bolts, fuel filters and the makings of engine and head work. While counting rolls of toilet paper and paper towels are at the forefront of my activities, he faces the more important decisions as to what will be needed for the workings of the entire boat.

Our Micrologic GPS isn't getting fixes and the new Traxar handheld has never functioned. We recently had a Garmin GPS shipped in from West Marine. It is small and has so many functions it may well become our main GPS.

Boats in The Europa Round the World Rally arrived here about a week ago. The entire Rally, Gibraltar to Gibraltar, takes 1.5 years! Don and I were invited to a party for the Rally members last week, a very nice buffet and a lovely evening.

Interesting people from the Rally are seen about the marina every day, some cruising couples like us. Some are crewing for owners not aboard but who fly into designated stops for the parties. Many of the crew members are young people. There are young men with long, shaggy hair who don't appear—or smell—to have combed or washed their hair or their clothes in some time—and those who take more pride in their appearance as guests of this very nice club that is hosting them royally.

Most of the Rally members are busy doing repairs and provisioning or ferreting out boat parts—not exempt from the problems that plague the rest of us! It is unusual that they have the opportunity to spend a whole week in one spot, and the smaller, slower boats often make it to designated ports just in time to refuel and take on water and provisions before setting off once again.

On one side of us we have an Italian boat, crewed by young people who are either a mixture of female and male, or else are all male. So far, it is impossible to tell. They do like loud music on deck late into the night. Are we showing our age? Certainly after the grueling schedule, everyone enjoys the opportunity to let their hair down.

On our other side we have a nice young British couple who, with a non-functioning autopilot as well as an inefficient wind vane, have been hand steering since Australia—and plan to do so for the remainder of the Rally back to Gibraltar. Youth is definitely for the young!

After paying $25,000.00 to join, a lovely British couple about our ages is facing serious equipment and engine problems. Repairs won't be done in time to catch up with the Rally in Phuket—so they are out of the Rally. Many join with the idea of safety traveling in numbers, an understandable thought. One lady assumed that they would be in sight of each other out on the ocean!

The NE monsoon is arriving and it has rained on and off for the past two weeks, along with the early thunder and lightning storms that come in and out as a squall, one terrific storm sending lightning down at us for several hours. Three of the Europa Rally boats in the marina, all of the tugboats, and two of the freighters anchored out in the Strait were hit and lost every piece of electronics aboard, some melting down to nothing. With the short stay for the Rally boats, frantic attempts to get everything replaced in Singapore was a rather daunting task, and we felt for the crews who were hard pressed to do so.

It was important to us to see people up in Port Klang and the Royal Selangor Yacht Club one last time. But we don't want to take the boat upriver to Port Klang when passing through Malaysia. We took a bus from Singapore and stayed with our British friends in K.L. A lovely dinner was shared with friends at the Yacht Club, where the people have been so dear to our hearts and such a memorable part of our cruising life. It was very difficult to make yet another goodbye.

The new Yacht Club is nearly finished and is just beautiful. It will be open for the Raja Muda Race near the end of the November.

November 11, 1994
Raffles Marina
Singapore

Happy Thanksgiving and a Merry Christmas,

Memories of blazing fires and all the Christmas trimmings make us nostalgic for home, but I have purchased another little decorated tree just the right size, to come out in Phuket where we plan to spend our Christmas.

Since our departure is imminent, we are in the usual frenzy, readying for the big push in the months ahead. Not likely to see the likes of a marina and dockside water again in a long time, I am busy keeping my buckets and toilet plunger busy. Don tells anyone who will listen that I have a fear that I will never see fresh water again.

Captain seems to muddle through his days attending to his own concerns, most of which have to do with checking out every system on the boat without a thought to these domestic necessities. First mate here has been ready to jump ship at any moment in recent days, feeling terribly sorry for myself. Captain says that she does this every time we are readying to leave, but one's standards are one's standards!

Yesterday, this first mate went into the city for last minute provisioning— which follows last minute provisioning done by both of us two days before. After spending considerable time perusing the aisles and choosing with such care, I looked around before taking my wallet out to count my cash. All was in order and I had carefully kept track of every item's amount. I put the wallet back into my purse, zipped the purse and turned to the shelves just once more before heading up to the cash register where all was checked through.

Imagine my surprise and horror when I opened my purse to pay— and found my wallet was missing! I was taken to the manager's office, where I dissolved into tears. He kindly arranged for tissues and such and handed me S12.00 for cab fare back to the marina.

The lesson learned: Keep your purse over your shoulder—not in the cart—even in Singapore where it is so easy to relax one's vigilance! How could I be so lacking in judgment?

The cabdriver spoke some broken English and with me sobbing in the back seat, repeated all the way to Raffles Marina, "It all right, Miss. It all right."

But it wasn't! Not only was the cash gone, but credit cards and my driver's license were gone as well. Cash that we couldn't replace and missing cards that had me gasping for breath.

On my arrival, Don was duly concerned when I could only sob, "Something awful has happened." Sob, sob sob.

Frankly, when I was finally able to tell him that my wallet had been stolen and I had lost all of the provisioning money—again—he was so relieved to know this was all that was wrong he didn't go into the state of shock I fully expected. Of course, the little matter of the credit cards would have to be faced.

This was to be our last day here and we were to be off the next morning. I had lost every last dollar of our provisioning money.

For our last night's stay at Raffles Marina we had been given a complimentary dinner in the fancy restaurant upstairs—whose door we had never darkened—as well as a luxurious Garden Room in which to spend the night. It was such an unexpected gift and we had been terribly excited about it for days. Our excitement was dampened now by our fears about the missing money, cards and driver's license—the last being the least of our worries.

This is how we spent our night: After getting ourselves all gussied up for the restaurant we attempted to enjoy a Chinese meal that was very different from any of our prior experiences, consisting of Chinese dishes not often seen in our everyday street world and that were all new to us. The atmosphere was very posh.

Then we went to our lovely Garden Room where, due to the time difference, we spent the entire night making phone calls to Visa and Master Card and to our bank, doing a lot of explaining. I felt like an idiot. We had so looked forward to snuggling down into the luxurious bedding, but no sleep was to be had in our lovely Garden Room after all.

Fortunately, we were able to pick up an emergency Visa card the next day at a hotel downtown. It would be good for thirty days. The permanent card would be sent to Wendy and we made calls to her with instructions to DHL it to Phuket for us to pick up on arrival there. As for the back-up Master Card, we have learned not to keep it on us but to hide it on the boat. It isn't much good as a back-up if it's gone along with the Visa.

We have met two American cruising couples here at the marina and expect to see more of them on down the line, since our paths will be about the same. They are Dick and Penny aboard *Gray Eagle*, and Jerry and Joanie on *Lady D*, whose homeport is Spokane! Who would have thought anyone else from Spokane would be bouncing about out here! *Investigator*, with Faye and Max from Australia, passed through here for a few days and we are anxious to see more of them as well.

"On the Hard" in Singapore

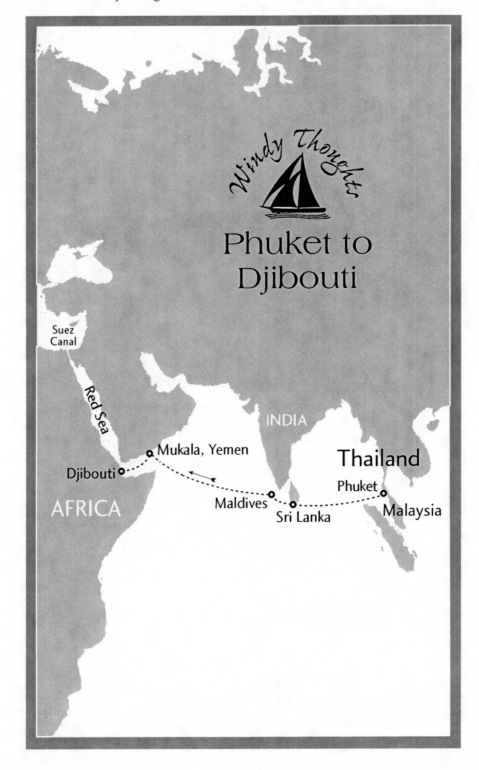

Phuket to
Djibouti

Suez
Canal

Red Sea

INDIA

Mukala, Yemen

Djibouti

Thailand

Phuket

AFRICA

Maldives

Sri Lanka

Malaysia

Chapter 11

Goodbye Southeast Asia, Hello Indian Ocean

The amount of time that a person spends sailing is not deducted from his life span. —Anonymous

After 4.5 years in Southeast Asia and more memories than we could ever have imagined, we were ready to be off and on our way for parts unknown.

It had at times seemed that we were to never leave SE Asia, almost as if something intangible was holding us there. Nevertheless, the years had provided us the opportunity to get to know people, a time to explore and a time to travel the Malacca Strait from Singapore to Phuket and back—as well as south from Singapore to Bankka Island, Indonesia, and back.

We felt privileged to glimpse a part of the world filled with gentle people, peaceful living and amazingly good food. The area offers the cruising sailor one beautiful anchorage after another, an abundance of remote, traditional villages contrasting with the vibrant cities and luxurious resorts. Above all, the welcome from people here is unlike any place in the world. When asked what part of the world is our favorite, it is SE Asia that holds a special place in our hearts.

All engine problems remedied, provisioning completed, all systems checked and re-checked, hull and topsides gleaming, we awaited proper weather before heading north toward Phuket, where we would celebrate Christmas before heading westbound across the Indian Ocean. We were ready to anchor in some peaceful little hidey-hole, to meet new people, see new lands and share new adventures.

The first Commodore of the Royal Selangor Yacht Club, a Brit married to the Sultan's cousin, had told us about a legendary curse placed upon British rubber plantation owners in earlier times. The British men, alone in Malaysia would often form a relationship with local Malay women. When the plantation owners returned to England, it was generally without the company of the Malay women—who would invoke the curse and tell the men that they would never make it out of the country alive. As the story goes, many Englishmen didn't make it out of Malaysia alive.

The story of the curse carries on today and it is said that those who spend time in Malaysia will be destined never to leave. We often laughingly referred to this curse as causing our breakdowns so that we could never really leave Malaysia. We weren't about to test its merits and weren't going to make a stop-over in Port Klang when moving north! We loved Malaysia but our time to move ever westward held precedence, and we had taken the bus to Port Klang for those final goodbyes.

Leaving Singapore for good on November 25, 1994, was a milestone for us. In the generally fairly mild Malacca Strait we encountered two days and nights of nasty storms with thunder and lightning that rattled our nerves. Heavy winds and miserable seas rolled and bashed directly on *Windy Thoughts'* nose, making progress slow and unpleasant.

We dropped anchor on the third day behind an island just outside the entrance to the Klang River, where we had anchored before in the superb mud bottom. After a few hours on the hook, the wind dropped and there wasn't a breath of wind or a ripple on the water all night.

Awakening about midnight, I peeked out of the porthole to discover that we weren't where we were when we went to bed! *Windy Thoughts* was happily drifting about in the shipping lane, amongst many big ships and tankers moving in and out of the Strait and others sitting at anchor awaiting river pilots. She had gone walk-about for a whole mile across the channel and into the middle of all of this shipping activity.

We flew out of our bunk, threw on the spreader lights to light the boat up as much as possible, hit the starter switch on the engine and took our places at the helm and the anchor windlass. The anchor happily dragged along at the end of the chain, not doing a bit of good.

It didn't take us long to get the anchor up and secured on deck, and then to get underway, not to return to the anchorage! Don remarked, "I told you so. That curse is trying to get us again."

There wasn't a reason in the world that we should have dragged in a dead calm, with the anchor set in a good mud bottom. Of course we truly don't believe in curses, but we don't leave on a Friday either—an old sailor's belief.

By day's end we joined up with friends on *Oz* at anchor off Pankgor Island. Along with Mike, Jo and young Jenna, we watched monkeys cavort on the beach, snorkeled, ate our fill of chicken rice at local spots and rented motorbikes to explore the villages on the island.

One late afternoon we all stopped at the very fancy Pan Pacific Hotel. The guards let us in and we made our way to the restaurant beside the pool. After enjoying two cold drinks each, the bill arrived. When we read the total it sent shock waves down our spines—$97.00—a huge contrast to our lunch in the village that came to $14.00 for the five of us! Perhaps we'd best leave the resort life to the tourists from now on!

Conditions on the Malacca Strait were now lovely with clear skies. We were moving into the dry NE monsoon season and the squalls of the wetter SW monsoon season were behind us. The sun bore down as we lounged under the bimini cover, ate all of the Ritz crackers from Singapore, most of the Nature Valley Granola bars, and Don finished up his treasured red licorice while we listened to hour after hour of our favorite music.

In company with *Oz* we made our way toward Phuket, stopping at Langkawi Island to make our clearance from Malaysia and to breathe in all that had been so special to us here one last time. We said our goodbyes to Malaysia at this beautiful island.

Windy Thoughts sailed into Thai waters within a few miles after leaving Langkawi Island. The distinct hull designs of local fishing boats from both countries constantly fascinated us as they busily plied the waters. It was easy to distinguish the Thai boats from the Malay boats, both by the colorful housing and the hulls. Sometimes a boat came near us just to wave hello.

For several days we meandered through the spectacular islands, snorkeling in the perfectly clear turquoise waters and enjoying the beauty surrounding us. Jagged limestone formations rose up as if reaching for the sky. Vegetation is lush, the surroundings tranquil, with a beauty unlike any other place in the world. The busy city life of Singapore and all that it had offered was forgotten as we became exhilarated by cruising once again.

The folks on *Oz* were deciding whether to cross the Indian Ocean or head for Hong Kong to find jobs for the final two years before the changeover to Communist rule. They had just spent two years working in Kuala Lumpur, and Jenna had finished her third grade in the International School. When we reached Phuket, Mike and Jo flew to Hong Kong for a few days to check the city out before making a final decision.

Happily using the anchorage off Ban Nit Marina on the island of Phuket as our base, we were in familiar grounds and it was good to be back.

Don rented a motorbike for the duration of our stay. When we learned of a young fellow with a T-shirt shop who did screen-printing, we jumped on the bike and headed there with our *Windy Thoughts* logo in hand. The minimum order was fifty T-shirts, twenty five for each of us! Our order was given to us in two big plastic packages, and we made it back to the boat with me holding onto Don with one arm around his waist, and the other around one big package. The second big package was tied onto the bike.

We liked our T-shirts so well that we ordered twenty-five polo shirts. The cost was minimal and though it was a challenge to stow seventy-five shirts, in the coming years we found them the mainstay of our wardrobes—possibly the best investment we have ever made!

Christmas in Phuket was celebrated with a giant potluck at Ban Nit. It was a merry crowd, with boats at anchor up in Patong Bay on the western shore sailing down to join us. Our toes dug into the sand as we sang Christmas carols and relished the joy of the season. Another Christmas without snow, blazing fires in the fireplace and families, but one celebrated with friends and full of the Christmas spirit that comes from within.

Days were clear, sunny and hot, with cool nights that stayed in the low eighty degrees. Amongst a fresh group moving through Southeast Asia there were many new people to meet, as well as a few who had lingered. Most were busy getting ready to make the Indian Ocean passage, but others would spend another season in Southeast Asia. Some choose never to leave, finding the area beautiful with unparalleled cruising grounds, easy living, perfect weather and genuinely friendly and welcoming people. In addition—good food!

Don and I celebrated our twenty-seventh wedding anniversary on December 30, 1994, with the folks on *Oz*, *Lady D*, and *Investigator*. Both *Lady D* and *Investigator* were on similar paths as *Windy Thoughts* and we would often bump along

together in the future. For our special night, we crammed into one taxi and chatted and danced the night away at a restaurant with a Filipino band singing American songs.

After the New Year's celebration, *Windy Thoughts* moved over to Nai Harn Bay, the southernmost bay on the west side of Phuket. Farther up the coast, busy Patong Bay was replete with hotels, tourists and lounge chairs on the beach. Quieter Nai Harn Bay was a favored spot of ours with its beautiful sugary white sand beach, the Yacht Club Hotel and a few small restaurants scattered amongst the palms.

Several spectacular bays indent the west coast of Phuket Island from north to south. One of our favorite forays was a motor bike ride over to Kata Beach, south of Patong Bay. An American woman ran a bookshop at Kata and we loved browsing the shelves and picking out new books to add to our ship's library. Knowing our interest in the books written by Tristan Jones, she informed us that he would be coming into the bookstore the following day.

Tristan Jones, a Welshman who single-handed into many unusual spots under hardship conditions, including several months icebound in the Arctic Sea and several weeks up the Amazon, has written books of both adventures as well as his many others. Well known and respected, he often spoke to groups of cruising folks around the world. Tristan lived in Phuket at this time, had lost both legs and was experiencing rapidly declining health.

The following day Don sat and visited with Mr. Jones for over an hour, a real privilege for

Don, as Tristan rarely left his home anymore. Within two years, Tristan Jones passed away, leaving a legacy of love for the sea that is unmatched.

The winds were from the easterly quadrant now, and each day several cruising boats set off west across the Indian Ocean. We were ready for our planned departure on January 12, needing only fresh provisions and fuel and water topped off. The next stop would be Sri Lanka, 1150 nautical miles west and a nine- or ten-day ocean passage.

We had arrived at Nai Harn Bay with a hole in the new raw water hose. Don replaced it and the time had come to top off our diesel tanks from a fuel barge sitting at anchor on the west side of the island.

After taking on fuel and spending the night, we tootled back to Nai Harn Bay. As usual, Don had his head in the engine compartment checking things over while we were underway. To his horror, he found that things had begun to fall apart—again!

The hook went down and Don went to work, immediately discovering big problems. The pin through the shaft was sheared off and the rubber doughnut fastened to the flange had three hairline cracks in it! This latest development was a real down moment for both of us.

Don and I got *Breezy* down and went to shore to head into Phuket Town on the motor bike. On our return to *Breezy*, we found Max and Faye from *Investigator* sitting in the restaurant. Don's spirits were at an all time low, a fact that he was trying to disguise. When he and Max began to talk engines, Faye piped up and announced that Max would have a look at it! Aren't wives great?

Max is an excellent diesel mechanic, and, though not his line of work Max likely often felt it was, because he kept *Investigator's* engine going over the years. Faye, who would become a dear friend, often stated that she didn't know why they had to sail the boat around the world—because Max saw little of the world with all of the time spent in the engine compartment. After all, he could do that without ever bothering to leave home.

As for Faye, she had spent three weeks in Nai Harn Bay varnishing lovely *Investigator's* britework. She intended to be the first woman to varnish her way around the world. Cruising was a labor of love for her Max.

Meanwhile, Max earned Don's title "Sailor's Angel". Once Max had his head in *Windy Thoughts'* engine compartment, he was able to help Don set things right. If Max can't fix it, it probably can't be fixed—and he surely was an angel sent from above!

New and longer bolts had to be procured for the engine mounts and a new flange had to be fashioned. In three days Don and I made many frenzied trips back and forth to a machine shop in Phuket Town on the motor bike. Fortunately, one of the fellows spoke some English, was very competent and understood our problem.

Our sailor's angel wasn't done yet! Max and Don spent considerable time realigning the engine. This entailed raising the engine several times with our come-along—the same one so laughed at when Don originally put it aboard back in Seattle at the beginning of this grand adventure. Don loved his come-along.

Don and I upped anchor and spent three days running up and down the coast to test everything out. It seemed that all was going well until Don began his engine check as we re-entered Nai Harn Bay. Once again, the pin through the flange was sheared! Our hopes sank. Were we destined never to get out of Southeast Asia, after all?

Starting over again, Max and Don put their heads together, and Max determined that it had to be thrust from the propeller that was shearing the bolt. Don got the flange off and we hopped on the bike and rode back to the machine shop. A shoulder was welded to the damaged flange and a plug was welded into the other to keep as a backup. In order that all be 100 percent right, the mechanic wanted Don to bring the shaft in so it could be trued with the flange. This meant diving on the boat while *Windy Thoughts* sat at anchor.

The procedure was difficult without scuba gear because there was no room for both the tank and Don between the rudder and the stern. With the tank, Don wouldn't be able to brace himself against the stern in order to break the shaft loose from the stern gland and slide the shaft out. Surfacing continually for air and then heading back down, it took him over two hours.

The bike took us back to the machine shop, where Don had extra keyways made for the flange. With Max's good help, the shaft was put back in on January 18 and we would run the engine with the damaged flange and the plug. The new flange that Don had ordered while still in Malaysia had never arrived, so he called Seattle and reordered yet another.

Oz returned from Hong Kong, and having found well-paying jobs readily available, Mike and Jo would soon set sail from Phuket to Hong Kong. We would miss them, but were happy for them. After all, what is life if not an adventure?

The flange arrived; we paid 100 percent duty, and we anticipated that we would be ready to leave Phuket when both *Investigator* and *Gray Eagle* returned from a few days in the Similan Islands—with plans to keep a radio schedule as we all bobbed along toward Sri Lanka.

A German fellow repaired electronics in his home and we hoped he could fix our autopilot—our faith in it shaky, as well it might be. In addition, the radar wasn't working, so we tackled the challenge of getting ashore in the dinghy with both pieces of equipment intact. The surf created in Nai Harn Bay at the time made dinghy landing very challenging and getting back out through the surf even more so. After a successful landing, we arrived on the beach soaked to the bone ourselves but with both a dry autopilot and radar!

Though the German fellow couldn't fix the autopilot, he was able to repair the radar and we were very happy for that.

When we arrived back at the beach we discovered that *Breezy* had been caught in the breakers of an unusually high tide, and tumbled violently about. No damage, but everything we left in her was washed away, including our

Teva cruising sandals from Seattle that were irreplaceable here. We searched up and down the beach and amongst the rocks, and though we found both of mine we found only one of Don's.

Many tourists lounged on the beach within only feet of *Breezy*, but had paid no attention to her battle with the breakers. Rarely did we leave anything of importance in the dinghy, but we had felt safe there with so many people around. Put in perspective, it was only a sandal, but one from a pair most useful in our cruising life.

When *Investigator* returned, we took Max and Faye to dinner at the nice Yacht Club Hotel ashore, much more elegant than the usual digs we frequented. Were it not for Max, we wouldn't be leaving Southeast Asia, and nothing could truly repay him for his help. It was a lovely evening with good food and good friends, a fitting goodbye to Phuket.

On the morning of January 26, 1995, *Windy Thoughts* finally hauled anchor and pointed her bow westward toward Sri Lanka. The flange had arrived the day before and we were off. Most everyone else in our group had left, as had most other boats heading west.

Goodbye, Southeast Asia. Hello, Indian Ocean and new adventures ahead!

We kept radio schedules with *Gray Eagle*, *Investigator*, *Lady D* and *Exodus*, another American boat with a young couple aboard. The other boats were all off two days earlier. There was a loud hurrah when we came up on schedule that morning. *Windy Thoughts* had made it out of Southeast Asia! *Ponderosa*, an American boat with Craig and Mark aboard, called to let us know they had just left Patong Bay and were ten miles behind us. Down the line we would all meet up and share land excursions.

Boats that left earlier in the month reported light winds, but by now the winds were northeasterly at fifteen knots right on our quarter. By day two, winds had increased to twenty knots and we were all barreling along with the help of a westerly current. The winds tended more easterly than northeasterly and we were sailing dead downwind with a very heavy roll from side to side in the bigger seas. It would stay this way for the full 1150 miles to Sri Lanka, twenty to twenty-five-knot winds behind us and a fast sail that gave each of us record days.

Sailing again and on our way to new lands! What would the morrow bring?

With favorable wind and current giving us optimal speed, we approached the Sombrero Channel separating the Andaman and Nicobar Islands just north of Sumatra. We wished a stop were allowed at the Nicobars, where there were still working elephants, but good friends had attempted a stop and were held there for two days. Don opted to take a chance and shoot on through the channel that was off limits. We were on a roll and *Windy Thoughts* was headed for the barn when Channel 16, the radio hailing channel, suddenly came alive with a voice commanding, "Sailboat in the channel, come in immediately."

My heart stopped. We could see no boat within our sights or on the radar and Don told me not to answer the radio. *Windy Thoughts* rolled right on through without further notice and we breathed huge sighs of relief, not used to such risky business! Sri Lanka, here we come!

Radio schedules both mornings and evenings provided the chance to share our day's experiences, advice about whatever was broken down on any one of our respective vessels, and puzzles for thought read by *Exodus* each morning. It was always a race to the finish to see which boat could first solve the mystery presented.

We commiserated on our high levels of discomfort as the seas met at differing angles and caused heavy rolling for everyone. It may be a sleigh ride, but it wasn't comfortable!

We compared breakdowns and Don and I felt fortunate to be unscathed for the moment. *Investigator*'s spinnaker pole broke the third day out. *Ponderosa* lost both banks of batteries and *Gray Eagle*'s wind generator broke down the second morning.

Of most concern was Jerry on *Lady D*, who was experiencing severe abdominal pain that had everyone very worried. Fortunately, *Lady D* had crew aboard—Rosie and Jonell from the Philippines with little one-year-old Paulie. They joined *Lady D* in Hong Kong, where Jerry and Joan had worked for a year. Rosie took care of the meals and tended to Paulie, and Jonell and Joan handled the boat while Jerry was down.

This Filipino family crept into all our hearts as we got to know them over the next months, truly an integral part of *Lady D* until she reached her final port—and all three continue to be family to Jerry and Joan today.

After two days Jerry rallied, the pain lessened considerably and there was much relief from all boats keeping a close watch on this potential medical crisis. Radio calls to Phuket were frequent, with queries as to an available rescue service if Jerry needed to be lifted off the boat.

Don was tending the mainsail at 3 a.m. and using the spreader lights for visibility in the darkness. While I was tending the sheet, the spreader lights suddenly went out. At the same time, the rod holding our Hustler antennas broke off, catching on the lifeline just long enough for me to grab it before it went overboard. As I struggled with the antenna with one hand and the sheet with the other—and Don was busy with sails—the spotlight cord burst into flames in the cockpit. Fire on a boat throws you into heart-pounding red alert, but the fact that the fire was in the cockpit well was our saving grace. Five minutes later, the depth sounder packed up.

When order was restored, Don went below to sleep and I relaxed for my watch. All in a night's passage.

To pass the time and keep awake I counted stars, checked out constellations, hummed tunes and sang old songs to myself. It wasn't long before I heard a sound directly aft of the cockpit. Thinking about the tales of sailors who heard voices at sea, I wondered: did we have an unseen passenger aboard?

As the noise increased, I climbed up onto the stainless framework of the stern rail, looked over the top of the bimini and came face to face with a big bird that didn't even flinch on coming face to face with me. He was still there to greet Don when he came up for his watch and rode along with us until morning before deciding to continue on his journey west, perhaps in search of Sri Lanka. The bird left us happy that *Windy Thoughts* had provided a respite during his long journey.

Don got out his fishing gear with high hopes of getting a marlin on his line. Though the marlin didn't materialize, Don did hook a yellowtail tuna that gave him the fight of his life.

We were rolling down big seas coming directly from behind, Beethoven's Fifth Symphony booming—our favorite music for boisterous and crashing seas—the day was beautiful and Don had a smile that stretched from ear to ear. After two hours of working the fish, it was within sight just below the surface of the water and just aft of the boat. Exactly when the fish surfaced within two feet of the stern, the new pole broke in two. Undaunted, Don grabbed the end of the pole with the fish attached and didn't let go. No matter that he had to dive below the seat across the back of the cockpit to hang over the cap rail.

We sailed in ten-foot seas on top of a five-foot swell, and I held the video camera with one hand and grabbed his leg with the other to keep him from going overboard. Somehow, Don worked the pole around the stanchions, under lifelines and to the gate on the starboard side, all the while screaming at me to open the gate. He threw himself over the cap rail and hung over the side with me holding onto both legs now, camera abandoned.

How the two of us wrestled the fish into the boat is a mystery to us; adrenalin apparently kicked in when needed! Because we had no way to keep what was probably all of 100 pounds of fish fresh, Don pulled out the hook and let this wonderful fish over the side and into the sea, to happily live out the rest of his life where he belonged. The entire episode was an exciting one and quite a diversion to our days at sea, certainly a high point of the passage and something to talk about for days after.

Having a huge whale play around and under your boat when thousands of miles from land can also be a thrill—depending on how you look at it. While we were surfing along one day with the sun blazing down on us, we glanced behind us to see the huge giant no more than 200 feet from our stern and closing in on us fast. As he charged through the water toward *Windy Thoughts*, he looked bigger than the boat, and our mouths hung open with wonder and terror. Wonder as to his majesty—and terror that we may be about to meet our demise when this grand beast collided with us!

 Slicing through the seas, water poured over his head as he came at us. Just when he was very close behind the boat, he dove underneath to surface on the opposite side. We could easily have reached down and touched him! While I was still rapt with the wonder, Don was still rapt with the terror—because the whale was much bigger than the boat and the next course of events could be a sinking in a very short time.

About ten minutes later we looked astern to see the whale charging down the surface of the big waves and coming directly for us again. Should we grab the life vests and play out our abandon ship procedures—or was he just playing with us? He roared toward us like a freight train—only to dive underneath the boat again and reappear on the other side.

For the next four hours, this same sequence played itself out repeatedly as he circled back behind us and merrily played his game of touch and go. Though I felt a distinct kinship with him, Don never quite lost his wariness of the situation—as well he shouldn't. But there was magic in the air for those four hours. Living this life had given us boundless moments of nature's blessings and this giant had given us those blessings in both excitement and wonder to remember, always.

Seven days and ten hours after departing Phuket, Thailand, *Windy Thoughts* was approaching Galle Harbor, Sri Lanka. It was 5 p.m. on February 5, 1995, and we were in the middle of a huge squall. Visibility was so poor that I went out on the bowsprit in attempts to see the big red bell buoy that was to mark the entrance. I glanced down toward the water to find that the dolphin striker—or bobstay—was dangling from the end of the bowsprit—broken off from the boat at the bottom attachment!

The bobstay, a half-inch stainless steel rod running from the fore end of the bowsprit down to the hull at the water line, supports the bowsprit, and it had detached from its heavy-duty connection to the boat. The forestay connects to the bowsprit and runs to the top of the mast, holding the mast up. How in the world did we escape losing the mast as we ran wing and wing in heavy seas?

When we couldn't find the entrance buoy, we called *Investigator*, who had been in for two days ahead of us. Max informed us that we couldn't find the buoy because it wasn't there. It was ashore being painted. Max came out in his dinghy and guided us to the spot they had ready for us amongst about twenty other sailboats off the town of Galle.

There was no room for swinging at anchor and everyone was tied bow and stern to the wall or to buoys and one or more other boats. Jerry from *Lady D* jumped into his dinghy and joined Max, taking our lines and tying us bow and stern between two buoys as we ran other lines to other boats. This circus entailed much untying and retying of lines from the maze of boats here at Galle. In the end we seemed quite secure, if not in a position for a fast get-away!

There had been little sleep during the seven day passage and, while a great sail, it had been a tiring and uncomfortable one. The others in our group had arrived in the same fatigued condition but had two days on us to rest up. We were ready to crawl into our bunk when a call for *Windy Thoughts* came on the VHF radio.

Investigator's Faye had dinner all ready for us! Dick, from *Gray Eagle*, would be our boat-to-boat chauffeur with his dinghy. More sailing angels in the way of good friends, and with lamb chops from Faye's freezer, along with a glass of Max's red, we were once again amongst the living. But we slept the sleep of the dead when we got back to the boat.

The folks from *Investigator*, *Gray Eagle* and *Lady D* had planned a trip inland to see Sri Lanka that included us. Sunil, a young fellow who ran a vegetable stand at the market and spoke some English, had talked them into hiring him as a guide for the trip. Sunil knew a man with a van and someone else would be the driver. All we had to do was be ready—and we were determined to be.

So there was no rest-up for this little crew of *Windy Thoughts*. First of importance was our clearance into Sri Lanka and then the problem of the broken bobstay to solve, before departing on this grand sojourn with our friends.

The first issue was taken care of early the next morning with a call to the Harbor Master, who came out to the boat to start the procedure. Then we headed into town to the home of Don Windsor, a native Sri Lankan who had for years acted as an agent for yachts and kept his home open for cruising folk to gather. Everyone used his service to make their clearance and though he had passed away, family members carried on the agency service.

We continued on into Galle from Don Windsor's home in a little "tuk tuk". Cows wandered in the streets amongst people doing their daily produce shopping, and bullock carts carrying vegetables on the way to the market bumbled along. Galle is very rural in character and easy to walk about. Smiling faces greeted us and made us feel welcome. Dodging the sacred cows, we wound through narrow, dusty streets.

Don headed for an auto store known to be of help to boaters that might be his only chance to find chain to replace the broken bobstay. With turn-buckles onboard and new chain welded at the auto shop, a replacement bobstay could be fashioned. The auto shop could get chain from Colombo and it would be in the next morning.

The problem seemingly solved for the time being, we were off for the produce market. A jumble of stalls piled high with local fare greeted us, each stall manned by vendors with smiling faces, wanting desperately to lure us in. Every shop that we passed had an owner who did his best to encourage us to make a purchase.

It was late afternoon before we were back to the boat, and at 6 p.m. we headed back ashore to a surprise birthday party for Dick. Penny had found a restaurant inside a home set in lush tropical surroundings and had arranged for a dinner party for eighteen. The entire family joined in the planning for the wonderful dinner of Indian cuisine. Sleep would have to wait.

Don took the turnbuckles to the auto shop the next morning and showed them the welding needed. The work would be completed while we were on our land excursion. We hoped for the best.

The bobstay work underway, Don made several trips back and forth from the dinghy dock to a water spigot about 300 feet away, filling our water jugs and ferrying them out to the boat. He hired *Lady D*'s Jonell to jerry-jug diesel for us while we were on our inland tour of Sri Lanka. Jonell and Rosie planned to stay aboard to watch the boats and get *Lady D* ready to be off on our return.

I organized and packed for our trip, planned for five or six days.

At 7:00 the next morning we rowed ashore, tied *Breezy* securely to the rickety dinghy dock, and were ready with the folks on *Investigator*, *Gray Eagle* and *Lady D* to meet our van and set off to see Sri Lanka. The van arrived right on time and had seats for Sunil and the driver in front and four rows of seats behind, enough for everyone.

The driver said nary a word for the next five days, so we never knew if he spoke any English. He could drive, however, and kept us on our toes as we sped around curves, dodged bullock carts, the occasional working elephant and big trucks met on the road. Roads in Sri Lanka are not always in good condition and at times it could take several hours to go fifty miles. There were few cars, a luxury not affordable to the majority of people.

The countryside is indescribably lush; many believe Sri Lanka was the original Garden of Eden. The Strait between Sri Lanka and India is named Adams Reach—a fact we found intriguing.

Our van and driver carried us up into the mountains, where we stayed our first night at a small, rustic inn. Our rooms were simple, but immaculate and inviting after the long day's drive.

After settling ourselves in, we all gathered around one big table for dinner at the inn's restaurant, where we were the only patrons that evening. When our dinners hadn't arrived after an hour, we politely inquired about how long it might be, and were assured all would be ready soon. Fully another 1.5 hours passed before our meals arrived, and eight hungry people devoured Indian curries that awakened us with their spiciness. The lively dinner conversation and good company marked a happy beginning for our sojourn into Sri Lanka.

Full and content, we headed for our respective rooms. In the mountains the temperature dropped to sixty-five degrees at night and even with blankets on the beds we nearly froze. My, those tropical climes had a hold on us! Hot temperatures during the day had us wiping the sweat from our brows and the contrast during the night hours was significant.

Sunil had made plans for us to visit a tea plantation and the next morning we all piled into our van to head further into the mountains. We watched women returning from higher ground carrying baskets full of tea leaves atop their heads, and were invited to sit inside and enjoy hot and delicious tea to our heart's content. Everyone left with Ceylon tea to take back to our boats.

As our van worked its way back down the mountain a boy ran along beside us, carrying flowers that he eagerly attempted to sell. Each time the van made its way around a sharp switch-back the boy was there once again, having run straight down the side of the mountain. He chased us through five switch-backs just to sell us that little bunch of flowers! Happy to oblige, we gave him a big bonus for his enterprising efforts and he continued on down the mountain, still plying his trade.

Our next stop was the city of Kandi, where Sunil guided us to another inn for the night. After another good dinner of Indian cuisine we were invited to sit in a circle to enjoy local dancing. The dancers wore traditional colorful dress and their dance was fascinating to watch, quite acrobatic and painting many symbolic stories.

Kandi is an interesting small city and we would have enjoyed looking around more the next day, but after a visit to the well-known Kandi Temple that intrigued everyone in our group, it was time to move on. Sunil had planned busy days for us, and we were finding that the actual hours in a day didn't quite provide enough time for all that Sunil felt we should accomplish in a day!

It was after a very interesting stop at a temple, beneath which the original Buddha's tooth is said to be buried, that Sunil shepherded us back into our van, to escort us to one of his happiest surprises, a captivating visit to an elephant orphanage.

A boy expertly guided a herd of young elephants down to the river for their baths, and we all followed along to watch the bathing that these big fellows seemed to enjoy so much. Their joy was infectious and everyone wanted to get right into the river along with these mammoth animals.

As we drove along roads taking us through spectacularly scenic countryside, we passed working elephants on the road, their masters skillfully directing them. When we crossed a bridge two of the giants were taking their baths in the river just below us and we all got out to watch them frolic in the water, enjoying their baths every bit as much as those at the elephant orphanage. Sri Lanka's culture is fascinating, as is this stunningly beautiful country.

Sunil's plan included visits to two ancient cities whose ruins dated back 2,000 years, and we spent several hours wandering about each, Sunil passing on tidbits of historical information that made it all the more interesting. When the van was driving away from one site, Don noticed men working at the entrance and excitedly called to the rest of us, "Look guys, they're building more ruins!" Filled with exuberance and away from the realities of making passages for a few days, our time spent together was filled with laughter.

We climbed to the top of Sigiriya (Lion Head), the fifth century marvel and the rock fortress of King Kasyapa who reigned from 479-497 A.D.—and where the King held off his enemies. It was a long climb to the top along footholds and paths cut into the side of the huge rock sticking 400 feet above the landscape. Along the way we passed the world-renowned mirror wall, a sheltered pocket with graffiti and frescos of heavenly maidens painted on the rock many centuries ago. At the top, the huge rock flattened out to provide a vast area for the King's fortress and its ruins remain there today. King Kasyapa was said to have kept many concubines at his fortress.

Once we had been deposited at our quarters for the night Sunil and the driver disappeared, to emerge again early the following morning, ready to set off for the day. We guessed that they spent the nights in the van. Sunil did an admirable job of telling us about the sights, though we weren't always sure that his facts were correct. By the end of the first day we had realized that his disappearances during the day while we were looking about were not for sleeping on the job, as we originally suspected. It was soon apparent that he was imbibing something stronger than soda pop.

The Tamil Tigers were active at the time and while we were riding along one day four who were armed and in full camouflage ran out from the foliage, dashed in front of our van and quickly disappeared up a hill on the other side of the road. We had time only to gasp and then they were gone.

Throughout our five days of traveling through Sri Lanka we passed many small villages and farms and people everywhere waved to us. We marveled at row after row of perfectly stepped and perfectly spaced crops on the mountainsides, not a square foot of land wasted. Our accommodations were always good at small, inexpensive local inns. Meals were excellent, inexpensive and a high point of our day.

Our excursion nearly over, the men wanted to stop at Colombo, and it was 9 p.m. before we were on its outskirts. Sunil had an inn in mind but it was full for the night. We continued on into the city, making very slow progress as traffic increased, surrounded by honking horns. It was soon obvious that we were in an area unfamiliar to both Sunil and the driver and we were not at all sure that Sunil actually knew of any alternative accommodations.

Suddenly, a huge, multistoried Hilton Hotel loomed up ahead!

"Stop here!" we yelled in unison.

A Hilton would be far out of our budgetary constraints, but we were unable to bounce about any longer. We had the driver pull up to the front portico and stop in front of the big glass doors. Dick was nominated to go in and negotiate prices—even though the cost per room was higher than the group's total spending for the previous four nights, including meals!

The driver was instructed to take the van down the drive into an underground parking garage. Apparently, neither he nor Sunil had ever ventured into such a structure, and there was much discussion between the two of them in their native language along with lots of arm waving—the first we heard the driver utter a word during the entire trip.

As we made our way down the ramp the van suddenly jammed between the floor and the ceiling, proving to be too tall to clear the entrance. The driver stepped on the gas and attempted to lurch ahead and free the van but only wedged it in further.

Sunil issued directions, "Eight people out. "

We obeyed, the men tried to give helpful suggestions, but no one was listening. The driver, red in the face, huffed, puffed and shook his head in exasperation. By now, several other men had gathered about and there was a good deal of excited discussion about our problem, not a word that we could understand, but all intent was very clear.

Soon Sunil directed us, "Eight people back in van."

With the luxurious Hilton only steps away, we dutifully climbed back into the van. The men who were gathered around us jumped onto the bumpers and jumped up and down while the driver gunned the engine. Nothing happened.

Sunil gave further directions, "Eight people out with all baggage."

We shuffled our bags out of the van and stood aside. The men again climbed onto the bumpers—and again jumped up and down as the driver revved the engine and Sunil shouted orders. This time the goal was accomplished and the van rolled free and on down the ramp.

As for the eight of us, we lugged our bags up the ramp and back up the drive to the front entrance, ready to retire to our nice accommodations. But we made a 180-degree turn when we discovered three very nice restaurants in the hotel. Italian met with everyone's immediate approval and we agreed to meet there at 10 p.m. after freshening up. Enjoying a fine meal and an evening to remember full of more laughter and good conversation reminded us that, yes, the cruising life is good!

For the women, our conversation centered on the inviting rooms just upstairs with beautiful, smooth, cool sheets, big luxurious bath towels waiting to soak up the water from a hot shower or bath—and the thoughts of room service at our beck and call.

Making an ocean passage can seem days of deprivation when compared with a normal day lived on land. Out on that ocean your world is sailing and navigating, often accompanied with varying levels of discomfort. The normalcy that we take for granted as we go about our day in the comforts of our homes can seem like another world entirely—because it is.

After our dinner, Faye announced that while the men got up early to ferret out a hardware store, she intended to have breakfast served to her in bed. When morning came, she admitted to getting up in the night just to walk about the room and touch the furniture, the drapes and those thick towels in the bathroom. Imagine—a real toilet that flushed and didn't have to be pumped! We commiserated on the luxury of a long, luxurious bath, running all the water we wanted— such decadence!

That afternoon the van was loaded and we headed back to Galle, a distance of about sixty miles and taking 3.5 hours to negotiate. We stopped at the auto shop and picked up our parts before going back to the harbor. It was time to say goodbye to our Sunil and we collectively shared in a very generous tip for both him and our driver by way of thanking them for giving us five wonderful days.

We trudged to the dinghy dock with our bags and with good memories filling our heads, the dock bouncing up and down heavily with every step. Rowing out to *Windy Thoughts*, we knew that the good times shared had been special, but that it was time to get ready to set for sea again.

During our last three days in Galle Don fixed the bobstay, worked on antennas, and we changed the engine's oil. Our laundry was done by hand by a fellow who hung it to dry under the trees and I picked it up on our last day. It was time to prepare our sea berths with clean bedding and clean the boat for one last time before setting off.

We were ready once again to set to sea, westward bound in the Indian Ocean and headed on the leg that would take us to the Maldives. What would the morrow bring, and what treasures might lay ahead?

March 1, 1995
At sea
Indian Ocean passage

Hello Susan,

Everything heard or read about this Indian Ocean passage has proved to be true for us, and the placid seas permit me to sit below at the table in our little cabin as I write. The days are sunny and restful, much like being out on a big lake and without even the big swells to roll us about.

Windy Thoughts was the first of our group to reach the northernmost atoll of the Maldives. We anchored behind the island of Uluguma off a very remote and beautiful Muslim village, deciding to skip the southern islands where the tourists are gathered. The others arrived shortly after.

The Maldives are known for the magnificent diving, and *Windy Thoughts* was anchored off an exquisite reef just waiting to be explored. We had perfection at our doorstep—with beautiful turquoise blue water in which we could clearly see the anchor sitting on the bottom in fifty feet of water. Blue skies, sunshine and perfection in this thing called cruising. It doesn't get any better than this. Have we said that before?

Having motored about 75 percent of the time from Sri Lanka, the one concern shared by our entire group was diesel consumption. Just after settling in at anchor a man in a small boat rowed out to us and introduced himself as the Judge. We didn't have permission to go ashore (the Port of Entry is in the southern islands) but we were assured that "if we needed something" we were welcome to go ashore. We were also assured that arrangements would be made to get diesel for all of us.

At 3:00 the next morning one of the local boats set sail for another island, returning at 5 p.m, with five barrels of diesel, one for each of us! The sludge from the barrel bottoms was disturbed during transit, so the  barrels were stood upright on the beach overnight to settle.

The next day the men undertook the task of jerry-jugging the diesel from the beach to the boats. Yes, our division of labor definitely has its advantages at times!

The Judge was our guide as we trooped ashore to visit the village of about 400 people—one of the most remarkably lovely and immaculate villages we have seen. Homes were built of coral with yards of white sand that was swept clean each day. The island is heavily wooded and in-cluded fruit trees along with towering palms. Streets are laid out with perfect symmetry, with thick, beautiful hedges  and an obvious attention to detail. Each yard has a row of three or four chairs made from tree limbs, with a sling-backed macramé rope seat—beautiful, comfortable and ingenious.

Women and little girls shied away from our cameras and we were very careful not to offend anyone. In contrast the men and boys loved the cam-eras—and it wasn't long before Max had all the little boys involved in a game of cat and mouse and then taught them leapfrog. Language barriers are never an issue with kids! The little girls held back on the sidelines, obviously want-ing to join in and smiling in delight.

Uluguma was a bright spot in the middle of the Indian Ocean and our three days at anchor went all too fast. As always, it was soon time to venture on and we continued our voyage toward the Red Sea.

I have said it—the Red Sea. I am trying not to obsess about it, and I am certainly glad that our passage since leaving Thailand has been so delightful.

The winds finally picked up and we know we can make Selalah, Oman, though it is presently Ramadan and cruisers at Selalah cannot leave their boats until after sundown each day. Though none of us have harbor charts for Mukala, it is closer and we do have coordinates and a good description shared during radio contact with a boat whose crew recommends it.

Windy Thoughts was under power for fifty hours until the winds finally filled in, light winds at about ten to twelve knots—enough that our GPS shows a speed of 6.5 knots over the ground on this placid ocean with nearly non-existent seas. Yes, it is as good as it gets!

Yesterday Don dug out his special lure in hopes of getting a marlin on the line. He was lucky, but the marlin soon took the new lure and departed for better company, as has happened before. I think Don should be fishing for something for dinner.

A large group of pilot whales played about the boat today very much like dolphins, crossing back and forth in front of the bow wave effortlessly as we skimmed through the water.

Last night two big birds rode along up on top of the bimini, squawking all night long, odd company for each of us on our night watches that both Don and I have thoroughly enjoyed. As we move about this earth the night sky is always changing, and it is amazing at sea without any lights from land to dim its wonder. Don describes our passage across the Indian Ocean as just ghosting along, his favorite expression.

Today I baked three loaves of bread. There is just nothing better than the aroma of fresh bread baking in the oven, even though it is so very hot out and using the oven only adds to the discomfort. Fresh bread is a wonderful treat out here with thousands of miles of ocean surrounding us.

The wind pipes up to about fourteen knots now and then and we heel over a bit. My reverie broken for a moment, I wonder if perhaps the whisker pole should come down; a mere fourteen knots only seems so much more in these perfect seas.

March 9, 1995
Mukala, Yemen

Hello again,

Yemen probably doesn't conjure up images of white and salmon-colored buildings sitting invitingly on the hillside, even though a very barren and brown hillside. After all, it is about 300 miles east of Aden. That isn't east of Eden.

However, this is just the image we had as we made our approach, the town so quaint- looking after thirteen days at sea. It definitely wasn't quaint or pretty as we drew closer and we realized that picturesque isn't the word to describe Mukala—not an attractive spot, but certainly an interesting one.

Though we had no chart for Mukala, we had coordinates for the latitude and longitude of the western tip of the breakwater—along with navigation tips to offset the fact that there are no lights and no navigational aids. It was recommended not to go in at night and to be very wary of long floating lines from the Somali boats in the harbor. Look for rocks along the coast, see the town on the hillside and see the sunken ship that looks like it is at anchor. Keep this ship to port and the stone wall to starboard.

Eden it definitely isn't, but everyone has welcomed us with smiles accompanied by the ever-present machine guns and daggers. Officials came out to the boat to do our clearance, quite pleasant and certainly very curious. *Ponderosa* and *Lady D* went on to Aden and *Investigator* and *Gray Eagle* sit bobbing about near us. There is considerable sea swell in here and we actually roll from gunwale to gunwale. They are putting out stern anchors, but we don't want to bother—so we roll.

Our foreign flags fly along with those of a few goat boats from Somalia sitting next to us, and we hope that we aren't entangled with any of their long lines that do run every which-way! A distinct odor occasionally wafts our way, but we attempt to pay it never mind.

Don was left behind as the rest of us excitedly made our first sojourn into Mukala. The bilge pump alarm came on just as we were stepping down into the dinghy and Don stayed aboard to ferret out the problem, a hole in the raw water line. After thirteen days at sea he was as anxious as I was to join the others and explore ashore, but insisted that he could work better on his own. Still, it wasn't as enjoyable knowing that he was missing out on the fun. Not that there is a lot of fun to be had in Mukala. But just getting off the boat and getting together with friends rates as a good time. And we would be exploring a new place!

Our first guns were encountered when we stepped ashore to be met by a guard stationed at the dock and brandishing an automatic weapon. The guard asked for our shore passes, and we were soon to find that guns are carried openly—and virtually all carry daggers. We hear from friends up ahead in Aden that Mukala is much nicer. This doesn't bode too well for Aden.

Nothing read or seen in pictures quite prepared us for the utter visual desolation of this part of the world. Think brown, brown and browner without a blade of grass, a tree or a flower in sight. Instead, a vast area of rocky, brown rubble as far as the eye can see. Garbage is strewn all about and goats roam the streets, eating on discarded cardboard or whatever else lies about. The locale creates a very forlorn picture, but perhaps my attitude about our upcoming Red Sea passage clouds my vision.

Women peer out of doorways but slink away inside when we come near and are never seen out on the streets. All wear black in entirety, including their hands—and are veiled so that only their eyes peek out. It seems so uncomfortable in this intense heat. How I would like to make eye contact and share a smile in communication. The men are eager to talk to us and we so wished the women shared this privilege as well.

The street scene was even more deplorable than could be imagined from the boat. Everyone was anxious to find a place to eat and we eventually found a sidewalk restaurant, open onto the dusty street and so unappealing that I couldn't bring myself to order food—but did settle for a soda in a bottle and some fresh papaya with lime. Everyone else in our entourage delved happily into local dishes that honestly looked delicious, using their fingers as is the custom. Certainly, I do need to loosen up! We were a curiosity for everyone around us.

The men were armed with machine guns and carried hand guns in holsters, all carried openly. One fellow happily tossed his machine gun to Max to take a look at it. Knives that Don tells me are famous and smuggled in from the north are carried in a fancy scabbard. Very interesting dinner companions and I knew that Don would love to have been part of it.

Everything closes from noon to four in the afternoon. We were told that the many buildings that looked to have crumbled or been bombed out had simply fallen apart from rain. Rain? What rain here in this brown world? My descriptions are leaning heavily toward the negative—because the close proximity to the Red Sea is clouding my world! I do need to appreciate the here and now.

After lunch a fellow offered to take us to a hotel that we were anxious to check out for future restaurant possibilities. He returned a few minutes later with an old car, carrying a loaded machine gun and a handgun in a holster. We jumped in, the loaded machine gun propped on the seat between him and Max, its barrel pointing toward the back seat and directly at Dick's head.

Adel, our new-found friend and driver, lived in Aden. He was visiting Mukala and wouldn't even consider traveling unarmed. When a group of risky-looking characters passed by in a van, Adel explained that they were an extremely dangerous group—but we shouldn't worry because everyone who lives here is armed—and he himself was prepared. I decided, on the spot, to feel well protected.

After following the coastline for a few miles, we came to the hotel, which looked pretty up-market after downtown Mukala. Instead of stopping, Adel drove right on past, explaining that he wanted to first show us some local sights.

As the road stretched further and further from civilization, I began to wonder if we weren't going to see that hotel after all—but instead were being kidnapped. How I wished that Don were with us! How soon would he begin to wonder where we were if we didn't return? What could Don do back in Mukala, the only foreigner in a city full of armed men and goats?

To our relief, Adel did take us to see some very interesting 3,000-year old buildings that jutted out of the rocks. When we turned back to the hotel, we found it clean and bright after what we had seen so far—the restaurant appearing to be a good spot to return to for a meal.

While we spent our day sightseeing in beautiful downtown Mukala and its further outskirts, Don had his head in the bilge. He did, however, have the opportunity to chat with a few local boys out fishing for cuttlefish in the bay, but thought them such pretty little things that he politely declined those offered him and wonders if we have missed a treat.

The next day was finally Don's turn to observe Mukala and we went in ahead of the others to have his walkabout. When our group was all together again, we managed to flag down one of the few cars on the street and asked, "Are you a taxi?", sure that the driver would consider himself one to earn a few bucks.

We took pictures of Max brandishing the driver's machine gun before piling in for a ride to the hotel that sat on a cliff overlooking the sea. It was downright scenic after downtown Mukala.

We had a very good lobster lunch for $8.00 apiece and watched a few children and adults swimming in the pool, happy to see two women enjoying the water, fully covered in the burkka and black gloves covering their hands.

The month-long observance of Ramadan had just ended and many shops hadn't yet reopened, though none looked particularly interesting. A few scraggly-looking vegetables made up the market and were on display on some pieces of rags on the ground along the street.

Alexander, who has an office just inside the harbor gate where we come ashore, has evidently made himself the yachtsman's go-fer and arranges fuel. We paid $.03 per liter for diesel, for a total of $10.00 for the same amount of fuel that cost us $100.00 in the Maldives! Ah ha! Something very positive!

Alexander was not happy that we had chosen our own driver, evidently assuming that taking care of visiting yachties is his territory. So, he paid the driver and set us up with his nephew who would show us "some sights". The nephew is fifteen years old, so we were told, looked no more than twelve and didn't speak a word of English. Nevertheless, we piled into the car and off we went, the boy barely able to see over the wheel even when sitting on a big cushion.

Our drive took us a long distance along a road lined with occasional block buildings that looked like apartment buildings still under construction—and sat in the middle of nowhere without a soul in sight. It was possible to look right through the buildings to the opposite side.

We arrived at an ancient village where people live in hovels made of stone, wattle and sticks. The ever-present goats rummaged about and shared the dwellings with the families. The women were open and friendly, even eager to have us take their pictures. What fun it was to pass out sweets to the children who happily trooped about with us. Though very interesting, this place was also very depressing, so barren and bleak and nearly impossible to describe. The smiles of the villagers, however, warmed our hearts.

We had been strongly advised to not tarry on land after dark and our boy driver drove rapidly to return us safely in daylight.

Everyone came over to *Windy Thoughts* for a dinner and Max brought his wine along. *Investigator* left Australia with five stainless steel tanks built

in just for red wine, each with its own pressure gauge—planned for that glass of red every night with dinner. Max claims that everyone has his priorities, don't they?

The men went ashore the following morning to take care of our clearance from Yemen, but found the officials eating breakfast and were asked to return at 6 p.m. We went to the hotel for lunch, getting a ride with a nice fellow who had escaped Kuwait when Saddam Hussein invaded. He shared horror stories about Hussein, stories that chill the blood.

This is a very lonely part of the world and it has been such a joy for us to bump along together—and will mean even more when we head up the dreaded Red. (Sea, that is)

March 13, 1995
Djibouti, Africa

Bonjour,

Though we were to make a stop at beautiful downtown Aden, we were having a good sail from Mukala in twenty knots of wind with a favorable current that would have put our arrival at Aden about midnight. Advised against a night entrance into Aden (not Eden), our three boats all bypassed it, sailing the 130 miles across the Gulf of Aden, to Africa. No lions and tigers, but we are in Djibouti.

Windy Thoughts arrived at 10:30 last night. The waypoint set with the co-ordinates listed for the anchorage wasn't the anchorage after all and we could see nothing. Jerry, on *Lady D* could see our light and talked us in on the radio. It was confusing and the green light that Jerry advised us to keep to starboard was never visible. Though out for only three nights, it was nevertheless very relieving to get in and just let go.

The Raja Muda was here on a beautiful Swan that replaced his Beneteau before we left the Royal Selangor Yacht Club. It is his dream to be the first Malay to sail around the world, and we are happy to know that the voyage is underway. We had given him Jimmy Cornell's *World Cruising Routes* before we left Malaysia and we hope it has been as valuable to him as it has been to us. We hoped to dinghy over this morning to say hello, but they pulled out at first light. [He has since become the next Sultan of Selangor, Malaysia. His full title is now Duli Yang Maha Mulia Sultan Sharafuddin Idris Shal Al-Haj ibni Almarhum Sultan Salahuddin Abdul Aziz Shah Al-Haj.]

Don took the big Genny down today and a huge job followed when we worked to fold it and then pack it properly into the big sail bag. It was replaced by the Yankee in preparation for the Red Sea, to have a smaller sail area against the coming northerly winds.

We are right at the mouth of the Sea now and when we leave here it will be to set north right into those dreaded waters. Going south to north can be a rather miserable beat into very nasty seas that are often bang on the nose—and notorious for offering up short, steep seas that make tacking back and forth a very slow and laborious process and an extremely uncomfortable one.

While in town, I saw a French doctor's sign hanging outside a building and headed through his door. After explaining that I was about to head up into the Red Sea on a sailboat and no longer felt I could do it, the doctor prescribed some pills that I am to take each day. Don refers to them as my happy pills. The fact that I have resorted to this tells you quite a bit about my emotional state at present. I am not the only one feeling some anxieties about this Red Sea. This too shall pass!

Djibouti is barren looking and very unattractive. The French are still here by way of the military. A supermarket that we heard discussed on the SSB grapevine and said to knock your socks off is the main reason we all made a stop here. Lovely French cheeses were purchased along with several other items that seemed like a mirage in the middle of this desolation. *Investigator's* red wine tanks were topped off and we all topped off our diesel tanks.

Somalian women refugees sit alongside the streets, selling their beautiful, brightly colored basketry. Little children with snapping black eyes play at their side as the women work, the baskets stacked next to them. Don and I purchased some baskets, their colors the only bright spot in an otherwise bleak world here in Djibouti. As I speak of the grimness of this part of the world, there is always the plight of the people. While we are seeing it only in passing through, we are unable to close our eyes to the stark realities of life here.

With only three days in Djibouti we were very busy with the sail change, making the supermarket run and topping off the diesel, the process of refueling taking Don all of one day. Max was elated when a young boy ashore offered his services to haul diesel for him. Max, our sailor's angel, gave him $100 and all of his jerry cans right up front. He never saw the cans or any diesel again. Good-hearted Max didn't complain, figuring the boy needed the money more than he did.

My attitude jumped about 300 percent when I discovered a Laundromat in town where I could drop off laundry—though I encountered a shocking bill of $84 for the one bag when I picked it up! I tried one of my pills after that just to see if it slowed my heart rate down a bit. I decided not to mention this to Don—no sense in raising his pulse as well. But the laundry was done. There are priorities in this cruising life.

Our water tanks were topped off with fresh potable water available to jerry-jug from shore. There is nothing left to hold us back from heading out into the ole Red Sea.

Windy Thoughts will take off alone, as the other folks are taking a land trip to the Anwar Dam and we have decided to forego it for a day of rest aboard before starting out. With larger boats and longer water lines, they will soon catch us and we will be together again. About fifteen boats sit at anchor here in Djibouti, with many others already in the Sea and more behind us.

The first 300 hundred miles of the Red Sea should be good, with strong winds behind us before encountering the northerlies blowing hard down from the Mediterranean. Luxor and Cairo loom on the horizon as the icing on the cake near the end of the line, not to mention the Mediterranean itself.

Don has assured me that we won't have one bad day—and I know that this is a noble thought. We have planned our strategy well and will not head out when it is blowing like stink—but will hole up in the many anchorages offered along the west side of the Sea, to take whatever time is necessary to make it to the top unscathed. That is the plan.

I look back on all of the magic and try to remember that this is an adventure, not an ordeal.

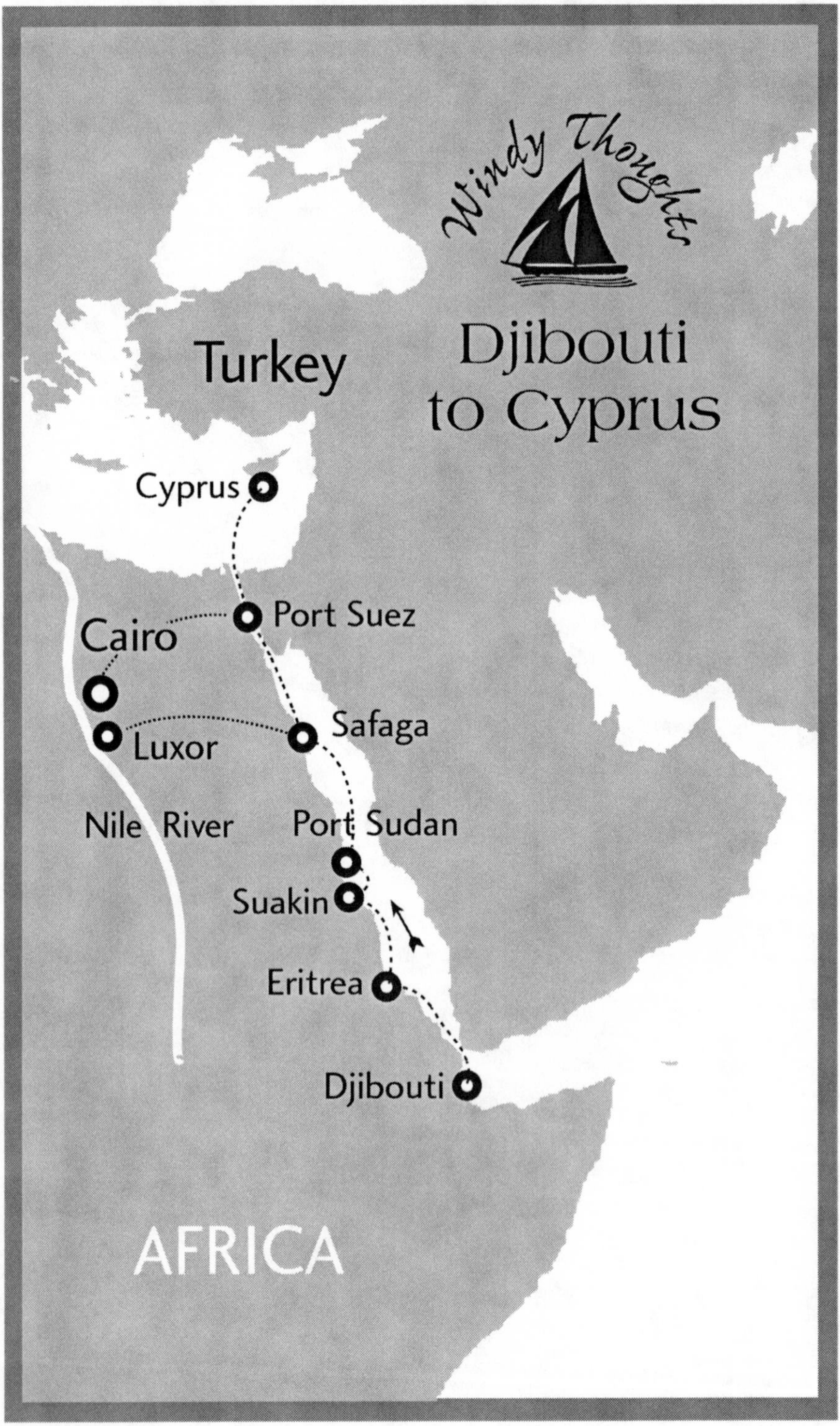

Windy Thoughts

Djibouti
to Cyprus

Turkey

Cyprus

Cairo   Port Suez

Luxor   Safaga

Nile River

Port Sudan

Suakin

Eritrea

Djibouti

AFRICA

Chapter 12

The Dreaded Red

Adventure is never an adventure while it is happening. Challenging experiences need time to ferment and adventure is simply physical and emotional discomfort recollected in tranquility. —Tim Cahill

The time had come to head into the Dreaded Red. The refrigerator was filled with delicious French cheeses, fresh vegetables and fruits. Lockers were ready to burst their seams with more canned goods and crackers found in the supermarket in Djibouti.

Djibouti itself had been a town of opposites: the excellent supermarket and French restaurants contrasting sharply with the dusty, unkempt and depressing atmosphere—the poverty of its people along with the plight of the Somalian refugees living on its streets. If not for the opportunity for provisioning and fuel, there would be little reason to visit.

However, to see our world is to experience all of its realities. We have acquired a perspective not possible had we not ventured to these faraway places. And we feel very blessed to be able to return to our home country fully appreciating its freedoms and its opportunities available to anyone wishing to pursue their dreams.

Before daylight on March 14, 1995, we hauled anchor and pointed *Windy Thoughts* outward bound. It had been a dark entry into Djibouti and it was a dark exit.

My heart pumped frantically but Don seemed to approach the day with his usual steadfastness and perseverance. Don was excited about seeing the Valley of the Kings and the Great Pyramids, as was I. With a 1,200-mile stretch ahead of us, we anticipated two months making our way north while holing up for the worst stuff—and finding enjoyment in the rest.

As we set out into the open waters of the Gulf of Aden, headwinds made the first hours very uncomfortable as the bow plunged into the oncoming seas, providing a glimpse of what was to come.

But first there would be a hiatus. We were heading toward the Strait of Bab El Mendab, the "Gate of Tears", forming the narrow southern entrance to the Red Sea. Following winds could be expected in the Strait, southerlies that can continue as far as the Hanish Islands, about 300 miles north, before the much dreaded headwinds blew their wrath from the Mediterranean.

The first day we bumped along uncomfortably and it was dark by the time we made our course change into the Strait. The welcoming southerly wind was there for us, very strong at thirty knots. The wind kept us on our toes in the black of night and we had a rip-roaring sail, keeping us busy navigating the heavy ship traffic. Even though the seas were big and boisterous, we were making good time and clocking off the miles in our quest north—miles with the wind behind us!

During the dark of night we often sat together in the cockpit, holding on as *Windy Thoughts* rolled, each of us with a wary eye to all about us and with very careful checks on our navigation. There was little sleep, but we welcomed the following winds. Our hearts raced right along with the winds that carried us past the Hanish Islands. We shot on just off the coast of Ethiopia, glad that the gunboats that patrolled the shores were apparently gone for a time. We were bound for reported good shelter in Massawa, Eritrea.

The wind came around into the northerly quadrant on the third day, and with each passing hour it stayed northeast between the bow and the beam. *Windy Thoughts* likes a close reach, so the situation was quite palatable. We turned on the engine to motor-sail—pointing as close to the wind as possible. We were on a mission! Nearly every boat making passage north in the Red Sea was doing the same.

On March 17, 1995, we arrived at Massawa, just three days after leaving Djibouti. The town is heavily influenced by Italian architecture from the nineteenth century. The ravages of thirty years of war were evident everywhere. Bombed-out structures were the only remnants of lovely buildings from the period when Eritrea was known as part of Italian East Africa. There was one paved road along the waterfront, the rest dirt. Massawa's economy was very poor.

Investigator joined us in Massawa and Faye and I took pictures of beautiful children as we walked the streets, so many charming little ones with those big snapping black eyes—and with smiles and laughing voices as they gaily romped along with us. Massawa was a relaxing stop, a place to catch our breath and to ready ourselves for the coming days, about which we were all somewhat anxious.

There were few publications detailing the Red Sea written prior to 1993. We carried aboard the British Admiralty and other countries' pilots written for big ships, plus Alan Lucas' helpful *Red Sea and Indian Ocean Pilot*, written for the yachtsman, but missing a lot of detail and somewhat out of date.

A fellow yachtsman had compiled every bit of information available before reaching the Red Sea in 1992, much of it photocopied, incomplete and written by other yachtsmen who had cruised through the area in the late 1980s and early 1990s. He made his own additions to these original notes and put his collection together in a publication with sixty-five pages of photocopied notes, eleven pages of sketches of various anchorages, a table of contents and an index. Don and I came upon this compilation of notes in Phuket.

The author emphatically writes, "These notes only scrape the surface of what cruising the Red Sea is all about; they are far from complete and I regret, in many places either greatly lacking in detail or perhaps even quite inaccurate. However, they are presented in the hope that they will be of some assistance to future yachtsmen visiting this fascinating area."

The author expected yachtsmen would have the British Admiralty charts on board and information about anchorages found in these charts wasn't repeated. Don and I had everything available, but found the *Red Sea Notes* to be our primary source of information.

The eastern coasts of Sudan and Egypt offer an abundance of safe places to find shelter. Because some beaches were believed to be mined still, we went ashore only at recommended anchorages. There are few small ports like Massawa, but good shelter can be found behind small islands, and many hidey-holes inside marsas dot the western coastline. Marsas are lagoons reached by a break in the extensive reef found in the western edge of the Red Sea. A channel leads from the entrance into the lagoon. Marsas make for superb protection from the seas, if not from winds—and we would be thankful for their welcoming shelter on many occasions.

We watched our weather faxes carefully and learned to predict when a low pressure system might bring calm seas for several hours or perhaps a day or two. High pressure systems are generally welcomed for the good weather and low pressure systems are usually unwelcome. However, Red Sea weather is largely influenced by the high pressure systems that cross the Mediterranean, and an approaching high produces strong winds often up to forty knots. Lighter conditions occur with a fall in the barometer as the center of the high passes to the east of Cyprus, after which the wind will start to come in again from the north, building daily until the next high arrives.

We didn't have a dedicated weather fax, but we did have a computer AXA weather fax program that, integrated with the SSB, brought up weather faxes on designated frequencies, and we knew the times for faxes originating from differing areas in the world. Both twenty-four hour surface analyses as well as thirty-six hour prognoses were available. Both provided valuable information, with isobars indicating the high's location.

Our life centered upon compiling information from every possible source and extrapolating what might be ahead. Generally, the southeast sector of an approaching high meant strong winds and the southwest sector of a passing high meant lighter conditions. The operative word was "generally", but a falling barometer could usually be counted on to mean lighter conditions. However, conditions could change very rapidly and the radio buzzed as cruisers shared localized conditions. No one wanted to head out if the calm may not last long enough to make it to the next shelter.

As we worked our way north, we learned to better read the idiosyncrasies and patterns and to sense what we might expect in the coming hours. It was the coming hours that we thought about always. If a weather fax was scheduled to transmit during the night, our alarm was set and we were up—alert and eyes glued to the computer screen.

Sundown was rapidly approaching on our second day out as we neared a shelter behind the island Khor Nawarat. Don turned off the autopilot and steered the last miles, sailing close to the reef, to reach the approach in daylight. My job was to watch the water's color as we galloped along and to keep one eye on the depth sounder.

We jogged along nicely and anticipated having the anchor down soon, when the depths suddenly plummeted alarmingly to shallow numbers—and the water rapidly showed the telltale brown color of reef just below the surface. We scrambled to get the boat headed off as we watched the numbers on the depth sounder creep up again—and caught our breath, realizing that we had done little breathing in the interim!

Just as the sun was giving up its last rays of light, we dropped the anchor behind Khor Nawarat, giving shelter that night to thirteen of us. *Gray Eagle* was already in. *Investigator* was five miles behind us but Max pulled out all the stops, squeaking in with little light left.

Other boats weren't so fortunate. Out there and moving north when the winds came, the sailors faced a miserable night at sea. Most of us had thus far avoided the notorious winds. We had all tacked against strong winds before—but we were so relieved not to be caught out in the rapid, short and steep seas, with bows slamming into the next wave before coming off the last.

After a restful night's sleep we awoke to find very grey skies and dead calm. Eerie conditions and my first thoughts were "the calm before the storm". We scurried about our morning routines, ate a good breakfast and discussed whether or not to go, all the time proceeding with preparations to set off.

While I was setting order to our cabin below, Don was up top calling over to Max, "What do you think, Max?"

Max's reply was matter of fact, "Oh, it'll be right, mate."

Gray Eagle called on the VHF to report they were staying put and everyone else was as well. *Investigator* was hauling anchor. Don and I hoped the calm would last a few hours and we planned to duck into a little hole about ten miles north.

Investigator pulled out as we hauled anchor and a slight northerly breeze began to niggle at the shrouds. Here it comes!

Windy Thoughts slowly made her way out of the anchorage a few hundred feet behind *Investigator*. By the time we cleared the end of the island, heading into the open sea, the breeze picked up alarmingly and the water began to rapidly bubble. Just as her bow turned north, *Investigator* plunged deeply into the oncoming seas and heeled well over. It was beginning to boil out there and the wind was coming dead out of the north.

Sorry, dear friends, we're turning tail to await another day. A radio call to *Investigator* to let them know that we hoped to see them up the line elicited Max's response, "Good on ya, mate."

Every boat was on the move whenever there was a break of a few hours and *Investigator* was a jump ahead of us for several weeks. We missed their company enormously but kept in radio contact.

The winds blew fiercely for five days as we sat behind Khor Nawarat. The anchorage was very choppy and the water had cooled to about eighty degrees. We had anticipated snorkeling and diving while sitting out northerly blows, but the tropical latitudes had spoiled us and we didn't want to get into that choppy and "cold" water! However, there were boat chores to occupy our time, books to read, camaraderie and meals with others shared back and forth in each other's cockpits.

The weather break came five days later, fast and within minutes on the morning of March 29, 1995. The wind and the seas lay right down. Everyone raced forward on deck to get anchors up, wanting to make whatever forward progress possible before the next change. We all moved north in this manner—duck in, wait it out while staying glued to barometers and weather faxes, then race out under power to make progress north during the calm periods.

Our overall approach was conservative, with a desire to avoid overnighters. But we found times when our strategy changed—allowing for remarkable progress that would have taken days or weeks were we to have adhered to the original plan.

One young single-hander decided that he was going to beat his way to the Suez Canal and get the passage over with as quickly as possible. Everyone followed his progress on the morning radio net, eager to hear how he was doing. Each morning the net operator called on him with the familiar, "And now for our report from our man on the scene. Michael, are you still out there?"

He made slow progress tacking back and forth across the Red Sea against the wind—moving north, traveling miles when it was dead calm and only miserable inches when it wasn't.

About three weeks into his trek, Michael reported that the lack of sleep and the beating had finally worn him down. None of us had aspirations to visit the Saudi coast, but Michael's present tack was carrying him there with hopes that he would reach shelter before sunset, no longer caring how he might be welcomed in Saudi Arabia—he just wanted to get in. We listened to his progress throughout that day, suspense building as sunset neared and Michael sailed close to the wind on his course toward his port of rest.

When the disappointing news came that he was not going to make it on his final tack after all, there was a resounding "Oh, no!" Michael tacked back out in the waning daylight hours, delaying the anticipated welcome night asleep in his berth.

A few days later we were sitting at anchor in one of the most interesting spots in all of our travels. We were heading for Port Sudan to make clearance—but heard via radio that officialdom was easier and faster at Suakin, located about fifty miles south of Port Sudan.

With sails rolled in and the mainsail tied to the boom, we motored through the channel leading through the reef, making our way toward the town. On our starboard side we passed an island with buildings resembling ancient, crumbling ruins. When the British conquered Sudan, they forced residents to relocate to Port Sudan, but allowed the citizens to demolish the buildings and take the stones with them. This original city, once called the Venice of the East, now looked like a movie set. Suakin has a fascinating history and was the last slave trading port in the world.

As we moved farther in, we weren't surprised to see a number of other cruising boats swinging at anchor. We had learned in Djibouti that our delayed departure from Thailand hadn't really left us far behind the others after all. There were waves of greetings to old friends and new. More boats were further north at various points, so the morning cruiser's net kept all in touch with one another and provided updates about weather conditions. There was a close community connection as everyone shared information about individual progress made, interesting stops, problems faced and the best ways to get into shelters.

Five days of strong northerly winds held us at Suakin, five days that felt like we had stepped hundreds or even thousands of years back into history.

Breezy took us to the causeway leading from the old town and we walked to the market, passing very primitive surroundings that seemed to have changed little since biblical times! Very simple structures of wattle and mud formed the few shops and homes. A donkey cart rattled down the dirt path, piled high with twigs used as firewood for cooking. Camels snorted at us as they stood or lay about in the hot sun. Goats roamed at will.

Nomads in their flowing white robes and carrying daggers and swords rode into Suakin on their camels each morning to sell vegetables or goods at the open market in the center of town. Nomads live as they have for centuries and won't spend a night in Suakin itself, preferring to make their encampments farther inland. War and troubles have come by way of the sea.

At the market, both camel and goat milk is sold in camel bladders. Nomads make yogurt to mix with maize as their main diet. The fresh produce offerings weren't very inviting, though there was an abundance of beautiful, big, juicy tomatoes spread out on the tables.

Local people mingled with the nomads, and scrawny camels that to us looked none too well-fed lay about waiting for their masters.

Don and I noticed a stunningly beautiful silver armband on a woman who was sitting on the ground with the nomad entourage. The armband was

about six inches in length with several rings of silver bands worn on her upper arm. With many hand gestures, Don attempted to negotiate a purchase, but the price asked was so high that we decided it belonged on the arm of that lovely lady—adorning her in a way that it never could me were I to wear it.

Men squatted on the ground before small fires, forging daggers and knives from iron as in ancient times. Don was fascinated and determined to purchase a dagger. Every man carried one, the nomads brandishing swords as well—all hand forged by simple and ancient methods. While we were watching, a little fellow of nine years, dressed in the long white garment of men and boys, sidled up to us and began a conversation in English.

Such was our introduction to Taj, a remarkable young fellow who became our interpreter and guide—and our friend. Taj, the boy we would never forget and one we have held in our hearts all the years since, often wondering about his fate in this inhospitable and poverty-stricken part of the world. Taj had learned English in school on those days that he attended. Taj was very bright and we felt that he would always make his way in this barren and primitive part of the world.

Taj latched onto to us, taking Don to have coffee while I purchased tomatoes. Coffee with the men—the two of them seated on an old bench at the local coffee shop. It wasn't the western world's idea of a coffee shop, but a simple business with a rickety lean-to structure covering a few benches. Several older men in long white attire sat around the tables, discussing the day's topics. Don was apprehensive about eating or drinking anything, but wouldn't let on and with Taj, imbibed the strong black liquid in the questionable cup.

Taj thought Don may be hungry and suggested he buy a local dish of camel meat in a flat pocket bread. Don explained that he had just eaten, but asked if Taj was hungry. He looked longingly at the food but said that he had already eaten that day. No amount of encouragement would change Taj's mind. Pride and dignity in a nine-year-old boy who wasn't looking for handouts even while living a very hard life. Don bought one anyway and Taj proudly tucked it into his robe to save for dinner.

Taj took us to the officials for clearance procedures in and out of Sudan. Taj flagged down an old truck with an open bed, filled with bearded men in flowing white garments. We climbed into the truck bed and hung on for dear life as we rode along at breakneck speed. Privately, Don and I both had thoughts that we might not be headed for any official offices. We didn't know these men, each carrying a dagger and a sword—but we put our trust in a nine-year-old boy, our new friend, Taj. He is pictured on the right.

Taj led us to the Harbor Master's office and waited for us as we began the long process. Taj acted as our interpreter as the Harbor Master finally gave us his attention. When we finished, Taj took us to Immigration where we waited in the hall for forty-five minutes until the Immigration officer finished reading the paper, looking up occasionally to see if we were still waiting. When it became clear that we weren't leaving, the officer eventually motioned us in and with Taj's help, we managed to get through the paperwork.

Another hour was spent at Customs, negotiating red tape as we endured the sullenness of the Customs Officer. The entire procedure took three hours, but Taj stuck to us like glue and managed to explain and interpret for us whenever necessary. Taj easily got us a ride back into town in another broken-down truck.

Both pounds and dinars are commonly used in Sudan and when we had difficulty figuring out which to use, Taj stepped right up and counted our money for us. Our banker as well! It hardly seemed that this little boy—this little man, really—whose company we so enjoyed could so comfortably manage the adult world. His daily existence depended on his ability to use his innate intelligence and Taj seemed to do it very well.

Taj was anxious to show us where he lived and we were surprised when we walked along with him back to the demolished town, where he proudly stopped in front of a very primitive lean-to made from old boards, propped up to form three sides. The structure sheltered his bed, a rickety affair made from a few boards without benefit of springs, mattress, or covers.

Next door was a small stone structure. An old man with a long beard came outside to greet us, and we later learned that he watched over Taj in a way, though Taj was left largely on his own.

Taj introduced us and explained that Don was interested in buying a sword. The old man took us into his home, one room with a wooden chair, a table and a bed. He pulled a sword out from a scabbard in the corner as Taj explained that our host was willing to sell it. A price was negotiated, and when we left Don was brandishing the beautifully made, hand-forged sword that was likely to have an interesting history behind it, were we only to know!

Don was also interested in acquiring a dagger and, while ambling about the market, saw a particularly nice one hanging from one fellow's belt, and stopped to inquire if he might be interesting in selling it. A successful bargain was negotiated.

There was nothing for me to stow away as a remembrance other than pictures that I would love to have of the smiling people, and particularly of our Taj. But pictures were a problem. We wanted to film the town, its people, the camels that loped along or lay lazily in the sun awaiting their master and the market ac-

tivity. On our first day, Don had just lifted the video camera to his eye when three men suddenly came up close and wildly waved their arms in front of him.

Their heads shook a definite "no" that we may not have understood in words, but their actions were very clear. Don immediately put the camera away, and we were happy that we had a few pictures taken with the 35mm camera. Though our welcome was warm in Suakin, there were customs about which we lacked knowledge, and we did not bring the camera out again.

Thrilled as he was with his dagger, we had just started down the street when Don saw a more interesting one worn by a scraggly looking fellow loping along on his camel. Don held up his dagger and gestured that he was interested in making a trade.

The fellow thought Don had something else in mind and he quickly brandished his own dagger in a confrontational manner. While our hearts beat furiously, we smiled the biggest smiles we could manage. Don shook his head and somehow managed to communicate that he wasn't interested in fighting but rather in purchasing the fellow's dagger. Ah! The fellow hopped off his camel to show the dagger to us, and once some dinars were offered in addition to Don's dagger, the trade was completed. Both the sword and that dagger are special remembrances to Don, crafted locally and part of the everyday attire of Suakin's men.

Taj would have loved to come out to our boat but such visits are not allowed by the police. Along with our leftover dinars, we gathered some smaller T-shirts and a couple of baseball caps to give Taj. As we left Suakin, Taj was standing on shore wearing one of each as he waved goodbye. The sight tore at our hearts, because Taj was someone we would have  loved to gather in our arms and take along with us. It was a very sad goodbye on the day that the winds calmed down.

Another cruising couple asked us about Taj when we met up again in the Caribbean. They had been touched by Taj and they had contacted the Sudanese government in hopes of doing something to help him. Sadly, nothing came from their efforts, but Don and I have always had faith that a little guy as enterprising as Taj is destined to make his place in his world. We think of him often, with prayers that he is all right and that perhaps his life has taken a turn for the better.

The morning the winds dropped off we headed out on a fifteen-mile jaunt. Our destination was an inviting marsa. Once through the pass, we dropped the hook and set up housekeeping for what we hoped would be only one night. *Voyager* was already sitting at anchor. We had met Jill and Mike over the radio when in Suakin and their good directions helped us get safely through the entrance.

Breezy was left securely tied to the topsides of *Windy Thoughts* and there was no visiting back and forth this time, for we were all anxious to move on as soon as possible. We chatted with *Voyager* on the radio and naturally, the key topic was the weather. We all continued to get every weather fax available and we put our four heads together. It appeared that the winds would calm overnight and we planned to be off in the morning.

As morning dawned, we sleepily reviewed the overnight weather faxes and decided it was a go. *Voyager* stayed right behind us and once into the open sea, we pointed our bows north.

We weren't planning to stop at Port Sudan as clearance in and out required several days. Our sights were set on Sanganeb Reef, about eight miles north.

Jogging along on calm waters with engines roaring and *Voyager* a few miles ahead of us, we were a few miles south of Port Sudan when our comfortable jaunt abruptly ended. The winds blew with vengeance on *Windy Thoughts'* nose and forward progress slowed to a snail's pace as we crashed against the seas. A marsa was located just a few miles north, but a boat reportedly was forced out at gunpoint and we didn't feel comfortable heading for it.

Don radioed the Port Authority to ask permission to anchor in Port Sudan overnight. If we didn't set foot on land, perhaps we could avoid the clearance procedures. We received permission and changed course to head through the entrance channel.

We were almost half way through the Red Sea! All had gone well and we were more than elated with our progress.

Voyager decided to press on to Sanganeb Reef, radioing that the last four miles took almost three hours. It may have been easier to run back to Port Sudan, but going backwards in the Red Sea is almost more than one could bear!

It was April 7, 1995. Good anchorage was found near another sailboat just off the city. No sooner did we get the hook down than we heard the radio come alive with the call, "This is the Port Authority calling the yacht *Windy Thoughts.*"

The call was repeated as Don went below to answer. Don was told that we would have to complete the official clearance procedures after all. Knowing that this would require hiring an agent and take several days, Don decided that we may as well use the agent to our full advantage and top off fuel. It was Friday, the Muslim holy day, and all business would wait until the morning.

The other sailboat had been in for a couple of days and we chatted back and forth from our cockpits. They passed along information about shore sights and places to find things.

Don arranged for an agent to arrive at 7 a.m. After a good night's sleep we were up early, untying jugs from the deck in readiness to get to shore and find diesel. From our vantage point we could see camels wandering the streets and we looked forward to seeing the city.

By 8 a.m. the agent hadn't arrived and the winds suddenly dropped right off to nothing. The radio was abuzz with boats calling in from points all the way to the top of the Red Sea, reporting calm conditions expected to last for two or perhaps even three days! A dissipating high was directly above the Red Sea and the isobars were closing—a good sign! Every single boat was on the move north.

I sputtered about how we couldn't just leave since the officials had alerted us of the necessity to make clearance—but Don said there was no way we were missing the weather window. So, we dashed about getting the jerry jugs and the dinghy back aboard and tied down.

The fellow on the other boat called over, "Don, I don't think it's a good idea to leave. You could be in big trouble."

My heart pounded. As we got the anchor up, my mind conjured up any number of scenarios that may take place imminently—a patrol boat chasing us and Don and me ending up in a Sudanese prison being foremost.

Windy Thoughts headed out of Port Sudan, continued into the channel and neared the Port Authority buildings immediately to starboard. Never a brave sailor, I went below to hide out, telling Don that when they called us on the radio he would have to talk to them. I knew nothing.

It wasn't long before he called below, "Joyce, get the shotgun! There's a patrol boat coming for us!"

From my hideout below came my very plaintive cry, "Oh no!"

We were doomed, right here in this Godforsaken part of the world! Within seconds, Don was laughing uproariously—but neither of us was at ease until we were well out into the sea! I told Don that his humor wasn't necessary with a first mate already on pins and needles!

Windy Thoughts made three hundred miles during this calm weather, further north than we could have expected, miles that might very well have been covered over a period of weeks. Our third day carried us to a shelter behind Fury Shoal, a reef located out in the open water and found by waypoint. An unbroken reef gave protection from the northwest and numerous bombies hiding just below the surface of the water gave us protection from the southeast. It was an idyllic spot, and we made it in within an hour of the change to northerly winds.

It was now mid-April, and thirteen boats sat at anchor for four days. Mike and Jill on *Voyager* were in and we enjoyed their special company.

With the water at seventy-nine degrees we suited up in full wet suits for diving and snorkeling. The reef that we took such measures to avoid while underway took on new meaning when viewed from beneath the water's surface—until a couple of sharks found the divers to be good company, or perhaps unwelcome company. There were other diversions however, and the large group of boats allowed for lots of visiting back and forth, the anchorage a welcome respite.

The seas calmed by first light on the fourth morning and *Voyager* led the entourage of sailboats out through the reef, Jill high in the mast to watch for the coral bombies—aptly named, as hitting one could really ruin your day.

Our hopes were to reach Safaga, Egypt, by sunset on the second day. This was the first destination to which we had really looked forward, with a trip inland to Luxor to visit the Valley of the Kings. This was to be one of the best destinations before reaching Port Suez, when we would be through the Red Sea and celebrating with visits to Cairo and the Great Pyramids. Safaga was also well north in the Red Sea and would mean that we were almost to the top!

So far all had gone well for us. I was nearly paranoid with concern that we make our moves at the right time, but we hadn't had one bad day yet. Wasn't that what my captain had promised me? It could be almost over!

On April 17, 1995, we made Safaga just before sunset. Friends radioed information on the ins and outs of arrival. We tied to a wharf to await a doctor who gave us our health certificate at a minimal charge of $6.00. After receiving the all clear from the health department, we moved very carefully two miles north to join everyone at anchor off the Paradise Hotel, its name conjuring up visions of everything that we hadn't seen in months.

Clearing into Egypt took most of the first day while we walked to Immigration and Customs. There were no harbor dues or immigration charges, though an agent would be required to handle customs charges and paperwork if taking on fuel or water—but we needed neither.

Then we were free to wander about Safaga and poke our noses into the various shops, all the while keeping an eye out for some fresh produce. Safaga didn't look like the Paradise Hotel, which in truth wasn't exactly a four-star place, but in the midst of such desolation, it seemed upscale to us.

We walked past shops with the day's fresh meat displayed outside—camel legs hanging from big hooks. It was fascinating to observe the culture in Safaga. People smiled welcomes and busily hawked wares and special deals, "just for you, sir." There wasn't a touch of greenery, not a tree or flower in sight, and the entire town was the dead brown color seen for hundreds of miles.

But our moods were happy, because we were about to see the Valley of the Kings! Off the boat, without constant attention to the next weather fax and free to walk about without any thought to night watches or wind!

A taxi was arranged for the next morning. Craig and Michael on *Ponderosa* and Jill and Mike from *Voyager* would join us for three days in Luxor. We were ill at ease at leaving *Windy Thoughts* at anchor unattended, but protection was good and the Valley of the Kings awaited us!

Don and I were up early, with backpacks packed, and bursting with excitement for the excursion. The wind had risen sharply and the anchorage was boiling with a steep and heavy chop, all bows jumping up and down furiously.

A German boat had arrived the night before and anchored so close to us that we weren't comfortable leaving for three days the with possibility of the boats swinging into one other. Before heading to shore, we re-anchored farther out. If *Windy Thoughts* dragged, she would drag further out and not into any other boats. This was our only consolation as we headed into shore, looking behind at *Windy Thoughts* bobbing heavily in the chop. We were going to enjoy ourselves. Hard to do when our little home and solace for our souls was left alone at anchor, winds blowing at thirty knots.

However, Safaga was our first milestone and we had so looked forward to visiting Luxor; we just couldn't bring ourselves to give up the Valley of the Kings! And we would be staying in a hotel! Life would be lived away from the rigors of the Red Sea for a few days and I would try not to obsess about what may be going on while we were away.

The six of us crammed together into the old taxi that awaited us. The drive along a two-lane road passed through dull brown landscape for about two hours until we neared the Nile River, where the first glimpses of greenery and palm trees began to appear and the barrenness gave way to a genuine beauty.

Sitting on the Nile, Luxor is a lovely town. Horse-drawn carriages carrying a few tourists and cars traveling here and there in town greeted us. Two tourists had been killed recently and tourism was suffering. The big riverboats that cruise the Nile with passengers from all over the world sat forlornly tied up along the shore. We subscribe to common sense when it comes to security concerns, but security was everywhere and our well-being seemed a genuine concern of the people we encountered. We pressed on with our glorious plans.

With abundant available rooms, we chose a small hotel, modestly priced, and after checking into our rooms we were quickly off on a walk to the well-known ancient Karnack Temple.

The Karnack Temple, the glorious legacy of Seti, has 134 huge columns. The ancient Egyptians perfected the art of cutting stone to build temples and tombs but never mastered the arch for interior space. If a big room was needed, many columns or pillars were used. Standing amongst the pillars, we looked in awe at hieroglyphics covering the stone from bottom to top. Yes, this really was ancient Egypt and it was hard to believe that we were finally here.

Back at the hotel we shared a good dinner on the terrace above the Nile River and we appreciated the evening breezes that cooled us after a hot day. Don and I put *Windy Thoughts* out of our minds. Surely she was doing fine and we intended to enjoy ourselves. After dinner, what luxury to climb between cool sheets, not to wake until morning—and without thought to what was going on other than our plans for the day.

After breakfast, we took a cab to the dock where a foot ferry would carry us across the Nile. The ferry was crowded with men dressed in the traditional long white garments—and it leaned heavily to port. Not a soul seemed concerned. The engine sputtered and coughed as the ferry made its way across the brown Nile. People hung over the rails while visiting. We looked about for any sign of safety measures—like small boats and life vests. There were none. We reminded ourselves to go with the flow as we wanted to see this world!

The world's most famous cemetery, the Valley of the Kings is located in a vast desert area extending farther than the eye could see. The taxi delivered us to the entrance, and we got out in front of several wood stalls hawking tourist souvenirs.

"Mister! Mister.! You buy! Precious treasures from the tombs, just for you!"

With smiles and continuous claims of no thank you, we made our way through the hawkers so anxious to take our money.

Visitor tickets for the tombs were sold in lots of five. We paid for one lot and set off walking toward the first tomb.

With all it had taken to get here, we felt like something magical had transported us to this faraway place. But it wasn't magic that allowed us to see these ancient Egyptian treasures. It was our own perseverance and our own *Windy Thoughts.*

Tomb entrances were reached through long tunnels with walls covered in ancient hieroglyphics—and paintings whose color was faded but visible. Often, a false entrance had been constructed to divert attention from the actual entrance, but even the false one was difficult to discover.

Crude wooden steps led us up or down within the tunnels and we had to bend over in the small space as we moved toward the tomb. Not a place for the claustrophobic! Light bulbs dangled along the way with some in the tomb itself. At the tomb, excavation had exposed a large area with walls highly decorated with hieroglyphics and paintings of the Pharaoh's life.

The more notable Pharaohs were honored with larger tombs, given the most elaborate chambers and were buried with the most riches. Because most of the discovered tombs have been plundered, the tomb of King Tutankhamen, found with its contents still intact, holds great interest. Most of the treasures from Tut's tomb have been relocated to a museum in downtown Cairo. Tutankhamen was a lesser king with a smaller tomb, but one no visitor wants to miss.

When we worked our way toward the tomb of King Ramses I, we were given strict instructions that photos were not allowed. When Jill thought no one would notice, she attempted to video the beautiful paintings on the walls of the passageways as we crept along. We were more careful after she was caught and sternly chastised. It was difficult to carry only memories but we all understood the request and did not tempt fate again!

Several hours later we came to the end of the tour, our heads filled with ancient wonders as we made our way along the path leading back to the entrance. As we neared the hawkers we had bypassed earlier, three men stopped

Don. He was offered a choice piece of artwork, promised to have come from a tomb itself!

It was a lovely rendition of Nephritite, painted on a piece of plaster—rough cut around the edges to look like it was chiseled from the wall of a tomb. Because Don loved the piece, we shot a video of his intense bargaining and the video has brought many memorable laughs since. That piece ended up on *Windy*
Thoughts, securely stowed and carried the rest of the way home.

When our circumnavigation was over and we were building our house and our life on land, we had the piece framed. Don paid $15.00 for it in Egypt, but that small price was multiplied many times over when it was beautifully set in a dark frame and positioned on a burlap background under art glass, setting it off perfectly. An art dealer visiting the frame shop took an avid interest in it, thinking it was a very valuable piece! It does have value to us, a treasured memory that reminds us of our day at the Valley of the Kings.

The Valley of the Kings is not the only burial grounds in this vast area. The Valley of the Artisans honors the people who spent untold time creating the artwork and hieroglyphics found along the entrances and inside the tombs. Walking amongst stone foundations that are the ruins of their homes, we openly wondered at the labor-intensive and time-consuming work these men had completed.

In the Valley of the Queens stands the era's most stunning archeological feat, the Temple of Queen Hatshepsut. Dedicated to the only woman pharaoh, the temple stood out in its splendor against a limestone cliff with several lavish terraces.

Queen Hatshepsut reigned as pharaoh after her husband's death, from 1479 B.C. to 1457 B.C. At the time, the temple was the most lavish monument in the world, and is unique in Egypt. Approaching its terraces, we made our way to the main temple to walk about its hallways and

vast public rooms, wondering at the Queen's life so long ago and wishing that we could interpret the hieroglyphics on the walls and columns.

It was overwhelming to experience so much antiquity, to walk along the stone pathways and to touch the walls that pharaohs and artisans had touched so many thousands of years ago.

On our way back to Luxor, a stop was made at one last temple. When we walked under the stone entry, we met with three men in their long white garments sitting cross-legged in the shade, eating lunch from a small cloth on the ground. Fingers provided utensils and we weren't at all sure what they were eating.

The men greeted us with smiling hellos and graciously offered us some of their food. Don and I, along with Jill and Mike, generously thanked them—but we demurred, rubbing our stomachs to say that we had already eaten and were full. The fellows from *Ponderosa* happily took a handful of the mixture from the dirty cloth and proceeded to eat, profusely thanking the men. There is a limit to how much culture we are willing to experience! In the end, we were glad that Craig and Mike had the kindness to be the recipients of such generosity.

Before leaving Luxor, Don purchased a solid gold cartouche with my name written in ancient hieroglyphics. The ancient Egyptians believed that the name of the person inside this special design will be protected. Don told me the cartouche was his gift to me for battling the Red Sea with him.

It was time to venture north again, once back to Safaga and the anchorage, all progress bringing us closer to the Suez Canal. But there was another good stop ahead of us at Hurgada, an area known for its rich diving and one visited by people from all over the world.

While underway, radio contact passed on very sad news concerning the fate of *Dream Weaver*, the boat that had sat next to us at the Raffles Marina in Singapore.

Dream Weaver was dismasted in the Indian Ocean and had drifted for about six weeks. Food provisions were in such short supply that the first mate died from starvation and the captain put her overboard. The captain was picked up by a Japanese freighter and taken to Australia. The article also told of investigations into his story. The news stunned all of us and we feel for the tragedy of *Dream Weaver*, a sad story and one that we would never learn more about.

Hurgada was a place to plan our final leg to the Suez Canal. There were only about 180 miles left before reaching the Canal, and we were all filled with a definite sense of exhilaration that Port Suez and the Suez Canal could be reached very soon.

Before heading into the Straits of Gubal, along with *Voyager* we made a short jaunt that brought us to rest behind a small island for the night. That evening we all studied every weather fax that we could pull and discussed the possibilities of making Port Suez in one last jump north. It would be an overnighter and we needed our window to last long enough. It looked good.

By first light on the morning of April 26, 1995, we were on our way, anticipating that we could be tied up at the Port Suez Yacht Club within the next twenty-four to thirty hours. Think of that! We watched the miles roll under our hulls as we motored on an amazingly calm sea. By afternoon our extrapolations indicated there was a good chance that the low-pressure system would not be pushed out for possibly another twenty-four hours! Should we take our chances and keep pushing through the night to get this passage over with—or should we be conservative and duck in?

Before dusk we had motored our way right into the Straits of Gubal that form the very narrow southern entrance to the Gulf of Suez—a place where the wind generally blows like stink. Locals in Hurgada had told us that God is believed to have parted the Red Sea here as Moses led his people out of Egypt.

We were in very busy shipping traffic for the night, sharing the narrow Strait with the many oil tankers and with many oilrigs as well. *Investigator* had passed through the Gulf just a few days earlier, beating into thirty-knot headwinds all night with a considerable amount of tacking back and forth between ships and oilrigs. Their battle was finished and they were already at the Yacht Club in Port Suez. A spirited vigil was kept as the night wore on, and we were grateful for the nearly unheard of calm conditions. As the miles ticked off, our excitement and thankfulness for our good fortune grew.

When morning came we were still pushing it for all it was worth—and it was our last day in the Red Sea! It is difficult to describe our feelings, feelings that every single one of us out there shared when reaching this point. The change in conditions could be expected at any time.

At exactly 10 a.m. the change came as the wind went from zero to twenty-five knots in ten seconds flat. Rapidly building, heavy chop greeted our bows, but protection of the northern Gulf kept the seas from building, and the apprehension of the past weeks melted away. A feeling that we hadn't experienced in a long while seeped into our beings. Normalcy was returning.

Voyager radioed resounding cheers of happiness and we were overcome with the pure joy of being almost to the Canal. I busied myself with cleaning *Windy Thoughts'* interior, anxious to arrive looking as decent as was possible. There wasn't anything to do about the layer of brown dirt and dust that covered the topsides. That chore would have to wait for lots of water and a hose. Every boat arrived in Port Suez in the same condition. Don just beamed from ear to ear, exhilarated that new horizons awaited us now and that the quest for the Suez Canal was finally coming to a close.

Side by side with *Voyager*, we took pictures of one another jogging to-

ward the Canal. Both
crews would likely have
been jumping up and
down with joy had not
the boats been doing
their best to meet the
heavy chop without los-
ing one inch of way—and
doing the jumping up and
down for us! Surely, the
spirit of *Windy Thoughts*

understood inherently that she had reached an all-time milestone and felt the
excitement right to the bottom of her keel.

When we were within a few miles from the entrance of the Suez Canal,
we called for the required pilot boat and spent the next hour looking for it
amongst the ships around us, continuing along and talking the entire time to
the pilot boat that couldn't find us.

At 5 p.m. on April 28, 1995, we entered the basin of the Suez Canal Yacht
Club and were met by Jerry, from *Lady D*, who took our mooring lines. Huge
sighs of relief and joyful silliness overtook the crews of both *Windy Thoughts*
and *Voyager* as we secured our moorings.

The concerns of the past six weeks dissolved into memories stored away
for later, waiting to be joined by memories from the new adventures ahead.
Our memories of the Red Sea would never fade but would, in time, become
less ominous. They could be pulled up at will, but without the dread that had
accompanied every inch of the way north.

And in truth, my captain had been right in his promise that we would
not have one bad day. Like Mark Twain, I had suffered a great many trials that
had never occurred—and as Don would say, paying debts that were never
incurred. Joanie, on *Lady D*, told me that her way of coping when things were
most dreadful was to curl up in her sea berth in the fetal position.

Nearly wilted with relief at making Port Suez and refusing to think about
leaving, my happiness was shared with Don's. Our minds focused on Cairo
and the pyramids, plans for the Canal transit and what for us was a little R
& R—but mostly a time for celebration. While others had some hair-raising
experiences during their passages, we had been very fortunate. Ah, what a
wonderful feeling it was to be here at the Suez Canal!

Truth be told, had we not made this journey on our *Windy Thoughts*, it
is unlikely we would ever have seen this fascinating part of the world. Never
would we have experienced a culture so vastly different from our own. A land
that had seemed so very uninviting truly held rich history and interesting
people. In no other manner could we have had the opportunity to experience

the region's daily life. Nor would we have met that special boy, Taj.

Today we look back at that time as a very special segment of our cruising life. Life does teach lessons of patience and endurance and the Red Sea passage was a major one. We had been blessed with a good six-week passage and many memories. In retrospect, all of the good memories came to the surface and we could look back on the time as an exciting and wonderful experience. As so often in life, it was the mundane and simpler experiences that reached our hearts and the recesses of our memory banks. And all of my personal agonizing about what might happen had been for naught. Was there a lesson to be learned from this as well?

And now we were tied to a mooring at the Yacht Club! Such luxury it was, not in the literal sense, but the luxury of a strong sense of security and well-being. The Yacht Club is located in a basin right off the Canal and we watched ships transiting a few hundred yards from us. The water was flat calm no matter how hard the wind blew. Such simple blessings to be thankful for! The Yacht Club may not have been elaborate, but it had welcome moorings for visiting boats.

The others in our group had all arrived within the past few days. Some had made their visits to Cairo and were making arrangements for their Canal transits. Other boats sat leisurely on moorings, everyone feeling the ease of being at rest. Two boats were stuck 100 miles back, sitting at anchor for what would become four very long weeks before a break in the wind set them free again. One, hailing from England, had already rounded Cape Horn on a previous circumnavigation, and its captain emphatically stated that he would take on the Cape again before ever setting foot in the Red Sea!

Nothing could keep us from joining the others for dinner and celebration at the Yacht Club that evening. There were twelve of us, ten who had bobbed along in company since Thailand—all filled with stories to share and plans to make. *Gray Eagle* and *Investigator* had both scheduled their transit date for two days later. Since being separated several weeks ago, we had much to catch up on, no matter that we had kept daily radio contact.

Investigator and *Gray Eagle* went on to Israel for a short visit. *Investigator* planned to spend the winter in Italy and we anticipated crossing paths somewhere along the way in the Mediterranean. *Voyager* was headed on the fast track home. Don and I thought we would likely cruise Turkey for the summer months and perhaps spend the winter there. *Gray Eagle* was planning a similar path. With the Red Sea behind us, it was time to look forward to "cruising time" again.

Canal transit was a main topic of conversation as the others shared the ins and outs as learned thus far. Canal transits are made through an agent, and the busiest agent was the Prince of the Red Sea.

Our transit would wait, however, until we made a much anticipated visit to Cairo. We rested one day before setting off in a taxi for the city, with Jill and Mike along with us.

It was a two-hour drive from Port Suez, and our driver, who spoke some English, filled us in on the sights and told stories about the Gaza Strip and the troubles he had seen and experienced in this area of the Middle East. We passed several military checkpoints along the way, and at each we presented our passports after the driver spoke to the armed soldiers. Before reaching the outskirts of Cairo, we stopped at yet another military checkpoint and learned that a military escort was required for the trip into Cairo, intended for our safety. A military truck led in front and a jeep with three armed soldiers followed behind.

As we ventured into the city's outskirts, we asked the driver if we might stop at a place where we could get cold drinks. He rapidly veered off from the escort and pulled up to an Egyptian coffee shop amongst the many small shops lining both sides of the street. Inside, several men sat at tables, reading the daily paper and drinking coffee or tea while sucking on the mouthpiece of a water pipe rented for use.

While we enjoyed our cold drinks and observed the daily activities, the commanding officer from our military escort came in and spoke sternly to our driver. We weren't to have left the escort and were to have remained in our cars until deposited at our hotel. After some stern words and frowns, we were directed on our way. Stammering apologies, we returned to our taxi and headed to our hotel further into the city.

Cairo is a vast city immersed in the brown color of its buildings, streets and often colorless clothing. By the time we reached our hotel, we found ourselves in a rather nice part of the city that we would find lovely to walk about before we saw the last of Cairo—as this wasn't to be our only trip into this fascinating city before transiting the Suez Canal.

Our five-star hotel had been arranged for through the Prince of the Red Sea and offered to us at a generous discount. Our room was located on the eighth floor. Mike and Jill had a room right next to ours and after transiting the nerve-racking Red Sea on a small sailboat, the hotel and promises of all of Cairo to see was a long awaited pleasure!

Our deck overlooked the Nile, muddy brown below us. While Don and I gazed down at the lovely hotel pool, the landscaped grounds and the Nile in all of its glory, we heard Jill and Mike call from their balcony, "*Windy Thoughts. Windy Thoughts.* This is *Voyager.* Over. "

We could easily see them on their neighboring balcony and continued the talk of the ever familiar radio contact,

"*Voyager*, this is *Windy Thoughts.* Over."

"*Windy Thoughts*, are you as hungry as we are? Over."

"Roger that, *Voyager.* Let's have ourselves a good meal. Over."

"We can be dressed and ready to go in fifteen minutes. How about you? Over."

"Affirmative. Meet you in the hallway in fifteen minutes! *Windy Thoughts* is clear."

"*Voyager* is clear."

And we did treat ourselves to a grand meal, made even better by the good company and the joy that we all felt at having forged ahead to this auspicious spot on our globe.

After a long and relaxing time at the table, we strolled along the streets in the early evening, accompanied by the persistent honking of horns. The tree lined area we were now in awakened us to the fact that we were in a very different environment than experienced in Egypt so far. This was the great city of Cairo, with all of its glory and culture. Armed military stood at nearly every street corner, and we chose to feel quite safe with their presence as we planned our next day's events.

After a lovely breakfast in the hotel restaurant, we were off in another taxi, bound for the Great Pyramids! The city appeared to be one giant brown environment, but a fascinating and busy one. Changing lanes seemed to be the ongoing goal of each and every car and we were surrounded with the incessant sound of blaring horns. Perhaps we were just more aware, because our world was lived so far from the sounds of traffic and the daily life of a bustling city. The occasional camel loped alongside the cars, its master comfortably atop, both seemingly unaware of the cacophony.

The Great Pyramids can be seen in the distance from downtown Cairo, so great is their size. When we reached the outskirts of the city, we found ourselves in a business courtyard of sorts. This was our destination. The taxi driver let us out and would return for us in a few hours. He had been hired for the return trip and would be paid at the end of the trip. From this courtyard, we would continue our journey to the pyramids, less than a mile away.

A few camels lazed about in an open area, their masters all young fellows eagerly offering rides to the Pyramids. Two very tired horses stood nearby, having seen better days. The fellows bargained with the camel drivers a bit but when I learned the cost for the rides, I balked.

But Don in his wisdom stated that we were at the Pyramids for the only time in our lives and were going to see them properly! Don was overjoyed at the prospect of riding a camel. The camels snorted and growled at us and I had visions of a runaway camel, me high on his back, holding on for dear life as we fled across the desert. The camels smelled and the thought of my bare legs against dirty camel hair was revolting.

My hesitation was met with great astonishment.

"Do you mean that you sailed all the way up the Red Sea and now you're afraid of a camel? Hey, we're only going this way once."

Right again, of course.

Don chose a camel by the name of Ali Baba, who snorted and growled exceptionally noisily and seemed to prefer to lie in the sun. However, Ali Baba's young master had him up onto his knees in no time, giving instructions to Don on how to get aboard. Mike had chosen his camel as well and we were in hysterics watching the event and filming it for posterity.

Don climbed onto the seat and grabbed onto the front of the platform, tilting way forward as the camel went to his knees. The young fellow rapped on the camel's knees and Ali Baba came up off his knees, rising quickly to his full height so that Don was tilting back in the saddle.

"Whoa there, Ali Baba. Ride'em, cowboy!" Don gleefully yelled.

The boy laughed and told Mike that his camel's name was Michael Jackson. We never really get away from it all, do we? Michael Jackson did the same as Ali Baba when the boy tapped on his knees and soon Mike was tall in the saddle, on the riding platform. Jill and I chose the two horses. The men were rightfully disappointed in us, but we agreed that we would ride the camels on the return trip, not to miss this great opportunity. We could worry about that later on.

Our spirits were high as we set off on our steeds for the Great Pyramids. Ali Baba was directly behind me, determined to keep his big lips nearly touching my shoulder, breathing his unpleasant breath, snorting the entire way and baring his teeth. My horse ambled along with no desire to move faster than a slow jog. The men claimed to find their  camel rides comfortable, but we were here for the adventure of it all.

While Jill and I withstood the lumpy old steeds, we joked and laughed as we merrily approached that wonder of wonders, the Great Pyramids, looming before us like a storybook come to life. The camel boys led us on, walking on the hot sand with bare feet in ill fitting rubber thongs that flopped about, barely staying on their feet.

As with everything, pictures of the Great Pyramids had not done them justice. To stand and gaze up at them in close proximity took our breath away.

After exploring the Pyramids, we mounted our respective steeds and took a ride up a slope to a vantage point that provided a wonderful vista of this magnificent location. Giddy with excitement at being here and with having the Red Sea ordeal behind us, our joviality continued. After taking pictures of us in front of the Pyramids it was time to head back for the barn, as it were—and time for Jill and me to trade our horses for the camels.

There was great merriment over our getting aboard, and I made my camel boy promise he would hold tight to Ali Baba's lead and that we would walk the entire way. I had heard stories from *Investigator* and *Gray Eagle* about camel races! That group had been in the same celebratory moods we were. Apparently, at a full run, Dick's camel came to a dead stop on all fours, sending Dick flying over his head onto the ground, no short distance. Fortunately, Dick only sprained a finger and we laughed delightedly, knowing that he hadn't seriously injured himself.

Ali Baba snorted the entire distance and I had grave concerns about my camel boy's hold on him until we arrived safely back at the square and our waiting taxi driver.

The boys began in earnest to renew bargaining upward the already negotiated price. Though baksheesh had been included in the original agreement, Don felt good-hearted about it and wasn't going to argue about the extra bit of baksheesh. The boys had done their best to show us a wonderful day and it would end that way.

Baksheesh is asked for and expected in Egypt for any and all number of things. It is demanded on many occasions and you cannot walk down the street without calls for baksheesh coming at you from all directions. When in Luxor, baksheesh had been demanded when we paid our hotel bill, when we paid our restaurant bill and when we purchased any item whatsoever. Baksheesh is not a gratuity given by the happy receiver of services rendered—you don't have to make a purchase to be on the rather unwelcome end of these demands.

On our second morning we were off early to meander around the Citadel before heading to the eagerly anticipated Cairo Museum. We had wished for two full days there. In reality, we found that the one day was enough to satisfy us. It was just so overwhelming!

Don and I took a short break midday to leave the museum and relax for a bit with a cold drink at a nearby café. We found the cataloging in the museum to be rather poor and for the most part of little help. We were disappointed that few or no descriptions were provided, other than the occasional small index card nearly hidden near the bottom of a display. Wandering aisles of ancient stone statues of Pharaohs and the like, we had little idea of dates or their significance and could only guess in historical generalities. It seemed to us that everything was more warehoused in piles, or simply lined up in a way to fill the space, than displayed with any intent to make it understandable. Perhaps others more schooled feel differently.

As we sat at a little table with our cold drinks and watched those around us with their water pipes, we were discussing just this. A local gentleman next to us spoke up and explained that he couldn't help overhearing.

He introduced himself as a local archeologist and wanted us to know that he shared our sentiments exactly. A big issue with him and many others in his field was the total lack of thought to preservation of any of the antiquities in the museum. Little was placed in hermetically sealed glass casings, and as the years passed, light from the windows was doing harm to many of the displays. Though the archeologists were greatly concerned, they were unable to convince the curators to take any interest in the matter. There were plans to move the museum to a new building in future and we sincerely hoped any problems might be solved.

When our trip was over and we were deposited back at the Suez Canal Yacht Club, our friendly driver came alive with demands for more money. The Prince of the Red Sea had established a price for the taxi that included the driver's baksheesh as well.

Don understood that it was the practice to try to get more money than agreed upon and kept the dialogue friendly as he explained that we would not be paying more than the agreed price, though he included some additional baksheesh. Mike and Jill made their complaints to the Prince of the Red Sea on our return.

Two evenings later the four of us were invited to the home of the Prince of the Red Sea for dinner, fully cognizant of why the invitation had been extended. While we enjoyed a good meal, we were aware that our taxi driver was sitting in the foyer. We felt a tension in the air and worried for the man's job. Nothing was said about the incident until dinner was over. Then Don spoke up, doing his best to smooth over the situation and expounding on the great day the driver had provided for us. By the end of the evening the matter had been resolved and the driver still had his job. He could sleep well that night and so could we.

On our return to Port Suez and the Yacht Club, we said our last good-byes to Jill and Mike, who would make their Canal transit the next day. Our paths wouldn't cross again and we wished them well as they continued their adventure homeward. It is always difficult to say goodbye to people who are a special part of our memories and who have shared many good times.

Before making our transit we made another trip into Cairo, hoping that a city of its size would have a replacement transformer for our computer. Ours had packed up several weeks ago and Don had jerry-rigged one to keep it going, necessary for getting our weather faxes. We pictured ourselves lounging about the pool and luxuriating in our surroundings before getting back to cruising and getting through the Canal and into the Mediterranean.

Our trip was very relaxing though there were no movies on the TV in our room, necessitating that we spend our evenings doing more interesting things. All of Cairo awaited us!

Wares were hawked in the packed and busy narrow streets of the great historical market. Pieces of colorful material hung above our heads, as did baskets, clothes and anything that didn't fit at ground level. Every manner of wares was for sale, so much so that we could barely take it in as we wound our way through the little warrens, making way for the many busy shoppers that crowded the spaces.

Donkey carts shared the streets with cars and the occasional camel. With no designated traffic lanes, every vehicle's driver simply laid on his horn as he pushed his way into any space available, be it in oncoming traffic or not.

Determined to solve the problem of the computer transformer, we set off in a taxi to find a computer business suggested to us by the hotel staff. A small shop awaited us and it was eventually determined that one of the young fellows could get the part for us in another part of the city if we would wait for him. Eagerly obliging, we sat on the steps outside while a young fellow hopped aboard a motorbike and zoomed off.

Though it was an hour's wait, he did have a transformer for us, one that we were reasonably sure wasn't a new one and cost significantly more than a new one should—but we had our transformer.

Another important matter of business was taken care of in Cairo with a visit to the United States Consulate. Don would have a birthday soon, qualifying him for Social Security, and we filled out necessary forms—hoping that the wheels of government would surprise us with a check in the not too distant future.

Then it was back to the business of our Suez Canal transit, set for two days later, May 10, 1995. We were instructed to pull onto a small dock on May 9. We could spend the night and our pilot would meet us in the morning. The Prince of the Red Sea arrived to sit in our cockpit and explain the procedures—and to get our payment for the transit.

We were well versed on the subject of baksheesh for the canal pilots. Amongst the shipping community, the Suez Canal is known as the Marlboro

Canal and the big ships transit with several cartons of Marlboro cigarettes as baksheesh, the preferred tip here in Egypt. By the time we got to Port Suez we knew the procedure.

It was recommended that we put ten dollars in one dollar bills in an envelope and show the envelope to the pilot at the onset of the transit—letting him know that for every bit of trouble he caused, one dollar would be taken out. The baksheesh would be whatever was in the envelope at the end of his time on the boat.

This may seem a rather rude procedure, but the problems canal pilots can cause for boats are well known, and there was a general sense of dread in dealing with the pilots. The pilot's baksheesh was included in the fee, but we were ready with our envelope, as well as one carton of Marlboros purchased in Port Suez.

All of us who made our way north shared the same battle with the dust and sand. Now that a hose and running water were available on the dock, we relished the opportunity to get every niche and cranny spick and span. When we finished several hours later, *Windy Thoughts* gleamed like the little lady that she was.

Excitement filled the air as we woke up the following morning. Our pilot arrived at 10 a.m., and three minutes later we cast off the lines. One other sailboat was transiting that day.

The Suez Canal is basically a big ditch too narrow to accommodate big ships passing north and southbound at the same time. Small boats must wait and transit behind the big ships in the northbound convoy. The southbound convoy would transit in the afternoon. Our pilot was a capable as well as a congenial fellow and we had no problems as some reported. The previous day, we had watched a pilot put a sailboat aground before even entering the Canal itself!

We entered the Canal behind the last big ship of the northbound convoy. The ship literally loomed up in front of us! The day was beautiful and we motored along in the flat water of the Canal, Egypt on our port side and the Sinai on our starboard side. The autopilot steered most of the time, and when it was necessary to hand steer, the pilot allowed Don to take command.

We met none of the demands or surliness or rudeness with which others had to contend in their pilots. It was a very pleasant, if unexciting day, motoring along in this big ditch. There was little scenery to observe along the banks, only the barren desert. About the only diversion came when we were radioed to pull into a side basin to await the southbound convoy in the afternoon.

By 5 p.m. we arrived at the center of Great Bitter Lake, located in the middle of the Canal, north to south. Because our speed didn't allow us to make the entire transit in one day, we anchored here for the night. A rather rickety powerboat with five fellows hanging off its sides approached us and pulled alongside to pick up our pilot, who had said nothing about baksheesh the entire day—and we presented him with not only Marlboros, but the envelope of money with our sincere thanks for his work.

After a quiet night's sleep we awaited our next pilot, who arrived on another rickety boat. To our good fortune he also was a very pleasant fellow, said nary a word about his baksheesh and produced his own Marlboros for his smokes.

Late in the afternoon on the second day, we were pulling into Port Said. We had made it to the top of the Red Sea!

The pilot directed us alongside a stone wall on our port side where he was given his baksheesh and Marlboros before yet another pilot boarded us, required for the transit through Port Said. Ours was an older and more seasoned pilot who generally piloted the big ships.

With better weather reports for the Mediterranean predicted for the following day, we decided to spend a night at the Port Said Yacht Club before setting sail for Cyprus, only three days distant. The Yacht Club was a small facility located in an equally small basin to our starboard in the Canal. It was time to conquer Med-style mooring, and our first time was in twenty-five knots of wind right on our beam.

Few marinas offer dock space in the Mediterranean. Instead, the bow anchor is dropped well out from the dock or quay and the boat backed down into the space available, generally squeezing between other boats already there. There was one small space available on the dock between two local boats. With her full keel *Windy Thoughts* doesn't back up easily, but we had prepared for the Med mooring well ahead of time.

Our plan was to drop a stern anchor and drive the boat forward for better control. Don had a stainless steel ladder built that would attach to the bowsprit, allowing us to climb down onto the dock or stretch it out like a boarding platform. Since we weren't allowed off the boat, we didn't bother with the new ladder or make any flying leaps from the bowsprit. Instead, we concentrated on a good night's sleep. Few cruising boats stop here, so anxious is everyone to get out of the Red Sea—but instead exit the Canal and head directly into the Mediterranean Sea.

Words simply cannot describe the excitement we felt at being out of the Suez Canal and sailing right into the Mediterranean at first light the next morning, bound for the island of Cyprus. It was so good to be at sea and sailing *Windy Thoughts* again—sailing with winds that were manageable! Only three days later, on the morning of May 13, 1995, we were tied to the breakwater wall on the outside of Larnaca Marina, on the beautiful island of Cyprus.

The marina was full of boats, many of them local and many others cruising sailboats like us. Another sailboat was to leave within the hour, freeing up a berth inside for us, and very soon *Windy Thoughts* was tied up in her new home for the coming months. Securely tucked into a corner that looked impossible to get out of again, we knew that concern could wait for another day. At the end of a pontoon, with a high wall on one side of us and a smaller sailboat on the other, it was a quiet spot with little foot traffic.

There would be no worries about contrary winds and weather for awhile now, and no weather faxes to pour over—just lovely Larnaca, Cyprus, to explore and happy reunions with friends.

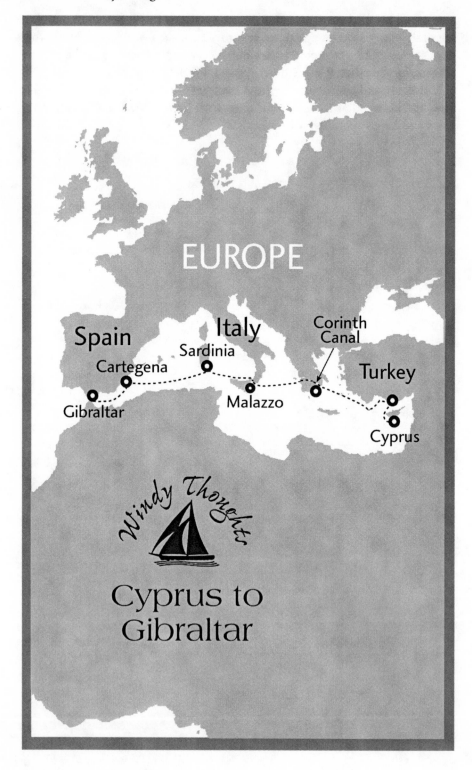

EUROPE

Spain

Italy

Sardinia

Cartegena

Corinth
Canal

Turkey

Gibraltar

Malazzo

Cyprus

Windy Thoughts

Cyprus to
Gibraltar

Chapter 13

Plans Change Once Again

Be patient, for the world is broad and wide.
—William Shakespeare

May 15, 1995
Larnaca Marina
Larnaca, Cyprus

Hello Susan,

Hallelujah—we have made it into the Mediterranean! We transited the Suez Canal a few days ago and are firmly tucked into Larnaca Marina on the beautiful island of Cyprus. There is absolute exhilaration at being out of the Red Sea, and all cares and woes have melted away as we enjoy the pure ease of life while tied into a very secure corner of the marina.

We have entered the world of Med mooring, though our spot is at the end of the pontoon and between the big breakwater wall and the sailboat next to us. A Marine Police Boat is moored directly at our stern and we consider ourselves to be in good company!

Our neighbor is Clarissa, from Vancouver, British Columbia, Canada! She has lived here for three years and her husband is often away working on offshore drilling platforms. She has a garden of flowerpots on the pontoon and a little dog, Skippy, who is adorable. Her flowers are the first we have seen in so long!

Windy Thoughts is in bow first and we can either climb down over the bowsprit onto the pontoon, or climb up the wall—our preference, and not difficult if we stand on the cabin top, hold onto the stay, and step directly on top of a stanchion with one foot and onto a nail sticking out of the wall with the other foot—and then swing up and onto the top of the wall. Since the stanchion is 1.25 inches in diameter, it presents a little challenge. But we have mastered the art of gymnastics necessary to accomplish this maneuver and can do it now in seconds flat.

Nothing separates us from our neighboring boat but our fenders. Fortunately, Clarissa is a great neighbor, is accustomed to life here and is giving us good information on where to go and where to find things.

Larnaca is lovely, and a walk out of the marina gate takes us directly to the waterfront promenade, lined with beautiful restaurants and shops. Everything seems so clean, so wonderful—a mixture of both the quaint and the modern with its winding streets of old lined with shops filled with stylish and modern goods.

The change in atmosphere from our past six weeks is almost overwhelming. One needs to have experienced the Red Sea to truly understand the enormity of this for most of us. Don and I wander the streets and peer into the shops with childlike delight. We might have been let out of prison after years of confinement, so happy are we. And to be able to leave the boat without thought to the wind—to just climb up onto the wall and wander off at our will! We haven't paid the weather or weather faxes any mind since arriving two days ago. Nor must we concern ourselves with navigation duties—we have only to find our way back to the marina on foot!

We will await our mail sent from home, and anxiously await news after no mail for the past three months.

June 7, 1995
Larnaca Marina
Cyprus

Susan,

Our much awaited main package arrived just today. Not able to make further plans or transits, we had become very concerned. Our noses have been pressed to the pages of your letters and clippings before reading anything else.

We are both laughing hysterically over your Hal's exploits with the bagpipe lessons. Such a smart shopper to emerge from the bagpipe store without all of the paraphernalia—but who spends his money on single malt scotches instead! Even though he has been put into remedial bagpiping, his practice sessions are sure to result in greater degrees of excellence.

Our pictures were just developed from Phuket and we have one of Don attempting to blow on the bagpipes on New Year's Eve, at Ban Nit. He couldn't produce a sound, but says that Hal must be full of a lot more hot air than he has ever let on.

Larnaca is just what the doctor ordered after the apprehension of the past months. Everything closes up for the entire afternoon and it takes acclimating to the slower lifestyle, one that we surely should be accustomed to by now!

We have just returned from a three-day trip by rental car with another American couple, Anne and Jerry, on *Lovely Lady*. The four of us drove into the mountains, where we basked in the beauty of the villages.

Cyprus is a relatively small, but fascinating, island with coastal beaches—as well as mountains, that even sport a ski resort in the winter. In truth, the snow base is never more than bare minimum. Don was reminded of his own dearly loved mountains and we breathed in the mountain air with homesickness biting at our heels!

The quaint little village of Kakapetria clung to the side of the mountain in a storybook setting. The hotel was as quaint as the surroundings, inexpensive, immaculate and with a grandpa and grandma in charge. Breakfast was included, prepared and served by the same sweet couple.

Narrow winding streets led to lovely homes. Small restaurants abounded and we sampled the delicious village wine and the food, our dinner in a perfect setting in an old mill with a three story water wheel. Everything about it created an evening to remember.

We drove down out of the mountains to the coastal village of Pathos, an old port town chock full of old ruins that has become a major tourist attraction in the past years, its old port front now dotted with hotels and hundreds of restaurants.

Outside of Pathos we stopped to visit the original castle of Richard the Lionhearted that is still intact, small, but fascinating. The ruins of an ancient amphitheater intrigued us and Anne was able to give us good historical background on everything, adding immeasurably to our enjoyment.

Marina life is very easy. The waterfront promenade greets us the moment we step out of the marina gate. A number of restaurants line its walkway, with tables outside to beckon us as we pass by.

We sit outside, under an umbrella, gazing at the seaside as if we were tourists having an annual vacation by the sea. Almost as if the sea weren't our home and we were banking memories of the moment, to call up when we are back to everyday life. However, we are banking memories as well, aren't we? In front of us are exciting new surroundings, a new historical culture to embrace and an easy life for which we are so ready.

There are many small groceries in town, almost mini-supermarkets with many different foodstuffs carried on the shelves. The closest big supermarket is a twenty-minute walk, and if too much is tossed into our cart we simply take a taxi home. Our feet have carried us all over Larnaca, up and down narrow streets winding hither and yon and full to bursting with shops.

Almost daily, I walk to the open market located within a huge, covered building. Inside, many stalls are filled to overflowing with all sorts of beautiful produce and wares. I have already picked my favorite butcher from the several available, and he presents me with big delicious pork chops and mince (hamburger ground to order right before my eyes), lamb and chicken.

Greek salads are on the menu aboard nearly every day, with fresh greens, cucumbers, red onion, tomatoes that are not hot house, and beautiful local feta cheese that is so abundant. The local red wine vinegars grace our salads of fresh greens, as does the Cypriot olive oil, pressed right here on Cyprus. I cannot imagine ever taking such things for granted when cruising life is over.

The large variety of Greek dishes offered in the local restaurants fascinates our palates. Beef, pork, chicken and lamb are slow cooked, lending themselves to such mouthwatering dishes as stifada and souvlaki. Don refers to the delicious roast potatoes, and green beans slowly cooked with bacon as "Grandma's cooking." In addition, we have found what might be the best Pizza Hut in the world—perhaps it is the Greek influence! Our stomachs are loving Larnaca.

A PHONE CALL MAKES ALL THE DIFFERENCE

Along with the wonderful feeling of being on an R and R, it was a busy time in Larnaca. Don had the usual repairs and the preparation for setting off for Turkey. Though no cruising guides were available in Larnaca, others shared guides for the Mediterranean, and much of my time was spent at a local copy shop. Each day brought us closer to pushing off.

After four weeks in Larnaca, we were ready to set off for Turkey the following day, well provisioned, fuel topped off and the excitement of the entire Mediterranean awaiting us. We climbed the stairs to the Harbor Master's Office and completed the clearance procedure from Cyprus. With this last piece of business finished, we spent the last of our Cypriot money in the small store below and then sat outside sipping cold drinks. All was at the ready.

Suddenly, the loud speaker heard throughout the marina came to life. "*Windy Thoughts*. Telephone call."

This was repeated several times as we leapt back up the stairs to the Harbor Master's office, our hearts beating overtime. We learned that there were personal business matters needing our attention at home and we returned to *Windy Thoughts* with sinking hearts, to ponder just what we should do, quickly deciding that there was no choice but to return to the States.

And so, our plans made an about face again. We would not be heading through the Strait of Gibraltar by summer's end and would not be home in one year after all. Going home wasn't a whim that we could easily satisfy at a moment's notice and would take a big chunk out of our budget. Many things that we wanted to see and do in the Mediterranean would now have to be set aside when we returned and resumed our voyage.

The decision was made to go home for the summer and return to Cyprus to spend the winter before making our way across the Mediterranean and toward the Strait of Gibraltar. With heavy hearts, we headed back to the Harbor Master's office to request that we clear back into Cyprus—and to leave our boat in the marina for the few months.

It was with mixed feelings that we headed back to the boat, where we began the process of ridding ourselves of every fresh vegetable and fruit, all of the delicious cheeses, anything that would not keep. Arrangements were made to fly to Seattle, and during the next few days we kept very busy with the myriad things that must be done in preparation to leave the boat for several months. Though we would be changing course midstream, the inevitable visit back home was beginning to stir excitement in us.

We left Cyprus in a week's time, *Windy Thoughts* safely tied between Clarissa and the wall. After the long flight, our plane dropped down in Seattle. We had been without a car for eight years and we set off in a rental car to visit car dealers, heading toward an area known for both new and used car dealerships. As we pulled into the first one, Don spotted a well-used gray conversion van, viewing it as the perfect answer to our transportation problems. When he learned its price, it became even more perfect for us.

Old Gray Bell, named after the conversion company whose name Grey Bell was on the back of the van, became ours within minutes. Don's eyes lit up with its possibilities. The back seat made into a bed and trips could be taken! A television and reading lights were additional amenities that put stars in his eyes. Four big seats were overly comfortable and the fact that a little of the paint was peeling slightly on the exterior didn't deter him at all. My Don, who loved spiffy cars in his past land life, had changed priorities during the cruising life. He fell in love with the van at first sight.

"You've got to be kidding!" was my only response.

Since money doesn't grow on trees and we didn't belong to the working world anymore, we were in the driver's seat and on our way before we knew it. The van's exterior wasn't really that bad, but may have belied the condition of the inside—which seemed rather plush to us.

Old Gray Bell provided us with thousands of miles of adventure and exploration that summer, from the west coast US to the east coast and back again. At each day's end we stopped at a campground or RV park, where fresh showers were always available, and every night on the road was spent sleeping on the comfortable bed. Long distances were covered in a matter of hours instead of days! Rolling about and night watches were not a part of this kind of travel—and the only navigation to be concerned with was reading a road map, elementary in comparison to navigating oceans and reefs.

At the end of the day, Don put on the emergency brake and sat back to leisurely remark that the anchor was down and secure. With no thought to wind and waves for the night, we slept like babies without a care in the world. It was a very relaxing and restoring six weeks that we spent on the road. What would *Windy Thoughts* think if she knew how much we were enjoying Old Gray Bell?

Much of our excursion was a trip into the past for me. On the way east we stopped in Michigan to visit my dear friend Jolene Curry and her John and daughters. Jolene and I went back a long way—we were roomies in college and this was a wonderful and nostalgic stop. When visiting my hometown of Ischua, in western New York, we were graciously given a bed at the home of Aladine Kessler, who remained the lovely lady that she always was—some things don't change! A highlight of our trip was a visit with my aunt and uncle, Margaret and Larry Upton, in East Rochester, New York, where we caught up on family memories that tugged at my heart.

Up and along the St. Lawrence River, and then on to Maine, where we meandered the coastal towns and ate lobster. Maine's coast was exactly as we anticipated it should look, with the beautiful greenery and trees, quaint homes and the little hidey-holes that boaters love to duck into when cruising the local waters.

Heading south to Florida to see Don's daughter Patti and her Jim, we stopped in Virginia to visit my childhood friend Terry Meyer and her Joe, high school sweethearts. These were a wonderful and nostalgic few days, and just before we left they asked where we planned to leave the van when we flew back to the Mediterranean.

We had thought to find storage in Florida. Once we transited the Atlantic Ocean, we might sail the boat up to Florida and stay there for a bit, then traverse the Inland Waterway north and go through the Great Lakes to Duluth, Minnesota—where we could ship the boat west to Seattle. At the time, it sounded like an easy plan when compared to alternatives.

The Meyers suggested that we drive back to Virginia after our Florida visit and leave Old Gray Bell in the airplane hangar on their property. This very generous offer was agreed to and we said our goodbyes, knowing that we would see them again in the next weeks.

We loved our time with Patti and Jim in Stuart, Florida. They treated us royally and it was so good to have time with family—something we had little of during the past few years and we treasured the opportunity. Dr. Jim gave us physicals and pronounced us both physically fit. The pterygium that was removed in Malaysia had grown back again and needed to be removed soon. Because the ophthalmologist at Jim's clinic was on vacation and we were leaving the country soon, I would have it removed on Cyprus.

Voyager was back in Florida, and though Jill was off visiting family in another state we took a day to drive over to Ft. Lauderdale to visit Mike at the marina that we had in mind to return to with our *Windy Thoughts*. Interestingly, we now found that the Inland Waterway no longer appealed to us, realizing that its only attraction was that it had seemed an easy way home after years of cruising.

Perhaps this was the reality check that boosted our energies and desires to do what would always be the right thing for us—complete our circumnavigation. We reminded ourselves that we would have the chance only once and we'd best make the most of the opportunity. There was so much more yet to see and once our cruising years were over, a special lifestyle would be over as well.

It was time to head back to Virginia and leave Old Gray Bell with our dear friends Terry and Joe Meyer, who drove us to the airport in Washington, D. C.

Windy Thoughts was awaiting us in Larnaca. But we would take a short diversion and would fly from Washington, D. C. to Istanbul, Turkey for a wonderful five days.

WINTERING ON CYPRUS

October 30, 1995
Larnaca Marina
Cyprus

Dear Susan,

Three months away from *Windy Thoughts* and suddenly, as of two days ago, we are back aboard, all is in miraculously good order and such a difference from our return to Malaysia and the weeks of restoring the boat to decent living conditions there. Cyprus's dry climate during the summer months presented none of the mildew problems that took over in the more tropical latitudes. Just a pail of water and Murphy's Oil Soap was all that was necessary to give a cursory wipe-off to the cabin below, and today the hose gave a quick wash-down to the topsides.

Clarissa is gone for three weeks, but little Skippy is aboard with willing people watching over and feeding him. Clarissa has put a covering over the entire boat to provide shade and a log book in the cockpit to be signed by those who take Skippy for a walk. Everyone stops for a chat so he doesn't lack for attention! Skippy is a quiet little dog and only barks a bit if cats appear in the night or when someone walks by, but never incessantly—a good little watchdog.

Five days in Istanbul, Turkey, were probably some of the most enjoyed ever. Istanbul is immaculate and so wonderfully full of historical sights.

Our hotel was recommended by old cruising friends in Seattle—Jan and Dave on beautiful *Moulin Rouge*, a Hans Christian Hansa 33, like yours. The small hotel was family-run, filled with antiques, and located amidst all of the most interesting sights in the old section of Istanbul. There were only eleven rooms and everyone visited together in the small dining room where excellent fare was served family style.

Because our location was central we could walk virtually everywhere. An entire day was spent at the spectacular and well known Topkopi Palace. Ancient mosques and wonderful museums drew us in. It was obvious that much care and pride is taken in their antiquities—and we were fascinated with the national treasures. It seemed that a million or so carpet stores might be within our immediate area, though we heard that the best buys are away from the coast and in the small towns inland.

After making our arrangements in Florida, it suddenly occurred to us that getting back into Cyprus from Turkey would be a problem. And for two reasons: you saw how much luggage we were carting back, and we contemplated seeing Turkey before returning to Cyprus. Don had no intention of carting luggage throughout Turkey on public transportation—even the superb bus system offered in Turkey.

Since Don would be carrying the heavier load, his wiser opinion won out and we instead decided to fly from Istanbul to Cyprus. Now, we realized that we could not fly directly from Turkey into Larnaca, Cyprus—but we could fly into the Turkish occupied side of Nicosia, the capital of Cyprus. Once your passport is stamped in Turkish-occupied Cyprus, you cannot come directly into south Cyprus.

This meant we would have to fly back to Athens, Greece, and from Greece we could fly directly to Larnaca. The cost to do this was as much as flying from Florida to Istanbul!

But off we went to Athens. One of the brothers who own the hotel in Istanbul also has a travel agency. He made our arrangements and reserved a room for us for four nights. It was a spot that lacked charm, but we learned on our last day it was in the nicest section along the beach.

After completing the proper officialdom and awaiting our flight in Istanbul, a voice suddenly came over the loudspeaker, calling for Mr. Green to come to the gate where luggage is loaded on the lower level. It seems that the stern gland, securely packed with stuffing around it, had set off alarms and initiated a search. Officials had found the stern gland and removed it from our luggage.

Don spent several minutes explaining what it was and, given the language barrier, finally drew pictures of a sailboat and engine. Along with interjection from the flight captain himself, the officials finally understood what the part was. Though they were most polite, several policemen surrounded Don, and when all was settled everyone had a good laugh. At this airport everyone was body-searched, and every bag closely inspected and carefully searched before being stowed on the plane.

After Istanbul, Athens was somewhat of a letdown. We signed up for a tour on the first morning; by the end of that day we learned we could have taken a bus downtown for fifty-cents—and walked to everything that we saw on the tour for $70.00.

The Acropolis was the tour's main destination; it was fascinating to walk amongst the ruins and attempt to comprehend the historical significance. However, as the bus made its way along the road leading into the city, we were put off by the garbage strewn about everywhere, even in the vicinity of the Acropolis!

We walked a short distance down the hill to the Plaka, the main shopping area in the old section of the city and also the touristy spot—fairly charming in character. Food was rather expensive, but when in Greece, do as the Greeks do; eat, drink and remember that we are storing memories of this ancient city.

Archeological sites that we had only read about surrounded us. Statues seen in photos now stared at us through the maze of traffic and the busyness of city life as our bus drove along the streets. And the trash that often surrounded these antiquities quite amazed and perplexed us, an obvious disregard for these national treasures—such a contrast from what we saw in Turkey. In our opinion, we prefer Istanbul, such a fascinating city is it and in such a beautiful setting. However, we will vouch for Greek culture and food!

Cyprus appeals to us every bit as much as it did before returning home—and we eagerly look forward to wintering here. On our first evening back we strolled out to our favorite restaurant and had our fill of stifada and potatoes, sitting at a sidewalk table and gazing at the ocean just across the street from us.

As it is a popular haven for wintering over, a large contingent of British boats along with their owners will stay in Cyprus—as well as boats from the States returned from summer cruising in Turkey while owners leave the boats in the marina and fly home for the winter. We will attend a Halloween BBQ tomorrow night and see just who is about.

Don installed the new VHF radio, and the refrigerator is perking along fine now after giving it a few shots of Freon. Don is preparing to install the Ham radio tuner and the new Hustler antenna. He recently purchased a battery charger, and we expect to purchase an electric heater for the cabin during colder days in December, some days getting down into the fifties!

Nesting again keeps us busy and it is good to be back in our own little home. The marina laundry sports three stainless steel washing machines and though no dryers, I hang all on the boat's lifelines to dry within an hour. Tomorrow, a trip to the market will provide us with the makings for big Greek salads—along with the local peasant bread that we dip into the delicious Greek olive oil and Cyprus's red wine vinegar.

We read of a new haul-out facility in the northern part of the Sea of Cortez that handles trucking boats back into the States. Since we will have completed our circumnavigation when we reach La Paz, we have no desire to beat all the way north to Seattle!

If not feeling too pushed, we are determined to cross the Atlantic Ocean in December of next year. We feel so close to home now, though there is the matter of 2,500 miles of the Mediterranean to cross, the entire Atlantic Ocean, the Caribbean Sea and then the west coast of Latin America up to Mexico. But after all of the miles under our hull, this route really doesn't seem daunting at all! We are nearly there and there is so much more yet to see!

November 26, 1995
Larnaca Marina
Cyprus

Hello again,

Thanksgiving has come and gone and we look back to last year, when on this date we had departed from Singapore five days earlier. It was the beginning of several months that carried us thousands of miles, when oceans of water passed under the hull. Life on Cyprus has been slow, easy and domestic and we remain very content.

Our refrigerator is perking along beautifully but won't shut off, which means that the evaporator box is in its freezer mode constantly. I will take my good fortunes when they come because this means that I have the use of the freezer for the first time in years!

We are well into our winter mode, with a change from shorts just last week to daytime temperatures sometimes down into the fifties, warming up to the sixties as the day progresses. By 5 p.m. it is dark, and evenings find us tucked below, all comfy and cozy with a movie rented from a video store in town—perhaps a favorite book from the many aboard. Isn't this just the picture of domesticity?

Nicosia is about a forty-five minute bus ride from Larnaca. The DMZ zone, referred to as the Green Line, separates the city into the northern Turkish-occupied part and the southern Cypriot part. When in Nicosia, we often walk about the buffer zone and peek through the wall from the Nicosia side, where all is buzzing with shoppers. The scene just a few feet away on the Turkish occupied side is one of desolation—taken in 1974 and still looking like a forlorn, deserted city. There are pictures of Cypriot loved ones posted all along the wall on the Cypriot side, those who didn't make it out and whose loved ones long for information about them—as well as pictures of those who have lost their lives. It is a haunting place to be.

About two weeks ago there was a bit of a rhubarb when a Cypriot soldier caught smoking a cigarette with a Turkish soldier in the buffer zone was taken prisoner by the Turks—and is yet to be released. This caused a fair amount of media attention and students protested for the first week, throwing rocks back and forth. The Turkish Air Force also violated air space by flying over several spots in southern Cyprus, including Larnaca, during the episode. The "Cypriot problem" is always present and many people in south Cyprus are refugees in their own country.

The owner of a Ham radio shop in Larnaca has befriended us and invited us to his home for a lovely dinner with his wife and children. They lived in a formerly lovely city in northern Cyprus before the 1974 invasion. Because he was a radio operator in the Army, he learned of the invasion right away and was able to rush home and get his new wife and his mother out. Their flight to Larnaca and safety was made with only the clothes on their backs.

Now they drive to a point on a hill and look down at what was once their home. The story of how he had to start a new life over for himself and his family was so typical of the many who suffered the same fate. He has worked hard to build a well-run business in Larnaca.

January 12, 1996
Larnaca Marina
Cyprus

Happy New Year!

Christmas has passed and for us it was a lovely one. A late afternoon dinner with the other boaters wintering here was celebrated in a Tavernna. The owners cooked traditional turkey, potatoes, rice dressing, Cypriot vegetables, village bread and Christmas pudding with brandy sauce for dessert.

A white elephant gift exchange topped off the Christmas excitement with everyone bringing a no-longer-needed item, and a very nice winch handle was the jackpot. After the gift exchange, Greek dancing began with an explosion of hand clapping and foot stomping all about the tables. Christmas music filled the Tavernna, mixed with Greek music performed by a merry group of fellows with instruments.

New Year's Eve arrived, and we elected to stay home on *Windy Thoughts*. Unfortunately, at the stroke of midnight Don and I were sound asleep—and not even the blaring of ship's horns or little Skippy doing his best to bark in the New Year woke us up!

Last week Don took a much deserved break from boat projects and we took a bus sojourn to Ayia Napa, a lovely village about an hour away along the southeast coast of Cyprus. Our guide was Walter, who lives in Austria and spends his winters on Cyprus.

Caught in a squall just as we arrived in Ayia Napa, we ducked into a restaurant that was the perfect venue to enjoy delicious moussaka for break-fast—seated in front of a blazing fireplace with steaming cups of strong, hot coffee laced with brandy that warmed both our hands and our insides. The weather outside was nasty, and Walter declared this the appropriate way to start our day before ambling though beautiful old churches from the Byzan-tine era in the absence of the summer crowds.

Orange and lemon trees are laden with fruit that is at its best now. Greek olives purchased from big crocks are so delicious that we are devouring them in huge quantities, and we are eating well.

A bad tear is developing along one of the zippers in the window of our dodger, another is forming on the top, and it is time to replace the entire dodger. Though duct tape has been known to hold many a boat together, a friend from New Zealand accompanied me to Nicosia to purchase Sunbrella material. We will attempt to set something up in the spring with a lady who does sail and awning work and lives on Kastollorizo Island, Greece.

Yesterday was Epiphany, the day the three kings were to have arrived in Bethlehem, according to the Greek Orthodox Church. The celebration took place here on the public wharf, only about 200 feet from *Windy Thoughts*. The Archbishop led a procession from St. Lazareth's, a beautiful, ancient church where Mary's brother is said to be entombed—and a place that Don is fre-quently drawn to when in town. In preparation for the ceremony, the en-tire length of the wharf was strewn with olive branches in the early morning hours.

Three boys were chosen to dive for the three crosses thrown down from the wharf by the Archbishop. It was a very moving ceremony and a big crowd attended. Clarissa was able to get us into the small wharf building that houses officials and we had front row seats.

February 10, 1996
Larnaca Marina
Cyprus

Susan,

Don has just called me up into the cockpit to see the installation of the new radar that is interfaced with the GPS and presently mounted at the cockpit station. It works!

One project that is very frustrating is the replacement of the propane system. Safety demands a solution for an elusive leak whose origin Don has yet to find—though he has found extensive corrosion.

An anticipated shipment from Doc's includes a new BBQ that should help with the cooking until all is remedied. Meanwhile, Clarissa has provided us with a small propane burner on which I can boil water and make soup and eggs, much like camping! Greek salads with lots of feta cheese, along with the wonderful village bread and fruit, make very good meals possible as well. The weekly Sunday BBQ is an opportunity to cook a chicken for the refrigerator, and with Pizza Hut nearby, being without the stove has not been quite the survival mode that I make it sound.

A bug is running rampant through the marina and, along with many others, Don and I have been laid low for the past week. Clarissa has surprised us with complete dinners handed over the lifelines. Last night was pesto pasta with antipasto and garlic bread; the night before we enjoyed onion soup with salad and peasant bread. Though I am rallying in the galley, Don continues to inquire from Clarissa about tonight's menu.

A local fellow who does excellent stainless work is making us a new framework structure for the cockpit. Louie has also made a small outdoor grill with legs that fold up for storage. We anticipate beach gatherings and picnics, but are likely as excited about its prospects for camping back home.

A friend on a nearby boat is making us a new sail cover and will also make the new slipcovers for the cabin. The lady from Kastollorizo Island, Greece, will be at the marina at the end of the month to look over the dodger work. Several boats have recommended her, but I am a bit nervous about the whole thing because they say she is a bit chaotic—explaining that this means she drinks a lot.

Don has just come below and lit several candles that along with our little heater keep us quite toasty and warm—while wearing a sweatshirt, a fleece jacket and another heavy sweater on top. The thermometer reads sixty-eight degrees, and it is impossible to remember that our cruising to date has been in dastardly hot climates where our highest priority was keeping the fans running. We rather enjoy the experience of not perspiring twenty-four hours a day.

At present I have been appointed to wage a fight with Federal Express. We paid $300.00 in shipping charges for our new radar, to arrive in five days—but after three weeks it hadn't arrived. Another $100.00 was spent in phone calls and faxes attempting to find our package. Fed Ex doesn't offer tracking service here. Though we finally got the package, we felt somewhat miffed that these charges were incurred.

The secretary for the local manager told me that it was no use trying to reach the manager because he wasn't the kind of boss who "wants to listen to anyone's complaints"—and that it would do no good to call headquarters in Nicosia. Instead, she gave me the phone number of the regional office in Dubai, swore me to secrecy as to where I got the number, and told me to keep her posted. The offices in Dubai are not interested in our problems either.

Another shipment is coming from Doc's but this time was sent via DHL service. Just making the phone call is a hurdle as we must go to the telephone company and wait our turn for a booth. Nothing is easy. Ah, but the adventure of it all!

February 24, 1996

Our shipment did arrive in four days. But after installing all new line, regulator, etc., that elusive propane leak is still with us. Don has spent three entire days checking every fitting again and again and now thinks the stove may need replacing. I doubt that I would ever have another stove like my Dickenson Marine Stove, so this is not good news.

The turbo on the boat's engine needs cleaning but the manual doesn't explain how—and Don doesn't want to face a turbo uneducated. A diesel mechanic recommends that we have a number of spare parts ready when he tears it apart, as chances of a ring or something needing replacement are about fifty percent. Some of these parts are not in Don's spares supply, so Don called Doc's—and learned that they are not in stock. It will take a special order and the additional time to ship them here.

The good news is that Don had Louie make a mount for the new BBQ that, thankfully, has a burner plate. Without the stove, we do need the BBQ to accomplish any real cooking.

Most of my major disasters on this journey around our world have occurred in supermarkets rather than at sea—and I faced another today. You might remember that I lost several hundred dollars in Singapore a few years ago in a supermarket—and again, just two days before leaving Singapore for the final time.

Today I set off to the Metro supermarket in search of gas canisters for both the new BBQ and the little ring burner. I had the valve for the new BBQ with me to be sure the canister fit. Though the canisters weren't available at the Metro, with my cart piled high on my way to the checkout counter I had the inspiration to ask if someone might know where I could find the canisters. It was now 12:30 p.m. and the man kindly drew a map and called a taxi so that I might get there before everything closed at 1 p.m., not to reopen until Monday.

I helped the checkout girl throw things into the sacks and rapidly tossed the sacks into my cart. As I paid the bill and raced to the door, with a quick check in the cart I found that the important new valve for the BBQ wasn't there. My heart stopped.

I dumped every grocery bag out onto the floor, expecting some miracle to happen and the valve to appear before my eyes. People looked at me with either pity or disgust; this poor woman must be deranged or just ill-mannered. But they didn't have to go home and tell their Captain that another valve must be ordered—at considerable expense as well as a long wait for its arrival. Meanwhile we couldn't use the BBQ, we had waited so long for naught—and he would again have to make do with the little ring burner and soup for dinner.

Clarissa was sitting in her cockpit when I arrived back at the boat. After all of Don's frustration with the propane system and now having a new BBQ that we couldn't use, I felt sure this news would be the final straw. She decided that it was a good time to head to the showers.

But my hero and captain took it quite calmly—and though the cruising life does have its ups and downs our little world remains a happy one.

The cruising life also requires a certain amount of patience, sometimes beyond one's endurance level. Our shipment didn't include several items ordered for the propane system, requiring yet another fax to Seattle. Don keeps a stiff upper lip, and elation overcomes him with the recent discovery that the propane leak is between the solenoid and the stove! Now, to find its precise location.

Ah, for those halcyon days when we first returned to Cyprus, with all of that glorious time stretching ahead of us. Don maintains that right now he could strangle the person who "invented boats".

March 28, 1996
Larnaca Marina, Cyprus

Hello Susan,

Though we had planned to set off from Cyprus and be on our way this next week, we still await the order from Seattle, sent by mail rather than DHL as we requested.

The weather blows up between late morning and noon each day, never less than twenty knots and with very steep and sloppy seas that will be right on the nose for our passage along the south coast of Cyprus.

Everyone tells us that "the Devil is not out of the Mediterranean until after April 27." But we must get on our way if we expect to make Spain by fall and see a bit of anything at all along the way. We hope to follow the European advice and head out in the early mornings to get as much distance under our belts as possible before the wind comes up against us in the late morning. Small bites at a time. That's how to eat an elephant.

Next day:

Last evening our Cypriot friends picked us up for a lovely dinner at their home—a traditional Cypriot dinner of roast pork, roast potatoes, village salad and lots of various dolmades with stuffed grape leaves, tomatoes, zucchini and onions. Their home is lovely, the lower floor built when they first arrived as refugees and the second floor added about a year ago. The son and his fiancée joined us. A June wedding is planned and a baby is expected in August. Clarissa explained that being with child at the wedding is not uncommon and is considered proof that the wife is fertile.

It is a beautifully warm and sunny day, going from cold yesterday to hot overnight when a squall came through. Our thermometer reads a lovely eighty-three degrees and it is very dry, without the humidity of the tropics.

Topsides are polished and gleaming, including the teak; winches are greased, all lines have been soaked and washed, sails are washed, and the new bimini top and new stainless steel framework is installed—along with the new radar, new VHF radio, new antenna tuner, new antenna and new BBQ.

A new mainsail cover graces the boom and new slipcovers brighten the cabin below. Louie made a stainless base for the toilet that should last for perpetuity. Two new aluminum propane tanks were purchased at a marina jumble sale last fall, American-made and never used! New line is run for the preventer and new sheets for the sails. Don made a new cover for the Life Sling (which we considered dispensing with since we "never use it"). A new mattress is being made locally for our master berth, to arrive in two days—and we feel brand new!

We are now looking at jumping off by mid-April, just a couple of weeks away, as soon as our parts arrive from Seattle. British friends who have sailed this Mediterranean many times advise us to get to Gibraltar by end of July, so it will be a mighty push ahead.

A few days later:

We have had no luck in getting parts for the oven from New Zealand, but a local fellow has located a stovetop oven for me. His mother used one just like this when he was a child. Just having the burners of our stove back in business has changed life aboard about 180 degrees, but to have an oven now just puts me over the top. It works great for biscuits and small items and I have even baked a pie.

There are so many social occasions that accomplishing every chore has been difficult. Two days ago Clarissa invited us to go to the United Kingdom Club for a luncheon. I slapped the first coat of bottom paint on the dinghy before we set off, assuming to return to add the next within a couple of hours. Not so, as we ended up stopping to visit a lovely little grand dame of ninety-one years of age who runs a small inn nearby. This meant sipping more wine, and by the time we arrived back on *Windy Thoughts*, both Don and I were finished for the day.

Yesterday we were invited to dinner with friends newly returned from winter in the United States. Today, after going to the veggie market and then to the video shop, I made a big salad for a BBQ tonight in honor of two birthdays here in the marina. Life is busy!

About thirty boats are expected in from Israel over the weekend for a race held during Passover. A few are already in and we are hailed with "Shalom" as we go up and down the dock. It should prove to be an exciting weekend and one with excellent winds for racing.

April 18, 1996

The weather has been horrible! A big blow lasting two days finally passed through last night, and another is predicted to set in today with thirty-five to forty knots of wind by mid to late morning—and all directly on the nose for heading for Turkey. Another system is coming behind this one and there are many small lows popping up all over the Mediterranean. It is early in the season yet and the weather patterns are not settled until well into May.

Our departure must be timed for a calm night to get around the westernmost cape on Cyprus, and then hope to have a close reach on to Turkey. Unable to make clearance on the weekend, we are looking at Monday.

In preparation, this morning Don and I tackled the problem of turning around in our little spot. As Don and I attempted to walk the boat backward, the wind was rising with alarming speed, and the water was so shallow that we managed to get stuck hard on the bottom. Two American couples came to our rescue and it took fully one hour of melodrama before we finally broke loose. Impossible to get back against the wall, Don fended off and attended lines while I raced up to the marina and requested another spot—with tears in my eyes. Did that work?

Windy Thoughts now sits in one of a handful of finger berths—and we step from the boat right onto the dock! It wasn't easy getting in with the wind at thirty knots and there is no chance that we are leaving here until it abates. As we wait out the weather, we are eating up the cheeses and meats stocked for our coming passages. But we look outside the breakwater just a few feet away, see the boiling seas and are not at all anxious to leave our comfortable spot.

Cyprus has been so good to us. What a perfect little oasis after the Red Sea! We look back at our arrival here and remember how overjoyed we were to be tied so securely in this marina, to feel safe and to throw all cares to the wind as we let the Red Sea settle to the back of our minds, to take its place as an exciting part in the tale of our adventure.

JOURNAL OF *WINDY THOUGHTS*

April 29, 1996

No one leaves Cyprus at noon this time of the year—but today we did just that! It wasn't planned, but rather we expected to leave in the early evening when the headwinds let up, to clear the southwest point of the island by late the following morning—knowing after that we would take what we got. However, we had an easterly blowing, as if a miracle had popped up just for us. We needed about forty-eight hours to get across the southern coast of Cyprus, around the western end and up to Turkey.

It blew thirty knots right up our tail all day; it was in the Indian Ocean that we last had such a good sail. We subsisted on crackers, peanut butter and apples today with little rest for either of us, our sea legs not quite yet acquired. Nevertheless, *Windy Thoughts* is at her best and loves taking this on.

May 1, 1996:

The easterly continued blowing thirty knots dead behind us all night. How did we get so lucky? We rocked and rolled along, with our eyes wide open after the comfort of the marina for so long, and it takes us about ten times longer to do anything—but we are getting our sea legs again.

We weren't the only ones who like better weather. A little bird flew into the cockpit around midnight last night and tucked himself under the dodger, seeming not to mind our presence at all. Is he Cypriot or Turkish? My, he's far from home; no wonder he's so tired.

He stayed all night and we gave him some breadcrumbs and some water in a jar lid. Don placed it down ever so gently and just as gently tucked a small washcloth around him for a little nesting feeling. He didn't fly off, but stayed to ride along with us. This afternoon he perked up and decided that he would take flight for the rest of the way to Turkey. We miss him and wish that he had stayed aboard all of the way.

Sometimes I wish that we could take flight. Will he get there before we do?

This morning the wind lay down and we're motoring in very uncomfortable seas that remain big and lumpy. *Windy Thoughts* appreciates the ride much more when she can cut through the sea balanced out under full sail. Surely, that little bird is more comfortable in flight than he would be with us.

May 3, 1996:

We pulled into the Kekova Roads Bay on Turkey's southwest coast at 9:00 yesterday morning. It wasn't until we got the anchor down that the wind started snorting at twenty-five- plus knots. We sit in a very large and well protected bay with no one else about, and we crawled into bed and slept most of the day before enjoying a dinner of Greek salad with fresh tomatoes, green peppers, cucumbers, lots of feta cheese—and more of the Cypriot village bread.

This morning, after a great night's sleep gently rocking in the winds, we faced repair day. The salt-water pump lost its prime and Don tackled that first. Before changing the masthead light, he worked on the sticky engine problem that had kept him busy during our second night out.

Mountains and greenery surround us. We won't go ashore, but will have a good night's sleep again and be off in the morning, bound for Kas, up the coast just a short distance.

May 5, 1996:

It was only a three-hour jaunt to Kas, a delightful village that so perfectly fits the definition of picturesque.

Down came the dinghy, and we were off to shore to walk into the little village that has a quay with other boats moored Med style to it—but we prefer the quiet anchorage. The village is full of sidewalk cafes and quaint little shops. After finding the proper offices, we made our clearance into Turkey. It cost us U.S. $100.00 for the visas, transit log and other officialdom.

Don continued investigating the engine problems; though the fuel tanks were kept topped off in Cyprus and preventative additive used, Don found algae in the fuel. He pumped 100 gallons of fuel from the tanks with the little hand pump, an all day job, and we jerry-jugged it to shore in the dinghy to waiting fishermen who would readily use it up.

Meanwhile, a diesel fuel truck came to the anchorage and waited for us to finish all of the pumping and going back and forth with our fuel cans. The diesel cost $4.00 a gallon, but also cost us a lot in energy by the time we cleaned the fuel tanks as best we could, nearly crawling into them to do so, and then poured new fuel into the tank one six-gallon can at a time! This alone took hours. Yes, we are back in the business of cruising, all right—exhausted but ready for the next adventure!

LETTERS TO SUSAN

May 10, 1996
Fethiye
Turkey's southwest coast

Hello Susan,

Welcome from big, beautiful Fethiye Bay, where we sit after spending time at the most charming village where we ate good food in the little cafes—and nearly exhausted ourselves working on the boat.

While Don's days were spent with his body contorted over the engine,

I was in the dinghy working on our decal. The edges of the vinyl were peeling back and I used a razor to carefully cut off every little bit, unfortunately necessitating removing much of the light gray shadowing effect—but it does look better.

After four days, we left Kas at 5 a.m. on May 8, for the run up here to Fethiye, sailing past the infamous "Seven Capes" without a hitch. There are about a bazillion charter boats here and many tourists—though the tourist season doesn't really peak until June.

The streets are dotted with shops and sidewalk cafes, a lovely welcome. The Turks seem genuinely friendly people.

"Have a beer in my garden café. No, please, no money. Just sit and visit."

Every shop that we walk into nearly forces Turkish tea on us. The apple tea is glorious. We have purchased spices at the open spice market, all wonderful and inexpensive—everything imaginable available in huge containers. People stop us on the street to chat, asking where we are from and to please, come back and have tea with them tomorrow. Yes, we will try!

Fethiye is enchanting, but we must get moving—though no one has ventured out with the very strong winds experienced since our arrival. Many who are not planning to move across the Mediterranean stick around here for weeks at least, and often for most of the cruising season.

We made our clearance last Friday, intending to leave on Saturday night after the wind settled down and head for Rhodes, Greece, only a forty-nine mile run—to get there in the morning before the gale blew again. We loaded the dinghy, tied it down before dark and got lines and sheets ready. At 9 p.m. we upped anchor in settled weather and started out of Fethiye Bay. We had been underway only a few minutes, when the wind began to rise. Capes are always a bummer, and we were sure that it would be better once rounding the cape.

By the time we reached the cape two hours later, it was twenty-five knots bang on the nose. Hauling in tight, we laid her over and made a gallant dash to round the cape in less than pleasant conditions. It only got worse around the cape—with much bigger seas that met *Windy Thoughts*' bow like a brick wall. Turning tail, we headed back, dropping anchor again about 2 a.m. We would bide our time.

British friends have been our nightly weathermen, calling us on the radio about 9 p.m. with an update from the Nav Tex that gives an audio of the winds and weather several times a day for all areas in the Mediterranean. Local weather changes every few miles and one really never knows quite what to expect.

For the next three days, we loaded the dinghy at day's end and hoped for the best that night. Still, it continued to blow thirty-five to forty knots. Were it behind us as we wended our way westward, we would be off and flying—but this Aegean Sea was living up to its reputation.

Meanwhile, we are enjoying old friends as well as new amongst the many boats sitting at anchor. Don has had good rest and I remind myself of our good fortune, to appreciate the blessings that we have experienced in being out here and from whom these blessings come.

Ralph Waldo Emerson did say, "Adapt the secret of nature; her secret is patience." Surely patience on our part is a small price to pay.

Our delayed departure gives us time for good exploration of Fethiye. Beautiful Turkish charter boats line the quay, looking to us like colorful pirate ships of old. Ancient ruins surround us everywhere, many antiquities of 2000 BC and older; amphitheaters, tombs and castles enchant us. Ancient sarcophagi lie about in helter-skelter fashion and might be used for watering troughs or perhaps nothing at all. Yes, the world is our oyster!

Two days ago we took the bus over to Gocheck, a lovely small village on the other side of Fethiye Bay sporting shops, cafes and even a chandlery of sorts. The southwest coast of Turkey offers a bonanza of fabulous cruising grounds, the lagoon by Gocheck with thirty-two anchorages in one eight-mile area itself. We met up with American friends Jim and Sue, off *Sea Shanty*, and enjoyed a nice lunch together at a sidewalk café.

At a shop in Gocheck we purchased a beautiful plate by Mehet Geshing, a well-known artist from Istanbul who makes pottery according to traditional and ancient customs. The design is from the Ottoman period, three sailing vessels in blue on a white background, and is one of a kind, as are all of his works. I picture it in our future home—and home is only about 9,000 miles away now, a guesstimate off the top of my head, as I only want to focus on the wonders to see along the way.

It is easy to understand why this entire spectacular coastline is such popular cruising ground, with the scenery, the people, the culture and many fine marinas—best of all, so many beautiful anchorages. The Meltemi wind sets in during July and many boaters don't venture farther north, but instead leave boats in one of the well appointed marinas and take land trips to Istanbul, Ephesus and Cappadocia.

May 17, 1996
Simi Island, Aegean Sea
Greece

Hello Susan,

A big Greek hello! Yesterday we loaded the dinghy again, early in the day this time and just after a trip to the market for more of the delicious bread—ready to jump off for Rhodes at last.

Our British neighbor gave us the nightly Nav Tex weather report and last night's forecast was for Force 4 WSW, probably about as good as it would get. When all seemed quite calm at 1:30 a.m. we decided to make hay while the sun shines—and wouldn't some sun be nice for setting off rather than the dead of night?

Up came the anchor and we silently made our way past others who were sound asleep aboard, peering through the darkness for anchor lights and shapes of hulls like shadows on the dark waters of night. It took a couple of hours to work our way out to the Cape again.

As *Windy Thoughts* poked her nose around the Cape, welcoming flat calm conditions stayed with us and we motored straight through the night. When conditions held this morning, we knew we could make Rhodes before the headwinds came up.

As we approached Rhodes we passed castles and old forts. With a continuing dead calm we decided to keep moving and make west while we could, crossing the Rhodes Channel without a breath of air and pulling into a small bay at Simi Island, Greece, a port of entry, just a few hours later. Three other boats sit here with us. One left Cyprus just two days after us and experienced thirty-five knots of wind right on the nose for the first seventeen hours! Don was right again. Do you suppose that I will ever listen to him?

White buildings ashore beckon us with their brightly painted doors and their flower boxes overflowing with both flowers and color. This morning, we took a mini bus about one-half mile over the hill to make clearance into Greece at Simi Town. The bus wound uphill and downhill on a road with room for only one vehicle. When we met an oncoming vehicle, one or the other had to back up. The short trip took a half hour and we soaked up the local culture. A Greek Orthodox priest in traditional black garb boarded, greeting us with a warm smile and a handshake for both of us. A tourist who spoke English told us about some of the best bargains in the village. We felt at home already!

As the bus reached the top of a hill, we looked down at the harbor and little town below. Before us was the quintessential Greek harbor town as seen in paintings, with whitewashed homes and buildings tumbling down the otherwise brown hillsides surrounding the harbor—each building made bright and colorful with its flowers, and the doors painted the Mediterranean blue that so matches the water here. Sidewalk cafes winding along the main quay mix with shops butting right up to the sidewalk. Fishing boats bob gaily up and down and pleasure boats, charter boats and ferries vie for space, squeezing in where it seems impossible there could be room.

Very narrow old streets ramble and wind up and down hills, most having room only for walking—or for motorbikes or donkeys. Front doors open right onto the cozy little streets and those beautiful flowers tumble and pour out of colorful window boxes. Music is playing and the sun is shining in the always clear blue Mediterranean sky. Perhaps we are in a painting!

Before any leisure activities, we had to complete clearance procedures. Unaware that it was Saturday, we were fortunate to take care of half of the proprieties at the Passport Office and the Immigration Office. We lacked the transit log that we were to have first purchased at Customs, so made our way around the little harbor only to find that Customs officials were out for awhile. When we learned that it was Saturday we fully expected that we would have to pay an overtime fee, or else wait until Monday to complete the procedure.

To bide our time, we sat at a charming little sidewalk café that was only one of several dotting the little harbor, leisurely enjoying cold drinks and Greek salads. To our good fortune, Don saw the Customs officials walking along the harbor wall and jumped right up from the table to greet them. He paid the $30.00 for the transit log on the spot and we had only to head back across town again to the Passport Police and were finished.

May 26, 1996
Still meandering westward in Greece

Hello again,

The two delightful days on Simi Island were a wonderful introduction to the Greek people and their culture, but we had to keep moving. After jogging along nicely for about thirty miles, the engine sputtered and quit. I wished for wind, even against us, as we could at least sail back to Simi. Don worked on the engine while we drifted about one mile offshore, a bit disconcerting to be so close without power and no wind for sailing.

The engine finally started and we set off, relief filling us, only to have our hopes sag when it quit again—this pattern continuing. We turned back and nursed our way five miles to an alternate anchorage on the Turkish peninsula. Though cleared out of Turkey, we didn't expect it to be any problem—until we got in and saw military in the anchorage. But no one bothered us and we hoped that engine problems would be sufficient reason to be without proper paperwork.

Don spent the day with head and body draped over the engine. I provided moral support and sustenance from the galley.

Heading out the next morning, we limped our way to Kos Island and are happily in Greece again. It seems that along with the gunk found in the fuel when in Turkey, we have air in the fuel lines. Don has replaced some lines but finding the air lock is elusive and rather a trial and error process. A reliable engine is necessary in this Mediterranean!

The next day we made it to a very small and well protected all-weather anchorage. Soon, another boat showed and squeaked into a spot not far from us. A British fellow and his wife, from the lovely *Quo Vadis*, rowed over for a wonderful chat. Three other boats arrived; all was very tight but it worked.

When a charter boat with four German men aboard arrived and dropped their anchor not more than five feet from us, it took some anxious explaining by Don as to how dangerous this was—not only for us, but for all the other boats in the anchorage. They told us where we could go, and it wasn't out of the anchorage. While they settled in, others stared in disbelief. But when they suddenly hauled anchor and pulled out, everyone called over to us to say that had the boat not left, they were ready to assist Don in persuading them to re-anchor safely.

The next day was a rather nasty experience and the last fifteen miles were spent with Don below, bleeding the engine constantly until we made it to our next destination, a lovely big bay, by the skin of our teeth. Bleeding the engine would be much easier with an electric fuel pump, and Don plans to purchase one when we get to Piraeus, near Athens.

After an energizing lunch, *Quo Vadis* arrived and Semra and George rowed over. George offered words of empathy, knowing air locks can be so difficult to trace. Don spent the afternoon changing hose fittings and hoses and checking fuel lines—but we went to bed without a solution. Without an engine, we would have to sail when the winds came up—a nasty beat to weather. I had visions of beating all the way to Gibraltar, and the Mediterranean suddenly lost much of its allure.

Quo Vadis pulled out in the early morning, but before long, George called on the radio to tell us that in good conscience they couldn't leave us alone with our engine troubles, George having fought the same difficulties for a long time himself. These good people were willing to jog along with us not only to offer their good company, but to offer any assistance that may be needed—moral support for sure!

George is from England, is retired and has lived aboard for several years. Semra is much younger and comes from an influential family in Turkey. We marvel at their shared love of life aboard a very well kept boat that doesn't sport all of the electronics and gadgets that most do. *Quo Vadis* has been home for the nine years of their marriage.

Headed for the Corinth Canal and Prevaris, on mainland Greece, *Quo Vadis* would travel with us to Piraeus, near Athens and considered the place to get boat parts and boat work done.

Don promised me that we would not leave Piraeus without solving the engine problem. Don's vista had so long been limited to the engine compartment that he was ready for some fun. These recent engine sniffles had us wishing that we could sprout wings and fly across the Mediterranean. Where is our quest for cultural adventure now?

Force 6 conditions came at noon and remained through the next day, so we stayed put. The next morning we got the dinghy down and Don put the Yamaha motor on for the first time since having it serviced in Cyprus. The motor refused to start and Don discovered that a bolt was stripped.

Along with *Quo Vadis*, we rowed about a mile across the bay. George and Semra had given up their motor years ago when costly fuel didn't fit their budget, and they tell of loving the hours spent rowing together. Fuel is not the inexpensive commodity that it is for us at home. With diesel cans in our cart, we walked uphill a good distance on a goat path to the dirt road and then three miles into a fishing village.

All buildings were freshly painted white, with blue or red trim on the doors and windows. Picture-postcard perfect again. As in all of the islands, every street is narrow and winds up and down hill, some only steps that go up and down, with houses and buildings sitting directly on the street around the harbor. Our lunch under a grape arbor was wonderful, and fresh baked bread and beautiful bright tomatoes were purchased—just perfect for our Greek salads! All was a welcome relief from troubles of the engine compartment.

Much of the long walk back with the twelve gallons of diesel was uphill and George helped Don pull the cart. Don would have stopped for a breather now and then, but George just happily galloped along. By the time we reached our floating homes, the wind was blowing fiercely, about thirty knots and gusting higher. If only this were behind us, just think how we could fly west to Gibraltar!

Waiting for better weather, we invited George and Semra to share a movie and popcorn that evening, snuggling down in our cozy cabin and counting our blessings; we were enjoying friends, we were safe and the world could go by.

The next afternoon we were actually able to sail with the wind on our beam after a nasty beat all morning. The mainsail went up, the headsail was rolled out, and *Windy Thoughts* became a sailboat again to thread our way through some rocks and into the bay of our destination—where we sit in total peace and tranquility.

Several boats sit in the anchorage with us and a beach beckons us ashore. Looking through the binoculars we note that everyone on the beach is completely nude! A charter boat pulled in next to us with two men aboard who are lying on top and reading—without a care in the world—and without a stitch of clothing on! Do we relax in our cockpit and pretend that we don't notice, or do I just stay below? I'll just go on as usual and attempt to adapt to local custom, but with eyes averted.

Don claims that when we get this boat home, the closest he intends to go anywhere near a boat is the ferry system in our San Juan Islands. He claims that he doesn't even want his canoe anymore. Thank goodness for his sense of humor! We know what charms those islands of home hold and we cherish the pristine cruising and boating offered there.

May 31: Naxos

Waiting out weather seems to be the more typical way in which the Mediterranean is cruised—and that is what we are doing here on the island of Naxos, though we have made both northerly and westerly progress. Though southwest winds are not to be expected this time of year, sure enough, by 8 p.m. when the winds usually die down, in comes a southwesterly.

Windy Thoughts and *Quo Vadis* headed across to the other side of the bay, to duck behind a breakwater in front of the Navy station that provided total protection, a dandy little spot where we sat for two days.

Semra and I walked uphill to a small village, where we had sliced pork cooked on a spit and stuffed in pita with tomatoes and onions in the quaintest mom and pop café. Pop sang Greek songs in a booming baritone voice while he was cutting up a side of beef—live music while enjoying the most delicious lunch imaginable. Don stayed aboard while he and George worked on the electronics, men time for the two of them.

June 4, 1996

Quo Vadis' autopilot packed in a year ago, so they prefer short daily jaunts that suit us just fine, and we are certainly not pushing as hard for Gibraltar had we not met them. After a night at anchor off the island of Paros, our course was set for only a twenty-mile hop in rising wind on a near beam reach. Uncomfortable seas with their wild pattern of square waves were still welcomed, for we were sailing again, headed to a little bight on the island of Kithnos. And little it was!

Just as we entered, the depth sounder packed up. It flashed radical readings only three or four times, none of which we trusted for accuracy. So we got out the "ole lead line" again. Columbus would be proud of me.

Two French boats were readying to haul anchor as we worked our way to the head of the bay. Once the hook was down and we fell back, we discovered that if there was as much as four or five inches under the keel, we were lucky!

We pulled up anchor, snagging the anchor of a small fishing boat as we did so. Everyone drops anchor out in the middle of the bay. The wind was howling as we struggled to free the anchor and our bow didn't want to come around against the wind. Don finally managed to back out, having no choice but to will *Windy Thoughts* to do what she won't do under normal and easy circumstances. Thank you, *Windy Thoughts*!

We radioed *Quo Vadis* to hold off until the French boats left before entering the little finger, when there would soon be more room. Both our boats swung from one side of the bay to the other with the current—and with only a few feet between us and the rock walls on either side. Stuck here four more days, we became accustomed to our little spot and contentedly set up housekeeping.

With thirty-knot winds, we shared anchor watches with *Quo Vadis* the first night, but by morning knew that we were dug in good. With only two feet under the keel, when we didn't hit bottom while bouncing in the heavy chop we decided to sit back and enjoy the wait—though we used our time wisely.

One of Don's days was spent wiring in a spare depth sounder using the "transducer inside the hull" method, prior to spending the past two hours re-wiring the Auto Helm depth sounder—and it seems to work! Don has his head in either the engine compartment or in the Yanmar engine manual. I expect that by the time we reach home he might have the manual memorized.

Ashore and just up a hill, an ancient water spigot offered good, potable water. Don spent all of one day jerry-jugging 120 gallons out to the boat, carrying two five-gallon cans at a time.

Semra and I spent two days at the spigot doing laundry—feeling that we lacked only a tent as we chatted away while working under the glorious hot sun. Our laundry blew dry on the lifelines in no time. There is nothing better than fresh laundry, full water tanks and the anchor hooked solidly to the bottom while the wind blows thirty knots twenty-four hours a day.

Bread and groceries, including the excellent local feta cheese, were available in a village about a fifteen-minute walk away. With our fresh bread, fresh produce and fresh laundry, what more could one ask for in life? A little olive oil and red wine vinegar for dipping our bread, fresh Greek salads piled high with juicy blood-red ripe tomatoes (that are not hothouse), cucumbers, green peppers—and topped with feta cheese and all the Greek olives that we want—all to the accompaniment of music playing softly in our cockpit—this is what life is all about.

This morning's forecast was finally good with north-northeast winds at force four to force five, the best we could ask for since we're headed northwest. *Windy Thoughts* and *Quo Vadis* actually sailed thirty miles, the last two hours in the shelter of mainland Greece.

Sitting at anchor thirty miles east of Piraeus, we are ready to head there tomorrow, where we'll seek out another electric fuel pump, do more provisions shopping, and hope to be out again in three days. The engine hasn't quit now for the last 80 miles!

The local people are so very friendly and welcoming, the villages lovely, and the anchorages for the most part have been good. There is much for which to be thankful.

Don celebrated his sixty-third birthday on May 21—and though he has the health, the energy and the will of a much younger person, it is not getting any easier as we move along. Don put so much time into the boat in Cyprus, going over everything, installing new equipment and making us almost new again. It is discouraging to have to spend his time working on the boat now when he would like time to enjoy it all a bit more. We often feel that we are not so much cruising the Mediterranean as forging our way westward in our quest for Gibraltar.

Windy Thoughts is in the Gulf of Corinth now, where the winds should tend to be north-northeast as we move into the Ionian Sea, where sailing conditions are far nicer and a complete turnabout. And we will be thrilled to see greenery again. Of course, the rest of the Med will be west-northwest winds. Whoops, negative me again. Our goal was to get to the Corinth Canal before the Meltemi sets in and we are safely in the area with time to spare.

George and Semra have been such enjoyable company. We admire them for the way in which they live well and happily without the frills others find so necessary. George is a true seaman as he lives life aboard, knowing what is important. Both have been excellent role models. Two highly educated people who don't consider riches important, and who love the life they are living together aboard their beautiful *Quo Vadis*.

During our first five years of cruising, we too pinched every penny—and when others were eating $25.00 lunches out in the South Pacific, we were eating aboard. We didn't notice because we were living our dream on a well equipped boat that provided a beautiful home for us.

It isn't a vacation but a lifestyle that we chose and we have always done what was necessary to maintain it. Though our pockets don't jingle with lots of extra change, we are thankful that a few things that were considered a luxury during those first years can be a part of our lives now.

June 8, 1996
Piraeus, Greece: Near Athens

Huge Piraeus Bay provides the vista as we sit in arguably the best well-protected spot yet.

Many small marinas are near us, with big Zea Marina about a half-mile across the bay, all full to overflowing. Four boats sit at anchor with us and their crews have shared directions for getting into Piraeus, a few miles away.

Don and I immediately got *Breezy* down and, with bus directions in hand, headed ashore, to ferret out chandlers and the like. Rather than trusting our directions, a local fellow advised us to get off the first bus with him, but after a twenty-minute wait for a bus we learned that we could have stayed on the first bus! It is 2:20 p.m. by time we get to town, needing to exchange money, but we learn that the banks had all closed at 2 p.m.

The afternoon is spent trying to find the elusive chandlers. Don can't make headway with the electric fuel pump, but has been advised to go to the Land Rover dealer. The only other option for parts is Malta and we aren't headed in that direction! We also want about three meters of stainless steel chain to replace the galvanized chain used to replace the broken bobstay in

Sri Lanka. After hoofing it a long distance over a hill to a place that handles stainless, we find the shop closed for the day. By now it is late afternoon—and nothing is accomplished. But a Greek dinner lifts our spirits before heading back to the anchorage—where we find that the thirty-five knot winds have blown all day while George and Semra kept busy with chores aboard.

With winds still howling the next day, George and Semra join us to check out the chandlers at the main harbor. After hours of walking about, Don finds an oil pump that looks able to do the job, and is thrilled to purchase three meters of shiny 3/8 inch stainless steel chain for the bobstay. George comes up empty-handed on his search for underwater silicone needed to sandblast his hull.

Land Rover is our goal the following morning and Don and I leave amidst the blowing gale, but the anchorage has excellent holding ground and by now we aren't as concerned. Once ashore, a taxi scoots us into Athens to the Land Rover dealership, where several men are sitting behind a counter, each smoking and reading the newspaper. Patiently waiting until someone looks up, Don asks about an electric fuel pump. The fellow replies that he can't help us and goes back to reading his paper. I whisper to Don to persevere. We are *not* leaving without our fuel pump! Eventually, we are told of another place that may have one—they are just too busy here.

Fortunately, a taxi driver standing behind us is given explicit directions and off we go to an auto mechanic shop, where I have been instructed to start sobbing when Don pokes me if it looks like we aren't going to have any luck here. But they have a fuel pump—not exactly at the shop—and the young fellow takes off on his motorbike while we sit on the steps awaiting his return for an hour and a half.

The pump doesn't look as Don expected and he is skeptical, especially since it costs $250.00 and he has never paid more than $30.00 for others. A hose for the pump is an additional $40.00. Knowing that we have few alternatives, we pay up and head back to Piraeus. At the anchorage, we learn that it is exactly the same pump that George has used successfully for the past twelve years—though he paid only $30.00 for his.

The men were left to their respective boat projects again today while Semra and I continued our domestic chores, this time in search of water for laundry. We hit the jackpot when one of the nearby marinas allowed us to use their hose. Though Semra was too shy to ask and felt that we were imposing (nor will she go into a store unless planning to buy something), I have no such inhibitions. Under the sun, we slosh and swish in our buckets—and sit under the trees enjoying cold drinks before heading back to our boats to hang all in the breeze.

After diving on the prop this morning and completing more boat chores this afternoon, Don takes a nap and feels quite chipper by the time we row over to *Quo Vadis* for a lovely dinner. Earlier, George brought over one of Semra's lemon meringue pies, to keep in our refrigerator until dinnertime—a wonderful treat!

Aboard *Windy Thoughts* we have just eaten the last of our vacuum-packed meat. Don says no more, as temperatures are quite hot now and he worries about the fridge failing and meat wasted. I believe that he is getting anxious about one more breakdown before we get home!

Our plans are to leave on Tuesday morning, anchor nearby the Corinth Canal and make our canal transit on Wednesday morning. Once through the Canal, we will be clear of the Aegean Sea weather patterns and ready for good sailing again—as well as greener scenery!

June 29, 1996
Lefkas Island
Ionian Sea

Hello dear friend,

The greenery that we so looked forward to, as well as islands that are so very different from the Aegean side have welcomed us on the Ionian side of Greece—where for the past week we have resided leisurely at anchor off Lefkas Island.

The three-mile Corinth Canal was the most expensive canal experience we have ever had, or will ever have, for the distance traveled. Very early on the morning of our transit, *Quo Vadis* tied to a wall with us while we went up to pay our fees and arrange for the transit.

The history of the Corinth Canal is interesting, as the idea of a canal was first conceived as far back as 602 B.C. Julius Caesar entertained the idea of digging a ditch, but it was never finished and eventually fell to oblivion. Others throughout the ages also courted the idea of a canal, but it wasn't until the completion of the massive Suez Canal in 1869 that the opening of the Isthmus of Corinth was finally legislated. The project was assigned to French contractors. Even then the project was stalled for twelve years until a Hungarian general took over and started construction. Funds ran short and a Greek company didn't complete the Canal until 1893.

The canal cuts the Isthmus of Corinth and makes our trip much shorter! It is 63,456 m. long, and the canal width is 24.6 m. at the waterline and 21.3 m. at bottom level. The depth ranges from 7.5 to 8 meters. Interestingly, the flow of water changes course every six hours and the usual current speed is 2.5 knots.

Quo Vadis led the way when the light signaled go, putt-putting along with us right behind her. It took a full hour against the current and following in *Quo Vadis'* very slow wake, but we emerged into the Ionian Sea, feeling that we might have moved through the looking glass! Greenery surrounded us and gentle breezes called for raising the sails as we headed for Trevonia Island, the jewel of our Greek travels so far.

At tiny Trevonia Island we tied *Breezy* up to the dock inside a break wall. Wouldn't we just love to be behind this big and lovely break wall with *Windy Thoughts*? Fishing boats bobbed in the waves on the outer harbor in front of the most charming village, and everywhere we looked were olive trees and flowers.

For three days boat chores were abandoned while we enjoyed the village and took walks out to the old Greek Orthodox Cemetery, up and down hills—and frequently ate in a little café only a few feet from those bobbing fishing boats.

Trevonia Island captured our hearts and we will likely always remember it as the highlight of our time in Greece, truly a very special spot.

Sailing on to Lefkas Island took us past Ithaca, the home of Ulysses of Homer's Odyssey and the ruler of the island Kingdom of Ithaca. This small Ionian island reached its prime around 1000 B.C. Archeological finds from this period seem to support and correspond with Homer's epic as literal descriptions of historic events. Don loves the long-believed-to-be-mythical story of Ulysses—and that many interesting facts seem to validate the tale. Myth or fact?

Windy Thoughts also jogged along past Onassis's Scorpio Island before slipping into Lefkas harbor—which is full of other boats, many that we know, so it was like a homecoming, all of us shouting hellos and catching up with one another.

After two days here, sad goodbyes were said to *Quo Vadis* as they set off twenty miles north to Prevaris. Their plans for the summer include getting to Italy to pick grapes. This is the hardest part of cruising—saying goodbye to people whom you will most likely never see again. George gave Don a book about the Battle of Trafalgar as a goodbye.

Lefkas is the center of boating activity in this area, and a nice small town caters to charter boats, with several restaurants and small grocery stores. It is a social community of boaters here after the Aegean and everyone is reveling in the joy of being in new waters.

Our plans to attend a BBQ on a nearby island were curtailed when the toilet plugged up—of course, when I was pumping it. It wasn't a simple matter of righting things and was instead two days of rather miserable work, Don and I remaining quite sure that the boat was built around the head.

With little time for "shore leave", Don remains busy and has installed a new Nav Tex that we purchased here, a system used by the Europeans that we hoped would give us up-to-date daily weather reports for the rest of the Mediterranean. The proprietor of the shop assured us that the antenna could be installed anywhere—inside the cabin or outside, sideways or upside down. Don has changed position of this antenna five times in the cabin area and even changed it to a number of different positions outside—and still we get no broadcasts at all! We are told that it doesn't work because we are an American boat, and the fellow refuses to take it back. [We were able to sell it later on down the line.]

As for me, a hotel ashore allows the cruising boats use of its laundry facilities with three washing machines. Good as this was, my experience with Semra ashore using the water spigot back at Kithnos Island was culturally more significant and memorable!

July 4, 1996
Salina Joniche
Italy

Buon Giorno,

Our Independence Day finds us at the toe of Italy and inside a breakwater at Saline Joniche. As we ran up the Italian flag, we paid our due respects to our own United States flag, proudly flying in the breeze below the Italian flag. We know there will be no fireworks and that no one here is aware that it is a special day on our calendar.

We departed Lefkas Island on July 1 and had a great passage with two nights out. Lining ourselves up to enter through the breakwater of Saline Joniche, we slowly began working our way in when suddenly, right in the middle of the entrance, was a beach—complete with people sunning themselves on the sand! The Pilot didn't mention this!

After very carefully making our way between this sandbar and the wall, we were soon inside a man-made basin with a breakwater around it. Though a safe harbor, it is not an attractive one, with storage tanks ashore and all rather industrial looking. The greenery is missing again and we look at brown landscape.

This breakwater was obviously built at great expense, but nothing ever came of its intended use. No one seems to know exactly what this use was, but there are rumors that it may have been a bit nefarious. It is a good spot for boaters in transit through the Messina Strait. Fewer anchorages are found in Italy and laid moorings to the quay are common. It was an easy procedure to pick up a mooring behind us and come on in to tie the bow off.

Another day will be necessary here to change oil and get diesel before heading north twenty miles to the exit of the Messina Strait.

When we communicated that we needed to get to a bank to exchange money before we could pay for our diesel, the dock hand called a taxi for us so we could get to the bank before it closed. The driver tried to charge us

30,000 liras ($21.00) for a ride taking less than three minutes! Don handed him 20,000 liras and said no more, in spite of the driver's complaints.

Our sights were set on lunch and we were the only patrons at the one restaurant that we found. The lady easily interpreted our gestures, and we were sure she understood that pasta and tomato sauce would be just fine for us.

Before long two big plates of antipasto were placed on the table, one for each of us. A superfluous abundance of pasta followed, along with a basket of bread. Her son joined us and offered to drive us back to the dock—a big relief because we didn't want to have to face the only taxi driver in town. Lunch was very expensive, but it was our celebration for being in Italy.

Back at the boat we invited our driver aboard for a visit. Incredibly, he was well informed about our Northwest, recounting various Indian tribes and speaking at length about the Seattle Seahawks and the Sonics. Yes, it is a small world!

Fuel tanks were topped off at $3.80 a gallon, and between our taxi ride, the expensive lunch, mooring fees and fuel costs, we have had a very expensive introduction to Italy—but we have full stomachs and full fuel tanks.

British friends on *Helios* and German friends on *Anna Maria*, both met in Larnaca, arrived here yesterday and it is like a little reunion. We were planning to head up the west coast of Italy and through the Bonafacio Strait separating Corsica and Sardinia, thinking we might have a better slant on the wind heading to the Balearics. *Helios* has done this numerous times before and Joe advises that a course from here across the north coast of Sicily is more direct and much easier on the boat.

We will go from northern Sicily to Sardinia, wait for a window there, and make tracks for the Balearics.

July 5, 1996
Milazzo, Sicily

Buon Giorno,

Up early this morning to face the Messina Straight; my jitters were for naught once again when we made it through without a hitch. Another boat left two days ago in relative calm, but was unable to get through the Strait with forty knots of wind on the nose, and had to turn back to Saline Joniche. Do you suppose I worried?

The wind whistles down from the north in the summer and the Pilot states that conditions are worst at springs, with winds and the biggest currents forming whirlpools and eddies that a small yacht shouldn't be out in. Full moon was two nights ago. Don reminds me that we are a blue water boat, just in case our westward journey around the world has somehow eluded me thus far.

At 3:00 a.m. with only a breeze playing about us inside the breakwater, *Windy Thoughts* was making her way through the black of night out through Saline Joniche's entrance, fully aware of the sandbar this time. When *Windy Thoughts* made her way outside and turned to starboard, she very soon faced eighteen knots of northerly wind bang on the nose. Surprisingly, there was little sea, however, and we made good time. When the sun rose, blue skies appeared and the water sparkled around us. By 8:30 a.m. we were through the Strait, the last five miles flat as a pancake!

We sailed along the north coast of Sicily for twenty-three miles, past old towns with older forts sitting on hillsides almost within our reach. It was a lovely day, with light and pretty breezes that gave us a beautiful sail right to Milazzo, Sicily.

As we neared Milazzo, we could see a good-sized town with the same dun-colored buildings as Salina Joniche. Closing with the harbor, we pointed our bow in the direction of the boats on the quay. It looked to have only one spot open for our first Med tie.

Anchor ready, we lined ourselves up, carefully dropped the hook off our stern and headed in bow first, playing out the anchor line as we went. Squeezing between two boats was eased when some fellows on an adjoining boat grabbed our lines while Don sorted things out. Nothing to it this time! Bow first did not give our neighbors the entertainment that stern first would have provided. European boaters are used to these procedures, as the convenience of a dock is not common in the Mediterranean.

A rather large wash from passing ferries makes the boats jostle about, so boats must keep well back from the quay. Once tied and adjusted, we found that we could climb over the bowsprit rail and make a flying leap to the quay several feet away. It takes gymnastic efforts to get grocery bags up onto the bowsprit when the boat is about five feet from the quay, to say nothing of getting ourselves up there. Once aboard, we let more line out to keep us farther off.

Shops close for the entire afternoon, not to reopen until 5 p.m. Bars with pastries and ice cream seem to be popular and restaurants don't open until 9 p.m. We must change our schedules! In honor of being in Italy we did have pasta for dinner, but ate aboard.

Next day:

A trip to the supermarket and a walk about found the town far more interesting than it first appeared. Our stomachs responded favorably to the aroma of fresh bread, and our noses found the bakery before our explorations took us to visit the citadel, a loaf of bread under each arm. Fresh garlic bread for dinner was delicious!

Both *Helios* and the German-owned *Anna Maria* have arrived. Our barometer has dropped about nine millibars, the weather reports are not encouraging, and we all watch the situation carefully, though nothing developed today.

This afternoon we visited *Helios* and traded information on things ahead of us. They feel as we do: move as fast as possible to Gibraltar, and leave quickly while the weather is best for the run south to the Canaries. *Helios* has done this numerous times before and advises us to get to Gibraltar by August to avoid being blasted with a southerly storm out in the Atlantic.

July 8, 1996

Our three boats planned to be off this morning, but weather reports and faxes led to predictions of Force 7 winds blowing on the nose as we headed west. Unsure that we would make the next port sixty-five miles ahead of us before things piped up, we stayed put.

Everything in town starts to hum after dark and hundreds of people young and old alike stroll along the promenade that runs along the waterfront, with people sitting and chatting on the park benches. Don and I joined in the strolling one evening when we managed to hold off the hunger pains long enough to enjoy a good dinner in town.

Yesterday we had a ferry excursion to Lipari Island in the Aeolian group. The sun was bearing down in the wall-to-wall blue that defines the Mediterranean, and when the ferry stopped to let passengers off at Volcano Island, we stood against the deck rail and watched the sulfur rising above the volcano's crater. It was a busy ferry; everyone was in a holiday mood and eager for a taste of these little islands.

Lipari Island was an absolute delight, with a town that was very much "old Sicily", even though highly touristy. Narrow streets winding up and down hills, charming architecture and a nice lunch on the waterfront gave us a beautiful picture of the town to store in our memory banks forever. The harbor is small and very crowded with fishing boats tied to the quay in complete disarray, all bobbing heavily in the swell.

While we await the right weather window, there has been no end of excitement to keep us busy. Our anchor was pulled up yesterday when another boat snagged ours as they pulled out. They re-dropped it and a few hours ago we discovered that it had been re-dropped over *Helios'* anchor. Anchors tangling is a common occurrence for boats packed together like sardines and getting ours untangled took fully two hours. Med mooring does not appeal to us.

With the poor holding ground, the prospects of the predicted gale are not inviting. All boats are about eight feet from the quay and every ferry wash sends them flying forward. The European boats have boarding planks. Don had a boarding ladder made in Cyprus that attaches to the bowsprit, allowing us to climb down or fold out a platform to leap on or off the quay.

Later:

It has been a busy few hours here with the wind coming beam-on, pushing all bows off and threatening to drag anchors. Our German friends are hearty, strong swimmers who swam for an hour in the ocean each day all winter in Cyprus! Niklas courageously swam a 200-foot line from our neighbor to the quay that meets at a ninety-degree angle at the end of the line of boats, and another line from *Helios* on to our other side. Hopefully, this should keep the entire line of boats from dragging. Don and I have helped an older German couple to get tied securely.

Latest report is Force 8, though our barometer is rising a bit. Everyone has spent the afternoon preparing for the worst and every boat has lines tied off in every direction.

Don tells me not to think about it anymore because we have done everything that we can and are not out at sea. Of course he is right, but much damage could easily be done right here without sea room to ride it out. And so, I obsess. Are you surprised?

July 26, 1996
Costa Brava
Cartagena, Spain

Hola,

Just 225 miles from Gibraltar now! So much progress has been made in the past couple of weeks. *Windy Thoughts* sits in a very new marina in Cartagena, on the Costa Brava of Spain.

The gale that we braced for in Milazzo wasn't so bad after all, though the time spent tying off was worth it because we did get heavy winds! Everyone was on alert and watching lines very carefully for the duration, adjusting when necessary until the storm blew itself out.

The following morning we left Milazzo and jogged along the north coast of Sicily, arriving in Palermo by late afternoon. *Anna Maria* had a guest berth at the Yacht Club, arranged by Italians met previously. *Windy Thoughts* and *Helios* found spots on the main quay in the commercial harbor that is safe, though quite unattractive. The Yacht Club was expensive at $90.00 a night and nothing to write home about. A $25.00 fee per day for the main quay, plus $25.00 for fifty gallons of water however, made that Yacht Club sound better! Diesel at $4.50 a gallon is also a jolt to the budget. Thank goodness these boats don't operate on gasoline!

Over the weekend, we were spectators to a festival in honor of Santa Rosario, Palermo's patron saint. Amidst the watching crowd, the Cardinal led an impressive procession to the cathedral. A young man climbed to a balcony high above the crowd to place flowers at the statue of Santa Rosario. It was a festive occasion and one that seemed revered by everyone there.

Palermo's history is interesting, the architecture of the city fascinating, and we tried to see as much as possible in our short visit.

On July 14, *Windy Thoughts* set off for the southwest coast of Sardinia to take advantage of a high pressure system sitting over the central and western Mediterranean. Goodbyes were made to both *Helios* and *Anna Maria*, *Helios* to leave the next morning on a similar path and *Anna Maria* to head to the southwest coast of Sardinia and up through the Bonafacio Straits.

Motor-sailing at about thirty degrees off a light wind of only ten knots, we enjoyed a lovely two-day run, making landfall at the old town of Calaforte, on San Pietro Island—without question one of the most beautiful towns we have ever seen.

Pastel-colored buildings with lovely wrought iron balconies line the streets. Restaurants with tree-shaded sidewalk seating along the harbor's waterfront called us in for a delicious meal of pasta. Tree branches made a bower over us and their arms enveloped us while we dined in style. Our waiter gave us two plates with the name of the restaurant printed on them. They will be treasured for the memories of this beautiful spot. The town quay was free, though we paid $10.00 for three gallons of water needed to do a bit of laundry.

After three memorable days we set off for Mallorca, in the Balearics, an expected two-day passage. When the wind came around easterly to stay right behind us during the second night out, we continued on through to the mainland coast of Spain, running wing and wing. With three good nights out, we arrived here in Cartagena about 8 p.m. on July 22. Wind behind us—wow!

Cartagena's harbor is big, with a commercial area as well as a naval area and a new yacht basin. As we entered, we had some difficulties. Don was trying to maneuver in thirty-knot winds when the throttle cable broke. We got the anchor down immediately but drifted about, rapidly coming near the other boats and two big red bell buoys. Three fellows rushed over to assist us and I threw a line to them on the breakwater, where they fended off the boat.

Two jumped aboard *Windy Thoughts* while the other came around in a dinghy with a forty-horse engine to keep us off the breakwater wall. One fellow adjusted the throttle in the engine compartment below, Don shouting directions down to him, while I ran around tying on fenders. With the dinghy alongside to assist, we managed to get into a berth with tailed lines to the dock. Out came our boarding ladder for the bowsprit!

Don spent yesterday getting the old cable out, today attempting to replace with new—a very difficult task as the cable has to be threaded behind the steering cable in the binnacle. The space is very tight and the work seems impossible. He also dove on the boat today, believing something was wrong with the raw water intake.

Cartagena is the old historical city from which the Spanish fleet left for the Battle of Trafalgar, and is the home to a Spanish naval base. Cartagena's city center is just across the street from the marina. It is closed off to all traffic and pedestrians can easily walk to stores and restaurants.

The wind increased in the late afternoon, with the barometer dropping ten millibars in the past three days. A weather report predicts Force 8 tomorrow. With this lovely new yacht basin costing us only $10.00 a night, we are happy to be here until all is clear again.

As in Italy, evenings are devoted to strolling while young and old alike swarm the streets and along the quay. After dinner aboard we joined the families strolling on the esplanade.

We felt very cosmopolitan sitting at an outdoor café with ice cream and coffee and reading the International Herald Tribune. At 9 p.m. we strolled home to *Windy Thoughts*, but no one else was even contemplating their dinner at this early hour! Yawn. How did we manage those late nights in our younger years?

Happy with our progress, we don't feel as pushed as we did in the eastern Mediterranean. Our hopes are to get into a new marina at Almerimar, on Spain's southern coast. A British neighbor relates that it is very nice, inexpensive, and has a great yard facility. We are contemplating hauling the boat there, do the bottom painting and check on thru-hulls.

August 1, 1996
Almerimar, Costa del Sol
Spain

Hola!

Just 130 miles from Gibraltar! We arrived at Almerimar two evenings ago. The boat is on the hard and I am heading for the supermarket just outside the boatyard and only 200 feet away—one of four supermarkets in this massive man-made harbor that is a complete marina/condo/apartment lifestyle complex. Can you imagine how pampered I feel?

On arrival at Almerimar we picked up a tailed mooring and secured to the dock with our bow in first. Yesterday, we were up early to head over to the boatyard. After dropping our tailed line we waited for it to drop deep into the water before engaging gears. Even with this precaution, the line wrapped around the propeller when we backed out. Red alert again!

Don dashed below to grab his knife and was over the side of the boat in only moments. While he dove on the boat, I attempted to keep us from hitting the other boats all about us as *Windy Thoughts* did her best to drift about and say good morning to all in a more personal way than was necessary. I dashed about in attempts to keep us off her friends while we had absolutely no control over her fun.

 Don worked furiously for a full forty-five minutes to cut the line free, frequently coming up for air and returning below to keep at it. He emerged with blood dripping down both arms from multiple cuts and I was relieved to find that none were more than surface cuts.

While we muddled about getting it all sorted out, a boat last seen in Cartagena, when we were muddling about without a steering cable and also trying to keep from hitting any boats—came ambling by as they exited Almerimar, staring at the same two people who were in a jam again. At least Don was underwater. Only I endured their heads shaking in amazement to see us drifting about precariously, a second time.

Then followed the drama of getting into the boatyard. Told that we would have to un-step the mast to enter the travel-lift in the forward position—and not willing to undertake this troublesome work—the yard agreed that we could enter the lift stern first. Don had to maneuver the boat onto the travel-lift backwards but managed it, the mast cleared and we were lifted out of the water and plunked safely down in this beautiful yard. Whoever thought that I would be referring to a boat yard as beautiful!

Having planned to do the bottom work ourselves, we had psyched ourselves up for a few days of drudgery. Putting on our oldest clothes that could be thrown away when we were finished, we gathered our supplies and started scraping the bottom. After two hours of very hot and sweaty work, Don decided that he was a bit done in from his morning's excursions underwater, and the hundreds of cuts were stinging like scorpions.

Don headed into the office and hired the yard to complete the work. Echoing my sentiments exactly!

The past four days have been spent cleaning and polishing the topsides and stainless, while yard workers have been scraping the bottom and applying anti-fouling paint. This project won't face us in Gibraltar now and we will be ready to head off for the Canaries.

Radio contact with another boat informed us that *Investigator* was just thirty miles east of us at Almeria! This was exciting, as we hadn't seen them in so long. As soon as we got off the hard, Don and I rented a car and took an excursion up into the Sierra Nevada Mountains and on to Granada. Strong westerlies were predicted for the next few days, so *Windy Thoughts* would stay put while we enjoyed the trip and paid a surprise visit to *Investigator*.

It was good to be in the mountains again though the Sierra Nevadas were not the lush, green mountains of home. Granada was capital of Moorish Andalusia, and tops on our list was a day at the fabulous Alhambra, the best preserved of several Arabian palaces in the area. It is a huge and fascinating complex, with the many ninth century gardens of the Gereralife as well as a very impressive military fortification. Our breath was taken away time and time again, as we took in the grandeur and the rich cultural history.

When we left Granada we detoured to Almeria and drove straight to the harbor, where we could see *Investigator* sitting on dry land in the yard—a bit like a huge fish out of water. Our hearts were beating with excitement before we even found a place to park! Faye and Max were working on *Investigator*, covered in grime and bottom paint and sweat dripping from every pore. They had our sympathies for the huge job that they were undertaking.

We strolled up and stood back watching for a few moments before Don called to them, "Is this boat for sale?"

They turned around and were as surprised to see us as we were happy to see them. After leaving Port Suez last year, *Investigator* spent the winter in Italy, and Faye and Max took a land tour throughout Europe in a camper van that they keep in England. It was a great reunion with these good friends and we hope to meet up again in the Canaries, when it will be time to head down the African coast and across the Atlantic Ocean—bound for Panama and those gates back into our dear Pacific Ocean.

Once back in Almerimar, we began to ready for the short jaunt to Gibraltar. The strong westerlies had blown themselves out, there wasn't anything more to hold us, and we set out for the overnight run.

The short voyage went well, with a slack pressure gradient and variable light winds that turned stronger and against us only for the final ten miles, when we sailed into some rather thick fog. A small, open boat approached us while we bumped along, pulled up beside us, and the two men aboard began urgently trying to tell us something. Finally understanding that they were headed to Morocco and didn't know where they were, Don got out our chart and showed them our exact position. He also gave them a handheld compass that he had owned for years. If they headed in the right direction, they should hit Morocco.

Our quest to make Gibraltar was over when we finally sighted the Rock through poor visibility, about four miles out. The mighty Atlantic Ocean was just a very few miles distant.

Windy Thoughts rounded the Rock and headed into the harbor and the lovely new Queensway Quay Marina. Gibraltar at last!

Whoever controls Gibraltar controls the Strait of Gibraltar, so it is easy to understand why it remains a territory of the UK under English law—and we are enjoying this place that stands at one of the world's strategic crossroads. Gibraltar is a bit shabby around the edges and a funky little spot, but very popular and with a happy atmosphere. It is only a short walk into town, where the main street is closed to traffic and the streets are filled with people.

This morning we were off to Customs at the frontier border to pick up three big mail packages. Not having had mail since Cyprus, it was so exciting and good for our souls to get so much news from you and to hear from others as well. Mail is our lifeline to home and we so appreciate the time that you and others take to keep us in your hearts and thoughts.

August 26, 1996
Queensway Quay Marina, Gibraltar

Hello Dear Friend,

Don is attempting to rally from a cold and flu that is running rampant through the marina. We expect a six or seven day passage down to the Canaries with the wind behind us, the first good sailing in a long time. Meanwhile, we await the weather window, as getting through the Strait of Gibraltar westward bound is not just any small thing. It generally blows right in from the Atlantic—and mighty hard at that. Our neighbors left this morning to head out through the Strait after waiting here for an entire month.

Occasionally during the summer months a Levanter, an easterly wind, blows. One blew two days ago—at fifty knots for twenty-four hours, so everyone stayed put. Perhaps it might be our luck to have another Levanter, not quite so fierce. The currents, tides and winds have to be just right to make it through the Strait and the combination doesn't happen frequently. It is only about fifteen to twenty miles before you are out of the worst grip of the current, but it is a challenge getting through!

Both Don and I have just finished reading "The Adventures of Huckleberry Finn", and enjoyed lapsing back into this wonderful tale so enjoyed in our youth. At present, we are watching the movie of the same while slurping chicken soup for both health and soul. The movie version seems to have the character of Huck looking far too young, too clean cut and too upper- establishment to possibly be the same Huck that Mark Twain so artfully created!

Few days later:

We have been to the top of the Rock and cavorted with the world famous Gibraltar apes—actually tailless monkeys. Not sure how friendly they might be, we were somewhat cautious, but they didn't seem to mind people at all and, of course, enjoyed any tidbits of food thrown at them.

The vista from the top gave us a spectacular look out at the Strait of Gibraltar and over to Morocco, and we gazed wide-eyed at the waters through which we would very soon be moving. Don has picked up his personal "piece of the Rock" to keep with him, having many such small treasures that are remembrances of special places around our world.

Don particularly enjoyed the gun batteries of Gibraltar, and we visited the 100-ton gun at the Napier of Magdala Battery. Built in 1870, it took three hours for it to build up enough steam to operate, but the shell could penetrate up to twenty-four inches of steel! It is good that ships moved slowly then because it could fire one shell only every four minutes—and it took 450 pounds of gunpowder to fire the 2,000 pound shell up to eight miles!

The famous Battle of Trafalgar is commemorated at the Trafalgar Cemetery every October. Commanding twenty-seven ships, the British national hero Horatio Nelson defeated the combined French and Spanish fleet of thirty-three ships off the coast of Spain, assuring his place as Britain's greatest naval hero.

Lord Nelson being *Windy Thoughts'* namesake, Don attempted to explain the significance to *Windy Thoughts*, a proud Lord Nelson boat—but she just nestled alongside the dock and seemed not at all interested. She was much too busy having an R and R for a few days before taking on the mighty Atlantic Ocean.

Don is feeling better but still not 100%. A Levanter is blowing again through the Strait, fifty knots for the past four days, and no one is moving. Probably the most challenging part of our next leg will be getting out of this marina.

Columbus used the Canary Islands, about 700 miles south of Gibraltar, as his jumping-off spot when he left on his voyage to the New World. The islands provide a hiatus between the Mediterranean and the Atlantic while waiting for the best weather conditions. We will follow in Columbus's wake as we head for the Canaries to await the proper time to move on.

Reading about Puerto Madero Marina on Gran Canaria Island had put stars in our eyes, but when I faxed to arrange for a berth we learned that the marina was fully booked for the coming months. The ARC Rally leaves from Gran Canaria in mid-November and those boats, numbering about 100, are arriving in the islands along with all the cruising boats. Panic!

We can find only one anchorage in all of the Canaries, on Lanzarote Island, the most northern in the group. The anchorage is described as rather "grotty".

However, a new marina on Lanzarote Island has, to our good fortune, one berth available—and it has been secured for us!

September 7, 1996
Atlantic Ocean bound

Canaries, here we come! This morning we took on the Strait of Gibraltar and are on our way. It is about 9 p.m. on my watch and we're sailing along in the Atlantic Ocean with about fifteen knots of wind—at last!

The Levanter slacked off for two days, making a perfect window to get through the Strait. Don was still feeling puny but decided that we'd best get moving, as Force 3 to 4 westerlies were predicted in the Strait, about as light as it gets.

Don and I had studied everything we could about timing a transit through the Strait. Working from at least four different theories, including local knowledge, in the end we went by Don's theory: leave in the early morning if it is calm and turn on the engine to manage the always adverse current. In a short fifteen miles we would be free from the grip of the current and to a point where we could bear south toward the Moroccan coast.

This was the calm morning and Don's theory would prevail. I came close to a nervous breakdown in anticipation of the Strait of Gibraltar. Will I never learn?

Two days ago a boat arrived from the Azores, expecting to have westerlies blowing them through the Strait—but having just the opposite—fifty-knot Levanter winds that hit them just ten miles west of the Strait. The first mate feels that she will be recovering from the experience for some time yet. With her story, told while still rather shell-shocked, still in our minds we were heading off. All was quiet and few were up and about, because no one else was attempting the Strait this morning. Do you suppose that I fretted?

After all of the theorizing, discussing and planning, the mighty Strait of Gibraltar proved to be in a meek and mild mood for us! The Atlantic Ocean was just a hop, skip and a jump ahead. We would be sailing again and *Windy Thoughts* would be doing what she was meant to do. As we were changing course to head southwest, the winds began to fill from the west, but *Windy Thoughts* danced right along as she hadn't in some time. When we headed into the Atlantic Ocean, she leapt to attention, knowing that she was ocean-bound again.

The expected north-easterlies haven't materialized and winds have stayed more westerly. However, with a course set for Lanzarote Island, we've remained on a close reach with about fifteen knots of wind, the optimum amount in our opinion. You can do just about anything in fifteen knots of wind. *Windy Thoughts* and I are comfortably bouncing along and Don is asleep below. It has been a glorious day of sailing, outward bound in the Atlantic Ocean and headed southbound on a 700-mile leg to the Canary Islands. All is well with the world—and all is well with our souls.

The lights of Casablanca beckoned to us during the night as we sailed along Africa's coast, and we tipped our hats to Bergman and Bogart as we passed by.

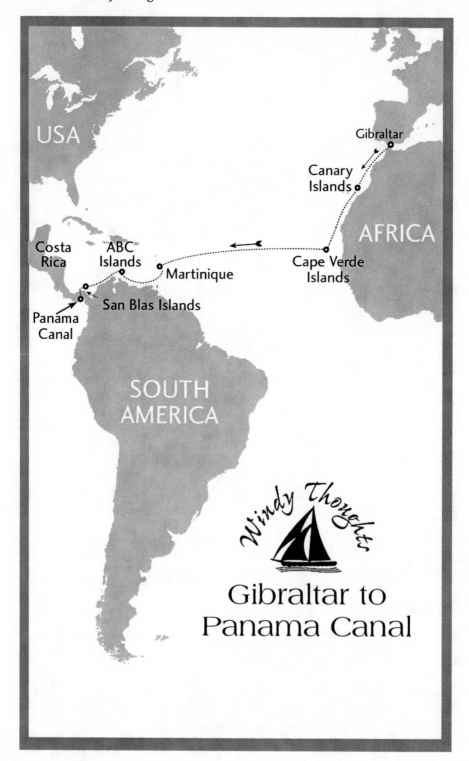

Gibraltar

Canary
Islands

AFRICA

USA

Costa
Rica

ABC
Islands

Martinique

Cape Verde
Islands

Panama
Canal

San Blas Islands

SOUTH
AMERICA

Windy Thoughts

Gibraltar to
Panama Canal

Chapter 14

The Canaries Sing For Us

I have learned to be content in whatever state I am.
—Philippians 4:1

A perfect five-day sail carried us southwest to Lanzarote Island, the north-ernmost of the Canary Islands. Perfect, because the winds were neither light nor strong, holding between fifteen and eighteen knots and suiting us just fine. Perfect, because we were making excellent time, with little sea run-ning as we hugged the coast of Africa. Perfect, because *Windy Thoughts* was under sail again. Perfect, because we were setting off for new adventures and new horizons. Perfect, because we were together for the halcyon days, rolling along, reading, navigating, sailing, eating well and happy to be moving ever southwestward.

On September 12, 1996, our last day at sea, we sailed along Lanzarote Island's east coast, peering through the glasses at pristine white buildings dot-ting the landscape, buildings that stood out against the brown that formed the mountainous volcanic island. As we neared our waypoint for the Puerto Calero Marina that would become our home for the next three months, we could see several beautiful homes along the banks.

Passing through the entrance to the new marina under a blue sky that didn't have any room for clouds, we were entranced by a beautiful white oc-tagonal building just to port, a restaurant. Ahead were beautifully kept docks and a few smaller buildings that housed shops. The stark white buildings sparkled in the sunshine and the gleam of beefy and perfectly polished brass bollards along the quay were signs that we were entering a special place for us.

Most boats were local and several others were without crew aboard, waiting to take part in the

ARC Rally in November.

Our first impressions were that we were going to like Lanzarote Island if things were as good as they looked! The marina was first-class and we stepped onto the dock from our own finger berth. Our surroundings were spotless and we soon learned that the restaurant passed when coming through the entrance offered fine cuisine—and the small El Tomato café served less expensive but superb meals. A dive shop located at the top of our dock was run by a young Australian couple who had moved here from Gran Canaria Island. They found Lanzarote to be the nicest of the Canary group and to offer the most to see and do. How fortunate we were to get the last berth available!

The town of Puerto del Carmen was three miles up the coast, and without bus service we considered a motorbike rental—until we found it to be four times as much as a car rental. Don found what back home might be called a Rent a Wreck, and he bargained for a small white Opal that could be ours by the month. Living on Lanzarote Island took on a whole new character!

Our little Opal was four years old, without any visible dents and looking like every other car on the island in a variety of colors. Bubble gum cars, we called them. Lacking any amenities such as air conditioning, power windows, or radio, it was luxury to us. We had wheels!

Lanzarote Island is a popular vacation destination for Europeans and Puerto Del Carmen a resort town. Many day trips about the island took us to quaint villages and the many attractions that draw people to this fascinating island, rich in culture and history. In Puerto Del Carmen we roamed the many nice shops along the oceanfront, stopped for cold drinks or a bite to eat in one of the many excellent restaurants, and searched out items on our to-do list.

There is an ease to life on Lanzarote. With a car, the big Hypermarket five miles from the marina was convenient, and had everything that we could want when it came time for provisioning for an Atlantic crossing. With water on the dock and blue skies that never seemed to find a cloud, *Windy Thoughts* was effortlessly kept glowing, and she preened as she glistened in the sunlight.

Lanzarote's climate is moderate, with average yearly temperatures in the low eighty degrees and 300 days of sunshine a year. With its lack of humidity, we felt it as perfect as it gets.

During the winter on Cyprus we had entertained thoughts of going up a river in Gambia, said to be spectacular—but information about it had come to us fifth-hand. A powerboat in the marina was said to be heading for this same river. Anxious to find out more, we walked down the dock and knocked on the hull, introducing ourselves to a British gentleman. We were welcomed aboard and he kept us laughing as he described why the boat would be going to Gambia—but without him. The sixty-five foot yacht was from England and was skippered and fully crewed, his job the corporate man who was to oversee the voyage to Gambia.

The voyage from England to the Canaries had been his first and only experience on boats and he had managed the stretch from England to Gibraltar just fine. But trouble began as the boat headed down the Moroccan coast. When they stopped to take on fuel in Casablanca and properly declared weapons aboard, they were all detained under armed guard for a full week. Following this indignity, they were kicked out of the country just as weather faxes predicted bad incoming weather. Weather that was a full-fledged storm with huge and wild seas endured for three days.

No one slept during the storm, and each crew member—other than the British fellow who knew nothing about handling a boat—took one-hour turns at the helm because a new autopilot installed in Gibraltar had failed. He described what he was sure were fifty-foot seas into which they desperately tried to keep the bow pointed to prevent being hit beam-on and rolled.

Claiming to have been fairly fearless prior to this experience, he was wide awake with terror—just waiting to die and trying to figure out the quickest way to do so. We laughed with tears running down our faces as he described the trauma of getting into a pair of jeans in a boat that didn't know which way was up—jeans that he felt would protect him from the fish that he knew would be biting him while he was drowning.

The boat was being repaired from the damage it suffered during the storm and he was about to fly home to England. Having reached Lanzarote Island intact and not down with the fishes after all, he had no intention of ever setting foot on a boat again.

He hadn't a clue about Gambia, but did have a tourist brochure that was of little help to us. With concern for water, fuel and preparation for the Atlantic crossing, we soon lost interest and decided to forego Gambia. But we loved his story.

Our days were happy ones that generally started with a walk in the early morning. Just outside the marina entrance we veered off to walk through quiet streets of houses—villas in the several-million-dollar price range. All were of masonry and painted a pristine white, with much attention paid to landscaping. Each home was set off by courtyards of fine-ground lava rock, filled with cactus, palms and flowering bushes pleasingly arranged. In turn, large setbacks lining the roads around the island were landscaped beautifully as well.

Devotion to the artistic attraction of the island is credited in large part to Cesar Manrique, who had passed away only two years before. An enterprising man, he was also a genius of sorts in his field of artistry. It was his vision that made Lanzarote so attractive with landscaping lining the roads on the island—and his drive to enact an ordinance that all buildings be kept freshly painted white. Five very special attractions on Lanzarote Island are creations of Cesar Manrique, each unique and beautiful.

Mr. Manrique's home is managed by the Cesar Manrique Foundation and is open to visitors. Built above five underground bubbles formed from earlier lava flows, the upper exterior is inspired by Lanzarote's traditional architecture. The home is entered on the ground level. Stairways lead down through the bubble-formed rooms with walls of lava, each room made more interesting with innovative furniture and lighting. Some of the volcanic bubbles are open to the sky and sunshine. Along one walkway the vista below is a beautiful pool, built to look as though it was naturally formed.

Our car gave us the freedom to drive about the island and see all that it had to offer. On the north coast we ate fish in our favorite village, away from the tourist spots. A Saturday arts and crafts market drew us to the small town of Teguise, the ancient capital of Lanzarote. Some of the craftsmen flew from Morocco to present their wares along with those of the locals. Teguise is a lovely town, with beautiful churches, elegant palaces and spacious houses in stone and brick, with white walls and large windows with picturesque balconies.

On our walks we admired the name signs on both the homes and many of Lanzarote's businesses, each sign presented on beautifully crafted tiles. One day, when we were walking about the Saturday market, Don discovered an artist who created tiles in the old Spanish way. We commissioned her to make a set of eight tiles for us, each tile eight inches square. Together they make a scene of three Spanish galleons, with "The Greens" written below. These tiles now form a name sign at the entrance to our drive on Orcas Island—and we never pass by without remembering the charm and beauty of Lanzarote Island.

Looking out from the keep of Santa Barbara's fifteenth century fortress that overlooks Teguise, we were spellbound by the wonderful view of the Teguise valley countryside, the coast, the sea, and the distant dark profile of Fuerteventura and the lesser islands. The fortress protected the island from marauders and had been attacked and destroyed several times, finally reconstructed in 1586 and largely unchanged ever since.

Cesar Manrique's works held us spellbound on many an occasion, especially the Jamos Del Agua Cuevas De Los Verdes, an underground grotto created when one of the giant volcanic bubbles formed a volcanic tube. The tube cooled and solidified externally as the lava continued to flow internally. As the lava flow streamed out, the walls collapsed to varying depths, forming caves of different size and length.

An underground walkway leads to the magnificent bubble that is the Cueva De Los Verdes, measuring two kilometers in length and thirty to forty meters in height. Bistro tables for snacks and drinks are tucked cozily into one area, and pathways wind through volcanic gardens of cactus, with organ music softly playing in the background.

Vistas were ever-changing, and pools with waterfalls bubbling through glens gave the entire area a surreal feeling—as though we might have been in the Land of Oz. With technology that was never obvious to the eye, an amazing system of artificial lighting helped nature to show itself in its splendor, with Cesar Manrique's unseen artistic hand ever present.

In the lower section of the tube, the Jamos Del Agua hosts an underground lake that joins to the sea beneath its surface, its fauna hidden from the sun for 3,000 years. Though seemingly incongruous, the Jamos Del Agua has been turned into a unique night club that provides an incomparable setting for musical events while still protecting the tube's natural beauty.

Mr. Manrique's use of nature's landscape and the fascinating forms created by the underground volcanic bubbles crafted beautiful settings unlike anything we had ever seen.

A drive to the northern tip of the island led us to the Mirador del Rio, another of Manrique's works, a very unusual scenic overlook created right out of the side of a mountain and perched atop the Punta Faraones cliffs. After climbing a series of stairways, we emerged into a natural cave setting that is the Mirador del Rio.

A vast curved glass fronted the outlook, forming a huge picture window—offering a view down to a nearby small island and the beautiful surrounding ocean waters glistening in the sunlight. The turquoise water and island might have been a painting, so amazing was the vista.

The Lanzarote landscape is very unusual, with many indications that the island was formed by volcanic activity. The volcano itself is a popular attraction and the Timanfaya National Park is a natural landscape unlike anywhere else in the world. A visit to the Park is a unique experience, and one of the favorite ways to travel up the mountain is by camel. Don and I chose to drive our car, having already had the privilege of riding on Ali Baba when in Egypt.

The park is a vast area of volcanic cones, craters, ash and lava flows that solidified into the strangest shapes. A few meters below the surface of some sections the temperatures reach 400 degrees centigrade! Surprisingly, lichens have colonized on volcanic rocks and a large number of plant species reproduce within the park. One of the more amazing plants is the bulrush that survives on moisture carried in on the sea breezes and retained in the volcanic ash.

The glass walls of the beautiful El Diablo restaurant encased the view, and the kitchen is probably the only one in the world that cooks meals using heat coming from the very center of the earth. The Devil indeed!

The island's many beaches are a combination of white sand and volcanic black sand. The windward side of Lanzarote presents a far different vista than does the leeward side, and we frequently stopped to explore the smaller, more remote beaches of both—often dashing into the water and then drying off on the hot sand. Windward beaches are tucked into rock formations with waves crashing, while beaches on the leeward side of the island offer more peace and calm.

A knock on our hull surprised us one day in mid-November and a voice called below, "Is this boat for sale?"

It was Max and Faye, our dear friends from *Investigator*. They were at the anchorage in Naos, about ten miles north, following a horrid sail down from Spain with weather not conducive to happy passage-making. At the time, our barometer had taken a seventeen-millibar dive, alerting us that something big was coming—and while we were happily tied securely to the dock, they were out in a Force 8 southerly on the nose.

Shortly after our visit in Almeria, Spain, *Investigator* was left on the hard while Faye and Max went to England to pick up their camper van for six weeks of touring Norway and the Scandinavian countries. On their return to the boat, they found very serious problems from salt water in the engine. Max spent a solid month working on it from first light until bedtime.

When Don asked him why he didn't just replace the engine with a new one, Max looked at him in astonishment—a new engine on his *Investigator*? Not on your life! This was the original and he wouldn't think of anything else!

Faye explained that Max had a unique relationship with his engine, developed over many years together as Max worked to keep it going. The engine was Max's labor of love for his boat.

When Don asked Faye where they were heading next (Gran Canaria Island), her quick reply was, "Sydney!" She had told Max at the outset of their cruising that he could go anywhere he wanted as long as he got her home in four years. Cruising was her labor of love for Max.

The ARC Rally headed off on November 24, and *Investigator* was able to get space in the marina at Puerto Calero for a few days before they left for Gran Canaria. We enjoyed a goodbye dinner at a favorite spot located in an ancient Spanish farmhouse, where we dined in one of four rooms that surrounded the original courtyard. The food was exquisite. The restaurant had its own winery and the atmosphere was very special, as was our evening with these two dear friends. We planned to stay in radio contact across the Atlantic and meet up in the Caribbean.

The last weeks flew by quickly as we attempted to avoid "harboritis" by not setting up serious housekeeping and trying to remain in the preparation-to-leave mode. The trade winds blew with a strength that created big seas, and two cruising boats were knocked down as they sailed past the area. Looking out each day at the seas beyond the breakwater, thoughts of leaving could easily be put on the back burner.

Everything on the boat was always in the best working order when we were on the move. In all of our years of sailing and cruising, we never lost the rigging, the mast, or had to replace sails. It was always equipment and mechanical problems that plagued us.

Don was discouraged to find algae growing again in the fuel tanks, and additive wasn't available for purchase. He went to the airport and was taken through security to the mechanical area, where he was allowed to purchase the chemical additive. Don pumped out every bit of diesel with the little hand pump as we had in Turkey, and replaced it with new fuel and additive.

During the last two weeks in Puerto Calero I was busy making provisioning trips in our bubble gum car, while Don attended to the boat and made sure that all was in readiness. Returning from the Hypermarket one day, I found Don sitting on the curb in the parking lot, waiting for me with a very stricken look on his face.

We had *big* problems! Don was greasing the steering quadrant when he found it cracked through the ring where it was bolted on. Stainless steel bolts with an aluminum quadrant equaled electrolysis. While Don was pondering how to solve the problem, I was merrily making my way up and down the aisles of the Hypermarket. Don thought he could perhaps take the quadrant to England to have another manufactured. First, he would check into local help, but didn't hold out high hopes of solving the problem here.

Hope does spring eternal, and within a few days Don found a young French mechanic who spoke both English and Spanish fluently, was trusted to do good work, and could manufacture a new quadrant out of stainless steel. Even better, he would try to have it finished within ten days!

The ten-day plan actually materialized, but we waited for another week for a fellow at the marina to complete some welding before the quadrant could be installed. It was the first week of December when the new quadrant was finally in the boat.

On our last evening on Lanzarote Island, the couple who owned the dive shop, along with two other couples who lived in the area, treated us to a wonderful dinner out in the very nice restaurant located in the marina. With soft music playing in the background and an excellent meal shared with people whom we would never see again, we once again wondered how it was that we were so blessed to be the recipients of such amazing generosity.

The wind had turned around, blowing steady at twenty-five to thirty knots out of the northeast every day—good winds to carry us south. Our food lockers were overflowing. We had baskets of apples and oranges, juices, crackers and cookies secured behind the table with a bungee cord. Ready to be outward bound again.

ATLANTIC BOUND

December 8, 1996, dawned beautiful and sunny, as does every day in the Canaries. It was our departure day and there wasn't anything left to hold us back. A big stretch of the Atlantic Ocean lay ahead, about 2,500 miles at an average speed of five knots an hour. In a twenty-four hour period, an average of 120–130 nautical miles was good. This wasn't our first ocean and we attacked it with the feeling of old salts in our veins. We could make it and face anything that the Atlantic threw at us. Homeward bound!

As we pulled out of Puerto Calero Marina just after first light, we raised the mainsail and rolled out the Yankee. *Windy Thoughts* jogged along nicely in fifteen knots of favorable wind out of the northeast, less than had been blowing for the past days but very comfortable for us. As we looked back toward our home for the past three months, a perfect rainbow stretched the full arch, so vivid that Crayola might have colored it for an advertisement. The pot of gold at the end of the rainbow was our ultimate destination, our Orcas Island. But there would be much more of this world to see between Lanzarote and Orcas Island!

The second day brought lessening wind and then wind so slight that we drifted along, not wanting to use our engine so early in a long ocean passage. Eventually giving in we putted along at lower RPMs to conserve on fuel, unsure of what might lie ahead.

By the third day, southerly winds at thirty knots set in against us and *Windy Thoughts* hove-to for two full days, waiting for favorable winds rather than beat to weather. Time dragged, but patience is a virtue and we worked on our virtuousness. By day six, we had made just 300 miles. It was beginning to look like a very long passage.

Boredom was broken when a weather fax showed a horrendous low-pressure system off England that extended down to the Canaries. The bottom edge sat at our latitude and the isobars were closing fast, an indicator of unpleasant things to come. No waiting around now! The engine came on in attempts to stay below the low, moving south right toward us.

Radio contact with boats making their westward passage toward the Caribbean reported light to no wind. Where were the northeasterly trades that we hoped for? Not knowing what to expect on our passage to the Caribbean, we decided to top off our diesel with a stop at the Cape Verde Islands, off the coast of Africa about 700 miles south of Lanzarote Island. Sao Vicente Island was described as having the only all-weather anchorage in the islands and the only spot to take on fuel alongside a wharf.

Two hundred miles north of the Verdes, the northeast trade winds finally set in with twenty knots of wind on our quarter. Though very tempted to keep sailing, before dark on our tenth day out, we pulled into the anchorage off

Mindelo, a city of about 50,000 people. Fifteen other boats sat in the anchorage, all making passage across the Atlantic Ocean.

While we were anchoring, a dinghy approached. A fellow yachtie was rowing and a local man was waving papers at us. It was Lewis, who introduced himself as a boat boy for us. Lewis would come back at 9:00 in the morning.

True to his word, while we were having breakfast in the cockpit, we saw Lewis swimming out the long distance from shore, papers held in one hand high above his head.

Lewis became our right-hand man during our time in Mindelo. As each boat arrived, he swam out to offer his services for hire. Having had several recommendations from others in the anchorage, we hired Lewis to be the "watcher" for our dinghy when ashore, and he would be available for other help as well. Lewis was a kind and wonderful man who was supporting a wife and little boy on the wages from this entrepreneurial enterprise. Our cost was 300 Escudos a day, or $2.40.

Lewis went ashore in *Breezy* with us, landing on a beach quite filthy with broken glass and garbage strewn about—water that we waded through as we pulled *Breezy* up on the beach. We were off for the Harbor Master's and Immigration offices, accomplishing our clearance efficiently and painlessly.

It was interesting to note the architecture of the old buildings as we walked along streets of old cobblestone. Hordes of young local men hung about on the streets, foreign aid seemingly the backbone of the economy. The main language spoken is Portuguese, along with some Creole frequently spoken in the more southern islands of the Verdes group.

One of these young men guided us to a restaurant where we found manna from heaven. This was Pici-Pau, a little hole-in-the-wall place that looked spotless and offered seafood dishes with lobster, crab and shrimp. Notes written on the walls by visiting yachties said that this was the place. Don refused to imbibe anything, feeling the establishment questionable. We invited the young man to join us and when our beautiful seafood dishes arrived, Don capitulated and ate half of mine.

Don and I went to the Shell fuel offices on the commercial pier the following morning, where we made arrangements to purchase our fuel, duty free. When we returned to *Windy Thoughts* we were thrilled to see *Investigator* sailing into the bay, and they followed us to the pier to make arrangements. Lewis went along with us, taking his position quite seriously and changing into a pair of shorts that Don gave him, as well as an older pair of sandals given him by Max. He was great help in the entire procedure.

That evening a French boat arrived with two fellows aboard who were making a boat delivery to the Caribbean. They had no dinghy and asked Max, our sailor's angel, if they might borrow his in the morning to go ashore to make their clearance. Max didn't see his dinghy again for the next two days while the fellows went about their business and pleasure. When the French boat left to go to the fuel pier, Max decided it might be wise to ask if he might have his dinghy back—worrying that they might be leaving port!

Lewis met Faye and me on the beach the next morning and took us to the laundry, helpfully carrying each of our laundry bags over his shoulder. Laundry was done for us in the only machine. It was a Saturday morning and we could pick up our clean laundry at noon on Monday. OK, we would stay the weekend. Then, off to the large produce market where little looked tempting—other than the delicious bread that we didn't pass up. At the supermarket we purchased paper towels, boxed juices and boxed UHT milk. Lastly, we stopped at our Pica-Pau restaurant to order dinner to pick up that evening.

Rather than leave our boats unattended after dark, the four of us would enjoy dinner aboard. One boat had been broken into the previous evening when the crew was ashore at Pici-Pau. Much was stolen, including all of the electronics. Our men went ashore to pick up our dinners, Max guarding the dinghy while Don picked his way through the pitch dark, stepping over men lying in the streets. There was lobster, shrimp, calamari and other things that we couldn't identify, all enjoyed aboard—a bounty at remarkably low prices!

While Faye and I were in town during the day, Don dug out the Christmas decorations and decorated the boat with stockings, our little tree and stuffed reindeer—giving it a festive atmosphere. How nice to return to this surprise! Busy with preparations to set off across that big Atlantic Ocean, I likely would have foregone Christmas decorations this year.

A woman on a boat from the Netherlands came aboard for a visit, and told of the awful passage down to the Verdes when they lost their mast in high winds and seas. Tears welled up in her eyes when she told of the several Pan Pans put out over the radio, none answered. They had been here for three weeks awaiting a new mast shipped to Sau Vicente. Another boat was awaiting engine parts and others were in states ranging from the serious to "just the usual" disrepair. Don was happy to have "just the usual" variety of repairs and maintenance jobs for a change. Max had discovered a problem with the hydraulics pump that served *Investigator*'s refrigerator and main engine batteries. With Lewis's help, Max located a hydraulics mechanic who made a temporary repair, but the pump would have to be replaced in the Caribbean. Cruising is making repairs in exotic ports—as has been said so often.

Along with Faye and Max we went to Pici-Pau for lunch, during which

Lewis came in four different times to tell us something thought to be vitally important—or to ask if he could use our dinghy as boats arrived. We knew he was hoping that we would ask him to join us—and we were filled with guilt for wanting this last time for ourselves. To this day, Don and I can't think about that meal without remorse, having placed our time together above sharing the company of Lewis and treating him to a meal as well.

Later that day, we paid Lewis for his services and gave him some clothes, a T-shirt and a $20.00 bill as a Christmas present for being so kind to us. His eyes lit up and he couldn't stop grinning. I wanted to cry. Would that we could go back to Sao Vincente and start the day again—and have this gentle man, who asked for nothing but a few escudos to keep our dinghy safe, join us at Pici-Pau and honor him for the kind and decent man that he is.

With winds steady at twenty-five knots daily, we were anxious to get moving and planned to leave Tuesday, December 24, deciding that spending Christmas at sea would be just fine with us. That early morning dawned with lovely fifteen-knot winds. *Windy Thoughts* had brought us 700 miles from Lanzarote to the Verdes and could now begin her passage westward to the Caribbean. *Investigator* would be another day awaiting the hydraulics pump, but would soon catch up.

It takes us about three days to fully adjust to the passage-making life. Soon sleep patterns interrupted by watches become a natural part of life at sea—and the rhythms of the body, mind and sea begin to meld into a unique world of nothing but sailing and the surrounding water.

Our Christmas was a quiet but joyful one as we sang Christmas carols together in the cockpit on Christmas Eve—and felt the promise of peace brought us on the first Christmas night. The night sky was so clear and full of stars and it seemed the entire universe was welcoming the Christ child. We had one of Faye's chickens for our Christmas dinner, along with a boxed dressing, mashed potatoes and gravy, canned green beans and the wonderful fresh bread from Sao Vincente. I made a peach cobbler in the little stovetop oven. Though we were celebrating Christmas alone, we had plenty of time to consider the "reason for the season".

This final stretch of the Atlantic Ocean was the longest one, 2,000 miles yet to go and a seventeen-day passage that provided excellent sailing each day. Steady trade winds between twenty and twenty-five knots gave us one of our best passages. During the first days we were on a broad reach, our favorite point of sail with quartering wind. When the wind began to come around behind us we made leisurely jibes downwind every few days—keeping the comfort level quite decent.

One night we were plagued by continuous squalls with higher winds that switched 180 degrees in a split second so frequently that using the autopilot seemed to risk jibing the boat accidentally—so Don steered the boat. There were other times when the sameness of our days was interrupted by a sudden event that took our breath away and reminded us that the sea makes no promises and is ever changing! During the leisurely days we sat up on our "back patio" to have our morning coffee and visit. The liveliest days found us spending more time below, flat on our backs on our sea berths, and cabin fever would tend to set in. Patience!

It is often said that sailing oceans is leisurely and peaceful time interrupted by moments of absolute terror. This was proven true one night when we rolled along with the big Genny poled out. Don was on watch listening to a book tape—his peaceful reverie interrupted when the boat lurched violently. Wham! A sudden squall came in the black of night and hit with a ferocity that instantly whipped up the seas and nearly put the leeward rail in the water. I was awakened by Don's urgent, "Joyce, I need you up here *now!*"

Conditions were such that it seemed we might broach at any moment, as the wind filling the big Genny held us over. I stumbled out of the comfort of my sea berth, my own reverie broken by the realities of ocean sailing.

"Grab the safety harnesses!" Don yelled to me.

I tossed Don's safety harness up to him and frantically put on my own. *Windy Thoughts* is a heavy displacement blue water boat and doesn't easily heel to this degree—and it seemed that we were roaring along at ninety miles an hour. Both Don and I hooked into the eyebolt in the cockpit with both tethers of our safety harnesses. It started to rain, pouring rain.

The roller furling line was run to a starboard winch and through a block at the stern, leaving the main port winch for the sheet that I was working and Don to the winch for the roller furling line. At the very moment when I released the first of four wraps around the main port winch—the sheet ripped right out of my hands, flying off with a mind of its own. With the Genny flying free, Don worked furiously until the pressure quickly came off the sail that was working to force a knockdown—and *Windy Thoughts* righted herself considerably, the dangerous situation suddenly under control.

Don always tied the whisker pole between two shrouds, allowing us to roll the Genny in or out without having to take the pole up or down; we would deal with it in the morning. We bumped and bounced throughout the night under main and stay sail, maintaining top speed while continuing to face off against the mighty Atlantic. Radio contacts informed us that *Investigator* and two other boats had all broken whisker poles during the onslaught. Though the experience was an eye-opener for a few days, we were soon lulled into a more mundane routine, and it wasn't until we were about two-thirds of the way across the Atlantic that we saw our first ship.

A second electrifying occurrence came during another squall when the wind rapidly changed direction—again during the night. The one-half inch stainless steel bailer on the boom broke, allowing the boom to swing violently across the boat, causing an accidental jibe. It was a very dangerous situation, and Don used a one-inch dock line to jerry-rig a preventer. Several slides had broken free from the mainsail track during the accidental jibe and Don wrestled the mainsail down. When the wind slackened to twenty knots two days later, we replaced the slides with the six we had as spares, just the number needed for all but the largest one at the very top.

Don kept a pole rigged for marlin, and it was an exciting day when a beautiful huge marlin jumped completely out of the water in a spectacular show, skipping across the water on its tail. Unfortunately, after this display the marlin disappeared, taking the lure and breaking the line—a blow to Don— but the thrill of getting the huge marlin on the line at all made up for any disappointment.

Our twice-daily radio schedule with *Investigator* was the high point of our days and gave us something to look forward to other than watching our position line move slowly westward on the charts. The anxieties that usually plagued me were non-existent and my worry level was very low.

Our twenty-ninth anniversary was celebrated aboard, on December 30, 1996. Though a quiet celebration, it was certainly an anniversary that commemorated many adventurous years together. Years that had brought us closer than we could ever have imagined when, with stars in our eyes, we took our vows in the little white church next to my family home in Ischua, New York. This anniversary didn't require anything special to make us happy beyond being together. After all, when would we again celebrate our anniversary in the middle of the Atlantic Ocean aboard our *Windy Thoughts*?

The next evening would ring in the New Year of 1997—but any celebration was quietly ignored. At midnight and time to radio *Investigator*, Don was sleeping so soundly that I decided to forego the celebratory contact. I wanted him at his best when the going got tough!

All in all, we both felt that this was one of our best ocean passages, with good winds the entire time. Books or books on tape provided us with a welcome diversion and the days were largely uneventful.

Those already in or through the eastern Caribbean didn't give especially glowing reports about the cruising there, but reports were more positive as one moved further west. Don and I had loved the tropical weather when visiting the Virgin Islands and Puerto Rico many years ago. This time we would be visiting the Islands with the cruising sailors' perspective, understanding that it would be a very busy cruising ground.

We have always believed that each place has something to offer, an introduction to another culture or lifestyle. This is what makes the cruising life so special. Don has always maintained that if you stay three to four weeks minimum, you become not yet a local, but not quite a tourist. Our time wouldn't allow us to spend that long in any one place in the Caribbean, but we would get a glimpse of the islands as we passed through.

On a cruising sailboat, new people are met and you must learn where things are and become accustomed to local practices as you begin to feel somewhat at home. Some might perceive our life to be a privileged one—others just the opposite. Privileged, yes—beyond measure for the two of us. Privileged, because we have met wonderful local people who have become friends, and have been welcomed into others' lives and shared cultures and built friendships.

As *Windy Thoughts* made for Martinique, *Investigator* made for Antigua, north by three islands in the Windward chain. Three days before making landfall, Faye was thrown across the cabin into the chart table, badly breaking three ribs. She spent the days on her sea berth, suffering from the boat's heavy downwind roll. Breathing was difficult and very painful.

On arrival at Antigua, *Investigator* was allowed to tie to a wharf and a medical person came aboard to examine Faye. X-rays would be necessary to confirm broken ribs, requiring a long and bumpy ride to town, not attempted since Faye couldn't even get off the boat. Faye radioed that Antigua looked beautiful, at least what she could see from the porthole. *Investigator* would meet up with us on Martinique within the next two weeks, and we planned to cruise together to Panama.

On the morning of January 9, *Windy Thoughts* crashed through seas whipped up by thirty-knot winds, sailing under a reefed main as we came around the south end of Martinique. Our landfall was Marin Bay. With eyes riveted to our waypoint, we searched for the elusive, charted buoy that was to mark safe entrance to the bay. When it appeared that the buoy didn't exist, we slowly made our way in toward the head of the bay.

Marin Bay is huge, with the town at its head. It was 10:30 a.m. on a Friday morning as we worked our way toward a multitude of other boats at anchor—more boats than we had ever before seen in one spot! Further in was a very large marina that was also full to overflowing with boats. Green hills surrounded the bay, and after seventeen days at sea with nothing but water as our "landscape", terra firma looked mighty good to us!

Our plan had been to stay aboard the first day and sleep for about twenty-four hours, but Don was definitely getting his second wind—and suggested heading to shore for a good breakfast and some exploration of Marin. After getting the anchor down and set, we cleaned up lines and tidied up the cabin below. Our little home was back to normal.

We decided to take a short nap and go ashore in time to treat ourselves to a late lunch instead. We laid our heads down at 1 p.m. for just a short nap—and didn't awake until fifteen hours later at 4:00 in the morning! Because the wind had lessened considerably, we jumped out of bed and went on deck to take the Genny off the track and tie it securely to the deck. The sacrificial strip needed re-sewing and we would look for a sail loft ashore—but first back to bed to pass out for several more hours.

In the morning we felt very refreshed and certainly ready to head to shore. A steel cable and a lock secured the dinghy to the marina dock and another steel cable secured the engine to the dinghy. Thievery runs rampant in the Caribbean and locals were known to climb aboard boats at night, go below, and steal whatever they could without the sleeping crew ever being aware of the thieves' presence.

Clearance was an unusually simple procedure right at the marina and involved only Customs. No one asked to see our passports and only the crew list was required.

Needing francs, we headed into town, only to find that it was a Sunday and banks were closed. Fort du France, the biggest town on the island, had a money exchange. A taxi driver agreed to take us there for $40.00, one way. No thanks.

Downtown, with traffic passing us in both directions, we decided to thumb a ride into Fort du France, but no one stopped or gave us a glance. We eventually discovered a collective taxi, a van that takes as many people as can cram into it. The drive to Fort du France took forty minutes along a super highway lined with home centers, supermarkets and car dealers. This was the Caribbean?

Fort du France was much larger than we expected. Told that it was just like Paris, we failed to see anything that might be reminiscent of Paris—of course, we had never been to Paris! We did get our francs and enjoyed a delicious lunch—the French certainly know how to cook!

Sail repair was our priority while in Marin and we found a sail loft that could do the work. Unable to find a slide in the correct size to replace the top slide on the mainsail track, Don purchased a larger one and took it to a metal shop to be shaved down a few millimeters. The broken traveler could be re-welded at another shop.

The cruising guide had our mouths watering with its descriptions of the superb provisioning and we had big expectations. The French supermarkets in Djibouti, Africa, had been excellent, and we were prepared for magnificence here in the hub of civilization, surrounded by busy tourists and charter boats—and in such close proximity to the United States. How disappointing to find that the stores in Marin weren't like those in Djibouti, Africa, after all.

Paper towels, butter and other basics were readily available, but good fresh produce wasn't. After sorting through a small bin of tomatoes, we found only five that were suitable—if eaten right away. The fresh baguettes did meet our expectations, however, and were a highlight in eats. Food provisions were plentiful aboard but fresh vegetables would have been a welcome addition.

When *Investigator* arrived in Marin Bay, we were happy to find that Faye was able to be up and about as long as she took it very easy. *Investigator* had started the short sail to Martinique with the dinghy trailing behind in calm conditions. Max had elected to forego the procedure of loading the dinghy, as Faye wasn't able to help. Unfortunately, the wind came up with a vengeance—and with it roughening seas that soon parted *Investigator* and the dinghy. Unable to retrieve it, *Investigator* arrived without transportation to shore.

Martinique gave us respite for two full weeks while our repairs were completed, and we shared trips to shore with Faye and Max. It had been a lovely stop, one that we thoroughly enjoyed. *Investigator's* problems were solved and they left with us, bound south for the lovely green hills on the island of St. Lucia—just twenty-two miles distant.

Rodney Bay was our destination at St. Lucia, but we found both the marina and anchorage space full to the brim. The chart showed a little lagoon just past the marina, where we found a few homes dotting the shoreline and only two other boats at anchor. It might have been waiting just for us!

The lagoon was quiet and removed from the bustle and activity of the hundreds of boats nearby, and within close dinghy distance to the big bay, where we could tie *Breezy* to the marina docks. It was yet another blessing, a place to hang our hats for a few days, another spot for *Windy Thoughts* to have a bit of an R & R. We had experienced cloud cover for most of our time in the Caribbean so far—but our anchors went down, the sun peeked through the clouds, beaming rays of sunshine down on us—and the Caribbean took on a whole new light!

In our travels we often purchased something small enough to store on the boat that we would treasure when our cruising days were over. In the lovely town of Castries, I found a watercolor painting of an open market scene with local women in their bright garb offering baskets of fresh fruits and vegetables under colorful umbrellas that shielded the produce from the sun. The women's lovely ebony skin tones contrasted sharply with the bright colors and the clear blue sky. In a sense, it was a picture of our life for the past years when we frequented the open air markets around the world.

Finding the pictured bounty in the Caribbean proved to be rather elusive, and it wasn't until reaching Bequia, in the Grenadines, that we found a market that surprised us with its abundant fruits and vegetables.

Faye and Max were wonderful companions as we explored St. Lucia. Faye hung in there, even though pain in her ribs was ever-present. Still, each week was better than the previous and she was showing much improvement.

The marina at St. Lucia accepted mail for cruising boaters and we stopped in daily to check on our package of mail sent from home by Lindy, who had taken over as our "mail lady"—only to find Federal Express packages for others, but none with our name on it. In an attempt to track our package, we went to the Federal Express office and spotted our large envelope of mail right on the counter! Instead of picking it up, we politely asked if we may please have our package. No, we would be required to hire an agent—an agent who charged a $150.00 fee to hand the package over to us. No one else had to hire an agent!

After several trips between the marina and the Federal Express office in attempts to reduce the cost, we paid the full $150.00 to the lady behind the desk—who didn't budge an inch.

Australia Day is a big event "down under" and it was a big day for the Australian contingent cruising here on St. Lucia. An Australian living near the marina invited the Aussie cruisers to his home for a BBQ, and Max and Faye invited Don and me to come along.

After the Aussies sat spellbound around the television to watch a national cricket match, all were off to the beach for a lively game of cricket. When it was Don's turn, he was handed the bat, and when he asked what he was to do, was told, "Run!"

"Run where?"

"Back and forth! Back and forth!"

In a game dear to Aussie hearts but one that we didn't understand at all, we were in gales of laughter as Don ran back and forth between the pitcher and what we only know as home plate, a quizzical look on his face. Faye pulled out two huge flags, the Australian national flag and the official flag of the 2000  Olympics to be held in Australia. The flags were hung from the trees and the Aussies were near tears. Our Faye had come prepared!

It rained on and off every day, and other than the occasional burst of sunshine we saw little other than gray clouds. Occasional surly attitudes of locals, constant guarding against theft, hassles with boat boys and water a bit cool for diving added up to an experience not quite as anticipated. Visitors didn't seem overly welcome and we wondered if it might be because there were so many tourists as well as boaters here. Someone else's experience may well be different, and in the following days we would find our attitudes much more agreeable to Caribbean cruising.

Moving south through the Grenadines, we stopped at lovely Bequia, where old friends aboard *Sea Shanty* joined Faye and Max for lunch aboard *Windy Thoughts*. Jim and Sue had sailed the Grenadines before and hosted a walking tour of the rural village. A small open-air market selling good vegetables was the first seen to this point and we were ecstatic. The highlight of our day was lunch at the Frangipani Hotel, a quaint old place with charm dripping from its rafters. We said goodbyes to Sue and Jim, who were sailing home to Florida, and we would continue westward to the Panama Canal.

Don and I moved to a lovely spot beneath the Pitons of Canoun Island—a perfectly spectacular setting. The anchorage sat below two verdantly green mountain peaks, and for $15.00, an enterprising young fellow in a small boat took our lines for the laid mooring to shore.

It was a busy and noisy spot with lots of partying that didn't quite fit with the serenity of this beautiful place, but we took the good with the bad and attempted to focus on the good.

We discovered that *Windy Thoughts'* bottom was covered with tubeworms down to the bottom of her keel, something never seen before. It astonished us how quickly they made us their home after the Hemple bottom paint was applied in August; the same bottom paint used in Singapore had lasted the two years.

A good cleaning was in order and lovely Mayreau Island, just a short sail away, provided the place for us to don skins and scrape the hull. The bay was large, with only a few boats at anchor and a surrounding stretch of sandy beach. When we jumped into the water, we both let out squeals of surprise at the cooler temperatures—yes, we had been spoiled! But the anchorage was a beautiful setting, a serene spot, and we were content.

Starting after breakfast, we worked hard for two entire days to get those pesky little tubeworms off *Windy Thoughts'* bottom—but those tubeworms would come back to haunt us on a regular basis. While working beneath the water, we discovered that an important rod for the wind vane was missing. Sure that it must have disappeared while there, we spent considerable time scoping out a big circle around the boat, hoping to find it on the bay's bottom. Unfortunately, our search was in vain.

A few homes dotted the hillside ashore and Don and I took the dinghy to the beach and walked uphill to a village. Children smiled and called out to us along the way and waves greeted us from doorways, their welcomes warming our hearts. A small school not in session sat at the top of the hill and we peered through the windows to spot rows of tables for desks, and benches behind each table. It was always fun to peek into the schools to see how classrooms were arranged, what was available, and to appreciate the abundance that our schools enjoy at home.

Further along, we stopped for lunch at a hilltop restaurant where we were the only patrons—and sat looking down at our *Windy Thoughts* far below, bobbing about in the bay. The serenity and peacefulness of the day will be remembered for the gift that it was to us.

It was mid-February of 1997, when *Windy Thoughts* and *Investigator* sat together in the large harbor of St. George's, on the southwest side of Granada. Caribbean sailing was brisk, with rather lively winds and seas that somehow managed to often come at us right on the nose no matter the direction we wanted to go—and St. George's calm anchorage was appreciated by everyone.

A new dinghy for *Investigator* had still not been found and we were sharing *Breezy*. Don found a place to weld the replacement rod for the wind vane. While it appeared that Max finally had the hydraulics working, those same gremlins that he had worked so hard to drive out of his engine in Spain had returned.

Faye and I went to the Venezuelan Embassy to apply for the required Venezuelan visas while the men attended to boat duties. As so often happens, our simple task turned into several hours of "taking care of business". Stamps had to be purchased, requiring a trip to the post office, where we didn't have the exact amount and change could not be made. It was two trips back and forth and finally a long wait at the Embassy before all was in order.

Visas handled, we turned our attention to making arrangements for a tour of Granada the following day.

The four of us headed ashore in *Breezy* at 7:30 the next morning, to join two other couples from the hotel who were also taking the tour. Our driver was Mandoo, who was well informed and did an excellent job as our guide.

Our tour included a hike to a waterfall, more difficult than we had imagined. The British woman had recently had hip surgery and found the hike enormously difficult. The other couple was American, the lady a psychiatrist who never stopped talking—and her husband, a professor at Duke University who was very opinionated and constantly questioned Mandoo's knowledge. To his credit, Mandoo held his own, giving us a grand talk on Granada's plentiful nutmeg trees and going out of his way to show us a good time.

When we arrived back at the hotel at 6 p.m. the American couple had a long talk with Mandoo, insisting that he lower the cost of the tour since they expected it to be just four people. The doctor turned around to the four of us and stated that we were the highlight of the day—and paid the fare of the unhappy couple. One would be hard pressed to find anyone more fun to have along than Max, who charmed everyone—as did our Faye. We all thought the day a huge success.

One of the delights of Granada came from Patrick, a young man who came out to the boats in the anchorage each day, his small boat piled with the day's produce. Patrick loved to accompany his sales with a song and a smile. Hanging alongside, he broke into dramatic song in his sweet singing voice, not a bashful bone in his body. How could we ever forget Patrick, with that smile that stretched from ear to ear?

Fully five years after our experience in Granada, we were watching the travel channel on the television at home—and suddenly heard the undeniable singing voice of our Patrick. Could this possibly be? Sure enough, there was that same big smile on the screen—and our Patrick now had his own restaurant on Granada.

Winds and seas just outside the harbor kept all boats in the anchorage while we were at Granada. On February 17, 1997, weather faxes showed the system moving on and we upped anchor to make our way out of St. George's harbor. It was just before dark, and with a two-knot favorable current, we set off for an overnight sail to the Venezuelan island of Les Testigos, about ninety miles distant, making landfall during the morning daylight.

Already in, Max talked us through the coral that was impossible to read with the morning sun right in front of us. Once the anchor was down we discovered a delightful and peaceful spot—well removed from the busy easternmost islands.

Our next stop would be Margarita, another overnight sail, its name conjuring up visions of the salty song that made us yearn for the Caribbean paradise.

When we were off Margarita the next day, both *Windy Thoughts* and *Investigator* anchored amongst several others near the good-sized town of Polomar— in a very open anchorage that had us rolling from gunwale to gunwale. We picked up Faye and Max and the four of us held tightly to *Breezy's* sides as we made our way to shore—where we tied up to a wharf open to the swell and equally as bad as the anchorage.

We were headed to town in a taxi to both the Caribe and the AB dinghy dealerships, but Max and Faye were unable to find a dinghy at either—disappointing, since this was the main reason for stopping. But we did find interesting shops and shared a delightful lunch together.

At first light the following morning, both boats set out into the open sea again. Still in search of a dinghy, *Investigator* headed south to Puerto la Cruz, on mainland Venezuela, a very popular spot for cruising boats. We pointed our own bow westward, planning to meet up again at Tortuga in just a few days.

Some journeys are themselves peaceful; others offer peace at the journey's end. Making our way to the west side of Margarita to anchor for the night, our last two hours were a beat against strong headwinds that made those last three miles hard gained—and our peace came at the journey's end.

Though we had a good night's rest, we were anxious to get off, and we left Margarita to sail west to Tortuga, approaching the island under full sail and under a blue sky that stretched from horizon to horizon in sunshine that bathed us all day. Securely anchored behind the reef's lee side, we listened to the pounding surf just in front of us on the windward side. The long stretches of Tortuga's sandy beach were behind us.

Because you can't always do things when most convenient—and often must take care of chores before planning leisure activities—we donned skins and snorkels and jumped over the side to spend hours scraping the tube-worms that were trying their best to devour *Windy Thoughts'* hull.

While we waited for *Investigator* on their way from Puerto la Cruz, Don and I thoroughly enjoyed the tranquility and the absence of the "freeway cruising" conditions that prevailed in the eastern Caribbean. Even our work scraping tubeworms didn't dissuade us from the good feeling that comes from sitting idyllically at anchor in a pristine spot.

The next day we happily watched *Investigator* arrive, their anchor go down and a very small soft dinghy put into the water. Soon, Max and Faye were alongside *Windy Thoughts*. The dealership in Puerto la Cruz had nothing for sale, but they were fortunate to purchase this dinghy from a European boater. *Investigator* had transportation again!

There were 800 miles of ocean between us and the San Blas Islands that we were looking forward to seeing before reaching the Panama Canal. We planned to stop along the way at the Netherlands Antilles, known as the ABC islands—Aruba, Bonaire and Curacao.

Brisk winds and confused seas made for a lively sail as we wended our way westward to Bonaire. On our arrival, we found a berth in a small marina that was simply first class, part of a hotel complex and a real treat for us. The irony was that Bonaire offered the most beautiful anchorage seen in a long time—with perfectly clear, turquoise waters along its coast. But the luxuries of a marina won out!

Bonaire is a beautiful island surrounded by crystal-clear waters that make it a popular diving destination. Bonaire is not the semi-tropical terrain as found further east, but is a dryer climate with a desert terrain, contrasting sharply with the pure turquoise waters surrounding it. The sun beamed its welcome rays down on us and we enjoyed the absence of rain and squalls—even if we were safely tied up at the marina and could pay them never-mind.

The town of Krelendink with its Dutch style pastel buildings was beautifully clean and orderly, with many lovely shops and good restaurants. Our favorite was the Green Parrot, where Parrotfish as well as other tropical varieties swarmed about in the lighted water just feet from our table—a beautiful sight after dark.

Don surprised me with the purchase of a silver piece of eight set in gold that came from the Spanish galleon *Atocha*, found by Mel Fisher after his devoted eleven-year search. Don said it was his gift to me for crewing with him across the Atlantic. Don is an old softie at his core and always surprises me with something straight from his heart.

In twenty-five knots of wind and uncomfortable and confused seas we made next for Curacao, only thirty-five miles from Bonaire, sailing right for the bay called Spanish Waters with its many arms reaching in several directions and providing an abundance of room to anchor. *Windy Thoughts* found her rest amongst the others, including *Investigator* who had arrived the day before.

Max and Faye advised us to do both the entry and exit procedure at the same time—the practice of most boats as they sat in Spanish Waters awaiting the weather window to head out again. Weather reports predicted gale warnings, with an increase in winds in the next few days in the entire Caribbean. We wouldn't be racing toward the San Blas islands quite yet, but we were in a great spot with excellent all around protection, and all of Curacao awaited us for exploration.

It is always exciting to venture into a new place, to explore and to gain a peek into the lives of another culture, and we soon found ourselves on the half-hour bus ride to Willemstad. Our stop at Curacao gave us a wonderful opportunity to touch base with those from other cruising boats as well.

When we left Curacao we made for Aruba, the last of the ABC islands. *Windy Thoughts* zoomed along in lively winds that were never less than twenty-five knots, the seas rushing along and trying to get to Aruba before we did.

During the black of night, Don and I were watching a ship about a mile away when we received a call on VHF radio, asking that we stand by for boarding. The seas were large and a boarding procedure would be very difficult under the conditions. Don explained that we were American citizens and answered any number of questions about *Windy Thoughts*, our intentions and our destination. Don asked that they not attempt a boarding since it would cause damage to *Windy Thoughts* and be a dangerous procedure. They were insistent at first, but eventually complied and we sailed off into the night.

In the morning light we entered Aruba's anchorage in high winds, *Investigator* to join us within the hour. Getting dinghies down and going ashore wasn't at all inviting in the rough water. Three other boats sat at anchor and all were staying aboard. They had already been ashore and felt that we weren't missing much. This we will never know!

Aruba was our final spot to await a weather window for our passage to the San Blas Islands. We needed about 4.5 to five days of good winds and wanted to take advantage of the first good window that came along—as did all others waiting here. This next leg was known for possible monster seas that are generated in long distances of open water eastward. Some even advised trailing warps behind the boat to slow it down. We knew crews on two of six cruising sailboats that suffered total knockdowns on this run in the past week and we were relieved to know none suffered major damage.

Herb's Net, a very popular weather net covering the Caribbean area and the west coast of America, was available on single side band radio. It was our lifeline because we weren't getting good weather faxes in the Caribbean. The coming leg was one for which we wanted his expert reporting. He had a reputation for always calling it right, garnering his weather faxes from several different sources. Each boat was given an individual weather analysis. Herb told us that, although it was blowing a steady thirty knots at the time, the wind would settle down in a couple of days.

Lessening winds weren't common nor of long durations at this time of year. Knowing that better conditions lay ahead, we decided that now was our window.

At first light the following morning, *Windy Thoughts* and *Investigator* upped anchor and made their way out of the pass, meeting big seas and big winds, favorable for our sail but extremely bouncy. While Don put up and trimmed the sails, I was white-knuckled at the helm, attempting to keep the boat under control while we set our course and got underway again. When the autopilot took over, *Windy Thoughts* dipped to each wave and crashed through the seas in the rhythm set for us for the next days.

Safely away from land, my tensions were again released. We were back to passage- making after just a twenty-four hour respite—and on the most worrisome leg. The other boats in the anchorage at Aruba were staying put, but we reckoned we could take a bit of hammering at the outset, knowing that it would very soon change for the better—and we wanted long enough during that "better" to make landfall in the San Blas Islands.

Herb's Net did us right and our first two days continued with the brisker winds, settling down along with the seas to twenty knots as promised and making our passage to the San Blas Islands a good one. As we neared the Columbia coast, contact with Herb advised us to head south about two degrees to avoid an area of very heavy and uncomfortable seas. This was good advice and within the next twenty-four hours we were back to better conditions again in our preferred twenty-knot range. During the worst period we passed very close to Cartagena, Columbia. *Investigator* made a stop for two days to see this famous walled city.

Max and Faye had nine days before meeting Aussie guests who would fly into Porvenir, on the westernmost of the San Blas Islands and only fifty miles from Panama. Porvenir had a little airstrip and the visitors would puddle-jump from Panama. With a few days' sail to get to Porvenir, along with some time in Cartagena it would be tight, but their friends' visit had been planned for months and *Investigator* would be there!

Don and I considered our options and decided to continue on in the excellent weather. *Investigator* would sail from Cartagena on to Porvenir and return 100 miles east with their guests to Hollendes Cay, where *Windy Thoughts* would make landfall and be awaiting them.

PARADISE ONCE AGAIN

San Blas is made up of many islands off the coast of Columbia, and stretches eastward from Panama for 100 miles. On a glorious sunny day of March 19, 1997, *Windy Thoughts* made her approach to Hollendes Cay. After taking sails down and turning on the engine we slowly conned our way through the coral on the leeward side of the island. The vista ahead of us intrigued us like none other had in a long, long time.

Six little thatched-roof huts dotted the landscape on tiny Tia Tupa Island, where palm trees swayed in the breeze. Tia Tupa was separated from an equally tiny neighboring island by a coral reef that gave excellent protection from the seas to both islands. Our anchor went down off the reef and not another boat was in sight. Just in front of us, on the windward side, surf pounded hard on the reef.

This tropical paradise might have been in the Pacific, or in the islands of Southeast Asia. Hordes of charter boats and most of the cruising boats were left behind back in Granada. The

scene was picture book perfect with clean, clear, warm turquoise waters that invited us to jump right in. The thatched roof huts let us know that we were in a remote and peaceful spot. Our first reaction? Love at first sight!

Since leaving the Canary Islands in December it had been such a push, and now we were almost to Panama. There was time to lie back in this perfect little paradise and just let the tranquility of our idyllic surroundings sink in.

Investigator arrived three days later with stunning tales of Cartagena, where they spent two days before leaving to pick up their guests on Porvenir. Timing was right down to the minute and as they dropped the hook off Porvenir's beach, they watched the little four-seat puddle-jumper touch down on the landing strip just a few hundred feet away.

Max and Faye's guests had left Australia six weeks before, and faxes had kept them up to date on *Investigator*'s progress and whereabouts. It isn't easy to match cruising schedules with planned vacations when weather and other factors rule a sailboat's progress. The folks took a long excursion that included touring Ecuador and Peru while they attempted to match the timing of *Investigator*. There was much joshing with Max about how his sailing had caused them to hop all about the globe to find them, and the couple was the great fun that we had been told they would be.

The San Blas Islands are home to the Cuña Indians, who have remarkably retained their culture, dress and heritage. It is an area unspoiled by tourists with only a spattering of cruising boats passing through, most whose crews appear to honor the serenity of the islands and to make themselves as inconspicuous as possible. The Cuña women dress in colorful sarongs and wear several inches of colorful beadwork bracelets on both their upper arms and on their legs. Bright scarves cover their heads and rings in their noses complete the attire.

The Cuña people are known for making intricate molas—panels of material sewn into the fronts and backs of blouses. The panels are like a reverse appliqué, most often with a final layer of a burgundy colored material. Varying colored layers are turned back to produce color on the final layer, several layers making up the finished mola. Tiny hand sewn stitches are required to create intricate designs that represent natural surroundings such as birds, fish and corals. The best designs are very detailed and can easily take six months to complete.

Locals in hand hewn canoes arrived at the boat with a mola selection the moment we arrived, some coming from more distant islands. Molas ranged in price from $10.00 to $15.00 for the least detailed; most common were the more detailed ones for $30.00—and the most outstanding pieces were priced at $100.00.

Enticed ashore on Tia Tupa our first day, *Breezy* took us to the white stretch of beach that formed the edge of this paradise. Warm wavelets lapped on the shore as we landed and greeted an older gentleman who appeared to be in charge. About six thatched homes peeked out from the palm trees onto the beach, each hut with hammocks for sleeping or sitting, but no other furniture. Possessions appeared to be few, life relaxed and idyllic. All food was prepared in a larger hut that was the community kitchen.

The few women, children and the men folk

gathered about at the home of the older gentleman, where we sat about under the thatched overhang. A little albino boy held out two beaded change purses that he had made, and we purchased them for our little grandnieces back home before turning our attention to the molas that everyone wanted to show us. The quality of the work can vary significantly and, though warned not to buy the first ones we saw, we were excited and wanted to honor their invitation by making a purchase from them.

And more molas there were! The following day, two canoes operated by the men pulled up alongside with Cuñas from an island ten miles distant. We welcomed the couples aboard and sporting broad grins, they climbed up into our cockpit. The molas came aboard with them. Don and I settled in to peruse each one with intense interest. After about two hours, we succumbed to their artistry and purchased several, all carefully chosen.

Another canoe arrived the next day. One "woman" wanted lipstick and I readily dashed below to find some. Don poked his head below to tell me that the lipstick was for a man—I told him that he was wrong. Dressed like a woman, with the right attire and hairdo and complete with a ring in the nose, he/she presented the most beautiful mola work, all done in great detail. Not able to decide on just one, we happily said goodbye to more of our dollars and purchased several.

Our he/she was grinning from ear to ear as they pulled away—the lipstick eagerly spread on his/her lips. We were to learn that the few he/shes in this society were known to produce some of the most intricate mola work.

The Aussie guests had the time of their life. No one wanted to move on and we spent a full relaxing week in our private paradise. Two other boats arrived and each evening we shared a BBQ on the more uninhabited beach so as not to disturb those in the tiny village. Don brought his stainless steel grill, made by Louis on Cyprus, to set over the campfire and the air was pungent with the fragrance of good food cooking—and excitement as we viewed the comet Hale Bopp, so clearly visible to us.

These evenings were magical. Under a dark tropical sky that had erupted with millions of sparkling stars, we laughed, ate, and softly enjoyed ourselves in a way that is still dear to our hearts. The sixteen year-old son on one of the boats brought his guitar ashore and we sang old camp songs. On our last evening together he sang "Amazing Grace" for us in the silence of the moonlit night. It was poignantly touching and there wasn't a dry eye in the group. It was a piece of heaven that we shared. How much we had to be thankful for.

These very special islands provided an idyllic end to cruising with our dear friends on *Investigator*, knowing that soon we would part ways at the Panama Canal.

On March 29, we made our way toward Panama. At the end of a beautiful day sail we stopped for the night between two of the westernmost of the San

Blas islands. Two little boys and a little girl paddled a canoe out from the beach to come alongside *Windy Thoughts*. They clung to our cap rail, big smiles spread across their faces. Now just what would please young children? A package of cookies, of course! When we handed the cookies down, the smiles became even brighter and with  giggles of happiness they eagerly paddled back to shore.

Six other sailboats sat at anchor with us, all making for the Port of Cristobal at Colon, on the eastern side of the Isthmus of Panama. After a very peaceful night, each boat left at first light, headed on the fifty-mile leg to Portobello. From Portobello, it is a short twenty miles to the Port of Cristobal where we would prepare for our Canal transit. So very close now!

After studying the charts carefully we elected to sail part of the distance behind an extensive reef that, by staying in adequate depths, gave us a fast sail in calmer waters—and *Windy Thoughts* made excellent time. The winds stayed steady at twenty knots under blue skies carrying us through the sparkling waters. This glorious day brought to an end the Caribbean chapter of our Atlantic Ocean experience.

When we pulled into the deep and well protected bay of Portobello, fifteen other boats sat peacefully at anchor, their crews all aware that they were about to achieve an important goal—transiting the Panama Canal, a significant milestone for each of us.

Portobello is a sleepy town of less than 5,000, rich with history and once visited by Columbus. The town was founded in 1597 and developed into a thriving colony connected to Panama City by a stone highway. Spanish treasure fleets shipped riches from the Spanish Pacific domains between both ports.

Portobello was believed impregnable. Sir Francis Drake died of dysentery before he could capture the city and was buried in the bay inside an iron coffin. English buccaneers sacked the town in 1601, 1688, and again in 1739. After this, fleets switched from calling at a few ports, to smaller fleets that traded at a large number of ports, a fundamental change in trading practices. Fleets also began traveling around Cape Horn to trade on the west coast.

Portobello's economy was so damaged by the English raids that it didn't recover until the Panama Canal was built, and has never again been the thriving community it once was.

The anchorage sat just off Fort San Lorenzo, declared a World Heritage Site. We went ashore in the afternoon to walk amongst the fascinating ruins, imagining the treasures and the battles passed through here. Ready to continue on our journey toward the Canal, we had a quiet and restful night at anchor before making the last push toward the Port of Cristobal.

Chapter 15

Stuck in the Panama Canal

Do what you can, with what you have, where you are.
—Theodore Roosevelt

The next day was Easter Sunday and, deciding to forego the Easter egg hunt planned by other cruising boats, we made for the Port of Cristobal. Blue skies, moderate winds right on our quarter, slight seas, and excitement bubbled up right from our toes.

The push across the thousands of miles terminated with our arrival at the Panama Canal Yacht Club just a few hours later. We would arrange for our transit here. The Australian and the American flags flew proudly beneath the Panamanian flag—and the Aussie guests couldn't help picking up on our excitement.

Windy Thoughts was about to transit from the Atlantic to the Pacific Ocean, back into familiar waters. We felt almost home.

There was silly revelry on board *Investigator* as the men danced their happiness across her decks to the accompaniment of music from below. Three lively men with arms across each other's shoulders and legs kicking in a kind of can-can as they celebrated our auspicious arrival in Panama—the culmination of thousands of ocean miles and many years of magic.

This world's crossroads was a personal one as well. *Windy Thoughts* and *Investigator* would part ways after the Canal transit. Our joy at arriving here was bittersweet.

The Panama Canal Yacht Club was older and had seen better days. Still, the club served as an oasis for the small boats moving through the Canal. We were thankful that the Club was still open, as the word was that it would likely close anytime. Within the next year, the United States would transfer the Canal to Panama, as required by the Carter administration treaty of 1979.

The restaurant was good, inexpensive, and the Yacht Club a safe spot in a not very safe Colon. A larger anchorage known as the flats, not far from the club, provided safe rest for those not wanting moorage at the Yacht Club. Every boat was in preparation for the transit.

As Colon was not considered safe to walk about, the next morning the six of us taxied into town for the check-in procedure. After four hours and much paper work, our mission was accomplished. The Aussie guests were good sports, patiently waiting for us outside and fanning themselves while the rest of us perspired profusely inside a variety of official offices.

With the most important business handled, we were primed for a good lunch. One of the officials highly recommended a spot for great local food, but did mention that it wasn't in the best part of town.

While we were searching for a taxi, a local lady who sat at the wheel of her car nearby asked us where we were going. On hearing the restaurant's name, she told us to pile in. She strongly advised against the restaurant as it was in an area in which even the police wouldn't venture. Instead, she drove us to restaurant outside of town, where she was our guest. It was a wonderful lunch shared with good company and accompanied by the quick wit of our newfound friend, Lumi.

Investigator's guests flew home two days later. It would be a much longer voyage for *Investigator* before it, too, reached Oz again. But wonderful cruising grounds between Panama and Australia awaited them and Max and Faye still had magical times ahead.

Colon is not a lovely city and is very much like a big slum. Though the Yacht Club was near to town, we made use of a taxi whose driver was kept busy by all moored there as we wrangled with all the details of our transit, making many trips to various offices.

An appointment for an ad measurement of *Windy Thoughts* was necessary before arranging an actual transit date and must be made by phone. The only available phone was in the Yacht Club bar and worked only about thirty percent of the time on a good day. When the phone was not working, the taxi driver took us to the Intel office in Colon, where we stood in a line of locals waiting to use one of two phones available—a long, hot and humid wait. The ad measurer would arrive at the boat the following morning.

Ad measurement clearance is required to determine a boat's fee for the Canal transit. Each ad measurer has a university degree and the Panama Canal Commission position is a highly paid one. We were anxious about the transit, and our ad measurer was patient and helpful as he explained just exactly what would take place, doing much to allay our concerns.

After measuring the boat topside here and there, he went through the entire locking procedure. We were given a choice for how we would like to be locked through: we could be tied to a tug, rafted to another sailboat, or center locked by ourselves. Scuttlebutt about the Club was that being tied to a tug was easiest, but we agreed to accept any of the three methods.

In a Panama Canal transit the big ships are given priority scheduling. The locking procedure is quite complicated, timely, and costly so isn't done for small boats alone. Small boats are locked through directly behind the big ships, and the strain on lines caused by the turbulence of powerful engines only a few feet in front can be tremendous. There were rampant stories of damage to small boats in the locks.

Windy Thoughts had heavy-duty bronze cleats that were thru-bolted to the hull and our lines passed through heavy-duty bronze scuppers. We weren't too worried about our own boat, but did have some concern about being rafted up to a boat with small cleats only bolted or screwed to the deck.

Don and I enjoyed Lumi's and her daughter Maricruz's kindness throughout our time in Colon. Maricruz attended University and lived with her mother. Lumi had recently lost her husband and invited us to her home to see the memorabilia collected while he worked for the Canal Commission. Lumi chose a big ship's lantern to give us. The lantern was very special to us and today hangs outside in our home's entry, converted to electricity. We often contemplate what ship in the distant past carried the lantern—and we treasure the lantern because it was a gift from Lumi.

Lumi and Maricruz provided the cook's tour of the Panama Canal Zone and drove us to the Gatun locks, the first that we would pass through, giving us the opportunity to see the operation prior to taking it on ourselves. And what an impressive operation it was! Lumi joined us for several lunches and dinners, took us to a local fair one evening, to Panama City on the other side of the isthmus on another day, and for a visit to a military fort as well.

One day Lumi introduced us to Colon's duty free zone, whose entrance was insignificant amongst the many doorways on the street. Just inside we were required to show our passports before passing through another door that literally opened into another town! It was like stepping through the looking glass into this bright and well ordered shopping area. Streets of shops and stores replaced the dirty, rundown and unsafe Colon.

Lumi's friendship took us away from the hectic transit preparation procedures and gave us memories of Panama beyond those of the boat and our scheduling tasks—a very special person who just dropped into our lives on our first day in Colon.

Never having been to the United States, Max and Faye decided to leave *Investigator* at the Yacht Club and fly to Eugene, Oregon to visit Max's cousin, and would take along the autopilot for repair. They would be gone for two weeks, so we said our sad goodbyes and enjoyed a last dinner together the evening before they left, expecting to be gone by their return.

It hardly seemed possible that we would never share an anchorage again, or share the company of two of the finest people we had ever had the privilege to know along our way. A lot of water had passed under the keels of both *Windy Thoughts* and *Investigator* together and it was very difficult to say goodbye. Little did we know that fate would bring us together again, much sooner than we could have imagined.

The taxi driver took us to a tire dump where we purchased six old tires to use as fenders inside the locks. The tires would be covered by large garbage bags to protect *Windy Thoughts'* hull. The driver understood our needs, having driven many a sailor on this same quest.

Lumi drove us to the Canal Commission to pay our $475 transit fee, and the resident taxi took us to various offices to pay other fees totaling $100.00. There were visas requiring another $75.00 each, but little did we know that our pocketbooks would be lightened considerably more before the transit was complete. Much paperwork was required, as was procuring line handlers for the locking process. Each day we made progress toward our transit date, set for April 7.

I would be one of four line handlers required in addition to the helmsman. Many boaters took turns helping one other as handlers, but problems occurred when scheduling transit dates. We ultimately decided to hire three young men who were sons of a Club waitress, considered "pros", as they had been handlers numerous times before. The fee was $50.00 each, whether the transit was completed in one or two days. We were prepared to host the line handlers overnight and plan meals for a two-day transit.

Four 130-foot lines were required, available for rental at $15.00 each, to be returned on the Pacific side. The costs were adding up. But we had no idea what was ahead of us. It would be more than a two-day transit for *Windy Thoughts* and at far higher costs.

On our last day we washed down the boat and made a final visit to a nearby supermarket. Our visas came with a forty-eight-hour extension that allowed for a stop in Balboa when we reached the other side, giving us time to return lines, do produce shopping and prepare for the big blue Pacific Ocean.

Don coiled the big lines on deck—two forward on either side of the bow and two in front and on opposite sides of the companionway. The line handlers could be kept comfortable overnight, with cushions ready for one in the cockpit, the other two put up in the main cabin below. I purchased enough food for breakfasts, lunches and dinners. There was deli ham and chicken, fresh bread, snacks, soda pop, fruits, cinnamon buns and much more.

Lumi arrived at the Yacht Club to join us for lunch on this last and very busy day. Not only had Lumi given us the ship's lantern, but she wanted to give Don an old ship's bell. Not being able to remember the English word for bell, Lumi called it Don's ding-dong. How did we deserve to meet this jolly and happy lady who so generously took us under her wing? More goodbyes, sad ones for sure—but oh, the happiness and memories Lumi had given us.

We were ready. The morning would bring with it the beginning of our transit through the waterway separating the narrowest point of land between the Atlantic and Pacific oceans. Homeward bound!

The Panama Canal first opened on August 15, 1914, and has had far-reaching effects on the economic and commercial development for the region throughout the century. The transit service is generally rapid and efficient, and large vessels complete the transit process in slightly less than twenty-four hours. It is a remarkable level of performance, and the people who provide the transit service and around-the-clock maintenance are absolutely critical to the Canal's efficiency and effectiveness. About 23 percent of the thousands of oceanic vessels that transit each year are Panamax-size vessels, the largest vessels the Canal can accommodate. To see these big vessels maneuver between the sides of the locks with literally only two or three inches between their hull and the sidewalls is a breathtaking sight.

The Canal is constantly dredged to ensure a year-around draft of 39.5 feet. The operations of this remarkable locking system go on twenty-four hours a day. It takes about nine hours for the average vessel to transit the fifty miles from deep water in the Atlantic to deep water in the Pacific. The canal uses four separate locking systems, an absolutely astonishing engineering feat.

Discussion amongst the Panamanian people about the Canal's transfer to Panama was interesting, in that many locals were unhappy about the change of control. People liked the United States' efficient running of the Canal and the thousands of good paying jobs available for Panamanian people. The ramifications of the change were already felt, as many jobs had been eliminated. People were concerned with what might happen to the great and vital connection between the Atlantic and Pacific. Only time would tell if fears were justified; we sincerely hoped not.

Our hearts raced with excitement over the transit experience and the awesome responsibility to deliver *Windy Thoughts* safely through the locking procedures. We were up at 4 a.m., awaiting the line handlers who arrived at 5 a.m., all nicely dressed young men who changed into shorts once aboard. One spoke English and all were polite and professional. I was a bit nervous about my own line-handling duties; this would not be the Hiram Chittenden locks in Seattle! Leaving the marina, we moved into the flats to motor about while waiting for our pilot.

While Don attended to important boat matters, I served fresh pineapple rings and slices of fresh mangoes, oranges, and peaches along with cinnamon buns, cold juice and hot coffee. Busy with cooking and serving tasks kept the butterflies in my stomach at bay. Don was in great form, if a bit on edge. This was no small feat ahead of us!

At 6 a.m. our pilot boarded *Windy Thoughts* and we were off!

Early as it was, we weren't the first boat scheduled, as friends on three other boats left at 4:30 a.m.! Our pilot was a very polite young Panamanian with a master's degree, working his way to Step Eight when he would be able to pilot the larger ships. Pilots complete two full years of intense training on the smaller boats, so we felt very confident. His yearly salary was $135,000, a well-paying position. The pilot immediately calmed my butterflies by telling me to just sit back and relax. I would have nothing to do, as our three line handlers knew exactly what to do and when to do it. Things were looking up!

As for Don, his responsibilities would get more and more demanding when all wasn't as smooth as planned.

The Canal transit begins at sea level in Limon Bay, on the Atlantic side. We putted along for an hour through the 500-foot-wide, six-mile channel in a mangrove swamp only a few feet above sea level. As we neared the Gatun Locks, we slowed our progress. Soon a Swiss sailboat about our length joined us. We would raft together for the locking procedure. The pilot instructed Don to keep the boat moving about in a small area.

Don, the pilot and the three line handlers worked to raft-up properly, with the Swiss helmsman, his pilot and own crew as line handlers doing their part. Rafting had to be executed perfectly so that neither boat's spreaders would hit as we rocked in the violent surges to come. I was a lady of leisure, providing cold drinks and snacks.

With the two boats rafted tightly, one helmsman would be appointed to take the boats into the locks. Don was the appointed helmsman and it was his job to keep both boats in position until the pilots instructed us to move ahead. This was no easy task as we waited for an hour for the ship that we were to be locked behind. I had nothing to do, so I did what I do best—fretted about what was to come.

Finally, the huge vessel moved into the locks and we were given the go-ahead to move into the locks behind it. We moved forward to the center of the chamber that could take a 103-foot beam vessel, leaving two inches on each side. Two inches is precisely what the large vessel had between its sides and the lock walls. The line handlers were very busy. Fellows high above at the top of the lock walls threw down four monkey-fists, pitched like baseballs with perfect aim onto *Windy Thoughts'* deck. Our three line handlers grabbed the monkey-fists, to which were attached small lines that were then tied onto our 30-foot lines.

The procedure was similar to what we had been accustomed to in Seattle, but on a much grander scale. The long lines were drawn up by the fellows above and our three handlers worked to adjust the lines with the right amount of tautness. We were center-chambered and the pilot continuously instructed Don to keep the boat first in reverse and then forward again.

The locking procedure had begun. *Windy Thoughts* was a mere ten feet behind the giant vessel that loomed ahead of us like a skyscraper. The turbulence directly behind this giant was tremendous—we might have been in huge tumbling waves at sea! The line handlers worked hard adjusting lines, the pilot again giving Don constant instructions of hard reverse, then hard forward.

The giant ship with our two tiny boats behind it was raised a total of twenty-seven feet in the first of three stages in the Gatun Lock. It is a vulnerable time and the strain on the lines is enormous as the locks fill with water. The men worked diligently to keep each line released and then tight-

ened so that our position in the locks was stable and constant. Don continued his hard reversing and hard forwarding as directed—very concerned about the effect on our engine.

My only job was to stand by—and fret. On the chamber walls a unique system of mechanical locomotive cars provide the muscle for handling the large vessels' huge lines, moving lines back and forth to keep the vessel in place.

This was first of three lock chambers in the 1.5 mile length of the Gatun Lock. When locked through all three chambers, the larger vessel, with us directly behind, would be raised eighty-five feet. It was the most interesting experience, with something happening every second, and intense attention needed to see us safely into the next chamber.

All was fine through the first chamber. As we moved into the second chamber, Don battled the turbulence and worked at keeping us centered directly behind the vessel in front of us. Suddenly, it seemed that *Windy Thoughts* had reduced power and the turbulence from the vessel's huge propellers made controlling the boat increasingly difficult for Don.

An abrupt clunk, heard above the noisy turbulence, aroused everyone's attention. The Swiss helmsman thought the horrific sound came from his boat—but after four more loud clunks, *Windy Thoughts* was suddenly without gears! This couldn't be happening right in the Panama Canal!

The Swiss helmsman immediately took control to get the boats through the next two chambers. Each step was like the first one, requiring great attention to detail and line handling. Don was horrified at what might have happened and we were sick at heart.

As we exited the third chamber, we moved into manmade Gatun Lake, twenty-five miles from the next Pedro Miguel Locks. The lake was beautiful and would have seemed more so, were we not so stunned.

There would be no moving on to the Pedro Miguel Locks for us. With excellent instructions from his pilot, the Swiss captain got us immediately to port as we exited the Gatun Locks. We untied all of our rafting lines and while the others went on their way, *Windy Thoughts'* anchor went down.

Our pilot radioed for a boat to pick him up and Don rowed the line handlers to shore. We were anchored off the Gatun Boat Club where there were no boats, but a guard let the fellows into the Club to call a taxi. Don paid them each the $50.00, providing taxi money as well. It was agreed we would be in touch when we could finish the transit.

Never pay up front!

Here we sat—broken down in the Panama Canal.

Don tore off the companionway steps to expose the engine compartment, where he discovered that the rubber doughnut in front of the flange had cracked completely through in four places, its four bolts stripped completely and one missing. But we had a spare rubber doughnut! He worked for the rest of the day before heading to bed, only to get up before dawn to work all morning replacing the rubber doughnut.

Ready to go ashore ourselves, we both jumped into the welcoming fresh waters of Gatun Lake for a cool-off and a bath.

The Canal Commission Dive School was next to the Boat Club, but nothing else in the area as far as we could see. After tying to the Dive School dock, we went inside and were allowed to use the phone to call a taxi. A chain link fence topped with concertina wire enclosed the Dive School and the Boat Club. Within the Panama Canal Commission, we were in a safe place. We could use the dock at the Dive School for the dinghy, but since the school closed at 3:30 p.m., we would have to return in time to get back through the gate.

The taxi took us back to the Panama Canal Yacht Club that we hadn't expected to ever see again. We had the 520 feet of heavy line to return; it hadn't been an easy task to get the line down into *Breezy*, up the ladder at the Diving School and then out to the taxi. By the time we hefted it to the rental place in the heat and extreme humidity, we were quite done in.

Boaters at the Yacht Club gave us information about a crack American diesel mechanic who lived aboard at the Pedro Miguel Boat Club—located near the Pedro Miguel Locks that were yet ahead of us and within the Panama Canal system. Jim was presently working on a boat at the Yacht Club and he would come to our boat that night when he finished work, but said that it might be 8 p.m. before he arrived.

Don and I took a taxi back to the Dive School, jumped into the dinghy and headed over to the Boat Club to investigate how we were going to get Jim in through a locked gate. We searched the fencing and found a spot where Don could work enough loose to squeeze Jim through. As darkness dropped fast, a close watch was kept in the cockpit for any headlights ashore.

We saw nothing as the hours passed. Finally, at 10 p.m. car lights approached and Don jumped into *Breezy* and headed to shore. Don made his way through a rugged area to the front gate holding his flashlight directly in front of him—the dark nearly impenetrable. Suddenly, a flashlight met up with Don's, not three feet in front of him! Both lights flew up in the air, as did two very frightened men who each thought he had met his end.

It was the guard on duty, his hours and days seeming to vary. Don hurriedly explained, in sign language, that he was off the boat at anchor and that he was meeting a fellow at the gate.

Jim stayed until well after midnight investigating our problems. His diagnosis was a bent shaft. The cracks in the rubber doughnut didn't look new. It seems that the very hard clutch work in the Canal had been the breaking point, the same assumption Don had made.

Jim assured us that he could make it right, but he had many boats scheduled ahead of us. He could better fit us into his schedule if we could get through the Gatun Lake and the Pedro Miguel Locks to the Pedro Miguel Boat Club. As we sat now, it was a two-hour's drive for Jim, one way. He felt certain that with the work that Don had done so far, we could make it.

Jim gave us a tip about re-scheduling our Canal transit; we wouldn't be locked through without paying a fee for breaking transit—and we should pay this fee before trying to do anything further. Our spirits lifted. We would get through the Panama Canal yet! But it would be three more weeks right inside the Canal before we saw the Pacific Ocean.

Another taxi took us back to Colon to begin the paperwork required to re-schedule our transit. We set off first for the Port Captain's office to take care of the delayed transit fee that Jim told us would be necessary.

The Port Captain wasn't in and our Spanish was very limited. No problem. Someone from the street was brought upstairs to the offices to interpret for us. The Port Captain was at a funeral and we were invited to sit down and await his return—because even after lots of interpretation, no one knew what fee we were talking about.

After an hour's wait, the Port Captain returned and listened to our plight as interpreted by the kind fellow off the street. We wanted to pay our delayed transit fee. The Port Captain didn't know anything about a delayed transit fee. We insisted there was one and were determined to pay it in order that there be no snags in the remainder of the procedure.

The captain disappeared for a bit and came back to tell us that no one else knew anything about a fee either. Well, could he please write a letter stating that we had *tried* to pay the fee?

He agreed, and we would return after lunch, giving him time to write the letter. The kind interpreter had endured the whole procedure and we invited him to lunch, but he declined and happily went on his way, likely wanting to avoid more contact with these two dunderheads.

Rudy, the taxi driver we knew well by now, was enlisted to take us back to the Port Captain's office. When he heard our story, we learned that we had spent all morning at the wrong Port Captain's office! We had been at the one used originally for clearance procedures—and should have been at the Panama Canal Commission Port Captain's office!

Rudy took us to the correct offices, where we met with the correct Port Captain. How could we have been so ignorant?

We had $200.00 with us, having been told by Jim that the fine could be hefty. It was heftier. When the Port Captain sternly announced that our fine for delaying the transit was $400.00, I dissolved into tears. The kitty was eroding before our eyes. My burbling away didn't help at all and I seemed to have reached the end of my rope. The banks were closed for the day, but we would be allowed to come back the next morning to pay up.

Meanwhile, the other Port Captain had two confused people in his office all morning trying to pay him a fee that he knew nothing about—and he had just spent a good deal of time composing a letter for us. So we trudged back to get it. The letter was in Spanish and we had no idea what it said, but we profusely thanked him for his kindness and left with the letter, uttering not one word about our mistake but choosing to leave well enough alone.

Back at the boat we dove into the clean, warm and inviting water for a swim and a bath, doing wonders for us. We dipped buckets over the side to gather more good water for laundry that was washed in the cockpit and hung on the lifelines to dry in the hot sun. Baths and fresh laundry both put an air of normalcy back into our lives.

Off to Colon the next morning, first to a bank to get United States currency and then to the proper Port Captain's office to pay our fine. Following this indignity was a long taxi ride to the Treasurer's office and another back to the Port Captain with our receipt from the Treasurer.

Finally we were at the Club waiting for our turn at the phone. Once we found ourselves at the front of the line, a call to the transit scheduler was successful and our transit could resume on Friday morning, just two days away.

With the phone now deciding it was done for the day, we taxied into Colon to stand in the customary long, hot line to use the phone at the Intel office. Patience! Don called our three line handlers to tell them that we could resume the transit. The men were ready to continue—for another $150.00. We had an agreement that the first $150.00 was for the entire transit, reassured us when we put the line handlers in the taxi back at the Boat Club after we broke down. It had been foolish to pay before the transit was completed.

A fellow at the Club commiserated with us and promised to get two new men to handle the lines for us—for $150.00. He would go along himself as the third line handler. Even though this meant an additional $150.00, Don was not going to give it to the first three men. Another $60.00 to rent the four 130 foot lines again was also necessary. We were starting over.

As so often happens, our delay was not wholly without merit—because it meant the possibility of seeing Faye and Max upon their return. We stuck several notes through *Investigator*'s hatch with updates. With plans to stop at the Pedro Miguel Boat Club, we might meet up with them again. There were many bright spots in the big picture of things!

The schedulers bumped our transit ahead a day to April 12, 1997, requiring more trips to the Intel office in Colon and telephoning line handlers to let them know of the change, hoping they would still be available. Not being able to reach everyone on the first try, we took several taxi rides before we were finally finished. Rudy, our friendly taxi driver, delivered the men to the Diving School at 6:00 on the morning of our transit and we were set to go.

There was much trepidation concerning the temporary engine fix and its ability to hold all together long enough to get across Gatun Lake and through the locks.

We had heard glowing reports of the Pedro Miguel Boat Club that sits within in the Panama Canal Zone itself—an older club, small but reportedly filled with warmth that made it so popular and well known. Cruising people helping one other sounded like the haven we needed just then.

One of the line handlers spoke English, which was very helpful to us. The pilot arrived soon, another young gentleman who was very business-like, with a newspaper to keep him company. Though he wasn't as sociable as the first pilot, he was very competent and we had confidence in his piloting.

The 23.5 miles through Gatun Lake to the north end of the Gaillard Cut was a fascinating and beautiful trip. We might have been out on any lake for a day of leisure, but for the attention needed to stay within the prescribed channel and avoid submerged trees. I served a breakfast like the first and had deli meats for lunch sandwiches, various fruits and homemade chocolate chip cookies baked in preparation. Until we reached the Pedro Miguel Locks there was nothing for the line handlers to do but to sit back and enjoy the ride, with Don at the helm.

The Gatun Lake covers 164 square miles, formed by the earthen dam across the Chagres River adjacent to the Gatun Locks. The spillway and the two wings of the dam are a length of 1.5 miles, the dam one-half mile wide at the base. The dam narrows to a width of 100 feet at the crest, 105 feet above sea level and twenty feet above the level of Gatun Lake.

The Gaillard Cut is an eight-mile cut through rock and shale and gives one the impression of being in a big ditch. This cut was the site of the principal excavation, where the devastating slides took place during construction. The cut slices through the Continental Divide, one reason it holds so much interest for passengers on cruise ships—as well as for the crews on small boats.

The pilot was on the radio when we reached the Pedro Miguel Locks and it was determined that we would be rafted to a tug when locking through. This was a simple procedure requiring us only to tie securely to the tug—while the tug's crew kept busy handling lines and keeping to the center of the chamber. Our line handlers had only to continue to ride along as we all enjoyed the locking procedure.

Windy Thoughts was lowered thirty-one feet in one step to Miraflores Lake, a small man made body of water a mile wide separating the two sets of Pacific Locks. When the locks opened to let us pass through, our pilot directed us to the Pedro Miguel Boat Club, very close by.

Prior to resuming our transit we had made arrangements with the Panama Canal Commission to make the stop, and had received permission from the Pedro Miguel Boat Club to moor there. Instructions were to call the Boat Club on the radio while still in the locks because it is impossible to get in to the Boat Club without assistance. Until then we were to just hold off the Club until a dinghy came out to us.

Many lines were handed from other boats and there was much maneuvering assistance offered. It was quiet, safe, and big ships were transiting just 200 to 400 feet from us. Double-enders like *Windy Thoughts* surrounded us and we found that most were from the Northwest, beefy boats meant for blue water sailing.

The Boat Club was simple and plain, an older two-story wooden structure. Upstairs, windows on all four sides opened to breezes and the big room served as the social meeting place. A community kitchen was the center of the room, with a refrigerator housing food from each boat. Tables and chairs surrounded the kitchen, and well-used couches and chairs at one end provided comfortable spots to relax with one of the many good books or magazines available. Everyone from the moored boats cooked here, avoiding humid and hot boat galleys. We joined in and prepared our dinners alongside the other busy cooks.

Everything we had read and heard about the Pedro Miguel Boat Club proved to be true. This little spot just reeled us in. The Panama ceiling fan and cozy atmosphere, with everyone sharing stories and conversation, has to be experienced to fully understand the unique camaraderie there. Camaraderie amongst cruising people is common, but something about this club was special. Everyone had boat projects, many were held up, and all shared information on where to go for various things and how to get there.

We also learned that our mechanic, Jim, was indeed excellent and promised to take care of everyone. But Jim's workload was backlogged more than we had understood. Another Seattle boat had been there for three months waiting for Jim. Their work would be extensive and time consuming—and we were hoping to get out of there in a few days. Help! The calendar was passing quickly, and if we were to make it up the Central American coast to Mexico safely before the hurricane season set in, we needed to sail very soon.

April 21 arrived and we were still at the Boat Club. Don started his days at 6 a.m. attempting to remove the flange. Temperatures hovered at a very hot and humid ninety-five degrees. When Don emerged the winner, the flange finally off after several days of hammering, he wilted with relief. Don's ball peen hammer and the flange were completely ruined—but we had another flange.

Jim had left the country for a few days to renew his visa, and we didn't hold out hope for his getting to our needs very soon. Our neighbor on a beautiful Hans Christian Mark 2 had been there for two months, waiting for Jim to work on the refrigeration.

Jim had planned to do the machine work himself and didn't recommend anyone else in the area do it. But we heard otherwise from the American Club manager who offered to take Don to a machine shop that he felt was a good alternative.

Both the prop and shaft had to be pulled and the shaft taken to the machine shop. The Gatun Lake water had been very clean, but the water where we sat now was brown and murky. To top it off, the water was home to *crocodiles!* Don had pulled the shaft several times before, but he definitely didn't want to get in this water!

Fortunately, our neighbor loaned Don a hookah that he had fashioned from a vacuum cleaner hose—and as good luck would have it, *Investigator* arrived during the week and we talked over the radio. Thrilled that we would see them again, Don was also thrilled that our Max volunteered to come to the Boat Club to personally plug the shaft's hole to keep the boat from flooding. Both of us welcomed Max's assistance, as it meant my not being responsible for sinking the boat during the procedure.

Seven geese made the boat basin their home and squawked greetings to everyone walking about the grounds or near the water. The night before Max arrived, we were reading in bed when we heard a huge splash. One of the geese met his demise when a crocodile chose him for his dinner, and we counted only six geese amongst the resident gaggle the next morning! Don wasn't excited about joining the crocodiles in the water. Though this was one of many jobs shared in the past, I was satisfied this time to call this job men's work.

A few days later, we were on the bus to Colon and the Panama Canal Yacht Club, to handle lines for *Investigator*'s Canal transit. After a nice dinner, we sat in the cockpit to remember old times together, realizing that these old times were again coming to a close. Faye had berths made up for us, and that night when we crawled in we felt like two people on a charter boat.

We were up before dawn getting ready for the big day ahead—more than a little excited about our duties aboard *Investigator*, her fifty-foot length seeming like a ship to us. A local man who was hired as the fourth line handler boarded at 5 a.m., after which we headed to the flats to await the pilot.

Investigator was center-chambered by herself through the three Gatun

Lake Locks behind a huge freighter. It was a constant battle to keep the boat in control and sighs of relief followed each time that we cleared a chamber and moved on to the next. Faye was one of the four line handlers and we all kept very busy during the intense locking procedures.

After moving part way through Gatun Lake, the pilot had us drop anchor in a pre-arranged area. He left the boat but would return the next day to resume the transits through the Pedro Miguel and Miraflores locks.

Dinner was grilled lamb chops from *Investigator*'s freezer, done on the BBQ and accompanied by grilled potatoes, salad fixings, vegetables and bread—and of course, a glass of Max's red. The line hander said that he had never had better food aboard any other boat. Surely this was a charter cruise!

After a sound sleep for all, with Don and me in the forward V-berth and the line handler in the cockpit, we were ready for the adventure of moving *Investigator* into the Pacific Ocean.

Though everyone was up early, the pilot didn't show. As time wore on and he learned that the pilot wasn't coming, Max's usual calm demeanor fled and he made it very clear on the radio that he wasn't waiting another day. A pilot was sent out immediately and the transit continued as planned.

And suddenly, *Investigator* was moved into the mighty Pacific Ocean!

Investigator dropped the hook off the Balboa Yacht Club, and we took a water taxi to shore to catch a bus back to the Pedro Miguel Boat Club. Final goodbyes weren't necessary yet.

Two days later, we would finish our own transit. More 130-foot lines were rented, and three more line handlers were located—an easy task this time when three men at the Pedro Miguel Boat Club offered their services. It would be just a few hours transit of the Miraflores Locks, there would be no need to overnight and the final leg would be easier than the first.

After the drama of our transit so far, the final section went so smoothly we could barely believe our good fortune. There was no need to handle lines because we were rafted securely to a tug through both locks—and Don was able to enjoy the entire locking process.

The waters of the mighty Pacific Ocean were finally under our hull, a milestone long anticipated. Our pilot was picked up as we pulled in front of the Balboa Yacht Club, and we radioed for a water taxi to pick up the line handlers, who offered to return the rental lines for us. We didn't even drop anchor. Though allowed forty-eight hours here, we no longer had any need or desire to go ashore on this side.

Setting sail, we headed under the Bridge of the Americas and right into the open Pacific Ocean. Don and I were positive that we could feel *Windy Thoughts* bubbling with glee as she bent to the breeze, knowing that she was on her way home. We planned to meet up with *Investigator* at an island just ten miles away.

Two hours later the hook went down near *Investigator*. A birthday dinner for Max marked the
last dinner that we would
share together. It was the
last time ever that we
would sit bobbing at an-
chor together.

As first light soft-
ly broke the following
morning, we were on deck
and ready to haul anchor
when Faye called over to
us, "Let's go home now."

It was necessary to sail 125 miles south in the Gulf of Panama until rounding the southwestern point at Punt Maia—a sail against southerly winds for
about twenty-four hours. Once around Punta Maia *Windy Thoughts* could sail
north and *Investigator* west toward our respective homes again. Punta Maia
has a reputation for dismal weather that can be especially uncomfortable, and
we sighed in relief after we rounded the point in the black of night.

For the final time we caught glimpses of *Investigator's* sails during the
day and her masthead light at night.

On May 2, 1997, *Windy Thoughts* and *Investigator* parted ways. I could
not stop the tears from flowing. Another chapter in our lives had come to an
end—but we knew that a bright new chapter lay ahead. We were truly on our
way home now.

Don and I were headed straight up the Central American coast. Any
thoughts of enjoying Costa Rica, Nicaragua, El Salvador and Guatemala were
set aside as we hastened to reach Mexico before the hurricane season arrived.
Beautiful islands in the Gulf of Chiriqui on Panama's coast beckoned to us as
we passed by that second morning out, islands that would have drawn us right
into their charms, to explore if we had more time.

As the second morning stretched into midday, we turned on the engine
and rolled along in light air. Our course was a straight shot north that kept us
offshore just a few miles. Don didn't want to add one unnecessary mile on this
leg home! A close watch was kept both day and night. Crossing from Panama
into Costa Rica, we were happy that the notorious Papagayo winds don't generally blow across the Isthmus of Panama after April lst.

Continuing light airs and gentle seas had us feeling lazy and we felt more
or less in the clear as we ghosted along on day three. We should be safely
between the Papagayo winds and the hurricane season. Thoughts of being in
Puerta Vallarta in about a week brought eager anticipation as we entertained

the idea of sitting in a marina for the winter with luxurious amenities!

When we first sailed into the South Pacific those many years ago, the North Star sunk rapidly toward the horizon. Now, as we gained latitude north, Don's personal star began to rise in the skies again, letting him know that his heaven, Orcas Island, was waiting for us.

Knowing that we would be there soon and that all was going well, at one day's end we headed into a large bay and found respite for the night behind a huge reef extending from north to south. Once the anchor was well set, we sat in the cockpit to enjoy a relaxed meal along with cold glasses of lemonade that quenched our thirsts in the sultry climate.

Don decided to give the engine a check again—our confidence could easily be shaken at the least little quirkiness and we were treating the engine with kid gloves. Don's heart nearly jumped out of his throat when he found that the pin going through the flange and shaft was broken clean through—and the only thing holding the flange on was the keyway! If the keyway gave way, the shaft would just spin and we would be without an engine. With all of the motoring since coming up from Panama, this wasn't good news.

But the good Lord had always been sitting on our shoulders. Flamingo Bay was just fifty miles north of us, with a small marina—the only one on the Costa Rican coast. If we could get in there with the keyway still intact, there was hope. It would take about ten hours to reach Flamingo Bay and we planned to set off in the morning if there was wind to sail.

With the latest developments, we knew that we wouldn't be cruising in our San Juan Islands during the coming months after all—and we wouldn't be preparing our property on Orcas Island for building our home. If we made it to Flamingo Bay, we would have to leave the boat there, fly home with the shaft and have a new one made. The perfect weather window would be lost and we wouldn't be able to continue on until the hurricane season was over in November.

Mentally shifting gears had been done before and could be done again, so we sat back and contemplated what lay ahead. We hoped the Flamingo Bay Marina had room for us, that it would be a safe place to leave the boat and that we could work things out from there. Far worse things can happen. We were quite safe. The boat wasn't sinking. The end of the rainbow wasn't as close, but we believed there must be a reason that we weren't destined to sail the final leg of our journey home just yet.

We thought of all our blessings and we were thankful. The only marina in Costa Rica was just up the coast! We enjoyed good health. A beautiful, cozy boat that was our home had given us more adventure and happiness than we could ever have imagined. And we were together. The latest mechanical difficulty was just a glitch in the adventure that wasn't ending just yet.

In truth, when the adventure resumed it would include cruising Mexico's mainland coast, with glorious stops that we wouldn't have made on our current fast track. We would not head up into the Sea of Cortez until spring, giving us another year of cruising! It would also mean facing a late-season hurricane that would give us something to remember. But that part of our story's ending was still to come. Yes, there was still plenty of adventure ahead!

And so we tucked ourselves into our sea berths for a good night's sleep. At 3 a.m. we were awakened with very high wind that we thought was a sudden squall. We leapt into the cockpit to find the wind speed indicator hitting forty knots, and it remained steady for more than an hour. OK, God, we did ask for wind. Always be careful what you ask for. It wasn't raining and the wind's long duration wasn't typical of a squall. The sky was alive with stars.

Any other time, we would have been happy that a squall was coming from land, because should our anchor drag we would be blown out to sea. However, the reef behind us extended a long distance between us and the open sea and couldn't be navigated safely in the dark. After two hours, the wind eased to fifteen to twenty knots. If the wind held we could sail at first light.

As the sun lazily crept over the horizon, we slowly made our way out of the bay under full sail, clearing the reef and setting our course north. The wind was coming from shore, as Papagayo winds do, and we were uneasy, but the seas were slight. There were only fifty miles to go. For the present, conditions were perfect and we would take any wind that we could get. So we thought.

Yes, do be careful what you ask for. The weather conditions began to change rapidly. The wind increased within minutes to forty knots plus. We now understood the force of Papagayos.

In Panama we had talked to many boaters who had sailed south in fifty-knot Papagayo winds for hundreds of miles. Sailors are very familiar with the fierce winds of Mexico's Tehuantepec Bay that also blow from land, but few are as experienced with the equally ferocious Papagayo winds blowing from the Caribbean Sea over the lakes of Nicaragua, and pushing far out over the Gulf of Papagayo on the Pacific Coast.

We turned off the autopilot and Don took over the helm, sailing the boat with one foot on the beach. Though this kept us out of the bigger seas building very close in, it forced us to move in and out from shore to avoid rocks that were charted but not seen. It was a constant struggle as the huge seas built just yards from shore. Oh, for the safety of sea room!

Wrestling the wheel under the circumstances took every ounce of Don's strength. Constant attention to our position, charting it precisely, watching for the fathom line that would keep us safe and passing information on to Don kept me busy. And I could privately fret while Don had the more difficult job, focusing intently upon sailing the boat.

Around noon a powerboat just north of us called on the radio to inquire about conditions south. He reported that conditions worsened further north and suggested an anchorage seven miles below Flamingo Bay. Costa Rica's coast doesn't offer many good anchorages and the ones that do exist are generally open to southerly swells. Several local boats were on moorings and though the water was very choppy, it was safe and well protected. The hook went down in fifteen feet of water and the change from being fully "on" to being entirely "off" was dramatic. Our alert and anxious attention dissolved into more restful thoughts.

It was a rip-roaring sail that following morning of May 6, 1997, in forty-five knot winds as we sailed the boat close to the beach again. When only a few miles from Flamingo Bay, we called the marina on the radio and learned that, though the marina was full, we could anchor in the outer bay until a slip opened the following day.

Feeling better about everything already, we happily laid *Windy Thoughts* over, pulled out all the stops and began tacking in—rather enjoying the thrill of it as it would be a short beat to windward and we were almost to shelter! When we were just outside the breakwater to the marina's entrance we rounded up, dropped sails and the hook—and it was over—until the next fall.

Flamingo Bay Marina is a small marina with Med style mooring with lines for the stern or the bow. This is prime big game fish area and the marina was filled with charter fishing boats. Jim McGee, the American manager, was most helpful and would make room for *Windy Thoughts* for an extended stay—and would help us to get into the slip the next day. Jim wanted us stern-to, requiring us to back in when we couldn't put the boat into reverse. We would cross that bridge the next day. For the present, we took *Breezy* inside to tie up at the marina docks and to scope out what would be *Windy Thoughts'* home for the next three months.

The manager pointed to a small building up the road, home to the only other business in the area—a travel agency! Just exactly what we needed to make our arrangements to fly home!

Within an hour we had made plans to leave Flamingo Bay five days later, on May 12. We were booked on a puddle-jumper to the main airport in San Jose, and would fly out of a little airstrip that snuggled into a cow pasture a few miles down the road. The agency made hotel accommodations for a night in San Jose and booked a flight to Seattle on May 13, 1997. This was almost too easy!

Up the road from the marina were a few small restaurants. Nice homes sat on the hill nearby. Outside the bay was a huge white sandy beach. A few hotels were located close to the marina and we could use any of their pools. Immediately, we felt it a safe place to leave the boat.

Though very disappointed with our sudden change in plans, if this life taught us nothing else, it taught us to take all in stride. A safe haven had been provided—just when we needed it.

The next day a fishing boat helped to maneuver *Windy Thoughts* between two cruising sailboats whose owners had left for visits home to the United States. Jim and seventeen other men gathered on the dock to assist in the continuing forty to forty-five knots of wind. The entire procedure was challenging, but after a fire drill of sorts, *Windy Thoughts* was safely tied up and ready for her R and R.

The next few days were spent in a frenzy of preparation for leaving the boat for the summer. Jim's fifteen year-old son was hired to clean and air the boat out weekly. I busily packed bags and cleaned everything out of the fully packed refrigerator. Lovely big cheeses purchased in Panama, including some aged Parmesan that was hard to part with, all had to go. All of the refrigerator's contents and bins of potatoes and onions were given to a cruising boat just arrived and sitting at anchor with two little boys aboard.

The shaft had to come out, and the prop had to go home with us. It wouldn't be the first time that Don had faced these chores without the benefit of a haul-out. He would do the ole diving routine again, and when that was done he moved on to the unwelcome job of tearing the toilet apart. It had chosen to plug up once we were nicely in and secure, naturally not wanting us to abandon the boat to landside pleasures without reminders of its importance.

There was a long list of things to do in preparation for leaving the boat unattended. Topsides, we put all in order, and had no time to try out any of the hotel pools—that pleasure would come in the future. The night before our departure we took showers under the hose on the dock, all ready to head out in the morning.

The plane carrying us to San Jose would leave at 6 a.m. and we arranged for a taxi to pick us up in front of the marina at 5 a.m. We were up before the crack of dawn, with nothing left to do but to get everything off the boat—not as easy as it may seem.

We had been climbing over the stern rail and down onto the wind vane—leaping across the five foot void that stretched from the vane to the top of a dock box. This morning the boat bounced up and down with the swell, and getting from the boat securely onto the dock box with both shaft and prop in hand was worrisome. Everything was hauled over *Windy Thoughts'* lifelines and onto a vacant sailboat six inches away, and we leapt from its stern rail right onto the dock. Don took responsibility for the shaft and the prop, and one by one each bag came off. It took three trips to get everything up the ramp in the dark—and in air so hot and humid that we gasped for breath.

Then Don reached to open the gate at the top of the ramp—only to find it locked!

Where was the night guard? Were we destined to miss our plane? After calling and calling to him, we finally woke him. He stumbled out to unlock the gate, everything was hauled out to the road and we settled in to await our taxi.

Five o'clock came and the taxi didn't show. Five-fifteen and then five-thirty came and still no taxi. We were in a panic. There was no phone.

About that time a young couple came up the dock carrying a bag each, obviously headed for the airport and having made arrangements to get there. A power boat had arrived the previous day and anchored outside in the bay. The boat belonged to the young man's parents and the couple was heading home after a week aboard.

Relief flooded over us and we introduced ourselves. There wasn't so much as a smile as they introduced themselves—and indeed they were awaiting a taxi to the airstrip. Don explained our dilemma and asked if we might share their taxi. The answer was no. No explanations.

Don had gotten us safely into Flamingo Bay Marina, had taken out the shaft and the prop and had spent one full day working on the toilet—and wasn't about to miss this plane, come hell or high water. We nearly begged. We would be more than happy to pay the full fare for all four of us if only they might reconsider. No reaction.

We weren't giving up. When a roomy taxi van pulled up we begged for the final time. Without even looking at us, the couple said there wouldn't be room.

The driver spoke up to say that there was more than enough room and started putting our gear aboard. Don and I jumped into the back seat, paid the total fare along with a healthy tip for the driver and we were on our way home!

Not even the uncomfortable feeling of sitting inches away from people very unhappy to be sharing a taxi could erase our excitement. Our plans may have changed, but the adventure continued as we contemplated going home.

About five miles down the road the taxi pulled onto a side road next to a cow pasture. When the taxi stopped, we were at the airstrip. Two Costa Rican boys about eight years old were waiting and with big smiles took on the job of getting our bags out of the van. The young couple considered it begging and stated emphatically that they weren't about to give a tip. Don happily gave the boys an extra tip for the help that they were to all of us.

When the bags were lined up on the ground the taxi pulled away—and we were left standing in the cow pasture with these people who still didn't want to engage in conversation. But the boys were a joy and we entertained ourselves with them.

Before long the two little boys jumped about in excitement, pointing to the sky. Our small plane soared overhead and then dropped down onto the cow pasture and taxied right up to us. The six-passenger plane had both a pilot and a co-pilot. We boarded, Don and me sitting behind the young couple. The boys busied themselves, honored to load our baggage. Before long we were up and away, leaving Flamingo Bay and *Windy Thoughts* behind for the summer.

An hour later we touched down in San Jose, the capital city that stretched as far as we could see. A taxi deposited us at the nearby Hampton Inn, waited for us to check in, and then took us into downtown San Jose for a tour of the city that reminded us of a bigger Tijuana.

The next day we were suddenly back in our United States again, deposited in Virginia where good friends Terry and Joe Meyer picked us up at the airport. A wonderful few days were spent with them before we jumped into Old Gray Bell, waiting so long for us there. *Windy Thoughts* had always sailed west-about to reach home and Old Gray Bell carried us west-about to Spokane, Washington.

Our niece, Kelly, opened her home to us. We visited with friends and took care of some personal business before driving over the mountains to Seattle. Lindy and Mike McCollum kindly hosted us in their "mother-in-law" quarters in their home, northeast of Seattle. Mike went out of his way to find the best place to get a new shaft made and we found a place to have a new prop manufactured. It concerned Don when a computer analysis determined that the new prop required a different pitch from the original.

Two wonderful weeks on Orcas Island were spent hiking the beautiful trails, and walking our property to picture just where our house would sit. Don talked to the excavators about putting in the septic system on our return, as well as planning the driveway. There was no doubt that we loved it there and preferred the quiet island life to an urban one—and we looked forward to our new life.

We returned to Spokane to spend two weeks at our friend's condo on a lake just east of Spokane while they spent the summer at their lake place on Coeur d'Alene, Idaho. Our bags lay open on the living room floor and considerable time was spent distributing boat parts between them, this part of a home visit still a big part of the cruising life. We relaxed in the quiet surroundings before returning to Costa Rica for our final leg—to bring *Windy Thoughts* home for good.

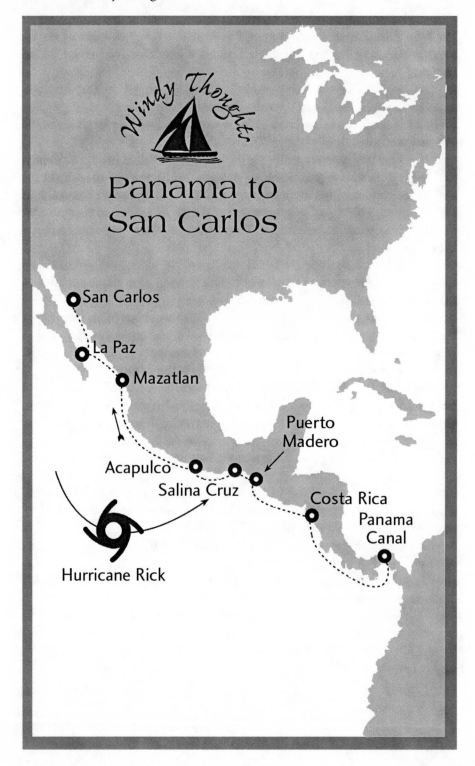

Windy Thoughts

Panama to San Carlos

San Carlos

La Paz

Mazatlan

Puerto Madero

Acapulco

Salina Cruz

Costa Rica

Panama Canal

Hurricane Rick

Chapter 16

Just One Hurricane From Home

To reach the port of heaven, we must sometimes sail with the wind and sometimes against it. But we must sail and not drift, or lie at anchor.
—Oliver Wendell Holmes

When we exited the small plane at Flamingo Bay's tiny airstrip in the cow pasture, we stepped into such heat and humidity there was no doubt that we were again in tropical latitudes. Wilted, we strengthened our resolve as we hauled our bags, shaft, propeller and computer to the taxi that sat in wait.

It was September 3, 1997 and we had been gone from Costa Rica for three months. The heat felt oppressive after the long time away, but our home was just a few miles away and we were anxious to see how she had fared in our absence.

The marina basked in the sun and heat, as laid-back as when we left. The taxi driver helped us to unload our gear in front of the marina office. Don and I made several trips up and down the dock getting everything to the boat.

Windy Thoughts looked fresh and clean and she was smiling at us! All was deposited in the cockpit for later attention while Don unlocked the companionway doors and swung them open, eager to see if our home was as welcoming as she appeared.

She was indeed! The manager's son had kept her clean and aired out and had prepared for our return! Cushions were back in place and it was obvious that a heartfelt attempt was made to welcome us. We were home again—and our wilted spirits lifted. A single flower in a glass on the table nearly put me over the edge. Yes, *Windy Thoughts*, you have carried us to magical places, full of people who never cease to amaze us with their generosity and kindness.

We set about unpacking and planning the repairs that needed to be completed before we could leave Flamingo Bay in mid-November.

September passed, and things progressed for us in the heat and humidity. The rainy season returned suddenly while we were enjoying quesadillas in Maria's restaurant, and we walked home in a deluge. Following its abrupt onset, the rain came daily in a sudden torrential downpour. Then, as fast as the rain had come it would leave. Even with daily rainstorms the area was experiencing a drought, though everything was green and lush. Could this really be drought conditions?

As we settled into life back on the boat and the routine of our days, my need to keep in touch with my friend Susan returned full force.

September 27, 1997
Flamingo Bay Marina
Protrero, Costa Rica

Hello Susan,

It seems that the months in the Northwest never really existed, so entrenched are we in boat life and preparations for leaving. We jumped from one life to another in a matter of hours—so different that we think we are in a fairy tale and hoping for a good ending!

Immediately on our return we found problems with the head, and Don spent the first week working on the toilet lines that are impossible to reach—just where he was prior to our return home. The repair kept Don down below where the heat and humidity are at their worst. The toilet sat in the cockpit for the week while Don and I spent literally hours working new lines through the bilges, a frustrating procedure that tests our patience but one that we have accomplished before and knew we could do again.

Ah, back to the cruising life! How could we have become so complacent about flush toilets during those three months back home?

Don moved next to installing the new shaft and prop, doing most of the work himself with the help of a local diver. The new prop's pitch was changed by computer in Seattle, and this change is Don's biggest concern right now. We returned to a horrid knocking sound in the engine and Don suspects valve problems.

Flamingo Bay, or Protrero, is a beautiful area with lovely beaches and surrounding jungle. Our daily routine starts at first light when we set out on our daily walk, taking advantage of the least oppressive time of the day when the temperatures drop one or two degrees. Unfortunately, we haven't experienced any drop in humidity!

Some mornings we walk two miles down the beach to a very small store where we can often find lettuce and tomatoes for salads, as well as some very nice fresh fruit. We don't pass by the fancy tourist establishments; we just meander under the palms and pass a few local homes along the beach where people are slowly starting their days—and we much prefer this route.

After making our purchases, we often sit outside the small restaurant next door and have our breakfast. The beach stretches in front of us, lovely white sand leading down to the water's edge where we look out across the vast Pacific Ocean, knowing that we will venture out there in a just few more weeks. Time to go cruising again!

Other mornings we walk in the opposite direction around Flamingo Beach, listening to the howler monkeys in the trees. The creatures certainly have earned their name, making the most horrendous howls and sounding like a huge band of gorillas on the attack. Actually, the monkeys are sending their morning greetings and are quite harmless.

The terrain is absolutely thick with vegetation and lots of vines hanging down. We feel like Tarzan and Jane. I have to dissuade Don from flying though the air on one of the vines just to see if it really works as it did for Tarzan.

Several Canadians and a few Americans make this area home. The marina manager refers to many expatriates as either the "wanted" or "unwanted", but we located a nice Canadian lady who will make us a new dodger. The old dodger has been deposited at her home to use as a pattern—one thing underway. She lives with her husband in a scattering of homes under the palms near other ex-pats and they love it here. A boa constrictor killed her cat yesterday, just to give you an idea of our surroundings.

While the slow pace and simplicity of life is enticing, the area doesn't really attract us as a permanent residence. Perhaps because we have our own paradise awaiting us in the San Juan Islands and are getting so close to home now. The infrastructure here is very poor, with roads frequently in deplorable condition, and the typical conveniences are few and far between.

Don and I are both affected by an ominous feeling about this area. Something that we can't put words to hangs over us in the same way as does the oppressive heat and humidity. When we learn that Flamingo Bay is a preferred area of the country, we try to look at it in a new light. We are enjoying the beauty of the area and the opportunity to experience the country's many interesting aspects, as well as the culture of its people. After all, we won't be passing this way again—as you have reminded me every now and then as we meander about the globe.

We have arrived back from the States to find other live-aboards on the dock, though the little marina is primarily filled with charter fishing boats. Everyone has passed on information on where to find groceries, as well as how to get there. This means bus trips to either the town of Liberia or Santa Cruz—and already, we've made bus trips to both. It is an all day jaunt for each, close to three hours one-way to Liberia and a little over two hours to Santa Cruz.

The smaller Santa Cruz appeals to us more, reminding us of a Mexican village, and we found two small grocery stores that carry American products. Disappointing was finding that the fresh produce stands leave much to be desired. The bus lumbers in and out of every little village along the way, along those deplorable roads. Still, we get an opportune glimpse of village life. Don is happy to find a hardware store and I am happy to find groceries.

Everyone tells us that just about anything can be found in San Jose, but that is a four-and- a-half-hour drive one-way—or a seven and a-half hour bus ride. It would be like going from Spokane to Seattle for a bottle of catsup! Ok, so perhaps I am losing my sense of adventure as our nearness to home looms ever closer.

Convenience and the cruising life do not go hand in hand. You just cannot have the joys of cruising with convenience wrapped up all in one nice package. This is the joy of seeing our world and certainly part of the adventure—even though I am not willing to jaunt to San Jose for something I need, just yet! One bonus of our lengthy bus rides is the glimpse into daily life in Costa Rica. It is beautiful farming country and Don is excited to see so many men on horseback in their western style hats—and real cowboys they are! Local people are most friendly and welcoming and we enjoy their warm personalities.

There are several hotels in the immediate area around Flamingo Bay, though few tourists. We're told that the area is overbuilt and that the present government is friendly to crime, making Costa Rica unattractive to visitors. It is so hot that after about four or five hours of working on the boat, we have our choice of which pool will be our salvation for our afternoons. Though we have spent years in latitudes closer to the equator, somehow this place seems to attract and hold in every bit of heat and humidity that exists on this planet.

This is our daily schedule: we walk early and are back to the boat by 7 a.m., to work until noon. After lunch we head just up the road to the Flamingo Beach Hotel with its Olympic-sized pool. Our marina group gives the hotel most of their business. The pool is much too warm from the sun itself for a refreshing dip, so we sit in the covered kiddy pool area after our swim to cool off. Don and I do laps in the pool for thirty minutes before visiting and reading our books, stretched out on lounge chairs around the pool—lazy beings after busy work mornings. At the end of the day we use the showers on the hotel's pool level, so much nicer than the low pressure hose on the dock.

By 6 p.m. it is dark, and we often stop at Marie's restaurant on the way home for the excellent seafood—with mahi-mahi, red snapper and rock scallops our favorites. Beans and rice are in abundance—and we are getting very attached to quesadillas stuffed with cheese and jalapenos, served with sour cream. We wonder why we have this odd, dark feeling about the area when it offers us a safe haven, good food and a nice pool where we are so welcome. Certainly, we are blessed to have found this beautiful spot on the chart.

This week we met two young women staying at the Flamingo Beach Hotel. The younger woman's parents are part owners of the hotel. Though the hotel had only four other guests, the girls had been given one of the least desirable rooms, without an ocean view. They had great difficulty upgrading to a room with an ocean view. The younger woman is planning to be married next year and is looking the place over as a possible honeymoon choice. The hotel is now crossed off her list.

The women had a rental car and invited us to spend a day touring the Arenal area, known for its huge, active volcano. It was a stunning 3.5 hour drive through miles of beautiful rain forest. The road between the town and where the volcano is best viewed is dirt and in many places has been washed out completely. The potholes are unlike anything we have ever seen and it was a jarring, slow-moving trek that took over 2.5 hours to cover ten miles in one stretch—this the main road in one of the most visited areas of Costa Rica!

The volcano is truly spectacular and worth the bumpy drive, the entire day a fascinating trip for all.

There are now five live-aboard boats, including our neighbors who have returned from California. They spent the last year in the marina in Puerta Vallarta. He tells us they are "real cruisers—unlike you, who move about all the time"—his exact words. Gads, here we thought we were cruising all of these years!

On our other side is David, a retired anthropologist and a single-hander, also out of California. A young couple is crew on a powerboat that plans to leave for Mexico about the same time we do. The owner jumped ship after getting violently seasick on the passage south and had to be lifted off by a United States Coast Guard helicopter based in Panama. His dream of taking the boat to Florida via the Canal has come to an abrupt end, and the couple will return the boat to Mexico.

Another couple has purchased a house in the mountains near San Jose, so are no longer officially live-aboards, but do come to spend time on their boat. This is our little village of cruising people on the dock at Flamingo Bay.

October 7, 1997
Flamingo Bay Marina
Costa Rica

Hello Susan,

Yesterday, we returned from five days visiting Nicaragua. Our neighbor David hired an American, Jim, to crew with him to Panama. Jim needed to renew his Costa Rican visa and suggested that we might enjoy joining him on his jaunt out of the country. The invitation came last Friday afternoon when we returned from the pool, and we left on Saturday morning.

David has sailed from Flamingo Marina three times in the last three months, only to return due to continuing engine problems. All is supposedly fixed now and David hopes to be off tomorrow. We have enjoyed him as our neighbor, a gentle man who we barely know is there.

Jim has been to Nicaragua several times and speaks fluent Spanish, and, as our tour guide, made the trip interesting and added immensely to our enjoyment.

Our destination was Isla Ometepe, on Lake Nicaragua—the tenth largest inland lake in the world and home to the only fresh water sharks in the world. A taxi was engaged to take the four of us from Flamingo Bay to the Nicaraguan border.

Jim got us through the legalities in a half-hour's time and a bus took us to the town where we could catch the ferry to Isla Ometepe.

This was all plan-as-you-go or perhaps go-as-you-plan—and without Jim's translation skills and former experiences, we couldn't have known where to go or what to do. We have discovered in our travels that things seem to work out best if not a lot of pre-planning goes into land excursions. Ask around about the best places to stay and just go for it.

Rambling along the road, we realized that the lamentable road conditions in Costa Rica were superhighways in comparison to these in Nicaragua. The contrast in the living conditions between Nicaragua and Costa Rica was like night and day. However, the countryside was absolutely lovely, with lush greenery everywhere. The bus was full to overflowing with local people getting on and off, stuffed right to the stairway at the front and then down the stairway, with the last two hanging on outside of the doorway—and all smiling and friendly.

While waiting for the ferry, we sat in a hotel courtyard and enjoyed cold drinks. The adjoining rooms were being cleaned at the time, so I wandered over to have a look in through an open door. It was very Spartan and looked a bit questionable.

I asked Jim about our hotel on Isla Ometepe. Was it like this? Yes, about the same.

Don suggested that I keep an adventurous spirit. But we are not nineteen-year-olds with backpacks on our backs, and I have my standards! I am being encouraged to loosen up.

The ferry was for passengers only, a very old and well-worn wooden structure that listed heavily to port as it sat at the rickety pier. A crowd of people and chickens, along with two goats lying on flour bags, piled aboard. When we finally boarded, the only seat left was a board stretching across the stern with just a small rusty metal railing behind us on which to lean, held on with only two rusty screws. We decided it might be wise not to lean against it.

Though the ferry was filled to capacity with people filling every nook and cranny, it still listed heavily as it pulled away. Because this is a huge lake and there was considerable wind, the water was very choppy, with generous whitecaps all around us.

We very gingerly stepped up to our seat to avoid a ten-foot square opening in the ferry's sole and right at our feet—big enough to easily fall into, and through which we could look right into the water below. The more interesting aspect was the bilge pump that was simply a big stick that a boy hand-pumped for the entire 1.5 hour trip.

But the boy kept the boat from sinking and we arrived at Isla Ometepe intact—though still listing very heavily to port. We embraced the adventure of it all and didn't obsess about stories of horrific ferry accidents periodically making news in some parts of our world. Yes, going with the flow is a necessary component of the adventure!

Off the ferry, we wandered into the center of the small town where Jim hailed one of perhaps four pick-up trucks that we saw during our five days in Nicaragua. Two young boys agreed to drive us to the hotel, ten miles distant and about a fifty-minute drive over roads truly difficult to describe. The four of us stood in the open truck bed behind the cab, holding on to the sides of the truck for dear life as the young fellows did all they could to show off their driving abilities—and the speed of their beloved truck.

Other than the bus, the usual means of transportation was on the back of the occasional horse, more often on the back of a cow or in a cart with wooden wheels pulled by horses or oxen. Little boys rode double atop both horses and cows, carrying machetes in one hand, with their little legs  sticking straight out—the front rider holding onto the horse's mane and his companion with one arm wrapped around his waist. Everyone smiled big, broad smiles and waved. We loved the people already.

When we reached our hotel we were pleased to find it tucked into the jungle and right on the huge lake. It was quaint and in an exceedingly picturesque setting, just as Jim had promised. David and Jim secured rooms in the hotel for $5.00 each, but Don and I upgraded to a cabin, the most exclusive quarters and costing us $16.00! Our accommodations were monastic, a light bulb hanging from the ceiling, a bed, and a bathroom with a showerhead in the ceiling. The sheets on the bed were considerably smaller than the mattress. I spent my nights in attempts to keep the bottom sheet under us so that we weren't sleeping on the mattress. A top sheet wasn't necessary in the heat. Don slept like a baby, as usual.

The island is formed by two volcanoes joined by an isthmus. A beach stretched out in front of us, unspoiled by beach umbrellas and sun bathers. Cows were brought to the water's edge each morning to drink the fresh water. Ladies stood up to their waists in the water, happily chatting while doing laundry. Thatched roofed huts and concrete structures dotted the roadside, many in very poor condition.

On our second morning, after breakfast on the veranda, Jim ushered us on a walk along the beach to catch a bus for an excursion to see ancient petroglyphs dating back to the Mayans. Don and I found a seat on the top of some bags of rice, sharing our little perch with some chickens. David and Jim stood in the aisle and hung on for the bumpy ride of a half-hour until we reached a small village. Several people hung on outside the bus, happy to be on at all.

Once off the bus, we stepped into a little store to purchase cold drinks that refreshed us. Several pairs of the prettiest white dress shoes were displayed in a glass counter—likely for women's Sunday best going to church—and looking rather incongruous amongst the store's other goods.

Jim led us on a hike uphill through a banana plantation and on into the mountains. Along the way we passed men and boys carrying machetes for work and women carrying loads of bananas on their heads.

After hiking for about an hour we reached the home of a family that Jim had last seen a year ago. The family lived here in relative isolation and in such desperate living conditions that it brought tears to my eyes. They were just overjoyed to see Jim.

Their home was an old barn that had the remnants of platforms along the walls that might have originally been for chickens, but were now used as the family sleeping area—without mattresses or bedding, just bare wooden platforms. The family didn't appear to have any material goods other than the clothes on their backs and a pot in which to cook rice over an open fire. We didn't see any dishes or any other traditional household items.

The parents, along with a sixteen-year-old girl, a little girl of about seven and a baby boy of about two, all lit up with bright smiles and laughter during our visit. The two girls didn't attend school—there was no money.

Jim carried on a lively conversation as the family filled him in on their life since he had last visited. We witnessed the reality of parents who could provide nothing for their children except a strong Christian faith that they shared by singing devotional songs for us—which both lifted our spirits and made us want to weep.

This humble and gracious man and his older daughter guided us even higher through the jungle, until we came to some large rocks on which the petroglyphs were carved. Jim interpreted for us as the father described one as a helicopter that he felt indicative of visitors from outer space. Other pictures showed animals and trees and stick figures of people. It was fascinating—as if these ancient pictures were the family's own private archeological site.

On our return to the family's home we gave them American dollars to thank them for guiding us. Jim suggested that a total of $20.00 would be appropriate, taking care not to offend. The money, more than they had seen in a long time, would feed the entire family for a good while. Don and I wished to give the children a gift, but all we had in our packs was a brush and a cap that we gave to the girls—and a small flashlight was given to the little fellow. For all the excitement over the items and the appreciation that they expressed, it would seem that we had presented them with manna from heaven itself.

We returned to our hotel feeling that we had experienced far more than the fascinating petroglyphs. These five people had showed us such joy amidst conditions that can only be described as desperate. It was an experience that we can never forget and it humbled us more than I can possibly express.

After three nights in our cabin on Lake Nicaragua, we went by local bus to another town for our final night. The bus was an old Russian truck bed with a bus body on top. It was crowded, as the buses generally are, and Don and I again found a place to sit on sacks of rice.

Our accommodations were in town at the Hotel Castillo, owned by eighty-six-year-old Don Ramon Castillo, who took us under his wing. Accommodations were much like our cabin— perhaps a bit more Spartan if that was possible, but certainly all that we needed.

A charming courtyard with tables for dining presented us with a lovely evening under the palm trees and the stars—and the food was pleasurably delicious. Don Ramon sat with us and we visited and enjoyed the moment, making another treasured deposit in our memory banks.

Don Ramon arranged for a tour of the island in a pick-up truck, providing plastic chairs for the truck's bed. We stopped at several spots, passed local people waving and shouting greetings to us, and were surrounded by beautiful scenery—and always, the volcanic mountains rising up nearby. Numerous pigs and chickens roamed amongst the yards and roads at will, and in and out of homes. It appeared that the area was open range for cattle or horses that were surrounded by this simply beautiful countryside.

We stopped at the home of a potter and took a picture of Don standing in the outdoor kitchen, the proverbial big hog lazily lying next to him, not at all concerned that he may be dinner someday.

All too soon it was morning and we were up at 5:00, to be transported in the back of Don Ramon's pick-up truck to the ferry. The ferry crossed Lake Nicaragua, again listing heavily to port, and the bilge was constantly hand-pumped just as on the trip over. Thus began our trek back to Flamingo Bay.

From the ferry landing we took a taxi to the border and then a local bus through the few kilometers of the frontier area. Jim whizzed us through the border procedures and we were soon on the long bus ride to Liberia.

Another long taxi ride transported us to Flamingo Bay. After depositing bags on *Windy Thoughts* at about 5 p.m., Don and I headed straight for "our" pool, followed by those wonderful showers, ready to resume housekeeping aboard our little home again.

My, how fresh and luxurious everything looks to us! How welcoming our own *Windy Thoughts* seems! After our little sojourn into Nicaragua, we both feel surrounded by luxuries. Marie's restaurant was like coming home, our pool was ever so nice and our own bed and our own little boat so appreciated.

How differently we look at everything after those few days! How much more we appreciate the ease of our lives, right here where we are. Perhaps we were becoming much too anxious for the conveniences of living on land again. Perhaps we needed to be reminded again of how blessed we truly are right in the here and now.

We will always be thankful for the opportunity to see beautiful Nicaragua—and especially to have walked into the life of that special family and been welcomed so warmly. Their happiness is a light amongst the many lives facing such difficulty in the aftermath of the Sandinistas. The struggle may never end for them and for so many others.

October 21, 1997
Flamingo Bay
Costa Rica

Dear Susan,

The mechanic finally arrived last week, suspecting that the valves needed grinding, as well as the head gasket replaced. Don went into a blue funk after that news, but we reminded ourselves that we're in a safe spot for facing problems.

Further investigation found that the noise seemed to be the injectors instead. Don had them cleaned and the engine now purrs along nicely. We will take the boat out in the next couple of days and give it a good run to check things out. It won't be easy to go out just for a spin, due to the way we're tied in here every which way!

Hurricane Pauline was awful. A fellow on a nearby boat has flown to the United States to collect clothes to take to his Mexican wife's village that was hard hit. Her mother is sleeping on the beach, having lost her home and restaurant. Of 1200 residences, we're told that only two homes were left standing.

We're keeping our fingers crossed for our trip north and watching weather very carefully. At present, we have the officials lined up to come to Flamingo Bay this coming Friday to clear us from Costa Rica and to get the boat out of bond. With any luck, we will be off on Saturday.

The pool remains our salvation each afternoon when we swim laps and then use the showers. Our social life includes enjoying the others on our dock. Ed and Virginia, from Chicago, have recently opened a BBQ restaurant on an old houseboat.

While all of this adds to our good life, we are most anxious to be moving on. Perhaps it is the nearness to home that prompts us to want to get to Mexico for the winter months—itchy feet that want to keep moving on toward home!

Tomorrow, we will take the boat out to check this prop pitch and afterward will anchor outside of the marina for our last few days; we will bring the dock lines back here to the dock to clean them, keeping the mess of doing so off the boat.

So far, the weather is a go and we wish we had been off this past week. The Papagayo winds seemed to have started to blow—which is a bit early. Fifty-knot winds are not uncommon, and we want to be on our way before they really start to snort. However, the marina manager reports that there should be no more than twenty-five knots of wind this time of year—and this would give us a good sail north. He has the availability of specialized weather information and assures us that though we may get Papagayo winds, we will not experience any hurricanes.

The next hurdle will be getting across the infamous Gulf of Tehuahtepec, only a few days north and just into southern Mexico. We are so close to home now. No more oceans to cross!

October 28, 1997
Update: About off!

Windy Thoughts sits at anchor out in the bay and we spent yesterday cleaning dock lines back at the dock. After ferrying the lines back and forth in the dinghy, we looped them over the lifelines to dry. Together we spent most of today diving on the bottom of the boat and it looks quite presentable again. *Windy Thoughts* does sail so much better with a clean bottom.

The officials were to be here on Friday, October 31, at 3 p.m., but the Port Captain's car wouldn't start. Their trip was aborted and we weren't about to wait until Monday. By getting off right away, we would miss the predicted strong Papagayo winds.

A man in the marina office took us to the Port Captain's office in Playa Del Cocoa, an hour away, driving so fast that even Don became nervous! After the long process involved in getting our clearance from Costa Rica, the racecar ride home no longer seemed so daunting. Hopefully, weather holding, we are off in the morning. Mexico, here we come!

November 5, 1997
Puerto Madero
Mexico

Hola,

With wall-to-wall blue skies and strong Papagayo winds reported to start within forty-two hours, we did get off in the early morning on November 1, knowing that those forty-two hours would put us north of any Papagayo threat. The timing seemed perfect.

Twenty-five knots of quartering northeast wind gave us one of the nicest sails ever, with slight seas and sailing in the lee. If the Papagayo is blowing at full strength, sailing in the lee would be of no help. The winds were steady, and with current with us we made 170 miles in our first twenty-four hours. The radio advisory warned boats to stay in harbors due to the strong fifty-knot winds, but we had sailed far enough north to be able to ignore any of the winds south in Costa Rica. Had we waited, we wouldn't have gotten out of Flamingo Bay!

Almost placid waters were the order of the day as we ambled north—and we rapidly became complacent about the good sailing conditions. Shouldn't we know better by *now*?

We sailed a straight course for Puerto Madero, Mexico, staying on the rhumb line as best we could, taking us out about sixty miles at our most distant when off Golfo de Fonseca and bringing us close into the northern coast of Guatemala after passing Nicaragua, Honduras and El Salvador. After our long R and R, it was good to be underway. We stood watches, ate, read books and did our navigation duties as we inched our way north on the charts.

The Gulf of Tehuantepec up ahead had me filled with apprehension.

However, I really tried to stay in the moment and enjoy the peace and the serenity of the sail, the blue skies and the surrounding seas. Cruising again and almost home! How bad could it be? The Tehuantepec should be one of the last of the big hurdles forever.

Never question how bad it can get!

Just after daylight on the third morning, we entered Puerto Madero at the southernmost part of the Gulf of Tehuantepec, just over the Guatemalan border. Tehuantepec storms are not known to hit until about ninety miles north following the shoreline of the bay.

The Gulf of Tehuantepec is about 250 miles across as the crow flies. But even good sized powerboats are advised not to attempt a direct crossing. It is considered best to take the long, but safer, route following close to shore up and around the Gulf—staying as absolutely tight in the lee as possible.

We had long ago decided to take the advice and follow the shoreline, even though it increased the miles considerably. The winds blow from land and create great havoc very close in, and we had no aspirations of tempting fate by racing across the Gulf to get it over with in a few days. If caught in a Tehuantepec storm, a boat is easily pushed out to sea for hundreds of miles.

Here we sit, at anchor off Puerto Madero where it is very quiet, well protected and peaceful. Just ashore we look at about fifteen restaurants, little spots with thatched roofs. Town is somewhere ashore.

Crackers, a British boat that had stopped in Flamingo Bay was sitting at anchor when we arrived. They were waiting for the present storm to abate in the Tehuantepec and shared information on how to get diesel.

We headed to shore in *Breezy* to find the lighthouse keeper's son, who was very eager to do the job—and he arranged for a truck to take us to the officials and to get diesel. Our pesos were secured after a long drive to the bank, than a stop at the small Mercado, and finally back to the beach. We have the refueling to finish before we will be ready to take on the Gulf of Tehuantepec.

Don is feeling just rotten with a sore throat and cold that he likely caught that day of last provisioning in Costa Rica, when several people on the bus were sneezing and coughing. Don says his throat hurts so much that he can't decide which is worse—not being able to breathe, or not being able to swallow. Of course, he's sweating bullets and doesn't know if it is due to the heat and humidity—or to a fever. He should be in bed.

While we were ashore, *Crackers* got an update on weather and felt the window had arrived. Winds are down to thirty knots in the Tehuantepec and they were readying to up anchor and head out. We are missing the window! Don and I shared information about staying as close to the shore as possible with one foot on the beach. We shared articles full of tidbits of advice to avoid the worst of the seas that build up fiercely very close in on a lee shore in these conditions. We said our goodbyes, hoping to meet up further in Mexico, and we set up a radio schedule for keeping contact.

Back at the boat, we found the depth sounder on the fritz again, and Don worked on it for about an hour. We will need the depth sounder in the worst way in the Gulf as we sail with the proverbial one foot on the beach.

Crackers took off early afternoon, and how we wish we were ready! But here we are, unloading fuel, hot and tired, with Don feeling just awful.

If the weather window holds, maybe tomorrow will be our day. The next stop should be Hualtuco, depending on how hammered we get. Then on to Acapulco, the crème de la crème, after which we should have no hurdles left.

Almost home—and such interesting and wonderful places yet to see!

November 19, 1997
Underway

We rather enjoyed our time in Puerto Madero, ate several meals ashore in one of the palapa restaurants, enjoying seafood and hoping that the pesky parasites don't decide to do havoc on our insides.

Twice a day for two days after *Crackers* departed, we went to the Port Captain's office to monitor weather in the Gulf of Tehuantepec. The reports were written reports, not pictures showing the isobars and pressure gradients—and we much prefer to see the isobars ourselves. In turn, we poured over our own weather faxes, comparing the two sources of information.

We were anxiously following *Crackers'* progress on our radio schedule. Two days after leaving Puerto Madero, the captain repeated several times, "Don, stay as close to the beach as you can possibly get! Yes, be sure that you can hear the dogs barking ashore!"

The lovely weather window fell apart when fifty-knot winds came right at them! After ninety miserable miles, they ducked into Salina Cruz, at the top of the Gulf, to get a good night's sleep. They radioed reports that Salina Cruz was a good port should we need to take shelter.

We would get to know Salina Cruz, but didn't know that yet. In fact, we would have much more than the Tehuantepecers with which to concern ourselves! But we didn't know that yet, either. Tehuantepecers were enough to set our hearts to racing.

The weather reports that we monitored seemed to have little to do with the actual weather conditions. Don and I were watching for a cold front to come down from Texas to give us the break that we needed. Two days later our own faxes finally showed our anticipated cold front—and yes, moving south from Texas! Just what we were looking for, and we knew that this was our weather window.

The next morning, November 8, we were off and heading into the unknown. I could tell that even Don was a bit uptight about the Gulf, imagining himself hand steering along the beach day and night without radar! Did I mention that it failed two hours out? And again, the depth sounder seemed to have forgotten how to find the bottom. No radar and no depth sounder—and planning to sail with one foot on the beach—and at night.

Well, we motored merrily along through the first day with no wind at all, the depth sounder reading a consistent twelve feet the entire time. That cold front was still moving down and we felt we should be good to go for awhile yet—and our window looked about perfect. Even I began to relax a bit and take it all in stride.

During that day the Mexican Navy stopped us. Six men from the big destroyer came alongside in a small tender, to board us for a very courteous inspection. Four of the men stood on deck with machine guns casually pointing in any and all directions as they visited amongst themselves. The head fellow and one other went below and opened a few lockers, but didn't really move anything about. I was planning on taking each and every thing out very slowly and then putting each and every thing back ever so carefully before moving on to the next locker, sure that the time involved to do this would deter them from wanting to search the entire boat—a daunting procedure because we have so much stuffed in everywhere.

We had been watching a low off central Mexico that was slowly moving north and we asked the men if updated information was available. The men left for a few minutes and then kindly returned with an updated weather report, suggesting that we take note. When we reviewed the report, we were in shock!

The low had turned south and become a tropical depression! It was 3 p.m. and our attention shifted rapidly from Tehuantepecers to this tropical depression. And what if the tropical depression deepened?

Our 6 p.m. fax showed that it had indeed deepened and was now a *tropical storm* and moving further south, the isobars closing! It is not encouraging to see isobars cozying up close to one another—and these isobars were alarmingly cozy!

I had long since given up on my relaxed attitude and was nervously counting the miles under our keel. By 10:30 p.m. we were off Point Arista. If a Tehuantepec storm was going to get us, it was likely to be here. We had no wind at all and continued motoring merrily along. Should I start relaxing now?

The sky had some lightning and there was a big ring around the moon, never before having failed its prediction of very foul weather to come. But having passed Point Arista with no winds, we were breathing big sighs of relief about Tehuantepec storms.

About five lows were popping up around us, but our big concerns were for the tropical storm bearing down on us as we pushed on through the night, constantly charting our position and peering through the dark for any obstacles that might tell us that the shoreline was closing in on us. Without the depth sounder and the radar, we did our best to sail the four and five fathom line on the chart, not exactly easy to do under the circumstances.

By morning, the 6 a.m. weather fax out of Norfolk, Virginia, shocked us to the core. The tropical storm had deepened and was now classified as *Hurricane Rick*—headed right for us and moving fast! Our stomachs turned over.

Knowing that Salina Cruz is an all-weather harbor, we pushed ahead for this safe haven at the northernmost part of the Gulf—and at the apex of the biggest winds in the Tehuantepec. And to think that I was so uptight about a Tehuantepec storm! Oh dear God, now we had a hurricane after us!

By noon, our weather fax showed that Hurricane Rick had moved 100 miles closer to us in the last six hours. We also had tons of rain all day, several squalls and horrendous looking skies. By now we had been hand steering for quite some time due to that little glitch in the autopilot, but we didn't mind, and Salina Cruz was close ahead. When a very light southerly set in we poled out the Genny to catch as much air for any lift possible. The southerly may have been welcome, but thoughts of what it may portend were not encouraging.

When we were an hour out of Salina Cruz we relaxed our vigil, knowing that we had it made. By mid-afternoon *Windy Thoughts* was entering the manmade outer harbor, offering excellent protection—but with the entrance open to the south. However, the breakwater extended out for about one-half mile at an angle and we felt that we were in good shape. The inner harbor doesn't offer moorage for small boats.

Under a horrid looking sky, we dropped anchor, set it hard and hunkered down for some good rest.

Hurricanes are not generally known to hit at Salina Cruz—famous last words.

Six hours later, at 9 p.m. the winds began to pick up alarmingly. Don was sleeping, but any little whisper of wind has me in red alert. Though we expected that we might experience some wind from the hurricane, we didn't expect anything very serious. There were no other boats about and we felt pretty much in the clear.

It got serious—very fast.

By 10 p.m. the wind was up to thirty knots and the southerly was becoming much perkier. The harbor entrance had now become the opening through which the Gulf of Tehuantepec was gushing in—and we were suddenly in seas causing the bow of the boat to plunge up and down quite dramatically, pushing us back toward the rocks.

I frantically wakened Don (who as always slept soundly, knowing I was ever alert). Don thought I was overreacting again—until he started up the companionway stairs to peer through the dark and saw the rocks very close behind us. As grogginess turned to instant reality, he realized that there was a reason the boat was jumping up and down like a rabbit—and it was looking like we might be in real trouble here.

I dissolved into tears of anxiety, assuming the boat would be on the rocks in a matter of seconds. Here we were within shouting distance of civilization, about to be in the water and unable to climb the steep rocks of the breakwater.

To be honest, for a brief moment after waking Don, I simply lost it. This was the end—drowning in the outer harbor with no one aware until morning, when what was left of *Windy Thoughts* would be seen strewn about the water. It wasn't even drowning that I was afraid of—it was the terror that I would experience as we drowned or were bashed against the rocks in an even worse demise.

It wasn't the time to fall apart. I had held up my end in far worse situations and have always done a good job of keeping my overwhelming feelings of vulnerability hidden. Don grabbed me by the shoulders to shake me, looked me straight in the eye and declared that I had to get a hold of myself—right then! I could fall apart tomorrow if I chose, but right then we had to take care of the boat.

I snapped out of it, my common sense returning as we worked to get the anchor up and move the boat immediately.

I was to keep the bow into the wind and the RPMs just high enough to keep the pressure off the chain while Don brought up the anchor. In the increasing winds it was becoming more and more difficult to keep the bow directly over the anchor. The bow just wanted to blow off one way and then the other. We weren't making any progress.

Don yelled through the screaming wind to ask if I thought I could manage the windlass while he took the helm. With Don controlling the boat, the anchor slowly but easily came up, he kept the boat off the rocks, and we bumped and bounced along to the narrow entrance into the inner harbor.

Oh, such a relief to be in relatively calm waters—but there was no place for us to go! Big ships were tied to high piers and were lit up like Christmas, running lights on and engines running—their captains knowing what was to come. With wind rising continually we circled the harbor, frantically looking for anything to tie to—and noticed a fuel barge tied up against a ship. If I jumped at just the right time, I could land on the barge and get the boat tied to it. I raced to get fenders and lines out as copious amounts of rain poured down on us.

The wind-speed indicator was reading fifty knots and was gusting higher—wind that would hit us beam-on the windward side, holding us off from the barge. Not the ideal situation since I had to jump onto the barge—and if I missed, I would be in the drink and Don would have more to cope with than just controlling the boat. Then again, fifty knots of wind bashing us against the barge wouldn't be a pleasant situation either.

Don was reminding me that I had a split second to secure the boat to the one big cleat that we saw on the barge. Once this was accomplished, we would hope to find something else to secure to. His was the more difficult job and he was concentrating on controlling the boat in the high winds, trying to get us close enough to the barge so that I could jump across to it. Well, jump up to it, to be exact.

Suddenly, we realized that a voice on the VHF radio, in accented but good English, was calling for the sailboat going around in circles out there. Gosh, that was us! A big fishing boat down at the other end of the harbor was calling us to come down and tie to them. They shined a high beam light to show us where they were located.

We high tailed it out of there and headed right toward that light, narrowly managing to miss hitting a shallow bottom near the fishing boat's stern as Don concentrated on maneuvering in very constricted space—in wind that was now sixty knots on our stern. Sixty knots behind us that could push us into other big fishing boats moored stern-to and perpendicular to the bow of our fishing boat. The entire crew of our helpful fishermen was up on deck in full rain gear and ready for our lines.

We came alongside the fishing boat with its sides looming above us, big tires hanging down. Don screamed at me to not grab onto one, instinctive as it would be to attempt to stop the boat in any way possible. It is impossible to stop a boat of our weight by grabbing onto anything.

Better to ram the boats in front of us than get an arm or body caught between the boats.

Five welcoming fellows on deck up above were ready for us when Don put the gear into reverse. All lines were at the ready, and I gave a mid-ship line a mighty hurl straight up, aiming right for the eyes of the waiting fisherman. A gal taught me this in Seattle when we first had the boat. Aim for the eyes. Don let go of the helm just long enough to do the same with the stern line while I made a second hurl with the bowline. Waiting hands grabbed our lines on the first try and before we knew it the lines were securely wrapped— and *Windy Thoughts* had come to a stop.

It was over.

There was much scrambling about to adjust lines and fenders, and the tires were let further down so they too would come between *Windy Thoughts* and the hull of the fishing boat. More lines were run back and forth—and when at last we were secure and the frantic scrambling about was finished, we called our heartfelt thankfulness up to the men above.

The fellow who spoke English called down to tell us that we weren't to worry—just get below. All was secure. Being the courageous person that I am, at that point I rushed below to collapse so as not to have a public nervous breakdown. No more worries. If anything happened to the boat in here, there were lots of strong men to assist Don. We would not succumb to the sea in the outer harbor after all.

Don assured me that I wasn't needed on top while he went up and down constantly to check on things as the winds increased, the inner harbor alive with the frenzied wind. The boat could not have withstood this onslaught out in the outer harbor. Below, it sounded like a freight train was barreling down on us and the noise was deafening. I curled up into the fetal position and let the world and this hurricane go by. I didn't have to be quite so brave any longer. Don wouldn't be alone.

When the winds peaked out at 100 knots, or 125 mph, Don had to put on diving goggles and crouch as low as possible to crawl forward along the deck against the wind. Our Mexican angel was up there, standing in the window of the wheelhouse. It was impossible to communicate by voice because of the noise of the wind, but he motioned to Don to go below where it was safer. They were keeping a watch on our lines as well as their own.

Angels were watching over us.

With the wind coming directly on our stern, *Windy Thoughts* didn't bash against the hull of the fishing boat. About midnight the eye of Hurricane Rick passed over, and all was eerily silent and quiet for a few minutes before the wind made its 180-degree turn to come directly on our bow, to blow itself out a few hours later. When it was finally over, both Don and I crawled into our berth to fall into the soundest of sleeps.

Windy Thoughts was safe at last.

A wonderful, soothing sense washed over us in the stillness, along with it a strong sense of gratefulness for having been so fortunate. All I could think about was that we would soon be home, no longer living on the edge. Things could have played out far differently.

Oh, the highs and the lows, they come and they go. Let it never be said that the cruising life is boring!

Amazingly, there had been no problems on deck. The bimini and the solar panels were still secure. Earlier in the afternoon we had made sure that all was tied down securely and Don had run line around the forestay, bringing the roller furling up as tightly as possible. Fortunately, this had prevented the sail from unfurling. We were stunned that we had experienced 100 knot winds and sustained no real damage!

Angels disguised as Mexican fishermen had come out of the dark and stormy night to beckon us to safety and we had survived the onslaught of Hurricane Rick.

San Andreas, the blessed fishing boat, wasn't, in morning's light, the most beautiful boat ever seen. But she was beautiful in our eyes and was the best kept in the harbor, a good and strong boat, immaculate and well run. Armando was the English-speaking fellow who had shepherded us in the night before. When we first stepped up into our cockpit, he was there above us, greeting us with a big smile of welcome. Armando invited us up and let down a ladder for us to climb aboard.

Armando, the cook and one of a crew of six, took us on a tour of the boat. It was very nicely finished inside, the pride that the crew took in the boat very obvious. Armando and the crew were happy to have us tied to them because it prevented other fishing vessels from doing so—most of which were big rust buckets. The *San Andreas* was in the harbor awaiting dry-dock time.

Our mutual friendship with Armando was immediate. Armando had worked as a cook in Seattle, thus his command of English! Armando's wife and fifteen-month-old daughter live up north in Ensenada and a new baby had been born a few days before we arrived. Oh, how Armando missed his family, and he called his wife every day. Armando hoped that he might get home for a week soon and wanted to take his wife and babies to Puerta Vallarta for a vacation. We were excited about the possibilities of meeting there this winter and we exchanged addresses.

Throughout the hurricane we had grave concern for *Crackers* at anchor in Hualtuco, sixty miles ahead and wide open to the south. When we got no response from several anxious radio attempts over the two days following the hurricane, we worried that the worst had happened. We were overwhelmed with relief when we finally made contact.

Crackers had ridden out the hurricane without any major damage! Expecting to take a direct hit but with several hours to prepare, the couple had set two anchors, removed every bit of canvas—sails, dodger and bimini—and sunk the dinghy. They now faced the chore of putting everything back together.

Salina Cruz is a working port with big ships and a large fishing fleet. After the hurricane we were anxious to go ashore for a look about town. The storm had caused some flooding that was already abating, but surprisingly, we saw little other damage other than some trees down and things blown about—a few windows out and a few damaged roofs. Most buildings were built from concrete and structural damage was minimal—at least what we could see. A big clean-up effort was underway.

Tacos, burritos and other savory delights were sold in the many sidewalk stands, looking inviting, and we ate on the streets. Will we be sorry?

Along with the fishing boats we stayed in Salina Cruz for eight days before the port was opened again. Armando joined us on our jaunts into town and we made visits back and forth between the *San Andreas* and *Windy Thoughts*.

When we were ready to head out, Armando insisted on filling our water tanks from the *San Andreas*—and urged us to wash *Windy Thoughts* with a hose hooked up just for us! The crew was very particular about their fresh water and didn't want us to haul drinking water from the town.

Don took our Auto Helm 7000 autopilot out and replaced it with the spare 5000. However, when we tested the 5000 it refused to steer correctly, wanting only to go to starboard, no matter how many adjustments Don made. No matter: we would hand steer to Acapulco, only about four days distant. We were past the Papagayos and the worst of the Gulf, and had survived a hurricane. The rest of our journey should be a piece of cake!

On the morning of November 20, we were up bright and early to motor through the harbor until clearing the outer breakwater. Sails were set in the wing and wing position for a downwind run with a very nice fifteen knot wind. About four miles out, Don took the companionway stairs off to check the rubber doughnut and the bolt that goes through the shaft.

Cracked again and in four places! The discovery turned our hearts and stomachs upside down. We turned around and tacked toward the entrance, turning the engine on only at the very last moment—to limp in with expectations that we would lose everything at any moment.

Don wanted to drop the hook in the outer harbor, sure that we wouldn't make it any farther. I had mental images of trying to fix the boat in this obscure Mexican port and not going home for a very long time—if ever—and begged Don to give the inner harbor a try.

Windy Thoughts did make it to the inner harbor and all the way to the *San Andreas* but no one was aboard, nor had we raised them on the radio. The plan was that I leap onto a three-inch ledge as we came along side, climb rapidly onto one of the tires, hurl myself over the top and get a line around something—one chance only. Don wasn't expecting anything below to hold up much longer. Don would slow the boat by putting the engine into reverse at precisely the right moment. But the ledge was too narrow and the wind was blowing us off.

At precisely that right moment, Don discovered that there was *no reverse*!

Windy Thoughts happily rolled past the *San Andreas*, her bow headed for the fishing boat moored perpendicular to the *San Andreas*—and only a few feet in front of us. Don let go of the wheel, leaped onto our cabin top and then up to the closest tire. He was up the rope and over the rail of the *San Andreas* in about one second flat, a mooring line in hand. Those few seconds provided enough time for *Windy Thoughts*' bow to crash into the boat ahead—leaving a dent in the stainless steel end of our bowsprit, and one in the fishing boat. But the strength of the bowsprit stopped us.

The fishermen aboard rapidly flew from below when we hit. I apologized profusely but they just smiled and motioned that all was OK. Quite frankly, there were so many dents on the hull that a couple more weren't noticeable. The men wouldn't discuss any compensation for the damage, so I baked them a cake the next day.

Don had managed to get a line around a cleat on the *San Andreas* and I quickly threw others up to him. Once secured, we sat down in the cockpit and nearly cried, feeling shaken and blue. We pictured a winter stuck in Salina Cruz rather than in Puerta Vallarta with cable TV and all the other dock amenities that we had been so looking forward to. We weren't ready to contemplate solving this problem here in Salina Cruz.

Angels to the rescue! Armando soon returned from town. Don was in his usual strategic position over the engine, setting to work taking off the doughnut. Armando came aboard with the *San Andreas*' nineteen year-old engineer and mechanic, assuring us that the young man could fix our engine. No worries! Our communication with the young man was entirely through Armando, who translated every word. But we both instinctively trusted Armando's judgment.

The young mechanic went to work on the engine and we were promised that it would make it all the way to Seattle. Thank the good Lord we weren't going that far! Don found the one spare doughnut that he had aboard and by day's end miracles had occurred.

In one day's time our moods swung from near depression to elation. Once again, as with so many things in our cruising life, the lows are so low and the highs are so high. We seem to vacillate between the two with fair regularity, don't we?

The next morning we set off for Acapulco on a good sail, with twenty-five knot winds for the first forty miles. For eight hours we kept busy hand steering in very lively seas, but when we reached the northern end of the Gulf of Tehuantepec the wind dropped instantly. It was necessary to use the engine for most of the remaining passage to Acapulco, keeping us on pins and needles. Worried about the doughnut, we would rather have been sailing.

As hours and days ticked off, our concerns about the young engineer's abilities abated.

Hand steering for four days wasn't difficult in the easy seas, just boring and certainly not on the list of the worst of things that could be encountered. We were almost home!

We continued our six-hour watch schedule and were thankful for easy conditions, though the boat rolled in the swell much more uncomfortably than when under sail. On my night watches I sang every song that I could remember to fill in the time. Don relates that on his night watch he contemplated about things, mostly about the engine.

December 12, 1997
Beautiful Acapulco
Mexico

Hello Susan,

Acapulco has stolen our hearts for the past three weeks. Entering Acapulco Bay just before dark on November 23, we were quite taken aback by the exquisite setting, with Acapulco glistening in the last of the sun's rays and the mountains rising up so majestically behind the city. Drawn in immediately, we knew that we would like it here.

A lovely new marina welcomed us, not far from the older one. It has a beautiful pool and a very nice staff, is somewhat pricey but Don has humored them into lowering the cost to some extent.

Life has been so good to us here and we have let go of the "hurry up and get to Puerta Vallarta" idea. After hearing how crowded it is, we are not as anxious to spend *all* of our winter in Puerta Vallarta, and have moved into vacation mode as the last hurrah of our cruising life.

The Auto Helm 7000 computer box was sent to the States from here and returned to us three days ago—but still didn't work! Don called the office in New Hampshire and we have now sent in the linear drive unit as well. We don't mind being here for a bit longer because we are thoroughly enjoying this lovely city.

There is absolutely no sign of Hurricane Pauline's havoc in Acapulco but we have listened to countless stories about how bad the hurricane was. A tremendous cleanup job was finished in just two weeks of hard work that was taken on by a good many of Acapulco's population. Everything looks beautiful and tourists are everywhere.

The marina is in a quiet area, and an inexpensive Volkswagen taxi (VWs that are made right here in Mexico) takes us to the main shopping area. We first set our sights on a Hard Rock Café hamburger, but it wasn't very good and we haven't returned. We took a peek inside Planet Hollywood with its weird music and decorations and knew that we weren't interested in that either. Are we getting old? There are movie theatres, any number of nice restaurants, good supermarkets and a huge public market that is closer to us.

The more traditional Acapulco appeals to us and we are eating our way through each day, filling ourselves with good Mexican fare. We amble about in the small shops and in the public market, amazed at the amount of produce and goods available.

Armando had told us about bus service from Acapulco to Mexico City. One late afternoon (the day before Thanksgiving) we made a quick decision to take the bus, and on Thanksgiving morning we were off. Truth is, we thought Thanksgiving had been the week before and weren't aware that it was turkey day.

The bus was nothing short of sheer elegance, with a stewardess at our service. An immaculate bathroom, a movie, reclining seats with foot rests, and cold drinks and snacks served made it all seem first class—so much nicer than any airplane. It was a five-hour trip to Mexico City, very scenic and very comfortable. We sat back and luxuriated in comfort and enjoyed the scenery outside our window. Someone else was doing the driving and we had no navigation duties, sailing duties or watches to keep. We felt so pampered.

Mexico City is a fascinating and cosmopolitan city! After the luxurious bus ride, a cab driver took us to a comfortable and economical hotel that he recommended that turned out to be a jewel in the middle of downtown. Our travel advice is, "Just ask the cabbies."

After settling in we were off to the streets and to a nearby restaurant—where we were handed a menu presenting a choice of traditional American Thanksgiving dinner along with the other fine entrees. Thanksgiving? This is how we learned that it was Thanksgiving Day! We celebrated with turkey, gravy and dressing—topped off with traditional pumpkin pie! It was the start of a wonderful few days for us.

The temperatures were cooler here, in the low eighty degrees and very comfortable. Nattily dressed business people scurried about their days in this upbeat and busy city.

We immediately fell in love with Mexico City and had two things that we wanted to see—the Anthropological Museum and the pyramids. There were art galleries to stroll through, lovely sidewalk areas with shops filled with beautiful items and many good restaurants.

Having visited the Great Pyramids of Egypt, we wanted to see the great archeological site at Teotihuacan, with the largest pyramids in the western hemisphere. It was about a forty-five-minute bus ride to the population center that rose around the time of Christ, a highly planned city that seems to have functioned as a well-developed urban center for centuries.

The Avenue of the Dead, the very wide main street (about forty meters in some sections, as much as ninety in others), divided the city into two areas with pyramidal structures forming apartment compounds. Rising on the east side of the Avenue of the Dead in the northern half of the city is the Sun Pyramid. Ritual activities are said to have been conducted in a cave here. The pyramid is 225 meters along each side and about sixty-three meters high—with five huge stepped platforms.

The Pyramid of the Moon is located at the extreme northern end of the Avenue of the Dead and faces south. Archaeologists are excavating this pyramid to discover if any other structures might be within its walls.

The Ciudadela is at the geographic center of the city, an enclosure whose main plaza could easily hold 100,000 people—and whose central pyramid is the Feathered Serpent Pyramid.

Teotihuacán is every bit as fascinating as the Great Pyramids of Egypt, vast in size and oh so interesting! We spent most of the day walking about the ruins of this ancient city.

Another high point of Mexico City is the Anthropological Museum. An armed guard stood at the entrance of a special display of pottery behind glass. A small bowl sat by itself in a place of honor. The bowl had the same three little rodent shaped feet and was identical to one that had most interested Don when perusing those treasures found by our innkeeper back on Isla Ometepe, in Nicaragua. The bowl was excavated in Nicaragua—and dated back 2,500 years. Perhaps that little treasure so intriguing at Isla Ometepe was from the same era!

On Saturday a "Walk of Silence" in downtown Mexico City protested crime, as well as corruption in the police force. The route was down the main street that was closed to traffic and we found that we couldn't get back to our hotel.

We set out on foot and walked along with the reported group of 50,000 people. It would have been easy to get caught up in the occasion and we might have joined right in with those who were shouting at the police—but thought better of it and trooped along until we got to our hotel. I did manage a sneer once just to test my wings, but Don quickly suggested that this wasn't our battle and that we'd best concentrate on reaching our hotel!

In beautiful Acapulco we continue to feel as if we are on vacation, the fabulous marina and pool like a five-star resort and a quiet and welcome place after our forays about Acapulco during the day. And our own home awaits us right here. Several years ago when we first entertained the idea of cruising, Don told me that it would be like having our own condo to take anywhere in the world with us. How very true! *Windy Thoughts* has made us the most comfortable home no matter where she rests.

December 29, 1997
Still in Acapulco

Merry Christmas!

Our Christmas was rather quiet, because after all of the bragging about our eating habits in Mexico, Don and I are both down with bad cases of amoebas. I have been sicker than a dog for what seems like forever and Don is starting to suffer in the past few days. We did eat on the streets in Salina Cruz and wonder if that was the source. But we have been eating out often in Acapulco, perhaps overconfident in the white linen tablecloths and napkins!

I spent an entire week in bed until the evening of December 21—so sick that Don got me dressed (doing a respectable job of picking out an outfit, far more capable than he lets on), dragged me up into the cockpit and onto the dock.

With bucket in hand he led me out to the road, where we waited for a taxi. I sat on the curb with head in my hands, bucket and purse beside me and barely lucid. I did know, however, that I didn't want to leave my purse behind on the boat. After all, what if I should need to comb my hair? Not that I cared a whit about hair right then, but one must always be prepared!

Off we whizzed to the hospital, where with Don on one side of me and the taxi driver on the other, they ushered me into emergency, the bucket swinging along with us. Emergency was full to overload with people waiting to be seen, but it was only a short time before we were taken into the examining area.

While lying on the table I had a few more lucid thoughts rolling around in my mind in sync with my rolling stomach—when I suddenly realized that I had no idea where my purse was. While I was thinking that it might be nice to see my maker rather than continue on, Don nearly went into apoplexy over my missing purse. *How could I just lose it?*

While Don went off to Admitting, in a frantic attempt to make himself understood that a purse was missing, I was getting hooked up to IVs and feeling quite poorly.

In Admitting, who should come walking in the door at that very moment but the cab driver with my purse in hand! Every peso was in my purse, as well as my Visa card and identification. More Mexican angels watching over us! Don gave the driver all of the pesos in my purse, so thankful were we for his kindness and honesty.

Tests confirmed that I had the bad amoeba, and I was led to a hospital room for the remaining twenty-four hours on the IV with its various medications. After settling in, I insisted that Don go to the boat and get some rest. I couldn't communicate with anyone and felt much too sick to enjoy my little R &R.

At 11:00 on the following night my doctor came in to see me. I understood that if I wanted to get out of jail right then I was free to go. He handed me several medications and within an hour I was discharged.

Though I felt very rocky, I got myself to the front entry, into a cab and back to the marina. As I stumbled into the cockpit, slid back the hatch cover and began removing the screens, Don awoke with a start. Who was boarding us in the middle of the night? It was just me. Nothing is better than your own bed when you're feeling like the pits.

I have spent the past week lying in bed twenty-four hours a day due to the strong medication—and perhaps feeling even sicker than before my sojourn to the hospital. The good news is that I am finally on the mend, even if not quite ready to kick up my heels yet!

When Don started with his symptoms a few days ago the marina manager mentioned a lab nearby; hopefully, his has been caught soon enough that he won't have a long bout. I am getting better but Don is just beginning the fight. In addition, that cold and cough in Puerto Madero chased us up here and we are passing the cough syrup back and forth.

The Auto Helm office in New Hampshire closed due to snow, but supposedly we are on the priority list. Their diagnosis is that something is seriously wrong. If the repair proves to be too complicated, we will have the unit shipped back as is and continue to hand steer from here. As much as we have enjoyed Acapulco, it is time to move on.

February 6, 1998
Las Hadas, Manzanillo
Mexico

Hello dear friend,

Another New Year has begun and we have no more oceans to cross, no more big passages. Just this meandering up Mexico's west coast and stopping at all of the wonderful spots that we have always heard so much about. So far, the autopilot is working fine, and we treasure our third mate.

Windy Thoughts sits at anchor off the beautiful Las Hadas Hotel, where for $4.00 a day we have use of every facility at this fabulous resort plus the privacy of our own home gently bobbing out on the water. Those beautiful white buildings of Las Hadas rise from the hillside and the atmosphere is quite posh for these two old sailors. *Breezy* takes us the short distance through the breakwater entrance to the small marina—where she rests at the dinghy dock while we lounge about the pool, use the showers, or wander off to town. Now that we are about to call it a day, we are on vacation and treating ourselves.

The weather is perfect in the mid eighties, with cold nights dropping into the mid- sixties—excellent for sleeping and no fans are required! Blankets are on our berth and we cozy down beneath them at night.

The only glitch comes when an occasional powerboat unloads the jet skis and races about the huge bay. Some of them are very insensitive to the serenity of an anchorage. Ashore most of the day, we are thankful to be away from most of the noise.

We left Acapulco after six wonderful weeks (discounting the two weeks of sickbay) and headed north to settle into the very nice marina just north of Zihuatenejo and around the point at Ixtapa, where potable water is advertised. From here, a fifteen-minute bus ride brought us into Z-Town (also referred to as Zihuat) each day.

Doesn't Zihuatenejo just have a ring to its name? Like Constantinople, the syllables just roll off your tongue. Christmas was a big celebration here amongst the cruising crowd and many headed here to anchor off Z-Town. We loved this small Mexican town with its shops and restaurants—and we played tourists to our heart's content.

Ixtapa itself is a bit sterile looking with everything so new and very up-scale. It could be any resort anywhere, but no complaints on our part! The tourists from the hotels seem to stick to the pools, seldom venturing onto the beautiful white sandy beaches that are absolutely pristine. We had the beach all to ourselves as we walked along, toes curling in the sand, breathing in cruising at its best—knowing there may be few times left to do so in this cruising life that is nearly over.

Excellent restaurants were only a jaunt up the dock. What will it be like where restaurants have doors and windows to hold us inside—instead of wide-open areas without walls, letting the breezes flow through? At one, the proprietor sold us four new plates that were hand painted with sailboats especially for the restaurant. The plates will be a very special remembrance of our days in the sun.

Nothing has broken down recently and Don has been playing tourist. Well, nothing except the windlass that he is presently working on.

Whoops! Don just called below to announce that something is wrong with the solar panels—that have never once given us an ounce of trouble. He is checking things out now. Don also reports that the refrigerator has suddenly decided not to work. Horrors! Must we revert to monastic cruising mode just when we consider ourselves on vacation?

The local Mexican people are very close to our hearts. Yesterday we joined four other cruising couples at a cantina in Manzanillo, well away from the tourist haunts. It was to be our "cultural experience" day and we had first headed to the Museum, only to find it closed. We would go to the cantina instead.

At the cantina, only drinks are purchased and the food just keeps coming all afternoon, with entertainment at 4 p.m. It was a very Mexican experience and we loved every minute of it. Ate to our stomachs' content and laughed and sang and joined in with the many moms and dads, children from babies on up in age and grandmas and grandpas—all packed into the cantina and all having fun. Surely, this was a far better and more interesting cultural experience than the Museum!

The renowned Las Hadas golf course is a destination for many avid golfers. One couple joined us for dinner at a mountaintop restaurant where our table sat out on a cliff—with the ocean waves crashing against the shore below and candles and lanterns lighting our vista. Music by Enya played softly in the background. It was an evening to remember, a very significant one near the end of our cruising life. Is it really almost over?

Don purchased the Enya CD and we listen to it on the boat—haunting melodies that will always bring back memories of our lovely evening—and memories of life aboard *Windy Thoughts* and the magic that she has brought us over the years.

Thoughts of arriving in the Northwest are becoming more real every day. Excited as we are at being in our islands for the summer, we realize that it won't be easy putting the boat back together after shipping it north. Our last five-acre tract on Lake Spokane just sold, the one on which sits the building storing nearly all of our earthly goods—so we must face getting our goods moved immediately. Don wants to get home as soon as possible to tackle these chores and still have some summer left to enjoy.

Life goes on, but we cannot yet contemplate how different it will be.

With all of the excitement of bringing *Windy Thoughts* home, realities are setting in that this special way of life is almost over for us. No more blue water sailing and no more sunsets at sea. No more peaceful anchorages, *Windy Thoughts* bobbing gently in the breeze as we gaze out at yet another new and special spot in our world.

After sharing with you all of my personal feelings and failings over the years, I am compelled to share that it will be the end of something very meaningful to Don and me, two people united together in a distinct and unique way.

February 14, 1998
Puerta Vallarta
Mexico

Hola and Happy Valentine's Day,

Puerta Vallarta Marina is home to us these past days, and we have only to walk up the ramp to be at a mini market. How convenient is that?

This marina is well organized, with shops, restaurants and condos surrounding it, so it is not exactly getting away from it all—but we are still in our vacation mode. It is very quiet and peaceful and we are away from the bustle of the touristy areas of Puerta Vallarta. A short bus ride takes us to the busy shopping area—and very busy it is!

After those fifteen wonderful days hanging off Las Hadas Hotel, we forced ourselves to up anchor and move on to Barra Navidad. And oh—what a very special little spot it is.

Well inside a large bay, negotiating an opening much like a small river channel was very much like taking *Windy Thoughts* through shallow rapids. Our hearts were in our mouths until we found ourselves in the calm and narrow waterway that leads well in to the lagoon anchorage. And what to our wondering eyes should appear just to starboard—but a new hotel and a brand new marina as well!

Make no mistake, it was Don who commanded his first mate to get on the radio and contact the marina. There were only two boats on the dock and we were given a choice slip for only $15.00! We forced ourselves to stay two nights while we lolled about the pool and took a shore boat over to the village that we found delightful. The hotel is a full five-star resort, impeccably kept and incredibly beautiful. We saw very few guests and felt that we had it all to ourselves.

Barra Navidad is a secret jewel known to a handful of Americans who come for the winter. There are not the crowds of people here, though some have purchased newly developed condos. Will the town change? Just the word condo seems to forebode changes to come.

Just to let you know that we are still cruising people and not marina hoppers, we did anchor out a few times on the way north. Tenacatita was a lovely bay in which to drop the hook and savor the gentle Mexican sunset—while sitting in the cockpit in total peacefulness, remembering that there won't be many more of these special times. We took the dinghy a long way up a river to a spot where we purchased cold drinks in frosted glasses, sold under a little palapa—a wonderful contrast to fancy resorts. Never has something icy cold tasted so good.

Puerta Vallarta's marina complex is very nice, even though it feels like we are in San Diego. Only a handful of masts are seen across the dock's horizon. This is a popular place for powerboats, primarily from the States, and there is no real cruising atmosphere. We would have missed so much had we just scooted north to Puerta Vallarta before we switched gears and lollygagged our way along.

It is fairly cool, but will eighty degrees ever seem cool to us when back in the Northwest?

The welcoming temperatures put us to work polishing the topsides. Unable to find a spot to get the rugs cleaned, we took them onto the dock, and with the cold-water hose, a soft brush and Woolite, brushed them clean. After much rinsing, we hung them dripping wet over the lifelines to dry—and they look professionally done.

Popping in and out of the tourist shops in Puerta Vallarta is fun. We were especially fascinated with a shop that features the beaded work done by the Huichole Indians from northern Jalisco and eastern Nayarit—in a mountainous region crossed by the Occidental Sierra Madra in elevations of up to three thousand meters above sea level. The Huicholes have their own language with only slight variations in the dialects.

Their narrative contains a good number of stories, among them stories about their own deities, the stars, floods, and legends of their heroes. They include their beliefs and culture in this colorful beaded work that is done on gourds. In their native villages they are often taken advantage of in the pricing of their distinct and labor intensive works of art.

When we found the particular shop that employs a few to do their art right there and gives them a very fair wage, we wanted to purchase a remembrance for ourselves. The Huichole art work is found in other shops in Puerta Vallarta, but in most cases the artist receives little compensation. We selected a bull's head, as well as a sun/moon piece signifying marriage.

Mazatlan:

Windy Thoughts has moved north to Mazatlan and sits ready to jump across the Sea of Cortez, back to our old stomping grounds in La Paz. It is hard to believe that we left there all those years ago. Did we dream the past years? No—the pictures are too sharp and too vivid in our minds to have been a dream.

Mazatlan has been a quiet respite after playing tourist at the resorts. And yes, we are luxuriating at another marina, a new one that, when completed, will have moorage for 1,000 boats. The docks, office and showers are completed and a few slips have electrical hook-ups and water. The rates are very reasonable. It is a 180 degree turn from PV, because the establishment targets cruising sailboats. There is a vastly different feeling, one of adventure and dreams of faraway places.

A former cruising sailor, the marina manager is attuned to our needs. Many use the office to plug in laptops and check on email. A mail drop is provided, as are any number of services. A vegetable truck comes every morning with beautiful produce, as well as eggs and fresh bread. An Italian restaurant truck comes on Wednesdays at noon and sets up take-out lasagna, calzones and enchiladas. Is your mouth watering yet?

We like using the term cruising people again and seem to have eased back into it naturally when we left the more international group—where the term yacht refers to a sailboat and yachtie to the sailor. Here, these words conjure up visions of grandeur, something not usually compatible with the cruising life! Or is it all just the way that you look at life? Because grandeur has befallen Don and me on an enormous scale, the grandeur of maintaining the cruising lifestyle so special to us.

Today is St. Patrick's Day and it has been years since we have celebrated this fun holiday. A big party was held here at the marina, with a roast pig, potatoes, cooked carrots and cabbage, salad, and bolillos, those wonderful Mexican rolls. And cake for dessert!

In the morning, a priest went about the marina in a small dinghy and blessed each boat. It was very touching and much appreciated. A special day surrounded by fellow cruising people again and sharing experiences, plans and stories. There are always stories to share!

While immersed in the delights of resort life over the past several weeks we have missed the cruising community. Give us a good ole cruising crowd any day to bring us back to our *Windy Thoughts* and all of the reasons that we chose this lifestyle. What a life it has been! I do believe that I am getting teary-eyed just thinking of how close we are now to swallowing the anchor. We both relish the thought—we are both saddened by the thought. Will we never be satisfied?

Much of our cruising gear has been unloaded here at Mazatlan. A young couple purchased the wind vane. The plastic Davis sextant that we carried in our overboard bag went to a couple who have the same stars in their eyes that we had all those years ago. Don's Tamaya Spica sextant is a keeper.

It was very hard to pass along our flags from countries visited, but the time has come. With us, the flags would likely go into storage, never to happily fly above someone's boat as it arrived in a new and magical country.

We sorted out the charts that are special to us and passed along the rest to a couple who were elated to get them. Cruising guides, we have kept. We can look back on them and dream about places and people that have been such a wonderful part of our lives over the years. The memories of storms, long night watches and the trials and tribulations that are a part of this life are now taking on the aura of true adventure. Oh, the stories to be told!

Surprisingly, not many boats are jumping off for the Pacific. Many are hanging about Mexico and some are hugging the coast south to Panama—to head through the canal toward the Caribbean. Wrong way! Go west, young man, go west! But each must sail his own boat and there are adventures ahead for all, adventures that most have only dreamed of.

We see the eagerness and the anticipation, as well as the apprehension for such an undertaking, and know exactly what they are feeling—because the feelings never end.

We leave in the morning to cross the Sea of Cortez toward La Paz. The northerlies haven't fully abated yet, but we think we can bump along on one tack and hope to be there in two days.

La Paz—the City of Peace. Was it eight years ago almost to the day that we left there to cross the Pacific Ocean? Did we really leave Seattle *ten* years ago? It is becoming so surreal. So much cruising gear off-loaded, La Paz so close and then just a short jaunt up to San Carlos—where *Windy Thoughts* can proudly take her bows and say goodbye to blue water cruising and come to rest at home in our islands. And oh, does she deserve a rest after all of the magic she has given us.

March 20, 1998
Pichilinque Bay
Just outside La Paz,
Baja, Mexico

Dear Friend,

At exactly 7:45 a.m. today we crossed our outward-bound track ten miles out of La Paz, at twenty-four degrees, sixteen minutes N latitude, 110 degrees, thirty minutes W longitude.

We have done it—circumnavigated the world! Just the two of us, with our beloved *Windy Thoughts*— and ten years of joy, terror and hard work. Yes, the highs were oh, so very high—and the lows sometimes oh, so very low. But the adventure that we shared together is something that we will cherish forever.

Don sprinted down below to emerge with a bottle of champagne hidden in the bilge. I am afraid that I somewhat spoiled the occasion with shock that he would consider opening this at 7:45 a.m. I feel bad that I reacted so when he was so very excited, as was I. After all, we are not likely to complete a circumnavigation ever again! None of this great adventure would ever have been realized were it not for him.

Rather than going right into La Paz, we pulled into the quiet bay of Pichilinque, a few miles out, in order to give the boat bottom a good cleaning. Good old Pichilinque. It is so hard to believe that we are really back here after so much water has passed under our keel. All of the recent months of feeling almost home, all of the excitement to get here.

We are both feeling very blessed to have safely made it all the way around and are not sure whether to shout for joy or cry with sadness.

I have shared so much with you as we bounced and bobbed along on this dream of ours, the good as well as the bad. A shoulder to cry on, the first person I thought of when there were wonders to tell about, and the person to whom I sat down and spilled out my heart when things weren't going well—

and all done at long, long distance. Thank you for being a dear friend.

Tomorrow morning, we will wend our way into La Paz.

March 21, 1998
La Paz
Baja, Mexico

Hola,

It is nearly impossible to express the joy of being back in La Paz. We are feeling quite privileged as we treat ourselves to a night or two in a berth at Marina De La Paz before moving out to anchor as we did all of those years before. We are on sensory overload after the luxuries enjoyed while vacationing on Mexico's mainland coast.

Mary is still in the marina office and La Paz doesn't seem to have changed a great deal. But we have cable TV here on the dock! The marina has a restaurant now as well as new laundry, showers and a chandler. All good changes, though maybe a bit posh compared to the "old days".

A new hotel sits just next door, with a breakwater and several nice restaurants along the water. We have chosen the one for our celebration dinner and plan to get ourselves all gussied up. Downtown seems about the same, other than some new paint in a few places.

Old Abe's boat isn't in the anchorage anymore and we suppose that he has gone where all old sailors go, as he was in ill health when we left.

We have already headed for lunch at our favorite fish taco spot downtown—still there, the same white cart and the same family running it, attired in their white aprons and hats. Best of all—the same excellent fish tacos, with the only change a price increase from twenty-five cents to fifty cents.

Don and I stuffed ourselves until we could eat no more—and then topped it off with a visit to the ice cream parlor, still there and unchanged. We truly enjoy La Paz after the glitzy tourism of the mainland and feel home again. We are so close now!

Our plans are to enjoy La Paz for about a week before setting off for San Carlos, about 300 miles north and on the mainland. Though it will be a quick trip north, we hope to take about three weeks, making a few stops for old time's sake. The northerlies may slow us down some.

Don called Barry McCormick in Seattle today. Barry commissioned *Windy Thoughts* when we first took possession of her. Cruising Yachts has changed hands since we left and Barry is working independently. He has been a lifeline whenever we needed something for the boat and will be available to help Don rig the boat and to do some special jobs on the boat for us.

Barry told us that he could get us a berth at the former Cruising Yachts, the same docks from which we left! His exact words were, "Just come home now!"

The boat will be trucked to the Canal Boat Yard just outside the Hiram Chittenden Locks. We have a little glitch in the engine to sort out, discovered as we came over from Mazatlan when power-sailing against the wind, pointing high enough to make it across on one tack. Don is checking over the prop pitch as I write, still concerned that the pitch is too high.

Don thinks we will be home in about a month. Home—imagine that!

Chapter 17

The End of One Dream

In the end, it is the magic that grabs a hold on you and remains imbedded in your soul forever.

This account of the spark to our imaginations that soon grew into the re-alization of our dream ends where it began. The phone call to San Carlos changed our plans for the celebration dinner in La Paz and for meandering visits to old favorite haunts. We dropped everything, threw off the dock lines and sped up the Sea of Cortez to San Carlos, where *Windy Thoughts* was hauled out—and then trucked the short distance to the boat yard.

As soon as we arrived in the yard, we worked feverishly, stripping *Windy Thoughts* of everything on deck. Don and I dismantled the solar panels and the bimini top, and we quickly moved to dismantle the framework. The hot sun blazed down on us and we accomplished as much as possible before calling it a day and disappearing into the showers—to refresh ourselves before settling down for a good dinner.

Up early the next morning, the feverish pitch continued. Antennas came down, lifelines and stanchions were dismantled and stowed, *Windy Thoughts'* deck stripped and her stays and shrouds dismantled.

And then her mast came down—and a big crane placed it on a huge trailer. She didn't look like a sailboat anymore—but she was ready to go home.

She had changed her demeanor in just those few hours, from ocean-going pride to landlubbing sadness. She had no mast, no sails and no lifelines, nothing to show what she really was. But we knew exactly what she was; to us, she had a soul of her own and had brought us safely around the world. She was our home, our magic carpet and our beloved *Windy Thoughts*.

At 5:00 on her second morning in the yard, *Windy Thoughts* was on her way home, Don and I right behind as we followed her to the border in the pilot car. We would not have believed that so much preparation for shipping could be accomplished in so short a time. But with the good help and hard work of the fellows at the yard, near miracles had been accomplished.

At Tucson, the truck pulled into a storage yard and *Windy Thoughts* was left sitting on the trailer while the truck returned to San Carlos. Another transport would pick her up in the morning. Don and I slept aboard in the storage area, surrounded by a chain link fence—a vastly different vista from those of our previous years. This was the final step in the culmination of the dream of a lifetime for us.

Excited as we were, it was difficult to see our *Windy Thoughts* stripped of her glory and removed from her element—no longer sailing oceans and taking us to places previously only dreamed about. We reminded her that she would soon be back in our Northwest waters with glorious surrounding vistas, mountains and beautiful greenery, with time to rest and savor her delightful past, time to glide across pristine waters with eagles soaring above.

Up early the next morning, we said goodbye to our home for a few days and we were off in a taxi to Tucson's airport.

Suddenly it was all over, much faster than it had all begun. There was much to adjust to as we stepped off the plane in Seattle and entered the landed world again.

Windy Thoughts came home a few days later. Don and I were anxiously waiting for her at the Canal Boat Yard, excited to see her. The proprietor only gave us a nod, not as interested in her arrival as we were. He murmured something about shipping schedules never being kept and not to expect our boat to arrive on time—or even on that day. The trucking company had set the estimated time of arrival at noon. The truck pulled into the boat yard, with *Windy Thoughts*, at 11:30 a.m., the driver apologizing for being a half hour early!

A few days later *Windy Thoughts* was back where the dream had begun—at the very same dock. We were home to stay.

We have built our home where new dreams await us on Orcas Island in Washington State's San Juan Islands, ninety miles north of Seattle. *Windy Thoughts* remained our home for two years, 1999 and 2000, the first year in Seattle with frequent visits to "our island" as we set all in motion for living there—and the second year on Orcas Island as we began clearing the land and building our home.

Windy Thoughts never sailed oceans with us again, but she rested at peace and on her laurels while we continued with other dreams, less adventurous dreams for us—but dreams that we are living and loving each and every day.

Though we never entertained the thought of giving *Windy Thoughts* up, expecting to spend many an hour bobbing about the waters of our beautiful islands—land life, as well as the rigors and the excitement of clearing property and building our home, left us little time to think of cruising.

And something unexpected had happened to us when we stepped off our *Windy Thoughts* in San Carlos. It was as if we had turned off the lights and closed a door. It was a bittersweet goodbye to our cruising years. *Windy Thoughts'* ocean-going days with us were over and we knew it; the grand adventure was completed and nothing could ever be the same again.

We couldn't justify paying monthly moorage while the boat simply sat in the quaint and quiet marina on Orcas Island, little used and not out on the water where she belonged, breezes filling her sails as she picked up her skirts and danced away. And so, in 2002, *Windy Thoughts* went to new owners, young people who spent a lot of money, time and sheer elbow grease restoring her to her original beauty. When their cruising dreams didn't materialize a year later, she sold again.

The boat's name has been changed twice now, but there will always be only one *Windy Thoughts* and only one adventure that was the dream of our lifetime. Such a perfect live-aboard blue water cruising boat, so safe and strong and so forgiving she was—and we hope she may give her present owners the same passionate ride that she gave us, wherever that passionate ride may take them.

As for *Breezy*, when we were first back to Seattle the owner of the marina had offered Don two months free moorage in exchange for *Breezy*. Remembering the thousands of times we had dragged her up onto beaches, and the job of getting her off and onto the boat, Don made the deal. A year had passed and I was saddened that *Breezy* was no longer a part of our lives. Without my knowledge, Don called her new owner and sheepishly asked if he might buy her back again.

Good friend Barry McCormick sailed his own boat, *Chubasco*, up from Seattle with *Breezy* happily bobbing along behind, making her way back to her home with us on Orcas Island. She is where she rightfully belongs now, proudly sitting outside our window on chocks under a big Madrona tree—there to remind us of the years that took us away and brought us back again—and she will be with us always.

Not a day goes by without Don and me talking about our cruising years, remembering the places we visited and the people we met along the way. It was a dream in the beginning and it often seems a dream now—one that we often cannot believe we really experienced—but one that changed our lives in so many ways.

A little six-year-old girl on another boat, met way back in the South Pacific, just about summed up cruising and its experiences when we sat in their cockpit visiting one day. In the middle of the adult conversation, she blurted out, "Boy, after cruising nothing in life will ever seem hard again."

We try to remember this and to keep life in perspective—because the best things in life are not necessarily easy. It often takes hard work to achieve and to sustain one's dreams. Sometimes it is just plain hard work physically; often it is hard work emotionally and sometimes it is overwhelmingly frustrating.

But always, there was for us so much pure joy. When all is said and done, it was pure joy given to us as we sailed *Windy Thoughts* to faraway places, a joy that gave her a soul of her own and a joy that we will never take for granted and will remember always.

Mark Twain said, "Happiness is not a thing in itself. It is only a contrast with something that ain't pleasant."

Things that ain't pleasant can be counted on to happen with fair regularity when sailing a boat to faraway places. Happiness can be counted on to pop up just when you thought you couldn't get through one more minute or one more crisis. Suddenly, all turns around and you are in wonder again, a wonder that lasts far, far longer than any unpleasant experience.

Happiness comes from yet another wondrous sunset at sea. Joy comes as you spend another starry night lulled by the sound of the bow wave slapping against the hull as you glide across one of our earth's vast oceans—and when you sail your own boat into a new anchorage or a new port—wide-eyed with child-like wonder and excitement to see what is on this new horizon.

Happiness arrives again when you come to rest for good on an island called Orcas that is the island of your dreams—and plan to live out the rest of your days where you have made dear friends and are surrounded by all of God's wonders.

Our horizon is now filled with islands and waters, mountains and spectacular sunsets, and our souls are content and at peace, the two of us together. None of this would ever have happened were it not for my captain—the one who always makes life adventurous and who always perseveres, no matter how difficult the challenge.

My captain still remarks on how it doesn't quite seem possible that we are really here to stay, that we won't have to up anchor someday and move on. This is our dreamland now.

> *There is some satisfaction*
> *that is mighty sweet*
> *to take,*
> *When you reach a*
> *destination that you*
> *thought you'd never make.*
> —Spirella

We have found our safe harbor. When the anchor comes up next, it will be for the final journey that will truly take us home. All is well with our souls. The best is yet to come.

HOME SWEET HOME

FAVORITE RECIPES ABOARD

ALEXANDER CAKE
    1 ½ cups margarine or butter
    3 cups sugar
    5 eggs
    3 cups flour
    2 Tbsp. lemon extract
    ¾ cup 7-Up

Cream sugar and shortening together and beat until light and fluffy. Add eggs, one at a time, and beat well. Add flour. Beat in lemon extract and 7-Up. Pour batter into well-greased (with oil) and floured Jumbo Fluted Mold.

Bake at 325 degrees for 1 – 1½ hours.

Does not need an icing.

BEST BOAT BREAD
    4 cups flour (1/3 of which may be oat bran or other cereal)
    2/3 cup powdered milk
    1 Tbsp. sugar
    1 Tbsp. dry yeast
    1 tsp. salt
    1 ½ cups warm water

Stir dry ingredients. Add water and mix. Do not knead. Grease bread pans or roaster. Sprinkle flour over grease. Install dough.

Set in warm place. Cover with a tea towel and permit to rise to double original volume (about 1 hour).

Bake in oven at 425 degrees about ½ hour. If not brown, remove from pan, invert and put back in oven until brown.

Breinigsville, PA USA
03 August 2010
242956BV00002B/1/P